Android Apps for Absolute Beginners

Third Edition

Wallace Jackson

Apress®

Android Apps for Absolute Beginners

ISBN-13 (pbk): 978-1-4842-0020-9

ISBN-13 (electronic): 978-1-4842-0019-3

Publisher: Heinz Weinheimer
Lead Editor: Matthew Moodie
Technical Reviewer: Chad Darby
Editorial Board: Steve Anglin, Mark Beckner, Ewan Buckingham, Gary Cornell, Louise Corrigan, James T. DeWolf, Jonathan Gennick, Jonathan Hassell, Robert Hutchinson, Michelle Lowman, James Markham, Matthew Moodie, Jeff Olson, Jeffrey Pepper, Douglas Pundick, Ben Renow-Clarke, Dominic Shakeshaft, Gwenan Spearing, Matt Wade, Steve Weiss
Coordinating Editor: Mark Powers
Copy Editors: Ralph Moore, Kezia Endsley
Compositor: SPi Global
Indexer: SPi Global
Artist: SPi Global
Cover Designer: Anna Ishchenko

Distributed to the book trade worldwide by Springer Science+Business Media New York, 233 Spring Street, 6th Floor, New York, NY 10013. Phone 1-800-SPRINGER, fax (201) 348-4505, e-mail orders-ny@springer-sbm.com, or visit www.springeronline.com. Apress Media, LLC is a California LLC and the sole member (owner) is Springer Science + Business Media Finance Inc (SSBM Finance Inc). SSBM Finance Inc is a Delaware corporation.

For information on translations, please e-mail rights@apress.com, or visit www.apress.com.

Apress and friends of ED books may be purchased in bulk for academic, corporate, or promotional use. eBook versions and licenses are also available for most titles. For more information, reference our Special Bulk Sales–eBook Licensing web page at www.apress.com/bulk-sales.

Any source code or other supplementary materials referenced by the author in this text is available to readers at www.apress.com/9781484200209. For detailed information about how to locate your book's source code, go to www.apress.com/source-code.

This Android book is dedicated to everyone in the open source community who is working so diligently to make professional application development software and new media content development tools freely available for all of us application developers to leverage in order to achieve our creative dreams and financial goals. Last but certainly not least, I dedicate the third edition of this educational book to my family, my life-long friends, and cool ranching neighbors, for their constant help and assistance, as well as for those smoky, savory, late night BBQ parties.

Contents at a Glance

Contents

About the Author

Wallace Jackson has been writing for leading multimedia publications about his work in new media content development since the advent of *Multimedia Producer Magazine* nearly two decades ago, when he wrote about advanced computer processor architecture for an issue centerfold (removable "mini-issue" insert) distributed at the SIGGRAPH trade show. Since then, Wallace has written for a number of other popular publications about his work in interactive 3D and new media advertising campaign design, including *3D Artist Magazine, Desktop Publishers Journal, CrossMedia Magazine, AVvideo/Multimedia Producer Magazine, Digital Signage Magazine,* and *Kiosk Magazine*.

Wallace Jackson has authored half a dozen Android book titles for Apress, including four titles in the popular *Pro Android* series. This particular *Android Apps for Absolute Beginners* title has been rewritten entirely from scratch three times, and this third edition is one of the most thorough and comprehensive Android titles found on the market.

Wallace Jackson is currently the CEO of **Mind Taffy Design**, a new media content production and digital campaign design and development agency located in North Santa Barbara County, halfway between their clientele in Silicon Valley to the north and in Hollywood, "The OC," and San Diego to the south. Mind Taffy also produces interactive 3D content for major brands around the world from their content production studio on Point Conception Peninsula in the California Central Coast area.

Mind Taffy Design has created open source technology (HTML5, Java, and Android) and digital new media content deliverables for more than two decades (since 1991) for a large number of the top branded manufacturers in the world, including Sony, Samsung, IBM, Epson, Nokia, TEAC, Sun, SGI, Dell, Compaq, ViewSonic, Western Digital, CTX International, KDS USA, KFC, ADI and Mitsubishi.

Wallace Jackson received his undergraduate degree in Business Economics from the University of California at Los Angeles (UCLA) and his graduate degree in MIS Design and Implementation from the University of Southern California (USC). His post-graduate degree, also from USC, is in *Marketing Strategy*. He subsequently completed the *USC Graduate Entrepreneurship Program* in USC's popular night-time Marshall School of Business MBA programs. The night-time USC MBA program allowed Mr. Jackson to work full-time while he completed his graduate and post-graduate business degrees.

About the Technical Reviewer

Chád Darby is an author, instructor, and speaker in the Java development world. As a recognized authority on Java applications and architectures, he has presented technical sessions at software development conferences worldwide (U.S., U.K., India, Russia, and Australia). In his 15 years as a professional software architect, he's had the opportunity to work for Blue Cross/Blue Shield, Merck, Boeing, Red Hat, and a handful of startup companies.

Chád is a contributing author to several Java books, including *Professional Java E-Commerce* (Wrox Press), *Beginning Java Networking* (Wrox Press), and *XML* and *Web Services Unleashed* (Sams Publishing). Chád has Java certifications from Sun Microsystems and IBM. He holds a B.S. in Computer Science from Carnegie Mellon University.

Acknowledgments

I would like to acknowledge all my fantastic editors and the support staff at Apress who worked long hours and toiled so very hard on this book to make it the ultimate *Absolute Beginner* Android title.

Matthew Moodie, for his work as the Lead Editor on the book, and for his experience and guidance during the process of making this book one of the great Android beginner titles.

Mark Powers, for his work as the Coordinating Editor on the book, and for his constant diligence in making sure I hit or surpassed my deadlines.

Ralph Moore and Kezia Endsley, for their work as the Copy Editors on this book, and for their close attention to detail, and for conforming the text to the current Apress book writing standards.

Chad Darby, for his work as the Technical Reviewer on the book, and for making sure I didn't make any programming mistakes. Java code with mistakes does not run properly, if at all, unless they are very lucky mistakes, which is quite rare in computer programming these days.

Frank Serafine, my close friend, the world's finest and most respected sound designer, and a popular rock musician, for contributing the audio samples used in this book. These audio samples are from his stellar (no pun intended) work on some of the world's most popular science fiction and action adventure movies and television shows, including but not limited to Star *Trek* and *Hunt for Red October*.

Finally, I'd like to acknowledge **Oracle** for acquiring Sun Microsystems and for continuing to enhance Java so that it remains the premiere open source programming language, and **Google**, for making Android the premiere open source operating system and for acquiring ON2's VP8 video codec and making it available to multimedia producers on the Android and HTML5 platforms.

Introduction

The Android OS is currently the most popular operating system in the world. The Android OS runs on everything from smartwatches to HD smartphones to touchscreen tablets to ebook readers to game consoles to smartglasses to ultra-high definition interactive television sets!

There are even more types of consumer electronics devices—such as those found in automotive, home appliance, security, robotics, photography, industrial and home automation markets—that are adopting the open source Android OS as their platform as time goes on. This book will show you how to develop applications for these new device type verticals as they emerge into the market.

Since there are literally billions of Android consumer electronics devices owned by billions of people all over the world, it stands to reason that developing great Android applications for all these people might be an extremely lucrative undertaking, assuming that you have the right concept and design.

This book will help you go a long way toward learning how to develop Android applications that will run across all types of Android-compatible consumer electronics devices, and across all popular versions of the Android OS, most recently the 32-bit Android 4 OS and the new 64-bit Android 5 OS.

Developing an Android application that works well across all of these types of consumer electronics devices requires a very specific work process, which I cover in this book.

I wrote *Android Apps for Absolute Beginners, Third Edition* from scratch, targeting those readers who are absolute beginners to Android yet are technically savvy, but who are not familiar with computer programming concepts and techniques.

Since 32-bit Android is currently using Version 4.4.4, this book will be more advanced than *Android Apps for Absolute Beginners, First Edition*, when Android OS Version 1.5 was released by Google for smartphones, or *Android Apps for Absolute Beginners, Second Edition*, when Android OS Version 3.0 was released for tablets. Since then, five revisions of the 32-bit Android OS Version 4.x have been released, including 4.0, 4.1, 4.2, 4.3, and 4.4, targeting all new iTV set and game console products.

Since the **64-bit Android 5.0 OS** was announced during the writing of this book, and is currently in beta, I will also include an advanced chapter at the end of this book called "**The Future of Android: The 64-bit Android 5.0 OS**." This comprehensive Android 5.0 chapter will cover what you can expect when 64-bit Android 5.0 smartphone devices are released during 2014, as well as when 64-bit Android 5.0 game consoles, tablets and iTV sets are released during 2015 and into 2016.

The first edition of this book was a mere 300 pages, as Android 1.5 was the first version to appear on Android hardware devices (smartphones), and a second edition of this book was 33% longer, at 400 pages. I've expanded this version of the book to include nearly 700 pages of information, the size of the first two editions combined. This third edition even contains chapters that cover how to develop for Android wearable devices, such as the popular Neptune Pine smartwatch, as well as covering the new Android Wear SDK using the new Android Studio and IntelliJ IDEA. This book also covers how to develop for rapidly emerging Android appliances using the new Android TV SDK.

I designed this book to be a more comprehensive overview of the Android application development work process than most beginning Android application development books, because, at this point, there is really no way to "sugar coat" the Android application development process. To become the leading Android application developer that you seek to become, you will have to understand, as well as master, XML mark-up, user interface design, Java programming, and new media content creation. Once you have done this, hopefully by the end of this book, you will be able to create the vanguard user experiences required to create those popular, best-selling Android applications.

Android apps are currently developed for 32-bit Android 4 with Eclipse ADT Integrated Development Environment (IDE) or for 64-bit Android 5 using IntelliJ IDEA. Android applications are not developed via IDE alone, but also in conjunction with several other genres of new media content development software packages. For this reason, this book covers a wide variety of popular open source software packages, including GIMP 2.8, Planetside Terragen 3.1, Sorenson Squeeze Pro 9, VirtualDub 1.9, and Audacity 2. These professional new media content production tools should be utilized in conjunction with developing your Android 5 applications, and this book will show you exactly how to accomplish this, as well as how to download, install, update, configure, and actually use each of these programs.

This comprehensive Android 4/5 application development work process will allow you to experience exactly how the use of all of these multimedia content development software packages needs to fit into your overall Android application development work process. This 100% comprehensive "soup to nuts" multimedia-centric Android app development approach sets this 32-bit Android 4.x and 64-bit Android 5 book title distinctly apart from all of the other Android application development titles that are currently on the market. This book covers the Android development process at a broader level.

Chapter 1 starts by covering downloading and installing the current Java SE 6 and Android 4.4 SDK as well as the Eclipse IDE and the Android ADT bundle, along with several popular open source content development applications. In Chapter 2, you will configure your Android 4 application development workstation, and in Chapter 3, you will create a basic Android 4.4.4 application. You will be adding more and more functionality to that basic Android application during the remainder of the book, as well as converting it into an Android 5 app during the final chapter of the book covering Android 5.

In Chapter 4, you learn all about the XML markup language, and in Chapter 5, you learn all about the Java SE programming language. Thus, the first third of this Android book is foundational material, which explains how the Android OS works together as a whole. In Chapters 6 through 8, you learn about the fundamentals of user interface design in Android, and how to make UI designs interactive.

In Chapters 9 and 10 you will learn about graphics design and 2D animation in Android, and how to use new media content production software in conjunction with Android development software and IDEs. In Chapters 11 and 12, you will learn how to implement digital audio new media assets as well as how to stream digital video new media assets from your remote video servers.

In the final four chapters of this book, you will learn about some of the more advanced development topics that normally would not be included in an Absolute Beginner title, but I included them so that all of the important topics regarding Android application development are in this one, single, unified book. These included advanced topics including threads, processes and databases, developing apps for smartwatches and iTV sets, and everything you would want to know about the new 64-bit Android 5 OS, including how to set it up, how to develop Android 5.0 applications, and all of its new features.

In Chapter 13, you will learn all about threads, Services and background processing for Android using the **Service** class, and in Chapter 14 you'll learn about RDBMS database theory and SQLite databases in Android, as well as how to use the Android **Content Provider** classes to access built-in databases.

In the last two chapters in this book, you'll dive into the future of Android application development, by developing applications for Android wearables and Android appliances, and learning all about Android 5.0. Chapter 15 covers how to develop Android applications for wearable devices and the Wear SDK, and Chapter 16 covers how to develop Android applications for Android appliances such as the iTV set using the Android TV SDK and the new Android 5.0 OS and Android Studio Bundle based on the IntelliJ IDEA and Java 7 on top of an all new 64-bit Linux Kernel and the new ART Android RunTime.

This book attempts to be the most comprehensive Absolute Beginners book for Android application development out there, by covering most, if not all of, the major Android classes that will need to be used to create leading-edge 32-bit Android 4.x and 64-bit Android 5.x software applications.

Some of these classes include the **View**, **ViewGroup**, **Activity**, **Menu**, **MenuItem**, **OptionsMenu**, and **ActionBar** classes, used for GUI and screen designs, the **FrameLayout**, **LinearLayout**, **RelativeLayout**, **GridLayout**, **TableLayout**, and **SlidingPaneLayout** classes, which are used for user interface designs, the **ImageButton**, **ImageView**, **NinePatch**, **NinePatchDrawable**, **BitmapDrawable**, **Animation**, **AnimationDrawable**, and **AnimationSet** classes, which are used for graphics design and animation, the **SoundPool**, **VideoView**, **MediaPlayer**, **Uri** and **MediaController** classes, which are used in digital audio and digital video applications, and finally, the **Service**, **Thread**, **Context**, **ContentProvider**, and **ContentResolver** classes, used for database access and more complex background processing tasks.

If you are looking for the most comprehensive, up-to-date overview of the latest 32-bit and 64-bit Android OSes, including Eclipse ADT (Android Developer Tools) IDE on top of Java SE 6, and IntelliJ (Android Studio) IDEA on top of Java SE 7, this is the book that covers the entire gamut.

This Android title covers everything regarding the XML markup langauge and the new media content development work processes which spans across both 32-bit as well as 64-bit Android development, as well as detailed knowledge about how to optimally use Android app technologies with the leading open source new media content design and development tools.

If you are looking for the latest Android title that covers everything about Android from the first version that Google released (1.5) up to the current version (5.0) and how to assilimate these app development technologies into your current content production workflows, this *Android Apps for Absolute Beginners, Third Edition* book will be of significant interest to you.

It is the intention of this book to take you from being an "Absolute Beginner" in Android application development, to having a comprehensive, solid, intermediate knowledge of both 32-bit Android 4.4 and 64-bit Android 5.0 application development.

You should be advised that this book contains a significant amount of technical knowledge and work processes that may take more than one read-through to assimilate into an application development knowledge base (your current Android knowledge "quiver of arrows" so to speak). This vast journey through 32-bit Android 4.x and 64-bit Android 5 will be well worth your time, however; rest assured.

Setting Up Your Android App Development System

These days, you see Android devices of every size and shape everywhere you look. They can be worn on your person, used in an appliance, are a part of your car, or provide you entertainment in your living room taking the form of an iTV set, a tablet, eBook reader, or an Android game console.

In this chapter, we will explore some basic facts about the Android operating system (OS), to give you a high-level overview of the history of Android, the benefits of learning Android application development, and which open source programming languages and OSs Android is based upon.

We will also need to get all of the tedious searching and downloads out of the way regarding to how to go about obtaining all of the various software packages, SDKs, and components, which together form a comprehensive **Android production workstation**.

Even though this is an "Absolute Beginners" Android title, I want to teach you how to put together a pro Android development workstation, so that you are all ready to get into the various *Pro Android* series of books from Apress (after you finish mastering this book, of course).

So that everyone experiences this book equally, this chapter will outline all the steps to obtain a completely decked out Android development workstation.

The History of the Android OS: Impressive Growth

Android OS was originally created by **Andy Rubin** as an OS for mobile phones; this happened around the dawn of this 21st century.

In 2005, Google acquired Android Inc., and made Andy Rubin the Director of Mobile Platforms for Google. Many think this acquisition of the Android OS by Google was largely in response to the appearance of Apple's iPhone around that same time. However, there were enough other large players, such as RIM Blackberry, Nokia Symbian, and Microsoft Windows Mobile, that it was deemed to be a savvy business decision for Google to purchase Android engineering talent and

Android OS intellectual property, allowing Google to insert their company into this emerging market, which was known as **Internet 2.0**.

Internet 2.0, or the **Mobile Internet**, allows users of consumer electronic products to access content via widely varied data networks, using portable consumer electronic devices. These currently include tablets, smartphones, phablets (phone-tablet hybrid), game consoles, smartwatches, smartglasses, personal robots, and eBook eReaders.

These days, Android OS–based devices can also include those not-so-portable consumer electronics devices, such as iTVs, home media centers, automobile dashboards and stereos, and digital signage system set-top boxes.

This ever-growing Android phenomenon puts new media content such as games, 3D animation, interactive television, digital video, digital audio, eBooks, and high-definition imagery into our lives at every turn.

Android is one of those popular, open source vehicles (the other one being HTML5) that digital artists will increasingly leverage in order to be able to develop new media creations that users have never before experienced.

Over the past decade, Android has matured and evolved, to become a stable, exceptionally reliable, embedded open source OS. An Android OS that started out with its initial Version 1.0 just a few years ago, once acquired by Google, has released stable OS versions at 1.5, 1.6, 2.0, 2.1, 2.2, 2.3, 3.0, 3.1, 3.2, 3.3, 4.0, 4.1, 4.2, 4.3, and, recently, the much-heralded KitKat Android version 4.4, currently at Version 4.4.4. As of the writing of this book, Android 5.0 is in beta at version 0.8.0, so that should show up in 64-bit Android devices in 2015 and 2016.

If you want to see the latest statistics regarding each of these Android OS revisions, directly from the Android developer web site, visit this URL:

`http://developer.android.com/about/dashboards/index.html`

Table 1-1 shown this progression of all the popular versions of Android OS that have been installed on the popular consumer electronics manufacturer products over the past decades. I wanted to collect all of this Android OS information together into one single infographic for you so that you could get a "bird's eye" view of the current historic progression of the Android OS. As you can see, there are certain Android market share "sweet spots."

Table 1-1. *Android Versions, Internal Codenames, API Levels and Market Share*

VERSION	CODENAME	API LEVEL	MARKET SHARE
1.5	Cupcake	3	0.1%
1.6	Donut	4	0.1%
2.1	Eclair	7	0.2%
2.2	Froyo	8	0.2%
2.3.7	Gingerbread	10	14.9%
3.2	Honeycomb	13	0.2%

(continued)

Table 1-1. (*continued*)

VERSION	CODENAME	API LEVEL	MARKET SHARE
4.0.4	Ice Cream Sandwich	15	12.3%
4.1.2	Jelly Bean	16	29.0%
4.2.2	Jelly Bean Plus	17	19.1%
4.3.1	Jelly Bean Plus	18	10.3%
4.4.4	Kit Kat	19	13.6%
5.0	L	20	0.0%

In case you are wondering what an **embedded OS** is, it is like having an entire personal computer on a motherboard, which is small enough to fit into a handheld consumer electronics device, and which is powerful enough to run applications (which are commonly known simply as apps).

Just like today's personal computers and laptops, the Internet 2.0 devices such as smartphones, tablets, eReaders, smartwatches, and iTVs now feature quad-cores (4 CPUs) and even octa-core (8 CPUs) computer processing power, as well as one or two gigabytes of system memory. This is approaching the power of a modern day PC, such as the workstation you are going to set up during the next chapter of this book, which you can get for $300 at WalMart. The mini-tower PCs feature quad-core 64-bit processors along with 4GB or 6GB of system memory, and a 500GB hard disk drive with Windows 8.1.

The Android OS contains the power of a complete computer OS. It is based on the **Linux Kernel** open source platform, and Oracle (formerly Sun Microsystems) **Java 6 Standard Edition**, one of the world's most popular programming languages. Android 5, coming out in products next year, will use a 64-bit Linux Kernel, and Java 7.

> **Note**   The term **open source** refers to software that has often been developed collaboratively by an **open community** of individuals, and is **freely available** for **commercial use**. Open source software comes with all of the **source code**, so that it can be further modified if necessary. The Android OS is open source, though Google develops it internally before releasing the source code. From that point on, it is freely available for commercial use by app software developers.

It's not uncommon for an Android device to have a 1.2GHz processor and 1GB of fast, computer-grade DDR3 memory. This rivals desktop computers of just a few years ago, and netbooks that are still currently available. You will continue to see this convergence of Internet 2.0 (mobile device) OSs with desktop OSs, such as we are seeing with Windows 8.1 and Google Chrome OS currently, as time goes on.

Once it became evident that Java, the Android OS, and open source software platforms were vanguard forces to be reckoned with, a bunch of the popular consumer electronics manufacturers, including Philips, Sony, HTC, Samsung, LG Electronics, and T-Mobile, formed, and joined the **Open Handset Alliance** (OHA). This was all done in order to put the momentum behind Google's open source Android platform, and it worked! Today, hundreds of leading branded consumer electronics manufacturers leverage Android as an OS on their consumer electronic devices. In fact, Android OS is used more than any other OS that has ever existed on the face of the earth.

This development of the OHA is a significant benefit to Android developers. Android allows developers to create their applications using a single IDE, or integrated development environment, and now this support by the OHA can enable developers to deliver their content across dozens of major branded manufacturers' hardware products as well as across several different types of consumer electronic devices, including smartphones, iTV sets, e-book e-readers, smartwatches, smartglasses, home media centers, settop boxes, and touchscreen tablets.

The Android OS affords its developers a plethora of powerful content delivery tools and platform support and device playback possibilities, to say the least! But then again, you must have realized this yourselves, as you are reading this book right now, so you can get in on all that power!

In summary, Android is a seasoned OS that has become one of the biggest players in computing today, and with Google behind it. Android uses freely available open source technologies such as Linux and Java, and open standards such as XML, CSS, MPEG, JPEG, PNG, MP3, WebM, WebP, OpenGL, WebKit, and HTML5. Android incorporates all of these open source resources so that it can provide the free new media content and application delivery platform to Android developers, and an OS platform to consumer electronics manufacturers. Can you spell OPPORTUNITY? I sure can: it's spelled **ANDROID**!

Advantage Android: How Can Android Benefit Me?

There are simply too many benefits for the Android OS development platform to ignore your Android applications development workflow, and environment, for even one minute longer. We are going to get you all of the latest apps and OS SDKs and components during this chapter so you'll have a valuable PC!

First of all, Android is based on open source technology, which was at its inception not as refined as paid technologies from Apple and Microsoft.

However, over the past several decades, open source software technology has become equally as sophisticated as conventional software technologies. You will soon see this with your professional level new media content software that you will be acquiring (for free) during the remainder of this chapter.

This is clearly evident with Internet 2.0, as the majority of the consumer electronics manufacturers have chosen Linux and Java over the Windows, iOS, and Macintosh OSs.

For this key reason, Android developers can develop applications not only for their smartphones, but also for new and emerging consumer electronics device ecosystems that include never-before-seen products such as glasses and smartwatches and 4K UHD iTVs that are network-compatible and available to connect to an Android Marketplace. The Android Marketplace was recently re-branded by Google as Google Play due to a lawsuit brought by Apple.

This translates to more sales on more devices in more areas of a potential customer's life and thus offers more incentive to develop for Android over closed technologies such as Windows and iOS and over less popular and less prolific PC OSs.

In addition to being free for commercial use, the Android OS has one of the largest, wealthiest, and most innovative companies in modern-day computing behind it: Google. Add in an OHA and you have more than a trillion dollars of megabrand companies behind you, supporting your development efforts. It certainly seems too good to be true, but it's a fact; if you're an Android developer (which you are about to be, in about a dozen and a half chapters), then you now have a supreme hardware and software sales and support team behind you.

Finally, and most importantly, it's much easier to get your Android applications published than those for other platforms that are similar to Android (I won't mention any names here, to protect the not-so-innocent).

We've all heard those horror stories regarding major development companies waiting months, and sometimes years, for their apps to be approved for the app marketplace. These problems are nearly non-existent on the open source Android platform. Publishing an app on the Google Play Android Marketplace is as easy as paying $50, uploading your Android .apk file, and specifying whether you are offering a free or a paid download.

The Scope of This Book

This book is an introduction to developing applications for Android. It is intended for absolute beginners; that is, people who have never created an application on the Android platform for a consumer electronic device. I do not assume that you know what Java is, or how XML works, or what styles or themes are, or what a codec, an alpha channel, color dithering, or an anti-aliasing algorithm is.

All I know is that by the end of this book, you're going to appear as if you are speaking a foreign language when you start talking about new media Android application development in front of friends, family, and clientele, which ultimately will get you hired, and hopefully well paid!

What is Covered in This Book

This book covers the basic and essential elements of Android application development, including but not limited to the following areas:

- The open source tools required to develop for this platform

    - Where to get this free software development environment, as well as professional new media content creation tools

    - How to properly install and configure the necessary tools for application development as well as new media creation

    - Which third-party tools are useful to use in conjunction with the Android development tools (ADT)

    - Which OSs and platforms currently support development for the Android using these tools

- The concepts and programming constructs for Java and XML, and their practical applications in creating Android applications

- How Android goes about setting up an Android application

    - How it defines the application user interface components

    - How it addresses and writes graphics to a display screen

    - How it can communicate with other Android applications

    - How it interfaces with data, resources, networks, and the Internet

    - How it alerts users to events that may be taking place, inside of and outside of your Android application

- How Android applications are published using the app Manifest

- How Android applications are ultimately sold, downloaded, and updated automatically through Google Play Android Marketplace

Realize that Android OS has more than 44 Java packages, which contain functionality that allows you to do just about anything imaginable, from putting a UI button on the display screen, to synthesizing speech, or accessing advanced smartphone features such as the high-resolution camera, Bluetooth, GPS, Gyro, Compass, or Accelerometer.

> **Note**   A package in Java is a collection of programming utilities or functions that all have related (and interconnected) functionality. For example, the **java.io** package contains utilities that deal with input and output (IO) to your program, such as reading the contents of a file, or saving data to a file. Later chapters describe how to organize your own Android Java code, into your own custom packages.

What does the plethora of Android Java code mean for an Absolute Beginner?

It means that even the most advanced pro Android books can't all cover the plethora of amazing things that this Android OS platform can accomplish!

In fact, most Android books will specialize in a specific area of an Android API. An API is an application programming interface, or a collection of programming code routines that allow software development. We will be learning about APIs in Chapter 5. There is plenty of complexity in each API, which ultimately, from the developer's viewpoint, translates into incredible creative power. What is the price of this power, you might ask. Your time spent in mastering each API is the only price you'll pay, as the Android OS is otherwise free for commercial use.

What is Not Covered in This Book

So, what isn't covered in this book? What cool, powerful capabilities do you have to look forward to in the next level book on Android programming?

On the hardware side, we will not be looking at how to control the camera, access GPS data from the smartphone, and access the accelerometer, or the gyroscope, which allow the user to turn the smartphone around and have the application react to the smartphone position. We will not be delving into advanced touchscreen concepts such as gestures, or accessing other device hardware, such as the microphone, Bluetooth, or wireless connections.

On the software side, we will not be diving into creating your own Android MySQLite Database Structure, or Android's real-time 3D rendering system (called OpenGL ES 3.1), although we will take a closer look at these areas so that you know how to utilize them, and how they fit into the overall Android OS infrastructure.

We will not be exploring speech synthesis and speech recognition, nor the universal language support that allows developers to create applications that display characters correctly in dozens of international languages and foreign character sets.

We will not be getting into advanced programming such as game development, artificial intelligence, image compositing pipelines, blending modes, and physics simulations. All of these topics are better suited to books that focus on these complex and detailed topical areas, such as the Apress *Pro Android Graphics* and *Pro Android UI* titles.

Assembling Your Android Development Workstation

In this section, I will outline the broad overview of what's needed to put together a complete Android development workstation that you can utilize throughout this book to create cool Android apps.

The first thing that you'll do is get the entire Java software development kit (SDK), which Oracle calls **JavaSE 6 JDK** (Java Development Kit). Android OS uses Java Standard Edition (SE) Version 6 update 45, as of Android 4.4.

> **Note**   Java Version 7 also exists, and is in parallel release with Java6, at Java7 u45. In the second quarter of 2014, there will be a Java Version 8 released, which will include powerful JavaFX APIs that turn Java programming language into a powerful new media engine. Thus, the future of open source development (Android OS, Java8, XML, HTML5) is here! In fact, Android 5.0, which should be available in 64-bit consumer electronics products in 2015 and 2016, uses Java 7 and a 64-bit version of the Linux Kernel!

The second thing that we will download and install is the Android Developer Tools (ADT), which we will get from Google's **developer.android.com** web site.

ADT Bundle 4.4 consists of the **Eclipse 4.4 IDE** (integrated development environment), along with the **ADT 4.4 plug-ins,** which **bridges** the **Android SDK** that is also part of the ADT Bundle download, with the Eclipse 4.4 IDE. This makes the Eclipse Java IDE into an Eclipse Android ADT IDE, essentially, although it could still be used for straight JavaSE 6 application development as well. An IDE is an integrated development environment, like a word processor tuned for writing programming code.

After your core Android development environment is downloaded, you'll then download and install external **new media asset development** tools, which you will utilize in conjunction with Android for things such as UI wireframing (Pencil), digital image editing (GIMP2), digital audio editing (Audacity), digital video editing (Lightworks), 3D modeling and animation (Blender3D), and even running your Android development business (Apache Open Office 4.1).

All of these software development tools, which you will be downloading and installing, will come close to matching all of the primary feature sets of the expensive paid software packages, such as those from Microsoft (Office and Visual Studio), Apple (Logic, Avid, FinalCut Pro X), Autodesk (Maya or 3D Studio Max), and Adobe (Photoshop CS6 and After Effects).

Each of these paid software packages would cost a couple thousand dollars each to purchase and maintain, so plan on paying ten thousand (your local currency unit here) to put together a similar paid software workstation to develop for the iOS or the Windows consumer electronics device platforms.

Open source software is free to download, install, and even upgrade, and is continually adding features, and becoming more and more professional, each and every day. You'll be completely amazed at how professional open source software packages have become over the last decade or two; if you have not experienced this already, you are about to, and in a very major way.

Android Development Workstation: Hardware Foundation

Since during the chapter you will put together what will be the foundation for your Android applications development system for the duration of this book, let's take a moment to discuss the Android development workstation's hardware configuration, as that's an important factor for your performance (speed of development), which is as important as the software itself.

This section will therefore cover a plethora of important systems hardware considerations that you should consider when assembling your workstation.

I recommend using at a bare minimum an **Intel i7 quad-core** processor, or an **AMD 64-bit hexa-core** processor, with at least **8GB** of **DDR3 1600** memory. I'm using the octa-core AMD 8350 with **16GB** of **DDR3 2000**. Intel also has a six-core i7 processor. This would be an equivalent of having 12 AMD cores, as each Intel core can host two threads; similarly, the i7 quad-core looks like 8 AMD cores to the OS thread-scheduling algorithm.

AMD has a 16-core processor as well, which is usually deployed inside of server architectures, but this CPU can be used in a client-side Android development workstation, which would greatly speed video compression or 3D rendering for your Android applications development.

There are also high-speed DDR3 1866 and DDR3 2000 clockspeed memory module components available. A high number signifies faster memory access speed. To calculate the actual megahertz speed at which memory is cycling, divide the number by **4** (1333=333Mhz, 1600=400Mhz, 1866=466Mhz, 2000=500Mhz clock rate). Memory access speed is the key workstation performance factor because your processor is usually "bottlenecked" by the speed at which the processor cores can access the data (in memory) that it needs to process.

With all this high-speed processing and memory access going on inside your workstation while it is operating, it is also important to keep everything cool so that you do not experience "thermal problems." I recommend using a wide **full-tower** enclosure, with **120mm** or **200mm** cooling fans (one or two at least), as well as a captive liquid induction cooling fan on the CPU. This type of CPU cooler has cooling tubes filled with water that touch the CPU and draw away heat, turning the water into steam, which rises up the tubes to the cooling fan, which cools this steam, condensing it back into water, which runs back down the pipe to cool the CPU. It's important to note that the cooler your system runs, the longer it lasts, and the faster it runs, which is important for Android application development.

If you really want the maximum performance, especially while emulating Android Virtual Devices (AVDs), which are used for app prototyping or testing, which you will learn about in the next chapter, using Eclipse, you'll want to make sure that your Android development workstation has a solid state disk (**SSD**) hard drive as its primary (C:\ "boot" drive) disk drive, from which your applications and OS software will launch.

You can always use more affordable hard disk drive (**HDD**) hardware for your D:\ (secondary) hard disk drive, for your data storage, which does not need the speed of operation as it is just used for long-term storage.

For my OS, I'm using a **64-bit Windows 8.1** OS, which is quite memory-efficient. Linux 64-bit OS is also extremely memory efficient. It's important to note that Windows 8.1 comes on most quad-core workstations in retail stores such as WalMart and Staples, and with an OS price of several hundred dollars if purchased separately, you could look at the hardware as being essentially free!

Android Development Workstation: Software Foundation

To create a well-rounded Android applications development workstation, you will be installing all of the primary genres of open source software covered later in this chapter, after you install JavaSE 6u45, Eclipse, and the ADT environment, which are also all the open source programming packages you'll need. Thus, we'll be putting together a 100% open source workstation for you (with the exception of your Windows 8 OS).

For those readers who have just purchased their new Android workstations, and who are going to put their Android development software suite together completely from scratch, I'll go through an entire work process during the rest of this chapter.

We will start with Java SE 6u45 as it is the foundation for Eclipse ADT as well as Android, and then we'll acquire the Eclipse ADT Bundle. After that, we'll search for and download your new media content development software, as well as user interface design software and a complete business software suite called Apache Open Office 4.1, originally created by Sun Microsystems, and acquired and made open source by Oracle, who owns the Java SE platform.

Java SE 6: Download and Install a Foundation for Android

Before you run a JavaSE installation, you should remove any older versions of JavaSE using your Windows **Control Panel**, via the **Add or Remove Programs** (XP) or Programs and Features (Windows 7 and 8.1) utility. To remove an older version of the Java JDK or Java Runtime Environment (JRE) select them and right-click on the selected entry and use the "Uninstall/Remove" option to un-install.

This will be necessary especially if your workstation is not brand new, so that only your latest Java SE 6u45 and JRE 6u45 are the sole Java versions that are currently installed on your new Android development workstation.

To install a new JDK:

1. The first thing that you will want to do is to visit **Oracle's Java Archive** web site, and download and install the latest **Java 6 JDK** environment, which at the time of writing this book was **Java SE 6u45**, as shown in Figure 1-1.

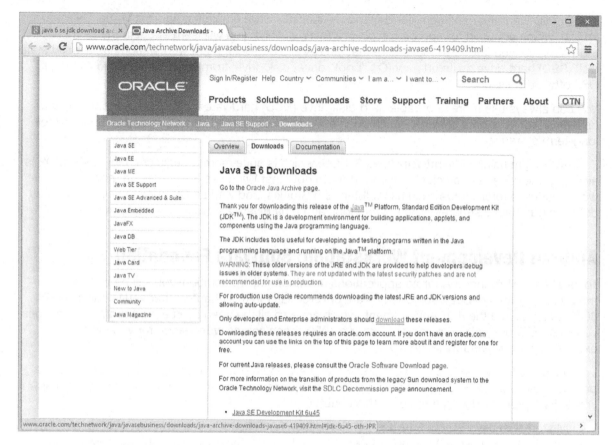

Figure 1-1. Oracle TechNetwork web site JavaSE6 Archive; scroll to the middle to find the JavaSE 6u45 JDK download

The URL is in the address bar of Figure 1-1, or you can simply Google **Java SE 6 JDK Archive Download**, which will also give you the latest link to this web page, which I will also put here, in case you want to cut and paste it:

```
http://www.oracle.com/technetwork/java/javase/downloads/java-archive-downloads-javase6-419409.html
```

You can pull the scrollbar on the right side of the web page down the page, until you see the **Java SE Development Kit 6u45 Download** button, which you can see on the very bottom of Figure 1-1. The first link in the long list of version links is the latest revision of the Java SE JDK Development Kit and since you want to get the latest bug-free version, this is the one you want.

Make sure that you use this **Java SE Development Kit 6u45** download link, and do not use a JRE download link. The JRE is part of the JDK6u45, so you do not have to worry about getting the Java Runtime separately. In case you're wondering, you will indeed use the JRE to launch and run your Eclipse IDE, and you will use the JDK inside of Eclipse to provide the Java core class foundation for the Android OS Java-based API.

Note The JRE is the executable (platform) that runs your Java software once it has been compiled into an application, and thus a JRE will be needed to run Eclipse, because Eclipse is 100% written using Java SE.

Make sure **not** to download a JDK 7u45 or the JDK 7u45 Bundle, which includes NetBeans 7.4 from the normal (non-archived) download page, because Android 4.4 uses JavaSE 6u45 and the Eclipse 4.4 IDE, **not** the NetBeans 7.4 IDE for its ADT plug-ins, so **be very careful** regarding this foundational install step.

I actually use a completely different workstation for Android development, which has Java SE 6u45 and Eclipse 4.4, and have another HTML5 development workstation that has Java SE 8u5 and NetBeans 8.0 (only) installed on it. These will be covered in my upcoming Beginner Java 8 Games Development title from Apress.

2. Once you click on the Java SE Development Kit 6u45 link, you will be taken to the Java SE Development Kit 6u45 Download section of this page, shown in Figure 1-2, where you will be able to select the OS you are using.

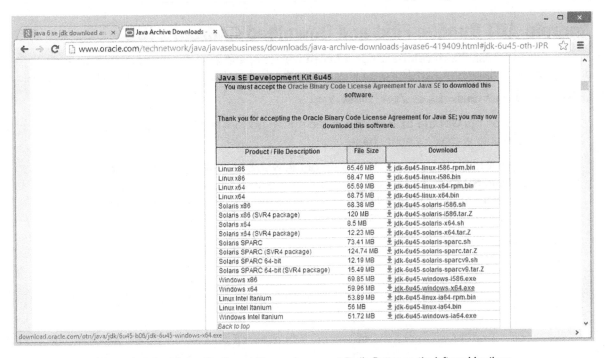

Figure 1-2. Java SE u45 download links after Accept License Agreement Radio Button on the left enables them

3. I am using what is described in these links as "**Windows x64**," which is the 64-bit version of Windows, for my Windows 7 and Windows 8.1 workstations. Once you click on an **Accept License Agreement** radio button on the **top-left** of this download links table, the links will become **bolded** and you will be able to click on the link for the OS version that you need to use.

If you're on Windows and your OS is 64-bit, you would use the **Windows x64** link; otherwise, you would use the **Windows x86** link. To find out what level of bit-depth your Windows OS is running at, open the **Start** menu, right-click on the **Computer** option, and select the **Properties** menu option. This will tell you all about your computer's hardware, including if it is using a 32-bit or 64-bit CPU and OS. Optimally, your workstation should match the bit-depth of the CPU with the bit-depth of the OS.

4.   Once the installation executable has downloaded, open it, and install the latest Java SE 6u45 JDK on your system by **double-clicking** on the **EXE** file.

Remember that the reason that we did not download the JRE is because it is part of this JDK installation.

Once Java 6u45 (or later) JDK is installed on your workstation, you can then download and install the **Android ADT Bundle** from the **developer.android.com** web site. You can also use that same Add or Remove Programs utility in your Control Panel that you just used to remove older Java versions to confirm the success of the new Java installation, and to remove any older versions of any Android development environments that might be currently installed on this Android development workstation that we're going to be assembling from scratch during the remainder of this chapter. Let's get back to work!

Android ADT Bundle: Find and Download Android's IDE

Now we need to visit the **developer.android.com** web site, and download and install the Android development environment ADT Bundle ZIP file from the /sdk/ folder of the site, at the following URL:

`https://developer.android.com/sdk/index.html`

1.   Click on the **Get the SDK** button found on the bottom left of the Android developer web site's home page.

2.   This will take you to the SDK section of the web site, which says "**Get the Android SDK**" at the top as shown in Figure 1-3, along with my Google search term: Android SDK (see top left browser tab), which is another way to find the Android developer SDK page!

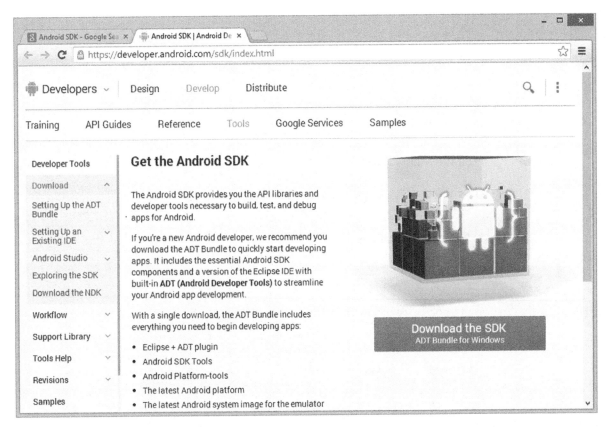

Figure 1-3. The `https://developer.android.com/sdk` *web site page and the Download the SDK - ADT Bundle button*

5. Once you are on the **Get the Android SDK** page, click on the big blue **Download the SDK** button on the middle-right to download an **ADT Bundle for Windows**, as shown in Figure 1-3. This will take you to the actual download page.

The actual SDK ADT Bundle download page, shown in Figure 1-4, contains a section at the top for the **end user licensing agreement (EULA)** specific to the **Android Software Development Kit**, as well as selections for either the **32-bit** or the **64-bit** IDE Android software bundle download.

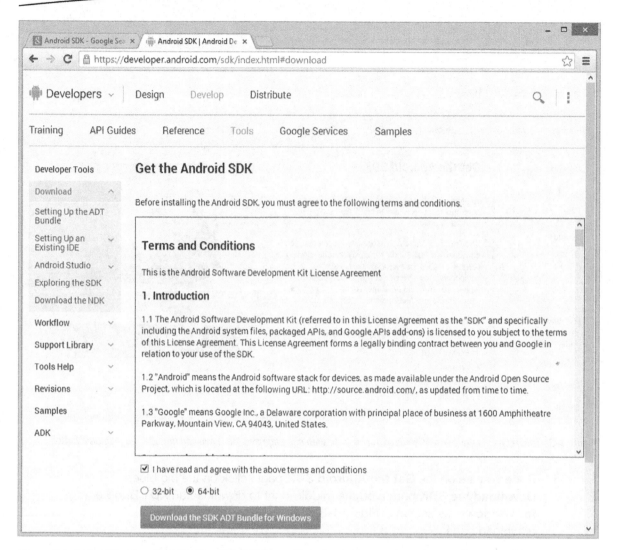

Figure 1-4. Android Developer site Download the SDK page where you click on the Download the SDK ADT Bundle button

6. Review the "**Terms and Conditions**" section of this web page carefully, along with your legal department, if necessary, and then click the check box next to the statement at the bottom that reads: **I have read and agree with the above terms and conditions**, as you can see in Figure 1-4. Once you have done this, the rest of your download options will become active (not ghosted) and you will be ready to specify which version of the Android ADT Bundle for Windows that you need.

I recommend using the 64-bit IDE on 64-bit Windows OSs and the 32-bit IDE on 32-bit Windows OSs. Hopefully, you will have a 64-bit OS that can access 4GB memory or even more (8GB or 16GB of memory). If you forgot how to find out at which bit-depth your OS is running, right-click on

My Computer" on the OS **Start menu**, and select the **Properties** menu option. This will reveal a multi-tab dialog containing all of your OS specifications.

7.   Once this check box has been activated (checked), you should now be able to select either the 32-bit or the 64-bit version of this ADT Bundle, which is essentially an Eclipse ADT 4.4 **ZIP format** software installation package that contains an Eclipse IDE with the Android ADT plug-ins pre-configured.

If you downloaded the Java 6u45 JDK for Windows x64 or Linux x64, you would select the 64-bit version; conversely, if you selected Java 6u45 for an x86 OS, you would select the 32-bit version of this SDK ADT bundle of software.

8.   Once this selection has been made, the actual **Download the SDK ADT Bundle** blue button will be activated and you may click on it to begin a download.

Once this download is complete, we'll **unZIP** the files in a development directory that will set up the Android OS and development environment (IDE) for use on your Android development workstation, which you will be creating during this chapter and then configuring for use during the next chapter.

PAST INSTALLATION

Before this Android ADT "Bundle" became available in Version 4, setting up this Android IDE was a complicated and involved process, taking some 50 or more steps, including installing Java SDK, then Android SDKs, then Android Plug-Ins, then configuring the Plug-Ins to "see" the Android SDK.

If you are familiar with the first or second edition of this *Android Apps for Absolute Beginners* title, you are already familiar with what used to be required to get a working Android development environment installed on your development workstation.

This new bundling approach accomplishes all of the Android SDK and plug-in configurations by including the Eclipse IDE, along with all of the Android SDK and plug-in components, in one single pre-configured "bundle."

This allows all the configuration work to be done in advance by the people at Google who work on the Android team, instead of by developers at home.

Install the Android ADT Bundle: Extract Android ADT IDE

1.   The first thing that you will need to do once your download is complete is to find the file that you just downloaded. It should be in your OS **Downloads** folder, or in my case, I specified my **Software** folder for the download, since I use a USB key to hold my open source software files.

If you don't know where your browser put your file when you downloaded it, you can also right-click on your downloaded file, located in the browser's **download progress** window, and select the **View in Folder** option. A download progress tab is generally located at the bottom "status bar" area for your browser, or accessible via a **download menu option**, or an icon in the upper right of the browser (usually three black bars/stripes indicating a menu).

Once you locate either the **adt-bundle-windows-x86.zip**, which you would use for 32-bit Windows XP, 32-bit Vista, 32-bit Windows 7, or 32-bit Windows 8, or the **adt-bundle-windows-x86_64.zip,** which you would use for your 64-bit Windows Vista, 64-bit Windows 7, or 64-bit Windows 8, you will then **extract** the contents of this ZIP file format into a folder on your hard drive.

9. **The ZIP** file should be located in your Downloads folder, unless you have specified a different folder during the download process. Once you find the ZIP file, **right-click** on it, and select the **Extract All...** option from the context-sensitive menu, as is shown in Figure 1-5.

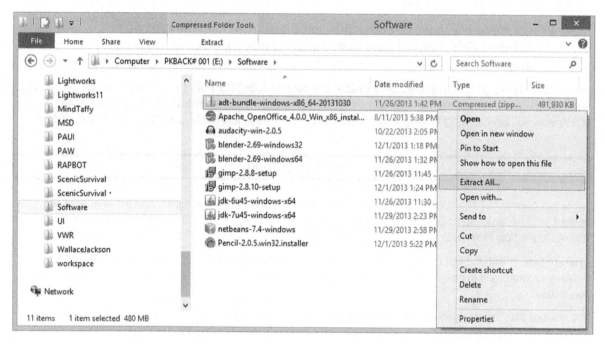

Figure 1-5. Right-click on adt-bundle-windows-x86_64-20131030.zip file and select the Extract All... menu option

10. In the **Select a Destination and Extract Files** dialog shown in Figure 1-6, place your cursor before the adt-bundle-windows part of the file name and then backspace over the Downloads folder, or in my case a Software folder. We're doing this because we don't want to locate a development environment in our software downloads folder, but rather under the **root** of our primary hard disk drive that is usually designated as **C:** and thus, the resulting install path is **C:\adt-bundle-windows-x86** or **C:\adt-bundle-windows-x86_64**, shown in Figure 1-7. Once your install folder is specified, click **Extract**.

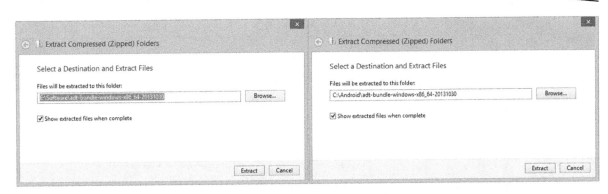

Figure 1-6. *Edit the Target Installation Extraction Folder to place the subfolder into the C:\Android\ HDD folder*

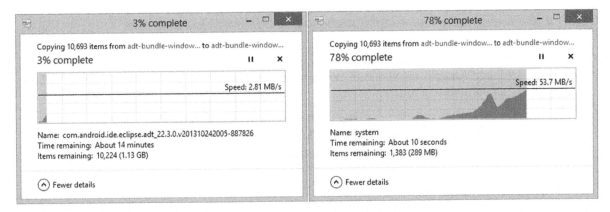

Figure 1-7. *Detailed progress bar showing installation in Windows 8.1 using More Details option at 3% and 78%*

Once you click the Extract button, you will get a **progress dialog**, as seen in Figure 1-7, showing the archived files being extracted into 1GB of data, spanning some 10,693 items, into dozens of folders and sub-folders.

Once everything is extracted, which may take a little while depending upon the data access (and write) speed of your hard disk drive and the computer processor speed, we'll be ready to create a **shortcut** for Eclipse.

11. Once this extraction process is complete, open your OS file management utility; for Windows 8.1, this is called **Windows Explorer**, and is shown in use in Figure 1-8, with the Android 4.4 ADT Bundle showing as extracted next to the older Android 4.2.2 installation I used for my *Pro Android Graphic* and *Pro Android UI* book titles that I wrote back in 2013.

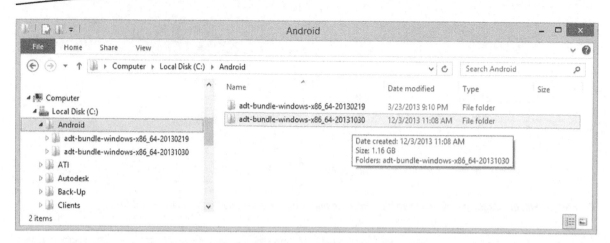

Figure 1-8. *An adt-bundle-windows-x86_64-20131030 folder (Android 4.4) next to the Android 4.2 folder*

It is important to note, as seen in Figure 1-8, that you can install more than one Eclipse ADT. Shown are Android 4.2.2 and Android 4.4 versions, so if I need to, I can launch a previous version of Eclipse ADT by using that **eclipse.exe** application to launch that (subdirectory) OS configuration.

12.   Next, you need to locate your latest **adt-bundle-windows-x86_64** folder, as shown in Figure 1-9, on your **C:\Android** hard disk drive path in the left side of the File Explorer, inside of your hard disk drive navigation pane.

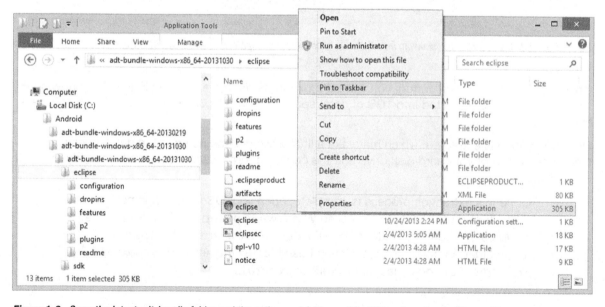

Figure 1-9. *Open the latest adt-bundle folder and the eclipse subfolder and find the eclipse Application and Icon*

13. Find your **eclipse** folder (it will be located under your **adt-bundle-windows** folder) and then click on it. This will show the **contents** (files and sub-folders) for this particular folder, in your **file management pane**, on the right-hand side of the File Explorer.

14. Find the **eclipse.exe** program **executable** file; it will have a **purple sphere** icon, as shown in Figure 1-9. Right-click on this eclipse executable file, and select the **Pin to Taskbar** option from the context-sensitive menu, which is always accessible via a right-click.

Once you select the **Pin to Taskbar** option, a **single-click** Eclipse software launch icon will be installed on the OS Taskbar, so that you can quickly and easily launch the Eclipse ADT software anytime you want to develop Android applications. Figure 1-10 shows your Eclipse quick launch application icon, along with some of the other applications that you will be installing later on in the chapter, and some useful OS system utilities that developers should have easy access to via these quick launch icons.

Figure 1-10. Taskbar with Quick Launch Icons for Eclipse, Pencil, Audacity, Blender, GIMP, Notepad, Calculator and Character Map

It is important to note that we did not need to install shortcuts for Java 6u45, as the JDK that we installed exists underneath the other application development tools. Java is a development environment infrastructure and is not directly accessed or run like Eclipse ADT or the other new media software development tools that we'll be installing next.

We'll be creating launch icon shortcuts for these tools as well on our OS Taskbar so that we can quickly and easily launch them at a moment's notice!

Let's install your digital image compositing and editing software package next. The current version of **the GIMP** (Graphic Image Manipulation Program) is 2.8.10 and it provides most of the primary features of Adobe Photoshop. GIMP 3.0 is expected out any day now, so if you are lucky, you will be installing the powerful new GIMP 3.0 for your content development workstation!

Digital Image Compositing Software: the GIMP

We will be using GIMP in the book to manipulate digital image assets that will be used for application icons and user interface elements as well as frame based animation. GIMP is a truly amazing piece of software.

As you can see in Figure 1-11, you can either enter "GIMP" into the Google search bar as is shown in the left browser tab, or you can type in the following URL for the web site:

`http://www.gimp.org/`

When the GIMP home page appears, you will see an orange **Download** button and a yellow **Downloads** link on the top-right of the page. You will click on either one of these to access the GIMP 2.8.10 /downloads/ page.

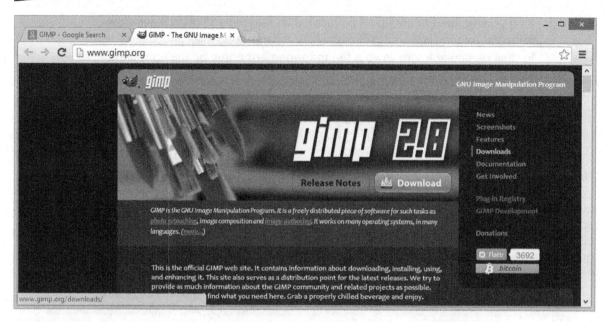

Figure 1-11. Go to the gimp.org web site and click on the orange Download button or on the Downloads link

Note   Until recently, GIMP was hosted on SourceForge, but the company made the decision to self-host on their HTTP servers, due to some activity regarding advertiser opt-ins that the creators of the GIMP didn't support.

As you can see in Figure 1-12, you can download GIMP via the GIMP 2.8.10 HTTP server, using this downloads page.

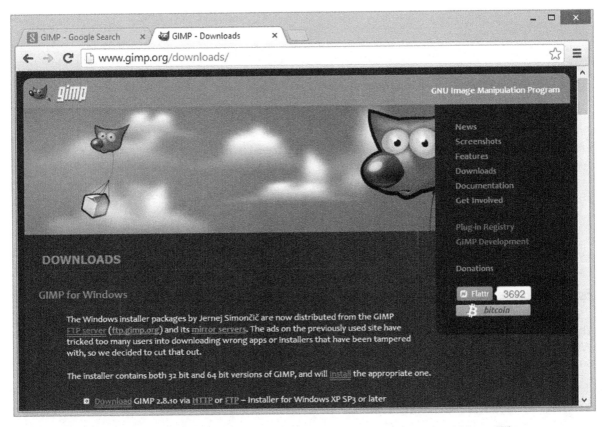

Figure 1-12. Click an HTTP link to download GIMP 2.8.10 from an HTTP server or FTP to download from an FTP

15. Once the download is complete, launch the installer EXE, which is actually visible in Figure 1-5, and should be named **gimp-2.8.10-setup.exe**, unless a later version has become available (version 3.0 is expected out in 2014).

3D Modeling, Rendering, and Animation: Blender 3D

3D modeling, rendering, and animation software is a valuable tool for a number of things that are included in Android, from application icons to digital imagery to frame-based animation to OpenGL real-time 3D rendering.

Next, let's go get one of the most popular open source software packages in the world, the Blender 3D modeling, 3D rendering, and 3D animation software package, which can be found on the Blender web site, at the following URL:

`http://www.blender.org/`

As you can see in Figure 1-13, there is also a blue **Download Blender 2.69** button on the Blender.org home page, which will also take you to a Blender download page, where you can select a 32-bit or 64-bit version of Blender for Windows. Blender is also available for Linux, Mac, Unix, and Solaris.

Figure 1-13. The Blender.org home page, where you can click on the blue Download Blender 2.69 button

This site will **auto-detect** the OS version that you are currently running, and since I am running Windows 8, you will see in Figure 1-14 that Blender for Windows is shown in the dark blue primary software download area.

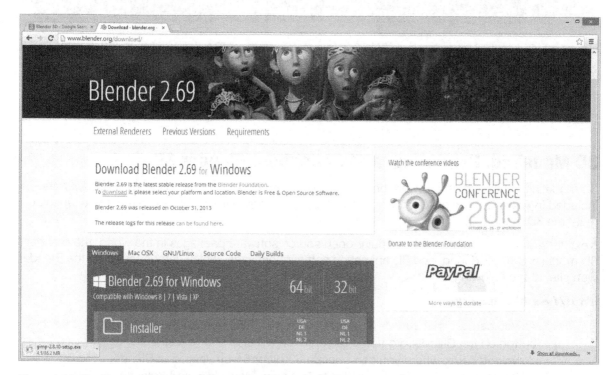

Figure 1-14. The Blender.org/download/ page and auto-detect of the Windows OS, and 64-bit and 32-bit options

Since I have new media content production workstations running Windows XP (32-bit), Windows Vista (32-bit), Windows 7 (64-bit), and recently Windows 8.1 (64-bit), I have downloaded both of these versions of Blender, as you can see if you look back at the screen shot in Figure 1-5.

16. Click on the version (the OS bit-level) that matches your OS configuration (32-bit or 64-bit) and then download the appropriate version of Blender 3D for your type of OS and your OS and hardware bit level.

17. Once your download is completed, launch the installer EXE, which should be named **blender-2.69-windows32.exe** or **blender-2.69-windows64.exe**, unless the later revision has become available (version 2.7 is expected out in 2014).

Open source allows designers to put together fully loaded media production workstations for all of their employees, as long as they can afford the cost of the hexa-core or octa-core workstation hardware itself, which can range from $650 to $850 each, depending on features and quantity purchased.

What this means is that putting together an Android development company is now affordable, at least from the Android content production workstation perspective, thanks to now mature and professional open source software packages such as the ones we're downloading and installing in this chapter.

18. Once your installation is complete, right-click on the icon, or executable file and select the **Pin to Taskbar** option to create the quick launch icon shortcut for the Blender 3D software.

UI Design and Wireframing Software: Pencil Project

Next, you will download and install a user interface (UI) wireframing and prototyping tool called Pencil, which is currently at revision 2.0.5. You can use this software to prototype UI designs for your Android apps.

Do a Google search for Pencil, or go directly to the following URL, as is shown in Figure 1-15:

http://pencil.evolus.vn

Figure 1-15. The pencil.evolus.vn home page, where you can click on the orange Download for Windows button

When the Pencil home page appears, click on the orange download button and download the 22MB executable file, which should be named something like **Pencil-2.0.5.win32.installer.exe** (also shown in Figure 1-5).

19. Once the download is complete, launch the installer EXE, and when it is finished, right-click on the icon or executable file and select the **Pin to Taskbar** option to create the quick launch icon shortcut for the software.

Next, we will install your digital audio and engineering software package.

Digital Audio Editing and Engineering: Audacity

The Audacity project is hosted on **sourceforge.net**, an open source software development web site, which you might find extremely interesting to search for software that interests you (if you didn't know about the site already, that is)!

Note   We will be using Audacity later on in the book, to add sound effects to your Android UI element objects, such as your Buttons and ImageButton objects.

To reach the Audacity project, go to the **audacity.sourceforge.net** URL and you will see a **Download Audacity 2.0.5** link, shown in Figure 1-16.

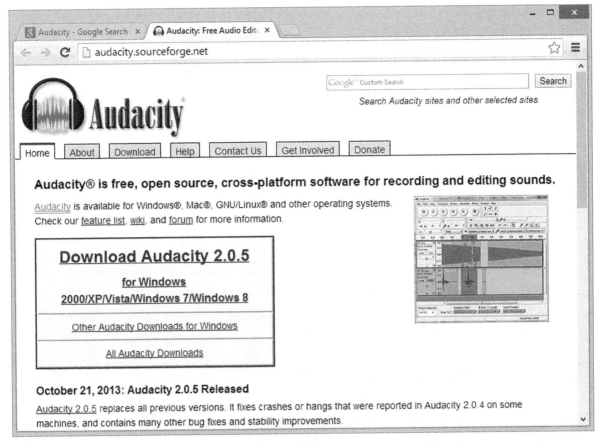

Figure 1-16. The audacity.sourceforge.net home page and Download Audacity 2.0.5 link for Windows OS version

Notice that the 32-bit Audacity supports decades-ancient OSs such as Windows 2000, well over a decade old, and Windows XP, now almost a decade old. I am hoping that you are using either a Windows 7 or a Windows 8 OS for your Android development workstations, as these two OSs, especially Windows 8, are almost as memory-efficient now as Linux is.

20. Once your Audacity installer file has been downloaded, you can launch it, and proceed to install this feature-filled digital audio editing software. The first thing that it will ask you is what language you want to run the software in. I selected the default, English.

21. Then I clicked the Next button and read the information given and then I clicked the Next button again, accepted a default installation location, and created the desktop icon, using an option in the next dialog.

22. Finally, I clicked on the **Install** button, and got the **Installing** progress bar dialog, as well as more information regarding the open source Audacity project, and a final dialog where I could click on the **Finish** button to exit the installer software.

Now that Audacity 2.0.5 is installed, you can launch the audio production software and make sure that it's working on your system.

If you like, you can follow the same work process that we did with Eclipse and place a quick launch shortcut icon on your Taskbar by right-clicking on the Audacity 2.0 icon and selecting Pin to Taskbar. You can reposition launch icons by dragging them into any position you prefer on the Taskbar.

23.   Launch Audacity via your quick launch icon, or by double-clicking the icon on your desktop or in your Windows Explorer utility. You should see a new blank project screen, as shown in Figure 1-17, open up on your desktop.

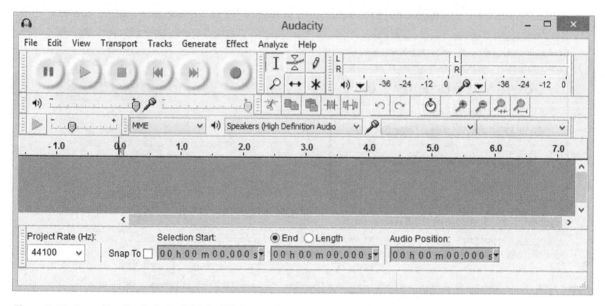

Figure 1-17. Launching the Audacity 2.0.5 for Windows software to make sure that it will run on your system

Next, let's go and download the leading open source digital video software package, EditShare Lightworks 11.5, which is available for Windows, Linux, and Macintosh, in both 32-bit and 64-bit versions.

Professional Digital Video Editing: EditShare Lightworks

EditShare Lightworks used to be an expensive digital video editing and special effects software, and to this day, it competes "head-to-head" with leading digital video editing packages (FinalCut Pro X and After Effects). Digital video editing software is useful for Android development, as the video formats it supports are also integrated into the Android OS.

You can find out more about this leading digital video editing FX software package on the EditShare web site at: www.editshare.com, or the Lightworks web site at: www.lwks.com, where you can also sign up to get a copy of the software and then download it. The home page is shown in Figure 1-18.

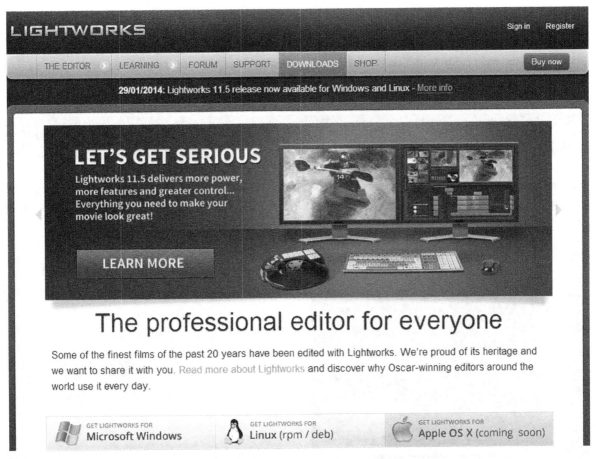

Figure 1-18. Go to the lwks.com web site, sign-in or register, and then click on the Downloads link at the top

When EditShare made Lightworks open source, it became the second free open source software (the first was Blender 3D) to be able to compete "feature-for-feature" with commercial software packages in its new media production genre (digital video editing, compositing, special effects, and compression).

> Once you register on the Lightworks web site, you will be able to create a video editor profile for your company and log in to be able to download a copy of Lightworks 11.5 for your content development workstation that you are putting together in this chapter. Since Lightworks is such a valuable piece of software, you need to register to get it, which is fine with me, given that this software used to have a four-figure price tag.

24. Once you are signed-up as a proud Lightworks 11.5 user, you will click on the **Downloads** button, located at the top-right of the site menu, and you will see all of the different versions and documentation for the software.

As you can see in Figure 1-19, you will have to again ascertain if you have a 64-bit OS or an older 32-bit OS, so that you can download the version of this video editing software that matches with your bit level capabilities of the workstation that you just purchased to do Android development. I'm hoping (for your sake) that it is a quad-core, hexa-core or octa-core with 64-bit modern-day specifications.

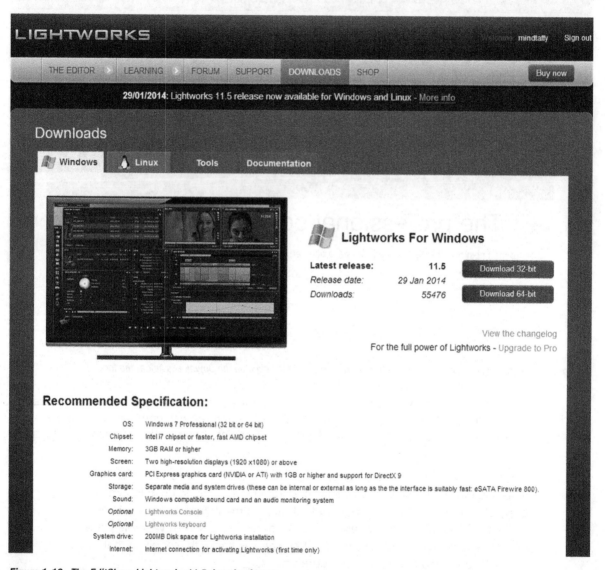

Figure 1-19. The EditShare Lightworks 11.5 download page

25. Click on the **Download 64-bit** button to initiate the download of the 64-bit OS version installation software, or the Download 32-bit button to get the 32-bit version of the video software installation executable (EXE) file.

26. Once you've downloaded an installer, install it using the default settings and create a quick launch icon for it. Run Lightworks to assure it's set up properly on your system, as you have done with your other new software.

Congratulations, you've assembled a professional-grade Android Application and New Media Content Development Workstation! You can now use your newest software development weapon to create Android UI designs, and develop user experiences as yet unseen. I hope you are excited, because I am!

Even though you've installed all of this amazing software and set up quick launch shortcuts for your future ease (speed) of development usage, you'll still need to configure Eclipse ADT for use and set up AVD Android Virtual Device emulators, which we'll be covering in the next chapter of the book.

Just to be thorough, let's install a business productivity software suite! We will do this just in case you need to assemble quotes, spreadsheets, and contracts for all of your future Android OS software development projects.

A Complete Business Software Suite: Apache OpenOffice

To make 100% sure that your Android development workstation has everything installed that you will need for your Android development business, let's finish off this run of professional software installation with yet another package originally from Oracle, the makers of Java, called **Open Office 4.1**.

Do a Google search for OpenOffice or go to the www.openoffice.org web site, as shown in Figure 1-20.

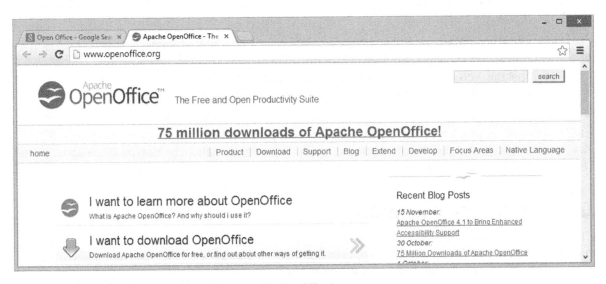

Figure 1-20. The OpenOffice 4.0 downloads button on the OpenOffice home page

Click on the **I want to download OpenOffice** link, to go to the OpenOffice 4.1 download page.

27. Once you are on the /download/ page, shown in Figure 1-21, click the green area to download the most recent version of the office suite for your OS.

Figure 1-21. The www.openoffice.org/download/ *page, where you can download OpenOffice 4.0.1 for Windows*

In my case, this was Windows 8.1, which the site auto-detected for me. This download is almost 140MB, and includes more than half a dozen productivity software packages, including a word processor, spreadsheet software, presentation software, drawing software, an equation editor, and a database engine.

28.   Once you have downloaded the OpenOffice 4.1 EXE installer, install it using the default settings, and then create the quick launch icon for it on your Taskbar. You should run OpenOffice 4.1 to assure it's set up properly on your system, as you have done before with your other new software acquisitions.

You have now set up a complete Android development and production business workstation, and can accomplish any task that may be required of you by a client! You can draw up contracts, edit digital video or digital audio, do 3D modeling, rendering, and animation, prototype UI designs, create digital image compositing pipelines, and of course, create Android applications!

Other Open Source Software

There are lots of other open source software packages that are available if you want to download and install them. Popular open source repositories include SourceForge.Net, GitHub, and Code. Google.Com if you want to go pan for open source gold.

Some of these other open source packages in the 3D software genre include: SketchUp (architectural rendering), TerraGen 3.1 (virtual world creation), Microsoft TrueSpace (3D), Wings 3D, Bishop 3D, POV Ray 3.7 (3D Rendering), and DAZ Studio 4.6 (Character Modeling).

There are also some very affordable 3D software packages, which you should take a look at as well, including NeverCenter SILO 2.2 (Quad 3D Modeling), Moment of Inspiration 3D 3.0 (NURBs 3D Modeling), TerraGen Pro and Bryce 7 (3D world generation), Hexagon 2.5 (Polygon 3D Modeling), and Auto-Des-Sys Bonzai (3D Modeling, all 3D modeling paradigms are supported).

In audio composition, production, and engineering areas, impressive packages include: Rosegarden (Music Composition, MIDI, Scoring) and Qtractor (Sound Design). The list of amazing open source software just goes on and on!

Summary

In this first chapter, you learned about Android, and acquired the software you'll need to be able to create a comprehensive Android application development workstation, which we will be configuring in the next chapter.

From Java SE 6, to Eclipse, to new media content production software, to UI prototyping to business productivity tools, you downloaded and then installed the most impressive open source software packages that can be found anywhere on this planet.

We did this to create a foundation for the Android application development work process that we will be undertaking throughout this book, and rather than install these software packages as we go along, I made the decision to get all of our readers set up with this amazing software right off the bat!

I did this in case you wanted to explore some of the many features of these powerful, exciting new media content production software packages before you actually use them during this book. I think that's only fair.

The best thing about the process was that we accomplished it by using open source, 100% free for commercial usage and professional-level application software packages, which is pretty darned amazing, if you think about it.

We started by downloading and installing Oracle's **Java SE 6u45 JDK** or **Java Development Kit**, which is the Java 6 Programming Language's SDK. This Java JDK is required to use Eclipse, as well as to develop application software for the Android OS for consumer electronic devices.

We then visited the **Android Developer** web site and downloaded and installed the **ADT Bundle**, which built an **IDE** and **Android Developer Tools** plug-ins on top of our Java SE 6u45 JDK programming software development environment.

Next, we downloaded and installed **GIMP 2.8.10**, your powerful digital image editing package, which is available for Windows, Linux, and Macintosh OSs.

Next, we downloaded and installed **Blender 2.69** a professional 3D modeling, rendering, and animation tool, available for Windows, Linux, and Mac OSs.

Next, we downloaded and installed **Pencil 2.0.5**, the popular UI wireframing and prototyping tool, which is available for Windows, Linux, and Mac OSs.

Next, we downloaded and installed **Audacity 2.0.5**, the open source, digital audio content editing tool, available for the Windows, Linux, and Mac OSs.

Next, we downloaded and installed **Lightworks 11.5,** a digital video editing and special effects package that was recently released as open source and is currently available as of 2014 for the Windows, Linux, and Macintosh OSs.

Finally, we installed Apache **Open Office 4.1**, just to make sure that you have a completely well-rounded open source Android development workstation at your disposal. Remember, your Android development business will require that you use a business productivity software package as well, so we cover all of the bases by finishing up with this Oracle business software suite.

In the next chapter, you will learn exactly how to set-up an Android workstation and how to create an **AVD emulator** for the Google Nexus Android device. We will also learn more about Android as well as review what will be covered during the course of this book.

Chapter 2

Configuring Your Android App Development System

Now that you have an Android development workstation assembled, with those valuable (but free), professional-level, open source packages installed on it, it is time to configure the Eclipse Android 4.4 Development Tools (ADT) integrated development environment (IDE) for what you will be doing over the course of this book. Eclipse now works "out of the box" thanks to the ADT bundle, a vast improvement over having to "wire" the Android SDK to Eclipse using plug-ins.

There are still a number of things that I want to teach you about in this chapter, however, regarding how to keep the Eclipse ADT up-to-date and create and install Android Virtual Device (AVD) emulators. Additionally, you'll get a tour of what is installed as a part of the "default" or initial ADT installation and how to install other Application Programming Interfaces (APIs), and other non-standard capabilities, such as Google Cloud Services of one type or another, for instance.

> **Note** You will be learning specifically about what an API is as well as about packages, classes, methods, and interfaces in Chapter 5, when we cover Java programming concepts and terminology in detail.

You've already configured your open source, new media content production software by installing the latest updates and creating a quick launch icon on your Taskbar, which was relatively easy. After we go over how to update, configure, and fine-tune Eclipse, I'm going to give you an overview of what you will be learning during the remainder of this book, so you have an overview of what you'll be learning in Chapters 3 through 17, and how it will all fit together. I'll make sure that the content gets more advanced with each subsequent chapter of the book; by the end, you will be well-versed in Android!

Updating Eclipse ADT: Check For Updates!

This is a simple work process, which is actually similar across many advanced software packages, so you may have seen what we are about to do before. There is a "Check for Updates" work process for making sure that you have the latest version of your operating system (OS), production, or development software. In fact, if you go into your Windows 8.1 Control Panel, you will see a Windows Updates icon at the very bottom that performs this exact same function. You can configure this to be automatic or you can run it manually, as we are about to do here, with your Eclipse ADT IDE.

Since we're focusing on Android's IDE in this chapter, we'll be doing this inside of Eclipse, so you can make sure that you are running the very latest version of your ADT IDE, including all of its many components. You'll always want to run the Check for Updates utility right after you install your Eclipse ADT software, and at least weekly thereafter.

This is the reason we are covering this here first, as this is a continuation of all of the installation work that you did in Chapter 1. If you have not done this already, out of sheer curiosity, launch Eclipse ADT using a single mouse-click on the Eclipse (purple sphere) quick launch icon, which you created in the previous chapter. Each time that you launch Eclipse ADT, you will be presented with the **Select a workspace** option, inside a **Workspace Launcher** dialog, right after you see your **Android Developer Tools** launch progress screen. Both of these are shown in Figure 2-1.

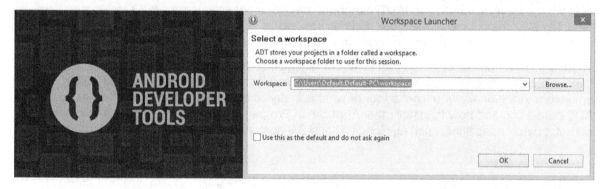

Figure 2-1. The Android Developer Tools launch progress (left) and Workspace Launcher dialog (right) on launch

You will probably accept the default **workspace** folder location for your Android project, although you don't have to, if you have another folder that you would prefer to use for your Android project.

I use the ADT suggested workspace folder, which is located under my operating system supplied **C:\Users** folder, and under my system-name sub-folder, which on my AMD octa-core workstation is named **Default.Default-PC**, a default (how can you tell?) folder name created by Windows 8, that I, to this day, remain too lazy to change! I should have named the book *Lazy Android Development*.

After you select (and thus set) the Workspace location, Eclipse will then open up with an introductory **Welcome!** screen, actually a tab, as shown in Figure 2-2. Click the close tab icon (or X) for now, it is located in the right side of the tab, and let's proceed to open a blank (empty) instance of the Eclipse ADT IDE.

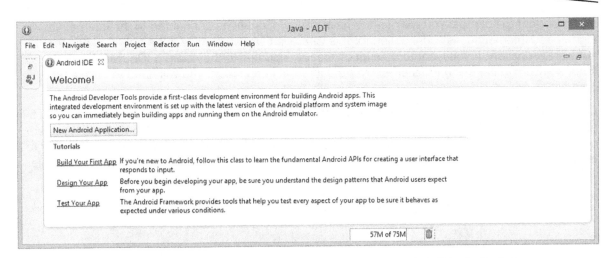

Figure 2-2. ADT's Welcome! Initial start-up screen, with shortcuts to tutorials and New Android Application button

The Eclipse IDE will open up the first time that you start it with no project open, and thus will not show any project data at all, just the blank IDE, as shown in Figure 2-3. Once we start creating projects, which we will be doing in the next chapter, these projects will "persist" inside of Eclipse, so that every time you launch the Eclipse ADT, you will see your current Android project exactly as you left it the last time you exited the Eclipse ADT IDE.

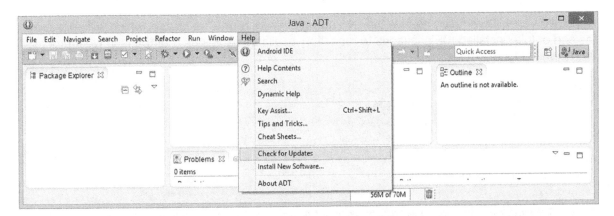

Figure 2-3. The Eclipse Java - ADT IDE on initial launch, showing no project data, and showing Help ➤ Check for Updates

Let's go ahead and perform the Check for Updates work process now. To do this, click the **Help** menu, as shown in Figure 2-3, and then select the **Check for Updates** menu option. Once this Check for Updates utility has been launched, Eclipse will reach out over the Internet to the server at Google that hosts the ADT **software repository**, and will then proceed to check your currently installed Eclipse ADT component versions against the latest versions that "live" on this Android Eclipse ADT IDE software repository. We will be getting into what exactly a software repository is and how it works in the next section when we access it using the Android SDK Manager software repository tool.

It is important to note that you will need to have your workstations connected to the Internet via high-speed Internet access connection for this Check for Updates utility to be able to reach the software repository. If you want to do a lot of "heavy" updates to the Android IDE, which entail a lot of software (data) being transferred over the Internet connection, you will need to have a fast connection speed.

Once you click on this Check for Updates menu command, a progress bar will appear, which will tell you what packages Eclipse ADT IDE is looking at, or comparing your current IDE against. If you are on a fast Internet connection and a fast workstation, you may have to be a speed reader in order to read fast enough as these blaze by! The dialog is shown in Figure 2-4, fetching the **content.jar** file.

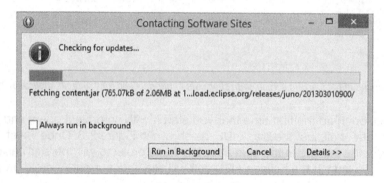

Figure 2-4. Contacting Software Sites dialog checking for updates

Hopefully, you will eventually receive the "**No updates were found**" message, which will appear at the end of this "installed IDE packages to repository available packages" comparison work process, as shown in Figure 2-5.

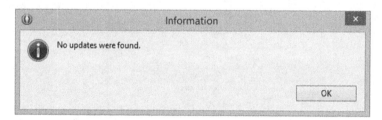

Figure 2-5. Information dialog showing that No updates were found

If for some reason new versions of any of the Android software components are available, you will be advised, and then asked to accept the licensing agreements so that you can install the new software.

After the updating process is accomplished, you can then proceed to take a gander at exactly what API components have been installed as part of the "ADT Bundle" Eclipse IDE that you installed in the previous chapter as well as in this chapter (if any updates were found, that is).

You're going to look at your **Android API installation** using the Android SDK Manager Tool next, so that you become more familiar with that tool and with your currently installed ADT utilities and Android SDK components such as APIs and documentation and emulation utilities.

Configuring Eclipse: Android SDK Manager Repository

Now that you've ascertained that you have the very latest Eclipse ADT IDE software possible installed on your Android development workstation, we can take a look at exactly what is installed, as well as options for other APIs, and things like documentation, which you can download to your Eclipse ADT environment from the Android Repository. You can do this conveniently from inside the Eclipse IDE.

A software repository is a specialized server hierarchy (folder structure across one or more servers) that is maintained by the software provider. In this case, that would be Google, and their Eclipse ADT IDE, which is customized specifically to (for) their Android OS software development kit (SDK) environment and everything that is compatible with it, such as plug-ins, documentation, emulators, hardware drivers, and similar things that would be used to enhance and support the Android OS.

This software repository is different from the download environments that you normally encounter, in as much that you cannot access it externally, using an FTP or HTTP, as you did with GIMP 2.8.10 or Blender 3D, for instance, in the previous chapter. Instead, the software repository will be accessed "internally" from within the IDE (or the OS environment, via its update utility) that you are working in.

Those of you who use a Linux OS are already familiar with this repository concept, as this exact same repository access functionality is an integral part of all the popular Linux OS distributions, or "distros." This repository methodology is how a Linux OS is upgraded, and how it adds in new OS features and bug-fixes, which is one of the key reasons Linux is perceived as a more complex operating system to work with. Windows also uses a software repository, but does not refer to it as such; instead it "sugar coats" the repository model by hiding it behind the Windows Update "front-end" Control Panel utility.

You are going to observe, and utilize, the software repository access work process here, using your Eclipse ADT IDE through its Android SDK Manager utility, which functions in the same fashion as an OS repository, but with a detailed front-end dialog that we are going to take a look at next.

Go to the **Window** menu, seen at the top of Eclipse, and select the **Android SDK Manager** menu option, as shown in Figure 2-6. This will open an Android SDK Management Tool that allows you to view the current Android development environment, as you should do after any new install, as well as to add features and functions to it, and to update any component that has a new version available.

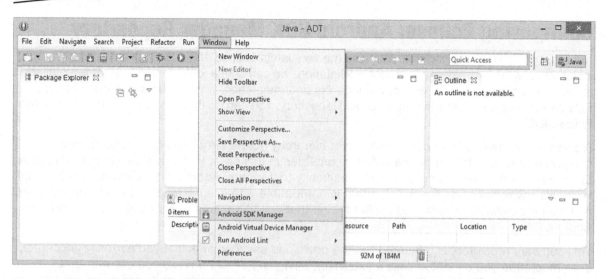

Figure 2-6. Use the Window ➤ Android SDK Manager menu sequence to open up the Android SDK Manager utility dialog

As you can see in Figure 2-7, the Eclipse ADT Bundle 4.4 installed exactly what you need to develop Android 4.4.4 applications, and nothing else. This is exactly what you'll want the ADT Bundle installer to do, and the ADT Bundle did it perfectly. As you can see in Figure 2-7, you have Android 4.4 Level 19 SDK Tools (left dialog, at top), and the Android Support Library (right dialog, in the middle), which provides backward-compatibility support for Android versions that came before OS version 4.4.4.

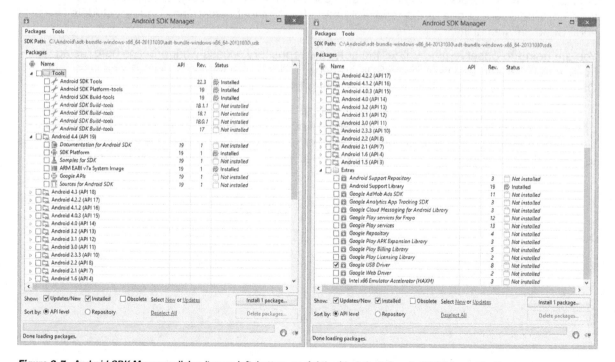

Figure 2-7. Android SDK Manager dialog (top on left, bottom on right) with default Google USB Driver selection

You may also notice on the right in Figure 2-7 that there is a default check mark that Eclipse has selected for you next to the **Google USB Driver**. This driver needs to be updated to a newer version, and to alert you to this, the Android SDK Manager has placed a check mark next to this software utility, in this case, a USB hardware driver. I am going to leave this check mark selected so that you can see the work process for "pulling" an Android component upgrade over to your Eclipse ADT configuration from the Google Android software repository.

You will also use this Android SDK Manager dialog to install any of the extras shown in Figure 2-7, including the latest Android SDK documentation, specialized emulators, earlier Android OS (called API or Level) versions, as well as external Google Cloud function libraries.

Let's do this now, and place your checkmarks in any of the other unchecked boxes next to functions you might need for your Android application. For instance, if you were going to create a messaging application, you would select the Google Cloud Messaging for Android Library option, in addition to the Google USB Driver, which is shown selected in Figure 2-7 on the right side of the screen.

Once you've selected the features you need, beyond the selections that the Android SDK will make for you automatically that it knows that you will need, then click on the **Install** (number selected) packages button.

It is important to note that you should not install any features or Android API libraries that you do not currently need for your currently open Android development project, as these downloads can be quite massive, and these APIs also get updated quite frequently. For this reason, you should download only those features, emulators, system images, and API libraries that you intend to use in the application development environment for the current project.

Later, you can add in older Android version API libraries, but only if and when you will need to utilize them to develop for targeted devices that only run these older versions of Android and need custom development. An example of this is the original Kindle Fire, which runs Android 2.3.7 API Level 10. The Android Support Library may not provide as "tight" a backward-compatibility result as simply using the API Level 10 API to create applications specifically for the Amazon Kindle Fire product line.

Once you click on the **Install 1 package** button, you'll be given the **Choose Packages to Install** dialog, which is shown in Figure 2-8, and which allows you to accept the license terms and conditions so that the Android software repository can (is willing to) install the latest USB driver revision (in this case, it is version 8, but will probably be a later version by the time this book is published).

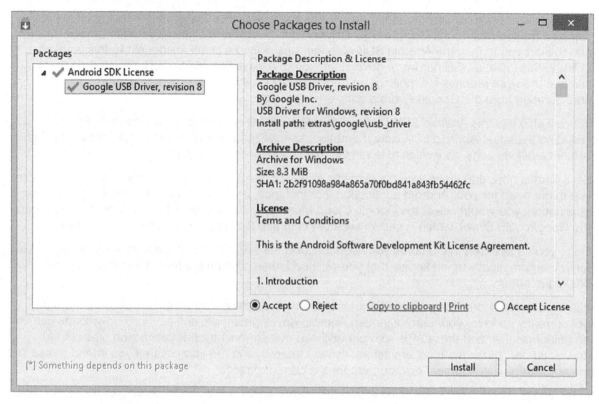

Figure 2-8. The Choose Packages to Install dialog and the Accept License Agreement

Once you click the **Accept** radio button or the **Accept License** radio button, click the **Install** button, and you'll get a progress bar at the bottom of the SDK Manager dialog, as shown in Figure 2-9.

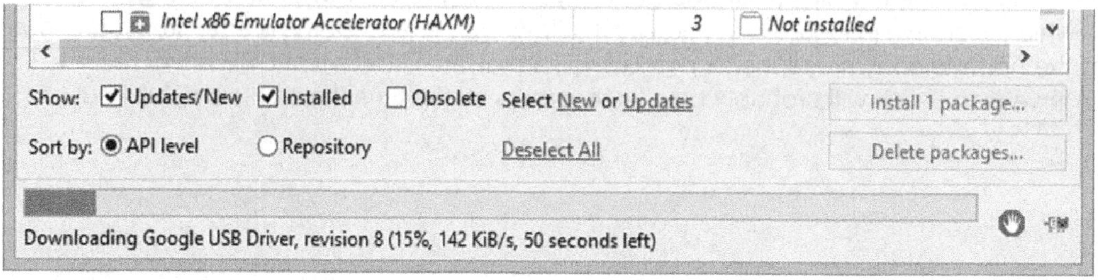

Figure 2-9. A download progress dialog bar located at the bottom of the dialog

Along with this progress bar, there is also information regarding what is currently being downloaded, as well as the percentage completed, what download speed is currently being achieved, and finally, the estimate for the remaining time that is left to completion, as shown in Figure 2-9.

Once your downloads are completed, the bottom of the Android SDK Manager dialog will then show that the Google USB Driver is now installed, along with any of the other Google API libraries that you have selected, the green progress bar will disappear, and you'll receive a **Done loading packages** message, all of which are shown in Figure 2-10.

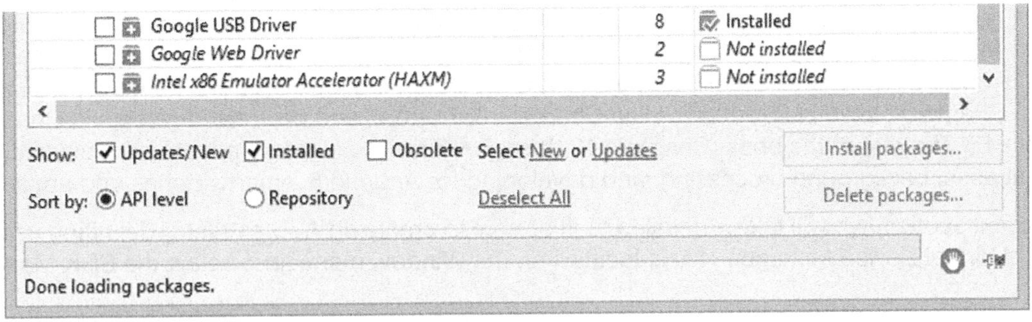

Figure 2-10. The Google USB Driver as installed after progress bar disappears

The next thing that we need to address in optimizing your Eclipse ADT IDE for Android development during the course of this book is creating and installing an AVD. AVDs will be used during the Android software development process to accelerate the development process. The reason an AVD accelerates development is because you don't have to go through the time-consuming process of transferring your application over the USB cable to the Android device every time you want to test!

You can create an AVD to serve as a software emulator for each of the Android hardware products or "devices" that you will be developing for, and need to test your application on. You can also create AVDs for device hardware that you don't own, which makes development and testing more affordable for everyone. Let's learn how to create an AVD and set it up for use in the next section of this chapter.

Android Virtual Devices: Creating the AVD

Eclipse ADT provides developers with a unique hardware emulation capability that speeds up your application development cycle of **design, code, and test**. This is done by allowing you to test your application using an AVD, which is a software emulator for any given Android hardware device (AHD).

If you are developing for the real-world market, you will eventually need to test your applications on all the real-world AHDs that you wish your application to run on. The AHD application testing process, as you might imagine, can quickly become an expensive and time-consuming proposition.

The reason that you don't want to test across these AHDs every time you want to test an upgrade to your app design or code is because that would involve connecting each of these AHDs that you want your application to support to your development workstation via USB, and then uploading a compiled **APK** (Android Package) to the AHD, and then test it using that hardware. You will learn all about the APK format in Chapter 5 when we cover the Java programming language in detail.

An AVD installed in Eclipse shortens this lengthy external device testing process to zero seconds! An AVD does this by allowing you to right-click on your Android app project folder in Eclipse, at any time during your development work process, and selecting the Eclipse **Run As ➤ Android Application** menu command sequence, which is accessed with a right-click on your Android project's root folder.

This work process will automatically compile and transfer your Android application into your currently active Android Virtual Device emulator, which we will be setting up in the next section of this chapter.

This will automatically launch both the AVD emulator as well as your Android application running on that AVD emulator on your workstation's desktop, so that you can test your app's XML markup logic, UI design, new media assets, and your Java programming logic. You will be learning all about XML in Chapter 4, Java in Chapter 5, UI in Chapters 6, 7 and 8, and new media assets in Chapters 9 through 12. The rest of the book (Chapters 13 through 17) will cover more advanced topics, relating to databases, background processing, and developing for Android 5, smartwatches and appliances.

In the next section, we will take a detailed look at how to create an AVD emulator definition using the Android Virtual Device Manager. This is located on the Window menu, just below the SDK Manager.

Creating AVDs: Android Virtual Device Manager

In addition to the Android SDK Manager, the other important menu command, which is also located under the **Window** menu in Eclipse, will access the Android Virtual Device Manager and its collection of dialogs. Access this using the **Window ➤ Android Virtual Device Manager** menu sequence.

This menu sequence, shown in Figure 2-11, will open up a dialog from which you can access several other related dialogs, all of which will be important for you to master as you learn the proper work flow for creating an AVD emulator completely from scratch.

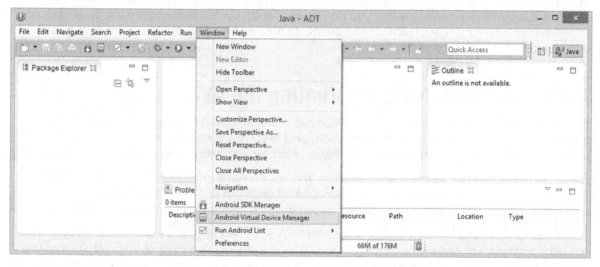

Figure 2-11. Use the Window ➤ Android Virtual Device Manager to launch a collection of dialogs for AVD creation

Once you select this menu sequence, the **Android Virtual Device Manager**, which can be seen in Figure 2-12, will open. As you can see, there is a **New** button to create the new AVD definition, and once this is done, buttons will be enabled to **Edit** (Editing), **Delete** (Removing), **Repair** (Fixing), as well as **Detail** (specifications) and **Start** (launching) the selected AVD. Using the **Refresh** button will update the list if any new AVD definitions have been added since the list was last refreshed.

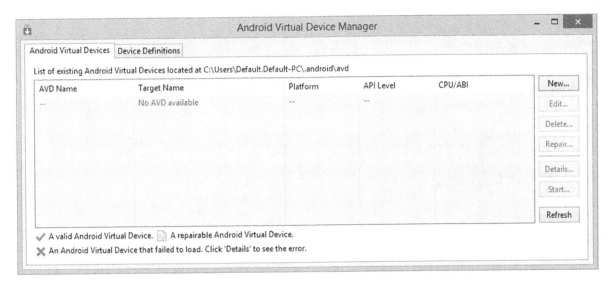

Figure 2-12. The Android Virtual Device Manager dialog before an AVD has been defined

In addition to the seven buttons on the right, there is a second tab at the top of this dialog that will access some preloaded device definitions that come with Eclipse ADT. We will take a look at these next, when we actually create an AVD for our use during this book.

There are two ways to create an AVD in Eclipse ADT, one is to select a "pre-configured" AVD device definition, and the other is to create your AVD "from scratch." We will do both in this chapter, so that you have a complete and thorough overview of exactly what functionality this AVD Manager offers.

Pre-configured (pre-defined) Android device definitions are accessed using the **Device Definitions** tab, shown as the right-hand tab at the top of Figure 2-12, which when clicked will display the currently defined device definitions. If you define your own AHD, which we will be doing soon, it will also be listed here along with the pre-defined AHD definitions that are provided with Eclipse by default. After I show you how to create a Nexus One AVD emulator using one of these existing AHD definitions, I'll then show you how to define your own custom AHD emulation specification from scratch, by using the **New Device** button, shown at the top-right of Figure 2-13.

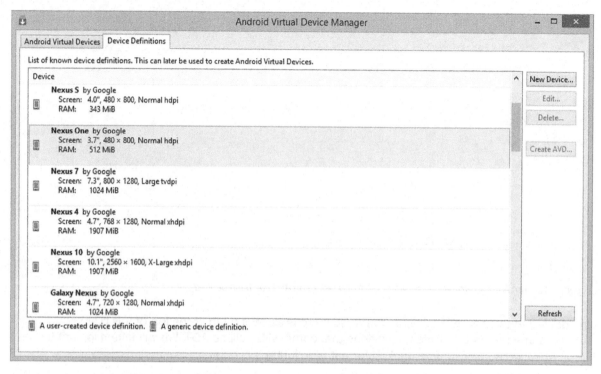

Figure 2-13. The default definitions in the Device Definitions tab, as well as the New Device... button

Creating an AVD from a Pre-configured Device Definition

Six of the pre-configured AHDs are shown in Figure 2-13. It will come as no surprise that many of the device definitions are Google's actual Nexus smartphone or tablet hardware products of one model or another. If you scroll down underneath those (not shown in the figure), you'll see more generic tablet and smartphone hardware device definitions that you can use to emulate general types of devices.

1. Let's click on the Nexus One shown highlighted in Figure 2-13 and enable the Create AVD button shown on the right.

2. Click the **Create AVD** button with this Nexus One AHD selected, and you will get the **Create new Android Virtual Device (AVD)** dialog shown in Figure 2-14.

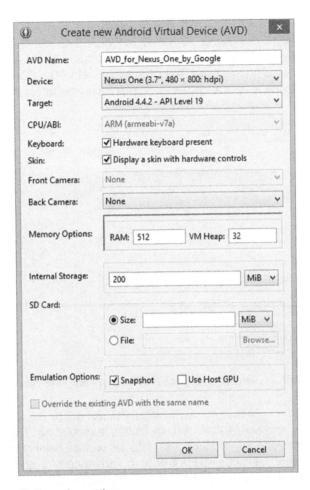

Figure 2-14. Create AVD dialog with Nexus One settings

3. The AVD **Name** and **Device** fields will be filled out for you by Eclipse, so first select the latest OS version as your **Target** using the drop-down selector UI element. This was **Android 4.4.2** at the time of writing this book, which is API Level 19, and is shown selected in Figure 2-14. The current Android 4.4 revision is at 4.4.4 at the time this book's publication.

4. Leave the Keyboard and the Skin options selected, since you have a keyboard and want an emulator skin on your AVD. A "skin" is a customized UI design that mimics the real AHD.

5. In the **Memory Options** areas, leave the default **512** MB of RAM and **32** MB VM (Virtual Memory) Heap and use an **Internal Storage** value of **200** MB. Since we are not using an SD Card, we can leave that blank. Finally, select the **Snapshot Emulation Option** and then click the **OK** Button.

Once you click the OK button, the Create AVD dialog will vanish, and you will see your new AVD in the Android Virtual Device Manager dialog, as shown in Figure 2-15. As you can see, the Android Virtual Device Manager dialog shows you quite a lot of information about each AVD that you might create, including the AVD name (in this case, AVD_for_Nexus_One-By_Google), as well as the Target Android OS version that device is operating under (in this case, the latest Android 4.4.2 API Level 19).

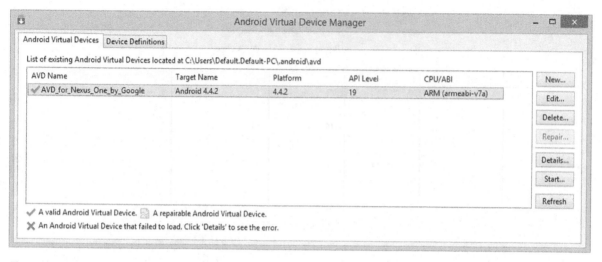

Figure 2-15. The newly created AVD_for_Nexus_One_by_Google AVD emulator with its primary specifications

There is also a column on the right that shows which CPU architecture (such as the Intel Atom, ARM, Cortex, AMD, nVidia, and similar) this AVD definition is emulating. This is because each CPU has a different way of processing instructions and data, as well as having different operating features and performance specifications. Discussion of this is too advanced for an Absolute Beginners title, but a device specification option (column) such as this allows developers to specify which CPU hardware that they are developing their application for, and allows them to emulate this using an AVD definition.

Even though in this book we will be using AVD emulators for more mainstream smartphone and tablet products such as the Nexus products from Google, in order to show you how to use the **New Device** button under the Device Definitions tab, we will need to also take a look at how to define one of these AHD definitions from scratch. We will do this so that we cover absolutely everything that this Android Virtual Device Manager is capable of, and to take a look at how to create an AVD for something really cool such as the Neptune Pine SmartWatch product.

Creating an AVD from Scratch: Pine SmartWatch

The first thing you will need to do in order to create an AHD definition for a Neptune Pine SmartWatch product would be to find out precisely what its technical specifications are. Fortunately, Neptune's Pine web site is very complete, and if you Google "Neptune Pine specifications," as you can see that I did in in the first tab in each screen shot in Figure 2-16, you can learn all about the Neptune Pine. The URL for the Pine Tech-Specs page is as follows:

`http://www.neptunepine/tech-specs.html`

Figure 2-16. Go to the NeptunePine.com web site, and its tech-specs.html page, to get SmartWatch product specifications

This Neptune Pine Technical Specifications Page is one of the most complete and thorough Android device technical specifications pages that I've ever encountered, and a very big thanks (and kudos) to Neptune for this from all of us Android apps developers! As you can see, this Neptune Pine product is nothing short of incredible, with just about every end-user feature that you would want to see in the Android device, especially one that is self-contained and worn on your wrist! Come-in, Dick Tracy!

6.   Open your Android Virtual Device Manager, using the menu sequence shown in Figure 2-11, and then click on your Device Definitions tab, in order to access the **New Device** button, as shown at the top right in Figure 2-13.

7.   Name the device **Neptune Pine SmartWatch**, as you can see in Figure 2-17, on the left side of the **Create New Device** dialog. Next, you would enter the **Screen Size (in)** specification, which is **2.4** inches, and the **Resolution (px)**, which is **320 x 240**.

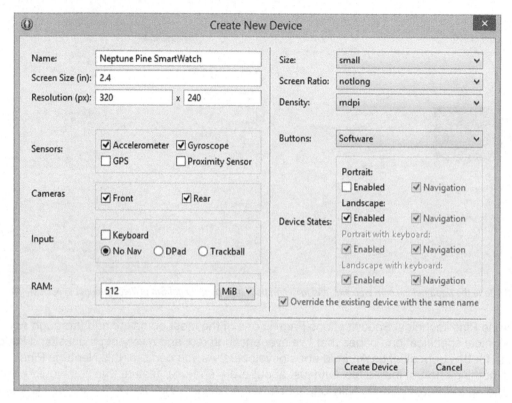

Figure 2-17. Create New Device dialog showing the Neptune Pine SmartWatch specifications

8. Next, you need to specify which **Sensors** the Neptune Pine has; the Pine has a **Gyroscope** and **Accelerometer**, as Figure 2-16 shows, so let's check these two checkboxes in the Sensors section on the left side of the dialog shown in Figure 2-17.

9. Next, you will specify what **Cameras** the Neptune Pine supports, and as you can see in Figure 2-16, on the right side of their web site under Camera, the Neptune Pine has both a front-facing as well as a rear-facing camera, so check both the **Front** and **Rear** check boxes. Even Dick Tracy himself would be proud to own this SmartWatch with these types of advanced features!

10. Since there are no **Input** devices included with the Neptune Pine (unless of course your user adds one, using the advanced Bluetooth 4.0 capability that the Neptune Pine features), you can leave your default **No Nav** radio button selected.

11. As you can see in Figure 2-16, under the Memory section of the Neptune Pine web site, the Neptune Pine SmartWatch product supports 512MB of memory, so enter 512 in the RAM section, and leave the drop-down selector set to MiB, which stands for MegaBytes! Why MiB? The only reason I can think of is that this drop-down uses GiB for GigaBytes, which would be a more accurate abbreviation!

12. The **Size** should automatically be set to **small**, and the **Density** to **MDPI**, so all you need to do is to set your **Screen Ratio** to **notlong**, since a Pine uses a 4:3 aspect ratio rather than a widescreen (long) 16:9 aspect ratio. We'll be learning about size, density, and aspect ratio in the graphics chapter.

13. Since the Pine has three hardware buttons, as shown on their product image in Figure 2-16, set your **Buttons** drop-down menu to reflect the presence of these hardware buttons.

14. Finally, in the **Device States** section of the dialog, **uncheck** the **Portrait Enabled** check box, since the Pine SmartWatch is intended to be used in the landscape mode, and leave the Landscape Enabled check box checked.

15. Once you have everything properly set up and configured, click your **Create Device** button, and you will have then created your new Neptune Pine SmartWatch hardware device.

Once you have created this Neptune Pine SmartWatch device definition, you will see it listed at the top of your Device Definitions tab in the Android Virtual Device Manager, on top of the Nexus S by Google, along with its primary specifications, as shown in Figure 2-18.

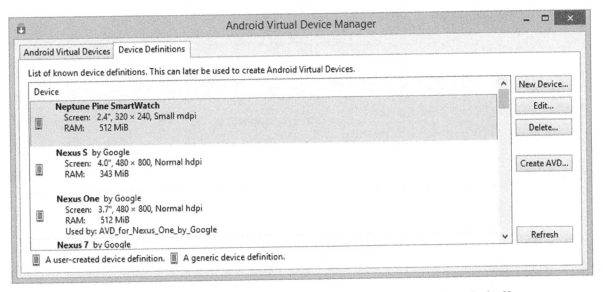

Figure 2-18. The Neptune Pine SmartWatch device in the Device Definitions tab of the Android Virtual Device Manager

As you can see, on the right side of the dialog, there are a number of other buttons that allow you to perform other AHD and AVD tasks. You have already used the Create AVD button to create your Nexus One AVD emulator, so let's look at the other two.

The **Edit** button allows you to highlight an AHD definition on the left side of the Android Virtual Device Manager screen, and then click the Edit button, which will take you back into the dialog that was used to create the Hardware Device specification data, which was shown in Figure 2-17. If you like, you can try this with the Neptune Pine SmartWatch device definition and see what I mean!

The **Delete** button allows you to highlight an AHD definition on the left side of the screen and remove it from the Device Definition list shown in Figure 2-18. Be careful when using this, as you can't get the device definition back!

It is also interesting to note that the **Create AVD** button on the right middle of this dialog accesses the same exact functional dialog that the **New** button, shown in Figure 2-15, does under the Android Virtual Devices tab. This is convenient; I just wish they had used the same button label in both tabs!

You can use either of these buttons to open up the Create new Android Virtual Device (AVD) dialog, which is shown in Figure 2-14, as well as Figure 2-19, and which you will be filling out next so that you can complete the creation of the Neptune Pine SmartWatch AVD emulator, which you will be using in Chapter 16 covering the Android application development work process for creating wearables apps, in this case for the popular Neptune Pine SmartWatch product.

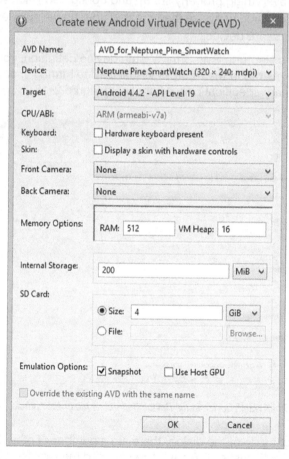

Figure 2-19. Creating the Neptune Pine SmartWatch AVD

16. Enter Neptune_Pine_SmartWatch into the **Name** field in the Create AVD dialog as shown at the top of Figure 2-19.

17. In the **Device** field, drop down the selector UI element and select the Neptune Pine Smart Watch (320 x 240: MDPI) device definition, which you just created.

18. In the **Target** field, leave the default Android 4.4.2 - API Level 19, since that is what the Eclipse IDE is running at currently and since you have the (backward) compatibility library installed. The Neptune Pine currently runs an Android 4.1 OS, which on an API level, at least for the APIs we will be using to develop apps for this product, there have been no major changes from 4.1.2 to 4.2.2 to 4.3.1 to just recently 4.4.4. We'll be discussing API levels in Chapter 4 covering the Java programming language.

Note The 4.x API revisions have implemented faster touchscreen refresh and graphics screen refresh rate increases for game developers. Also added were OpenGL ES 3.0 upgrades, speed, and efficiency improvements to the existing API methods, and an addition of cloud-related services, such as off-device printing and data storage on Google's various cloud services. In other words, all of the recent versions of Android, from 4.1 through 4.4 (released during 2013), have implemented what I'd term "user-facing" improvements, rather than developer-facing API updates. As you will see in Chapter 4, this means that none of those Java programming language elements of Android OS that developers use have changed much at all. Android 5.0, announced in the summer of 2014, will use Java 7 and a 64-bit Linux kernel when it becomes available in hardware devices in 2015 and 2016.

19. Let's get back to configuring an AVD definition for the Neptune Pine SmartWatch just to show you the complete work process from AHD creation through AVD definition and creation. **Uncheck** both of the **Hardware keyboard present** and the **Display a skin with hardware controls** check boxes.

20. For the **Front Camera** and **Back Camera**, you can select any of these three options that suit your workstation set up. If you have a webcam installed, you can use that to simulate the Neptune camera hardware on the Pine SmartWatch, you can simulate the cameras with the emulator itself, or you can simply select **None** for now, as I have done here.

Note Remember, you can use the Edit button at any time to change the settings you have set for the AVD emulator, so if you get a webcam or add camera features to your app, you can always change these drop-down selections at any time in the future, which is quite convenient.

21. I used a **512** setting for the Internal Storage field, and selected the **MiB** from the drop-down selector to specify megabytes, rather than gigabytes, which is designated as **GiB**.

22. For the **SD Card**, I specified **4GB** to make the emulator run more efficiently, even though the product supports a 16GB or 32GB MicroSD Card, which to the emulator would be the same as an SD Card.

23. Finally, for the **Emulation Options**, check the **Snapshot** option to speed subsequent AVD reloads for your testing cycle. This keeps a "snapshot" of the AVD environment in your system memory, so that each time you access the AVD emulator to test your application, it does not have to be reloaded. You can see the final result in Figure 2-20.

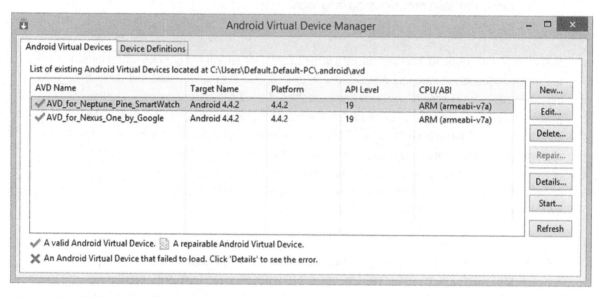

Figure 2-20. A Neptune_Pine_SmartWatch custom AVD once it has been created using the Device Definitions tab

Note   If you are creating interactive 3D OpenGL ES 3.1 applications, which use the OpenGL rendering engine that is part of the Android OS, you will alternatively want to choose the **Use Host GPU** option instead, to take advantage of your workstation GPU (Graphics Processing Unit) hardware. It is important to note that you cannot select both of these emulation options at the same time, so unless you are using OpenGL 3D technology in your application, select the **Snapshot** option.

Now that you have created AVD emulators for both a smartphone and a smartwatch, and are familiar with the work process involved, you can create your very own AHD definitions, which you can then use to create the final AVD definition. You are now ready for anything in the area of emulation that I can throw at you in the remaining chapters of this book, which cover how to develop applications for the Android operating system running on Android devices.

We'll be performing this same work process as needed in any chapters in this book that cover non-standard Android devices that are not listed (included) in the Eclipse ADT at this time (on the Device Definition tab) or that require us to add tablet or iTV set product definitions to our list of emulators.

What Will Be Covered in this Book

Since we downloaded, installed, and configured your Eclipse ADT and its Java foundation, as well as a plethora of professional-level, open source content production and business productivity software in the first two chapters, let's take a look at what will be covered in the rest of the book. I am doing this so that you have a comprehensive overview of what Android encompasses, and what you'll need to learn, in order to go from an Absolute Beginner to an intermediate level Android app developer.

I will progress from (relatively) simple concepts to more complex topics as the book progresses. However, don't expect any of this subject matter to be easy to master or even comprehend during the first go-round, because Android application software development is an extremely high-level endeavor. As you probably are well aware, Android software developer is a complete profession, as well as a high-paid career, and as such, will take you several years to completely master all of its complexities.

Introduction to Android Application Development Platform

In Chapter 3, you will learn the unique "lingo" for Android application design; that is, what the various components of an Android application are called, because Android uses its own terminology (or lingo) to describe things like messages and databases and background processing and app screen design. It is important to note that this "lingo," which is based on Android class names, will not change from version to version, which is why everything that you will learn about during this book will apply equally well to both Android 4.x and 5.x versions.

As you'll learn in Chapter 3, an Android application is "stratified." This involves how an app's function is spelled out via Java code, while its design is controlled with XML markup, and its privileges with an Android "Manifest," in a way that that is truly unique, modular, and powerful.

You will get an overview of all the basic knowledge of Android application development in Chapter 3, as well as learn how to create an application shell, which I call an application "bootstrap," in that chapter.

Android's modularity adds a great deal of extensibility, or development flexibility, to Android applications, but also makes it more difficult to learn initially. We will get a bird's eye overview of how all of these modules work together, to create your Android OS application development environment, and how everything comes together to create your application.

It's important to get this high-level view first, before we dive into each of the lower-level component areas of Android application development, as you will need this perspective to understand everything else in the book.

How Android Simplifies Design: Designing Apps Using XML

In Chapter 4, we will take a look at how Android uses the XML markup language to define the basic component design for your application, especially its visual (graphics) design and its UI component design. I look at XML as giving developers a maximum return on investment, as XML makes it possible for absolute beginners to develop robust and functional applications right out of the gate! That's what the book is all about, after all; getting up-to-speed on Android as rapidly as possible!

Writing XML "markup" is not technically programming, but rather consists of using **tags**, similar to the HTML5 tags that web developers use to format their online documents. These tags can also contain configuration **parameters** to fine-tune them for your exact application design usage.

XML is used in Android to define everything from UI designs, to constants, to styles or themes to data access, and even programming constructs like Java Object definitions, which we explore in Chapter 5.

XML markup tags are far easier for beginners to comprehend than complex programming languages such as Java. This is why I'm covering it first, right out of the gate, after the chapter after where we discuss how Android is structured and stratified. Because it's easier, we'll use XML throughout this book whenever possible, as Google recommends that developers do this.

Android Application Framework: Java Programming Primer

By the time you reach Chapter 5, you'll have built a rock-solid integrated Android application software development environment, and have acquired a basic understanding of all of the components that make up an application development project (XML markup, Java code, text, UI layout, UI widgets, images, audio, video, animation, and so on), and you will have learned how to upgrade a new (an empty, or a "bootstrap") Android application.

I will outline how Java programming logic or code and XML, along with any new media resources, are compiled, compressed, and bundled into Android's signature APK file type, and how the various Android application components "talk" to each other inside your apps. The majority of Chapter 5, however, will be dedicated to giving you a Java Programming "primer" in case you are unfamiliar with Java SE.

We will look at the various concepts in Java, ranging from the entire API to your own custom software "package" and the classes, methods, interfaces, variables, and constants that it may contain, which will be based on what your application programming logic is trying to accomplish.

We'll look at the concepts of **Object Oriented Programming (OOP)** so that you can understand how to visualize what we will be doing in the rest of the book. We will also put all this Java programming knowledge to good use and write our first Android class, called **Galaxy.java**, in Chapter 5.

Screen Real Estate: View and Activity Classes

Chapter 6 provides an overview of Android's Activity class and View class. These contain and define your "user experience," or UX, on the screen. I'll explain and demonstrate how an Activity works. We will take a look at the new Android application you created in Chapter 3, and turn your Java code from Chapter 5 into functional Android code. We will enhance the Java code inside of your application's Primary (Main) Activity class. You'll have learned about classes in the previous Chapter 5, so as I mentioned, we will always build on your previous knowledge base as we progress through this book.

We will also take a look at the Android View, which is the foundation for everything that displays on the Android display screen and inside of these Activities that you will create as an Android applications developer. Like the Activity, the View is another very high-level Android component, and we will take a close look at how the View is used to create UI elements and layouts (designs) that ultimately make your application easy to use, functional, and even fun!

You will learn how Android's Views are used to create the UI "widgets" in Android, which are the UI design elements that you will utilize to create your functional user interface design for your Android app inside of Android's UI layout containers, which are based on the ViewGroup class.

You will learn about the different screen resolution, density, orientation, and aspect ratio (width) issues in Android, which you will need to understand so that you can make your applications span across various Android hardware devices such as smartwatches, tablets, and iTV sets.

Chapter 6 explains how your UI is contained within the Android device display screen. Android device display screens are the way most users interact with their Android applications. In Android, your UI is written to the display using a mixture of Java (Activity class) and XML markup. This defines View and ViewGroup widgets and layouts, which controls the custom hierarchy of View and ViewGroup objects, which you've designed using nested ViewGroup layout containers (or using a single layout container).

These ViewGroup layout containers ultimately hold all the other graphics (Chapter 9) and UI content for your application in its proper place, and thus ViewGroup classes provide a foundation for Android application design. You'll want to learn these display screen (Chapter 6) and UI layout design (Chapter 8) concepts thoroughly, as they are core concepts to implementing everything else that Android can do. After all, without a proper UI, your user cannot access software functionality in the first place!

You'll revisit XML markup again in this chapter, as you will in almost every chapter in this book, and learn how XML allows you to define complex screen layouts and UI designs without writing a single line of Java code. You will learn about the different types of layout containers, and how each can be useful in different UI design scenarios, and you will continue to code a really cool Activity for your application, which is written almost completely using XML markup.

Interactivity: Using Android Intent and Event Handling

In Chapter 7, we'll start building interactive applications using Android's Intent class to make our application menu system functional. We will also make the UI screens for your application interactive, as you'll learn how to implement Android Event Handler and Event Listener capabilities.

We'll take a look at how to use Android's Intent class, and Event Handling capabilities, to launch new Activity subclasses and to make your UI design functional. Although this is fairly advanced material, we need to cover it fairly early on in the book, so that we can make sure all of the remaining chapters, which cover how to integrate new media and data external to your application with your UI design, can be made to function (be interactive).

The Android Intent and IntentFilter classes are used to communicate within an Android application, between components such as Activities and Services, as well as outside of your Android application. This External communication is usually with other Android applications, which are not part of your Android application, but which your application will need to communicate with, to synchronize with, or to exchange data with. Android is a very complex subject, so expect each chapter to become more complex!

UI Design: Adding User Controls to Your Apps

In Chapter 8, we will get into the plethora of facilities that Android provides to developers to design UI layouts containing UI elements (called "widgets" in Android), so that your app's users can "interface" with your application. That's why it's a "user interface!"

This design process is called **UI Design**, and you have already downloaded and installed the Pencil 2.0.5 UI design tool on your workstation in the previous chapter, so you can prototype UI designs!

In Chapter 8, we will focus on looking at Android's flexible UI design classes, which are based on Android's ViewGroup class. UI layouts can be "nested" within each other, or simply utilized on their own, in order to create any UI design, no matter how complex, that your application might require to "bridge" your application's functionality over to its users.

We will take a look at some of the most often used UI design classes in Android, commonly called "layout containers," and how these will allow developers to create UI designs quickly and efficiently.

Graphics Design: Add Visuals to Your Apps

In Chapter 9, we will start to get into adding new media elements to your Android applications by looking at static (fixed) graphics. These are implemented using digital images, and we will take a look at the basics of digital imaging as well as at the digital image formats that are supported by Android.

We will start building highly visual UI designs that incorporate graphic design elements, again by using the XML foundation that you will have learned during the previous chapters. As we are building one chapter upon another, this will continue to build on your newfound knowledge of Android Activity classes, XML markup, Android screen design, View widgets, and ViewGroup layout classes.

Because Android smartwatches, smartphones, tablets, and iTV sets feature Organic Light-Emitting Diode (OLED) wide video graphics array (WVGA, or 800x480) and high-definition television (HDTV, or 1920x1080) screens in the current market "line-up" of Android products, Android display screens are impressive enough these days to allow some amazing user experiences to be created using graphic design elements.

Since this is an area where Android development starts to get interesting, I decided to incorporate how to leverage new media assets in your Android applications, so that your work can stand far apart from the crowd. Android has a plethora of support for new media assets. Just because this is an Absolute Beginner title doesn't mean we should shy away from complexity!

We will look at several different image formats that are supported in Android and how they differ from each other. We will look at their strengths and weaknesses, and which are the preferred ones to use for your Android applications development. We'll look at why Android prefers certain image formats over others.

We will look at the class foundation for graphics in Android by learning about the Drawable class and its many subclasses such as BitmapDrawable and ShapeDrawable. You will also learn about foundational concepts in the area of graphics design and image compositing.

You'll learn how to create graphics assets, as well as how to create several different versions of those image assets that will scale well across different screen densities. You will learn about Android's scalable graphic classes, such as the NinePatchDrawable class, and learn about the 9-Patch tool that comes with the Android SDK. This is a chapter that will transform how your Android applications look, and the knowledge gained in this chapter will allow you to greatly increase an app's professionalism.

Animation: Adding Motion Graphics to Your Apps

In Chapter 10, we will build on those static (still) graphic capabilities we learned about during Chapter 9 by adding the **fourth dimension** of time, as motion, to these graphic assets, to create animation assets.

We will take a look at the Android Animation class, which you can use to create procedural, also known as vector or tween, animation, as well as the AnimationDrawable class, which is used to create frame animation (also known as bitmap animation or raster animation).

You will learn what the differences between procedural vector animation and bitmap frame animation are, and how to utilize the two completely different animation approaches together, in hybrid animation, to create a more impressive visual result than would be achieved by using them separately.

You'll implement animation assets using XML, so you will get even more practice designing and implementing new media assets using XML markup.

Digital Video: Captive or Streaming Video for an Application

In Chapter 11, we will look at the **digital video** type of new media asset, which is very different from the animation new media asset, because it is self-contained and uses a single file format. We will take a look at the concepts of URLs and URIs, which are used to define a path, or address, to your digital video asset.

We will also take a look at the Android **VideoView** widget class, which is a user interface element specifically designed and provided by Android for playing digital video formats. We will look at how this class works hand in hand with the Android **MediaPlayer** and Android **MediaController** classes.

We will take a look at the foundational concepts involved with digital video, and how they expand on what we learned about digital images, since digital video is simply a series of digital images. We will also take a close look at popular digital video formats, which are implemented as something called digital video **codecs**, currently supported in Android.

We will look at the two primary digital video formats that are supported in Android, MPEG-4 and WebM, how they differ from each other, their strengths and weaknesses, which are the preferred ones to use for your Android applications development, and which digital video formats you should use for various types of captive versus streaming implementations. You will create a digital video asset using Terragen, VideoDub, and Squeeze Pro and implement it in an Android application using Java code and XML markup.

Digital Audio: Adding Audio Media to Your Apps

In Chapter 12, we will look at the digital audio type of new media asset, which is the most well-supported type of new media in the Android OS, as far as file formats (codecs) are concerned.

You will build on your knowledge of the MediaPlayer classes that you gained in Chapter 11, as playing back audio files is quite similar to playing back video files, without the moving imagery, of course. We will also take a look at the more advanced Android **SoundPool** class, which is more suited to adding sound effects to an application as well as sequencing and mixing audio with an application, as well as the **SparseIntArray** class.

As an added bonus, in Appendix A we will look at the foundational concepts behind digital audio, as well as the plethora of different digital audio file formats (also known as codecs) that are supported in Android.

We will look at how the codec usage scenarios will differ significantly from each other. We will discuss different audio codec strengths and weaknesses, and which are the preferred ones to use for a given Android application, and discuss why you will want to use certain digital audio formats over the others that are available.

Services: Adding Background Processing to Apps

In Chapter 13, we'll take a look at the Android **Service** class. Services in Android are used to provide background processing, which is used when you want something done in the background (such as playing music) while your user works on something else using your app's Activity and its UI design.

To really give you a good feel as to what the Service class is doing, we will also have to cover some fairly complex OS concepts such as Processes, Threads, and Scheduling. Threads can be a very advanced area within any OS, and Android is no different, as Android is based on an open source Linux OS Kernel, as well as on open source Java, XML, CSS, HTML5, WebKit, and OpenGL.

We will look at the Android Service-related classes, as well as how to use Intent objects to create and control Services, which are launched and then operate in the background at the same time that your user is interfacing with your UI design (the UI layout and its UI widgets) in your Activity class. An Android app may never need to utilize the Service class, but it's part of our comprehensive coverage.

Content Providers: Accessing Stored Data Inside of Your App

In Chapter 14, we will look at the Android concept of **Content Providers**, which are "data stores" for the Android OS. These provide data to your application, and include things such as files on your SD card or an internal database.

The Android OS includes a popular open source database called **MySQLite**, which is the "Lite" or very basic version of the popular open source **MySQL DBMS** (DataBase Management System) relational database engine.

We will look at all of the different ways to provide data to an Android application, and we will take a closer look at the theory behind databases. We will revisit those concepts of the URL and the URI, which you will have utilized in Chapter 11 on digital video new media assets as well as in Chapter 12 on digital audio new media assets.

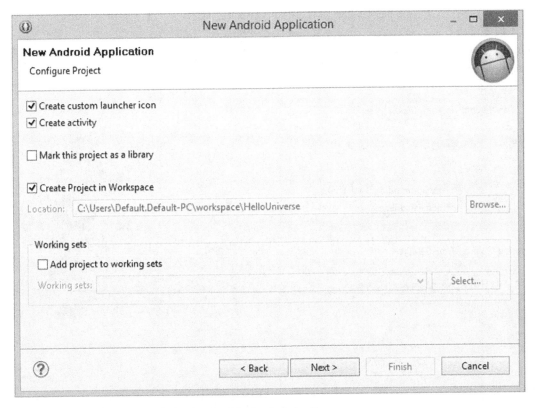

Figure 3-4. The Configure Project dialog, showing the default selected options

11. This dialog is much simpler and allows developers to select what the Eclipse ADT will create for the new Android application project. You will select the default settings for this dialog, which will create a **custom launcher icon** for your application, which you will learn how to modify and upgrade a bit later, and **create an Activity class** to hold your UI design and Java code. Finally, a **Create Project in Workspace** option will create the Android project for you in your Workspace folder, in the location that you specified when you started Eclipse ADT earlier in the chapter. This location is greyed-out as it is a combination of your workspace folder path and that the project name you specified in the first dialog.

We won't be using multiple libraries for this Android project (mark this project as a library option), nor will we be using working sets, an advanced feature that allows development of multiple versions of an app at the same exact time (too advanced for Absolute Beginners, I'm afraid; however, you can research it on the developer site).

12. Once you click on the **Next** button, you will progress to the third dialog in this series, which is the **Configure Launcher Icon** dialog shown in Figure 3-5.

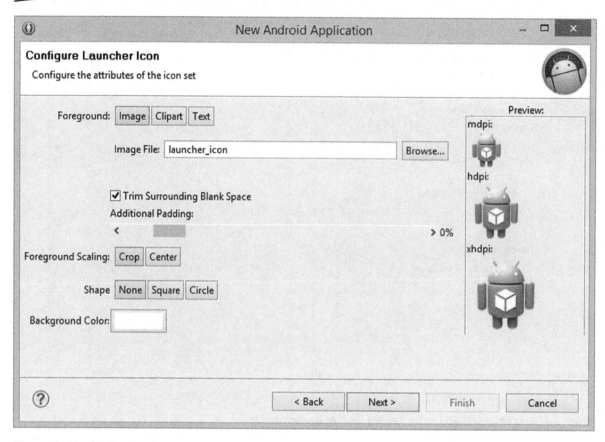

Figure 3-5. The Configure Launcher Icon dialog, showing the default selected options

13.   This dialog allows you to configure your Android application icon using an
       Image, **Clipart,** or **Text**, select a custom image file, automatically trim blank
       space around your icon, add additional padding, **crop** or **center** the icon,
       and determine the shape of your icon and the background color used. Since
       we are going to learn how to do all of this "from scratch" using XML and
       GIMP, as well as related concepts such as alpha channel support, which
       allows transparent areas around your icon, I am simply going to accept these
       default settings. We'll use the green Android robot for now as a placeholder
       until I can show you how your you can access your application icon content
       and settings from inside of your Android project.

14.   Once you click the **Next** button you will be taken to the fourth dialog in the
       series, which is the **Create Activity** dialog, which is shown in Figure 3-6. This
       dialog will allow you to specify what kind of UI design your Activity class will
       have installed in it, which will determine what Java code and XML mark-up
       Eclipse writes for you.

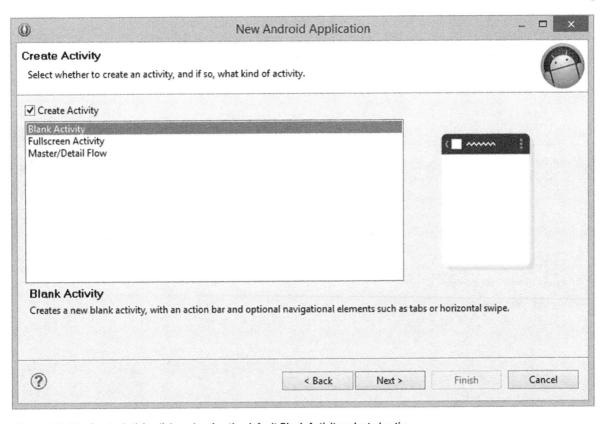

Figure 3-6. The Create Activity dialog, showing the default Blank Activity selected option

15. Since you're going to learn how to create your own custom Android Activity class, as well as your own custom UI design from scratch, I am going to select the first **Blank Activity** option, after making sure that the Create Activity checkbox is selected.

I am selecting this option so that you can see what the "minimum application bootstrap code" that Eclipse ADT will write for you will include, so that you learn how to code an Android application from the lowest possible level, and with the most control over Java code and XML markup that you yourself put into place.

16. Once you click on the **Next** button, you will be ready to fill out the final dialog in the New Android Application Project series of dialogs, where you will specify names for your Java code (Activity class), XML markup (UI design) and a UI navigation type. Let's do that now so that we can take a look at what Eclipse ADT creates for you using this series of dialogs, as that is really where you will start to learn how an Android app is structured!

17. After you click Next you will get the Blank Activity dialog, shown in Figure 3-7, where you will see the naming conventions for the "main" (the app's Home screen) Android **Activity Name** and UI **Layout Name**. I am going to accept the suggested names, and set the **Navigation Type** to **None** so that we can create our own navigation!

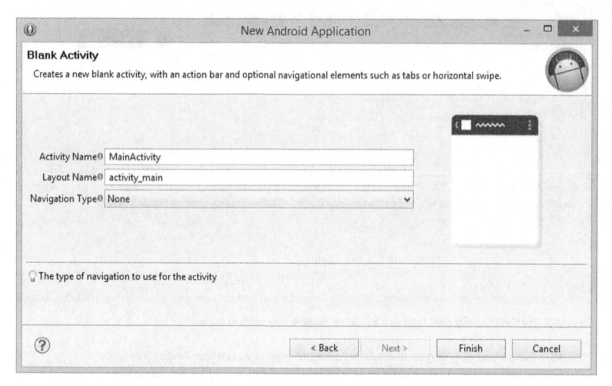

Figure 3-7. The Blank Activity dialog with Activity Name, UI Layout Name, and Navigation Type

You will see later (throughout the book) why I am accepting these suggested names and will be following these naming conventions that they embody. For now, just accept that your main application "home screen" is called "Main" and its Activity UI definition is referenced as **activity_main.xml**. We will soon see where this XML UI definition file is kept, and we will even take a look at its contents, and learn what it does, using XML markup.

18. Once you click the **Finish** button in the final dialog, the dialog will disappear, and you will see a formerly blank Eclipse ADT IDE filled with a complete, working Android application project, as shown in Figure 3-8.

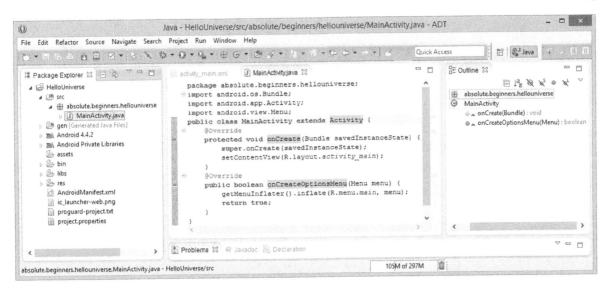

Figure 3-8. The bootstrap Android application MainActivity.java Java code for Activity, Bundle, and Menu

Eclipse has created a HelloUniverse project folder and sub-folder hierarchy (structure) as well as opened up your Java Activity class in a currently active (selected) tab and your XML UI definition in a currently inactive (ghosted or deselected tab), as you can see in Figure 3-8. There is also a "bird's-eye view" of your Java code hierarchy in an **Outline** pane on the right. The **Package Explorer** pane on the left is used to navigate the project infrastructure, as you are about to do next, so that you can learn about what assets go where in an Android application project!

We will be getting into what the Java code in the Eclipse central Editing pane does in the next chapter, so for now, let's focus on the Package Explorer pane and learn how to use that to navigate our Android project structure. As we do this, we will take a look at the various sub-folders and what components of our Android application need to be stored in certain sub-folders. One of the things you need to do to become an Android developer is to learn how Android projects need to be organized. It's really too bad there is not "forced organization" in more areas of our lives, because as you will soon see, Android is organized in such a way that it forces your app development to be surgically precise!

Navigating Around an Android Project

To close an open folder, such as the **/HelloUniverse/src/absolute.beginners.hellouniverse/** folder, containing your **MainActivity.java** file, shown highlighted in Figure 3-8, click on the downward-right pointing arrow at its left, called a collapse arrow, and it will close the folder, and will then display a right pointing arrow, called an expand arrow, instead of a downward-right arrow.

Conversely, to open up any folder, click the right pointing arrow, and it will reveal what is inside or underneath this folder, which will always be either another folder structure and/or a file or series of files. Let's do this to open your Android project's **resource** folder, named **/res**, which is shown opened up in Figure 3-9.

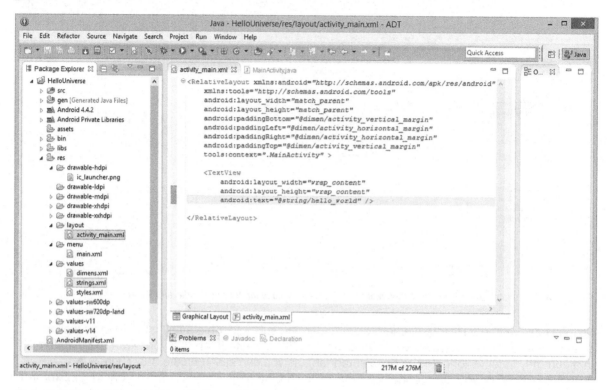

Figure 3-9. The bootstrap Android application activity_main XML mark-up, and project folder hierarchy

As you can see, there are a number of different types of folders present, which start with specific names, such as **drawable** (image, animation, text, or shape assets), **layout** (UI design XML definition assets), **menu** (menu design XML definitions) and **values** (value constants that define text, dimensions, styles, and themes).

You can also add other types of Android application project asset folders to this project folder hierarchy, which we will be doing over the course of this book, when we add assets such as digital video and animation to our HelloUniverse Android application project. Since these folders need to have specific names, which indicate the type of assets as well as their functionality to the Android OS, I will outline what these different asset folder types (indicated by the asset folder names) and naming conventions are within the next section of this chapter. I will provide them here in a tabular format in Table 3-1, just so that you have an overview of where everything goes in your Android project folder hierarchy first.

Table 3-1. *Android Project Directory (Folder) Hierarchy, Showing the Key Sub-folders We Will Be Using in this Book*

Project Sub-Folder Name:	What application assets this sub-folder will contain:
/src	Java source files (your Java programming logic)
/res	Project resources (your XML markup definitions)
/res/drawable	Digital image and digital illustration assets
/res/anim	2D animation assets (procedural or tween animation)
/res/raw	Digital video and digital audio assets
/res/values	Data values which remain fixed, called "Constants"
/res/layout	UI design layout definitions
/res/menu	Application menu structure design definitions

Android Resources: Asset Project Folders

If you want to add custom animation, custom themes, digital video, and digital audio to an Android project, you will have to add new folders to your project folder hierarchy. You will be learning how to do this during the course of this book, as you learn about how to create and add in these types of assets to your Android application.

For now, however, I just want to give you an overview of the different folder types and names that are possible to have in your Android application projects. This is so that you have a high-level view of what is possible in Android development as well as the types of Android assets you are going to learn how to incorporate during this book.

Your external new media assets (that is, those primarily created outside of Android, using software like GIMP and Blender 3D) are kept in the resources folder, shown in Figure 3-9 opened up to show all the sub-folders, and referenced as **HelloUniverse/res**. Other resource assets that are external to your Java code and XML markup such as constants, styles, themes, and user interface layout definitions, are also kept in this folder. **Externalizing resources** allows your Android development process to be more modular by nature, and to be more organized.

There are many different resource types in Android, and they either have their own sub-folders, under the **/res/** project folder, or their own files, under the **/res/values/** folder. We will go over the majority of these in detail in the next eight sections of this chapter. Primary types of resources include:

- **drawable** resources (graphic)
- **layout** resources (user interface design)
- **menu** resources (menu navigation)
- **values** resources (constant definitions)
- **raw** resources (video and audio files)
- **xml** resources (configurations and definitions)
- **string** resources (text values)
- **color** resources (custom colors)

- **dimension** resources (dimensions and units of value)
- **bool** resources (boolean true or false values)
- **integer** resources (numeric constants)
- **array** resources (collections of data values)

You can also provide something called **alternative resources** in the application project folder hierarchy. These **alternate resource folders** provide support for a wide array of device types or physical hardware specifications by grouping new media assets, user interface designs, and style and theme definitions into specifically named alternate resource folders. The **/res/values-sw600dp/** folder in Figure 3-9 is an example of an alternate resource folder, and holds assets that are specific to your application design for 600-pixel or greater screen dimensions. We'll be covering alternate resources as they relate to UI layout design a bit later on in this book.

At runtime, which we learned all about in the first part of this chapter, Android OS uses an appropriate resource, based on the device's hardware specifications. As an example, if you want to provide different UI design layouts that morph, or change based on the physical screen size, shape, or orientation (portrait or landscape), you can define different UI layout designs using different layout folder names, such as **/res/layout-land** for a landscape-specific UI layout design, or **/res/layout-port** for a portrait-specific UI layout design. We will be looking at all of this in greater detail in a future chapter on UI design principles and techniques.

As another example, you could define different string (a collection or array of text characters) values, which would be evaluated at runtime based on the language setting on the end-user's Android device. As you can see, there is a reason for the way Android organizes resources, and one of the major reasons is so that developers can create alternate resources (alternate resource folders) that can be accessed at runtime based on Android device characteristics. As this book progresses, I will show you how to reference and access these external resources from within your Java code and XML mark-up. We will get into how to set up alternate resource folders in the chapters covering user interface design, themes, and styles. Let's look at drawables next!

Android Drawable: Assets that Draw to a Screen

A "drawable" in Android is aptly named, as it is anything that can be drawn to the display screen. As you can see in Figure 3-9, Eclipse ADT created five /res/drawable subfolders, named **drawable-ldpi**, **drawable-mdpi**, **drawable-hdpi**, **drawable-xhdpi** and **drawable-xxhdpi** for your use. It is important to note that as of Android 4.2, there's also an **xxxhdpi** resolution density that has been added to Android to accommodate the new Ultra High Definition (UHD) (or Ultra High Density, in this case) displays, such as those found on 4K TVs, which have a 4096 by 2160 resolution, or the screen on the new Samsung Galaxy S5, which has a 2560 by 1440 pixel resolution screen. From smartwatch (ldpi) to 4K TV (xxxhdpi), Android has a density constant to fit any device!

You will be learning all about pixels and resolutions in Chapter 9, covering graphic design, but to give you an overview here of what these different DPI levels are for Android's screen resolution density constants, I have put all of the density constant data together here, in Table 3-2, for those of you who are already "pixel savvy."

Table 3-2. *Android Device DPI: Seven Levels of Pixel Density Constants Specifically Supported in Android*

Android Device DPI Constants Currently in the Android OS	Screen Size Constant	Pixel Density in DPI	Pixel Multiplier Index	Minimum Screen Size	Launcher Icon Size in Pixels	Action Bar Icon Size	Notify Icon Size
LDPI (Low Density)	small	120	0.75	426x320	36x36	24x24	18x18
MDPI (Medium)	normal	160	1.0	470x320	48x48	32x32	24x24
TVDPI (HD 1280x720)	HDTV	213	1.33	640x360	64x64	48x48	32x32
HDPI (High Density)	large	240	1.5	640x480	72x72	48x48	36x36
XHDPI (Extra High)	xlarge	320	2.0	960x720	96x96	64x64	48x48
XXHDPI (Super High)	xxlarge	480	3.0	1280x960	144x144	96x96	72x72
XXXHDPI (Ultra High)	xxxlarge	640	4.0	1920x1080	192x192	128x128	96x96

As you can see in Figure 3-9, I opened the first **drawable-hdpi** folder for you to show the **ic_launcher** graphic file, which the Configure Launcher Icon dialog shown in Figure 3-5 created for you in four different resolution density versions. If you are wondering what the pixel dimensions are for these ic_launcher files in the drawable subfolders that have arrows next to them (which indicates that there are files in the folders), take a look at the sixth column in Table 3-2. So the ic_launcher graphic I exposed in the drawable-hdpi folder is **72 by 72** pixels.

There are about a dozen different types of drawable objects in Android, each of which has their very own class. Some of the more important drawable types include: BitmapDrawable, ShapeDrawable, NinePatchDrawable, AnimationDrawable, LayerDrawable, TransitionDrawable, and StateListDrawable, to name a few. I will try and implement as many different types of drawables as I can during this book, so you will be well-rounded (no pun intended) when it comes to using graphics (drawables) in Android application design and development. If you wanted to dive into these graphics classes at a pro level, check out the *Pro Android Graphics* title, by Wallace Jackson (Apress, 2013).

There are several types of drawable assets that will need to be placed in the drawable folders for these assets to be visible to, and accessible to, the Android application. The primary one is **Bitmaps**, which we will be covering in Chapter 9, as well as media assets that are based upon (created with) Bitmaps, such as **Frame Animation**. Any assets that reference Bitmaps or Frame Animation in an XML definition file format would also be kept in this folder, as would any XML definitions creating **Shapes** (2D vector graphics).

> **Note**   **Vector graphics** are defined using math instead of pixels; if you're familiar with Adobe Illustrator (.AI files) or Scalable Vector Graphics (SVG files) then you are probably familiar with the distinction between pixel-based graphics (Photoshop and GIMP) and vector-based graphics (Illustrator and InkScape). I may have dropped the ball in Chapter 1, as I didn't have you download and install a vector graphics program! Google **InkScape** and go download this and install it, if vector graphics is an area that interests you (or just to get free software)!

Android Layout: Assets that Lay Out a UI Design

A "layout" in Android is also aptly named, as it is a definition of how your user interface elements and drawable assets are going to be "laid out" relative to each other on the Android device display screen. Once we get you up-to-speed on Java, in Chapter 5, you will be learning more about UI layout design during the rest of this book!

Chances are, if you want your Android app to have a custom design for each type of device (iTV, smartphone, tablet, smartwatch, and so forth), you are going to have a number of custom /res/layout folders, not just a /res/layout-land and /res/layout-port folder, as I gave as an example earlier. You probably will have complex **alternate resource** folders as well, such as **/res/layout-sw800dp-land** for tablets and **/res/layout-sw240dp-port** for smartwatches.

The **/res/layout/** folder, and any custom layout alternate resource folders that you create, will generally contain UI layout definition **XML files**. As you will see in Chapters 6 through 8, and over the rest of the book, UI layouts in Android are defined using **XML layout definitions**. These are hand-crafted by using XML markup, and stored in **filenamehere.xml** files in the /res/layout folder or one of the alternate layout resource folders that you create.

Since we are going to look at the XML for the UI layout that Eclipse created for us earlier in the chapter, and because we have a couple of chapters coming up specifically covering UI layout design, I am going to leave the /res/layout/ folder coverage at that, and move on to look at some of the other resource folder types next. If you are interested in the concept of alternate layout design folders, you can find in-depth coverage on the Android developer web site at the following URL:

```
http://developer.android.com/guide/topics/resources/providing-resources.html
```

Android Menu: Assets that Define Menu Options

A "menu" in Android is exactly what it says it is, and what you would expect it to be: a menu, or a list full of options, for your end-users to select from in order to navigate around your Android application infrastructure.

There are several different types of menus in Android, including pop-up menus, context-sensitive menus, and options menus. We will get more into menu design as we progress through this book, adding menu items to your application's menuing system. We will start this process during the next chapter when we customize the default menu XML markup and Java code that Eclipse ADT's New Android Application Project series of dialogs created for you.

Technically, the Android menu that your application uses, via a hardware MENU button on the Android device, or via those three vertical dots on the Action Bar at the top of an Android device (if there is no hardware MENU button) is called the **Options Menu**. The **Status Bar** is always at the very top of every Android device, and holds the battery power indicator, network mode (3G, 4G, 4G LTE, and so forth) indicator, signal strength indicator, and similar hardware operation indicators.

The **Action Bar** is located just underneath the Android Status Bar, which is the top-most OS bar containing your signal meter and the like. In addition to the options menu, accessed by those three vertical dots on the right end of the Action Bar, the Action Bar contains your application icon, application title, and if you code it correctly, either icons or text tabs that can access areas of your app.

The **/res/menu/** folder contains XML definitions of the **menu structures** that you create for your application, as you may have imagined. Notice in Figure 3-9 that Eclipse ADT created a default menu XML definition for you, in a file called **main.xml**. Notice the file naming convention here; the **main.xml** menu XML definition, and the **MainActivity.java** and activity_main.xml layout XML definition all match up, so you know they are related!

Android Values: Assets Defining App Constants

A "value" in the Android project folder hierarchy is what is known in Java programming as a "constant." Values in Java code are different than Java constants, as they are meant to change, whereas constants are meant to stay the same (that's why they're called constants). We will be getting into this distinction as far as Java goes soon, in Chapter 5, when we look at the Java programming language specifically. You will, of course, be required to understand exactly how Java works before we get much further into the book, as things will get more and more complicated with each chapter.

Android values (constants) are a bit more flexible than Java constants are, as Java constants define fixed (known as immutable) data values that cannot be changed, whereas Java values can be changed at runtime. The Android values we are talking about in this section also cannot be changed (they are actually constants, but are called values). So make sure not to get confused by semantics here. Of course, once your Java code places these initial constant values into memory, the application code (logic) may change them!

Let's examine the **/res/values** folder from the current application bootstrap project in more detail. This is where you (or Eclipse, in the case of the New Android Application Project series of dialogs) will place any predefined application values. These exist inside of (underneath) the **/res/values/** folder in the form of XML files. These XML files contain constant definitions that define constant names (x or y, for instance) and their data values.

The value constants that are defined inside of these XML files will later be referenced inside of your Java code, or via your XML markup. For example, these values might be **strings** (a collection of text characters), **styles** (how you want a UI design to be formatted throughout your app), **dimensions** (numeric size specifications), or other constants that need to be "hard-coded" values that your Java code or XML markup uses in your program logic or UI design that you do not want to change.

The logic behind having a /res/values/ folder involves holding all of your constant values for your application in one place. This is a similar concept to the repository we used in Chapter 2 to update Eclipse ADT, only the /res/values is a resource repository for value constants which are used in your Android application. The /res/values/ folder is therefore your application constants repository data (folder) structure, and its usage allows you to make your application constant changes in one single location. In this way, if you need to adjust your constant values during application development or testing, you can do this using XML files.

Figure 3-9 shows three examples of the types of constant value files that you can place into this values folder:

- **dimens.xml:** An XML file that defines dimension values, such as standard heights or font sizes for your UI. You can then use these values across your app, to ensure it is consistent.

- **strings.xml:** An XML file that defines text strings that are used in your application. For example, you can place any screen titles, or the app name, here and reference these in your code. If you need to change or refine these items in the future, you simply do it in this one central location, rather than in your Java code or XML markup.

- **styles.xml:** An XML file that defines UI design styles you can use across your application. These styling constants will be applied to the UI elements that reference the style constant definitions, allowing you to separate the look and feel of your app from the physical layout and UI functionality. This makes your app easier to refine, change, and enhance over time.

Some of the other types of value constant XML definition files you could create and place in your Android project's /res/values/ folder might include:

- **arrays.xml:** An XML file that defines a **series of data value constants** that are intended to be utilized together (known as an array) in your application. For example, this could be a list of icon files, a list of graphic layers, or a list of options to display to the user.

- **integers.xml:** An XML file that defines constant numeric **integer constant** values that will be used in your Java programming logic in your application.

- **bool.xml:** An XML file that defines **Boolean constant** values (true or false) that will be used for the default (initial) setting for the states (like switches) in an application. Examples of these would include states such as on or off, yes or no, visible or hidden, and so on.

- **colors.xml:** An XML file that will define the color constant values to be used in the app. These allow you to standardize the UI. For example, you could define your app's background color as a constant. Then, if you decide to tweak it later, you need to do the tweak in only one place and the change is implemented across your entire application. We will cover color theory and hexadecimal color values in more detail in Chapter 9, which covers graphic design.

Notice that Android uses certain file naming conventions for the different types of XML files in the /res/values/ folder, adding another level of complexity. It is important to note that you can also create your own customized XML files and file names in this folder, so you are not limited to the constant types that are discussed here. Next, let's cover the folder names that Eclipse ADT did not automatically create for you, and that you can optionally utilize to contain other asset types such as animation, digital video, digital audio, and XML data.

Android Anim: Assets Defining Tween Animation

Besides frame animation, also known as bitmap animation or raster animation, Android OS also supports **vector animation**, which it terms **tween animation**. This type of animation is what is known in the industry as **procedural animation**, and is created using Java code or XML markup parameter definitions rather than by "flipbooking" through a collection of images (frames) to create an illusion of motion.

Whereas Bitmap Animation in Android uses the BitmapAnimation class, Tween Animation in Android uses the **Animation** class, and thus the proper folder to contain resources or assets related to procedural animation is not the /res/drawable/ folder, but instead the **/res/anim/** folder, which you will have to create in order to utilize this type of animation in Android. Fortunately we will be covering this in Chapter 10, so you'll create this folder then.

Android Animator: Asset for Property Animation

There is a third type of animation in Android, called **property animation**, used to animate "properties" or "parameters" for any of your UI widgets or even your entire UI design. You can use this to obtain impressive special effects that entice your end-users. Property Animation XML definition files are held in the **/res/animator/** folder, and reference the UI elements that you want to animate as well as To and From values.

Android Raw: Pre-Optimized Video & Audio Files

The **/res/raw/** folder in Android OS holds your application's "raw data." Raw data in Android is not optimized (touched) in any way by the Android OS, it is simply played back (usually streamed) from this folder "as-is."

This is the folder that you want to contain your new media assets for which you have taken the time to optimize the data footprint (file size) to quality ratio. This would be done outside of Android using software packages such as Audacity or Lightworks, both of which you downloaded and installed during Chapter 1.

We will be looking at how to create and leverage this /res/raw/ folder a bit later on in this book, during Chapters 11 and 12, where I will cover the Android MediaPlayer and MediaController classes, as well as how to create and play back digital audio and digital video new media asset resources using this particular resource folder.

Android XML: Arbitrary XML and Configurations

The last resource folder that you should know about is the /res/xml/ folder, which is used to contain XML files that specify configuration parameters that are external to (outside of) the scope of your Android application, possibly relating to certain device hardware or similar. This folder can also contain custom XML files that have nothing to do with the Android application creation process, but that are "parsed" (read in) by your Android application using the Resources.getXML() method call. We will cover Java method calls in Chapter 5.

Creating a Custom App Launch Icon

One of the first things that any Android application developer wants to learn how to do is to create their own custom Android application launch icon for the Android OS desktop. This is because this icon represents the branding for the application, so let's learn about how to do this here, using the open source GIMP digital image editing and compositing software.

Creating a Launch Icon for Each Screen Density

The final thing that we are going to do in this chapter is give our application what Android OS terms a **launcher icon**. This is your application icon that will show up on your users' Android devices. Your users will use this to identify and then launch your Android application. This process is not as easy as you might imagine, so I am going to show you how to create custom launcher icons for every resolution density display screen type. We will do this using the GIMP 2.8.10 software that you installed on your workstations back in Chapter 1.

We will leverage what you have learned so far about defining alternate drawable resources by creating a custom icon in four different versions targeting medium (using the mdpi or MDPI constant), high (hdpi or HDPI), extra high (xhdpi or XHDPI), and super high (xxhdpi or XXHDPI) density resolution screens. It is important to note here that you can write constant values in Android OS either using all lowercase or all uppercase characters.

We will be modifying (updating or replacing) the appropriate launcher_ic.png files into their correct alternate drawable density resolution folders. These folders were provided by the New Android Application Project series of dialogs we encountered in the first part of this chapter.

By using these alternate drawable resource folders, we can assure that Android will automatically find and use the correct launcher icon image asset resource for mainstream types of Android device screen size and density:

- /res/drawable-mdpi for normal size, Medium Density in Dots Per Inch (MDPI) displays

- /res/drawable-hdpi for large size, High Density in Dots Per Inch (HDPI) display screens

- /res/drawable-xhdpi for extra large size, Extra High Density Dot Per Inch (XHDPI) screens

- /res/drawable-xxhdpi for super large, Extra Extra High Density Dot Per Inch (XXHDPI)

Not surprisingly, you do this by giving your icon an exact name and file format, and putting it into an exact directory. When Android finds an icon file there, it automatically puts it into play as your application's icon. These files must follow these rules (defaults) precisely:

- Be placed in the correct /res/drawable-dpi folder, which holds all of the drawable resources for that screen density resolution

- Be named launcher_ic.png (we will learn how to change this in the next chapter on XML)

- Be a PNG file with an alpha channel (transparency), so that the icon overlays on any system background wallpaper seamlessly

In this section, I'll use my 3D company logo and an Android green hue, but you can use any image that you like. Also, I will use GIMP 2.8 for this image editing example, since all readers will have it installed, but you can use any image-editing program you prefer, such as Photoshop CS6 or Corel Painter. So let's fire up the GIMP software package that we installed in Chapter 1 and create a PNG file with transparency. We will be getting into transparency (alpha channels) in detail in the graphic design chapter later on in the book.

Creating Transparency: Edit the Image in GIMP

The first thing we need to do is to put the logo onto a transparency layer, and remove the white color from the current graphic design. Here are the steps to remove the white background from the Mind Taffy Design logo:

19. Use the GIMP **File ➤ Open** menu sequence to open the MindTaffyLogoAndroidGreen.gif logo file. The graphic image is currently 200 by 200 pixels, and is actually the first frame of an Animated GIF file that is utilized on my WallaceJackson.com web site

20. Select the "Select By Color" tool (fifth in the toolbar) and set the tolerance at 15 (bottom-middle tool tab for Select by Color tool settings) and the Select By to Composite. Make sure the Anti-Aliasing option is checked as well and then click the white area to select it, as shown in Figure 3-10.

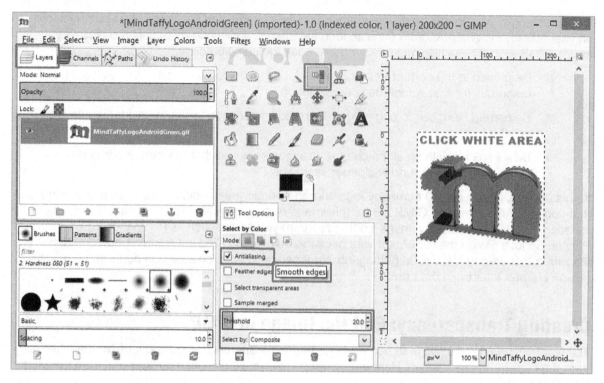

Figure 3-10. Logo open in GIMP including a Layers tab (left), Select by Color icon (middle), and settings

21. Right-click in the white area in the layers tab (upper-left, under the blue
     in Figure 3-10) that is directly underneath the selected layer showing the
     MindTaffyLogoAndroidGreen.gif image that you opened in Step 1, and select
     the "New Layer" option to open the New Layer Dialog shown in Figure 3-11.
     Name the layer "Transparency," accept the size defaults, and click **OK**.

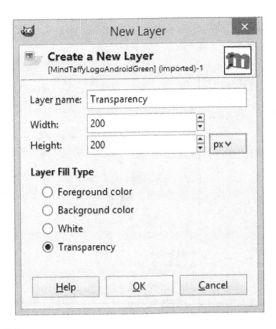

Figure 3-11. Create a New Layer dialog

22. Choose the **Select** Menu, and then the **Invert** menu option, shown in Figure 3-12. This will "invert" the selected white areas, deselecting them and instead selecting the logo itself. This cool technique will allow you to easily grab only the logo, since before only the white (non-logo) areas were selected, and therefore after the Invert operation only the logo pixels (non-white-area) are selected. The moral of this story? It's easier for the selection tool to select the (simple) contiguous white areas in the image than the complex shading gradients in the logo, so the proper work process is to actually work "backward," or in reverse!

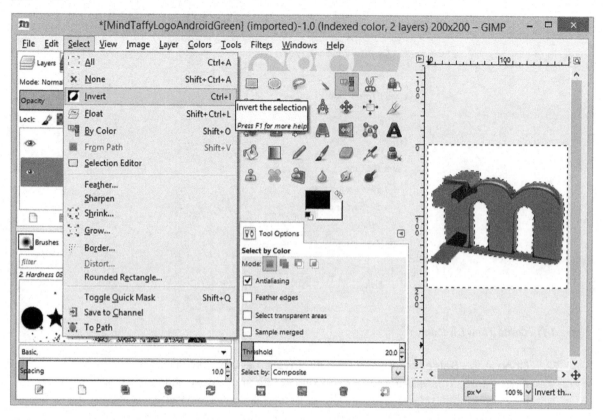

Figure 3-12. Use a Select ➤ Invert menu sequence to invert the selection so it selects the logo instead of white areas

23. Next, select the GIMP **Edit** menu, and then the **Copy** menu option shown
     in Figure 3-13. This will copy the currently selected logo image data to the
     clipboard. This is because the GIMP copy operation looks to see if there is
     a selection, and understands that if there is, that your intention is to copy
     the pixels inside of that selection area. It is important to notice the yellow
     pop-ups in many of these GIMP screenshots. These will appear in GIMP
     when you have your mouse over an icon, menu option, or tool setting, and
     they will tell you precisely what that GIMP UI element will do! I have included
     these pale yellow pop-ups in my GIMP screenshots during in chapter in
     order to make it easier for you to follow along with the work process we are
     learning about.

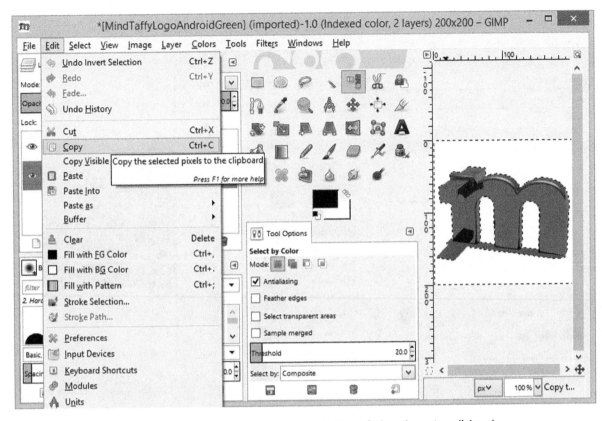

Figure 3-13. Use the Edit ➤ Copy menu sequence to copy the selected logo pixels to the system clipboard

24. Click on your **Transparency** layer on the left, which will select it (the layer will
     turn blue), if it is not selected already. You need to select this layer in order
     to paste the selected and copied logo above it. This is because the paste
     operation puts data above a currently selected layer, and not below it. If you
     left the original graphic layer selected, and then pasted, your transparency
     would be above your logo data, and not underneath it!

25. Next, hit the **Ctrl+V** keystroke combination, to paste the pixel data from the
     clipboard, or you can access the **Edit** menu and the **Paste** menu option,
     if you prefer a more visual work process. To see your logo on top of the
     transparency, you will need to click on the **Eye Icon** (turns a layer visibility on
     or off) next to the original MindTaffyLogoAndroidGreen.gif layer at the bottom
     of the layer stack. Once you do this, all that will be showing in your primary
     GIMP preview area on the right is the Transparency layer that you created
     earlier and the floating selection (the logo-only pixels that were copied from
     the clipboard memory) that you just pasted into the floating selection layer.
     The results of this work process are shown in Figure 3-14.

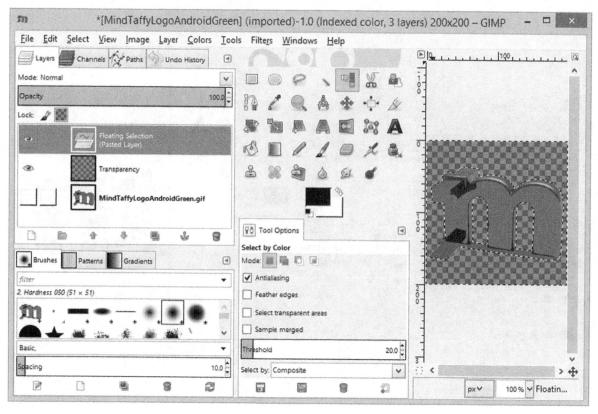

Figure 3-14. A floating selection layer over a Transparency layer; deselecting the original layer visibility

Note If you save out the file with GIMP configured in this fashion, what you see in the primary display area will be saved into the new target file that you specify, which we will be doing after we scale this graphic image to match the launcher icon size "rules" that I outlined in Table 3-2 earlier in this chapter. Once we do this scaling, you will be ready to save out your new app launch icons.

26.   Now that we have the launcher icon image in the transparent format we'll need in order to "composite" it (that is, to blend it seamlessly) with any Android desktop out there, we will use the **Image** menu and its **Scale Image** menu option, shown in Figure 3-15, to turn this 200 by 200 pixel source image into the Android-specified (required) target icon image sizes. If you remember from Table 3-2, the launcher icon sizes include 144, 96, 72, 48, and 36 pixels and you will need to use these icon sizes in your alternate drawable resources folders that Eclipse ADT created for you earlier in the chapter.

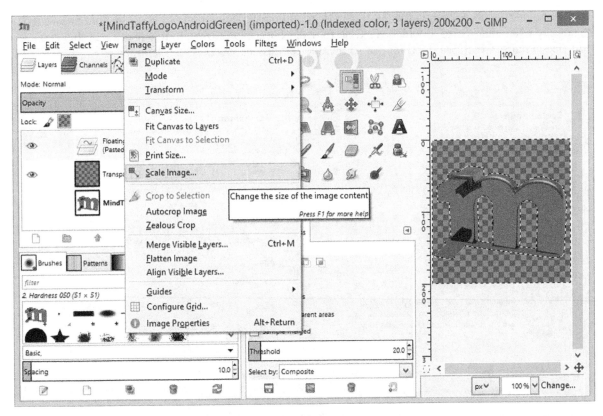

Figure 3-15. Use the Image ➤ Scale Image menu sequence to scale the 200-pixel graphic to be a 144-pixel icon

You have successfully finished the transparent Android launcher icon work process, in only eight steps. This is the basic work process necessary to extract your icon graphic elements and place them onto a transparent background.

Next, we will take a look at the work process to create all of the required resolution density assets (MDPI, HDPI, XHDPI, and XXHDPI; LDPI and XXXHDPI are not currently required) that you will need to have in place in order to properly support the wide range of Android consumer electronics devices in the marketplace, ranging from smartwatches to smartphones to eBook readers to tablets to laptops to iTV sets to 4K iTVs and probably beyond!

Creating Resolution Density App Launch Icons

To create the launcher icons needed for your Android application, we will use the GIMP **Image Scaling Algorithm** to "downsample" the 200 pixels in the current "source" image to the 144-, 96-, 72-, and 48-pixel resolution "destination" images that we need for the alternate resource folders.

Use the **Image ➤ Scale Image** menu sequence to do this in GIMP, as shown in Figure 3-15.

This menu sequence accesses the GIMP Scale Image dialog, shown in Figure 3-16, that allows us to specify what image size to which we wish to scale our Image down. In this first case, this is a 144-pixel image, which we need for our /drawable-xxhdpi/ resource folder location.

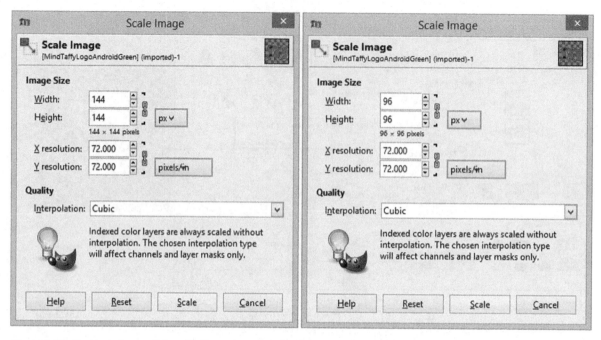

Figure 3-16. The Scale Image dialog with the settings for XXHDPI on the left, and for XHDPI on the right

As you can see, you will need to choose an **Interpolation Algorithm**. In GIMP, the "Cubic" (known as Bi-Cubic in Photoshop) interpolation algorithm will yield the highest quality level, so you will always want to use this particular algorithm. This is why GIMP 2.8 has this set as its default selection. GIMP 3.0 will be adding powerful new scaling algorithms, so make sure to get it when it becomes available!

Once you set your scaling parameters, click the "**Scale**" button to commit the scaling operation, and scale your 200-pixel source image into a 144-pixel extra extra high density Android device icon!

The technical term for scaling an image down in size is called "downsampling." In this particular case, we are downsampling an "indexed" or 8-bit color image, which is why you see the "GIMP Lightbulb" notification at the bottom of the Scale Image dialog shown in Figure 3-16.

This notification tells us that our image (and thus its layers) is using 8-bit indexed color depth, and that the Cubic interpolation will only affect **RGB color channels** (which we learn about in the graphic design chapter) and **layer masks** (transparency or alpha channel data, which our current image composite does indeed use). So we still need to specify **Cubic** since we are using a layer mask (an area of transparency) in our floating layer!

We will learn more about digital image concepts and terminology in an upcoming chapter on graphic design, where we will be creating "truecolor" PNG image assets and a truecolor application launcher icon, so that you will have experience working with 8-bit color, 24-bit color, and 32-bit color imagery in the Android OS.

Next, we will want to save this new 144-pixel image data into the launcher_ic.png file in our drawable resource folder to replace the standard green Android robot "placeholder" image that we had Eclipse ADT generate for us earlier in the chapter.

27. In GIMP, use the **File ➤ Export** or the **File ➤ Export As** menu sequences. The Export option in GIMP allows image data to be "saved out" using image formats other than GIMP's own **XCF** format, which is what you will get in GIMP if you use the **File ➤ Save** or **File ➤ Save As** menu sequences. Since Android uses **PNG** format (among others) but does not (yet) support the XCF format, we will be using the File ➤ Export As menu sequence shown in Figure 3-17.

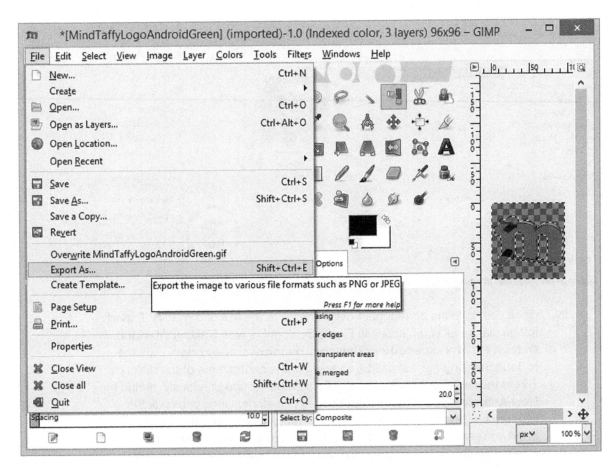

Figure 3-17. Use the File ➤ Export As menu sequence to export your downsampled icon to your project folder

Also notice that our transparent logo icon graphic has been scaled down from 200 pixels (shown on the right-hand side of the screenshot). The Cubic interpolation algorithm has done a great job, as the logo still looks really clean!

28.   In the **File Export** dialog, use the **Places Navigation Pane** (located on the left side of the dialog), and find your **workspace** folder, the **HelloUniverse** project folder, and the alternate drawable resources **drawable-xxhdpi** target folder, as shown in Figure 3-18, in the dialog that is numbered one, at the top, next to **Save in folder**.

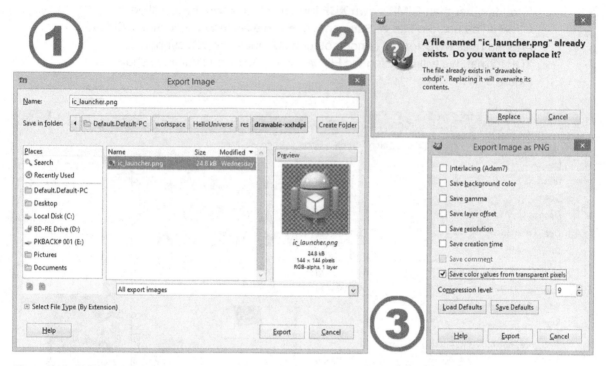

Figure 3-18. An Export Image dialog, the file overwrite warning dialog, and Export Image as PNG dialog

29.   Once you have the correct path diagrammed at the top of the GIMP Export Image dialog, as you can see in Figure 3-18, (mine was **C:\Users\Default. Default-PC\workspace\HelloUniverse\res\drawable-xxhdpi)**, click the **ic_launcher.png** file that will be showing in the central area of the dialog. This is the launcher icon that was auto-created for you previously, during the **New Android Application Project** series of dialogs. Once you click the **ic_launcher.png** file to select that file for replacement with the new icon asset you have just created, it will turn blue and you will see an image preview of what is inside of the file on the right-hand side of the dialog.

30.   When you click ic_launcher, that filename will be placed automatically in the top **Name** field, and the Save in Folder field will still show the proper path for saving (overwriting) this file to your **drawable-xxhdpi** folder on your C: drive! Once everything is configured correctly, click on the "**Export**" button to save out (to overwrite) your custom XXHDPI icon, which will replace the generic green Android robot that ADT auto-created earlier.

Once you click on Export, you will get two dialogs shown on the right side of Figure 3-18, the first confirming that you want to replace (overwrite) the existing ic_launcher.png launcher icon, and the second requesting File **Export Image as PNG** settings. These settings pertain to features supported by the PNG image file format.

To create the other three resolution icons, rather than going through the entire work process outlined previously from scratch, let's take a clever shortcut that involves the Edit menu and the Undo menu option, which is shown in Figure 3-19. This work process will save you almost a dozen iterative steps of production work!

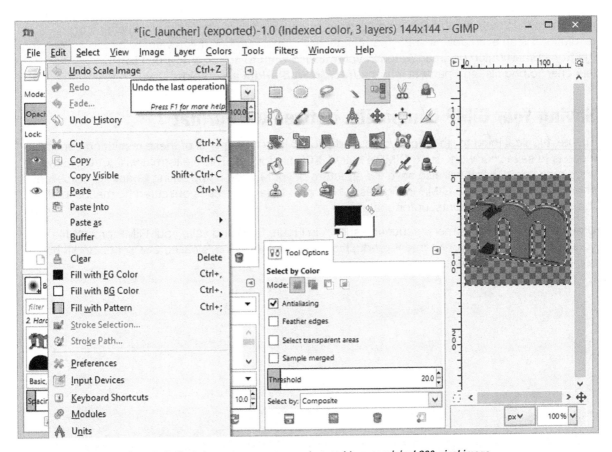

Figure 3-19. Use the Edit ➤ Undo Scale Image menu sequence to revert to your original 200-pixel image

All you need to do is utilize this **Edit ➤ Undo Scale** Image menu sequence, redo the last couple of steps (the image cubic scaling and the File Export dialog), and then do the same work process 3 more times to scale your original 200-pixel transparent image to 96, 72, and 48 pixels. Once you do the rescaling, you will then do the **File ➤ Export** and save (overwrite) your new launcher icon into the XHDPI, HDPI, and the MDPI alternate drawable resource folders under your HelloUniverse Android project master folder. This will replace the first ic_launcher.png file (Android robot) in each folder with the required resolution density equivalent of your new logo launcher icon. We will be replacing this later with a space-related truecolor (24-bit) HelloUniverse icon.

It is important to make sure that you scale down, or downsample, from the 200-pixel image each time you scale. So do a 200 pixels scale down to 96 pixels, a 200 pixels scale down to 72 pixels, and a 200 pixels scale down to 48 pixels. The reason for this is because the resulting quality will be significantly higher this way than if you utilized a work process where you scale from 200 to 144, and then 144 to 96, and then 96 to 72, and then 72 to 48.

This is because the more data you give the original Image Scaling Algorithm, the better job it will do; the algorithm will have more source image data to work with to create a good downsample quality.

Theoretically, to get the absolute highest-quality result, you would want to design your source image assets for your launcher icons to be 864 pixels! This is the resolution that Google actually recommends in their graphic design guidelines, because each of the Android launcher icon resolutions is an even downsample mathematically of that number. If you want to create an icon for the Sony SmartWatch or SmartWatch 2, you will also want to create a **36-pixel LDPI** launcher_ic.png file, and put that into the **/res/drawable-ldpi** asset folder.

Saving Your GIMP Composite: Native .XCF Format

The next logical thing to do before you spend a lot of time creating all of these resolution density icons is to save your work using GIMP's native .XCF file format. This file format will not only save your image data, but it will also save the structure of your image compositing "stack" or "pipeline" shown on the left side of GIMP in Figures 3-10 and 3-14 (and which is obscured by menus in all of the other GIMP screenshots, unfortunately).

Use the **File ➤ Save As** menu sequence shown in Figure 3-20 and save your GIMP project file on your hard disk drive in your content production assets folder. Mine is called C:\Clients, and it has sub-folders for each client.

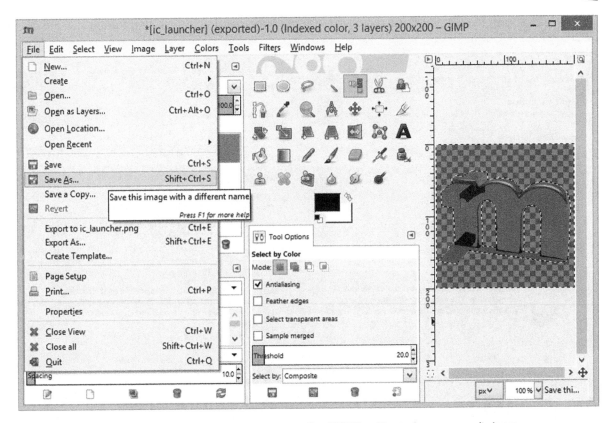

Figure 3-20. Use a File ➤ Save As menu sequence to save a native GIMP file with your image composite layers

Now that you have saved all of your hard image compositing work, it is time to go back and utilize what you have learned during this chapter to create all four (or five, if you are developing for LDPI devices such as smartwatches or flip-phones) ic_launcher.png assets.

In case you are wondering why all of these are called ic_launcher.png, ic_launcher is what is going to be referenced in your Java code and XML markup, and so that is the name you will need to use. What prevents these files from overwriting each other's different pixel resolution versions is the fact that they are kept separate from each other in different folder structures.

Then, at runtime, which we learned about earlier in the chapter (it seems so long ago, doesn't it?), Android will evaluate what hardware device it is running on as well as the physical hardware specifications of that hardware and decide for you what the optimal new media asset that you provided would be best served for that device!

Repeat the Work Process for the Lower Density Assets

Now, let's repeat the work process that you did to create your XXHDPI icon for the XHDPI, HDPI, and MDPI launcher icons. If you are developing for smartwatches, you can also create an icon to use for the 36-pixel LDPI density resolution specification. All of these resolution density folders have already been created for you by the Eclipse New Android Application series of dialogs earlier in this chapter, so hey, why not use them, and get in some much needed practice!

Figure 3-21 shown the **Scale Image** dialog in GIMP, with the parameters needed for the HDPI and MDPI icons.

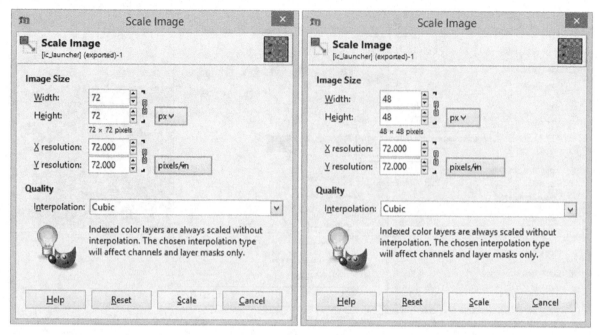

Figure 3-21. *Showing the Scale Image dialog with the settings for an HDPI icon on the left, and MDPI on the right*

Congratulations, you've just created a custom application icon for your HelloUniverse app, using GIMP 2.8.10!

Summary

In this third chapter, you learned about how the Android platform is structured, and about how it deals with the application at runtime, when one of your end users launches it on one of their many Android hardware devices. You learned that as of Android 4.4, the Android OS now has two different runtime environments, the Just In Time (JIT) Dalvik Virtual Machine (DVM) and the Ahead Of Time (AOT) Android RunTime (ART) virtual machine (VM). You looked at the pros and cons of JIT and AOT compilation as well.

Next, you learned how to create an Android 4.4 application bootstrap and Android project folder foundation by using the New Android Application Project series of dialogs in Eclipse ADT. Then, we took a look at the folders that comprise your Android application, most of which (besides your Java source files /src/ folder) are application resource folders. We looked at the various types of resource folders you can have in your Android app.

Finally, we learned how to create a custom Android application icon, which is always a top request from any new Android app developer. You learned how to use GIMP 2.8.10 to create a launcher icon with a transparent background, and how to save it in all the required screen density resolutions. In the next chapter, you will learn all about the XML markup language by taking an in-depth look at the Android application that you created during this chapter, including the XML files in the **/res/values/** folder as well as the **/res/layout/** folder and the **AndroidManifest.xml** file from your HelloUniverse project root folder.

Chapter 4

Introduction to XML: Defining an Android App, Its Design, and Constants

In this chapter, we will take a look at how the XML markup language allows application developers, and more importantly, application designers, to define their Android application's user interface (UI) designs, styling, themes, constants, permissions, icons, activities, services, and how they function within the Google Play e-storefront, all without having any knowledge of Java programming. Of course, I am going to teach you Java programming in this book, starting with the next chapter, but you could hire people to do just design and all they would have to know is how to use the XML language we are going to learn about during this chapter. It is important to note that these same XML concepts that you will be learning in this chapter apply to both the 32-bit Android 4.4 OS as well as to the new 64-bit Android 5.0 OS, which you will learn how to develop apps for in Chapter 16.

In the previous chapter, you created the foundation for your HelloUniverse Android application using Eclipse Android Development Tools (ADT) New Android Application series of dialogs. As part of this new application creation process, more than a half-dozen XML definition files were created. We are going to review all of these XML files during this chapter. We will do this so that you can learn the basics of XML markup, and also to show you how user interface design, menu systems, text values, styles and themes (global application styles), screen layout dimensions, and even your application configuration, using the Android Manifest, can all be easily implemented using only XML markup.

We will again take a closer look at all of the basic Android application components during this chapter, but this time, instead of doing this by looking at the Android application resource folder structure, we will do this by looking at the AndroidManifest.xml file. We will be learning about this Android Manifest XML definition file and its functions, structure, and its role in defining and controlling how your application will work within the Android OS, as well as within the Google Play e-storefront.

It is important to note that this AndroidManifest.xml application characteristics definition file works in exactly the same way, whether you are developing for 32-bit Android 4.x OS devices, or for 64-bit Android 5.x OS devices.

As you progress in your knowledge of Android, in this chapter this will be your knowledge of XML, you will continue to enhance the application foundation that you put into place in the previous chapter into something that is truly impressive, learning every corner of the Android OS as well as the Eclipse ADT Integrated Development Environment (IDE) in the process.

Extensible Markup Language: XML Overview

XML stands for **eXtensible Markup Language**. Extensible means that you can use it for whatever you like (think customizable); you could create your own XML set of tags for any purpose that you wish. It is a markup language because it uses simple "tags" to define what you wish to do. Most of you will be familiar with another markup language called HTML, or Hypertext Markup Language, which is used for creating HTML5 web sites and more recently for HTML5 application design.

Markup languages differ from programming languages in that they use **tags, parameters** (also called attributes) within these tags, and **nesting** structures to accomplish tasks that a higher-level programming language such as Java will implement using more complex programming structures, such as arrays, loops, and methods. We will be getting into Java and these types of constructs in the next chapter. You are really learning two programming languages, one that uses code, and the other that uses markup, over the duration of this book.

The reason for this approach, that is, using XML for everything that could possibly be construed as being design-oriented, is that using XML frees the members of your application development team who are designing the application's purpose, features, user interface, user experience, style and theme, graphics, and the like, from having to learn, or even understand, how the Java programming language works.

As you will soon see, when you compare this chapter to the next one on Java, XML markup is an order of magnitude easier to learn and leverage than Java programming structures and concepts are. For this reason, during this book, I am going to implement everything that I possibly can using XML markup, so that I can get you to an intermediate level of Android 4.x and Android 5.x application development in less than 700 dense pages of learning!

Although I'd like to take all the credit for this book being able to take you so very far from Absolute Beginner to Android Developer, the primary reason that this is possible is because Google Android OS developers allowed most of the advanced "front-facing" features, which allow you to ratchet up the wow-factor of your applications, to be designed and implemented entirely using XML, using only a line or two of Java programming logic!

Some examples of advanced Android design-related features that you can implement primarily using XML markup "definitions" include: multi-state graphics, skinned UI elements (custom graphic design UIs), frame or bitmap animation, vector or tween (procedural) animation, user interface layout design animation (UI parameter animation), options menus, pop-up menus and context-sensitive menus, dialogs, alerts, styles, themes, and more.

You can also implement less advanced design features using XML, including string (text) values for your app, integer (numeric) values, state or status (boolean) values such as on or off, visible or hidden, true or false, and screen spacing (dimension) values for your UI designs. Arrays, which are collections of data used in your app (sort of like a simple database) can also be created and loaded with their data values using XML files. All of this holds true for XML in 32-bit Android 4 and 64-bit Android 5.

XML markup is contained in **simple text format** files using an **xml** file extension. You can create XML files in a text editor, such as Windows Notepad; however, most programmers usually use a software editing tool with programming and markup design features, such as Eclipse, IntelliJ, or NetBeans. These XML files can then be read or "**parsed**" by the Android OS or your application Java code, and turned into Java object structures using the XML "definition" in each file.

XML Naming Schema: Tag & Parameter Repository

XML is comprised of "**tags**" and their "**parameters**." Parameters are part of the tags, and are used to **configure** and fine-tune what each of these tags accomplishes, as well as to **reference** any new media assets, or text fonts, or color values, or styles, or themes, or other XML definitions, and similar assets that might be required to "skin" or define how that application element appears to your users on their display screen.

The XML tags and parameters that you can use in a particular framework, such as in Android development, are specified using an XML "**naming schema**." This definition of the XML tags and parameters is stored in a **centralized repository**, similar to the one Eclipse accessed in Chapter 2, when you did a Check for Updates function. That repository hosted the latest Android SDK version and codebase, whereas the Android XML repository is located at a different URL location (a different folder) on Google's Android servers.

The reason that XML needs to have a naming schema is because this language is inherently designed to be "**extensible**." This means there is no "standard" version of XML; each version is customized for some required implementation (end use) by whatever person or organization needs to use it. In this case, Android's XML has been specifically customized for, and implemented for, the development of Android applications.

As an example, Android OS developers created the XML tag named **<RelativeLayout>** for designing Relative Layout designs that ultimately use the Android **RelativeLayout** Java class and define RelativeLayout objects. You'll learn all about what classes and objects are in the next chapter regarding the Java programming language.

The XML naming schema is referenced inside of each of your XML definition files, at the very top, so that the XML markup inside of that file can reference its XML naming schema (the customized XML specification) in order to make sure that all of the tags and parameters used in the XML definition are up-to-date and "**valid**."

This ability to reference the current XML tags and parameters definition (naming schema) is possible due to the ability to check the XML in the file against the "master definition" represented by the schema at the remote repository location, although Eclipse ADT does not do this in "real-time" currently, so you do not need an active Internet connection to be able to develop your XML markup. This process of making sure that your XML tags and their attributes or parameters are correct (in conformance with the XML definition) is called **XML validation**, and it uses an **XML naming schema** parameter to accomplish this XML validation.

In any custom extensible markup language, such as the one that has been created by Google for Android, this naming schema URL reference needs to be contained in the **first** (outermost) "**parent**" tag. This parent tag will usually contain other "**child**" tags, which are "**nested**" inside of (underneath) the parent tag. XML is so familial that way! The nesting of child tags, as well as tag parameters, are more easily seen if the XML programmer uses **indenting** to show which tags are inside of other higher-level (parent) tags, as you can see in Figure 4-1.

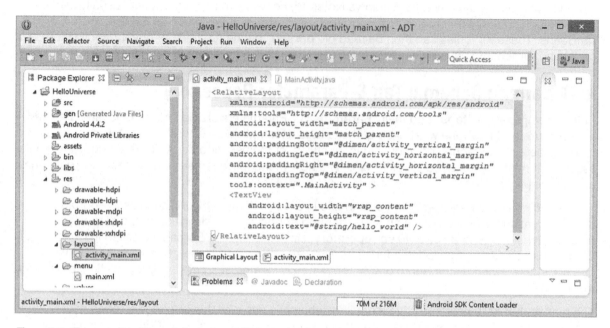

Figure 4-1. The contents of the activity_main.xml file in the /res/layout folder in the Eclipse editing pane

Let's take a look at the Relative Layout UI design in the **activity_main.xml** file, which Eclipse ADT created for you as a UI layout foundation to start building your UI design upon for the HelloUniverse Android application.

As you can see in Figure 4-1, the first line of the parent **<RelativeLayout>** UI layout container tag has an **xmlns:android=http://schemas.android.com/apk/res/android** parameter. This parameter defines the XML naming schema repository for Android OS as being in the **schemas** virtual server, on the **android.com** Internet address, in the **/apk/** folder, in a **/res/** sub-folder, and finally in an **/android/** sub-sub-folder.

In this case, the **<RelativeLayout>** container is the parent tag, and the **xmlns:android** is one of the parameters that configures this tag. This parameter will allow this parent UI layout tag to reference the XML naming scheme repository, and defines the prefix "**android**" as a short cut to reference this repository. Note that just because it "references" the proper XML definition repository does not mean that it is connecting in real-time to check this repository, as I pointed out earlier (it is used as a unique identifier). As you can see inside of the <RelativeLayout> tag, there are a significant number of parameters, a half-dozen of which start with **android:** and what this android: reference equates to is defined by that first xmlns:android parameter.

Essentially, what is happening here is that the xmlns:android parameter is defining a "shortcut" for all the other parameters that start with **android:** to be able to check themselves against the XML naming schema repository.

Thus, thanks to the xmlns:android URL definition parameter, the **android:width="match_parent"** parameter is actually short-hand for a **http://schemas.android.com/apk/res/android:width="match_parent"** parameter.

The same logic applies to the second **xmlns:tools** parameter and the **tools:context=".MainActivity"** parameter at the end of the <RelativeLayout> parent tag, also shown in Figure 4-1. These XML constructs (tags and parameters) are more complex, lower-level operating-system–related definitions such as the one here that sets the **Context** object for the RelativeLayout UI definition to the **MainActivity** Activity class, which Eclipse ADT created for you in Chapter 2 using the New Android Application Project series of dialogs.

As you can see here, Android OS really has two XML naming schemas (language definitions), in two different software repositories. The Android Package (apk) naming schema was designed for high-level (design-oriented usage) XML, and is at schemas.android.com/apk. It is also the one you will be using 95% of the time in your Android application development, and the one I will be covering throughout this book.

The Android Tools (tools) naming schema was designed to provide low-level (OS-related usage) XML, and is at schemas.android.com/tools. You can use it to do things such as declare a Context object using XML. You will learn more about Context objects in the next chapter when I cover Java programming concepts and structures as well as throughout the book as we use Context objects.

XML Syntax: Containers, Brackets, and Nesting

There are two ways to code (or to mark up, to be more precise) any XML tag, and which markup approach you use depends upon whether that tag is going to have any children (nested tags) or not. Attributes, also known as parameters, are inside each tag, and configure the tag and what it will do, but should not be considered "children" of the tag. Attributes that specify values or references will use quotation marks to do this, such as the **android:text="data value"** parameter shown shortly.

If an XML tag is a parent tag (this is, it has "nested" or child tags inside of it), it is said to be a **"container,"** just like the XML file itself is the container for the entire XML construct, which in Android is generally a **definition** of one type or another, as you will see throughout this chapter, as well as throughout the rest of this book.

Fortunately, our HelloUniverse bootstrap UI layout design, shown in Figure 4-1, shows both of these types of **bracketing** treatments, so I can simply describe the usage here and you can observe it in the screen shot (or in Eclipse ADT, if you have it running and on your computer workstation screen, which I am hoping you do).

Since the **<TextView>** UI element, which defines a Text UI element on the screen, as you may have guessed, has no children, and has parameters configuring its width, height, and text content, this tag is opened using the **<TextView** portion of the tag and is closed using the **/>** character sequence. So, with parameters inside of this tag, it would look something like this:

```
<TextView android:layout_width="OS constant" android:layout_height="OS constant" android:text="data value" />
```

The XML for this child tag, which is shown in Figure 4-1, uses **indentation**, for easy parameter views, as well as actual Android constants, which you'll learn about in the next chapter covering Java, as well as Java String references to a text data value, which you'll learn about soon in the chapters covering Java programming and UI layout design. For now, we are just going to look at the "syntax" of XML—that is, how it needs to be constructed or coded (written on the screen). We will look at how it all works together in the next section of this chapter.

Since the <RelativeLayout> tag does have a child <TextView> tag nested inside of it, it uses a different **bracket** configuration. At a high-level view, it will look like this:

```
<RelativeLayout> <TextView /> </RelativeLayout>
```

Once you put parameters inside of the parent and child tags, and indent everything, so that you know what level each of these tags and its parameters are supposed to be at, it will look exactly like what you see in Figure 4-1, which I will replicate here. We will be going over what all of this XML markup is doing during this chapter.

```
<RelativeLayout
    xmlns:android="http://schemas.android.com/apk/res/android"
    xmlns:tools="http://schemas.android.com/tools"
    android:layout_width="match_parent"
    android:layout_height="match_parent"
    android:paddingBottom="@dimen/activity_vertical_margin"
    android:paddingLeft="@dimen/activity_horizontal_margin"
    android:paddingRight="@dimen/activity_horizontal_margin"
    android:paddingTop="@dimen/activity_vertical_margin"
    tools:context=".MainActivity" >
    <TextView
        android:layout_width="wrap_content"
        android:layout_height="wrap_content"
        android:text="@string/hello_world" />
</RelativeLayout>
```

In summary, any tag that is used as a parent tag will have an opening tag **<RelativeLayout>** and a closing tag **</RelativeLayout>** with the tag name in both the opening and the closing tag. The closing tag will have a slash in front of the tag name to signify to the XML "parsing engine" (the code that is interpreting the XML markup and turning it into something else; in this case, Java objects) that this is a closing tag.

Alternatively, a child tag that has no children of its own will have the closing slash at the end of the opening tag, like this: **<TextView android:parameters/>** which allows a much more compact way of writing a child tag. You might think of this as an implicit closing tag, so a tag with no child tags nested inside of it will not have an explicit (backslash in front of tag name inside of < > chevron bracketing) closing tag like the </RelativeLayout> UI layout container has. Since a layout container is inherently a container and will always have child tags, it will always have an explicit closing tag at the bottom of the XML definition file.

It's important to note that tag nesting can be more than one level deep, so you can have the following structure:

```
<RelativeLayout>
    <LinearLayout>
        <ImageView>
        <TextView>
    </LinearLayout>
</RelativeLayout>
```

As you can see, the closing tags must be in the reverse order from the opening tag order, so that the XML tag structure exhibits proper nesting within its level hierarchy.

XML Referencing: Chain XML Constructs Together

XML files can also **"reference"** other XML files, so that you can create a "chain" where your XML definitions can be more **"modular."** XML file referencing is somewhat akin to XML tag nesting, but it **spans across files**. Referencing in Android uses the @ symbol, which is specific to Android XML file referencing.

If you were wondering what the **@dimen/** and **@string/** "prefixes" were in the activity_main.xml UI layout XML markup shown in Figure 4-1, these are references to XML tags and parameters in the dimens.xml and strings.xml XML definition files.

Android uses the @ character to signify that another XML file is being referenced, as you will see over the rest of the chapter, as we look at how to use XML markup to define values, dimensions, menus, styles, themes, and your Android Manifest, which controls everything about your application and how it works.

The @ character allows XML files to reference other XML files, allowing developers to create their own logical XML structures. This allows XML markup to be modular and allows developers to organize and optimize their XML definitions using multiple files. Without this referencing capability, XML markup would end up being all lumped together in one or two massive files. Referencing allows this XML "structure" to be created, such as the XML structure for your HelloUniverse application, which the Eclipse ADT put into place for you with the New Android Application Project series of dialogs.

We'll be looking at your application's current XML structure, and all of the files within it, as well as how these XML files reference each other. We will also be looking at how to change the tag parameter values within these XML files in order to customize your Android application during the remainder of this chapter.

Once we're all finished looking at each of the XML files that are currently in your bootstrap project, I'll include a visual of how all of these go together to for the foundational XML structure for your Android application that you will be building upon during the rest of this book. If you want to cheat, and look ahead in this chapter, you can go ahead and take a quick peak, the visual is Figure 4-17.

Let's take a closer look at the **strings.xml** file in the /res/values folder first, as this is one of the most often used XML files in Android application development. Open the **/res/values** folder by clicking the right-facing arrow next to it. Right-click on the **strings.xml** file and select the **Open** option from the context-sensitive menu.

As you can see in Figure 4-2, the strings.xml file does not need to reference the XML repository URL, as it just contains resource definitions, using the parent **<resources>** tag and, in this case, child **<string>** tags, defining each string value, and giving the value a (variable) name. We will get into variables in the next chapter on Java. The reason this file does not require an xmlns:android XML naming schema definition at the top of the XML definition is because the attributes or parameters used inside of the tags in this file do not preface themselves with something else. Notice in Figure 4-2 you are using **name="app_name"** and not **android:name="app_name"** and realize that if you were using android:name="app_name" that you would then need an xmlns:android naming schema definition in place before you used this parameter name convention.

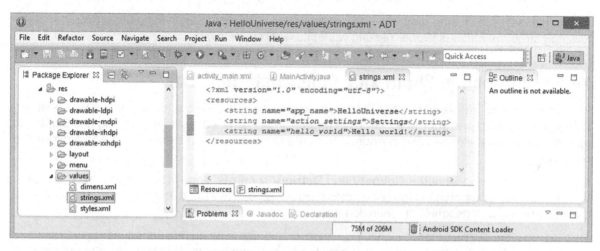

Figure 4-2. *The strings.xml file located in the /res/values folder and with three <string> constants defined*

The three <string> tags currently defined in this strings.xml file are named **app_name**, **action_settings**, and **hello_world**, and define the text strings for the application icon and title bar, currently **HelloUniverse**, as well as a menu item labeled **Settings** and the "**Hello world!**" message that your app writes to the display screen.

The way a <string> tag defines a string (text) variable is that the name parameter is used in the first part of the string value XML definition to define the string variable name, and the actual text value for a string goes inside of the **<string>text</string>**, as you can see in Figure 4-2. The app_name string XML definition would thus be:

```
<string name="app_name">HelloUniverse</string>
```

Next, we will edit our application name, by editing this XML <string> constant definition in this strings.xml file, so that there is a space between the Hello and Universe. Your AndroidManifest.xml file uses this app_name constant (as you will see in a later section of this chapter) to determine what the application icon name (under the icon graphic) and the title of the app in the title bar will be. Making this simple edit will make your app look more professional, and will be easier to read for your end users. Let's do this next, and then we can get into more complicated XML definitions after that.

XML Constants: Editing Constants Using XML

Click your text insertion cursor between the Hello and Universe in the first <string> tag's data value and hit the spacebar to add a space character, as is shown in Figure 4-3. This simple edit will change all of the instances of HelloUniverse in your application to be Hello Universe. After we look at the dimensions, styles, and OS themes defined by XML, we will run the Android application in the Nexus One Android Virtual Device (AVD) emulator and you can see this for yourself. For now, however, you will just have to trust me and the app modifications we are making.

Figure 4-3. The edited constant values in the strings.xml file located in the /res/values folder

Next, we will take a look at the dimens.xml XML definition file, which is used to hold the dimension constants and their data values used to define the dimensions, using pixel values to define layout spacing, for an Android application's UI design (or for more than one design, if you have defined multiple Activity classes).

XML Dimensions: Editing Dimensions Using XML

Let's take a look at the **dimens.xml** file in the **/res/values** folder and see what global application margin spacing has been set up for your Android application by the Eclipse ADT New Android Application Project series of dialogs. Right-click on the dimens.xml file and select the **Open** option from the menu, or alternatively, left-click on the file name and use the F3 function key at the top of your keyboard; either work process will work.

As you can see in Figure 4-4, there are two <dimen> child tags defined inside of a parent <resources> tag, just like you saw in the strings.xml file, but instead of <string> the child tag is <dimen>. These also use the **name=** parameter to name the dimension constants and set a data value of 16 dp, or **density pixels**, in exactly the same way that the text string values were set. Here is an example of the XML tag and parameter format used:

```
<dimen name="activity_horizontal_margin">16dp</dimen>
```

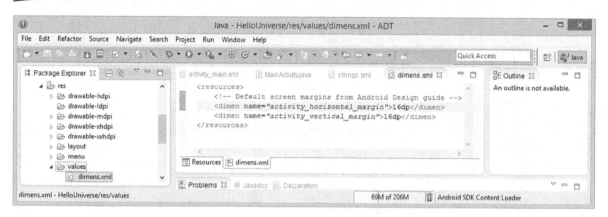

Figure 4-4. The dimens.xml file located in the /res/values folder and with two <dimen> constants defined

It is important to note that the tags for <string> and <dimen> are singular, as are the @string/ and @dimen/ referencing prefixes used to reference them, but the XML files that hold these definitions are plural.

In case you are wondering, the reason for this is that the assumption by the Android OS is that you are going to define more than one <dimen> or <string> and so the file names the Eclipse ADT IDE created for you to use are called strings.xml, dimens.xml, and styles.xml. The same logic applies to the <style> tag and @style/ prefix, as you are about to see in the next section where we cover styles and themes.

If you want to put a little more space between your UI design and content and the edges of your Android device hardware, you could edit these values and use something like 20dp or 24dp. Later, when we learn the AVD work process, you can edit these values and play around with the results of how close to or far away from the edge of the display screen you want your app content to be. I will be covering dp, also known as **device-independent pixels** (DIP) in later more advanced chapters on UI design and graphic design.

Next, we are going to take a look at the third and final XML definition file that Eclipse ADT created for you in the /res/values folder, the styles.xml file. If you are wondering why this values folder is not named value, or why the layout and menu folders are not named layouts and menus, I unfortunately don't have the answer to that one for you!

XML Styles: Editing Styles or Themes Using XML

Whereas text strings and density pixel dimensions are fairly straightforward, Android styles and OS themes, which are actually a collection of style definitions, are a bit more involved and farther reaching, and hence are more complicated. If you are familiar with web sites and apps created using HTML5 and CSS3, you are familiar with the concept of "styling" using a style definition that is separate from your code and content. Styles and Themes in Android 5 are called "Materials," and will be covered in Chapter 16.

What a style does is allow you to define in one central location how the design of your application is going to look as far as colors, spacing, and font characteristics (text typeface and size) are concerned. This allows you to extract the "styling" of your design from the actual content within that design, and from the programming logic behind how the design functions.

We are not going to completely cover styles and themes in this chapter, as that more advanced subject matter is better suited for the UI design chapters, but I am going to show you how the styles. xml files fit into your overall app structure and how to change the OS primary theme, so you can make your application "light" (white and light gray) or "dark" (black and dark gray).

Let's right-click on the **styles.xml** file in the **/res/values** folder, and select the **Open** option from the context-sensitive menu, or left-click and hit the **F3** key, and then we can take a look at the styles.xml file in the central editing pane of Eclipse, as is shown in Figure 4-5.

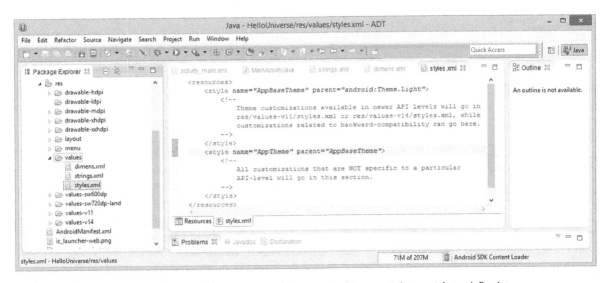

Figure 4-5. The default styles.xml file, located in the /res/values folder, with two <style> containers defined

As you can see, there are two <style> containers defined in the file, and both of these child tags are empty, although they are set up using the tag opening and closing syntax, which shows that they will eventually contain child tags (style definitions) of their own, which is why I am calling them "containers."

Another interesting thing in this XML definition file is that a second <style> tag named **AppTheme** references the first <style> tag named **AppBaseTheme**. This is done using a **parent="AppBaseTheme"** parameter, which makes the AppBaseTheme style the parent of the AppTheme style. As you can see, the **android:Theme.Light** OS theme is the parent of the AppBaseTheme, and since the AppTheme style is referenced as the theme for the app in the AndroidManifest.xml file, which we will be looking at a bit later in the chapter, the "chaining" that I talked about earlier between XML definitions would go something like this:

```
Android Manifest App's Theme > AppTheme > AppBaseTheme > android:Theme.Light theme definition
```

If you follow this chain of referencing through, you will see that for Android OS versions earlier than Version 3, your application is set to utilize the Android Theme.Light OS theme. If you wanted pre-version 3.0 Android devices to use a dark (black and dark grey) OS theme, you would change this to **android:Theme.Dark**.

As you decide what you want your application styles to be, you can add definitions in this /res/values/styles.xml file to affect Android versions 1.5, 1.6, 2.0, 2.1, 2.2, and 2.3. Styles for Android OS versions 3.0, 3.1, or 3.2 will go in the styles.xml file in an **alternate definition folder** called **/res/values-v11**, as you can see in Figure 4-6.

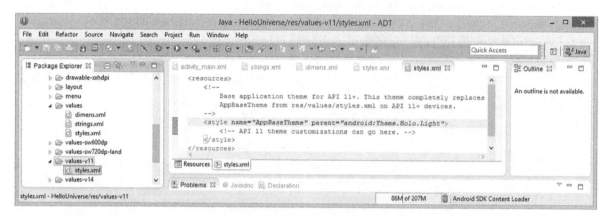

Figure 4-6. *The second styles.xml file, in the /res/values-v11 alternate folder with <style> definition container*

As you can see, there is a second styles.xml file in this alternate values folder! This will be accessed by Android OS if the device your application is running on is running Android OS version 3.0, 3.1, or 3.2. You will need to get used to this paradigm in Android OS where files with the same exact name also exist, with different content, in different (**alternate resource**) folder names. This can take some getting used to, but the logic behind it is that Android OS is allowed to select from different resources based on OS versions and hardware versions that your end users are utilizing. The reason the names have to be the same is that they are referencing the same asset in your Java code and XML markup. Once you understand what is going on and why, it will make complete sense to you and you will have that "Ah-Ha! moment" where (and when) you no longer question this strange practice.

You encountered this same file name with different asset contents for the first time in the previous chapter when you created the same ic_launcher.png file name with different image resolution versions of your icon graphic, in different /res/drawable-dpi alternate pixel density resource folders.

As you can see in Figure 4-6, Android OS incorporated a new theme in Version 3.0 and later called Holo, which also comes in Light and Dark versions. The reason for this "chaining" of <styles> will now become apparent to you, as the only link in the chain that needs to be changed to incorporate this change for V3 devices is the AppBaseTheme style, which gets changed to reference the parent style of android:Theme.Holo.Light. If you wanted Android 3.0, 3.1, and 3.2 OS devices to use a dark theme, you would change this to Theme.Holo.

So for Android Version 3.0, 3.1, and 3.2, the <style> XML definition chain still goes from the Android Manifest style assignment to the AppTheme style, and this first XML style definition link in the chain is located in your AndroidManifest.xml file as you will see a bit later on in the chapter. The style "link" from the AppTheme style to AppBaseTheme parent style still remains in place as well, as defined in the /res/values/styles.xml "root" style definition. However, for devices running version 3.0, 3.1, or 3.2, the AppBaseTheme style is defined differently due to the styles.xml file that is located in the **/res/values-v11** alternate folder. This same alternate style folders approach holds true for Android 5.x OS as well.

When the Android OS ascertains that your application is running on a hardware device that is running version 3.0, 3.1, or 3.2 of the Android OS, it will insert the API Level 11 folder **/res/values-v11** XML style definition(s), shown in Figure 4-6. Since this style definition (or definitions if you add any child styles in the empty container, as it is intended for you to do) features a parent of **android:Theme.Holo.Light**, the HOLO Light OS theme will be inserted into this XML definition chain, and this theme will be the one that will be utilized for the Android application whenever it is running on Android 3.0, 3.1, and 3.2 devices.

Figure 4-7 shows the **/res/values-v14** alternate folder, with a third **styles.xml** definition, which covers Android 4.0 and later OS versions, which would include 4.0.4, 4.1.2, 4.2.2, 4.3.1, and 4.4.4. The same logic applies here, and to implement the new HOLO Light Theme with a Dark Action Bar, all you need to do is change the AppbaseTheme style definition to point to the parent OS style of **android:Theme.Holo.Light.DarkActionBar** and the new XML style reference chain that will be utilized for Android 4.x devices will be as follows:

```
AndroidManifest Theme > AppTheme > AppBaseTheme > android:Theme.Holo.Light.DarkActionBar
```

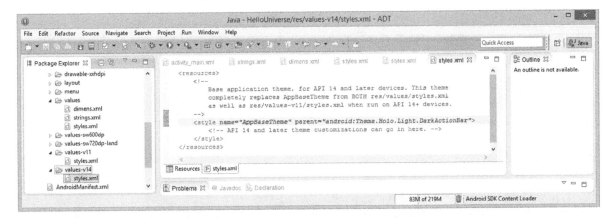

Figure 4-7. The third styles.xml file, located in the /res/values-v14 alternate folder with <style> container defined

If you want to change your OS theme for Android 4 and later devices to be a dark theme, which we will do in the next section after we learn how to launch and use the Nexus One AVD emulator, you would change this to be Theme.Holo, as the default Holo theme is Holo Dark. If you want to add a custom style, called a "material" in Android 5, it would go in a /res/values-v20 alternate folder.

Now that we have taken a look at the three XML definition files in the /res/values folder and alternate values folders, let's take a break from XML for a bit and run your HelloUniverse app using the Nexus One AVD. After that, we will change your OS theme to Holo to see what a Holo Dark OS theme looks like, and then we will take a look at XML definitions in the /res/menu folder. Finally, we'll look at the XML that is used to define your app itself inside of the AndroidManifest.xml file in the "root" /HelloUniverse project folder.

Running Your HelloUniverse App: Using Your AVD

The easiest way to "run" your Android application is to right-click on the HelloUniverse project folder, which will give you a context-sensitive menu containing all of the things that you can do in Eclipse relative to your HelloUniverse Android project.

As you can see in Figure 4-8, there is a "**Run As**" option two-thirds of the way down the menu, and it has a sub-menu with two important options. The first sub-menu contains the "**Android Application**" option. This runs your Android application in the currently active (selected) AVD emulator. If you have defined more than one AVD emulator, which we in fact did back in Chapter 2 when we defined the Neptune Pine smartwatch emulator to show you how to "scratch define" an unsupported AVD emulator, you can select which one you want to use using the **Run Configurations** sub-menu option.

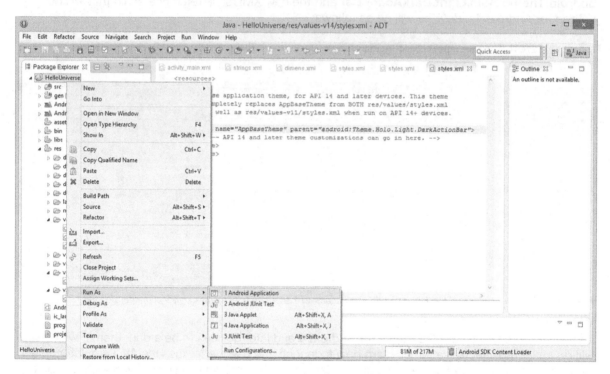

Figure 4-8. *Right-click on the HelloUniverse project folder and select the Run As ➤ Android Application menu sequence*

This is the reason that the other important sub-menu is the **Run Configurations** option, which opens the Run Configurations dialog that shows you all of the AVD emulators you have defined, and allows you to select which one you want to use and to set it to be your default or active AVD for your Eclipse ADT IDE.

If you use the **Run As ➤ Android Application** menu sequence, and the Nexus One AVD does not appear (for instance, if the Neptune Pine AVD pops-up), simply use this **Run As ➤ Run Configurations** menu sequence first. The Neptune One emulator is shown in Figure 4-10, in case you are wondering what it should look like.

Once you have launched the **Run Configurations dialog**, shown in Figure 4-9, click the middle **Target** tab, and then select the **Nexus One** as your default emulator. To do this, place a check mark next to **AVD_Nexus_One_by_Google**, which will deselect any other selected AVD emulator (in this case, that would be the Neptune Pine smartwatch). Once this is done, you can click the **Apply** button, which will set the Nexus One as your new default AVD emulator, so that it is now the AVD that will appear every time you use the **Run As ➤ Android Application** work process.

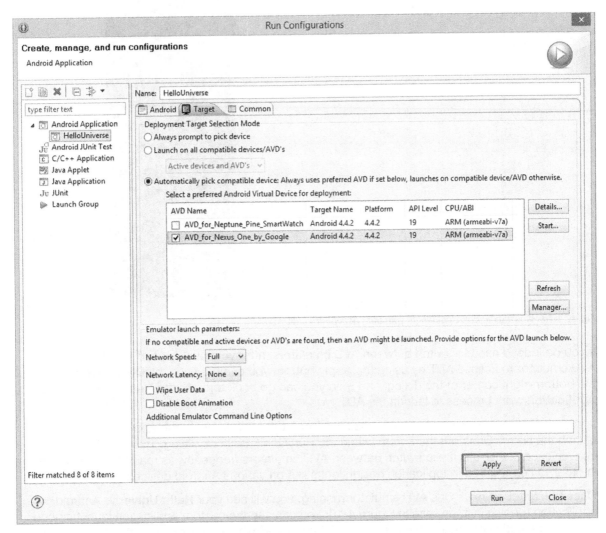

Figure 4-9. Use the Run Configurations dialog to select Nexus One AVD and click the Apply button to set it as your AVD

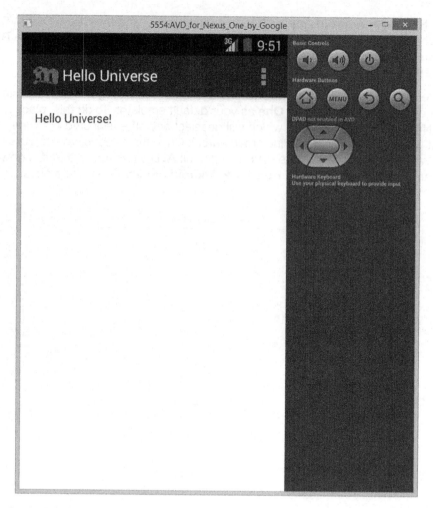

Figure 4-10. *Viewing the HoloLight theme with Dark ActionBar in AVD*

If you do indeed need to switch between AVD emulators, after you have applied the Nexus One AVD emulator to Eclipse ADT by using the Apply button, you can then use the **Close** button in the bottom-right corner of the dialog, and then you can go back and use the **Run As ➤ Android Application** work process to launch the ADT.

It is important to note that you can also use the **Run** button (underneath the Apply button) and launch the Nexus One right there from within the Run Configurations dialog. This is a great convenience, especially if you switch between AVD emulators frequently, as many developers do, in order to see what their application design looks like on various Android devices.

Once you get the Nexus One AVD emulator running, you will see your **Hello Universe** Android application running in it, as seen in Figure 4-10. You can see the custom application launcher icon that you created in Chapter 3 in the left side of the title bar, which is called the Action Bar in Android and is controlled by the Android **ActionBar** class. We will learn about Java classes in Chapter 5 and the Action Bar in Chapter 7.

You can see the text string modifications you made in the **strings.xml** file, back in Figure 4-3, in the ActionBar title, which is now attractively spaced, relative to your application icon. Your **app_name** text string now says **Hello Universe**, rather than HelloUniverse, and your **hello_world** text string, which is referenced in your UI design by the TextView UI widget in the **activity_main.xml** file shown in Figure 4-1, now gives a more logical greeting for the application relative to the application name. You can also see the Holo Light OS theme with the Dark ActionBar in this screenshot; this was defined in the **styles.xml** file in the /res/values-v14 alternate folder.

The first time that you use the AVD emulator in Eclipse, you will get an **Auto Monitor Logcat** dialog, which will ask you if you would like ADT to automatically monitor logcat output error messaging for your current application. This is a good idea to have available for your application "debugging" or error eradication work process, so select the "Yes" option and accept the default "error" level of notification set via the drop-down menu shown at the right side of the dialog in Figure 4-11. I clicked on the drop-down menu before I took the screenshot, so that you could see the various levels of error notification that the Android OS can give to you.

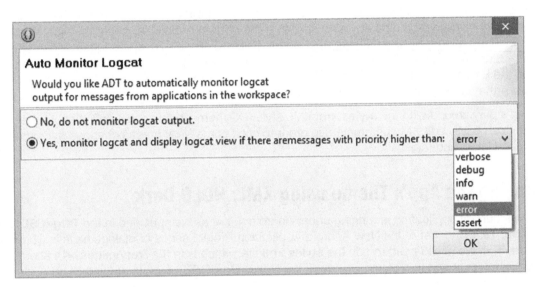

Figure 4-11. Setting the ADT Logcat to Auto Monitor error messages

If you look at the error and debugging related tabs at the bottom of Eclipse in one of the screenshots in this chapter before you select this Logcat monitoring option, such as Figure 4-7 being the most recent that shows this, you will see that there is no Logcat tab available. After you select this option, there will be a Logcat tab in Eclipse ADT, as you can see in Figure 4-12 when we begin to edit OS themes to change your application style.

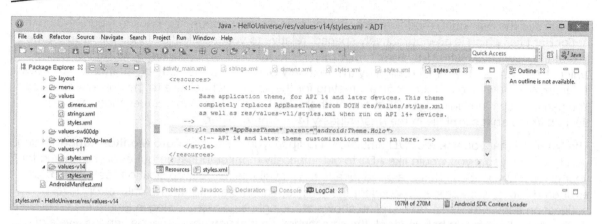

Figure 4-12. *Changing your application OS theme to the Holo (Dark) theme in the /res/values-v14/styles.xml*

In fact, Eclipse ADT also added a **Console** tab, as well as a **LogCat** tab, so now you have five different error investigation tabs at your disposal at the bottom of Eclipse, rather than just three! It is also interesting to note between Figure 4-11 and 4-12 that Eclipse ADT spells logcat three different (capitalization) ways: Logcat in the dialog title, logcat in the dialog text area, and LogCat in the tab used in the Eclipse ADT IDE. I prefer **LogCat**, as it stands for Error Log Catalog (for errors) and so I will used that capitalization during the rest of this book.

Next, let's play around with the **styles.xml** XML style (OS theme in this case) definition, to see how you can easily edit XML parameters in order to elicit some fairly drastic changes to how an application looks and feels!

Changing the App's Theme using XML: HOLO Dark

Since our current application is running under Android 4.4.4, as we specified in the **Target SDK** of **API Level 19**, in the first of the New Android Application Project series of dialogs back in Chapter 3 (Figure 3-3), we would need to edit the **styles.xml** file, which is in the **/res/values-v14** alternate resources folder to see this change inside of the Nexus One AVD, which is running as an Android 4.x device emulator.

Let's remove the Holo Light designation, and the Dark ActionBar, by setting the **parent=** parameter to simply refer to the **android:Theme.Holo** constant setting, as the default Holo OS theme is Dark as its default setting. This is shown in Figure 4-12, and simply involves back-spacing over the .Light.DarkActionBar position of the OS theme constant shown back in Figure 4-7. Once you run your AVD emulator again, which we are going to do next, you will see the change to the application's look and feel.

To test your new OS theme in the Nexus One AVD, use your **Run As ➤ Android Application** work process to launch the emulator, and check out your new "darker" application look and feel, which is shown in Figure 4-13.

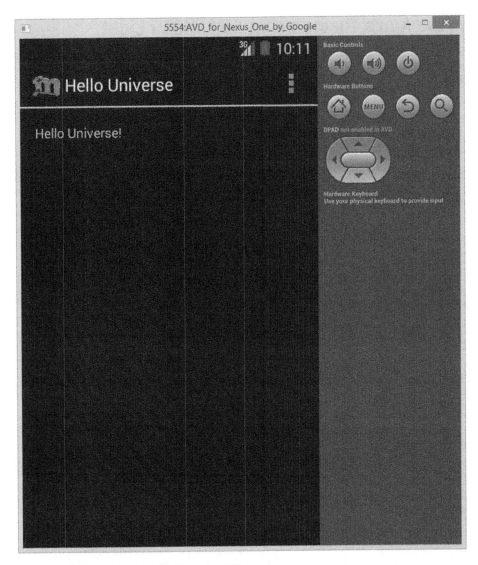

Figure 4-13. Viewing the Holo Dark theme in the Nexus One AVD

As you can see a "dark" theme uses **Black** as a background color instead of White, and uses **White** text instead of Black text. The same changes are applied to the ActionBar, which uses a **Cyan**-colored separator bar instead of no separator bar (see Figure 4-10). Next, we're going to try the Holo Light OS theme, so you can see some of the different looks you can get for your application, simply by changing one XML style tag **parent=** parameter!

Changing the App's Theme using XML: HOLO Light

Now let's take a look at the Android 4.x Holo Light theme, which is quite simple to do, thanks to Android using XML to define application resources, constants, and settings in such as organized and easy-to-code way. Add the **.Light** extension to the **android:Theme.Holo** constant in the <style> tag in the app's /res/values-v14/styles.xml XML style definition file, shown in Figure 4-14, so that this parameter now reads `parent="android:Theme.Holo.Light"` and then you will be ready to again use your newfound **Run As ➤ Android Application** work process to preview the results!

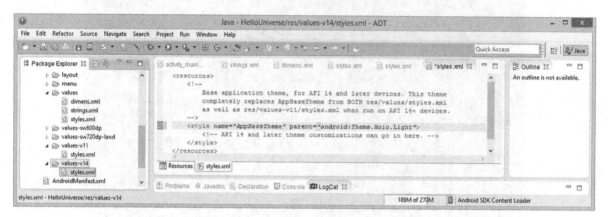

Figure 4-14. Editing the /res/values-v14/styles.xml AppBaseTheme style's parent theme to be Theme.Holo.Light

As you can see in Figure 4-15, the Android Holo Light OS theme uses a **White** background in conjunction with **Black** text, along with a **LightGray** ActionBar and **MediumGray** ActionBar separator, which looks quite nice!

Figure 4-15. Viewing the Android 4.x Holo Light theme in the Nexus One AVD, and showing the Options Menu

If you are wondering why I have been capitalizing color names during this chapter, such as White, Black, Cyan, LightGray, and MediumGray, it is because these are Android **Color Constants**, and I wanted you to get used to them in the format that you will be utilizing them in within your application design and development process.

Now let's take a look at how XML menu definitions are handled within the Android application development work process. To access the Options Menu, provided by the Android **OptionsMenu** class, click on the three dots on the right-hand side of the ActionBar to access this menu structure, which we will be adding to as we progress through the book. I have added a screen shot on the right side of Figure 4-15, to show this menu access visually.

XML Menus: Designing Menus for Android Apps

Let's take a look at the Options Menu bootstrap which the Eclipse ADT New Android Application Project series of dialogs created for you in the **/res/menu** folder named **main.xml**, after the Main Activity class. Android uses **lowercase letters and numbers** for file names, as a standard or "convention." You can also use an **underscore** character, as you have seen already, in the ic_launcher.png and activity_main.xml file names. Right-click on the main.xml file, and select the **Open** option to open this main.xml in the Eclipse IDE, as shown in Figure 4-16.

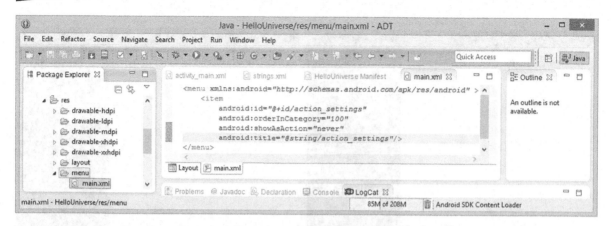

Figure 4-16. The /res/menu/main.xml file, with child <item> tag and parameters inside of parent <menu> tag

As you can see in Figure 4-16, an XML menu definition uses a **<menu>** parent tag to define an Android **Menu** (class-based) object, and inside of that Menu object, Android uses **<item>** child tags to define **MenuItem** (class-based) objects. Inside of the <item> child tags are parameters that set the MenuItem object's configuration data fields, for things such as a MenuItem object name (**android:id**), MenuItem order (**android:orderInCategory**), MenuItem ActionBar display mode, (**android:showAsAction**) and the MenuItem label (**android:title**).

As you can see, another convention in Android, as well as in Java, is that data field or parameter names will use "**CamelCase**," which uses internal capitalized letters, but start the variable (also known as data fields, properties, or parameters) names with a **lowercase letter**. This helps in readability, as you can see. An exception to this is Java Class names, which start with an uppercase letter. We will get into all of that in detail in the next chapter.

Now it's time to look at the most complicated XML file within the Android application, and the most important one as well: the **AndroidManifest.xml** file, located in your **/HelloUniverse** "root" (top-most) project folder. This Android Manifest XML file is used in the same exact way in 32-bit Android 4 and 64-bit Android 5.

This XML **application definition** file is the first XML file that the Android OS (runtime) looks at when your app is launched by your user on their Android hardware device. It defines everything about your application so that the Android OS knows exactly what it is dealing with.

The Android Manifest, as it is termed, specifies how many Activities, Services, and Providers are to be used in the application, as well as defining more complex constructs, such as Intent Filters, if they are needed by the application. You will be learning about all of these areas of the Android OS during the course of this book.

The Android Manifest also defines more simple and basic things such as API support, versioning, an app icon, name, and OS theme. These may be simpler to conceptualize, but they are no less important to the overall app.

XML Manifest: Configuring the Android Manifest

Let's open the Android Manifest in Eclipse's central editing pane by right-clicking the AndroidManifest.xml file and selecting the **Open** menu option (or left-clicking this file and using the **F3** function key). As you can see in Figure 4-17, the AndroidManifest XML markup is already nested several levels deep, and starts with the parent **<manifest>** tag, as would be expected, and contains two child tags.

Figure 4-17. Viewing the HelloUniverse Manifest in the Eclipse central edit pane using the AndroidManifest.xml bottom tab

The child tags describe the **<application>** as well as what SDK versions are being used for your application, via the **<uses-sdk>** child tag, which as you can see includes two parameters, for your **android:minSdkVersion** and **android:targetSdkVersion**, which you set back in Chapter 3 (Figure 3-3) at API Level 8 and 19, respectively.

The <application> XML construct or structure is more complicated, as expected, and references the icon that you created back in Chapter 3 as well as the **app_name** string constant and **AppTheme** style constant. There is also an **android:allowBackup** switch (Boolean) that is set to "on," which is indicated by a "true" value.

Nested under your **<application>** child tag is the **<activity>** child tag, so in a sense, the <manifest> tag has grandchildren, although Android does not use the terminology grandchild tag or great-grandchild tag. The <activity> tag has an android:name parameter that references your MainActivity.java file in your package, which is named **absolute.beginner.hellouniverse**, so the complete path to the MainActivity.java Activity class would be absolute.beginner.hellouniverse.MainActivity and would be referenced using the following parameter:

```
android:name="absolute.beginner.hellouniverse.MainActivity"
```

There is also an **android:label** parameter inside the <activity> child tag that is also set to **@string/app_name**, making this the same exact parameter as was used inside of the <application> tag, which is both a parent tag (to the <activity> tag) as well as a child tag (to the <manifest> tag).

You are probably wondering what the usage difference is between these two parameters. The app_name text string in the <application> tag is applied underneath the app launcher icon, as that is what labels the application.

The app_name text string in the <activity> tag is applied in the ActionBar, as that Activity (screen) title, and if you have more than one Activity (UI or screen area) in your app, this Activity title could be used to tell your users where they are in the app, or you can keep it as the app name for branding purposes. It's entirely your call.

This is a great example of how you can use a single XML constant value (in this case, it is a text string value) in more than one area of your application, and for more than one purpose. This is exactly why Android has set this modular asset and resource referencing up in this way, as when leveraged optimally by a developer, it will allow a more efficient and effective optimization of application resources by encouraging more modular and logical resource definition and usage. As you can see in Figure 4-17, there is a third level of nesting underneath the <activity> tag where an <intent-filter> child tag is defined, which launches the application from the main (icon) screen of the Android device. We will be getting into Intents and the IntentFilter class later on, in Chapter 7, when we cover event handling and processing Intent objects.

To describe what the <intent-filter> is doing here for you, so you don't have to wonder for several chapters, the <action> child tag (we are now at five levels of nesting) defines an Android Action Constant of MAIN, which refers to the Android MAIN screen, and the <category> child tag defines the category or "type" of action that should be taken (in this case, using the Android Category Constant of LAUNCHER, which tells the Android OS to launch the application). Essentially this is what tells the Android OS to launch your application when the user uses your app icon within their OS. Next, let's take a look at all this XML construction in a single view!

XML Application Structure: A Bird's Eye View

Before we learn how to edit these XML files **visually** inside of Eclipse ADT, which we are going to learn about in the next section of this chapter using the Eclipse **Graphical Layout Editor** (GLE), let's take a look at how all this XML that we've been looking at during this chapter fits together into the larger XML structural picture.

I am only going to cover the GLE in detail in this book because it is an **Absolute Beginners** book. I do not promote using the GLE in my Pro Android books, as an advanced developer should get used to thinking in and writing XML and Java code directly, but you can use the GLE as a shortcut for previewing some XML design work, including most UI design tasks, so that you do not have to use the more time-consuming AVD emulator as you are designing your UI design-related XML markup. There are some graphics features, such as blending modes and animation, that do not work in the GLE.

As you can see in Figure 4-17, as well as in the diagram in Figure 4-18, the AndroidManifest.xml file is where everything starts from (XML or otherwise) in an Android application. This is very similar to an index.html file, which will "bootstrap" or launch an HTML5 web site or an HTML5 application.

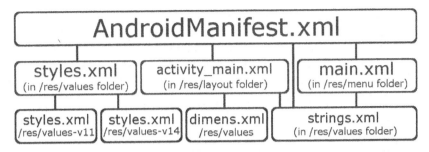

Figure 4-18. The HelloUniverse initial XML structure from the AndroidManifest.xml file on down the hierarchy

As you just saw in the previous section of this chapter, the **styles.xml** file is accessed using the **android:theme** parameter, set equal to **@styles/AppTheme**, and the activity_main.xml and main. xml files are accessed through a MainActivity.java reference, which is located inside of the <activity> tag, using an **android:name** parameter.

These XML UI and menu definitions are accessed through Java methods, which we will be looking at in the next chapter. These methods serve to "inflate" these XML definitions into Java objects, and so I include them in this graphic so that you can see how all of this XML markup affects and references each other.

The AndroidManifest also directly accesses the **strings.xml** file in both the **<application>** and **<activity>** tags, using the **android:label="@string/app_name"** parameter, which we learned does different things when used inside of different XML tags.

The **activity_main.xml** UI design layout XML definition accesses the dimens.xml file to get the app's screen dimensions as well as the strings.xml file to get text string constant values to display the Hello Universe message on the application's primary Activity display screen.

The **/res/values/styles.xml** file references the styles.xml files located in your alternate resource folders, named **/res/values-v11** and **/res/values-v14**, to set the OS theme preferences for your application. This depends upon if the end-user is using Version 3.x, Version 4.x, or legacy (earlier) versions of the Android OS, such as 1.6 or 2.3.

It is important to note that this diagram only includes XML to XML referencing, and not XML to new media assets referencing, most of which would exist underneath the activity_main.xml UI definition in res/layout.

Next let's take a look at the Eclipse ADT GLE, in case you have been wondering what that Graphical Layout tab at the bottom of the Eclipse ADT central editing page does whenever you are working on XML definition files that refer to UI design layouts, such as the activity_main.xml file does. I am including this in the XML chapter to give you an early preview of this feature as well as an overview of what it does, and how it can help the Absolute Beginner to quickly develop UI designs for their Android applications.

Using the Eclipse Graphical Layout XML Editor

You may have noticed the **Graphical Layout** tab, located at the bottom-left of the Eclipse central editing pane, when you were taking a look at the UI design XML definition at the beginning of the chapter in Figure 4-1.

I am going to show you how to use this now, as well as later in the book, as you can sometimes use it to **preview** UI designs that you create using XML, and can actually use it to create these designs visually. For the sake of learning XML and Android development in this book, I will be referencing this tab to create previews of UI designs using XML, so you don't have to go through the more time-consuming **Run As ➤ Android Application** AVD work process, which we took a look at a bit earlier in this chapter.

You can switch back and forth between XML editing view and the GLE by clicking the bottom-mounted tabs, which you can see in Figure 4-19, and are labeled with your XML file name for the XML editing view and the GLE name for the Graphical Layout view. Whatever you have your cursor clicked on (or inside of) in the XML editing view will be selected in the GLE when you switch over (in this case, a TextView).

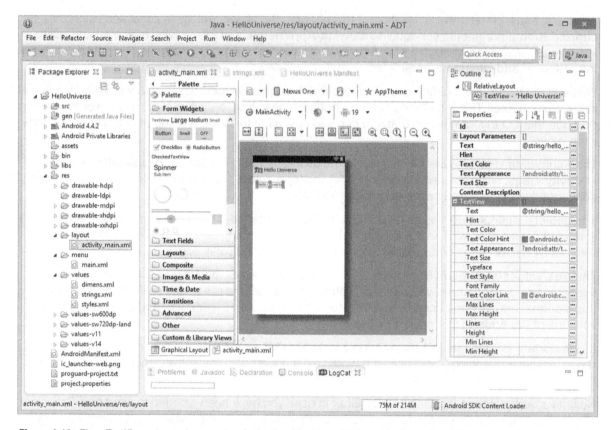

Figure 4-19. *The <TextView> tag and parameters in the Graphical Layout tab and its Properties Editors*

As you can see in Figure 4-19, there is a **Palette** pane on the left, where you can select and drag and drop UI widgets onto your design, as well as an **Outline** pane containing your UI design hierarchy on the right, and even a handy **Properties** pane, where you can set the properties (also known as parameters) for your UI element tags.

If you want to add parameters to your TextView tag, you can do it in the Properties pane and then switch back into XML editing mode to see the XML markup which Eclipse ADT has written for you. This is a good way to learn about the XML parameters that are available to you for any given UI element tag, so be sure and play with this GLE feature when you have a chance!

Using Eclipse's Graphical Manifest XML Editors

Eclipse ADT also has the equivalent of the GLE to edit your Android Manifest, except that it takes four tabs to cover all of the different types of Android Manifest editing visually. We will take a quick look at two of the primary Manifest editing tabs, the **Manifest** and the **Application** editing tabs, here; you can look at the others later on in the book, when we get into advanced topics covering permissions and instrumentation hardware.

The Manifest Visual Editor, shown in Figure 4-20, shows the parameters inside of your <manifest> tag in a visual environment. This includes your Java Package name, version code and version naming, and shared user information and installation location. Most of these fields are not needed for your Android application.

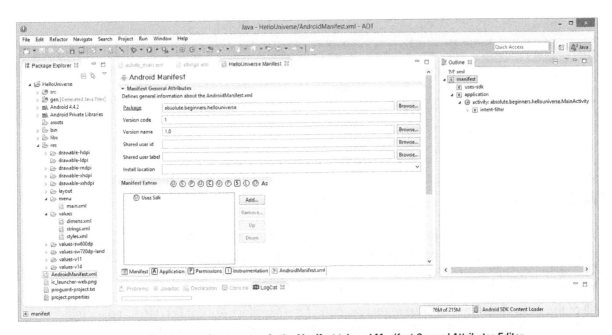

Figure 4-20. View the <manifest> tag and parameters in the Manifest tab and Manifest General Attributes Editor

The Manifest Extras interface allows you to add "extras" such as External Libraries, Compatible Screens definitions, Supported Input definitions, and other advanced features. This is accomplished by adding tags similar to the <uses-sdk> tag, to define support for various areas of your application hardware support features.

The next tab over is the **Application** tab, which shows visually the **Application Attributes** that you can assign to your Android application (see Figure 4-21). Those of these that have a drop-down menu next to them will show you every available setting for those parameters, which can again be an incredible learning tool.

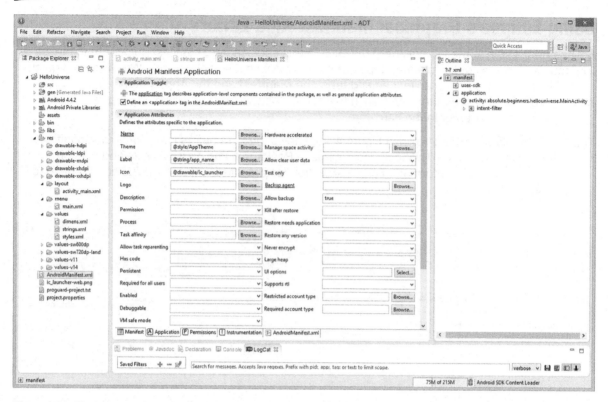

Figure 4-21. View the <application> tag and parameters in the Application tab and Application Attributes Editor

For instance, if you want to see every permission you can ask the Android OS to give your application, such as permission to use the camera, which is afforded by the **android.permission. CAMERA** constant, you can spend some time perusing the drop-down menu next to the **Permission** field, as it contains hundreds of Android OS permission constants.

All of the other drop-down menus in this section of the Manifest Application visual editor feature either a "true" or "false" value selection, so to learn what these do, you'd want to consult the developer.android.com web site.

Before we finish this XML chapter, I want to give you an overview of how XML and Java interface together, which is accomplished using a process that the Android OS calls "inflation." Inflation is simply a fancy term for "turning XML-compatible data structures into Java-compatible data structures," which is of course necessary due to the fact that your application programming logic is written using the Java programming language.

Let's take a look at XML inflation next, and after that we will summarize in greater detail how Android applications work on a more global level, by revisiting and refining the visual that I used back in Figure 3-1 in Chapter 3. After we do this, you will be ready to get into the even more complicated subject of the Java SE programming language and all of its various programming logic and data storage constructs.

XML Inflation: How XML Works with Java

Since we are going to get into Java objects, as well as classes and methods and the like, in the next chapter, I am going to briefly touch upon how all of this parameter-rich XML markup gets turned into Java-compatible data structures.

These XML definition structures that contain your parent and child tags as well as any parameters need to get transformed from XML-compatible data structures into Java-compatible data structures. This is accomplished by the Android OS using a process called "**inflation**," which you invoke using the **.inflate()** or findViewById() method in your Java programming logic.

The Java-compatible data structures that are created from your XML definitions via this inflation process are known as "objects," and you will learn all about what Java objects are, and what they are utilized for, in the next chapter, which covers the Java programming language.

Think of an empty Java object structure as a limp balloon, and your XML definition as the air that will inflate it! What Android does, more accurately, is to take your XML definition and create a Java object of the appropriate type using your definition; that is, by using the XML tags and parameters you defined in your XML file.

For instance, for a **<menu>** XML definition, the Android "inflater" will create a **Menu** Java object by using the Android Menu class **constructor**, and will then populate this Menu object with **MenuItem** sub-objects by using the Android MenuItem class. You will learn what a Java constructor is in the next chapter, so hold on tight!

These MenuItem sub-objects, which are contained inside of a Menu "parent" object, will have the configuration parameters for each of your Menu items (entries) set in exactly the way that you defined them within your XML menu definition. This is accomplished by using data fields within the MenuItem object that define each menu item in your menu using parameters (Android calls them "properties"), which you defined inside of each <item> tag in your XML menu definition.

Currently, this menu definition is contained in the **main.xml** file in the **/res/menu** folder of your HelloUniverse Android application project hierarchy or folder structure. Before we finish the chapter, let's add a level of detail into our How Android Works graphic that adds in what we have learned since we started Chapter 3.

XML's Role: Revisiting How Android Works

Now that you have learned a bit more about XML, let's revise Figure 3-1 from Chapter 3 and add in some of the things we have learned about XML. I also added the Dalvik Virtual Machine (VM) and the Android RunTime VM to the diagram just to be sure that I had everything covered, going from one layer to the next. The updated graphic is shown in Figure 4-22.

Figure 4-22. Android OS hierarchy from Linux Kernel, to Java Libraries, to XML Definitions, to New Media Assets

You can use XML markup to define a number of application new media assets, including 2D animation, called Animation and AnimationDrawable objects in Android, as well as digital images, or BitmapDrawable objects, and digital illustration, known as ShapeDrawable objects in Android.

XML object definitions get turned into Java objects using object inflation Java methods, and XML files that are not object definitions can be utilized by your application as well using XML file parsing methods such as the **.XMLparse()** method. The resulting Java objects and code is then run using one of the two Android runtimes.

Summary

In this fourth chapter, you learned all about the XML markup language, as well as how the Android platform utilizes XML markup to simplify the application development work process, so that non-programmers can get involved.

You learned about how XML uses tags and parameters to define XML definition structures, as well as how levels of nesting define what a parent and child XML tag is. You learned about the XML naming schema, and how this is defined at the beginning of XML definition files.

Next you looked at some of the primary types of XML files that are utilized in an Android application, by looking at the bootstrap XML files that were generated by the **New Android Application Project** series of dialogs in the previous chapter. You examined, and in some cases edited, XML files defining value constants, menu entries, application styles or OS themes, and the Android Manifest, which defines your entire application.

You learned how to use the **Run As ➤ Android Application** work process and **Run Configurations** dialog, and got used to compiling and running your HelloUniverse Android app using the Nexus One AVD emulator. You looked at all of the major Holo OS themes, and looked at the inter-relationships between all of these XML files at a high-level to see how they all relate to each other to create your Android application user experience.

Finally, you learned how to use the visual editors, including the GLE, in Eclipse.

In the next chapter, you will learn all about the Java SE programming language by taking an in-depth look at the Android application that you created in Chapter 3, including the java files in the **/src/** folder. You will also learn how to create Java objects, classes, methods, and interfaces from scratch for your Android application.

Chapter 5

Introduction to Java: Objects, Methods, Classes, and Interfaces

The programming language used for developing your Android applications is Oracle's **Java SE**, which was created by Sun Microsystems and acquired by Oracle. As you learned in Chapter 1, Java SE stands for Java **Standard Edition**, though many programmers shorten this to just "Java" to refer to this programming language.

Java is what is called an **object-oriented programming** (OOP) language, which you are going to learn all about during this chapter. It is important to note that all of these Java programming concepts, components, and constructs that you will be learning during this "Java Primer" chapter will apply equally well to both the 32-bit Android 4.4 OS as well as to the new 64-bit Android 5.0 OS that will be released by the end of 2014.

OOP is based on the concept of developing **modular**, self-contained constructs that are called "**objects**." These OOP constructs contain their own attributes and characteristics. In this chapter, you will learn a great deal about the OOP characteristics of Java, and the logic behind using a modular programming approach and OOP techniques to build applications that are easy to share and debug due to an OOP approach.

You will also learn about all of the other Java programming language constructs, such as packages and classes, methods and interfaces, loops and arrays, variables and constants, and application programming interfaces (APIs), which tie everything together into one coherent computing ecosystem, such as the 19 Android Java Platform APIs, which were discussed in Chapter 2. Android's 19 APIs are actually progressive collections of all of these Java programming constructs. The 64-bit Android 5.0 OS is the 20th API, and will be covered in Chapter 16, "The Future of Android."

Together these Java constructs will allow you to create the application's objects and then modify them according to the programming logic that your application will utilize to create a **user experience** for your end-users.

Finally, we will put much of this newfound knowledge to use, and will create our own HelloUniverse planetary tracking system, so that you get some hands-on experience creating your own objects, classes, methods, and the like. While we do this, we will also learn what the bootstrap Java code in your existing application is doing.

The Three Versions, or Editions, of Java

There are two other "editions," or versions of the Java programming language, in addition to the Java SE. These are called **Java EE**, short for Java **Enterprise Edition**, and **Java ME**, for Java **Micro Edition**, which was originally used for mobile application development, so a lot of people incorrectly assume that Java ME stands for Java Mobile Edition. Many mobile phones now use the Android OS, which uses the more powerful Java SE, instead of Java ME, due to the more powerful hardware utilized in today's HD smartphones.

Java EE was designed for use on potentially massive computer networks. These types of computing networks are used to run large "enterprises" or corporations with thousands of active users, and could be termed "server-side" computing.

Conversely, Java SE could be termed "client-side" computing, as the Java application, in the case of this book, an Android application, runs on the user's own personal computing device, which is termed the "client" in the computer programming industry.

The reason an enterprise computing network is considered to be a "server-side" scenario is because the "dumb terminals" used by workers are simply keyboards and display screens, whereas the memory and processing resources are centered in the powerful computers serving the network. Java EE was originally designed and optimized for this exact type of centralized computing scenario, which is still utilized today in many large corporate MIS and IT departments.

It is important to note that Java EE can also be run on smaller installations, as long as they have enough system memory and a couple of processing cores, and this is sometimes done in companies that are developing applications for use on Java EE installations, so that they can work in and simulate that type of environment for their testing. Java EE's differentiating feature to Java SE is that Java EE features a multi-user, scalable design, whereas Java SE is designed for use by a single user on a single computer system, say a home PC or a laptop, or better yet, on an Android device such as an iTV Set, eBook reader, tablet, smartphone, game console, or smartwatch.

Java ME was designed for low-power, embedded systems, to create highly portable computers such as mobile phones. It has fewer features than Java SE, so that it can fit onto a phone without using too much memory and resources to run it. Most mobile flip-phones run Java ME, but Android phones run the more powerful Java SE. Android phones can run Java SE because they have at least a half gigabyte or more of memory, and a 1GHz or faster CPU, so essentially today's Android devices are tiny Linux computers.

The Foundation of OOP: The Java Object

The foundation of OOP is, no surprises here, the **object** itself, because everything in Java is an object.

Objects in OOP languages are similar to the objects that you see around you every day, except Java objects are virtual, and are not tangible, since computers use zeroes and ones (binary) to represent things. Just like tangible real-world objects, Java objects have **characteristics**, called **states**, and things that they do, called **behaviors**.

One way to think about this distinction is that Java objects are nouns, or things that exist in and of themselves, whereas their behaviors are like verbs, or things that these nouns can do. As an example, let's consider that very popular object in all of our lives: the automobile. Some characteristics, or states, of the car might be as follows:

- Color (candy apple red)
- Direction (N, S, E, or W)
- Speed (15 miles per hour)
- Engine type (gas, diesel, hydrogen, propane, or electric)
- Gear setting (1, 2, 3, 4, or 5)
- Drivetrain type (2WD or 4WD)

The following are some things that you can do with a car, that is, the car's behaviors:

- Accelerate
- Shift gears
- Apply the brake
- Turn the wheels
- Turn on the stereo
- Use the headlights
- Use the turn signals

You get the idea. Now stop daydreaming about your new car, and let's get back down to learning about objects!

Figure 5-1 shows a simple "Anatomy of a Car Object" diagram of the Java object structure, using a car as an example. It shows the characteristics, or attributes, of the car, that are central to defining the car object, and the behaviors that the car object can perform. These attributes and behaviors serve to define the car to the outside world, just like your application's objects will for your Android application.

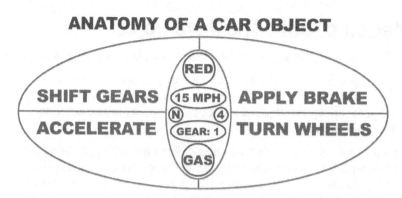

Figure 5-1. *Car object, showing the car attributes or characteristics (inner oval) and the car behavior (outer oval)*

Objects can be as complicated as you wish them to be, and Java objects can nest or contain other Java objects within their object structure, or object hierarchy. An object hierarchy is like a tree structure, with a main trunk, and branches, and then sub-branches as you move up (or down) its structure, and then leaves at the ends of these branches. A good example of a hierarchy that you use every day would be your multi-level directory or folder structure that is on your computer's hard disk drive (refer to Figure 1-9 back in Chapter 1, for a visual example).

Directories or folders on your hard disk drive can contain other directories or folders, which can in turn contain yet other directories and folders, allowing complex hierarchies of organization to be created. We saw another really great example of this back in Chapter 3, shown in Figure 3-9, where our Android HelloUniverse project folder was shown in the Eclipse Android Development Tools (ADT) Project Explorer pane, showing the project sub-folder hierarchy, with its source folder, and resource folder, and sub-folders for your layouts, menus, drawables, values, and the like.

You can do this same hierarchical construction using Java objects, which can contain sub-objects, which can themselves contain further sub-objects, and so on and so forth as needed to create an object hierarchy structure.

You'll see plenty of nested object hierarchies when you are working with Android, because nested objects are very useful for "grouping" related objects that are used together, but that are often used in more than one place, and for more than one type of usage. After all, the goal of modular code is to foster effective code re-use!

In other words, some types of objects are similarly useful to other types of objects in an Android app, so they are provided in a nested object hierarchy underneath the other object types. You will see many examples of this during this book, as we will be covering all of the primary Java classes (which as you will soon see are used to create objects) in Android in great detail during the course of this book.

As an exercise, you should practice identifying different objects in the room around you, and then break their definition or description down into states (variable characteristics and fixed or constant characteristics) as well as behaviors (things that the objects can or will do). This is a good exercise to perform, because this is how you will need to start thinking in order to become more successful in your OOP endeavors using the Java programming language (and even using the XML markup language, for that matter).

It's important to remember that you can use both Java program logic, as well as XML markup, to define objects for Android applications, as you learned in the previous chapter when you learned about object inflation. You have already defined a TextView user interface object, having several characteristics, in Chapter 4 using XML markup (refer to Figure 4-1, to see the XML tag and parameters defining the TextView user interface (UI) object definition).

OOP Terminology: Variables, Methods, Constants

Next, let's cover some of the technical terminology used in conjunction with Java objects. First, objects have data fields to hold **variable** data, **constants** to hold fixed data, and **methods** to define behaviors, as follows:

- Data fields that hold a Java object's **states**, or **things that can change** about an object's characteristics over time, are called "**variables**." Using the car example, the direction you're driving in, the gear that you're driving in, and the speed you're driving at, are all variables.

- Data fields that hold an object's **attributes**, or **things that do not change** regarding an object's characteristics over time, are called "**constants**." Using the car example, the candy apple red paint job on the car would be a constant, as is the car's engine type (unless you own an automotive paint and body shop, or are an auto mechanic, that is).

- **Methods** are programming logic, or program code routines, that operate on, and change, the object's internal data fields or states. Methods will also allow other Java objects that are external to the object itself to communicate with that object, as long as the method is declared to be "public." We will be getting into methods in greater detail a bit later on in the chapter, so I won't get into too deep a level of detail regarding how methods work here.

One of the key concepts of OOP is **data encapsulation**. In Java, data encapsulation is implemented by only allowing a Java object's variable data fields to be modified directly through that same Java object's internal (private) methods. This allows a Java object to be self-sufficient, or "encapsulated."

Using the car example, in order to turn the car, you would use the **.turnWheels()** method, shown in Figure 5-1 on the bottom-right of the diagram. This method would be comprised of Java programming logic that would correctly position the wheels of the car, ultimately causing it to move in the desired direction. You would not see the details of how the object's wheels turned, because of encapsulation. That detail is left to the private, internal functionality in the object.

> **Note**   Notice the empty parentheses I am using after my method names in the text. These are always used when writing about a method, so that the reader knows that the author is referencing a Java method. Additionally, since method calls are invoked using dot notation, I also preface the method names with a dot, further reinforcing that this is a method call, so that you can visualize it. You will see this naming convention used throughout the rest of this book.

With data encapsulation, you can build and test each object that is part of a larger object construct individually, without requiring data to be accessed from other objects, or modules, of your application. External data access can translate into "bugs," so encapsulation helps when developing complicated, large-scale applications.

Without data encapsulation, developers on your team could simply access any part of your object data and use it however they pleased. This could introduce bugs affecting the methods you have perfected to manipulate your object and to provide your encapsulated solution. So data encapsulation promotes the core concept in OOP of **modularity**. Once an object is created and tested, other objects can use it without worrying about its integrity.

Data encapsulation. thus allows code re-use, so programmers can develop "**libraries**" of useful objects that do not need to be rewritten, or retested, by other programmers. You can see how this might save developers time and money, by structuring only the work that needs to be done, and avoiding redundant work processes related to testing multiple code modules in conjunction with one another. Data encapsulation will also allow developers to hide the data and the internal logic of a Java object, if desired.

Finally, Java objects make **debugging** easier, because you can add or remove them modularly during testing to ascertain where bugs are located within the overall code. In the car object example, the attributes of our car are encapsulated inside of the car object, and can thus be changed only via the methods that surround them in each diagram. For instance, one would use a **.shiftGears()** method to change the Gears=1 field variable to Gears=2.

Java Constructs: Create Your Own Objects

In the next several sections of this chapter, you will learn about the primary Java programming "constructs," or code structures, that developers can create to be able to define their own custom Java objects. These custom objects will have their own attributes (constants), characteristics (variables), behaviors (methods), accessibility (access control modifiers), procreation (constructors), and rules of engagement (interfaces).

This is in large part accomplished using the top-level structure in Java, which is called a Java **class**. For this reason, we will start learning about classes first, since all of the other structures in Java are either created (nested) inside of the class or relate to its usage and implementation in some way.

The Java Class: Java Code Structure Container

In real life, there is seldom just one single type or kind of object. Usually, there is a large number of different object types and variations. For instance, for a car object, there are many different manufacturers, sizes, shapes, seating capacities, engine types, fuel types, transmission types, drive-train types, and so on.

In Java SE, you write something called a "**class**" that defines what your object can do (its methods), and what data fields it will possess. Once the class has been coded in Java, you can then create an "**instance**" of an object that you wish to use, by **referencing** the class definition. In architectural terms, the class is a kind of blueprint as to what the object will be structured like, including what states it will contain (its variables), and what tasks it can perform (the methods that it has).

> **Note** An **instance** is a concrete object created from the blueprint of the class, with its own states or unique data attributes. For example, you might have a (second) baby blue car instance that is traveling south and is in third gear. (In the example, our first car instance is red, and is traveling north, in first gear.)

To illustrate this further, let's construct a basic class for our car object example. To create a car class, you use the **Java keyword** `class`, followed by your custom name for the new class you are writing, and then curly brackets that will contain your Java code class definition, like so:

```
class Car {
    // Java code definition for the car class will go in here. We will do this next!
}
```

The first thing that you usually put inside of a class (inside the curly {} brackets) is the **data fields** (**variables**).

These variables will hold the states, or characteristics, of your Car object. In this case, you will have six data fields, which will define the car's current gear, current speed, current direction, fuel type, color, and drive-train (two-wheel drive or four-wheel drive), as was specified in the basic diagram shown earlier, in Figure 5-1.

To define a variable in Java, you must first declare its **data type**. An **integer** or **int** data type declares a variable to be able to hold a whole (non-fractional) number. A **String** data type declares the variable to hold a text value.

The next portion of the variable definition or "**declaration**" after the data type has been specified is your custom **variable name**, which you will use to refer to that variable later on within your Java programming logic. If you want to know technically what the Android OS is going to do with these variable declarations, it is essentially going to set aside, or "**allocate**" an area in the system hardware memory to hold this value for your application.

You can also (optionally) set a **default**, or starting, data value for your variable. This is done by using the **equal sign** and a starting or default data value. The variable definition is ended once it reaches, or is terminated with, a **semicolon** character. This is how the Android compiler in Eclipse, which is reading or "**parsing**" your Java code, knows that each statement or "Java structure component definition" is finished being defined.

> **Note** Semicolons are used in programming languages to separate each code construct, or definition, from the other code constructs within that same body of code (variable, method, interface, and so forth).

So, with the six variables from our Anatomy of a Car Object diagram shown in Figure 5-1 in place, your Car class definition will initially look something like this:

```
class Car {
    int speed = 15;
    int gear = 1;
    int drivetrain = 4;
    String direction = "N";
    String color = "Red";
    String fuel = "Gas";
}
```

Remember that since we specified a starting value using the equal sign for all of these variables, that these variables will all contain this default or starting data value. These initial data values will be set (in the system memory) as the Car class variable's data values.

Notice how the example spaces out the curly braces (**{ }**) on their own lines, as well as **indenting** certain lines, similar to what you did with your XML markup. This is done as a Java programming **convention**, so that you can visualize the organization of the code constructs that are contained within your Java class structure inside of those curly braces more easily and more clearly, analogous to a "bird's eye view" of your Java code construct.

The Java Method: Java Code Function Definition

The next part of your Java class definition file will contain your **methods**. Java methods will define how your Car object will function (that is, how it will "operate" on the variables that you defined at the top of the class that hold the Car object's current "state of operation").

Method "**calls**" can invoke a variable (state) change, and methods can also "**return**" data values to the entity that "calls" or "**invokes**" the method, such as data values that have been successfully changed, or even the result of an equation. For instance, there could be a method to calculate driving distance by multiplying speed by driving time, and this method would "return" this driving distance data value to the Java code that invoked this method.

You will see a bit later on exactly how a Java method is invoked or called; this is usually accomplished by using something in the Java programming language called **dot notation**. Next, let's take a closer look at how a Java method is **declared** and created inside of your Java class structure.

To declare a Java method that does not **return** any data values to the calling entity, and that only **invokes** some sort of state change in the object, you would utilize the **void** Java keyword before the method's name.

Note   In this chapter especially, but also throughout the book, you will be learning about a plethora of Java and Android "**keywords**." Keywords are **reserved words** that cannot be used in your own custom code (because that would confuse the compiler, which needs to have everything that is defined be 100% unique, and thus not ambiguous), because each keyword does something specific in Java or Android. As an Android programmer you will need to learn all of the programming language keywords and what they mean (do) and how to implement them properly, which we will be doing throughout the rest of this book.

You can see a good example of using **void** in a method that "triggers" something. This type of method would be used to trigger (invoke) a change in the object, and thus would not need to send any specific data values back to its calling entity.

If your method or function returns a data value, then instead of using the **void** keyword, you would use the **data type** of the data value that needs to be returned, say **int** or **String**. As an example, a simple, whole number addition method might return a number data value after finishing its sum calculation, so you would declare a data type using the **int** keyword.

After the **data type** keyword comes a **name** for the method (say, shiftGears). This is followed by the type of data (in this case, an int) and variable name (newGear) in parentheses, which is called the **parameter list**, and then finally the curly braces, which will contain the method's Java code, just like we used with the Java class:

```
void shiftGears (int newGear) {  The Java code which defines the method's functionality will go in
here.  }
```

The data variable's data type and name, seen within the parameter list, contains the data parameter that will be passed into the method, so the method now has this passed-in data variable to work with inside of the Java code that is defined inside of the method programming logic (inside of its curly braces).

> **Note**   The normal method-naming convention is to start a method name with a **lowercase letter**, and then to use uppercase letters to begin words embedded within the method name, called **CamelCase**, like this: **methodNameExample()**. Read more about naming conventions for Java at:
> http://www.oracle.com/technetwork/java/codeconv-138413.html.

Some methods, such as those that trigger something, will be "**called**" without using any variables, as follows:

```
turnCarOff();
```

To call the .shiftGears() method, you would want to pass the desired gear over using the parameter list as an integer data variable, so you would therefore utilize the following **method call** format:

```
shiftGears(4);
```

This passes over the integer value of 4 using the .shiftGears() method's **newGear** variable, which sets its value. This data value is then utilized in the interior of the .shiftGears() method logic (the part inside the curly braces), where it is finally used to set the object's gear (internal) field to the new gear shift value of 4, or fourth gear. If you wanted to set up your .shiftGears() method so that it does not require any integer data values, that is, if you wanted to set it up to be a method with no calling parameter, you will need to create a **.shiftGearUp()** as well as a **.shiftGearDown()** method. The programming logic inside of these methods would add (or subtract) a value of one from the current gear setting, instead of setting the gear value to the passed in (desired) gear value. In Java coding, there's always more than one way to skin a car! Or is it, there's always more than one way to shift a cat?

A common reason to use a method without any parameters is to invoke a state change in an object that does not depend on any data being passed in. In the case of this particular gear shifting example, this would also fix a potential problem of skipped gears, as you would simply code a `.shiftGearUp()` method and a `.shiftGearDown()` method, which would upshift and downshift by one gear level each time they were called, rather than change to a gear selected by the driver. If you have ever shifted from first into fifth gear on your car, you know that it does not work very well, and can cause a stall. This might be a smarter way to code this particular method, and then you would not need to pass a parameter in order to shift gears on your Car object; you would just call .shiftGearUp() or .shiftGearDown() whenever any gear shifting for the Car object was needed.

After the method declaration, the method's programming logic procedures are contained inside the curly braces. In this Car class and object definition example, we have four methods as defined back in Figure 5-1:

- The **.shiftGears()** method will set the Car object's gear to the gear value that was passed into the `.shiftGears()` method. You should allow an integer to be passed into this method, to allow "user error," just as you would when you are driving your car in the real world.

```
void shiftGears (int newGear) {
        gear = newGear;
}
```

- The **.accelerateSpeed()** method takes your object's speed state variable and then **adds** your **acceleration factor** to the speed, which causes your object to **accelerate**. This is done by taking your object's current speed setting, or state, and adding an acceleration factor to it, and then setting the result of this addition operation back into the original speed variable, so that the object's speed state now contains the new (accelerated) speed value.

```
void accelerateSpeed (int acceleration) {
        speed = speed + acceleration;
}
```

- The **.applyBrake()** method takes the object's speed state variable and **subtracts** a **braking factor** from the current speed, which causes the object to **decelerate**, or to **brake**. This is done by taking the object's current speed setting and subtracting a braking factor from it, and then setting the result of the subtraction back to the original speed variable, so that the object's speed state now contains the updated (decelerated) braking value.

```
void applyBrake (int brakingFactor) {
        speed = speed - brakingFactor;
}
```

- The **.turnWheel()** method is straightforward, much like the .shiftGears() method, except that it uses a **string** value of N, S, E, or W to control the direction that the car turns. When .turnWheel("W") is used, the car will turn to the left, when .turnWheel("E") is used, the car will turn to the right, given, of course, that the Car object is currently heading to the north, which according to its default direction setting, it is.

```java
void turnWheel (String newDirection) {
        direction = newDirection;
}
```

The methods that make the Car object function go inside the class and after the variable declarations, as follows:

```java
class Car {
    int speed = 15;
    int gear = 1;
    int drivetrain = 4;
    String direction = "N";
    String color = "Red";
    String fuel = "Gas";

    void shiftGears (int newGear) {
        gear = newGear;
    }

    void accelerateSpeed (int acceleration) {
        speed = speed + acceleration;
    }

    void applyBrake (int brakingFactor) {
        speed = speed - brakingFactor;
    }

    void turnWheel (String newDirection) {
        direction = newDirection;
    }
}
```

This **Car** class allows us to define a Car object, but only if we include a **Car() constructor method**, covered in the next section of this chapter.

Constructor Methods: The Java Object Blueprint

If you want to be able to make an object with preset values out of your class definition, then you need to include what is called a constructor method. This method needs to be named the same as the class name, in this case it would be the Car() method, and should be the first method that is defined inside of the class construct, after the variable definitions.

A constructor method is used to construct an object and to configure it, so the first thing that we will want to do is to make our variable declarations undefined, by removing the equal sign and initial data values, as is shown in the following code. A Car() constructor method will set data values, as part of the construction and configuration of the Car object, and thus the Java code for the Car() constructor method could be written as follows, where we specify the car name in the constructor's parameters:

```
class Car {
    String name;
    int speed;
    int gear;
    int drivetrain;
    String direction;
    String color;
    String fuel;

    public Car (String carName) {
        name = carName;
        speed = 15;
        gear = 1;
        drivetrain = 4;
        direction = "N";
        color = "Red";
        fuel = "Gas";
    }
}
```

A Java constructor method differs from a regular Java method in a number of distinct ways. First of all, it does not use any of the data return types, such as **void** and **int**, because it is used to create a Java object, rather than to perform a function. It does not return nothing (void keyword) or a number (int or float keywords), but rather returns an object! Indeed, that's why it's called a constructor in the first place; because its function is solely to construct or create the new Java object; in this particular case, that would be a Car object.

Note that every class that needs to create a Java object will feature a constructor with the same name as the class itself, so a constructor is the one method type whose name can (and will, always) start with a capital letter.

Another difference between a constructor and a method is that constructors must have a **public** access control modifier, and cannot use any non-access-control modifiers, so be sure not to declare your constructor as: **static**, **final**, **abstract**, or **synchronized**. We will be covering modifiers a bit later on in this chapter, so stay tuned!

In case you may be wondering how you would modify the previous **Car()** constructor method example if you wanted to not only name the new Car object using the constructor method, but also wanted to define its speed, direction, and color using that same Car() constructor method call, you would do this by simply creating a longer parameter list for the constructor method call. This revised Car() constructor method's Java code structure would look something like the following:

```
class Car {
    String name;
    int speed;
    int gear;
    int drivetrain;
    String direction;
    String color;
    String fuel;

    public Car (String carName, int carSpeed, String carDirection, String carColor) {
        name = carName;
        speed = carSpeed;
        gear = 1;
        drivetrain = 4;
        direction = carDirection;
        color = carColor;
        fuel = "Gas";
    }
}
```

It is important to note that this Car() constructor method will not do anything at all until you use it to instantiate an "instance" of the Car object. An instance is just what it sounds like it is; the Android OS will allocate system memory space to hold each particular instance of any Java object created by its class's constructor method.

A constructor method must be called or invoked in conjunction with the Java "**new**" keyword, which we will cover next. The new keyword creates a new object in a new area of system memory, so it's keyword appropriate!

Next, let's look at how you would create new Car objects in your current MainActivity.java class Java code.

Instantiating Objects: The Java "new" Keyword

To create an **instance** of an object, you **instantiate** it. Here's what it would look like if you added this code to the **.onCreate()** method of your current Android application. This shows the creation of two Car objects, as well as how you would use these Car objects along with **dot notation** to call the methods that would operate upon them. Refer to Figure 3-8 in Chapter 3 to see this bootstrap .onCreate() method code for the Android app.

```
public void onCreate(Bundle savedInstanceState) {
    super.onCreate(savedInstanceState);
    setContentView(R.layout.activity_main);
    // Two forward slashes allow you to insert comments into your code

    // Create new Car Objects using the Car() constructor method
    Car carOne = new Car("carWon", 20, "S", "Blue");
    Car carTwo = new Car("carTwoon", 10, "N", "Green");
```

```
    //  Invoking three methods on CarOne Car Object by using dot notation
    carOne.shiftGears(3);
    carOne.accelerateSpeed(15);
    carOne.turnWheel("E");

    //  Invoking three methods on CarTwo Car Object by using dot notation
    carTwo.shiftGears(2);
    carTwo.applyBrake(10);
    carTwo.turnWheel("W");
}
```

Upon launch or creation of our Android application, which is what the .onCreate() method is used for, we now have instantiated and configured two Car objects. We have done this by using the **Car()** class constructor along with the Java **new** keyword, which creates a new Car object for us, using the following Java code format:

```
Car carOne = new Car("carName", carSpeed, "carDirection", "carColor");
```

The syntax for doing this is very similar to what we used to declare our variables:

- Define the object type **Car**

- Give a name to our Car object (carOne) that we can reference in our class and method code

- Set the carOne object equal to a new **Car** object definition using four "state" value parameters (a String carName, an integer carSpeed, a String carDirection, a String carColor)

It is also important to notice that I have put **comments** in the Java code by using **two forward slashes**, which tells the Eclipse Java compiler to "ignore everything else on this line after these, as it is a **comment!**"

To invoke our methods using our new Car objects requires the use of something called **dot notation**. Once you have created and named a Java object, you can call methods off of it, by using the following code construct:

```
 objectName.methodName(parameter list variable);
```

So, to shift into third gear on the Car object named carOne, we would use this Java code statement:

```
carOne.shiftGears(3);
```

This "**calls**" or "**invokes**" the .shiftGears() method **off of** the carOne Car object, and "passes over" the gear parameter, which contains an integer value of 3. This value is then placed into the **newGear** variable, which is then utilized by the .shiftGears() method's internal code.

So, as you can see in the final six lines of code in the **public void onCreate()** method, we set the carOne Car object to third gear, using .shiftGears(3), accelerate it from 15 to 30 mph, by accelerating by a value of 15, using .accelerateSpeed(15), and then turn east by using the .turnWheel() method with a String value of "E" (the default direction is north, or "N").

Car two (carTwo) we shift into second, using .shiftGears(2), then .applyBrake(10) to slow it down from 15 to 5 mph, and finally turn the car west, by using a .turnWheel("W") method call, all using **dot notation**.

Dot notation "connects" the Java method call to the Java object, invoking that method on that Java object. Once you understand it, you will see it is actually really cool how Java works!

We will be creating a custom class for your HelloUniverse Android app during the second half of this chapter, and so you will be getting some excellent experience creating your own constructor method very soon.

Extend an Object's Structure: Java Inheritance

There is also support in Java for developing different types of custom objects, in this case it's a Car object, by using a technique called **inheritance**. Inheritance is where more specialized Car classes (more uniquely defined Car objects) can be **subclassed** using the basic Car **superclass**. The inheritance process is shown in Figure 5-2.

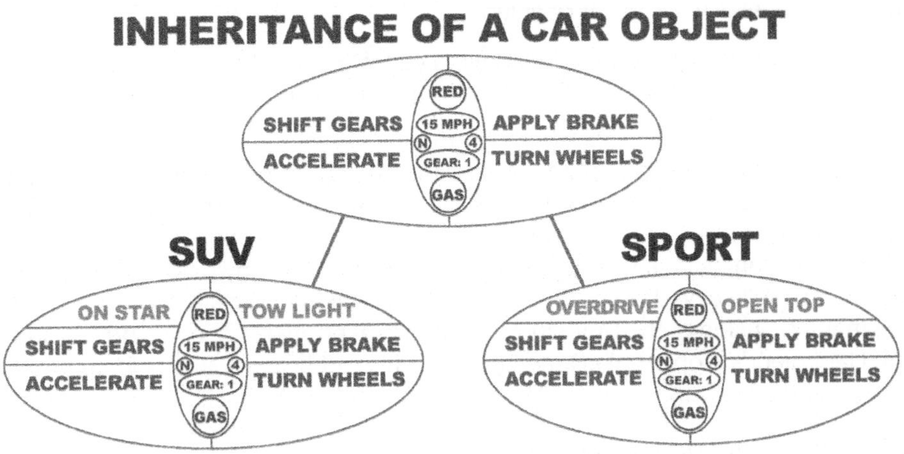

Figure 5-2. Inheritance of the Car Object superclass to create the SUV and the SPORT Car Object subclasses

Once a class is used for inheritance by "**subclassing**" it, it becomes a superclass. Ultimately, there can be only one superclass at the very top of the chain, but there can be an unlimited number of subclasses. All of the subclasses **inherit** the methods and fields from the superclass. The ultimate example of this in Java SE is the **java.lang.Object** superclass (I call it the masterclass), which is used to create all other classes in Java.

As an example of inheritance using our **Car** class, we could create the **Suv** subclass, using the Car class as the "master" class. This is done using the Java "extends" keyword, which **extends** the **Car** class definition, creating the Suv class definition. The Suv class will then define the attributes (variables) and behaviors (methods), which then apply only to an SUV type of car, in addition to **extending** all of those attributes (variables) and behaviors (methods) that apply to all types of Car objects, which is the functionality that the **extends keyword** provides to the subclassing (inheritance) operation.

The **Suv** subclass might have additional **.onStarCall** and **.turnTowLightOn()** methods defined, in addition to **inheriting** the usual Car object operational (basic car function) methods allowing the Car object to shift gears, accelerate, apply the brakes, and turn the wheels.

Similarly, we might also generate a second subclass, called the **Sport** class, which would create Sport objects. These might include an **.activateOverdrive()** method,to provide faster gearing, and an **.openTop()** method,to put down the convertible roof.

To create a subclass using a superclass, you **extend** the subclass from the superclass, by using the Java **extends** keyword inside of the class declaration. The Java class construct would thus look just like this:

```
class Suv extends Car {
    // Additional New Variable Data Fields, Constants, and Methods Will Go In Here.
}
```

This **extends** the Car class so that **Suv** objects have access to, essentially contain, all of the data fields and methods that the **Car** object features. This allows the developer to have to focus only on just the new or different data fields and methods that relate to the differentiation of the Suv object from the regular or "master" Car object definition.

Since classes create objects, given that they have a constructor method, the same hierarchy could be applied at the spawned object level. So logically, the Suv object will be more complex (more data fields and functionality) than a Car object.

To refer to one of the superclass's methods from within the subclass you are coding, you can use the Java **super** keyword. For example, in the new **Suv** class,you may want to use the master Car object's **.applyBrake()** method, and then apply some additional functionality to the brake that is specific to SUVs. You can call the Car object .applyBrake() method by using **super.applyBrake()** in the Java code. The following Java code will add additional functionality to the Car object's .applyBrake() method, inside of the Suv object's .applyBrake() method, by using the **super** keyword to access the Car object's .applyBrake() method, and then adds in additional logic:

```
class Suv extends Car {
    void applyBrake (int brakingFactor) {
        super.applyBrake(brakingFactor);
        speed = speed - brakingFactor;
    }
}
```

This code makes the Suv object's brakes **twice as powerful** as the generic Car object's brakes, which is again something that would have to take place in "real life" for an SUV to be safe for use. The reason this Java code doubles the SUV's braking power is because the **Suv** object's .applyBrake() method first calls the Car object's .applyBrake() method from the Car superclass using the **super.applyBrake(brakingFactor);** line of Java code in the **Suv** subclass .applyBrake() method, and then the line of Java code that comes next (again) decreases the speed variable, by applying the brakingFactor a second time, making the brakes twice as powerful or effective!

Be sure to use good programming practices and refer to documentation for your superclass's fields and methods within each subclass that uses the super keyword to reference these superclass programming infrastructures in one way or another. The Java class documentation should let users (developers) of your superclass know which of your superclass fields and methods are "public" and are available for use, since these do not explicitly appear in the Java code for the subclass, as only incremental code (methods and variables) appear in the subclass code.

The Interface: Defining a Class Usage Pattern

In many Java applications, as well as in the Android APIs, Java classes must conform to a certain usage pattern.

There is a specialized Java construct called an **interface** that can be **implemented** so that application developers will know exactly how to utilize the Java classes implementing an interface, as well as the methods **required** for proper implementation of the class. Implementing an interface will thus allow your class to become more "conformant" regarding those behaviors that your class offers for use.

Interfaces in essence are forming a "programming contract" between your class and the rest of the development world. By implementing a Java interface, the Java compiler can enforce this contract at build time. If a class "claims" to implement a public interface, all of the methods that are "defined" by that Java interface definition must appear in the source code for the class that implements that interface before that class will successfully compile.

Interfaces are especially useful when working within a complex Java programming framework like Android that is utilized by other developers who build applications on the Java classes that the Google Android OS developer team members have written specifically for that purpose. A Java interface can be used like a roadmap, showing developers how to best implement and utilize the Java code structure that is provided by that Java class within another Java programming structure. Basically, a Java interface guarantees that all methods in a given class will get implemented together, as an inter-working, inter-dependent collective programming structure, guaranteeing that any individual function needed to implement that functional collective does not get inadvertently left out.

This **public interface** that the class **"presents"** to other developers who are using the Java language and Android platform makes using that class more predictable, and allows developers to safely use that class in programming structures and objectives where a class of that particular end-usage pattern is suitable for their implementation.

In other words, a public interface is an **implementation roadmap** that tells your application what that class needs to do and how to implement it without your application needing to test that class's functional capabilities.

In Java terms, making a class conform to a usage pattern is done by **implementing an interface**. The following is an **ICar** interface, which forces all cars to implement all of the methods that are defined in this interface.

These methods must be implemented (exist) even if they are not utilized (that is, no code exists inside the curly braces). This also guarantees that the rest of the Java application knows that each Car object can perform all of these actions or behaviors, because implementing the **ICar** interface defines this public interface for all of the Car objects that implement the ICar interface.

The way that you would implement the ICar public interface for the methods in your Car class is as follows:

```
public interface ICar {
    void shiftGears (int newGear);
    void accelerateSpeed (int acceleration);
    void applyBrake (int brakingFactor);
    void turnWheel (String newDirection);
}
```

So, the Car class that implements this ICar public interface must implement all of the declared methods when implementing a Car class using this ICar interface.

To implement an interface, you need to use the Java **implements** keyword, as follows, and then define all of the methods exactly as you did before, except that the methods must now be declared using a **public** access control modifier, in addition to the **void** return data type. We will be covering Java modifiers in a future section of this chapter, after we cover the Java package and the concepts of APIs.

Here is how a Car class would implement this ICar interface using the Java implements keyword:

```
class Car implements ICar {
    int speed = 15;
    int gear = 1;
    int drivetrain = 4;
    String direction = "N";
    String color = "Red";
    String fuel = "Gas   ";

    public void shiftGears (int newGear) {
        gear = newGear;
    }

    public void accelerateSpeed (int acceleration) {
        speed = speed + acceleration;
    }

    public void applyBrake (int brakingFactor) {
        speed = speed - brakingFactor;
    }

    public void turnWheel (String newDirection) {
        direction = newDirection;
    }
}
```

Notice we added the **public** keyword before the **void** keyword, which allows any other Java classes to be able to call or invoke these methods, even if those classes are in a different package (packages are discussed in the next section). After all, this is a **public interface**, and anyone (more accurately, any class) should be able to access it.

A Java interface cannot use any of the other Java access control modifier keywords, so it cannot be declared as **private** or **protected**. We'll be learning about these access control modifiers in a future section of this chapter.

It is important to note that only the methods declared in the interface absolutely need to be included. The data fields that I have at the top of the class definition are optional and are in this example to show its parallel to the Car class that we declared earlier without using an interface. There is not much difference other than using the implements keyword, except that implementing an interface tells the compiler to check and make sure that all of the necessary methods that make a Car class complete (work properly) are included by the developer.

Logical Collection of Classes: Using a Package

As you know, each time you define a new project in Android, the Eclipse Integrated Development Environment (IDE) will create a **package** to contain your own custom classes, which you will define as you implement your application's custom functionality. In your HelloUniverse Android application, which you created back in Chapter 3, you named your package as **absolute.beginner.hellouniverse**. If you remember, that first dialog in the **New Android Application Project** series of dialogs asks you to specify this package name (refer to Figure 3-3 if you need to refresh your memory).

The Java **package declaration** is the first line of code in any Android application class, or in any Java class in any application for that matter. The package declaration tells Java how to package your application. Recall the first line of code in our Hello Universe application's MainActivity.java Activity class, as shown in Figure 3-8:

```
package absolute.beginner.hellouniverse;
```

After the **package** keyword and declaration come the **import statements**, which import existing Java classes and packages into your declared package. So, a package is not only for your own code that you write yourself, but also for all code that your application uses, even if it is open source platform code, or even code that has been written by another programmer or company, or, in the case of Android applications, Android API code, which serves up Android OS functionality that is only available within the Android OS.

Basically, a package naming strategy is similar to the folder naming hierarchy on your computer. A package is just a way of organizing or grouping Java code according to its functionality. As an example, Android organizes its classes into many logical packages, which we will routinely import and use throughout this book.

Each Android API Level (Level 19 for the 32-bit Android KitKat OS version 4.4, or Level 20 for the 64-bit Android 5 OS) contains a vast collection of functional packages that are utilized by developers to access the Android OS feature set. We will take a closer look at APIs in the next section of this chapter. In our Hello Universe application in the previous chapter, you needed the following import statement in your MainActivity.java file to be able to utilize the Bundle class:

```
import android.os.Bundle;
```

This is basically to address where the code for each `import` statement is located. Here is a generalization of how an **import** statement follows a path to the class:

```
import platform.functionality.classname;
```

The Android Bundle class import statement tells us the following information about the Bundle Java class:

- **android** indicates that this is an Android OS development package.

- **os** refers to the operating system utilities functionality inside of this **android.os** package.

- **Bundle** refers to the proper name of the class that we intend on using, or sub-classing.

Thus, the `Activity` class, which is the superclass for any Android Activity that you create, is found within the **android.app** package. This .app part says that this package logically contains classes that are necessary for the creation of Android applications, and one of these is the `Activity` class, which allows us to define UI designs. The **Bundle** class, which allows us to bundle together application variables into custom Bundle Objects, is kept in a different package for OS utilities as Bundle Objects can be used in any area of Android, not just Activity.

The API

You might be wondering if the package is the highest level of organization in Java. The answer is actually no, there is one even higher level, which is as you might imagine a collection of these packages themselves! This level is sometimes called the **platform** or **application programming interface** (API) level. An API for any given programming platform, like Android or Java, is a collection of all of the packages for that given language.

Thus, there is a separate API for Java SE, Java EE, and Java ME, containing all the packages for each specialized platform's implementation, as well as an Android API, such as you are using in your Hello Universe application currently. Android 4.4.4 KitKat API Level 19 is the 19th Android platform to be released so far, and Android 5.0 "L" API Level 20 is the first 64-bit version of Android, and the 20th Android platform, and will be released sometime during the fourth quarter of 2014.

For this reason, if you want to develop applications using any given programming language, you must go and get (and eventually learn) the API for that programming language in order to be able to develop an application using its API, which is simply a collection of all of that language's classes, methods, and interfaces, which have been logically grouped in packages. You'll essentially be learning about core classes used in API during the course of this book.

Modifiers: Data Type, Access, Inheritance

Java uses strategic keywords prefacing, or in front of, its major constructs, which include: variables, methods, and classes. These are also used in front of more specialized Java constructs, such as public interfaces or constructor methods, all of which we've been learning about in this chapter.

Since we have already looked at data type keywords in the chapter already, at least the void (signifying no data type used), String (text data type,) and int (Integer or whole number data), I will go over all of the other data type keywords that are used in Java and Android here, and then we will cover the more advanced access and non-access modifiers that are used in the Java programming language.

It is important to note that even though using a data type keyword in front of your variable names modifies the type of data that they are defined to contain, the more precise technical term in Java for this data type keyword is a data type **specifier** keyword. These two terms are often used interchangeably in Java; in the next section, the access control modifiers could indeed be looked at as access control specifiers, as they are indeed specifying the level of access control by prefacing a Java keyword in front of the Java programming construct.

Other types of data type specifier keywords used in Java (and thus in Android) include **float** or floating point numbers, which have a fractional component represented by decimal notation, for instance, 1.375, as well as **boolean**, which hold Boolean math "states" such as true and false. There are other data types in Java for holding more complicated (longer) numeric representations, such as the **long** and **double** data types, which have 64-bit accuracy and can accommodate extremely large or extremely small numeric representations. There is also a data type that can hold one single 16-bit Unicode character, called the **char** data type. The **byte** data type can hold one number from an 8-bit range (256, from -128 to +127) of numeric data values, and finally the **short** data type can hold one number from a 16-bit range (65,536, from -32,768 to +32,767) of numeric data values. Data types are relatively easy to understand in comparison to access and non-access modifiers, which we will cover next.

Java Access Modifiers: Four Levels of Access

Java has a number of **modifiers** that you can place before Java constructs to define what they are and who can see them. There are two types of Java modifiers, **access control modifiers** and **non-access control modifiers**.

In case you are wondering what I mean by **access control**, I'm talking about other Java programming constructs outside of a given Java class or package being able to reference and utilize Java assets inside of those packages.

You can apply access control modifiers to classes, methods, interfaces, constructors, and variables, and include the **public**, **private**, and **protected** Java access modifier keywords. Not using any access control keyword at all also defines a level of access control, so let's cover all of these concepts here in order from the most restrictive (closed) level of access control to the least restrictive (open) level of access control.

Table 5-1 shows the four different levels of access control modifier in one place.

Table 5-1. Access Control Modifier Keywords in the Java Programming Language and Their Functionality Definitions

Access Modifier Keyword:	Functionality Definition:
private	Access is allowed only within that class
protected	Access is allowed only to subclasses of that class and other classes in the package
public	Access is allowed to all classes even outside your package
unspecified	Access is allowed only to other classes within the package

As you might imagine, the **private** access modifier is the most restrictive, and if declared, only allows access to private variables and private methods from inside of the containing class. It is important to note that classes cannot be declared as private, unless they are inside of another class, in which case they are a special case and are called "**private inner classes**." Java interfaces, which we learned earlier, are public interfaces, and also cannot be declared as private since they are inherently public in their access control.

The next most restrictive access modifier keyword is the **protected** access modifier keyword, which is utilized in Java classes that are intended to be used as superclasses, and that need to allow access to their subclasses to protected variables, protected methods, as well as protected constructors. Protected access could be viewed as being protected from access by any class outside of the inheritance chain, keeping it in the family, if you will. Thus, other members of the same package can also access protected class members.

Like the private access modifier, the protected access modifier cannot be applied to any class itself, only to Java code elements inside of the class. Protected access cannot be applied to any Java interface definition, as these are required to be declared using the public access control modifier keyword. It also follows that methods and data fields (variables) within an interface definition also cannot be declared using a protected access control modifier keyword, as they also must always be declared using the public or the abstract access control modifier. If an access modifier is not explicitly provided for a method inside of an interface, it will default to be declared as public.

The next most restrictive access modifier is actually using none of the access control modifiers at all, which is the "norm" in Java, as we saw when we created our original Car class, using the data type declarations of void, int, or String without any public, private, or protected modifier in front of (before) them. Using no access control modifier allows visibility **throughout your entire package**, essentially, inside of your entire application if you have the entire Android application in one package, as we will be doing in this book.

The least restrictive access modifier, which removes all access restrictions, is the public access control modifier. This allows Java code in other packages to access your variables, methods, interfaces, and classes from outside of your package. It's like you are opening the door to your code and saying "come on in, folks!"

It is important not to confuse access control and non-access control modifiers with data type declarations, which are used before variables to declare their data type, and which thus look a lot like a modifier. In fact, modifiers and data type declarations are often utilized right next to each other, like in the **public void** shiftGears() method.

Java methods have their own rules regarding inheriting access control modifiers as classes that contain them are later subclassed and enhanced to become more detailed and refined subclasses. For instance, any method that has been declared using public access in a superclass must also be declared using public access in all subclasses. Similarly, any method that has been declared using protected access in a superclass must either be declared using protected access, or using public access, in any subclass. It can never be declared using a private access control modifier. A method declared without using an access control modifier is the only scenario where a method can be declared using a private access control modifier in a subclass.

It is important to note that a method that has been declared using a private access control modifier keyword is not inherited, because it is private relative to the class within which it is contained, and no others, including any subclasses. As you can see, although access control modifiers seem fairly simple and straightforward, you have to pay attention to what you are doing with them, especially where inheritance (superclasses and subclasses) is going to be utilized in your Java programming structure and package design.

Non-Access Modifiers: Static, Final & Abstract

There are also modifiers in Java that are not access control modifiers and not data type declarations. These are called non-access modifiers, and these are the most complicated ones to understand and implement in practical use. There are three modifiers that are frequently used in Java programming that we will be covering in this section of the chapter: the **static** modifier, the **final** modifier, and the **abstract** modifier.

There are also some more advanced modifiers such as **synchronized** or **volatile**, which are used to manage the use of **threads**, a topic that is beyond the scope of an Absolute Beginners level Android programming book.

The static Keyword

A static modifier keyword when used in conjunction with a variable will create a variable that will exist independently of any object instances created using that class. Static variables will be initialized only one time, at the start of the execution of the application, sometimes called the "app launch." The variables that use the static modifier keyword will be initialized first, before the initialization of any instance variables.

Only one copy of a static variable will exist in system memory regardless of the number of instances of the class that contains that variable are created. Thus, static in Java programming means a variable that belongs to the class and not to the object instances created by that class.

Objects created by that class can share that variable with the class and with each other, so use of static variables can optimize system memory. The opposite of static is "dynamic," and thus, any variable not declared as static would therefore be "dynamically" created (created at the time it is needed, not ahead of time as when it is declared statically), and system memory would be allocated for that variable in each object instance created by the class constructor method.

To use a variable from the Car class example, if you wanted all Car objects to reference the fuel variable, which is set in the code to "Gas" at the class level, and wanted that fuel variable to belong only to the class, and not to any of the Car objects that will be created using that class, you would declare the fuel variable as follows:

```
static String fuel = "Gas";
```

The static modifier keyword works in much the same way for methods that are declared as static, thus a static modifier would be utilized to create methods that are intended to exist independently of any object instances created using the class. This again "fixes" the method in place, so it is the only "copy" of that method that will be used by your class and objects from that class.

A static method can be referenced using the class name and dot notation even without an object instance of the class ever being created. For instance, if you declared the .applyBrake() method to be static, you could reference it using the code statement Car.applyBrake() even without having created a Car object using the new keyword.

Static methods cannot use any **instance variables** of any object instances created using the class in which they are defined, until one of those object instances has been created. Static methods should take all their data values from the incoming parameter list, and then compute something from those parameters, with no reference to variables, which are inherently not "static" because they're variable!

It is possible to access your class variables and methods inside of a static method. Use the class name followed by a period and then the name of the variable or method, so using your Car class example, you could access your Car object's speed variable using Car.speed, or its .shiftGears() method, by using for instance a Car.shiftGears(4) method call, similar to what you would do off of a Car object instance.

So to recode your .applyBrake(int brakingFactor) method as static and reference the class speed variable, you would modify your method to look something like this:

```
public static void applyBrake (int brakingFactor) {
    Car.speed = Car.speed - brakingFactor;
}
```

Notice that the access control modifier comes first, then the non-access modifier, and then finally the return data type declaration comes last in the list. This is the modifier and declaration ordering convention for the Java programming language. Next, let's look at the **final** modifier, which sometimes gets confused with the static modifier, as the final modifier also means that something cannot be changed, and is thus "fixed" as well! Java can be confusing in a number of areas, and this happens to be one of them!

The final Keyword

You can define a class using the **final** modifier keyword, and if a class is final, it cannot be subclassed. This is usually implemented for reasons of Java security, so tested, mission-critical Java code cannot be modified or changed. You will notice as we get deeper into the Android API and Java that many standard Java library classes are declared using the final modifier keyword. As an example, the java.lang.System and java.lang.String classes are declared to be final so that their functionality cannot be altered.

All methods in a final class are implicitly final. Any method that is declared using the final modifier keyword cannot be overridden by subclasses. This is also for security reasons and is used to prevent unexpected behavior from a subclass altering a method that might be crucial to the function or consistency of a class' functionality.

You can explicitly initialize a final variable only once. A reference variable that is declared as final can never be reassigned to refer to a different object, if the variable references an object, rather than a data value. If the final variable references an object, the data contained within that object can still be changed, only the reference to the object is "fixed," and is said to be **final**.

Thus, you can change the state of an object referenced by the final variable, but not the reference to the object, which is what is "locked" or final. With variables, the final modifier is often utilized in conjunction with the static modifier to make the class variable into what is considered a "constant" or an immutable fixed variable for the duration of the class.

As an example, the **<string>** constant named **app_name** that you defined using XML in the **strings.xml** file would have to be declared in your application's Java code by using the following single line of Java syntax:

```
public static final String app_name = "Hello Universe";
```

This shows how using XML to define constants is much simpler than using Java. Next, let's take a look at the **abstract** modifier keyword, which allows you to create classes that can be subclassed but not instantiated.

The abstract Keyword

A class declared using an abstract modifier keyword can never be instantiated, so it follows that a class logically cannot be declared using both an abstract modifier and a final modifier, because if a class cannot be instantiated or extended, it will not be of much use in the scheme of the Java programming language.

If a class is declared as abstract, then the sole purpose for that class is to be **extended**—that is, **subclassed**. If a class contains any methods that have been declared using the abstract modifier, then the class should also be declared using the abstract modifier. If a class contains abstract methods and is not declared as abstract, a compiler error will be "**thrown**" when you use the Eclipse **Run As ➤ Android Application** work process, which invokes the Android Java code compiler. Every time the compiler encounters an error, it "throws" it into the error log, which is now monitored in real-time by your LogCat tab in Eclipse. It is important to note that if your application will not compile, it also will not run!

An abstract class can, however, contain both abstract methods as well normal (non-abstract) methods, so the rule is if you want to put an abstract method inside of a class, make that class abstract as well, or you will get a compiler error. You cannot have abstract methods inside of a class that is not also declared as abstract.

Creating Your HelloUniverse Class: Galaxy

Now that we have gone over the main Java constructs and concepts, let's get some real-world experience with Java and code a Galaxy.java class for our Android HelloUniverse application. We will use our Hello Universe app as an example of how to create a functional Java class from scratch, and create a class that will define and manage our Galaxy objects, so that you can see these concepts in action! This Galaxy.java class will also be something that we can utilize and build upon as we progress throughout the book, so it is the perfect example.

Defining a Galaxy Class: Variables and Methods

First, let's define some of the attributes or characteristics of our Hello Universe app's Galaxy class (and thus of the Galaxy objects that will be created using this Galaxy class's constructor method) as shown in Table 5-2.

Table 5-2. Galaxy Class Data Fields (Variables) Along with Their Data Type Specifier Values

Class Variable Name	Data Type Specifier Used, and Information Held in the Variable
Galaxy Name	String data type containing a text value, such as "Milky Way"
Galaxy SolarSystems	An integer value representing the total number of solar systems
Galaxy Planets	An integer value representing total number of habitable planets
Galaxy Colonies	An long data value representing the total number of colonies
Galaxy Population	A double value representing total number of sentient life forms
Galaxy Fleets	An integer value representing a total number of starship fleets
Galaxy Starships	An integer value representing the total number of starships

As you can see, our Galaxy object(s) will need to have a name, number of solar systems, number of habitable planets, a number of habitable colonies, a population of life forms, a number of starship fleets, and a number of starships that are in that Galaxy object. This Galaxy object will help keep track of our "high-level" Galaxy information for each Galaxy object that we add to our Hello Universe simulation.

Next, let's define our Galaxy object behaviors, or functions, that can be attributed to our Galaxy objects, such as "getting" and "setting" the number of colonies in the galaxy, the total life form population, the total number of starship fleets, and the total number of starships in the galaxy, as seen in Table 5-3.

Table 5-3. *Galaxy Class Method (Behavior) Names, Along with Their Functionality Specifications*

Name of Method:	Functionality of Method:
Galaxy(constructor)	Constructor method, which creates each Galaxy object instance
setGalaxyColonies	Method allowing the number of Galaxy colonies to be set
getGalaxyColonies	Method that returns the current number of Galaxy colonies
setGalaxyPopulation	Method allowing the total population of the Galaxy to be set
getGalaxyPopulation	Method that returns the current total population of the Galaxy
setGalaxyFleets	Method allowing a total number of fleets in a Galaxy to be set
getGalaxyFleets	Method that returns the current number of fleets in the Galaxy
setGalaxyStarships	Method allowing the number of starships in the Galaxy to be set
getGalaxyStarships	Method that returns the current number of starships in a Galaxy

As you can see, these are behaviors or characteristics that each new Galaxy object can do, or can change, about its current existence (states or characteristics), including your Galaxy() constructor method, which can actually create and initialize a new Galaxy object, which will represent and track all the variables specified in Table 5-2.

Coding the Galaxy Class: Variable Declarations

Let's add to our Hello Universe application example from the previous chapters, and create a new Galaxy class that generates Galaxy objects for our existing Hello Universe application. To declare this new class, which we will call Galaxy, we will utilize the following Java class creation syntax:

```
public class Galaxy {  instance variables, constructor, and methods will go in here, between these
curly brackets  }
```

Just as is the convention with any other modern programming language, the first items that we will want to declare at the top of our Java Galaxy class are our **instance variables**, which we are going to use to hold the attributes or states of our Galaxy objects. In Java, this is done by using the following generalized format:

<data type declaration> <instance variable name> = <set variable value>;

So, for our Galaxy object state instance variables that we described in the previous section, we would write the variable description lines of code as follows, shown inside of the public Galaxy class definition code structure:

```
public class Galaxy {
    String galaxyName;
    int galaxySolarSystems;
    int galaxyPlanets;
    long galaxyColonies;
    double galaxyLifeforms;
    int galaxyFleets;
    int galaxyStarships;
}
```

We are not using any default values for these instance variables because that is something that we are going to want to do in our constructor method parameter list and constructor Galaxy object initialization code, which will create and initialize (set starting data values for) each Galaxy object we create using a Java **new** keyword. Normally, you would declare only the data types and variable names, and set the data values later, using your constructor method, which we will be looking at in the next section. If you wanted to set the data values as part of the variable declaration, here is an example of what that would look like with the galaxyName variable:

```
String galaxyName = "The Milky Way";
```

Coding Galaxy Objects: Constructor Method

Now let's look at adding some functionality to the Galaxy class by adding in methods using Java code that will start right after our variable definitions end. The first method we need to define is the constructor method that has the same name as the class, so it will be called public Galaxy(parameter list) and will create and initialize our Galaxy objects as we add them to our Universe.

The initialization code for the constructor method will live inside of the curly braces, which will always define the beginning and end of each Java method that you create (code). This first Galaxy() method is the very special type of method called the constructor, and this constructor method's Java code would be written as follows:

```
public Galaxy (String name, int solarSys, int planets) {
    galaxyName = name;
    galaxySolarSystems = solarSys;
    galaxyPlanets = planets;
    galaxyColonies = 0;
    galaxyLifeforms = 0;
    galaxyFleets = 0;
    galaxyStarships = 0;
}
```

Inside of this **Galaxy()** constructor, we take three important parameters for our new galaxy's name, number of solar systems, and number of planets, and we then **set** them using the = **operator** inside of the constructor method, where we will also be **initializing** the other Galaxy object instance variables to zero.

Creating Galaxy Functions: Coding Your Methods

Next, let's code our other eight methods, which perform functions that check on (called "polling" or "getting") and modify (called "setting") the state of our Galaxy's component attributes or characteristics. This will provide a number of useful "galaxy building" capabilities to the users of your Hello Universe application. We are going to use the .set() and .get() method naming format, which is commonly used throughout Android, so that you see the convention for how things are done in Java (and Android) at its most fundamental level.

You might be wondering: "Why not code an **.addGalaxyColonies()** method?" The answer is that then you would also have to code a **.subtractGalaxyColonies()** method call, for when any colonies were destroyed by starship fleets! By having a **.setGalaxyColonies()** method, we can add and subtract colonies in our gameplay code logic, and simply call a .setGalaxyColonies() method when we are done to update the Galaxy object **galaxyColonies** data value in either direction, up or down.

The first **.setGalaxyColonies()** method is much simpler than our Galaxy() constructor method, and it will allow us to set the number of colonies in our Galaxy object. The Java code for this method would be written as follows:

```
void setGalaxyColonies (long numberColonies) {
    galaxyColonies = numberColonies;
}
```

The **void return data type** that is declared before our .setGalaxyColonies() method name declares what type of data value will be returned by this method. In this case, the method does not return any data value at all, thus we'll declare it as being of the **void** return data type (that is, devoid of any data return type or return data value).

Also note that our method name begins with a lowercase letter, and uses uppercase letters for words that are internal to the method name. Inside the .setGalaxyColonies() method body, we'll utilize an **assignment operator** that sets the galaxyColonies instance variable to the value in the numberColonies long parameter.

In Java programming, assignment operators are how we set the values of instance variables, which we declare at the head, or top, of our Java class.

We will do something very similar with the **.setGalaxyPopulation()** method, which will look like this, once we code it in Eclipse ADT, which we will be doing a little bit later on in this chapter:

```
void setGalaxyPopulation (double numberLifeforms) {
    galaxyLifeforms = numberLifeforms;
}
```

Next, let's code our **.setGalaxyFleets()** method, which lets us set the number of starship fleets in our Galaxy objects. This method will set the galaxyFleets count instance variable, using the assignment operator, as shown in the following Java method construct:

```
void setGalaxyFleets (int numberFleets) {
    galaxyFleets = numberFleets;
}
```

Finally, let's code our **.setGalaxyStarships()** method, which lets us set the number of starships in our galaxy. This method will set the galaxyStarships count variable, using the assignment operator, as is shown in the following Java method construct:

```
void setGalaxyStarships (int numberStarships) {
    galaxyStarships = numberStarships;
}
```

The .get() methods do not involve any assignment operators, as they simply "**return**" the requested data field value, which is essentially the current variable value in the Galaxy object. The .get() methods use the return data type of the variable data type that is being returned. There are no parameters passed in the method call, so the parenthesis are empty, because a call to one of the .get() methods simply returns the requested value.

For instance, if you instantiate a Galaxy() object named theMilkyWay, to get the colonies would look like this:

```
theMilkyWay.getGalaxyColonies();    (this would return the galaxyColonies variable value at that
moment in time)
```

The .get() methods for the Galaxy class and object would thus be coded in Java using the following structures:

```
long getGalaxyColonies() {
    return galaxyColonies;
}
double getGalaxyPopulation() {
    return galaxyLifeforms;
}
int getGalaxyFleets() {
    return galaxyFleets;
}
int getGalaxyStarships() {
    return galaxyStarships;
}
```

Now we are ready to open up the HelloUniverse project in Eclipse ADT and create our new Galaxy Java class. We will write all of this code that we've developed until now into the Eclipse central text editor pane, so we can use it later on in the book in our HelloUniverse application to create, populate, and track our new Galaxy objects.

Creating a Java Class in Eclipse: Galaxy.java

Launch Eclipse ADT, if it is not already open on your Android development workstation, and close (using the x icon) the XML tabs at the top of the central editing pane, which will clear them out of the central editing area, making room for our Java Galaxy class programming coming up next.

1.   In the Package Explorer pane on the left side of Eclipse ADT, open the **/src** source code folder, the package sub-folder, and the MainActivity. java sub-sub-folder so that you can see your MainActivity.java class, as shown in Figure 5-3. Notice that the Package Explorer allows you to open up your MainActivity class structure as well, so you can also see the **void onCreate(Bundle)** method as well as the **boolean onCreateOptionsMenu(Menu)** method. You can also see the **LogCat** error message management tab that we added in the last chapter, which is shown at the bottom of the Eclipse ADT IDE, along with the other problems, error, and debugging-related tabs.

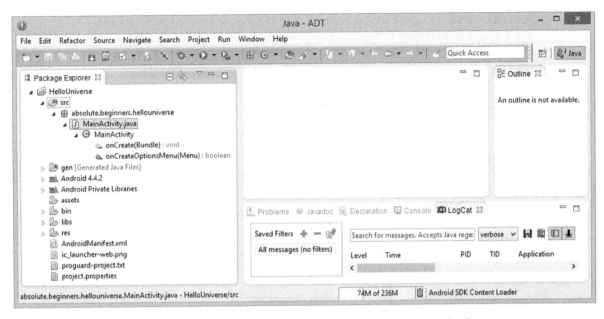

Figure 5-3. Eclipse with central editing pane cleared for Java editing, and /src folder open showing files

2. To create a **New Java Class**, right-click on the **/src** folder, as shown in Figure 5-4, and select the **New ➤ Class** menu sequence, which will bring up the New Java Class dialog, which allows you to enter all of the pertinent information needed for Eclipse to create a "bootstrap" Galaxy.java class infrastructure for you.

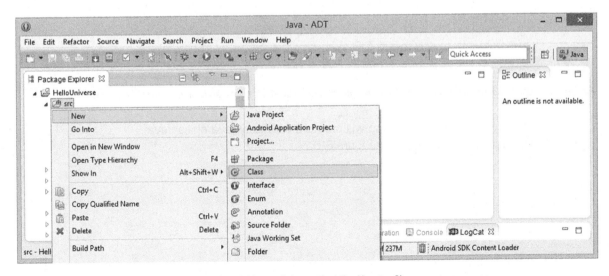

Figure 5-4. Right-click on the HelloUniverse/src folder, and then select the New ➤ Class menu sequence

3. As you can see in Figure 5-5, a New Java Class dialog allows you to click
    the Browse button next to the Package field to open the **Package Selection**
    dialog, where you can select the absolute.beginners.hellouniverse package,
    and click the **OK** button. Then all you have to do is to **Name** the class
    Galaxy, and then click the **Finish** button.

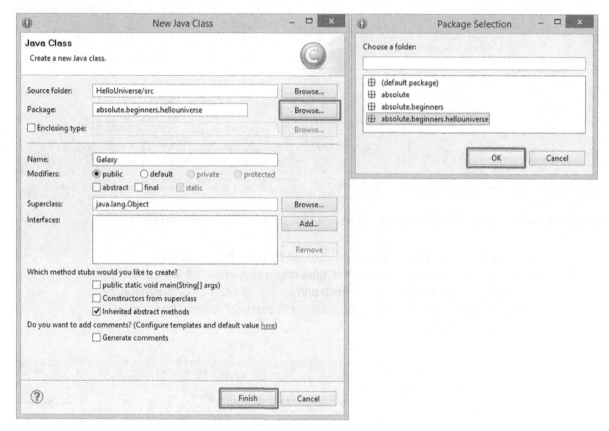

Figure 5-5. The New Java Class dialog and the Package Selection sub-dialog accessed using the Browse button

4. After you click Finish, Eclipse will create the **Galaxy.java** class Java
    structure, which is shown in Figure 5-6.

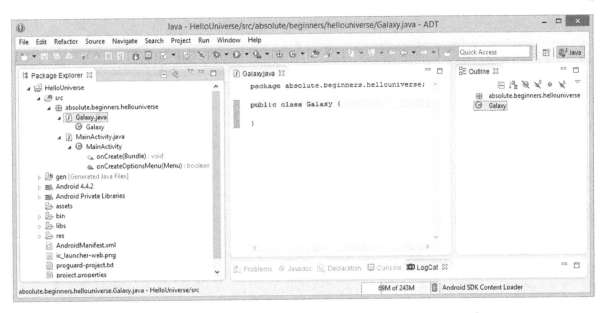

Figure 5-6. Bootstrap Galaxy.java public class definition that the Eclipse New Java Class dialog created

Coding Your Galaxy.java Class with Eclipse ADT

Now all you need to do is to type in your seven instance variable declarations at the top of the class, and then a Galaxy() constructor method under that, and finally the four .set() and four .get() methods, which I have paired together logically, as shown in Figure 5-7. If you type everything in accurately and all of your data types match, you will get the same error-free result that I did, which you can see in Figure 5-7. As you'll see during the book, Eclipse uses **red x icons** for errors and **yellow ! icons** for warnings, none of which are appearing in our Java editing pane shown here, so our Java code is error (and warning) free. Let's compile the app just to make sure!

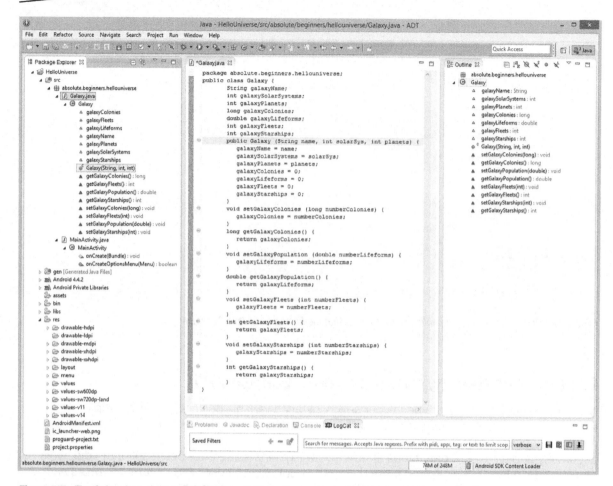

Figure 5-7. *The Galaxy.java class with instance variables, constructor method, and set and get methods*

Right-click on the HelloUniverse project folder and use the **Run As ➤ Android Application** menu sequence to run the Nexus One AVD and you will see the application launch and the Hello Universe screen shown back in Figure 4-15 (no need to duplicate screenshots unnecessarily here) will pop-up onto your screen. We are running the app here simply to make sure that the application compiles and runs, and thus that there are no errors in the Galaxy.java code. In the next chapter, we will use the Galaxy class to create Galaxy objects, which we will display in a user interface design.

Summary

In this fifth chapter, you learned all about the Java programming language, as well as how the Android platform utilizes Java to facilitate the application development work process, so the programmers can get involved too!

You learned about the various versions of Java used for enterprise, client, and mobile application development, and about OOP. You learned about the java.lang.Object that is the foundation of OOP and about how Java objects can define attributes, characteristics, states, and behaviors that allow Java programmers to mimic real-world objects in our "virtual" software development environment.

Then you learned about all the various components of Java programming structures, such as methods, constants, variables, classes, public interfaces, and constructor methods. You learned about the Java concept of inheritance, and how to use the **new** keyword to instantiate an instance of a Java object using a constructor method call.

Then you looked at the higher-level Java organization constructs called packages and how the total collection of packages in a programming language forms the API for the language.

Next, you looked at some of the data type specifiers and access control modifiers as well as the more complex non-access modifiers, and after that you were finally ready to design your first Java class, called Galaxy, to create Galaxy objects for your HelloUniverse Android application.

You designed the entire Galaxy class, including seven instance variables, one constructor method, and eight methods to get and set various attributes of the Galaxy object. Once this design was accomplished, you coded the variable declarations, constructor method, and the functional methods for the class, and then you typed them into Eclipse and compiled and ran the application to make sure everything was compiling and would run, meaning there were no code errors introduced.

In Chapter 6, you will start to learn about how Android handles the device display screen by using the Android View class, and all about the foundation of user interface design as it relates to the Android OS.

Android Screen Design: Writing to the Display Using Activity and View

Now that you've been exposed to the Android operating system, and have seen how it works from a high-level view, have learned about XML and Java, and how they are used in Android application development, the next thing we need to take a closer look at is how Android "addresses" or writes things to the device display screen.

In the new age of touchscreen devices, such as smartphones, tablets, eBook readers, iTVs, and smartwatches, the display screen has become the center of not only the visual feedback for your application but also for interacting with it. This chapter will cover those classes that allow your Android app to write things to the device display screen, such as Activity classes, UI elements, and of course, the app's primary subject matter content.

There are some very important Android superclasses, such as **Activity**, **View**, and **ViewGroup**, which provide a foundation for the subclasses that you will use to get your application content and UI onto the display screen. The superclasses are not used directly in the application, but you need to know about them nonetheless.

We will look at **Activity** subclasses, used for organizing your application's functional screens, which ultimately will provide the structure for your end user's workflow, let's call it the "use-flow," for your Android application.

We will look at **View** subclasses, used for creating your application's UI element components; these are also known as "**widgets**" in Android jargon, as you will soon see. We will look at the **ViewGroup** subclasses, used for creating your application's UI **layout containers**. Layout containers are used to contain View subclassed UI widgets, which make up the body of the UI design, providing the UI layout with its functionality.

Finally, we will put all of this newfound knowledge to use, and will create your first custom Hello Universe UI design, so that you get some hands-on experience in creating your own UI designs. We will create a Galaxy object using your code from the previous chapter, and populate an information screen for that object.

How Activity, View, and ViewGroup Relate

Before we look at the Android Activity, View, and ViewGroup superclasses and the functional subclasses (those classes that you will actually utilize to construct your apps) that are created with them over the next couple of chapters, it is important to understand how they all relate to each other within the context of your application.

The reason I'm not including the **Menu** superclass and its functional subclasses in this chapter is because menus in Android are "handled" separately from UI widgets (View) and UI layouts (ViewGroup), in as much as they pop up over the screen triggered by a hardware **MENU** button or the ActionBar Overflow menu. For this reason we are going to cover Menu objects separately, in the next chapter. The one similarity is that each Activity subclass also has its own Menu system, as you can see in Figure 3-8, set up via the second method, called **.onCreateOptionsMenu()**.

As you have learned already, the Android runtime environment resides on top of the Linux operating system (OS) kernel, and forms what is essentially the Android OS, under which your application executes (runs). Your application defines itself to the Android RunTime (ART, for Android 5.0 and later) or to the Android Dalvik Virtual Machine (DVM, for Android 4.4 and earlier OS versions) using the **AndroidManifest.xml** application definition XML file that we looked at in detail during Chapter 4.

For each functional display screen in your app, which will generally contain some sort of UI design, as well as related content, your application will define an **Activity subclass**. Your Hello Universe application currently has one of these Activity subclasses already, as you saw in Chapter 3 in Figure 3-8, with your **MainActivity.java** class, which as you now know from what you learned in Chapter 5 on Java is actually an Activity subclass, due to the **public class MainActivity extends Activity** declaration at the top of the class.

Each Activity subclass in your Android application will be required to have an **.onCreate()** method defined, and this method will in turn be required to contain a **setContentView()** method call, whose parameter list contains a reference to that Activity's UI layout XML definition. For the MainActivity.java class, this reference is **R.layout.activity_main**, which is Android "shorthand" to reference the **/res/layout/activity_main.xml** file, as you can see in Figure 3-8, which after our Java primer chapter should be making a whole lot more sense to you!

Android's shorthand resource "path" definition starts with an "**R**," which stands for "resources," and uses **period** characters (instead of slash characters) to reference the "**layout**" folder, and then the "**activity_main.xml**" XML file. Notice that Android references do not include any file extension, so R.layout.activity_main equates to your full Android project folder path as follows: **/workspace/HelloUniverse/res/layout/activity_main.xml**.

The **parent tag** in this UI layout XML definition will generally reference a **ViewGroup** subclass, such as the **RelativeLayout** class, which in the activity_main.xml file is represented by a **<RelativeLayout>** parent tag. The ViewGroup superclass in Android is used to subclass (create) custom layout container classes in Android, which we will be covering in detail in Chapters 7 and 8. There are a large number of custom layout container classes in Android, because these UI layout classes provide the foundation of UI design in Android.

Inside of a ViewGroup UI layout container parent tag are **child tags** representing **UI elements**, which are called "**widgets**" in Android. UI widgets are based on Android's **View** superclass. Each widget, like that **<TextView>** child tag you used back in Chapters 3 and 4, references an Android **TextView** widget class, which is subclassed from the View superclass. Inside each (View subclass) UI widget child tag, you can set parameters that **reference** the **new media assets** for your application, such as **drawables** (images and bitmap animation), **animation** (procedural, tween, or vector animation), **audio**, **video**, **shapes**, custom UI elements, and the like.

Thus, getting your new media assets onto the Android device display screen involves putting **parameters** in child widget tags inside of parent UI layout tags referenced by Activity subclass methods declared in your application's AndroidManifest XML file. This is all passed over to the Android RunTime engine, which then converts these into machine language, and then passes them over to the Linux Kernel, whose job it is to interface the software with the hardware and thus to write your application UI design and content to the Android device display screen hardware with pixel-perfect accuracy. Whew! The chain from Android Runtime to app resources looks like this:

```
Android RunTime > Android Manifest > Activity Subclass > ViewGroup Parent Tag > View Child Tag >
Resource Parameters
```

To make it even easier to visualize, I created a diagram shown in Figure 6-1 that shows layers (and connections) between your application's new media resources, the UI widgets that hold them, UI layouts that hold the UI widgets, and the Activity subclass that defines and controls your UI layout XML definition, by referencing it using the .setContentView() method call. It is important to note that since you can set the background image, or animation, for the UI layout container, a ViewGroup can also reference new media resources; thus, the new media resource area of the diagram in Figure 6-1 makes contact with both the View and ViewGroup subclasses.

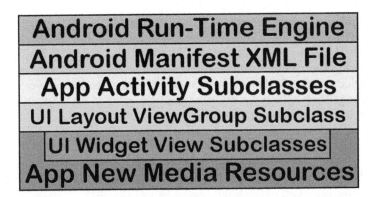

Figure 6-1. *The stratification of an Android application from new media resources up to an Android device screen*

As you learned in the previous chapters, your Android Manifest serves to define for the ART what Activity classes an application contains, as well as what your application is allowed to do, and other information about your application's version history, support, structure, permissions, communications, intents, and the like.

Next, we will take a closer look at the relationship between the ViewGroup (layout container) and the View (UI widget) superclasses in Android, since the ViewGroup superclass is actually a subclass of the View superclass. It is interesting to note that **a superclass can also be a subclass**! ViewGroup inherits characteristics like margin settings, which as you will see, are supported in both layout containers (ViewGroup subclasses) and UI widgets (View subclasses), thanks to Java inheritance, as well as to how Android has coded these superclass structures.

The ViewGroup Class: A Subclass of View

Even though the View widgets are nested inside of ViewGroup layout containers, the ViewGroup superclass is actually underneath (subclassed from) the View superclass in the Java class hierarchy. Starting with a Java Object master class, the inheritance hierarchy is structured as follows:

```
java.lang.Object
   > android.view.View
      > android.view.ViewGroup
```

The reason that the Android OS development team structured (coded) the View class hierarchy in this fashion is because some of the View class attributes, for instance, top, bottom, left, and right **margin** attributes (properties, or parameters), will also be available for use in a ViewGroup layout container, as well as in all View UI widgets.

Thus, the logical Java structure is to subclass ViewGroup from View, so that the ViewGroup subclasses inherit all of the same attributes and methods that the View subclasses will also feature. If you want to take a closer look at what this Android View superclass includes, you can see for yourself, by visiting the following URL:

```
http://developer.android.com/reference/android/view/View.html
```

If you look at the View class reference page on the Android developer web site, you will see that the View class has 11 **known direct subclasses**, one of which is ViewGroup. Some of the other common UI widgets such as the **TextView**, which you have already used in your app, as well as **ImageView** and **AnalogClock**, which we will eventually be using in your application UI design, are also subclassed directly from the View class.

> **Note**   A **known direct subclass** is a subclass that has been created from the class that is being documented on that developer web site class reference page. "**Known**" means it has been officially added to the Android API. If you subclass your own Android class, it would be called an **unknown direct subclass**, because it is "unknown" to the Android API. A **known indirect subclass** would represent any subclass of a known direct subclass. It is said to be **indirect** to the class being documented, because it is more than one level away from, and therefore not a direct subclass of, the currently documented class.

There are **63** known indirect subclasses of the View class, which are essentially subclasses of the 11 known direct subclasses. These are UI elements, known as widgets in Android, and you will be learning about some of these during the course of this book. Since ViewGroup (UI layout) subclasses are just as important as the View (UI widgets) subclasses that are contained inside them, the ViewGroup class also has dozens of direct and indirect subclasses with unique UI layout features or options. However, the ViewGroup class doesn't have quite as many subclasses as the View class does. Since referencing the Android developer web site page for the class you're using is always a smart thing to do, I'll provide these URLs. The ViewGroup class is located at this URL:

`http://developer.android.com/reference/android/view/ViewGroup.html`

If you take a look at this ViewGroup class reference page to see what the class is capable of, you will see that the ViewGroup class has **12** known direct subclasses, one of which is the **RelativeLayout** class that your XML UI layout definition is currently using for the HelloUniverse app currently. There are **30** known indirect subclasses providing more specialized UI design layout containers, because as subclasses get further down in the hierarchy they become more specialized. We'll be looking at several of the most popular ViewGroup subclasses in Chapters 7 and 8 covering UI layout design.

When using ViewGroup subclasses, termed UI layout containers in Android, and View subclasses, termed UI widgets in Android, the View widgets are contained **inside of** the ViewGroup layout containers, which is why the class is named ViewGroup, as it **groups** your View objects together into a UI layout design, as shown in Figure 6-2. The ViewGroup layout design is then referenced inside of, or contained in, your Activity.

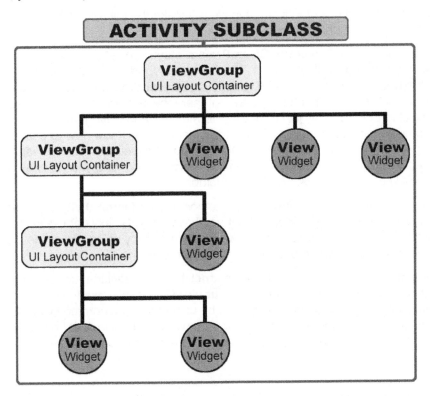

Figure 6-2. *Activity subclass contains UI design created with ViewGroup layout containers and View UI widgets*

It is important to note that even though a ViewGroup subclass must be used as the "parent" object in your XML UI layout design, ViewGroup subclass objects can also be "nested" underneath this parent ViewGroup object. We'll actually be nesting ViewGroup subclasses using a LinearLayout ViewGroup subclass later in the chapter. ViewGroup subclass objects can be both parent and child objects, whereas View widgets are usually just child objects.

Hands-on experience is the best way to show you all of this UI design theory, so let's integrate a UI design with a Galaxy object created using the **Galaxy()** constructor you built in the previous chapter. Let's use the Galaxy class you created in Chapter 5 to create a Galaxy object and utilize the **.set()** methods you created to establish its properties. Then we'll develop a UI design using the popular **LinearLayout** ViewGroup subclass that displays galaxy information on your Activity screen. Finally, we will "wire together" your UI design and the Galaxy object, so that the UI design displays the variable data in the Galaxy object's data fields.

Customizing Your UI Design: Galaxy Screen

Next, let's get right into learning how the Activity subclass, ViewGroup layout container, and View widgets are used, within the context of your current Hello Universe Android application. To do this, we'll continue building upon your Java programming work that you did in Chapter 5, and continue using your Galaxy class, to create a new Galaxy object in your MainActivity.java Activity subclass's **.onCreate()** method. Then, we'll create the UI design for this Galaxy Info Screen, which will display your Galaxy object's characteristics on the Hello Universe app screen.

During the next several sections of this chapter, we will make the following Hello Universe application additions and UI design modifications:

- Review the Eclipse **Project ➤ Clean Project** menu sequence, and learn the work process to **rebuild** a project. This is in case you ever open up Eclipse Android Development Tools (ADT) and find that your project is filled with errors that should not be there (that is, were not there the last time that you closed and exited Eclipse). This just happened to me, as I was writing the code for this chapter, so I am going to include this topic here so you know how to deal with it in case this ever happens to you. Opening up what you know is a "clean" project and seeing it filled with "red ink," or error highlighting everywhere, can be extremely unnerving to any Android developer.

- Review and enhance the **.onCreate()** method in your **MainActivity.java** class, to create a new Galaxy object, so that you have some Galaxy data values to display in the revised UI design that we'll be creating by using one of the most commonly used ViewGroup subclasses (LinearLayout).

- Edit and reconfigure the **activity_main.xml** UI layout definition, to use a more basic and memory efficient **LinearLayout** ViewGroup subclass to create a Galaxy Information Screen. We will also be using the most commonly used View subclass UI widget, the **TextView**, and we will take a look at how to "**nest**" LinearLayout ViewGroup objects, in order to create more complex UI structures.

- Install and reference **digital image new media assets**, to add an actual galaxy image to the background of your Galaxy Information Screen, to make it more visual and more professional.

- Further enhance your **.onCreate()** method, to create **TextView** objects so that the UI design can "**set**" its TextView objects to display the Galaxy object's attributes using the .set() method calls.

Eclipse Clean Project: Sanitizing Your Project

When I opened my Eclipse ADT and looked at the error-free code that I had left off in Chapter 5, I was startled to see errors in my project that I knew should not be there. To research what these were, I opened up the five **error-related tabs**, located at the bottom of the Integrated Development Environment (IDE), by placing my cursor on the tan divider area, above the error tabs section. I then clicked down (and held the mouse button in the down position) so that I could "drag" the divider upwards, to expand the area that holds these five error tabs. I then clicked on the first tab called "**Problems**," and then I clicked the right-facing triangle, next to the **Errors** line item, which revealed the two errors, "The project was not built since its build path" and "The type java.lang.Object cannot be resolved," which are shown at the bottom of Figure 6-3.

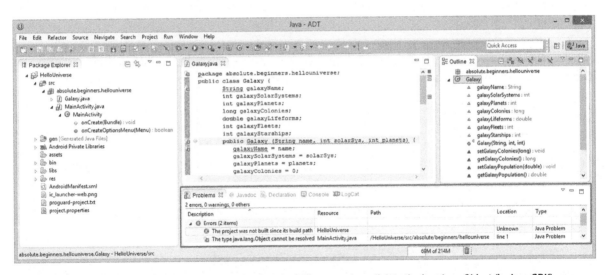

Figure 6-3. Errors on opening Eclipse, caused by Eclipse's inability to resolve a link to the java.lang.Object (in Java SDK)

Since Eclipse (and ADT) are constantly evolving, these software development tools themselves will also have "**bugs**" or errors in their code, just like your Android applications invariably will. This makes the software development process even more complex, but then again, the software development process is inherently complex anyway, so this is just something that you are going to have to be aware of, and deal with, in your software development work process. This is why I am putting what just happened to me, and how to deal with it if it happens to you, into this chapter, as its very own section.

You can see an error in the Eclipse programming code, in Figure 6-3, in fact. Notice that the **Galaxy.java** tab is clearly showing several errors in the code contained in it, but the Eclipse code is **not** putting the red error X next to the Galaxy.java class in the Package Explorer pane, which it should be, to show that this class has errors in it! This is an Eclipse bug!

As you can see under the **Problems** tab, these errors are stemming from Eclipse ADT's inability to reference, or "resolve," the **path** to the **java.lang.Object** master class, which is part of the Java SDK, also known as the JDK.

Let's utilize this Eclipse error in referencing the JDK to reinforce what we learned in Chapter 5, just to turn this negative experience into a positive one! As you can see in the editing pane in Figure 6-3, the **String** and **Galaxy** objects that are subclassed from the Java Object are the ones that contain the red underline, indicating an error. Since the **galaxyName** variable is a **String** object, it is also marked as an error. Thus these are not our own Java coding errors, but errors that are being generated by Eclipse's inability to "see," resolve, or reference, the Java Development Kit (JDK) and its Object superclass.

The easiest way to fix this is to simply click the red X exit icon at the top-right corner of the Eclipse IDE, or use a **File ➤ Exit** menu sequence, to exit Eclipse. Then restart Eclipse, accept the workspace, and wait for the IDE to load and reference the Java software development kit (SDK, also known as JDK), and after a while, the red error highlighting will vanish. I have seen online that developers have said that they had to exit and restart Eclipse several times before Eclipse saw the JDK again.

If this does not restore the link between Eclipse ADT and the JDK, you might need to "**rebuild**" your project. Use the **Project ➤ Clean** menu sequence, which is shown in Figure 6-4, along with the **Clean** dialog this menu sequence brings up, shown in the lower-right corner of the screenshot.

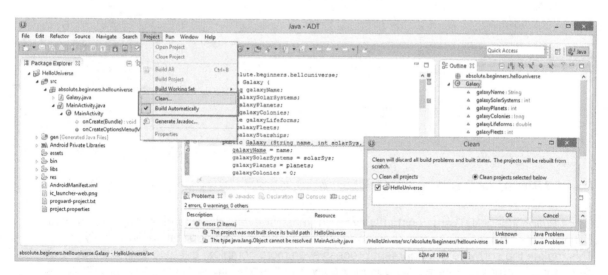

Figure 6-4. Using the Project ➤ Clean menu sequence with the Build Automatically option checked (underneath)

Make sure that the **Build Automatically** option on the **Project** menu has a **check mark** to the left of it, which it should, since this is the default setting in Eclipse. This auto-build option is directly underneath the **Clean** submenu option.

Once the **Clean** dialog opens up, click on the radio button next to the "**Clean projects selected below**" and then make sure that the check box next to the HelloUniverse project is checked, and then click the **OK** button, which will then "clean" and finally "rebuild" your Hello Universe project.

If this does not get rid of the errors in the IDE, which it didn't when I tried it, then exit Eclipse again, and restart it again, accept the workspace location dialog, and then wait for a few minutes for Eclipse to look for and to find the JDK on your hard drive. We know it's there, because we would not have made it past Chapter 2 of this book if it wasn't!

This finally worked on my workstation, and I finally got the clean project that I should have gotten in the first place, when I started working on all of this today. The clean IDE, shown in Figure 6-5 with zero Java code errors, which I knew to be the case, and the "empty" Problems tab shown at the bottom, shows me that Eclipse ADT has found, and is now referencing (I like to call it "wired up to"), the java.lang.Object class inside the Java SDK.

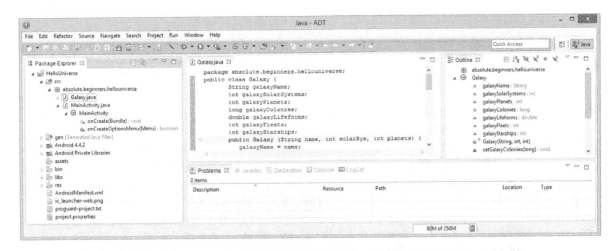

Figure 6-5. Once visibility to Java SDK (java.lang.Object) has been restored, all the incorrect error tags disappear

Next, let's construct the new Galaxy Object, and name it **milkyWay**, using the **Galaxy()** method, so that we can use the impressive code that you created in Chapter 5 for something useful in your Hello Universe application.

Using the Galaxy Class: Creating a Galaxy Object

As you learned in Chapter 5, the way to construct an object is by calling the **constructor** method; in this case, it is the **Galaxy()** method, in conjunction with the Java **new** keyword, utilizing the following Java code structure:

```
Galaxy milkyWay = new Galaxy();
```

As you can see in Figure 6-6, when you type this in Eclipse, the IDE will check your **Galaxy.java** class method.

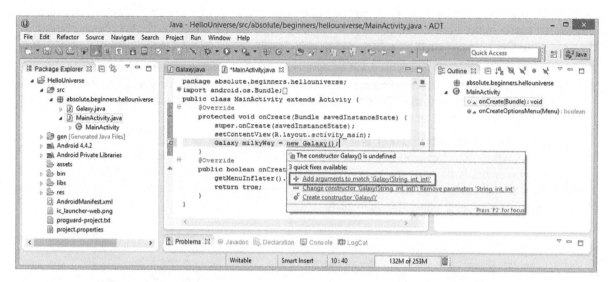

Figure 6-6. Constructing a Galaxy object named milkyWay using a Java new keyword and a Galaxy() constructor method

I typed the constructor method call in this incomplete way to show you that your Galaxy.java class is now a part of all of the Java language constructs that Eclipse checks all code against, and Eclipse will now tell you that you are not calling your constructor method correctly, and an error underline now highlights this **new Galaxy()** method call!

When you mouse-over the error highlight, you will get a **light yellow coding tips popup**, which will tell you what Eclipse thinks is wrong with your Java code; in this case, "**The constructor Galaxy() is undefined**" or more accurately, the constructor method call is not defined (configured) correctly. Eclipse is even nice enough to suggest "quick fixes" and as you can see the first one shows your constructor method call format of **Galaxy(String, int, int)**, which tells you that you need to pass some data values over inside of the method call parens (parameters area).

Let's add a galaxy name, number of solar systems, and number of inhabited planets now, and see if this removes the error. As you can see in Figure 6-7, I added the String "**Milky Way**," **511** solar systems, and **97** habitable planets to the constructor method call, and this removed the red error highlighting, but added some yellow warning highlighting. A **warning** means that the code will compile and run, whereas the error means that the code will not even allow you to attempt to compile (and run) your application until you fix that particular programming problem.

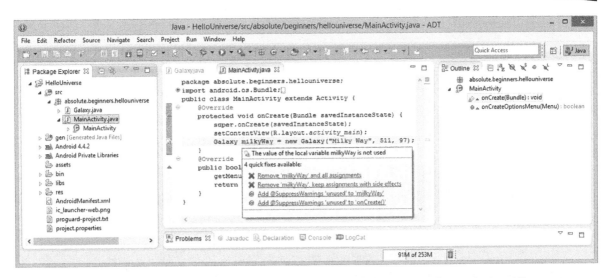

Figure 6-7. Completing the Galaxy() constructor method call parameter list and mouse-over the warning to get tip

To access the Eclipse warning helper popup to see what Eclipse thinks is a problem with the milkyWay object now that the constructor method call has been completed, mouse-over the milkyWay object reference in your code.

The warning message at the top of the popup will tell you that "**The value of the local variable milkyWay is not used**" because the milkyWay Galaxy object has not been used to do anything (call any methods) as of yet.

It is also important to notice that Eclipse is calling milkyWay a **variable**, and not an object name, telling us that milkyWay is actually a **variable** that's **referencing** that particular Galaxy object, created using the Java **new** keyword.

It is still OK for you to look at milkyWay as the name you use in your code to access this instance of the Galaxy object. I just wanted to point out the finer detail in how the Java programming language is viewing things here! The milkyWay variable, as Eclipse (Java) sees it, is a "pointer" or a **memory reference** that accesses the Java object instance (that is, in this particular case, a **Milky Way** Galaxy object definition and all its data values somewhere in system memory).

To remove this warning highlighting, make a method call, using dot notation, off of your new milkyWay Galaxy object. Enter a return character at the end of the Galaxy object constructor line of code, after the semi-colon, and create a new-line for your next line of code. Type in **milkyWay** and hit the period key on your keyboard. This will open a different Eclipse helper popup, which contains every method call that is compatible with this Galaxy object. As you can see in Figure 6-8, this includes the four **.set()** methods that you coded in Chapter 5, which we are about to use here, to set up the other properties of your milkyWay Galaxy object. We are doing this so when our UI design accesses this object, it has data values to display!

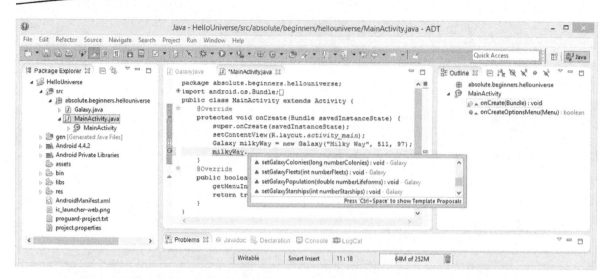

Figure 6-8. *Using a milkyWay object with dot notation to call the .set() methods, and get rid of the warning highlight*

Double-click on the **setGalaxyColonies(long numberColonies):void** method, which will insert the method into your code, and then enter **37,579,321** as the number of colonies for your new Galaxy object. As you can see, in Figure 6-9, this "throws" a red error highlighting indicator underneath your method call.

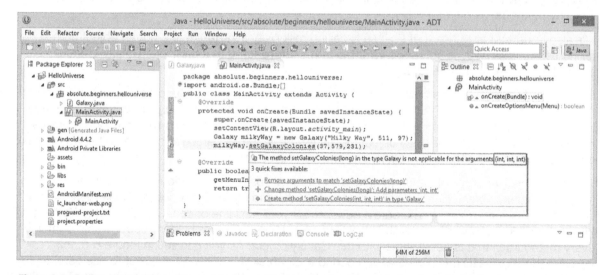

Figure 6-9. *Error message tip regarding using commas for the numeric parameter values in method call*

If you mouse-over the error, you will see that Eclipse is telling you that "**The method setGalaxyColonies(long) in the (object) type Galaxy is not applicable for the arguments (int, int, int).**" This lets you know Eclipse is evaluating those comma characters in your numeric designation as **value delimiters**, not as numeric formatting, which you were using to try and indicate (signify) a large (millions) numeric representation.

This means that Eclipse (and thus the compiler) will think you are passing **three integer values** into the method call, rather than one large, accurately formatted number! The solution to this is, of course, to not use commas in your numeric values in method call parameter lists, as parameter values are separated, or "**delimited,**" using Programmer speak, by using the comma character. We can always provide this numeric formatting once we pass a data value from the Galaxy object to each TextView, which we will be doing much later on in the chapter using Java code.

Note that none of these three "quick fixes" in this particular pop-up will solve the problem, so you will have to remove the commas yourself! Don't be surprised if someday Eclipse ADT features a higher level of artificial intelligence in their helper code analysis algorithm that will add in a fourth quick fix option of "Remove comma delimiters to create the required long data value." The reason I am generating these errors and warnings in this section is so that I can show you all these Eclipse helper popups and how to use them.

Once you remove these commas from your numeric data value, the error will vanish, and you can use this same work process of typing in the Galaxy object variable name of milkyWay and a period, and double-click on each of the remaining three method calls, to set the **population** at **1,967,387,132** (without commas, of course), set the number of **fleets** to **237**, and set the number of **starships** to **34,769**, without using the comma, as is shown in Figure 6-10. Note that all of the Java code is error-free and you have created and configured the milkyWay Galaxy object and all of its data fields (its characteristics) for your MainActivity.java class, using only five compact lines of Java program logic.

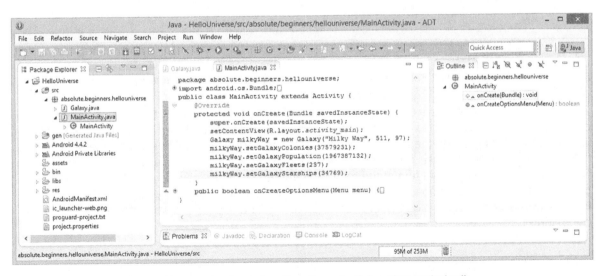

Figure 6-10. Completed Galaxy object construction and configuration using Galaxy class method calls

Next, we will create a UI design to display our Galaxy object characteristics (data values) using a LinearLayout class (ViewGroup subclass) as our layout container. Inside of the UI, we will use View subclass that we've been using so far in the book, the TextView class, to create an impressive Galaxy Information Screen UI design.

Using LinearLayout: Creating Linear UI Designs

Since we're going to cover the RelativeLayout class in greater detail in Chapter 7, I want to take the opportunity to teach you about the LinearLayout class in this chapter, so that we can focus on the advanced layout container classes in Chapter 8 regarding UI layout classes. To see how easy it can be to edit a layout container class reference using the parent tag in XML, change the word **"Relative"** to **"Linear"** in the opening and closing tags in the current **/res/layout/activity_main.xml** UI definition file, shown in Figure 6-11.

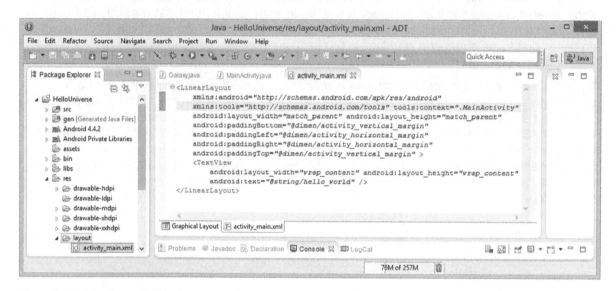

Figure 6-11. Changing a <RelativeLayout> parent tag to a <LinearLayout> parent tag and reposition parameters

To make room for some of the other child tags we will be adding, I also put the **tools:context** parameter next to (but after, as the xmlns:tools parameter defines the tools: prefix) the xmlns:tools parameter, and also placed the android:layout_width and android:layout_height parameters on the same line as well, to make the mark-up more dense and save us some space. Next, we need to change the Hello Universe! text at the top of the screen to be the new screen design's title, by editing the **hello_world** constant in the **/values/strings.xml** file to hold your new "**Galaxy Information Screen**" data value, which we will be using for a title for the new information screen's UI design.

Adding <string> constants for Your UI Labels

Once this has been edited, copy and paste this <string> constant definition tag seven times underneath itself, and then create text string constants for **galaxy_name**, **galaxy_solar**, **galaxy_habit**, **galaxy_colony**, **galaxy_pop**, **galaxy_fleet**, and **galaxy_ships** named constants, as shown in Figure 6-12, using the following XML mark-up:

```
<string name="galaxy_name">Galaxy Name:</string>
<string name="galaxy_solar">Galaxy Solar Systems:</string>
<string name="galaxy_habit">Galaxy Habitable Planets:</string>
<string name="galaxy_colony">Galaxy Colonies:</string>
<string name="galaxy_pop">Galaxy Population:</string>
<string name="galaxy_fleet">Galaxy Starship Fleets:</string>
<string name="galaxy_ships">Galaxy Active Starships:</string>
```

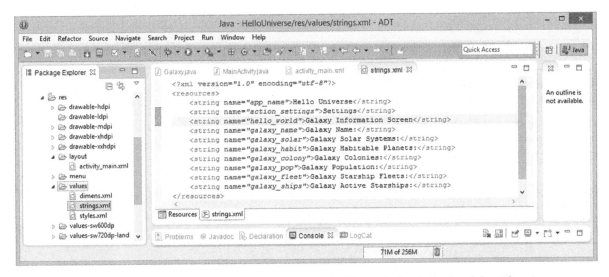

Figure 6-12. Change the hello_world <string> variable to a new screen title; create the eight galaxy info <string> tags

Using Parameters to Configure Your LinearLayout

Now that we have the galaxy information screen's data value holder string constants defined, we can configure the LinearLayout UI layout container. As you can probably infer from the class name, a LinearLayout class is used to create either **rows** of **horizontal** UI elements, or **columns** of **vertical** UI elements, as we are doing here with vertically stacked TextView UI elements (widgets). Let's tell the **<LinearLayout>** parent tag how to orient its child tag View UI widgets by adding the **android:orientation** parameter. To get the helper dialog containing all of the parameters that are available for use with the LinearLayout class, type in the word "**android**" and then type a **colon** and wait a second for the Eclipse child tag helper dialog to appear, as is shown in Figure 6-13.

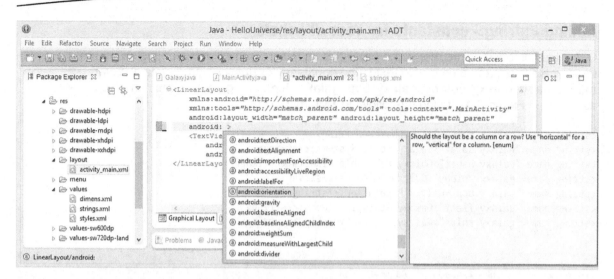

Figure 6-13. Use the android and colon work process to display a helper popup of parameters for LinearLayout

Find the **android:orientation** parameter near the bottom of the list and select it to see what it does, which will be shown on the right, and then **double-click** it to insert it into the parent tag.

Once the **android:orientation=""** appears inside of your parent <LinearLayout> tag, type the **vertical** constant inside of the quotation marks to complete the configuration of this parameter, which is shown in Figure 6-14.

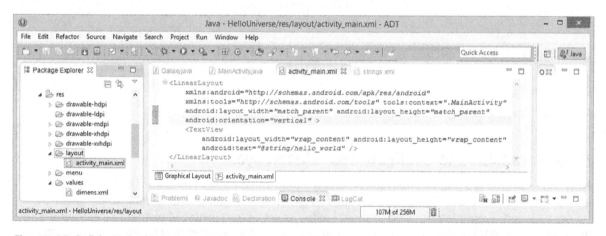

Figure 6-14. Defining the <LinearLayout> parent tag android:orientation parameter with a vertical constant value

Also, notice that I have deleted the **android:padding** parameters, since we are going to learn about how to use the **android:margin** parameters to control the spacing of our UI design on the Activity screen, after we add in the child <TextView> tags that will make up the galaxy information label portion of our UI design. First, let's use the **Run As ➤ Android Application** work process, and look at our UI design, shown on the left in Figure 6-15.

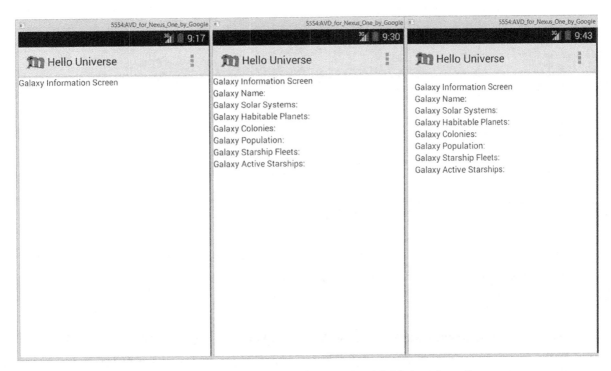

Figure 6-15. The Nexus One AVD with the changed title text, the added galaxy info labels, and margins

Let's create the seven **<TextView>** child tags the easy way. Select the **hello_world <TextView>** tag, and copy and paste it seven times underneath itself, as seen in Figure 6-16. Change the **android:text** parameters to point to, or to reference, the <string> tag name variables that you created in Figure 6-12 so that the TextView objects use the correct label data value. Leave the android:layout_width and android:layout_height set to **wrap_content**.

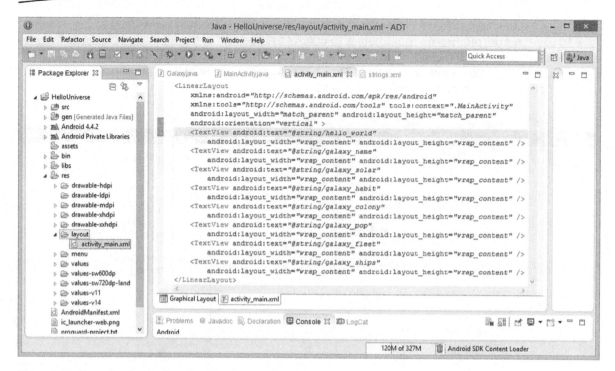

Figure 6-16. Reconfiguring the first <TextView> parameter, and then copying it seven times, to create text labels

> **Note**   These **android:layout_width** and **android:layout_height** are the only required parameters to have in both a ViewGroup (a parent tag) as well as a View (child tag) XML class reference. The reason these are required in ViewGroup is because they're required in View class inheritance scenarios, so essentially, every UI element must define a layout_width and a layout_height **constant**, either **wrap_content** or **match_parent**, which we'll be looking at over the next few chapters.

Once you finish these edits, use the **Run As ➤ Android Application** work process, and the Android application should look like what is shown in the middle part of the screen shot shown in Figure 6-15.

As you can see, since we removed the android:padding parameters that pushed the UI content away from the sides of the display screen, the UI design is now too close to (touching) the sides of the display. We are going to use the **android:layout_margin** parameter to space the UI design away from the sides of the screen next.

Although we could put these android:layout_margin parameters inside each of your <TextView> child tags in order to achieve this end-result, it would be far more efficient to use the grouping feature of the LinearLayout (ViewGroup) to space the entire design out by using a single parameter placed in the LinearLayout parent tag.

Inside of the end of your <LinearLayout> tag, after the **android:orientation** parameter you just added, type in **android:** again, display the parameter helper popup, and find the **android:layout_margin** parameters, as is shown in 6-17.

This android:layout_margin parameter puts space around the entire UI widget (if used inside of a View child tag) or around the entire UI layout container (if used inside of the ViewGroup parent tag), as you will soon see. If you want to put space only on one side, or only above or below your UI widget (View) or layout container (ViewGroup), you can use one of the more specialized layout_margin parameters, shown in the parameter helper popup in Figure 6-17. **Double-click** on the android:layout_margin parameter to insert it in your <LinearLayout> parent tag, and add a **12dip**, or 12 **density independent pixels**, value inside of the quotation marks. We will be learning all about this DIP (dip, or dp) constant, and how it relates to graphics, in Chapter 9, which will cover graphic design in Android.

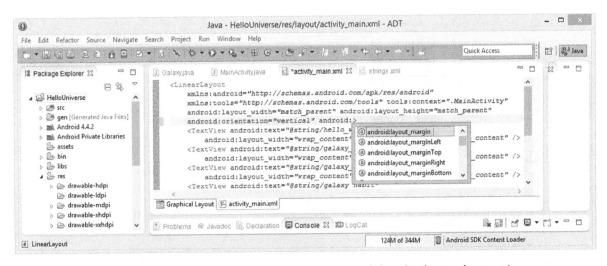

Figure 6-17. Use an android: work process to access LinearLayout parameter helper showing margin parameters

Let's see how this margin spacing around the perimeter of our design improves how it looks, and use the **Run As ➤ Android Application** work process. As you can see on the right side of Figure 6-15, an entire UI design is moved out using this single parameter, since we used it in the parent ViewGroup to move the entire UI design as a whole.

Since this is the Hello Universe application, and a Galaxy Information Screen, let's put a galaxy image from the NASA web site into the background of the UI layout container, before we start learning about how to refine and "tweak" our UI design using XML parameters, which is both easy and fun, at least compared to doing it in Java!

After you learn how to add this "**image background plate**" to your UI layout design using the **android:background** parameter in the parent <LinearLayout> tag, you will need to change your <TextView> child tag parameters to use a white text color and add some <TextView> UI elements to hold the default data values, and eventually the Galaxy object data values. Later on, once the UI design looks reasonably professional, we will go back into your MainActivity class Java code and create TextView objects and configure these with the Galaxy object data fields so that the actual data from your Galaxy object is referenced in your UI design.

Using Digital Imagery: Adding a Galaxy Background

I have prepared a **galaxyinfoscreen.png** digital image file to use as the background image, which is in the book assets' ZIP file. Open the ZIP file, or better yet, extract it to your hard disk drive on your workstation, **right-click** on the galaxyinfoscreen.png image, and select the **Copy** menu item. Then find your **/workspace** folder on your hard disk drive, it should be in a C:/Users/ComputerName folder. Right-click on the **/res/drawable-xhdpi** subfolder, and then select the **Paste** option, which will paste the image into that folder, as shown in Figure 6-18.

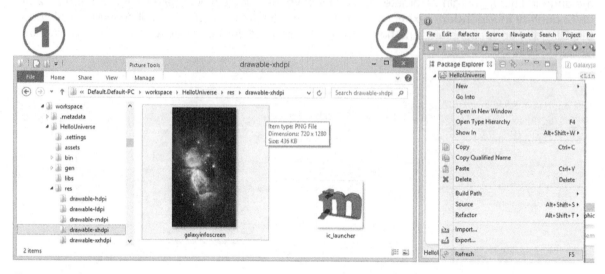

Figure 6-18.   Copy the galaxyinfoscreen.png file into the drawable-xhdpi folder; right-click and Refresh the project

Once you copy this digital image file into your /res/drawable-xhdpi folder using this procedure, you need to let Eclipse know that you have updated your project "outside" of Eclipse, so that Eclipse can **rescan** your project folder hierarchy and "see" any new files. This is done using the "**Refresh**" menu option. Access the Refresh utility by right-clicking on your HelloUniverse project folder in the Eclipse Package Explorer pane to access the context-sensitive menu, as shown on the right side of Figure 6-18.

Once you have copied the galaxyinfoscreen.png file into the drawable-xhdpi folder and used the Refresh tool, the file will appear in your Package Explorer pane as seen highlighted on the bottom-left of Figure 6-19. Now you are ready to add an **android:background** parameter to your parent <LinearLayout> tag that will place this background image behind every UI widget that you place inside of this container, giving your UI design a hip scenic background, and making your UI design more visually appealing.

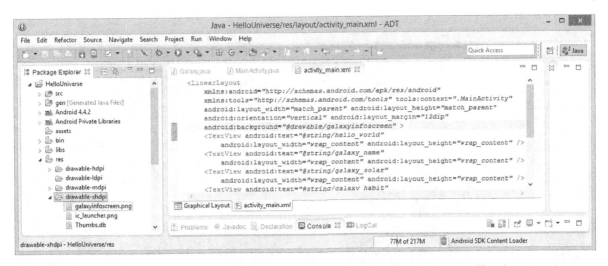

Figure 6-19. *Insert an android:background="@drawable/galaxyinfoscreen" parameter into the parent LinearLayout*

To add this parameter, you can type in **android** and the **colon** key, select the **background** parameter, and double-click it, or you can just type the entire parameter in along with the proper **@drawable/** path reference to the file, using the following XML mark-up:

```
android:background="@drawable/galaxyinfoscreen"
```

The reason we do **not** use **@drawable-xhdpi/galaxyinfoscreen** is because the Android OS will choose which drawable resolution density asset to use for any given Android hardware device screen specification. In the case where there is only one image asset available, such as this, it will simply use that. We will be covering how to develop multiple graphic image assets in Chapter 9, but for now, we'll just use one extra high definition (XHD) image asset.

Now let's use the **Run As ➤ Android Application** menu sequence, which can be accessed by right-clicking on the HelloUniverse project folder, or alternately via Eclipse's **Run** menu (Run ➤ Run As ➤ Android Application) and see how the galaxy image looks behind our current galaxy information screen UI design.

As you can see in the left-hand pane of Figure 6-20, the **contrast** between the dark gray UI text color and the galaxy space image makes the text quite difficult, if not impossible, to read, unless it is in front of a very bright star, like the "e" character that you can see is the only easily discernable character in the UI design currently!

Figure 6-20. Problems with dark text and parent layout_margin parameter (left); fixed (center) and refined (right)

Contrast is one of those graphics terms that we normally would save for Chapter 9 on graphic design for Android, but let's cover it here since we are encountering this problem now! Contrast is how much difference between light and dark there is in an image, and with text or UI widgets especially, influences how visible they are to a user (that is, how much they "pop" out, in the case of UI widgets, or are easy to read, in the case of text).

Maximum contrast would be achieved by using a black text color on a white background color, or a white text color on a black background color, while a minimum contrast scenario would involve a medium gray text color on a medium gray background color. The minimum contrast scenario would appear as though the medium gray background color was the only thing on the screen, as there is **zero contrast** between the medium gray text and medium gray background.

Let's fix this next by adding the **android:textColor** parameter to the <TextView> UI widgets, so we can crank the contrast back up near maximum, and make the UI readable again for our application users!

After we learn how to control the <TextView> UI widget textColor parameter, we will create the <TextView> UI elements that will hold the data values for our milkyWay Galaxy Object. If you want to peek at the result of the next two sections of this chapter, where you'll learn about **android:textColor** and **nesting** LinearLayout containers, you can also see this in Figure 6-20.

Creating UI Contrast: The TextView Color Parameter

Let's add a space character after the android:text parameter in our first hello_world <TextView> tag, and use the android: work process to bring up the parameter helper dialog. As you can see in Figure 6-21, I actually typed in **android:t** which "refined" the parameters displayed in this dialog, to only include those parameters that begin with the letter "t," which, as you can see, gives me all of the android:text related parameters!

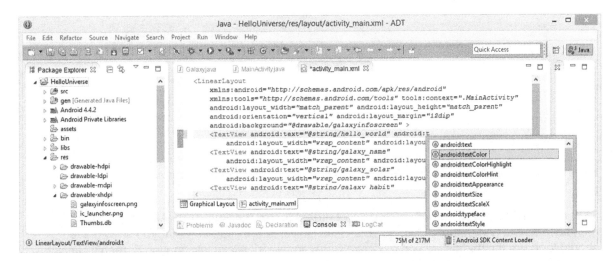

Figure 6-21. *Change the <TextView> textColor parameter from gray to white using the pop-up helper*

The second parameter is the one I am looking for, android:textColor. So, I selected that one, by double-clicking on it, so that Eclipse will automatically insert it into my XML mark-up for the hello_world <TextView> child tag, and all I have to do is to "**configure**" it, by using a color data value that the Android OS understands.

The android:textColor parameter takes a "**hexadecimal**" or **Base-16** color value, which we will be looking at in greater detail in Chapter 9 on graphic design. For now, all you need to know is the hexadecimal representation for the color white is **#FFFFFF**, and thus, that is the color data value you will need to utilize inside of the quotation marks, once Eclipse has written the empty parameter for you.

Once you have modified this first <TextView> child tag, as shown in Figure 6-22, you can copy just this one parameter (make sure to copy the space character in front of the parameter along with it) and simply paste it into the other seven <TextView> child tags in exactly the same location! Your XML mark-up is getting pretty dense and is about to get even more complex, as we have to add in seven more <TextView> tags, to hold data values!

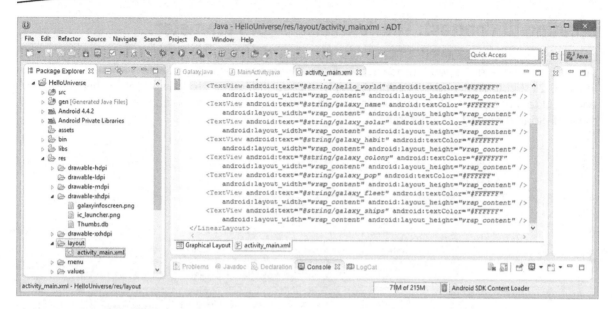

Figure 6-22. Add android:textColor="#FFFFFF" parameters to all eight <TextView> child tags in the LinearLayout

To confirm that you have solved your contrast problem, use the **Run As ➤ Android Application** menu sequence, and compile and run your Hello Universe application. What you should see should look like the middle section of Figure 6-20, and your Galaxy Information Screen's Galaxy characteristics text labels should now be readable!

Nested LinearLayout Containers: Creating a More Complex UI

To add in the <TextView> UI elements that will be updated by your Java logic (in the next section) to display the actual Galaxy object data values, we cannot simply add seven more <TextView> child tags into the existing <LinearLayout> parent tag, as that would put the values underneath the text labels, and not to the right of them.

The solution to this UI layout problem using <LinearLayout> containers is to **nest** two vertical LinearLayout child containers inside of a parent LinearLayout container configured as a horizontal layout, which will place two rows of (matching) text next to each other horizontally, kind of like a spreadsheet would. At a high-level tag overview, using pseudo markup, if you will, the basic XML structure that you will be building soon would look something like this:

```
<LinearLayout android:orientation="horizontal" android:background="@drawable/galaxyinfoscreen" >
    <LinearLayout android:orientation="vertical" android:background="transparent background" >
        <TextView>UI Labels</TextView>
    </LinearLayout>
    <LinearLayout android:orientation="vertical" android:background="transparent background" >
        <TextView>UI Data Fields</TextView>
    </LinearLayout>
</LinearLayout>
```

As you can see from my pseudo markup above, the parent <LinearLayout> is now configured to be **horizontal**, and thus will arrange everything inside of it from side-to-side instead of top-down. The parent tag still contains the digital image asset reference, as we want this image to fill the screen behind our UI design. There are now two child <LinearLayout> tags nested inside the horizontal parent <LinearLayout> both of which are **vertical**, and both of which have defined a transparency value for their background so that the parent background image will show through. If this is not done, Eclipse "throws" a warning that the parent background has been rendered useless because it is now covered up by the child layout containers. Inside of the vertical <LinearLayout> child tags are the seven or so <TextView> grandchild tags (no, they are not really called that), which are child tags of the child <LinearLayout> tags, hence the "nesting" terminology. Let's hope Dr. Phil never learns Android, or we may have to cover the psychology of Android parent-child familial relationships in a future version of this book.

Eclipse Tricks and Treats for Using the XML Editing Pane

Another Eclipse shortcut to get a **child tag helper dialog** is to use a **left-facing chevron <** character, to bring up the helper dialog, as is shown in Figure 6-23. Put your cursor at the end of the opening <LinearLayout> tag and hit the return key, which will auto-indent your code for you, and type a "<" character and wait for the pop-up to appear, with all of the child tags (widgets and layout containers) that are compatible with the parent <LinearLayout> container.

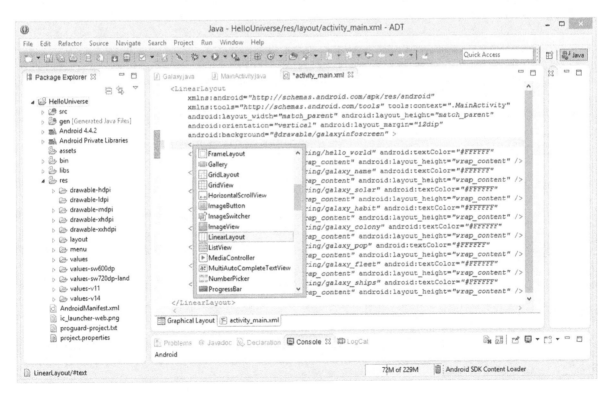

Figure 6-23. Use a left chevron < character inside the parent LinearLayout tag to invoke a child tag helper dialog

As you can see in the child tag pop-up helper (segment) shown in Figure 6-23, there are three layout containers: **FrameLayout**, which we cover in Chapter 11, **GridLayout**, which we cover in Chapter 8, and the **LinearLayout**, which we are covering in this chapter. The other 11 classes shown are UI widgets.

A slick way to calculate how many total class entries are shown in a helper dialog is to see how many times the slider-bar height divides into the total height (in this case, about 5 times, or one-fifth slider-bar height to total height ratio), and multiply that by the number of visible entries (in this case, 14), giving you an estimate of 70 or more classes that are supported inside of a <LinearLayout> parent tag.

Double-click on the LinearLayout selection shown in Figure 6-23 and insert the empty <LinearLayout> child tag into your activity_main.xml UI layout definition, so that we can start to configure these nested UI layouts.

Reconfiguring Your LinearLayout Container

The first reconfiguration that we will want to do is to move the android:layout_margin="12dip" parameter from the parent <LinearLayout> tag over to the child <LinearLayout> tag that you just added. This is to transfer the margin spacing for the <TextView> UI elements that are underneath the <LinearLayout> tag containing the text labels, which has now become a nested (child) LinearLayout.

The parent LinearLayout no longer needs any margin spacing, as it is now serving simply as a horizontal layout "organizer" of child vertical LinearLayout containers, which will now be "carrying" their own margin spacing configuration parameters. The movement of layout_margin from parent to child tag is shown in Figure 6-24.

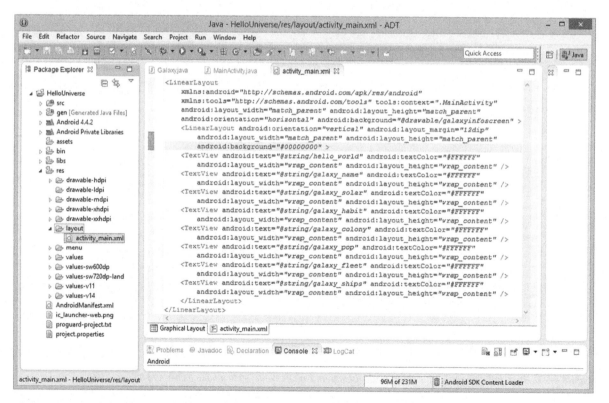

Figure 6-24. Configure a parent LinearLayout as horizontal and a child LinearLayout as vertical and transparent

Since the layout_width and layout_height parameters are required for every UI tag, copy these from the parent LinearLayout, and paste them into the child LinearLayout as well. We will get into what the exact difference is between the match_parent versus wrap_content constants after we define transparency for a child LinearLayout.

The next thing we need to do is to make your child LinearLayout container transparent, as far as its background plate is concerned, so the digital image asset that is defined in the parent LinearLayout container can show through. This is because the default (undefined) layout container background is white (Holo Light Theme) or black (Holo Dark Theme).

It is important to note that UI containers (and widgets) are stacked on top of each other from the ground (floor) up, just like you would build a skyscraper. Thus, the parent LinearLayout is on the bottom, the child LinearLayout containers are on top of that, and the grandchildren TextView widgets are on top of those.

The hexadecimal value for transparency in Android is **#00000000**, and the way that color and transparency are defined using hexadecimal values will be covered in detail in Chapter 9 covering graphic design for Android.

The android:background parameter can accept a reference to an image asset, to an animation XML definition, or to other Android drawables, such as a ShapeDrawable, for instance. The android:background parameter can also accept hexadecimal color and transparency values. To set the background to be 100% transparent (that is, not present at all), the android:background parameter would be configured using the following XML mark-up:

```
android:background="#00000000"
```

Once these parameters have been put in place in the child <LinearLayout> tag, as shown in Figure 6-24, use the **Run As ➤ Android Application** menu sequence and you will see the result shown in the middle of Figure 6-20.

Adding String Constants for Use in Your UI Design

Before we add the second nested LinearLayout container to hold the TextView UI widgets that will hold the actual Galaxy object data values, we must first create the <string> text constants for the default (pre-modified) values for the data value text UI elements. We will use "My Galaxy" for the default name and zeroes for the other default values, as shown on the right side of Figure 6-25.

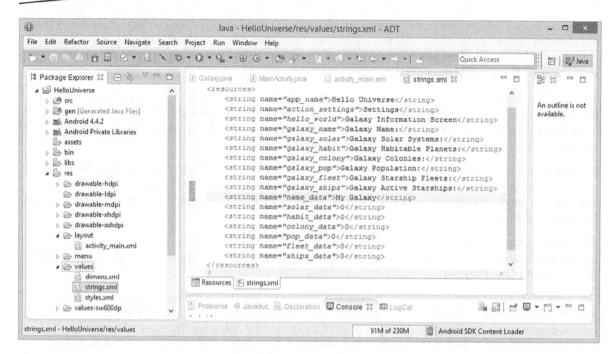

Figure 6-25. Create seven <string> objects to hold the seven data values (variables) for the Galaxy object

The easiest way to do this is to copy the galaxy_name through galaxy_ships string tag constants and paste them underneath themselves. Remove **galaxy_** from the front of the string constant name, and add **_data** to the end of the string constant name, so **galaxy_name** would become **name_data**, as shown in Figure 6-25.

Adding a Second Nested LinearLayout Container to the UI Design

Now we can create the second <LinearLayout> nested container, right after the first <LinearLayout> nested container. Since the parent <LinearLayout> container is arranging these horizontally, from left to right, the second <LinearLayout> content (nested TextViews) will appear on the right side of the UI design, as shown in Figure 6-20. Again, the easiest way to write all of this mark-up is to select the entire first nested child LinearLayout and all of its TextView children and copy and paste it underneath itself.

One of the concepts of fast program development is to copy, paste, and edit whenever possible! Delete the first hello_world TextView tag from the second nested <LinearLayout> and leave only the seven <TextView> tags that are needed to hold Galaxy object attributes (variable data values), as shown in Figure 6-26. Change the galaxy_ references to the _data references so the <string> constants you just created occupy those TextView UI elements. If you now use the **Run As ➤ Android Application** menu sequence and look at your UI design, you will see only what you saw after you added the first nested <LinearLayout> child tag, and you will not see the second nested <LinearLayout> structure at all. Why? It looks like it's time to discuss the UI layout constants!

Figure 6-26. Change child LinearLayout width and height constants to wrap_content; center hello_world TextView

The reason you can't see the second <LinearLayout> is because you have all of your <LinearLayout> structure **android:layout_width** and **android:layout_height** parameters set to use the **match_parent** constant.

What this match_parent constant tells Android to do for both the width (X axis) and height (Y axis) dimensions of the layout container is to expand the layout container to fill the UI layout container "above" it in the display hierarchy. For the first parent <LinearLayout>, this tells Android to fill the device display screen, which is what we want, and you can see by the background image filling the screen (once we removed the margins) that this is working as desired. The first nested <LinearLayout> is therefore also filling the screen, leaving no room for the second nested <LinearLayout> to display its contents, because it is also set to match_parent. The constant needs to be changed to a constant that tells it not to fill the screen, which is where the wrap_content constant comes in.

The solution to this is to change the "**match_parent**" constant in both of the nested <LinearLayout> containers to use the "**wrap_content**" constant instead. The wrap_content constant essentially does the **exact opposite** of what the match_parent constant does; instead of expanding to fill, or fit, the screen above it, it contracts instead and "shrink-wraps" the content below (contained inside of) it. As you can see in Figure 6-26, both of the nested <LinearLayout> containers use wrap_content constants in their parameter settings, and when you use the **Run As ➤ Android Application**, you get the result shown in the right-hand panel of the screenshot in Figure 6-20.

Next, let's add a couple of final android:layout_margin-related "tweaks," to fine-tune this UI design. The first thing we need to do is to space the data field TextView UI elements down next to their corresponding Galaxy attribute label TextView UI elements, using an `android:layout_marginTop="33dip"` in the second nested <LinearLayout> tag parameter list. The next thing we need to do is add an `android:layout_marginLeft="48dip"` to the first hello_world <TextView> tag in the first nested <LinearLayout> child tag to center the screen title.

Interfacing with UI Elements: The ID Parameter

There is one last bit of XML markup editing that we will need to do to the seven TextView UI elements in the second nested LinearLayout container, so they can be "wired into," or accessed by, the Java TextView objects, which we are about to create in your MainActivity.java class. In order to be able to transfer the Galaxy object variable data values into the data field TextView objects we have created in our UI design to hold and display these values, we need to create these TextView UI elements as **TextView** objects in your Java program logic.

The XML parameter you need to be able to reference a UI element (widget) or UI layout in your Java code is the **android:id** parameter, which gives an **ID** to the XML UI element definition, so that you can instantiate it and subsequently reference and utilize it in your Java code. The XML markup for this parameter is as follows:

```
android:id="@+id/name"
```

Create ID parameters for all seven of your TextViews as @+id/solar, @+id/habit, @+id/colony, @+id/pop, @+id/fleet and @+id/ships, which are going to display solar, habitable, colonies, population, fleet, and ships data respectively, as shown in Figure 6-27.

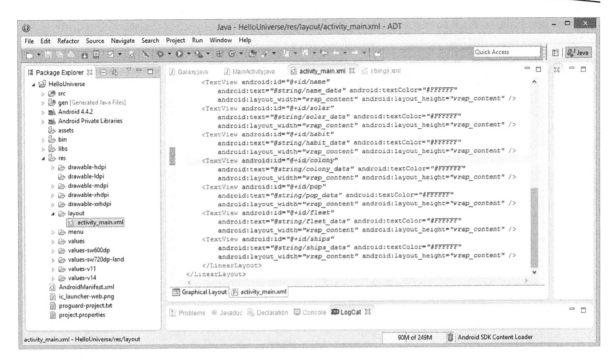

Figure 6-27. Adding the android:id parameter to the seven TextView UI elements which will hold the data values

Before I show you how to "wire up" your Galaxy object to your UI design in Java, so that your data display TextView objects display your Galaxy object characteristics, I want to first show you how to organize your Java code a little bit better, by creating your own custom methods in your MainActivity class, to organize your Java code according to task. This is primarily so that your onCreate() method does not turn into one huge Java code construct. Creating logical methods is called "**modularizing**" your Java code, and makes it much more elegant, organized, and logical, as you will see during the remainder of this chapter as you create three methods.

Creating Modular Code: createDefaultGalaxy()

Let's make our Java code more modular by putting the Galaxy class–related code into its own method, called **createDefaultGalaxy()**, so that all we have to call in our onCreate() method is a single createDefaultGalaxy() method call. We will perform the same modularization in the creation of the TextView UI objects later on, by using a method we will name **createUiTextViews()**. We will do the same thing for the transfer of the data field values from the Galaxy object to the TextView UI widget objects, via a method named **transferDataValues()**.

This modularization happens to be easy to do, which is why I decided to include it early on in this book. Since we just had the chapter covering Java, let's get some practice writing modular Java code right away, so you can build on what you learned in the previous chapter. First, create the empty method by typing the following code:

```
private void createDefaultGalaxy() { ... }
```

Then all you have to do is to cut and paste the five lines of Galaxy object code inside the curly braces, like this:

```
private void createDefaultGalaxy() {
      Galaxy milkyWay = new Galaxy("Milky Way", 511, 97);
      milkyWay.setGalaxyColonies(37579231);
      milkyWay.setGalaxyPopulation(1967387132);
      milkyWay.setGalaxyFleets(237);
      milkyWay.setGalaxyStarships(34769);
}
```

See, that was easy, as you can see in Figure 6-28. The createUiTextViews() method will be more advanced, and the transferDataValues() method will be more advanced, and you'll even learn how to "nest" Java method calls!

Figure 6-28. *Creating a private void createDefaultGalaxy() method to modularize our Galaxy object–related code*

Now we're ready to declare TextView objects for use, naming them while we're at it so we can instantiate them.

Updating the UI in Java: Using UI Objects

In order to have our Java program logic access or utilize our UI elements, we must instantiate (that is, create objects for) each UI widget or UI layout container that we wish to modify or control using Java program logic. There are two ways to do this, both of which we will take a look at in detail during the remainder of this chapter. To declare a TextView object for use and give it a name, simply call the TextView class and give it a name, using the following Java code, which looks a lot like your variable declarations, but it declares an object:

```
TextView nameData;
```

As you can see in Figure 6-29, the first time you use any class reference in your Java code that has not been specifically **"imported"** for use in your code, you will get the wavy red underline highlighting underneath it.

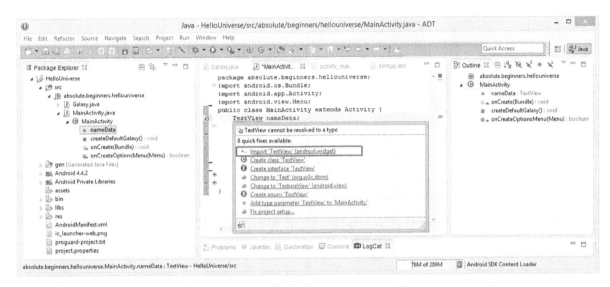

Figure 6-29. *Declaring a TextView object named nameData at the top of the MainActivity class to hold UI values*

If you place (termed "hovering" in computer speak) your mouse over the error highlight, you will get the pop-up telling you the TextView cannot be resolved, because Eclipse does not know what it is yet. The first of eight solutions to this problem happens to be the "correct" one, so click on Import 'TextView' (android.widget), which will instruct Eclipse to write this import statement for you.

As you can see in Figure 6-30, the Java import statement has been inserted (highlighted in light blue in the IDE) after the three existing import statements, and before the class declaration. As you will also notice, the error highlighting has vanished, and you are ready to copy and paste this first nameData TextView UI object declaration six more times underneath itself, which will create all seven "updateable" TextView UI widget objects, all of which are defined to "live" inside of your second nested <LinearLayout> container.

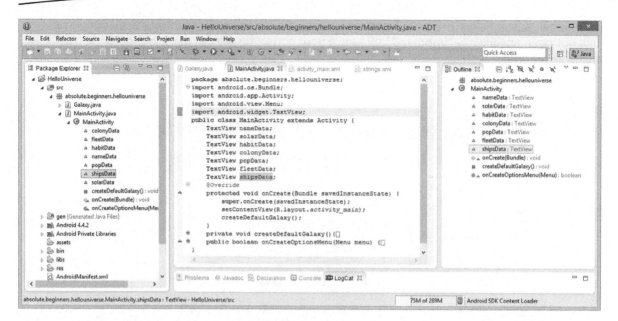

Figure 6-30. Collapse the createDefaultGalaxy() method to make room in the IDE; add seven TextView declarations

We will create all of the TextView object(s) instantiation code inside of a createUiTextViews() method so that all our onCreate() method will contain is method calls to Java routines or structures that create the Galaxy and TextView objects, and later on a call to wire them all together using a transferDataValues() Java code structure.

A UI Instantiation Method: createUiTextViews()

Now it's time to create the second method that will be called in the onCreate() method. Let's add a new-line in the onCreate() method after the createDefaultGalaxy() method call and type in a createTextViews() method call. As you can see in Figure 6-31, this is error highlighted; on mouse-over, Eclipse offers to write the code for you!

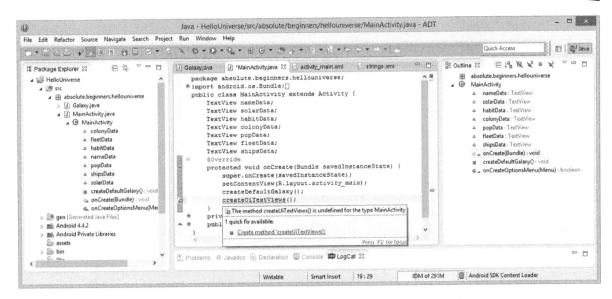

Figure 6-31. *Create a createUiTextViews() method call in onCreate() and allow Eclipse to create the method for you*

Inside of this "bootstrap" method structure that Eclipse will write for you, you will instantiate your nameData TextView object, which you declared earlier at the top of the class. This is done using the following Java code:

```
nameData = (TextView)findViewById(R.id.name);
```

If you type in the R.id part, and then hit the period key, Eclipse will display a helper pop-up containing all of the UI elements that have an ID attribute (parameter) assigned to them, as is shown in Figure 6-32.

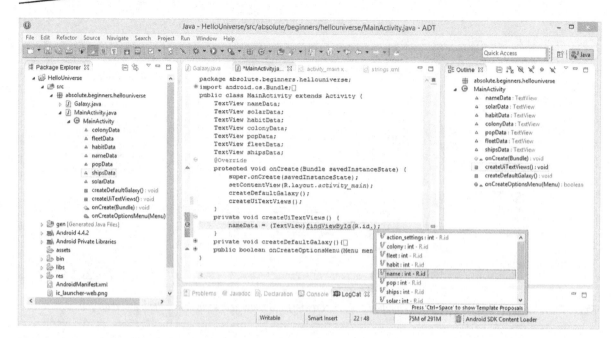

Figure 6-32. Instantiate a nameData TextView; use the findViewById() method and Eclipse helper pop-up to configure

Once this first line of code shows as being error-free, you can then copy it in its entirety and paste it, six more times, underneath itself. Make sure to change the **name** variable and TextView ID reference to be **solar**, **habit**, **colony**, **pop**, **fleet**, and **ships**, respectively, as can be seen in Figure 6-32.

Now you have the **createUiTextViews()** method coded, which instantiates all of your TextView objects and also sets them to reference their XML definitions by using the findViewById() method in conjunction with the appropriate resource area and ID value. You are now ready to create the **transferDataValues()** method, which will take the data values out of your seven variables in your milkyWay Galaxy object, and transfer those values into your seven TextView UI widgets, which you designed to display those values in your UI screen design.

Creating the transferDataValues() Method

By modularizing your Galaxy and TextView object(s) set up into logical methods, your onCreate() method has a mere two lines of code, as you can see in Figure 6-33, instead of a dozen lines of code. These method calls are logically named, so that anyone else who may need to read your code will know precisely what you are doing!

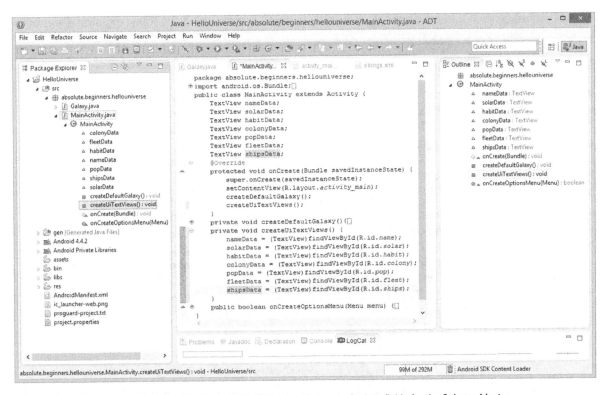

Figure 6-33. Duplicate the TextView UI objects instantiation for the other six data fields for the Galaxy object

Once you code your transferDataValues() method, which we are about to get into next, your onCreate() method will be quite compact, with only five key lines of code, and yet it will be doing quite a lot of work, thanks to the three methods that you have coded during this chapter. Your MainActivity.java class will have five important Java methods to use for your application functions instead of just the two that Eclipse created for you earlier.

Let's have Eclipse ADT write some more Java code for us, as it is always so much more fun watching someone else (or something else, in this particular case) do all of the work whenever possible!

Add a new-line under the createUiTextViews() method call in your onCreate() method, type in the name of your third method, **transferDataValues()**, and hit the **semi-colon** character to complete this Java (method call) statement, and watch the familiar wavy red error underline highlighting appear, as you had expected.

Mouse-over the red error highlighting, and bring up the Eclipse error message helper pop-up, and then select the **create method 'transferDataValues()'** option so that a method bootstrap code structure will be written for you.

Inside of the method, we are going to call a .setText() method off of your nameData TextView object to, as you might suspect from the logical method name, set the text value of this nameData TextView object. Since we want to use the galaxyName variable's data value to set the text with, we will reference this right inside of this .setText() method call, by using the following single line of (somewhat elegant, in my opinion) Java logic:

```
nameData.setText(milkyWay.galaxyname);
```

What this does is to pass over the milkyWay Galaxy object galaxyName variable as a parameter, referenced by **milkyWay.galaxyName** (ObjectName.VariableName), to the nameData TextView object that is utilizing the .setText() method call to retrieve and set this text (String) data value. This data value then replaces your default "Milky Way" placeholder text value, which you previously had set in the XML UI definition via an android:text parameter, so that you would have a text value to use to visually refine your XML UI design, prior to your Java coding.

As you can see in Figure 6-34, the milkyWay Galaxy object has error highlighting underneath it, which you discover upon mouse-over has an error reason that says "milkyWay cannot be resolved to a variable" (that is, Eclipse cannot "see" your milkyWay Galaxy object). The reason for this is that the Galaxy object is currently constructed inside of the createDefaultGalaxy() method, highlighted in light blue in Figure 6-34, so the object is considered to be "local" to that method. The same problem would have existed if you had left this code inside of your onCreate() method as well. The solution is to do what you did with the TextView object declarations, and cut the Galaxy constructor line of code outside of the createDefaultGalaxy() method and paste it at the top of your class above (or below) the TextView object declarations.

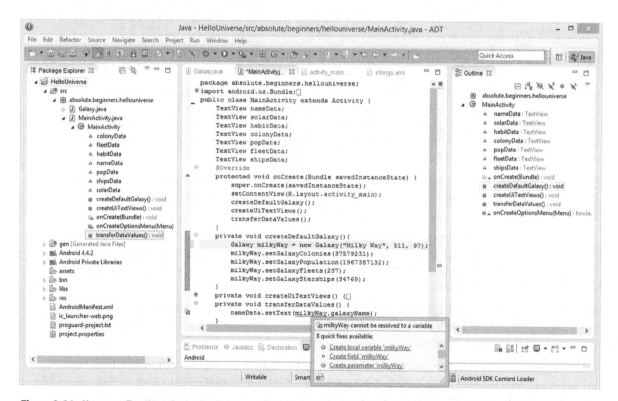

Figure 6-34. Use a .setText() method call off the nameData TextView object configuring it with galaxyName data

Doing this will allow every method in your class to now be able to "see" and reference your Galaxy object. The other code that sets your Galaxy object's attributes using dot notation to call your Galaxy class methods can stay inside of the createDefaultGalaxy() method.

As you can see in Figure 6-35, once you place this Galaxy constructor line of code at the top of your class, the error highlighting disappears, because the milkyWay Galaxy object is now visible to every method in the class.

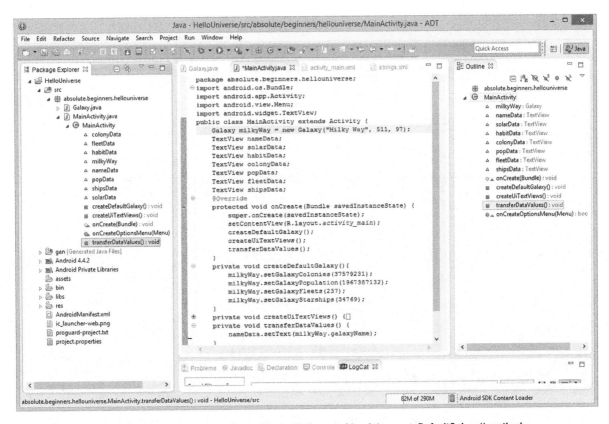

Figure 6-35. *Moving the Galaxy object declaration and instantiation outside of the createDefaultGalaxy() method*

If you remember earlier, I said I would show you two different ways to instantiate an object in Java, and now you have done this using one line of code (Galaxy object) in one location, or two lines of code (TextView objects) in two different locations (inside of, as well as outside of, a method). To clarify the difference, you could also split the Galaxy object instantiation using just the Galaxy milkyWay; part, called the object "declaration," at the top of the class and insert the milkyWay = Galaxy("Milky Way", 511, 97); part in createDefaultGalaxy().

You can try this second (split) coding as an "exercise" for this chapter, if you like; it is a cool way to make your object declaration(s) visible to your entire class, while actually instantiating the object inside of whichever method you wish to do so. On the other hand, the long-form (object declaration and instantiation all using one single line of code) uses less code, which is said to be more **"compact"** code, in programming terminology.

Testing and Debugging your Application

Now let's take a moment to use the **Run As ➤ Android Application** menu sequence, and we will see if your UI design now displays the "Milky Way" text data value, assigned using Java code, rather than the "My Galaxy" text data value assigned using XML markup using the <string> constant.

As you can see in Figure 6-36, the code thus far in your transferDataValues() method is working as expected, and the UI screen now displays the Galaxy object galaxyName variable's data value in the nameData TextView next to the "Galaxy Name:" labeling TextView.

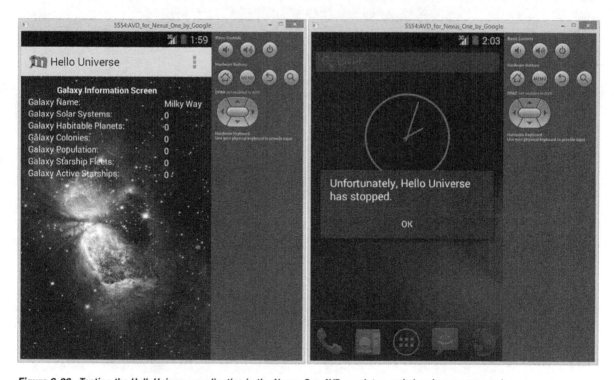

Figure 6-36. Testing the HelloUniverse application in the Nexus One AVD emulator, and showing an app crash

The next six data TextView UI widgets need to display numeric values (integer, double, long, and so forth) and so we can (and will) try to use the same code, and hope that Java will "cast" the numeric values into text values for us.

The concept of "casting" in Java is a process where the Java programming environment (the compiler) will auto-convert (cast) a data value from one format into another where it is logical and it is able to do so. So we will try passing a numeric data value type into the .setText() method call in the hope that the "type casting" (any actors out there?) will be done for us automatically. If not, then you are about to get to utilize your **LogCat** tool!

Copy and paste the nameData.setText(milkyWay.galaxyName); line of code underneath itself and change the nameData and galaxyName references to the solarData TextView reference and galaxySolarSystems Galaxy object variable references, respectively.

Next use the **Run As ➤ Android Application** menu sequence and see if you can get the application to run. As you can see on the right side of Figure 6-36, the Hello Universe application crashes (stops running, as per the error message in the emulator).

The probable cause of this crash is most likely passing a numeric value to the .setText() method call, which is expecting a String (text) value, and most likely Java is not "casting" the numeric value into a text value for you, and so the application crashes. When your application crashes, you can use the LogCat to investigate what happened. Let's do that next.

Using the LogCat

Let's use this as an opportunity to see how to use the LogCat error log catalog utility to see exactly what is crashing your application. Pull up the separator between the main editing pane and the error tabs at the bottom of the IDE, to give some room to the LogCat tab to display its results, as is shown in Figure 6-37.

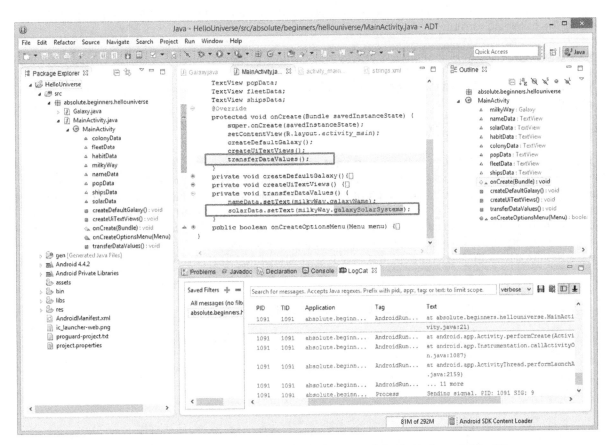

Figure 6-37. Using the LogCat utility tab to diagnose where the fatal app error is located in the code (Line 21)

I look for error messages that feature line numbers that I know are reasonable for the amount of code that I have written, such as the line of code annotated as **java:21**, shown highlighted in light blue in Figure 6-37.

Since I haven't written thousands of lines of code, I know the other error messages referenced are not in my code, although those errors are certainly **caused** by my code. What I want to see is what line of my code is causing the error, so I look at **Line:21**, which is shown highlighted in the screen shot, and references the latest line of code you just wrote, which attempts to pass an integer data value to a method expecting a text data value.

What we need to do to correct this error is add to our Java programming statement's structure in such a way as to convert the numeric value into a text value "on its way in" to the method call. In pseudo-code, this would be:

```
TextViewObject.setTextMethodCall( ConvertNumberToTextMethodCall(GalaxyObjectNumericDataValue) );
```

There is indeed a method in Java, in the String class that we have already used to create String objects, called the **.valueOf()** method, which will turn a numeric value into a String text value, by using the following format:

```
String stringVariableName = String.valueOf(numeric variable here);
```

In the construct we are using, we can nest this String.valueOf() method call inside of our existing Java structure:

```
solarData.setText( String.valueOf(milkyWay.galaxySolarSystems) );
```

Java is pretty cool in the way that you can **nest** and **chain** (using dot notation) constructs together to get dense code constructs; that is, to accomplish a lot of what I call programming "moves" using a single line of code. We will take a look at Java code chain constructs later on in the book as we get into more and more complex topics and code structures. This may be an Absolute Beginners book, but Android topics in it are inherently advanced. My apologies if you thought Android programming was ever going to be some sort of cakewalk! Once you have the solarData line of code working, replicate it for the other five numeric data values, as shown in Figure 6-38.

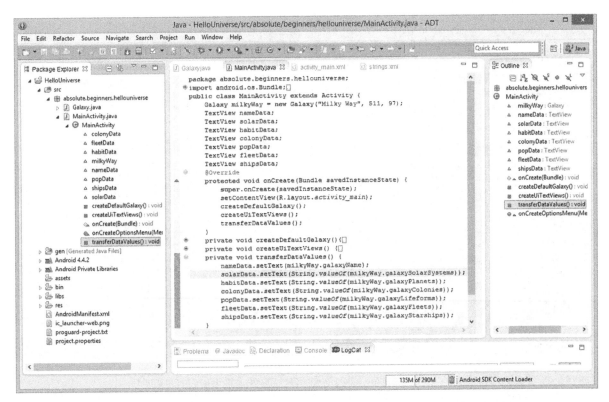

Figure 6-38. Using the String class's .valueOf() method inside of the .setText() method, to convert integer values

Now again use the **Run As ➤ Android Application** menu sequence, and see if your code will run, and is doing what you wanted it to. As you can see in Figure 6-39, everything is working, and the application runs and does not crash, but there seems to be an extra data variable listed on the right side of the galaxy information screen.

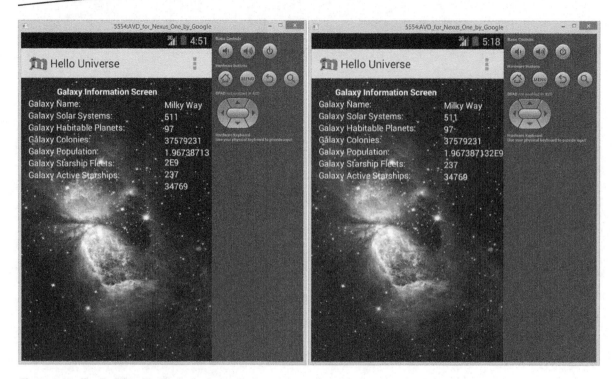

Figure 6-39. The TextView UI objects displaying the Galaxy object data values; fine-tuning the margins

Upon closer examination, it looks like Android is using "exponential" numeric representation for the population numeric data value. Instead of 1,967,387,132, or even 1967387132, Android is writing 1.967387132E9, part of which is wrapping to the next line.

To fix this, we will need to move the second nested (right side data values) LinearLayout container to the left, so that this long value will not wrap.

Since there is no margin parameter defined inside your second nested LinearLayout, it must be the android:layout_marginLeft parameter DIP value in the first (title) <TextView> that is pushing the second nested LinearLayout to the right, so let's reduce this by 20 DIP from a value of 48dip to a value of 28dip.

As you can see in Figure 6-40, the android:layout_marginLeft parameter value has been reduced to 28dip, fixing the problem with the Galaxy Information Screen <TextView> in the first nested <LinearLayout> container, pushing the second nested <LinearLayout> container too far over to the right, causing the wrapping.

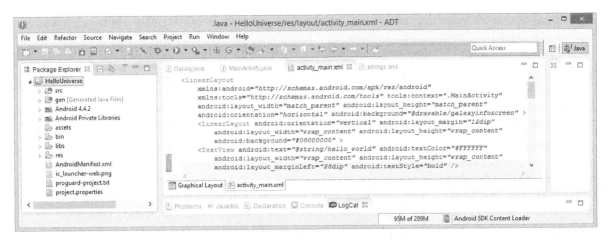

Figure 6-40. Reducing the hello_world screen title TextView from 48dip to 28dip, to pull second LinearLayout left

If you wanted to put this TextView above the nested <LinearLayouts>, you would need an even more complicated nested <LinearLayout> structure, such as the following (pseudo) UI layout container structure:

```
<LinearLayout android:orientation="vertical" android:background="@drawable/galaxyinfoscreen" >
      <TextView>UI Screen Title</TextView>
      <LinearLayout android:orientation="horizontal" android:background=" transparent background " >
            <LinearLayout android:orientation="vertical" android:background="transparent
            background" >
                  <TextView>UI Labels</TextView>
            </LinearLayout>
            <LinearLayout android:orientation="vertical" android:background="transparent
            background" >
                  <TextView>UI Data Fields</TextView>
            </LinearLayout>
      </LinearLayout>
</LinearLayout>
```

This is why we are going to learn about the <RelativeLayout> layout container in the next chapter, as it is always desirable to use a single UI layout container rather than using four layout containers and nesting as we've done here to achieve a fairly simple UI design result.

Summary

In this chapter, you learned all about several of the most important Android superclasses that are used to create Android applications and get them running on the device display screen. These include the **Activity** class, the **View** class, and the **ViewGroup** class, and the subclasses of these classes, which are actually used to create your Android applications, such as the **LinearLayout** class. You already know you have to write all the Activity subclasses yourself, but as far as the View and ViewGroup subclasses are concerned, Android has generously written all of the subclasses for you; all you have to do is to "include" them in your application code by using an import statement, and of course you have to implement their features correctly.

You learned about the relationship between the Activity class, the View class, and the ViewGroup class, and how these are used together to get your application UI design and content onto the device display screen. Then you used the Galaxy class you created in the previous chapter to create a Galaxy object to use in this chapter, where we create a Galaxy Information Screen UI design.

Then you learned about the LinearLayout class and how to create a UI design using this simple UI layout container designed for designing row-oriented or column-oriented UI layouts. You learned about the **Project ➤ Clean** work process in case you ever start up your application to a project filled with errors that you did not create, and how to go about restarting the IDE and/or using the Clean command to make sure ADT sees the Java SDK, or JDK, and the java.lang.Object class.

You learned how to reference digital image assets in your UI layout containers, how to use transparency, and how to nest LinearLayouts to create more complex UI layout designs. You also learned how to modularize your Java code by writing your own custom methods, as well as how to call those methods from inside other methods. You learned a couple different ways to declare and instantiate objects so that code inside all of your class methods could see them.

In Chapter 7, you will start to learn about how Android handles **Events**, uses **Intent** objects, and **Menu** objects by using the Android Menu subclasses, and all about how to make UI designs and Menu systems interactive, by using **Event Handlers** and **Intent objects**.

Making Apps Interactive: Intents, Event Handling, and Menus

User interface design is built upon the foundation of the Activity superclass as well as the View and ViewGroup superclasses, which you learned all about in the previous chapter. However, without any interactivity in your UI design, the usefulness of what you can do with your Android application is somewhat limited!

For this reason, I'm going to cover several fairly advanced concepts fairly early on in this book, such as how the **Menu** and **MenuItem** classes work in Android, as well as how **Intent** objects can be utilized to switch over to your Activity subclasses. Using Intent objects, you can switch between functional screens in your applications, each of which is defined using an Activity subclass that references a UI layout container (ViewGroup) subclass.

Besides covering Android's menu-related classes, we will also cover the broader concepts of **Intents** and **Intent Filters**, as they relate to Android. You first encountered Intent Filters in Chapter 4 (refer to Figure 4-17 near the bottom of the screen shot) when we looked over your bootstrap AndroidManifest.xml file in detail.

In this chapter, we'll implement an **"Edit Galaxy Info"** menu item in the HelloUniverse app, and make the menu item call an **EditGalaxy** class, using an Intent object. We'll learn more about the **RelativeLayout** layout class, developing a new UI design. This will allow users to update Galaxy objects via **Button** and **EditText** widgets.

Adding **interactivity** to your user interface elements, or widgets, will require that you learn what **Event Handlers** are, and how to implement **Event Listeners**, which are used to make the UI elements (widgets) interactive. Once the RelativeLayout UI design is completed and referenced using the onCreate() and setContentView() methods, we can instantiate your Button and EditText objects, and then attach **onClick()** event handler Java structures to them, so that your user can use them interactively to update the statistics for the Galaxy object. Since we are covering Menu, MenuItem, Intent, RelativeLayout, Button, EditText, and onClick() event-handling routines all in a single chapter, we had better get started right away. Hang on tight, you're in for an exciting journey through user interface land!

The Menu Class and Interface: Android Menus

An Android Menu interface was specifically created by the Android OS developers for creating **options menu** and **context menu** structures in Android. Android's Menu superclass has only two subclasses: a **ContextMenu** class and a **SubMenu** class. These subclasses are used to provide localized (context-sensitive) menu structures and sub-menu structures for both options menus and context menus.

The options menu is more of a "global" menu structure, as it is accessed using a hardware **MENU** key on your Android device, or, if the Android device does not feature a MENU key, using the ActionBar "**overflow**" menu icon, which is those **three vertical dots** at the right-side of the ActionBar, at the top of your Android device.

The Menu interface is used for creating Menu object structures, which hold your menu design, much like a ViewGroup holds your UI screen design. Just like a ViewGroup contains View sub-objects, the Menu object contains MenuItem objects, along with their configuration parameters, which you will define using XML mark-up.

As you have already seen, these parameters can include the MenuItem label or "title," as well as the order, ID, and various display characteristics, such as an icon, or whether the MenuItem is active (not dimmed or inactive) or is even visible, or whether it is checkable (can show a check mark next to it when it has been selected).

The three different types of Menu objects, options menus, context menus, and sub menus all have different characteristics. For instance, sub menus cannot have nested sub menus and cannot have MenuItem icons, and context menus also do not support MenuItem icons or shortcuts. In case you don't know what "shortcuts" are regarding menus, they are letter (android:alphabeticShortcut) or number (android:numericShortcut) definitions which the user can use as a shortcut for accessing that MenuItem more directly or more rapidly.

Options menus, which are the primary type of Menu object used in Android applications, and the kind we are going to focus on in this chapter, have their own set of rules, such as icon menus displayed within the ActionBar do not support MenuItem check marks, and will only show the MenuItem **condensed title**, if provided using the **android:titleCondensed** parameter.

You can access the expanded options menu, which will only become available if six (or more) MenuItems are defined, via the 'More' item in the icon menu or ActionBar overflow menu. This expanded options menu will not show MenuItem icons, and MenuItem check marks are not recommended for use either.

The Menu object defined by the Menu class and Menu interface will contain **MenuItem** objects defined by the MenuItem class, and as you will soon see when we create a working Menu and MenuItem in the Hello Universe application, both of these classes will have to be imported into your MainActivity class. There is another menu-related class, the **MenuInflater** class, which is utilized to turn or "**inflate**" your XML menu definition file into a Menu object in much the same way that your UI design is inflated.

The class hierarchy for the MenuInflater class is structured as follows, and this class was created "from scratch" from the Java Object master class specifically to inflate Menu objects using XML definition files stored in the /res/menu folder:

```
java.lang.Object
  > android.view.MenuInflater
```

It is interesting to note that you do not need to use an **import android.view.MenuInflater;** statement at the top of your MainActivity.java class because there is a method which is part of the **android.app.Activity** package called **getMenuInflater()** which provides access to the MenuInflater class's **.inflate()** method by using something called Java method "**chaining**" using the **getMenuInflater().inflate()** Java code construct. As you will see later on in the code which we will be writing in this chapter, the dot or period character **chains** the two Java methods together.

Designing Menus in XML Using <menu> and <item>

Your Menu object design is implemented using two primary XML definition files, specifically the **strings.xml** file, located in the **/res/values** folder, which contains the MenuItem object's label text (String) constant, and the **main.xml** file, located in the **/res/menu** folder, which holds the Menu object definition.

The first thing that you will need to do is to define your MenuItem object's "title," which I prefer to call its "label," in the strings.xml file. Right-click on this file in the /res/values folder, and use the **Open** command to open it for editing in Eclipse. Create a **<string>** child tag inside of the parent **<resources>** tag, with the name **edit_galaxy,** and give it a text (String object) data value of "**Edit Galaxy Info**" as is shown in Figure 7-1.

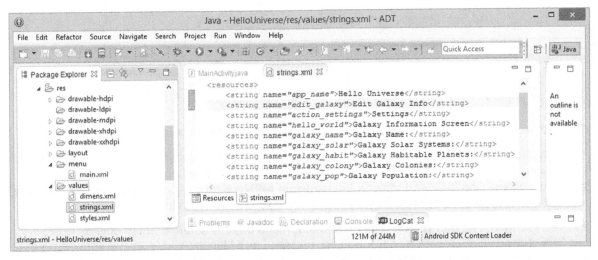

Figure 7-1. Add a <string> constant named edit_galaxy with a text data value of Edit Galaxy Info for use in an options menu

Now you are ready to edit your Menu object, which is defined inside of your main.xml XML menu definition file, which is located in the /res/menu project folder. Right-click on this /res/menu/main.xml file, and select the **Open** option to open this file in your Eclipse central editing pane.

Add a second MenuItem object by adding another <item> child tag inside of the parent <menu> tag which defines the Menu object. Just like MenuItem objects are "children" of the Menu object, the same hierarchy is reflected in your XML file definition, where your <item> tags are child tags of the parent <menu> tag.

You can further define and configure MenuItem objects using parameters within each <item> child tag, such as the android:id parameter to define the ID that will be evaluated (later) in your Java code, the android:title parameter, which will reference the edit_galaxy <string> constant which you just created for your MenuItem label, and other parameters defining MenuItem order and whether or not it shows up in the Android ActionBar.

As you can see in Figure 7-2, I placed the **edit_galaxy** MenuItem object above the action_settings MenuItem object, as Android menu design convention dictates that **Help** and **Settings** menu items should be last on the menu structure. This is similar to all software menu design guidelines, where help and settings menus are listed last, at the bottom of the menu.

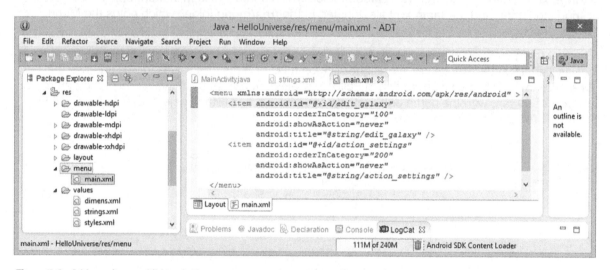

Figure 7-2. Add an <item> child tag in the <menu> parent tag which references the edit_galaxy <string> constant

To see your new Menu object design, use the **Run As ➤ Android Application** menu sequence and launch the Nexus One AVD, and click on the hardware **MENU** button, or on the **ActionBar overflow menu** (three vertical dots) to see that your menu now has two entries in it!

It is interesting to note that you can design and test Menu objects and MenuItem objects using this XML–based work process all day long and the Menu and MenuItem objects will show up in the AVD, which is a designer's dream! It will take some Java coding to make these Menu and MenuItem objects actually interactive (that is, do something when they are clicked on), but it is interesting that XML makes the application design possible using ZERO Java coding, which is the intent of extracting some of the application design functionality over to be done using XML markup.

When I used the **Run As ➤ Android Application** menu sequence, the Nexus One AVD launched, and the default Android (installed) OS application icons appeared, but the Hello Universe icon was nowhere to be seen, and the application start-up screen (MainActivity.class or MainActivity.java) did not show up, as it should have during a normal code-compile-AVD-test development cycle.

For this reason, I am going to add a section into this chapter here, much as I did in the previous chapter when I opened up Eclipse and got a gaggle of nasty red error highlights that were not even my fault! I will do this to show you what I do when the Eclipse AVD emulator "stalls," and does not complete its "lifecycle" and perform its necessary AVD emulation duties. Bad Emulator! Next, I am going to show you how I get around this emulator breakdown scenario, and how I get the AVD emulator to restart "from scratch," so that it will load the application, and then auto-launch the application in the way that it is supposed to launch the application for testing in the first place. After that, we will continue on exploring the **MenuInflater** class, as if this AVD glitch had never even occurred.

AVD Is Not Starting App: Using the Eclipse AVD Manager

To solve the "hung" AVD problem, I used Eclipse's **Run ➤ Android Virtual Device Manager** menu sequence, and opened up the **Android Virtual Device Manager** dialog shown in Figure 7-3. I selected a **Nexus One** AVD by clicking on it (it turns blue, as shown), and then clicked on the **Start** button. A **Launch Options** dialog pops open, with two selected (checked) options; **Launch from snapshot** and **Save to snapshot**. I then **de-selected**, or un-checked, these two options, as shown on the right-hand side of Figure 7-3, and I clicked on the **Launch** button.

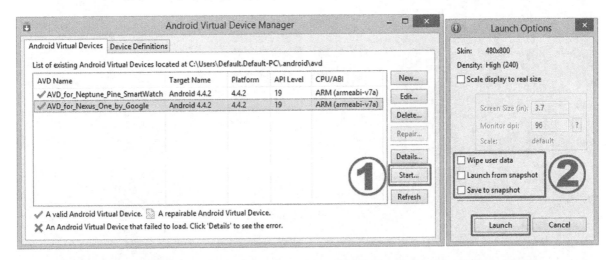

Figure 7-3. Use the AVD Manager's Start button, then deselect the snapshot options, before using the Launch button

This work process will launch the AVD "from scratch," and you will see the silver ANDROID logo "loader animation" reloading the AVD into your system memory anew (afresh?), which should "reset" or "restore" the connection between the AVD and the auto-loading of your project data into the emulator for auto-starting and testing.

My logic here in performing this work process is that somehow this "snapshot" of the app which was being saved (between subsequent launches of the AVD) had become corrupt, or otherwise was causing some sort of bug or error that was preventing the AVD emulator from continuing the part of its launch which accesses the app project (and icon) from Eclipse.

Thus, to allow me to do an "end-run" around this particular problem, I utilize the AVD Manager's Start button, in order to allow me to access this **Launch Options** dialog, so that I can disable these snapshot features. The Launch Options dialog allows me to be able to force a "fresh" AVD launch into system memory of whichever AVD emulator I wish to test with.

If the Android OS (or AVD) developers fix this particular AVD issue, which you at some point in time will most likely encounter in your Android app development work process, then this work process will no longer become necessary to fix this quagmire. However, I thought it wise to advise you regarding this work process, and my implementation logic behind it, in case you encounter this problem, and it brings you to a grinding halt in the application development coding-testing cycle! If you can't get your application to launch in the emulator, you can't test it as you develop it; thus, this is an important topic.

Once the animated Android logo stops loading the AVD into memory, you will see the screen shown on the left side of Figure 7-4. Click and drag the lock icon outward, until it circumscribes a circle, and then release it. After you do this your application (and your new menu structure) will auto-launch again, as is shown on the right side of Figure 7-4.

Figure 7-4. Drag to unlock the Nexus One; click the ActionBar options menu (three vertical dots) to open the menu

Next let's take a look at the **onCreateOptionsMenu()** method and see how it **inflates** your Menu object using the Android **MenuInflater** class in conjunction with your **/res/menu/main.xml** XML menu definition file.

Inflating the Menu: onCreateOptionsMenu()

Let's take a look at the Java code collapsing and expansion (plus + and minus –) icons on the left side of the IDE central editing pane. Click on the **plus +** sign, next to the **import** statements, to expand that section. This will turn the **+** next to the import statements section into a minus sign, as shown in Figure 7-5 at the top. This will allow you can see all of the import statements, including the highlighted **import android.view.Menu** statement, which Eclipse just provided (coded) for you.

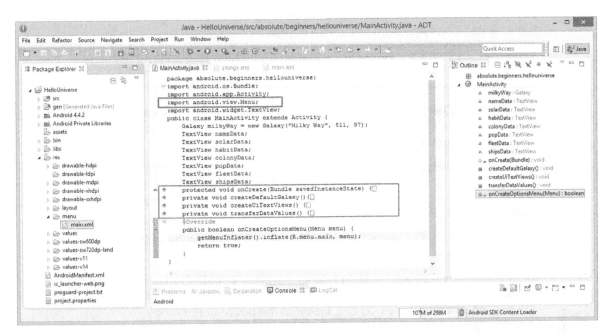

Figure 7-5. The getMenuInflater() method chaining to a .inflate() method referencing the main.xml menu

Use the **minus –** sign next to each of your MainActivity class methods, except for the onCreateOptionsMenu() method, for which you will click the plus + sign to open it up for observation, so we can go over what it does. The result of this is shown in Figure 7-5 and you will have four method names with plus + signs next to them! This is a handy way to "put away" your Java method code blocks when you are not working on them, so that you can focus on the code that you are currently writing, or in this case, the code in Figure 7-5 we are analyzing for learning purposes.

The **onCreateOptionsMenu(Menu menu)** method uses a Menu object named **menu**, which it passes over to the **.inflate()** method in the MenuInflater class along with the **R.menu.main** reference to the XML menu definition. The .inflate() method call is referenced inside the MenuInflater class using the Activity class **getMenuInflater()** method call, using a Java **dot-chaining** construct, like this: **getMenuInflater().inflate(R.menu.main, menu)**. Once this .inflate() method has been called successfully, the onCreateOptionsMenu() method will then **return** a **true** value, signifying the completion of the Menu object inflation process.

Now that your Menu object is inflated using the bootstrap method that Eclipse created for you back in Chapter 3, and which we just delved into the inner workings of how it stitches Android's Menu and MenuInflater classes together, we are going to finish implementing the Menu object and its MenuItem sub-objects via the following objectives:

- Learn how to declare multiple **TextView objects** in a single Java declaration by using commas.

- Create a **public boolean onOptionsItemSelected()** method to evaluate the **MenuItem objects**.

- Learn how to create a Java **switch** programming structure, using **case** statements to evaluate each MenuItem object.

- Instantiate an **Intent object** named **editIntent** using the Java **new** keyword, and then utilize that Intent object in order to call the **EditGalaxy.class**, passing over the current application **Context object**, by using the Java **this** keyword.

- Create the **EditGalaxy.java** Activity subclass, by using the Eclipse **New Java Class** dialog, and its related **Superclass Selection** sub-dialog to define an **android.app.Activity** superclass.

- Call a **.startActivity()** method from the Activity class and the android.app.Activity package, passing over the **editIntent** Intent object, which contains the current application Context and the binary representation of the **EditGalaxy.class** Activity subclass which you wish to start.

- Create a New XML UI Layout Definition, by using the Eclipse **New XML File** menu sequence.

- Create a **RelativeLayout** UI design, which contains both **Button** and **EditText** UI widgets, using an XML UI definition file, and then inflate that UI design using the **setContentView()** method call, inside of the onCreate() method, in the new **EditGalaxy.java** Activity subclass.

The MenuItem Class: onOptionsItemSelected()

In order to evaluate and process your MenuItem objects inside of your Menu object structure, you will need to create a **public boolean onOptionsItemSelected()** method, which will be the next step in your options menu implementation work process.

First, in order to make some additional room in the Eclipse central editing pane, let's turn your seven TextView object declaration and naming lines of code into just two lines of code, giving us back five lines of code. To do this, I will show you a **consolidation** trick by which you can declare the TextView object type and place more than one name after that declaration. This is done by using the comma character as a **delimiter** between the name values, as is shown in Figure 7-6. You can code seven TextView declarations and names using the following Java code:

```
TextView nameData, solarData, habitData, colonyData;
TextView popData, fleetData, shipsData;
```

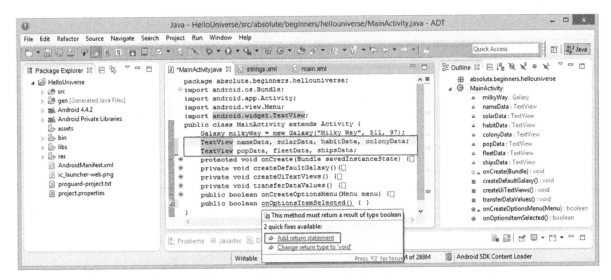

Figure 7-6. Add an onOptionsItemSelected() method and consolidate TextView object declarations with commas

You could also have done this using one single line of Java programming logic, by using the following format:

```
TextView nameData, solarData, habitData, colonyData, popData, fleetData, shipsData;
```

Next, collapse your five methods, as shown in Figure 7-6, and add the onOptionsItemSelected() method as follows:

```
public boolean onOptionsItemSelected() { ... }
```

Once you do this, you will get red error highlighting under this new method name, advising you that you need a **return statement**. Click on the **Add return statement** option, which will add the **return false;** Java statement for you. Later on, we will change this to return a **true** value; but for now, since the method does not do anything, false, which means nothing has been processed, would be the correct return value for the currently empty method.

Since the onOptionsItemSelected() method evaluates MenuItem objects, you will need to declare a **MenuItem** and name it **item** inside of the method parameter list area, because you will want to pass (or take) in MenuItem objects for evaluation, and inside of the method you are going to reference these using the name item. This is done using the following method declaration construct, as is shown in Figure 7-7:

```
public boolean onOptionsItemSelected( MenuItem item )  {  return false;  }
```

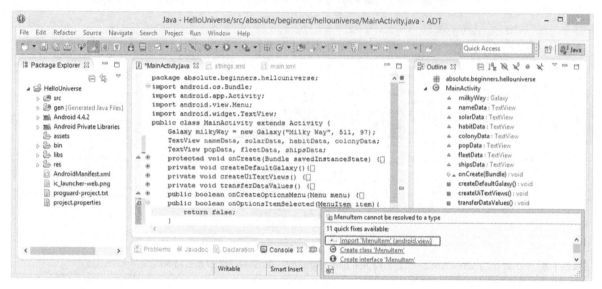

Figure 7-7. Add a MenuItem object named item to the onOptionsItemSelected() method, then import the MenuItem class

Mouse-over the wavy red error highlighting under the MenuItem class reference and select the **Import 'MenuItem' (android.view)** option to have Eclipse write the Java import statement for you.

Now that the method infrastructure is in place, we need to write Java code inside of the method that looks at the MenuItem object (named item) which is passed into the method, and puts this MenuItem object through some sort of evaluation structure, to ascertain what to do if the MenuItem conforms to certain characteristics—in this case, its **ID**.

The Java Switch Statement: Choosing a MenuItem

The Java programming structure to use in this scenario is called a "**switch**" structure, which will allow the Java code to switch between different code scenarios, based on a "case"-by-case evaluation structure, which you put into place. We are going to take a closer look at how to put together this type of Java code evaluation structure in this section of the chapter.

The first part of the evaluation structure starts with the switch keyword and something to evaluate on a case-by-case basis—in this case, that would be the MenuItem object named item. The switch statement, which is shown in Figure 7-8, would be coded as follows:

```
switch( item.getItemId() ) { case by case statements go in here }
```

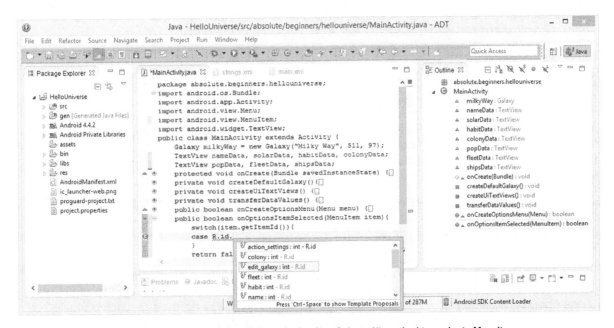

Figure 7-8. Add a switch statement to the inside of the onOptionsItemSelected() method to evaluate MenuItem

As you can see, we are again "nesting" Java constructs, with the MenuItem object named **item** calling the **.getItemId()** method by using dot notation inside of the switch() evaluation value parameter area. What this is evaluating is fairly obvious, as it is looking at each MenuItem object's ID value which comes into the method.

Inside of curly braces will go **case** statements, each of which will have an ID value and then a colon, as follows:

```
case R.id.edit_galaxy:  Java programming statements to process, these are exited by using a Java
break; statement
```

After all of the case statements, there is a **return** statement, which we will be changing to **true** once we add case evaluation statements. As you can see in Figure 7-8, once you type in the case keyword and the **R.id.** precursor, the Eclipse pop-up helper dialog will give you all of the ID values you have defined in your XML definition files.

Double-click on the **edit_galaxy : int** option shown highlighted in blue in Figure 7-8 to insert this particular ID for your edit_galaxy MenuItem object, for evaluation in this first case statement. Next, we will add Java statements inside of the case statement for the edit_galaxy MenuItem which will create, name, and load an **Intent** object, which will be used to launch an EditGalaxy.java Activity subclass which will contain our RelativeLayout UI container and an interactive UI design allowing users to edit and change the Galaxy object data field values.

Using Intent Objects: The Android Intent Class

An **Intent** object is used within the Android OS as a **messaging construct** that you can dispatch to request some sort of "action" from one of the other components within your Android application, or even within someone else's Android application, which is external to your own Android application. There are three primary uses for Intent objects in Android; launching Activity subclasses, starting Service subclasses, and sending messages around an Android application, or even to external Android applications by using Broadcast Receiver classes and methods.

Here's a basic diagram which shows how your Activity uses Intent objects:

```
Activity > Intent object containing start Activity Intent > Activity (launched) or:
Activity > Intent object containing start Service Intent > Service (launched)
```

As you know, the Activity subclasses each represent a single user interface screen within an app's functionality. You will start each new instance of an Activity subclass by passing an Intent object over to the **.startActivity()** method, which we will be doing in the next step in the menu implementation work process.

The Intent object passed into the .startActivity() method will contain data which prescribes which of the app's Activity subclass you want to start, and carries the Context object describing the current context for your application. We will go over the concept of Context within this chapter as well, as it is used often in Android programming.

You can also use an Intent object to start a Service subclass; we'll be covering Services in Chapter 13. A Service is an Android component which can perform operations in the background. These operations usually do not need a user interface, and can be performed "asynchronously," or out of sync, with the user's normal "flow of use" of your application and its purpose and objectives. An example of this would be playing a background music track.

You can also start a Service subclass using an Intent object in order to perform a one-time operation such as the downloading of a file, again by passing an Intent object over to a .startService() method call. This Intent should describe the Service subclass to start, as well as any necessary data that is needed for the Service to process.

You can also use an Intent object to deliver a broadcast across the Android OS, to anything running under it. A broadcast in Android is a term for any message that an app running on the same Android device as your app can receive. The Android operating system will deliver broadcasts for system events, such as when the system boots up, or when the device is plugged in and starts charging. You can deliver a broadcast message to other apps by passing Intent objects via a **.sendBroadcast()**, a **.sendOrderedBroadcast()**, or a **.sendStickyBroadcast()** method call.

There are two types of Intent objects you can create and utilize within the Android OS: **explicit** Intent objects and **implicit** Intent objects. Explicit Intent objects will specifically reference the Android application component to start, by using a precise application component name and component type. When you create an explicit Intent object to start an Activity subclass or Service subclass, the Android operating system starts the component specified in that Intent object.

In the next section, you will start your **EditGalaxy.class** using this fully qualified compiled class name. A fully qualified compiled class name would be referenced in your code as EditGalaxy.class, which is different than the fully qualified code class name, which would be referenced as

EditGalaxy.java. The difference is that your code is calling, or in the case of using an explicit Intent object, launching, a .class **compiled version** of your Activity subclass from within your compiled package (.APK or Android PacKage) infrastructure.

You will typically want to use an explicit Intent object to start a component within your own application. This is because you inherently know the class name of your Activity subclass or Service subclass which you want to launch, and so you can utilize, or "hard code," that component name in your Java code. For example, you would start your new Activity subclass in response to a MenuItem selection, as we are about to do in the next section, or you could also start a Service subclass, in order to start processing in the background, as we are going to do in Chapter 13 when we cover Services.

Implicit Intent objects do not name their target application component, but instead declare a general "**action**" to perform. This implicit Intent approach allows any application component, even from another Android app outside of your own Android app, to "handle" the Intent. The reason that Android also has Intent Filters and the IntentFilter class is for the processing, action determination, and handling of these implicit Intent objects.

For example, if you wanted to show your app's user a location on a map, you could use an implicit Intent object to ask, or "request," that another mapping-capable Android application show your application user that specific location on the map that your application is referencing. Implicit Intents allow Android apps to work together!

When you create an implicit Intent object, the Android operating system will find the appropriate application component (Activity, Service, Broadcast Receiver) to start up by comparing the contents of your implicit Intent object to the <intent-filter> definitions declared in the AndroidManifest XML file for other apps on the device.

If the implicit Intent object matches up with one of those IntentFilter definitions, the Android operating system starts that component, and delivers your implicit Intent object to it. If multiple IntentFilter definitions are found to be compatible on the same Android device, the Android operating system will display a pop-up dialog, so the user can pick which app to use. It is important to note that every user installs different apps, and thus different users' Android devices will invariably exhibit different combinations of installed Android applications, which will result in different popup dialog selection choices.

An **IntentFilter** object is an Intent processing definition construct which is defined using your Android application Manifest XML file. This <intent-filter> construct defines the structure for the type of implicit Intent objects that your Android application's components would like to be able to receive, and to be able to process. This is quite powerful (and quite complex as well), as it allows developers to create Android applications which do things (perform tasks) for other Android apps, which opens up an entirely new genre of Android applications that Android developers can create.

As an example, by declaring an IntentFilter object for an Activity subclass, as you have already seen done by Eclipse for your MainActivity class in your AndroidManifest.xml, you make it possible for other applications, in this case it would be the Android OS application launching screen, to directly start your MainActivity.class Activity subclass using a specific Intent object containing the **MAIN action** and the **LAUNCHER category**.

If you do not declare any <intent-filter> XML definitions constructing an IntentFilter object for any of your Activity subclasses, then these Activity subclasses will be "invisible" to outside Android applications, and will only be able to be started using an explicit Intent object. A great example of this is what we are doing in this chapter with your EditGalaxy Activity subclass, since we only want your MainActivity class Menu object to be able to start this private component of your Hello Universe application.

Finally, remember one important "rule" regarding the use of Intent objects in your Android programming! To ensure that your Android application is completely secure, you will always want to use an explicit Intent object when starting a Service object (Service subclass). This also means that you would not want to declare <intent-filter> XML constructs that create IntentFilter objects for your application's Service subclasses, since these are only utilized with implicit Intent object processing, and are not needed when using explicit Intent objects.

The reason for this "rule" is because by using an implicit Intent object to start a background processing Service class, you risk creating a **security hazard** within the Android OS on your end user's device. This is because the developer cannot ascertain what Service subclass will respond to an implicit Intent object, and the end user also cannot see which Service is starting on their Android device. This opens up the ability for a **destructive** Service to be created, which could be triggered by an implicit Intent object used to start a Service subclass. So don't create Services using implicit Intent objects!

Instantiate an Intent Object: An App's Context

Let's instantiate, name, and configure an explicit Intent object named editIntent, which will start the EditGalaxy Activity subclass, which we are going to create as the next step in this work process. This is done by declaring the Intent object for use, then providing a name, and then "loading" the newly named Intent object using the equal sign, while at the same time (in the same Java statement) creating an Intent using the Java **new** keyword, and configuring this new Intent with the class name which you will be starting.

All of this can be accomplished by using the following single line of Java programming logic:

```
Intent editIntent = new Intent( this, EditGalaxy.class );
```

So the **Intent** declares the object type, the **editIntent** gives it a name, the equals = sign signifies that we are about to instantiate it, the Java **new** keyword creates an instance of the Intent object, and finally the parameter list passes over the **Context** object for our MainActivity Activity subclass, using the Java **this** keyword, as well as the EditGalaxy.class Activity subclass that we want to start or launch using the **explicit** Intent object created with this Java statement. As you can see in Figure 7-9, we have some wavy red error underline highlighting in the code, which you will probably guess is related to creating either import statements or code structures which do not yet exist, but which are referenced within the Java code structure you are currently coding (you have seen both of these error scenarios before).

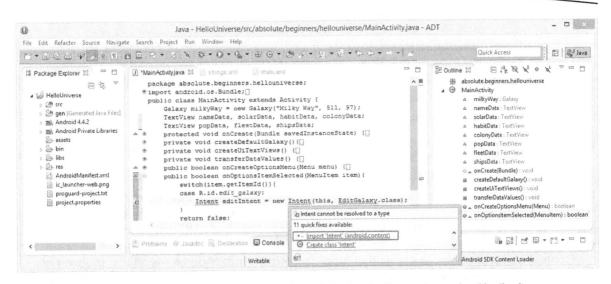

Figure 7-9. Declaring an Intent object named editIntent and instantiating it using the new keyword and loading it

Let's take care of the import statement for the Intent class first. Mouse-over the Intent error highlighting, either one will provide the same pop-up helper dialog, and select the **Import 'Intent' (android.content)** option. Next, we will go over what the Java **this** keyword and a **Context** object do for your Android application, and then we will continue our work process in the section after that, and allow Eclipse to create our **EditGalaxy.java** class.

Explaining Context: The Android Context Class

The concept of Context in Java programming is simple in its definition, and yet complex in its implementation. It is something that you will need to know what it is doing, and why it is needed, to be able to accomplish certain things in Android. It is not something you need to manipulate directly, at least not until you become an advanced Android developer.

The **Context** object, and the Java **this** keyword, which essentially passes over a Context object, is exactly what it sounds like it is! Android Context objects contain detailed "**contextual**" information regarding the application component which is calling over to the other application component to do something. If someone asks you to do something for them, you usually ask them what the context for the task is, so that you know what, and why, you are doing the task!

The reason for giving the receiving application component this "Context" (clever Java keyword pun intended) is that Context objects will allow a called application component to "see" or ascertain what the calling application component is doing, so that it can do the job (task) that it is being asked to do more efficiently, effectively and with greater precision.

When this "Context" object, which is filled or "populated" with information regarding the calling application component, is combined with the (inherent) "knowledge" of what the called application component is doing, it results in "Context," which, as we all know from real life, can be defined as the clear, overall view of the entire process which we are currently involved with. A Context object is similar to a Bundle object, in that it contains a lot of related information, all collected, or bundled together, into one complex object and sub-object hierarchy.

> **Note**   You have already used a **Bundle** object to save the current "state bundle" for your Activity subclass, with the Bundle object named **savedInstanceState** in your onCreate() method call. The Bundle class allows you to put together "bundles" or collections of variables and data, so it is not complex enough to merit its very own section in the book. That said, if you are really into bundling things, you can take a detailed look at the Android Bundle class on the Android developer web site, located at the following URL:
>
> http://developer.android.com/reference/android/os/Bundle.html

The Context object thus contains information about what your application component is doing, how it is set-up, what resources it uses, and all manner of information regarding that Android application component, essentially. Whereas the Android Manifest XML definition is used to provide some of this "global" information to the Android OS when it goes to launch your application, the Context object provides all of this technical-, systems-, and resources-level info for each of your application components, "local" information if you will, using the Context object while your application is actually running.

As I mentioned previously, you only need to know how to use an application component's Context (and the **this** keyword) properly to be successful in the majority of your Android application programming, design, and development endeavors, so I am not going to spend that much time delving into the **public abstract Context** class in this book.

If you'd like to learn more about this Android Context class, you can visit the following Android developer site URL:

http://developer.android.com/reference/android/content/Context.html

Now we can continue on in our work process for creating a working menu which launches a second EditGalaxy Activity subclass, and create a RelativeLayout UI design for that Activity, and make it functional using Events!

Creating Your Second Activity: The EditGalaxy Class

Now that you know what the Java **this** keyword is, which is used here to pass over the **Context** object for your MainActivity.class to the EditGalaxy.class, we can go ahead and mouse-over the wavy red underline highlight under the reference to the EditGalaxy.class (which does not yet exist), and select the **Create class 'EditGalaxy'** option, which will give Eclipse the go ahead that it needs to create this new Java class for you, as shown in Figure 7-10.

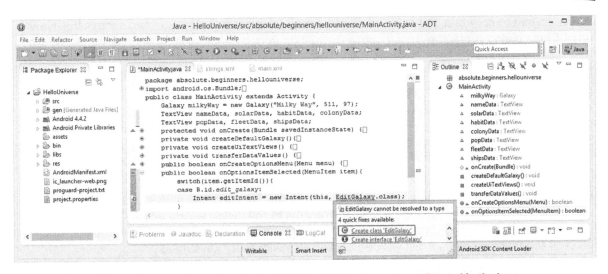

Figure 7-10. Using the Eclipse helper dialog Create class 'EditGalaxy' option to create your Intent object's class

This will bring up the **New Java Class** dialog, which is shown in Figure 7-11. This dialog is initially configured to create a Java subclass, by using the **java.lang.Object** superclass. In this case, since you allowed Eclipse to invoke this dialog from your code, the name (EditGalaxy) is already provided for you in the dialog, as is the project folder and package name, which Eclipse can also ascertain from the project you are working on.

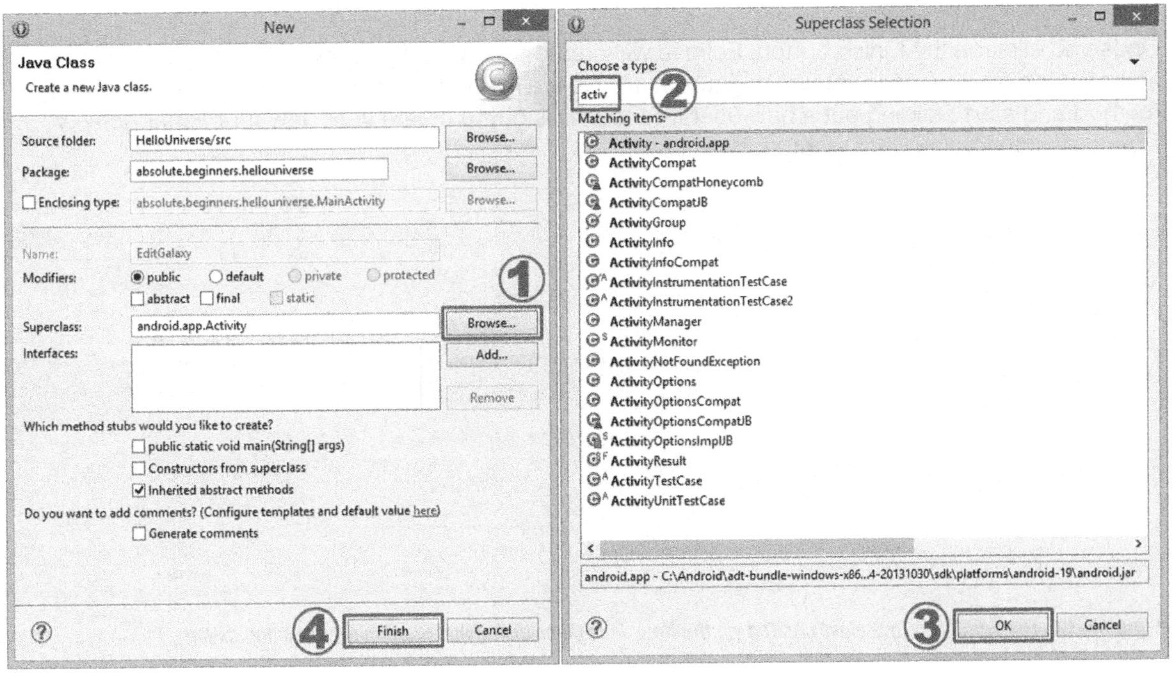

Figure 7-11. Browse for Activity superclass, select, click the OK button and the Finish button to create the new class

It is important to note that you can also create a new Java class; that is, you can access this **New Java Class** dialog yourself without Eclipse doing it for you, by right-clicking on your project's **/src** folder, and selecting the **New ➤ Class** menu sequence, just like you did in Chapter 5, shown in Figures 5-4 and 5-5.

Since you were creating your Galaxy class in Chapter 5, you accepted the "default" **java.lang. Object** superclass for the New Java Class dialog. However, since we are now creating a new functional screen and user interface for our app, this time we want the Android class that we're creating to be an Android **Activity** subclass, so you will need to click the **Browse** button next to the **Superclass** data field, which will open the **Superclass Selection** dialog, which is shown on the right-hand side of Figure 7-11.

In the **Choose a type** field, type in **"activ"** which will bring up all of the Activity-related classes in Android. Notice that as you type, the selection area of the dialog will be refined in real-time in response to every keystroke which you add. If you type the activ sequence of characters in slowly, you will see that the selection list will decrease in size with every keystroke!

Find the **Activity - android.app** package option; it should now be at the top of the dialog, and is the only option which specifies the package that it is in (because it is so commonly utilized). Next, select it, and click the OK button, or you can double-click on it, which will insert it as your new superclass selection.

Once you click the **OK** button, the Superclass Selection dialog will vanish, and you will be back inside of your **New Java Class** dialog, where you can now click the **Finish** button, since your class name was already defined in your Intent object constructor method call, and Eclipse filled out your **Source folder** and **Package** fields based upon the current project and package which you are working on (and in).

Once you click on the Finish button, Eclipse will create the **EditGalaxy.java** class bootstrap Java source code for you, as is shown in Figure 7-12. Now all you have to do is to add your onCreate() method and start building out a new user interface design, to create your new functional Activity screen design for your first menu option.

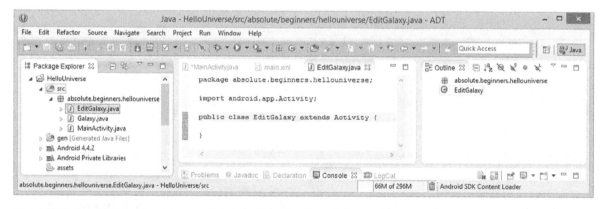

Figure 7-12. The EditGalaxy.java class created via the New Java Class dialog and Superclass Selection dialog

Before we start working on building out your EditGalaxy.java Activity subclass's Java code, let's finish up with coding the MenuItem **switch** and **case** statements we have been building first, so that we finish up with what we are learning about in this part of the chapter: how to create a working options menu inside of the MainActivity Activity subclass. The next step is adding a method call to the .startActivity() method, passing over the Intent we just created.

Starting an Activity: Using the .startActivity() Method

As you can see in Figure 7-13, now that the **EditGalaxy.java** Activity subclass exists, the error highlighting has vanished, and you are ready to call the **.startActivity()** method from your MainActivity subclass. This is done "off of," or using, your Activity subclass's Context object, which is named (using a Java this keyword "shortcut") **this**. Within the method you pass over the **editIntent** (explicit) Intent object which you created and configured in the previous line of Java code. This Intent passing construct is done using the following line of Java code:

```
this.startActivity(editIntent);
```

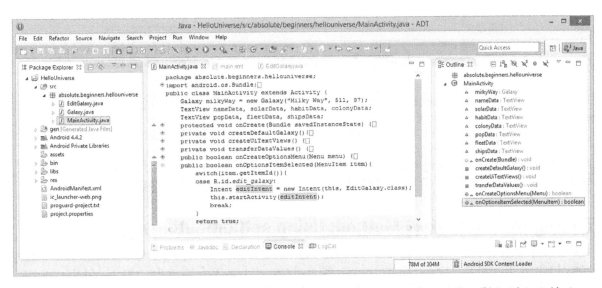

Figure 7-13. Calling the .startActivity() method off of the current Context object, and passing over the editIntent Intent object

This will call the android.app.Activity package's .startActivity() method, which is, as you can see, part of the Android Activity class, off of the current Context (this) object, and passes over as a parameter the editIntent Intent object. This will start your new Activity subclass (EditGalaxy.java, which will become EditGalaxy.class).

Figure 7-14 shows the completed onOptionsItemSelected() method structure, with the new edit_galaxy case statement and the action_settings case statement that was created by the Eclipse New Android Application Project series of dialogs. The default statement is triggered if none of the case statements are called (utilized) and passes (returns) control of the MenuItem Object back up to the superclass using the super keyword and the method name and item Object using the statement return super.onOptionsItemSelected(item); otherwise a return true; statement is used if any of the case statements were evaluated and completed.

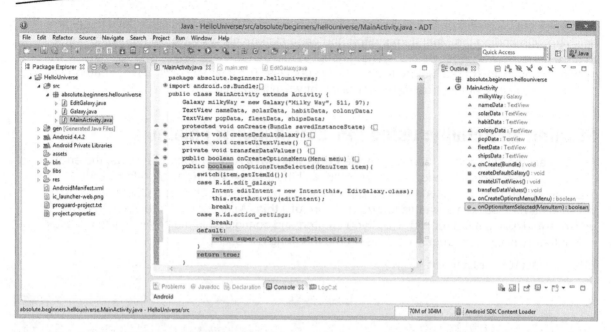

Figure 7-14. Complete onOptionsItemSelected() method structure showing (boolean) return statements selected in Eclipse

The next step in the work process is to create the "internals" of the EditGalaxy.java class, which when compiled becomes the EditGalaxy.class referenced inside of the Intent object. The EditGalaxy class needs to include the onCreate() method, a setContentView() method call referencing a RelativeLayout XML UI definition, and later on, we will add in some event handling structures, to allow the users to interface with the UI. This will allow the application's user to update the Galaxy object characteristics (its data fields, or variables) by using a series of EditText widgets.

Coding the onCreate() Method: Using setContentView()

The easiest way to add in the four lines of code that need to be in every Activity subclass is to simply copy them from your MainActivity.java class, as is shown in Figure 7-15 in the top half of the screen shot, and then change the reference to activity_main.xml to be one for **activity_edit.xml**, which will "throw" an error, initially.

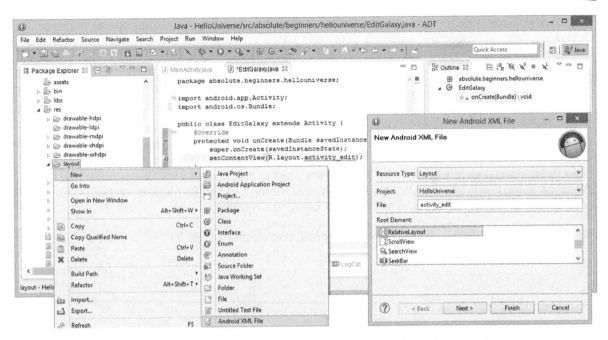

Figure 7-15. Copy onCreate() method from MainActivity, change UI XML to activity_edit, New ➤ Android XML File

It would be nice to be able to mouse-over this error and have Eclipse create the new XML file for you, just like it did on the Java side of things, but unfortunately, this option has not been added to the error pop-up yet, so we will need to create an XML UI Layout definition file for ourselves. You can also see the work process for this in Figure 7-15, which involves a right-click on the **/res/layout** folder and the selection of the **New ➤ Android XML File** menu sequence, which will bring up the **New Android XML File** dialog, seen on the right-hand side of Figure 7-15.

Since you right-clicked on the **/res/layout** folder, the **Layout** XML resource type is already set for you, as is the project name, so all you have to do is to name the file **activity_edit**, and select a **RelativeLayout** container type in the main (central) area of the dialog. After you configure everything, click the **Finish** button, and the file will be created for you, and will also be opened up for you inside of the Eclipse central editing pane.

Creating an EditGalaxy UI: Using a RelativeLayout

Since we learned about the LinearLayout class in the previous chapter, and since the **RelativeLayout** class is the next most commonly used layout container class in Android application UI design, we're going to use this class to design our Edit Galaxy Info screen in this section of the chapter. I want to cover more unique and advanced UI layout container classes in the next chapter on UI layout (container) design, so I am going to cover these two layout container classes in these first two chapters that include UI design topics in them. UI design in Android simply cannot be covered using one chapter; in fact, Apress has an entire book, called *Pro Android UI*, by Wallace Jackson (Apress, 2014) covering this topic alone! Thus, I will be covering some of the UI-related topics from this *Pro Android UI* book title during Chapters 6 through 12, including the different layout classes and many of the popular widget classes, resolution density assets, the popular Android **Drawable** classes, how to use alternate UI layout folders, styles, themes, UI graphics, UI animation, UI audio, and so on.

Using Editable Text Fields: The EditText Widget

To be able to enter a text value in a user interface design, you will need to use an **<EditText>** UI widget. As you know, the work process to find this widget is to add a new line under the opening <RelativeLayout> tag and use the left-facing chevron < character to bring up the UI widget helper dialog which is shown in Figure 7-16. Find and then select and double-click to insert the **EditText** (class) child tag inside of your **<RelativeLayout>** parent tag. Add an **ID** naming the EditText object **edit_colony** and a layout_margin value of **8DIP** using this markup:

```
<EditText  android:id="@+id/edit_colony"  android:layout_margin="8dip" />
```

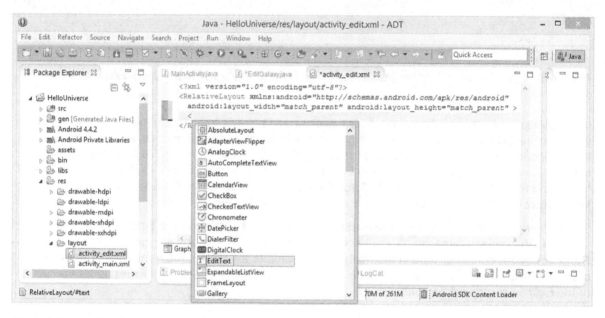

Figure 7-16. *Use the left-facing chevron to bring up a child tag pop-up helper dialog and find, select, and double-click EditText*

After we add the **<Button>** UI widget next, we'll add the other parameters which we'll need in this UI element.

We are going to add the Button UI element to this UI design so that when your user enters their new value into the EditText field, they can click an **OK** button when they are done making their entry, to tell your Java program logic that it is OK to now take that value and to update the corresponding Galaxy object data field (value) with that new numeric data value.

Using Buttons in UI Designs: The Button Widget

Add a new line underneath your <EditText> child tag, and use the left chevron **<** character to again bring up the UI widget helper dialog. Find the **Button** widget class, as is shown in Figure 7-17, and select, and double-click on, the Button widget in order to insert it into your RelativeLayout UI definition XML mark-up.

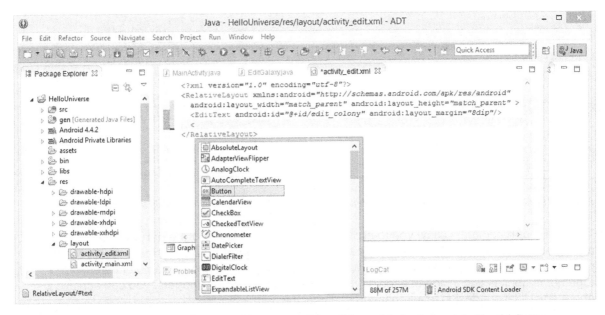

Figure 7-17. Use the left chevron to bring up a child tag pop-up helper dialog and find, select, and double-click Button

Add an android:id parameter named **submit_colony** so that the Java program logic can reference the Button UI element, using the android:id="@+id/submit_colony" parameter format, and then you will be ready to add in your RelativeLayout positioning parameters, which will position the Button UI element relative to the position of the EditText UI element. This "relative positioning" capability is what sets the RelativeLayout class and UI layout container type apart from all of the other Android UI layout container classes. Let's cover this concept in the next section and take a closer look at some of the most often used relative positioning parameters, using this UI design, which happens to be very well-suited for RelativeLayout positioning, as you will soon see.

Aligning Widgets Using RelativeLayout Parameters

After you add your android:id parameter in your <Button> child tag, type in the **android:layout_** characters and a pop-up helper dialog containing all of the parameters which are compatible with the <RelativeLayout> parent container type will appear, as can be seen in Figure 7-18. The first four, **above**, **below**, **toRightOf**, and **toLeftOf**, are used to specify relative layout **positioning**, and the next five listed in this dialog, **alignBaseline**, **alignLeft**, **alignTop**, **alignRight**, and **alignBottom**, are used to specify relative layout **alignment**.

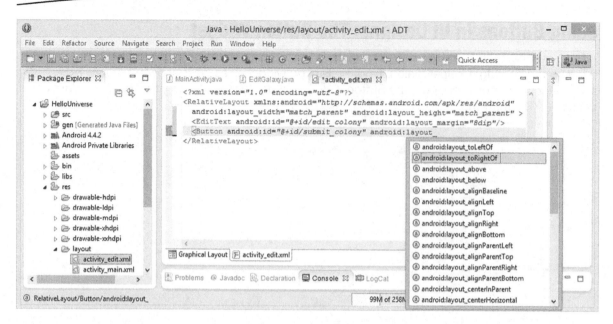

Figure 7-18. Add the RelativeLayout parameter android:layout_toRightOf inside the <Button> child tag UI widget

The next four parameters allow you to align your UI widgets relative to the **parent** UI layout container, and the ones listed after those will allow you to **center** your UI widgets, relative to their parent UI layout container. As you might well imagine, when all of these parameters are utilized together in conjunction inside of each of your component UI design widgets, you can achieve just about any UI layout design result that you can imagine.

What is really powerful about RelativeLayout is that when your user changes their Android hardware device's **orientation** from **portrait** (up and down, or vertical) to **landscape** (side to side, or horizontal), your relative layout design can "morph" to conform to the new display screen shape! Let's start learning about some of these relative layout parameters!

Since we want our <Button> UI widget to be located to the right of our <EditText> UI widget, the first UI layout parameter that we will want to implement inside of the <Button> UI element is the **android:layout_toRightOf** parameter. To tell the parameter what other UI element we want to lay it out relative to, we use an ID parameter to give it that reference point. So, to position the Button UI widget that you named submit_colony to the right of the EditText UI widget named edit_colony, you would use the following XML tag and parameter configuration:

```
<Button android:id="@+id/submit_colony" android:layout_toRightOf="@+id/edit_colony"/>
```

This will make sure that the <Button> named submit_colony is positioned to the right of the <EditText> named edit_colony. However, as you will soon see, it will not necessarily **align** these two UI elements attractively, nor will it position your UI elements in the Y axis (above or below) dimension, only within the X axis (side to side) dimension. This is why a number of RelativeLayout positioning and alignment parameters must be utilized in conjunction with one another in order to achieve a fine-tuned and professional UI layout design result.

Fortunately, these RelativeLayout UI alignment and positioning parameters all evaluate quite well in the Eclipse Graphical Layout Editor (GLE) tab, located at the bottom of the central editing pane, and so we will use this to save time previewing the UI design as we built it. Using a **Run As ➤ Android Application** menu sequence and launching the Nexus One AVD emulator every time you want to preview a UI design parameter will take about ten times longer (or more than ten times longer if you have a slow system) than simply clicking back and forth between the XML editing tab and the GLE tab!

Using the Eclipse Graphical Layout Editor (GLE)

As you can see in Figure 7-19, where I show the XML editing tab and the GLE tab output in the same screen shot, I have copied the required layout_width and layout_height parameters into the <EditText> and <Button> tags and set them to use a **wrap_content** system constant, and yet I still have the warning regarding a **hint** parameter, which we'll add in soon.

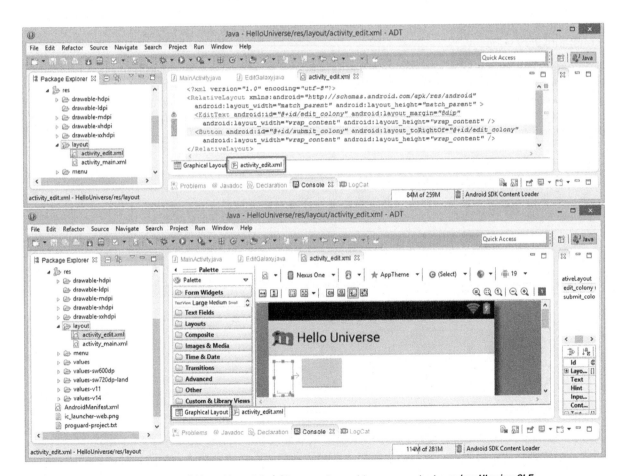

Figure 7-19. Add required layout_width and layout_height parameters set to wrap_content, preview UI using GLE

If you mouse-over the wavy yellow warning highlighting, the warning message informs you that Android wants you to provide a "hint" to your users using the **android:hint** parameter inside of your <EditText> UI widget, which we will learn about in the next section of this chapter.

As you can see in the bottom part of Figure 7-19, you can click on the **Graphical Layout** Editor tab and see the EditText UI widget, shown selected in light blue, and the **android:layout_toRightOf** parameter, shown using a green arrow pointing to the right, as well as the Button UI widget, shown highlighted using a light yellow color.

Giving an EditText Field a Hint for Your Users

The EditText UI widget class has a unique attribute or parameter called a "**hint**" which allows you to suggest to your user what needs to be placed into this data entry field, rather than just having a blank field next to the OK Button. This happens to be very handy for the UI we are designing here as this parameter will allow us to advise the user regarding what type of data we want them to enter into each data field. For the first EditView, the hint would be "Enter Number of Colonies:" The **android:hint** parameter references a <string> constant, so we will be creating hint <string> constants very soon.

Add a new line after your android:layout_margin parameter and type in **android:h** to bring up the helper dialog containing all of the parameters that start with an "h" and select and double-click to insert the hint parameter, as shown in Figure 7-20. Once you do this, the warning highlighting will disappear, and you can specify the hint <string> constant named **hint_colony** (which we will create next) by using the following XML parameter mark-up:

```
android:hint="@string/hint_colony"
```

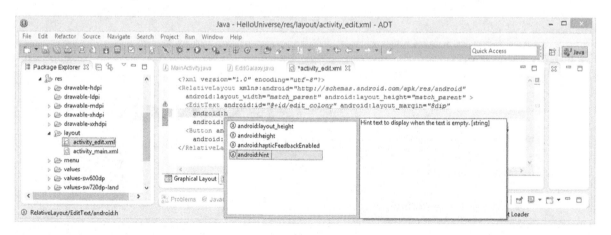

Figure 7-20. Add suggested android:hint parameter to suggest <EditText> field contents and to remove warning

Right-click on the **strings.xml** file in your **/res/values** folder, and add five <string> child tags in the <resources> parent tag, one for your **OK** Buttons, named **ok_button**, and four for the EditText UI widget hint text, named **hint_colony**, **hint_pop**, **hint_fleet**, and **hint_ships**, with the logical hint text values, as is shown in Figure 7-21.

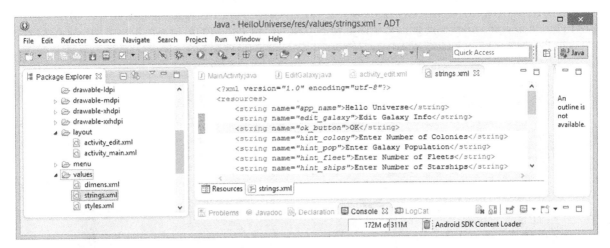

Figure 7-21. Create string constants in the strings.xml file for ok_button, hint_colony, hint_pop, hint_fleet, and hint_ships

Now your <EditText> child tag's android:hint parameter will appear error-free and you can add an **android:text** parameter to the <Button> child tag, using the following XML parameter mark-up, as is shown in Figure 7-22:

```
android:text="@string/ok_button"
```

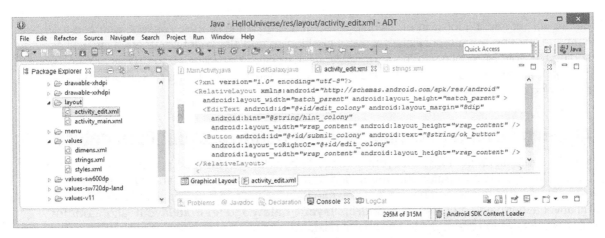

Figure 7-22. Reference hint_colony and ok_button string constants via android:hint and android:text parameters

If you toggle over into Graphical Layout mode (view), shown in Figure 7-23, you will see a drastic change in your UI layout design, which has just become an order of magnitude more professional in its appearance than it was before you added the hint and Button text label string constant value references. This great-looking result was achieved by using only one RelativeLayout toRightOf reference, and if we only had one EditText and Button UI element in the design, this would be a relatively (no pun intended) simple UI design. However, we have another half-dozen UI elements to incorporate into this UI design, not to mention some cool background image work that we will need to do to make this UI design match up with the "visual wow factor" within our MainActivity UI screen design.

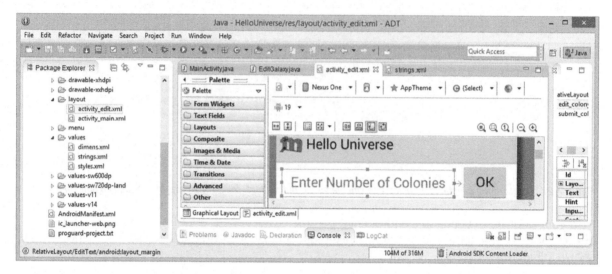

Figure 7-23. *Previewing the configured <EditText> and <Button> widgets using a Graphical Layout Editor (GLE)*

Before we get into the fun part of "skinning" the UI design using graphics assets, we need to continue learning some more RelativeLayout positioning and alignment parameters, as well as adding the EditGalaxy class to the AndroidManifest.xml file. You will need to do this at some point, so that your app will not crash when you decide to preview it inside of the Nexus One AVD emulator, by clicking on your "Edit Galaxy Info" MenuItem option.

Aligning Several UI Elements Using RelativeLayout Parameters

Now let's ratchet up the RelativeLayout complexity by adding in EditText and Button UI widgets for the Galaxy object **Population**, **Fleets**, and **Starships** characteristics, and align all of these UI elements relative to one another, so that you can gain valuable experience with some of the other RelativeLayout parameters, such as **android:layout_below** and **android:layout_alignLeft**, for instance, which you are about to implement next.

To duplicate the first <EditText> and <Button> UI construct, copy and paste the XML markup for these UI structures again underneath themselves, as is shown in Figure 7-24. Change the word "**colony**" to "**pop**" and add a new line in the second <EditText> child tag after the android:hint parameter.

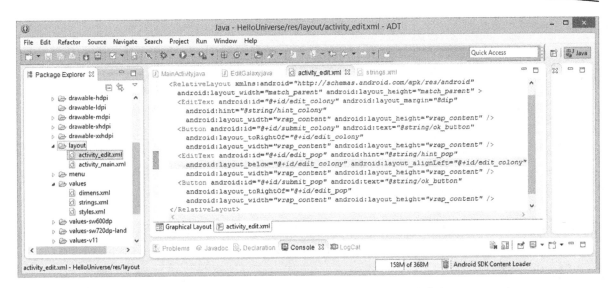

Figure 7-24. Adding a Galaxy Population <EditText> and <Button> widget, and using RelativeLayout parameters

Add an **android:layout_below** and **android:layout_alignLeft** parameter, and have each of them reference the **edit_colony** <EditText> UI element using **@+id/edit_colony**. This is done using the following XML markup:

```
android:layout_below="@+id/edit_colony"   android:layout_alignLeft="@+id/edit_colony"
```

The first parameter will apply RelativeLayout **positioning** to the second <EditText> UI element, positioning it **below** the first <EditText> UI element, using the **android:layout_below** parameter. The second parameter will apply RelativeLayout **alignment** to the second <EditText> UI element, aligning it using the **left** side of each of the <EditText> UI elements, using the **android:layout_alignLeft** parameter.

Let's click the Graphical Layout tab and preview what these parameters do for our UI design. As you can see in Figure 7-25, the EditText UI elements line up perfectly, but the second Button UI element is not **toRightOf** the EditText UI element as you specified. Or is it? In fact, the second Button UI element is to the right of EditText, according to the Y axis dimension; however, it is aligned with the top of the screen next to the other Button! This is the default alignment, unless otherwise specified, so we will have to add some RelativeLayout alignment parameters to the second <Button> UI element to correct this.

Figure 7-25. Preview the layout_below and layout_alignLeft parameters for the <EditText> widget using the GLE

We will use the same two parameters in the second <Button> UI element that we used in the second <EditText> UI element, since we wish to gain the exact same results. If you wish to utilize a speedy programmer shortcut, cut and paste the two parameters you just added to the <EditText> UI element into the <Button> UI element and change the edit_colony reference to instead refer to the **submit_colony** ID by using the following markup:

```
android:layout_below="@+id/submit_colony"  android:layout_alignLeft="@+id/submit_colony"
```

As is shown in Figure 7-26, you are positioning this second Button widget **to the right of** an **edit_pop** EditText widget, **below** a **submit_colony** Button widget, and using the **left** edge of the a **submit_colony** Button widget.

Figure 7-26. Using the layout_below and layout_alignLeft parameters to align the <Button> widgets to each other

If you now use the Graphical Layout tab, as shown in Figure 7-27, you can see your UI design is in alignment!

Figure 7-27. Previewing the layout_below and layout_alignLeft parameters for your <Button> widgets in the GLE

Since we are going to want to preview this RelativeLayout UI design and EditGalaxy Activity subclass in the Nexus One AVD emulator at some point here, before our curiosity gets the best of us, we need to take a quick break from UI design and add the <activity> tag and parameters for our new EditGalaxy class to the Android Manifest XML file. We will do this so that when this Activity is "called" using the Intent object we created for the application, the app does not crash! If you wish to see what that crash would look like were you not to add the Activity to the manifest, simply use your trusty **Run As ➤ Android Application** menu sequence now, and click on the Edit Galaxy Info MenuItem! Kah-Blamm! Let's do something to avoid this crash scenario!

Adding EditGalaxy to Your App: Editing Your AndroidManifest

Let's take a break and add the EditGalaxy class to your AndroidManifest.xml file, so that when we want to test this UI design in the Nexus One AVD emulator, the application won't crash. Since we use explicit Intent object Java code in order to launch the EditGalaxy Activity subclass, we will not need to define any IntentFilter object structures, such as the MainActivity features, so all that we will be required to add is the following XML markup:

```
<activity
        android:name="absolute.beginners.hellouniverse.EditGalaxy"
        android:label="@string/edit_galaxy" >
</activity>
```

You can add this either before or after the MainActivity <activity> definition, as you can see in Figure 7-28. Notice that we are using the MenuItem label <string> to label the top of this Activity subclass screen, so that users will know that it is the "Edit Galaxy Info" screen. If you want the application name (brand) on the top of the screen, you would simply leave the **app_name** <string> constant reference; that is entirely your call.

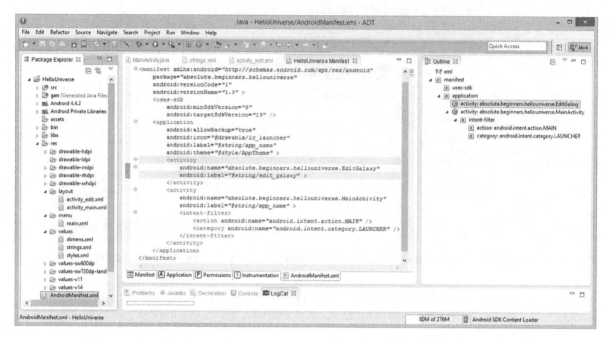

Figure 7-28. *Adding the <activity> child tag for the EditGalaxy class, and an Edit Galaxy Info <string> reference*

You could also use the short-form tag style, since there are no child tags inside of the <activity> parent tag, such as an <intent-filter> child tag, and thus, you could write this <activity> tag using the following XML markup:

```
<activity android:name="absolute.beginners.hellouniverse.EditGalaxy"
          android:label="@string/edit_galaxy" />
```

Now let's get back to adding the bottom half of our EditGalaxy UI design, which is not going to go quite as smoothly as you think that it might, and so we will have an opportunity to learn even more RelativeLayout alignment parameters which can be utilized to make your UI design absolutely perfect!

Finishing Up the RelativeLayout UI Design

Create your third set of <EditText> and <Button> UI elements by copying and pasting your second set of <EditText> and <Button> UI elements and change **edit_pop** to **edit_fleet** for the <EditText> UI widget and **submit_pop** to **submit_fleet** for the <Button> UI widget, as shown in Figure 7-29. Leave your android:text reference for the <Button> set to **ok_button** and the android:layout_alignLeft reference for the <EditText> set to @+id/edit_colony, so that all of the EditText UI widgets will align with the first EditText UI widget.

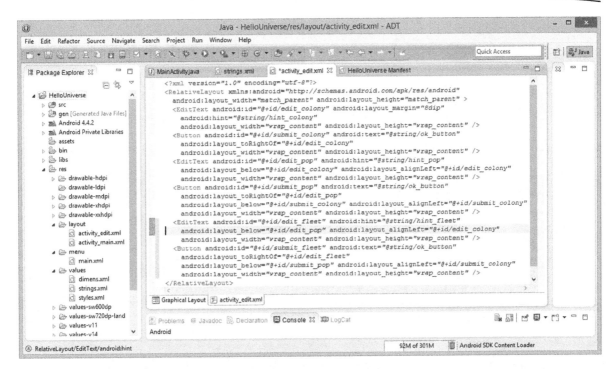

Figure 7-29. Adding the third <EditText> child tag and using RelativeLayout alignment to align it below edit_pop

It is important to note that you could also alternatively reference the layout_alignLeft parameter to the EditText ID of the EditText UI element above it (@+id/edit_pop), since that EditText UI element has already "inherited" the positioning from the edit_colony EditText UI widget's positioning. You can apply the same principle to the layout_alignLeft parameter for the third Button UI element; it could either reference the @+id/submit_colony or the @+id/submit_pop as both of these references will produce the same left-side Button alignment result.

Now click on the Graphical Layout Editor tab and preview the UI design, which can be seen in Figure 7-30. As you can see, the UI design does not look professional, as the alignment of the EditView UI elements and the Button UI elements is getting worse as we move from the top of the design to the bottom.

Figure 7-30. *Using the Graphical Layout Editor tab to check on your <EditText> RelativeLayout alignment results*

This means that we will need to add another alignment parameter to bring this UI design back into a perfectly aligned design. What we need is something that will align the bottom of the EditText UI widget with the bottom of the Button UI widget, or better yet, align the text inside of the EditText field UI element with the text label on the Button UI element.

As you can see in Figure 7-30, the Button UI elements already align quite well, so we should leverage that fact, by forcing the EditText UI elements to align with the Button UI elements in some fashion, either by using the **alignTop**, **alignBottom**, or **alignBaseline** relative layout parameters, and referencing the Button UI elements.

Since the alignTop and alignBottom parameters are fairly straightforward, and since the baseline alignment of the text in these user interface elements will provide a more professional visual result, we will go ahead and learn about **baseline alignment** next, using the **android:layout_alignBaseline** parameter.

The baseline of a font is the part of the font that sits on the line that most of the font characters sit on. There are a couple of exceptions to this rule, such as the "y" in Galaxy shown in Figure 7-30, which drops below the baseline, and some other characters, such as the "f" or the "j" and the "g" or the "q," which could also sometimes drop below the baseline, depending upon how they are drawn for any given font type or style.

Next, let's clean up the UI design alignment, by learning about the android:layout_alignBaseline RelativeLayout parameter, and then, once our UI design is back in perfect alignment, we can add your final pair of EditText and Button UI elements, and then we will be ready to add in the graphic imagery that will make your UI design really professional and visually appealing.

Using Baseline Alignment: The layout_alignBaseline Parameter

Add a new line inside of the third <EditText> UI widget after the android:layout_alignLeft parameter, and add in an **android:layout_alignBaseline** parameter that references the third **submit_fleet** Button UI ID value, using the following XML markup, as is shown in the top XML editing pane portion of Figure 7-31:

```
android:layout_alignBaseline="@+id/submit_fleet"
```

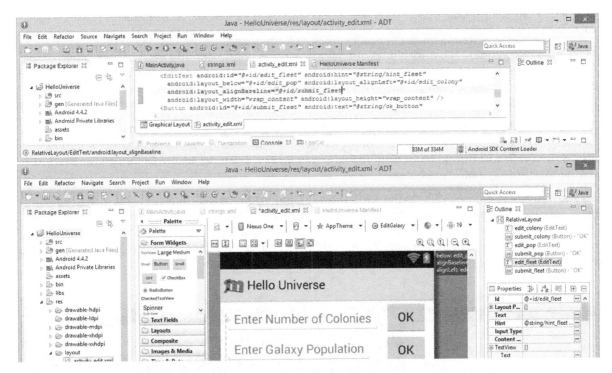

Figure 7-31. Using the android:layout_alignBaseline parameter to align your <EditText> widget with the <Button>

After you have added in this parameter, click on the Graphical Layout Editor tab at the bottom of the editing pane to switch over into visual layout design mode, and as you can see in Figure 7-31, the third EditText UI element is now perfectly aligned with the third Button UI element.

Also notice that all of the RelativeLayout alignment parameters are shown in the visual layout mode using **green arrows**. The green arrow pointing up shows the android:layout_below parameter, and the green arrow pointing to the left (on the left) shows the android:layout_alignLeft with the edit_colony EditText at the top of the UI design (which is indicated by a left pointing green arrow next to this edit_colony EditText UI element), and the android:alignBaseline parameter is shown by Eclipse drawing a dashed green baseline underneath all of the text.

The long green arrow coming out of the Button UI element and pointing at the EditView UI element is showing the **android:layout_toRightOf** parameter for the Button UI element, which references the **@+id/edit_fleet** ID for the EditText UI element, just in case you are wondering what that particular green arrow is referencing.

This **layout guidelines feature** in the Eclipse Graphical Layout Editor is a pretty cool feature, and makes it easier for me to show you what each RelativeLayout parameter is doing, and exactly where it is being applied!

Now you can copy and paste the third set of <EditText> and <Button> UI elements, and change the relative layout referencing to create the fourth and final set of <EditText> and <Button> UI elements. Change the edit_fleet to edit_ships, hint_fleet to hint_ships, and submit_fleet to submit_ships. The <EditText> UI element layout_below should reference edit_fleet and the layout_alignLeft can reference edit_colony, edit_pop, or edit_fleet, your choice, as these will all produce the same exact alignment result.

Make sure that you add the **android:layout_alignBaseline** parameter into each of your other <EditText> UI definitions, just to make sure that everything is being done in exactly the same precise way. Surgically precise UI design saves lives! We've created quite a complex network of relative positioning and relative alignment referencing in this design.

Now let's use the **Run As ➤ Android Application** menu sequence and take a look at the completed UI design in the Nexus One emulator, before we get tricky and add in a cool galaxy background image to take this UI design to an even higher visual level, so it matches the UI design we created for the MainActivity Activity subclass.

As you can see in Figure 7-32, on the left-hand side, the layout of the UI design now looks really nice, and was created using less than three dozen lines of XML markup, which is less than five lines of XML markup per UI element. The right side of Figure 7-32 shows the changes we are about to make, in order to bring this UI design for this Edit Galaxy Information screen into visual conformance with the MainActivity class's UI screen design.

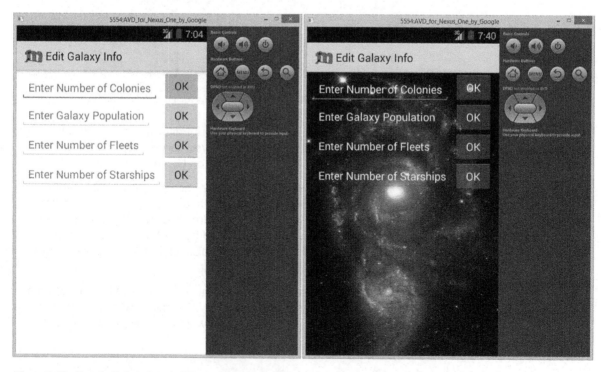

Figure 7-32. Test the RelativeLayout UI in the Nexus One AVD and add a background image and white textColor

Now it is time to add in yet another impressive background galaxy image, and change our <Button> UI widget's **textColor** parameter to white, as well as changing our <EditText> UI widget's **textColorHint** parameter to be white, in order to improve the UI design contrast and to make our UI design actually look like it is taking place out there in the HelloUniverse galaxy somewhere!

Adding a Graphics Asset to the RelativeLayout Container

Let's perform the same work process that we did in Chapter 6 to add an image to the LinearLayout UI container, except that we'll use a different **editgalaxyscreen.png** image, shown highlighted in the Package Explorer pane on the left-hand side of Figure 7-33. Since we are currently using dark text colors (a medium grey hintTextColor parameter default value for the EditText UI elements, and a black textColor value for the Button UI elements), we'll also need to add parameters for **android:textColor** and **android:textColorHint** to change these to white.

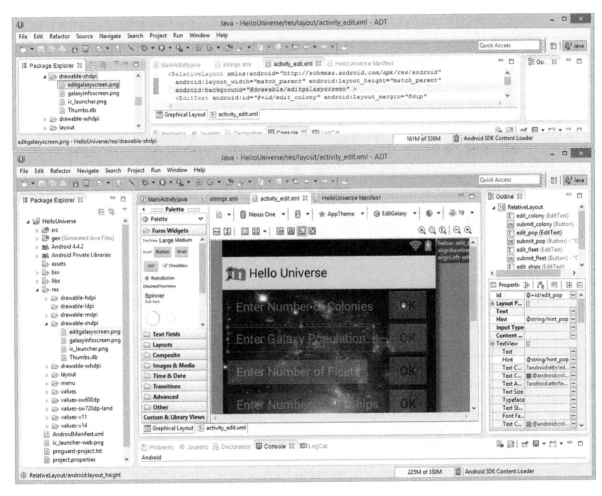

Figure 7-33. Add an android:background parameter to the <RelativeLayout> container and editgalaxyscreen.png

To put this new digital image asset into place, copy the file from this book's assets repository (ZIP) file and into the **/res/drawable-xhdpi** folder, where you installed the galaxyinfoscreen.png file, using the Windows Explorer utility. Then, right-click on the HelloUniverse project folder in the Eclipse Package Explorer pane and select the **Refresh** menu option, which will allow Eclipse to "see" that this file exists, and make it available for use, inside of the <RelativeLayout> parent tag using the android:background parameter. The XML markup looks like this:

```
android:background="@drawable/editgalaxyscreen"
```

As you can see in Figure 7-33, using the Graphical Layout Editor tab as a preview utility, the background image looks great, but causes contrast issues with the current textColor setting, which needs to be "flipped" from black to white, in order to be highly visible against this galaxy background image. Thus, we will again add a textColor parameter set to **#FFFFFF** (white), using the familiar android:textColor="#FFFFFF" parameter configuration.

We'll add in an **android:textColorHint** parameter set to **#FFFFFF** to also change your hint text color to white. We also need to add the android:textColor="#FFFFFF" to the <EditText> so the user can see text they type in!

The final XML markup for the entire eight UI elements in your final UI design should look like the following:

```
<RelativeLayout xmlns:android="http://schemas.android.com/apk/res/android"
   android:layout_width="match_parent" android:layout_height="match_parent"
   android:background="@drawable/editgalaxyscreen" >
  <EditText android:id="@+id/edit_colony" android:layout_margin="8dip"
     android:hint="@string/hint_colony" android:textColorHint="#FFFFFF"
     android:layout_alignBaseline="@+id/submit_colony" android:textColor="#FFFFFF"
     android:layout_width="wrap_content" android:layout_height="wrap_content" />
  <Button android:id="@+id/submit_colony" android:text="@string/ok_button"
     android:layout_toRightOf="@+id/edit_colony" android:textColor="#FFFFFF"
     android:layout_width="wrap_content" android:layout_height="wrap_content" />
  <EditText android:id="@+id/edit_pop" android:hint="@string/hint_pop" android:textColor="#FFFFFF"
     android:layout_below="@+id/edit_colony" android:layout_alignLeft="@+id/edit_colony"
     android:layout_alignBaseline="@+id/submit_pop" android:textColorHint="#FFFFFF"
     android:layout_width="wrap_content" android:layout_height="wrap_content" />
  <Button android:id="@+id/submit_pop" android:text="@string/ok_button"
     android:layout_toRightOf="@+id/edit_pop" android:textColor="#FFFFFF"
     android:layout_below="@+id/submit_colony" android:layout_alignLeft="@+id/submit_colony"
     android:layout_width="wrap_content" android:layout_height="wrap_content" />
  <EditText android:id="@+id/edit_fleet" android:hint="@string/hint_fleet"
android:textColor="#FFFFFF"
     android:layout_below="@+id/edit_pop" android:layout_alignLeft="@+id/edit_colony"
     android:layout_alignBaseline="@+id/submit_fleet" android:textColorHint="#FFFFFF"
     android:layout_width="wrap_content" android:layout_height="wrap_content" />
  <Button android:id="@+id/submit_fleet" android:text="@string/ok_button"
     android:layout_toRightOf="@+id/edit_fleet" android:textColor="#FFFFFF"
     android:layout_below="@+id/submit_pop" android:layout_alignLeft="@+id/submit_colony"
     android:layout_width="wrap_content" android:layout_height="wrap_content" />
  <EditText android:id="@+id/edit_ships" android:hint="@string/hint_ships"
android:textColor="#FFFFFF"
```

```
        android:layout_below="@+id/edit_fleet" android:layout_alignLeft="@+id/edit_colony"
        android:layout_alignBaseline="@+id/submit_ships" android:textColorHint="#FFFFFF"
        android:layout_width="wrap_content" android:layout_height="wrap_content" />
    <Button android:id="@+id/submit_ships" android:text="@string/ok_button"
        android:layout_toRightOf="@+id/edit_ships" android:textColor="#FFFFFF"
        android:layout_below="@+id/submit_fleet" android:layout_alignLeft="@+id/submit_colony"
        android:layout_width="wrap_content" android:layout_height="wrap_content" />
</RelativeLayout>
```

Now you are ready to make the Edit Galaxy Info UI screen interactive using event listeners and event handling!

Event Handling: Using Event Listeners

Android uses something called an "**event**" to allow the end users of your application to "**interact**" with your UI design. There are different events for button (or mouse) clicks, touchscreen use, and keyboard use, and your Java code must "**handle**" these events by implementing "**event listener**" code structures that "trap" these events as they move through your code. When a user "interfaces" with their Android device hardware, this will generate one of these events, and the Android OS will deliver this event to your Java code for processing, using your "**event handler**" Java code.

Creating an Event Listener: .onClickListener()

First, let's add Button and EditText object declarations at the top of the EditGalaxy.java class, as shown in Figure 7-34.

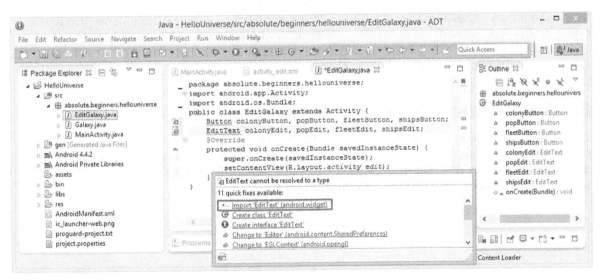

Figure 7-34. Add EditText and Button object declaration at the top of the class, mouse-over each, and Import each class

Mouse-over and import each class, then instantiate the objects using an **instantiateUi()** method, seen in Figure 7-35.

Figure 7-35. Create a private void instantiateUi() method, instantiate UI elements, and call method from onCreate()

Now that you have set up your UI elements as objects in your Java code, as well as practiced making your own instantiateUi() method to better organize your Java code statements, it is time to create an OnClickListener() event handling construct. I wanted to cover this as early on in this book as I could, as we will be using this type of event handling code structure throughout the book, so please pardon this lengthy chapter! We're almost done!

Creating an Event Listener: .onClickListener()

The **.OnClickListener()** constructor method (notice in Figure 7-36 that the method starts with a capital letter) is called off of the **View** class using the Java **new** keyword (since we are constructing a new View class OnClickListener object), inside of the **.setOnClickListener()** method called off of your UI widget. In this case, it's the **colonyButton** object.

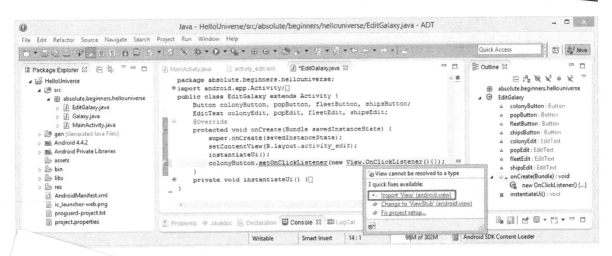

...ClickListener() method off colonyButton object and create new View.OnClickListener

...de produces error highlights, under the **.setOnClickListener()** method and

...ickListener(new View.OnClickListener() { Your .onClick() event handler code

My **rule of** ...... for dealing with multiple error highlights in Eclipse is to ascertain if any of them are under class names which may not yet be imported, and to mouse-over these, and generate the import statements first, as is shown in Figure 7-36. The logic behind why I do this is because the other error message in the same line of Java code might be rectified (fixed and removed) by the import of that class as well. This is indeed the case in this particular error scenario.

Now that we have erased the error highlighting under the .setOnClickListener() method, we still have a more complex error highlighting under the View.OnClickListener() constructor method call. Mouse-over this error, and you will see that all Eclipse wants to do is to create your .onClick() method structure for you, so this is a "good" error message, and you can go ahead and select the "**Add unimplemented methods**" option, which will save you some keystrokes! This will declare a **public void onClick()** method structure, inside of the .setOnClickListener structure you are creating, and will code an empty method for you (which you will fill later) using the following code:

```
@Override
public void onClick(View v) { Your Java program logic for processing the received onClick events
will go in here }
```

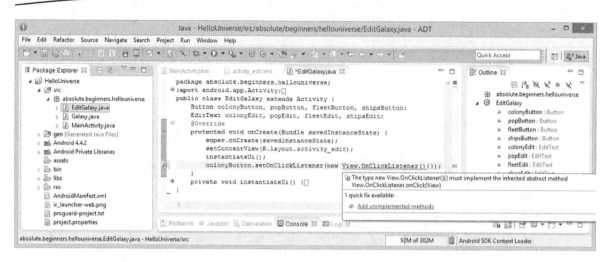

Figure 7-37. Mouse-over the View.OnClickListener error highlight, and select the Add unimplemented method option

Before we add our event handling code that will transfer the EditText object data into the Galaxy object data field, we will first need to go into our MainActivity.java Activity subclass and make our Galaxy object visible!

Making the Galaxy Object Accessible: Using The static Keyword

The Java **static** keyword, which we learned about in Chapter 5, will make an object **accessible** across your Android application. Open your **MainActivity.java** class in the Eclipse ADT central editing pane and add a static keyword before the Galaxy milkyWay object declaration and construction line of code. This is the very first line of code in the class, as can be seen at the top of Figure 7-38.

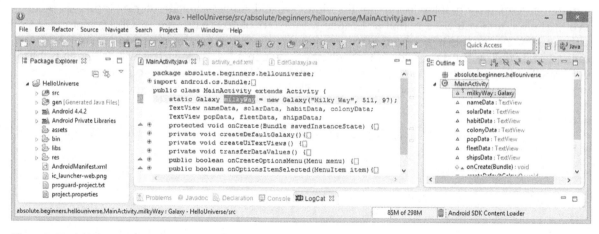

Figure 7-38. Add the static keyword in front of the Galaxy object named milkyWay in the MainActivity.java class

Now we're ready to get into the "meat" of our event processing (handling) code inside of the onClick() method, which will take the data value from the EditText UI object, parse the data, and write it into the Galaxy object variables (characteristics).

Transferring EditText Data to the Galaxy Object Using .parse() Methods

Inside of the onClick() method, set the Galaxy object named milkyWay **galaxyColonies** variable equal to the result of the **.parseLong()** method, which is passed the result of the data value which is obtained using method chaining to call a **.getText()** method off of the **colonyEdit** EditText object and then convert that data to String data using the **.toString()** method call. This is all accomplished using the following very dense line of Java code:

```
MainActivity.milkyWay.galaxyColonies = Long.parseLong(colonyEdit.getText().toString());
```

Working backward from the UI object, you get the text value from the colonyEdit EditText object using the .getText() method, make sure that the value is String data using the .toString() method, pass that String data to the .parseLong() method which will extract any number values from the String and make sure they are Long data values, and then set the Long data values to the galaxyColonies variable of the milkyWay Galaxy object in the MainActivity class.

The entire event handling Java code structure for the colonyButton object should look like the following code:

```
colonyButton.setOnClickListener(new View.OnClickListener() {
    @Override
    public void onClick(View v) {
        MainActivity.milkyWay.galaxyColonies = Long.parseLong( colonyEdit.getText().toString() );
    }
});
```

Now you can copy this event handling code structure three more times underneath itself, and change the colony UI object (Button and EditText) references to pop, fleets, and ships, respectively, as is shown in Figure 7-39.

Figure 7-39. Set the Galaxy object data fields equal to the EditText object data fields using .getText() and .parse()

Make sure that you use the **Double.parseDouble()** method call with your **galaxyLifeforms** variable, and be sure to use the **Integer.parseInt()** method call with your **galaxyFleets** and **galaxyStarships** variables. This is so that you make sure that you are matching up your numeric data types with the proper **.parse()** method call data type.

As you can see in Figure 7-40, your code runs well in the Nexus One emulator, and your numeric entries have good contrast, using the white text color and white hint color values.

Figure 7-40. Enter new data values into the EditText UI elements and click Button UI elements to call .onClick()

Note on the right side of the figure that the Android OS will provide an **insertion point guide** in blue if you go back to edit any of the data values. If you click the **OK** button after entering the appropriate numeric data value type, the **onClick** event will trigger the update to your Galaxy object's corresponding data fields, which we will visualize on your galaxy information screen during the next chapter, when we continue to refine these Activity classes as well as their user interface designs by using new UI layout classes, new UI widget classes, and new parameters for both. Learning Android can be fun!

Summary

In this seventh chapter, you learned all about how to make your Android application interactive by using **Intent** objects, **Event Listeners**, and an **OptionsMenu** object and its child **MenuItem** object structures. You learned about how to leverage the most popular layout container, the **RelativeLayout** class. You learned how to get the AVD emulator to launch an application if it gets stalled, by using an **AVD Manager** dialog and its **Start** button, and how to "clear" **snapshot** data in memory, to force Eclipse to "launch" a "virgin" AVD into system memory.

You created your second custom Java class, an Activity subclass called **EditGalaxy**, and designed its UI design from scratch, using two important new UI widget classes used for Android application design, the **EditText** and the **Button** classes. You learned some of the key configuration parameters for both of these important widgets, and you even installed an impressive galaxy background image, and adjusted your UI design's contrast using the **textColor** and **textColorHint** parameters. You also learned all about **event handling**, and how to implement an Android **onClick()** event listener Java code structure to process the click and touch events on the OK Button UI elements in your UI design.

Next, in Chapter 8, you will start to learn about some of the more complex Android UI layout containers, such as the **GridLayout, SlidingPaneLayout** and **ViewPager**.

8

Android UI Design: Using Advanced ViewGroup Layout Containers

The Android OS includes a number of ViewGroup subclasses that make advanced user interface layout design available to all Android developers, and fortunately this also includes the "Absolute Beginner!" This is precisely why I'm including this chapter in the book, and only halfway through the book, at that! To be able to implement advanced user interface layouts right "out of the box" is a testament to the quality and reach of the Android API.

One of the ways that I am "refreshing" this *Android Apps for Absolute Beginners* title in its third edition is the incorporation of many of the changes that have taken place with the Android 4.x versions and in the Android 5.x versions. One of the areas which has had the most change in Android 4 and Android 5 is the area of user interface design and user experience. Three powerful UI design layout container classes have been introduced since V4.0, so I added this chapter to the book in order to specifically cover the UI layout classes which were introduced in Android 4. I will also include a chapter at the end of the book which will cover the UI layout classes which are slated to be introduced in Android 5, so that you are completely up to speed as of 2015 and 2016 for your Android development.

In this chapter, we will be covering Android's more advanced user interface layout design classes, including the powerful, grid-based UI layout container class, **GridLayout**, and a sliding-drawer-based UI layout container class called **SlidingPaneLayout**. Both of these popular Android user interface layout container classes, which you have seen utilized in many of the apps currently on your Android devices, are built upon the foundation of the Android ViewGroup superclass, which you learned all about back in Chapter 6.

I covered several of the other basic ViewGroup subclasses, such as **LinearLayout** (Chapter 6), **RelativeLayout** (Chapter 7), and **FrameLayout** (Chapter 11) in the other chapters in this book, because there is simply no way I can effectively cover the primary user interface layout container classes which I need you to know all about as an Android developer within the span of one single chapter. By the end of this book, I will have covered most of those UI layout container classes that you will likely want to use in your Android 4.x and Android 5.x applications development.

In this chapter, we'll upgrade the RelativeLayout UI layout container design to a GridLayout UI layout container design, so that you can learn how to use the GridLayout class, and then we will create a new UI design using the ViewPager and SlidingPaneLayout classes. We will also take a closer look at the ActionBar class. Later on, we'll enhance this sliding UI design, which we will create using the ImageButton UI widget, using graphic design and animated UI elements which we will learn how to implement during the next two chapters covering graphics design and 2D animation.

Using the Android GridLayout UI Container

Android's **GridLayout** class was added to the Android OS in the Ice Cream Sandwich Version 4.0 release. As you saw in the previous chapter, the RelativeLayout class might also be used to create grid-like UI designs. The GridLayout class methods and attributes (parameters) are optimized for creating grid-like UI designs, while at the same time using the smallest amount of system memory possible. The Android GridLayout class has half of the number of parameters (**12** versus 24) than the RelativeLayout class has, making it more memory efficient.

Don't let the small number of layout parameters fool you into thinking that using a GridLayout is a cakewalk, as GridLayout is more complicated than it might seem on the surface; after all, using grids is simple, right? This UI class is actually more akin to a "**Grid Layout Engine**," if you will, and is complex in the sense that you will need to understand how it is going to process your parameters in order for you to design grid-based UI layouts using its dozen attributes (parameters).

Some of the advanced concepts I'll cover in this section include grid **flexibility**, grid **spanning**, grid **spacing**, and **multiple gravity constant** settings. It is interesting to note that this UI layout container class features more parent (global layout container) parameters, which are used to set GridLayout engine (processing) attributes, than child UI element parameters, which is fairly unique within Android UI layout container classes. This is why using the GridLayout class is more complicated, because you have to understand how the engine will process its settings.

It is important to note that multiple gravity constant settings are also available with some of the other UI layout container classes which support the concept of layout gravity, and we will cover this powerful concept here, because using more than one gravity constant at a time is quite useful in conjunction with all the features of a GridLayout container.

GridLayout Class: Grid-Based UI Layout Designs

The grid layout which is defined using the GridLayout class is comprised of a **collection** or **array** of "infinitely thin" **grid lines**. These UI grid lines, which are not really there, and which are not actually (visibly) drawn, separate the grid UI viewing area into something called "**cells**."

The GridLayout class hierarchy begins with a Java Object master class, and progresses from a View class to a ViewGroup class to the GridLayout class, and so the GridLayout class "inherits" all of the methods, constants, and attributes (parameters) of the View and ViewGroup classes. The class hierarchy can be visualized as follows:

```
java.lang.Object
  > android.view.View
    > android.view.ViewGroup
      > android.widget.GridLayout
```

The Android GridLayout class is a **public** class, extending the ViewGroup superclass. It is referenced by using the **import android.widget.GridLayout** statement at the top of an Android Activity subclass, as you will soon see.

Within the GridLayout class, your grid lines will be referenced using **grid indices**. A grid with a **Y** number of columns will have **Y+1** grid indices, which will be **numbered starting at 0** and run through Y as the last column index. Regardless of how a GridLayout is constructed, grid index **0** will be **fixed to the leading edge** of the layout container, and grid index Y will be **fixed to the trailing edge**, after any padding values are applied.

Using the rowSpec and columnSpec Parameters

A GridLayout's child UI widgets usually span one cell, but can also span more than one cell. This is defined by the **rowSpec** and **columnSpec** GridLayout class parameters. These parameters are specified inside of the child UI widget tags inside of the parent GridLayout tag. We will learn about all of the grid layout parameters next, when we cover the Java **nested class** which contains these. This class is called **GridLayout.LayoutParams**.

> **Note** Nested Classes in Java are classes which are defined inside of another class. If the class is defined using the **static** keyword, it is called a "**nested class**," and if not, it is called an "**inner class**." We will be creating an inner class later on in this book. Many of the View and ViewGroup classes use nested classes, which are declared as **public static abstract** classes, because they provide these parameters which are ultimately used in your XML definitions. The primary reason for a nested class is for organization, as nested classes in Android will often be viewed as "helper" classes, and need to be **logically grouped** together. The reason the class names are separated using a period character is because that is how the path is defined in Java, and so a class inside of another class, such as the LayoutParams class which is inside of the GridLayout class, would thus be referenced as **GridLayout.LayoutParams**.

You can use each of the GridLayout's "Spec" parameters to define a set of rows (android:rowSpec), or columns (android:columnSpec), which you define as being occupied by your child widget (View objects) tags. You can also specify how these child UI widgets are going to be aligned within the resulting set or "group" of grid cells.

It is important to note that while grid cells should not normally be defined to overlap each other in GridLayouts, the GridLayout class will not prevent child UI widgets from being defined in such a way, so widgets can occupy the same cell, or can span a group of cells. This allows UI designers a lot of flexibility for using the GridLayout container to create scalable (morphing to fit different screen sizes and shapes) grid-based UI layout designs.

Note that if you design with more than one child widget per grid cell, or with more than one grid cell per child widget (termed: **spanning**), there is no guarantee that child UI widgets will not overlap after the GridLayout UI engine evaluates your parameters in its GridLayout computation operation. For this reason, make sure that you test your GridLayout UI designs thoroughly using several different device emulators and device orientations.

GridLayout Location, Flexibility, and Gravity

If your child UI widget tag doesn't include any parameters specifying the row and column index of the grid cell which it intends to occupy, then the GridLayout class algorithm will assign its cell location for it automatically. This is done based on the GridLayout container definition parameters in a parent <GridLayout> tag, along with the GridLayout orientation, rowCount, and columnCount attributes or property (parameters) global settings.

White space between child UI elements in a GridLayout can be specified either by using an instance of the Android **SpaceView** class (i.e. a SpaceView object), or by using **android:layout_margin** parameters.

When the <GridLayout> parent tag (parameters in the parent tag signify that the parameter is a global GridLayout engine setting) XML parameter **android:useDefaultMargins** is set to a Boolean value of **true**, then default margins around child UI widgets are automatically allocated, based on the UI style guide for the Android platform running on the device at the time.

If you wanted to "toggle" this particular GridLayout parameter **dynamically**, you would do this using your Java code, by implementing the **.setUseDefaultMargins()** method call, passing a true or a false Boolean data value. The **UseDefaultMargins** attribute's value would be said to be set **statically** (the opposite of dynamically), if it's initial (starting) data value is specified by using the GridLayout XML layout definition. The reason that this is considered to be "static" is that the XML UI definition is evaluated during "inflation" before the application is put into use by the user, whereas the Java method is used in a "dynamic" fashion in response to the user's use of the application, and is therefore evaluated dynamically while the application is "in play," and not prior to its use.

It is important to note that each of the four (left, right, top, bottom) margin settings which will be automatically defined using the android:useDefaultMargins=true specification, may each be independently overridden via the assignment of one of these four margin parameters, allowing a GridLayout designer fine-tuned margin control.

It is important to note that the GridLayout class distributes excess space between child UI widgets based upon a **priority** principle, and not using the principle of weight, which is currently unique to the LinearLayout container type. For this reason, a child UI widget's ability to "stretch" is inferred from the alignment properties for its row and column groupings.

Grid cell alignment characteristics are set by specifying the child widget's **gravity** property (parameter) for each child UI element. This is done by using the **android:layout_gravity** parameter. If alignment is defined along a given X or Y grid axis, then that child UI widget would be considered to be "**flexible**" regarding that direction.

If no alignment characteristics are specified, then the GridLayout class will consider that child UI widget to be **fixed**, and thus to be **inflexible**. Fixed versus flexible grid cells are a consideration in how the GridLayout will scale or "morph" between different screen sizes and shapes; that is, between the different Android device types.

If you have multiple UI widgets inside of the same row or column grouping, the UI widgets will be considered to be acting together (that is, in parallel with each other). These groupings will be considered to be flexible, but only if **all** of the child UI widgets inside of the grouping are also configured to be, or deemed to be, flexible.

For example, if you wanted to make one of your GridLayout columns scale dynamically (to be stretchable), you would simply make sure that you define the android:layout_gravity parameter inside of each of your UI widgets which are contained within that particular GridLayout column. On the other hand, if you wanted to prevent any of your GridLayout UI columns from stretching, or in other words, make them fixed, or static, you would need to ensure that one of your UI widgets in that column does not define a setting for this android:layout_gravity parameter.

When a layout_gravity parameter-specified principle of grid flexibility is defined in a way that is interpreted by the GridLayout algorithm as being ambiguous (that is, able to be interpreted in more than one unique way), the GridLayout class's algorithm will prioritize flexibility for rows and columns which are closer to the right and bottom sides of your UI design. This would be the "end" of the UI design, since it starts in the upper-left corner, at pixel location 0,0.

The GridLayout.LayoutParams Nested Class: Parameters

The **GridLayout.LayoutParams** class hierarchy begins with the Java Object master class, and progresses from the **ViewGroup.LayoutParams** class to the **ViewGroup.MarginLayoutParams** class, and finally down to the **GridLayout.LayoutParams** class. A class inheritance hierarchy would be structured in the following fashion:

```
java.lang.Object
 > android.view.ViewGroup.LayoutParams
   > android.view.ViewGroup.MarginLayoutParams
     > android.widget.GridLayout.LayoutParams
```

This class provides parameters and constants which will be used in your GridLayout XML UI definition file, in order to create your GridLayout UI designs. We will go over these five GridLayout parameters here, as seen in Table 8-1, and we will utilize many of them in our GridLayout UI, which we will be creating during the chapter.

Table 8-1. Five GridLayout Attributes (Parameters) Along with Their Primary Functions (Used in Child UI Widgets)

GridLayout Parameter	Parameter Function Description
layout_column	Column boundary indicating left group of cells occupied
layout_row	Row boundary indicating top group of cells occupied
layout_gravity	Gravity specifying how UI widgets are to be placed in a cell
layout_columnSpan	Difference between left or right boundary delimiting cell span
layout_rowSpan	Difference between top or bottom boundary delimiting cell span

The GridLayout.LayoutParams class contains four **static** XML parameters shown in Table 8-1. These include: **android:layout_column**, **android:layout_row**, **android:layout_columnSpan**, and **android:layout_rowSpan**. There is also one **dynamic** Java method, **.setGravity()**, which can also be set or configured statically, using the GridLayout XML definition file, by using the **android:layout_gravity** XML parameter that I discussed earlier.

This is clearly a small number of configuration options for what is considered to be a complex and powerful UI layout container class. The reason I split these 12 GridLayout parameter options between the 5 that go inside the child UI widget tags, and the 7 which control how the GridLayout algorithm (I like to call it the GridLayout "engine"), is to point out how differently this particular UI layout container works from the other UI layout container classes!

The other seven XML parameters shown in Table 8-2 are used for setting how the GridLayout class's algorithm (engine) is going to interpret a given GridLayout definition. These therefore specify what I would term "global" GridLayout setting values, which will be used to configure this "grid alignment engine" which the GridLayout class creates for you. These global GridLayout parent parameters are included in this section so that we can keep these XML GridLayout parameters all together in one section (and one discussion). There are also two other nested classes, which deal with GridLayout XML parameters, which we will cover during the next two sections of this chapter.

Table 8-2. GridLayout Parent Layout Container "Configuration" Parameters, Along with Their Primary Functionality

GridLayout Parent Parameter	GridLayout Parent Parameter Function Description:
android:columnCount	A Max. Column Count to use when auto-positioning Views
android:rowCount	A Maximum Row Count to use when auto-positioning Views
android:useDefaultMargins	Uses auto-margin algorithm when no margins specified
android:alignmentMode	Sets how to align the grid, relative to View's margins
android:columnOrderPreserved	Force column boundaries to be in same order as indices
android:rowOrderPreserved	Force row boundaries to be in same order as indices
android:orientation	Sets orientation for grid (unused in layout algorithm)

The most often used parent attributes are the **android:layout_rowCount** and **android:layout_columnCount** parameters. These important parameters will allow you to define your GridLayout in a static (or fixed) fashion, which is more memory-efficient, because a fixed memory area can be established and optimized "up-front" for the grid UI layout. This is how we will be defining our GridLayout UI design during this chapter.

There are three **"flag"** (Boolean values, set to true or false) parameters, which can be utilized for turning on or off grid cell margins (the **android:layout_useDefaultMargins** parameter), preserving row order (the **android:layout_rowOrderPreserved** parameter), and for preserving column order (the **android:layout_columnOrderPreserved** parameter).

There are two **constant** parameters, which are used in conjunction with Android OS constants for specifying the GridLayout alignment mode (the **android:layout_alignmentMode** parameter) and the GridLayout's orientation (the **android:layout_orientation** parameter).

The GridLayout.Alignment Nested Class: Alignment Constants

The **GridLayout.Alignment** nested class hierarchy begins at the Java Object master class, and directly creates this GridLayout.Alignment nested class, which you can think of as containing the "**alignment constants**" for this GridLayout class, because that is what it does. This nested class therefore uses the following Java class hierarchy:

```
java.lang.Object
  > android.widget.GridLayout.Alignment
```

The Android GridLayout.Alignment nested class is a **public static abstract** class, extending the java.lang.Object superclass. This class provides the **nine** grid row and column alignment constants which you will be using to set the GridLayout **rowSpec** and **columnSpec** parameters that hold your grid definition settings for the child UI widgets contained in the grid layout.

The rowSpec and columnSpec parameters are actually objects, which are used to define the GridLayout overall layout algorithm functionality for the GridLayout design. These are defined internally to the GridLayout, using the **GridLayout.Spec** nested class, which we will be taking a look at briefly in the next section of this chapter.

These nine rowSpec and columnSpec alignment constants are shown in Table 8-3. It is important to note that you can use (define) one or more of the constants for each direction or axis, X and Y, for a GridLayout UI design.

Table 8-3. GridLayout Parent Container Alignment Attributes or Parameters, Along with Primary Functionality

Alignment Constants:	Alignment Constant Function Description:
TOP	Align the Top Edge of the View with Top Edge of other Views
BOTTOM	Align Bottom Edge of View with Bottom Edge of other Views
LEFT	Align the Left Edge of View with Left Edge of other Views
RIGHT	Align the Right Edge of View with Right Edge of other Views
START	Align the Start Edge of View with Start Edge of other Views
END	Align the End Edge of View with the End Edge of other Views
CENTER	Center all of the Views contained within a given cell group
FILL	View should be expanded to fill the entire cell group area
BASELINE	Views in cell group (rows only) should be baseline aligned

This alignment constant specifies how your UI widgets should be placed within the cell grouping, or how they should be scaled (resized) to fit the cell. Each X and Y alignment constant operates **independently** of the other constant. As I mentioned before, you can also combine these together, by using a vertical bar, like so: **TOP|LEFT**. Make sure **not** to use a space character between these constants and the vertical bar, because if you do, you will get a "**String Not Allowed**" error message. This is because Eclipse will then see the value as a **String** value and not a **constant** if it contains any spaces! Essentially, this vertical bar ties the two constants together, so that they will be considered to be one single constant value.

The GridLayout.Spec Nested Class: Horizontal and Vertical Spec

A **GridLayout.Spec** nested class hierarchy begins with the Java Object master class, and directly creates this GridLayout.Spec nested class. Thus this class could be thought of as being "scratch coded" to provide Spec object structures for the GridLayout class, which is why it is a nested (helper) class. You could think of a Spec object as **specifying** or **containing** the "row and column alignment structure." These Spec objects are used at the very core of the Android GridLayout UI class. A Spec object is used to define each of the horizontal or vertical attribute settings (parameters or characteristics) for a given group of grid cells. The GridLayout.Spec Java class hierarchy can be visualized as follows:

```
java.lang.Object
  > android.widget.GridLayout.Spec
```

The Android GridLayout.Spec class is a **public static** class, and it **extends** the java.lang.Object superclass. This class provides the Spec object which is used to define the core row and column definition and functionality for the GridLayout algorithm. This data is then used by the GridLayout engine to create the scalable Grid Layout UI design.

Since this Spec object is used internally, inside of the GridLayout class, we will focus in this chapter on your design of the GridLayout UI, and its parameters rather than get into the inner algorithm workings of the class.

The GridLayout Class Parameters: Default Settings

The GridLayout algorithm has a dozen primary parameters which are utilized in its grid layout engine algorithm, which is defined (using Java code) in the GridLayout class. These parameters (variables) in the GridLayout class need to have their **default settings** in place (initially defined), in order for the GridLayout algorithm to work correctly. This is done just in case developers, such as yourself, forget to define any of these parameters and settings, by using XML parameters in your GridLayout UI definition file.

These XML parameters should all be considered, and set, in your GridLayout UI design XML markup. Just in case you forget any of these, the GridLayout class will define default values for them. These default values are shown in Tables 8-4 and 8-5, and will be assigned in the case that any of these settings are overlooked, or so that they can be left set to their default settings. This is why I'm going over what these default values are in this section of the chapter. In this way, the GridLayout class algorithm will "throw" no errors or exceptions, as it will always have default values.

Table 8-4. GridLayout Row and Column Specification Parameter Default Data Value for Grid Cells (Child Widgets)

XML Parameter Used to Set:	Object Data Field Name:	Default Value:
android:layout_width	PARAMETER IS LEFT UNSPECIFIED	WRAP_CONTENT
android:layout_height	PARAMETER IS LEFT UNSPECIFIED	WRAP_CONTENT
android:layout_row	rowSpec.row	UNDEFINED
android:layout_column	columnSpec.column	UNDEFINED
android:layout_rowSpan	rowSpec.rowSpan	1
android:layout_columnSpan	columnSpec.columnSpan	1
android:layout_gravity	rowSpec.alignment	BASELINE
android:layout_gravity	columnSpec.alignment	START

Table 8-5. GridLayout Margin Specification Parameters Default Data Values (Based on useDefaultMargins Flag)

Margin XML Parameter:	useDefaultMargins=false	useDefaultMargins=true
android:layout_topMargin	0	UNDEFINED
android:layout_bottomMargin	0	UNDEFINED
android:layout_leftMargin	0	UNDEFINED
android:layout_rightMargin	0	UNDEFINED

As you can see, you do **not** need to specify **layout_width** or **layout_height** for child View objects in a GridLayout. The WRAP_CONTENT and MATCH_PARENT constants are evaluated in the same way, as they're considered to be the same thing in a GridLayout. You can thus consider these constants to be hard-coded in the GridLayout algorithms. Be advised that other than with GridLayout, you must always define layout_width and layout_height, so don't get used to this luxury unless you intend to develop UI designs only using the GridLayout class, which would be a shame, as Android has many more powerful layout container classes based on the ViewGroup superclass.

Row and column specifications can be left as undefined, as they will be automatically calculated by the GridLayout algorithm, if they have not been specified. These should be specified if you know the grid dimensions for your UI design, because defining a static (fixed) GridLayout dimension is more memory- and processor-efficient. rowSpan and columnSpan variables default to a value of **one**, which essentially equates to "**do not span**." We will implement a "**span**" in our example, later on in this chapter, so that you can see exactly how the GridLayout class's span functionality works.

Default alignment for rows is **BASELINE**, which is quite logical if you think about it, and the default alignment for columns is **START**, which is also the alignment constant that I would have guessed would be used as the default.

The GridLayout cell margins will always default to zero if you specify an **android:useDefaultMargins ="false"** parameter in your parent GridLayout tag. If you specify an **android:useDefaultMargins ="true"** parameter in the parent GridLayout tag, the margins will remain "**undefined.**" What undefined means is that your cell margins will be controlled by the GridLayout algorithm.

We will be using the **true** setting, so that margins are automatically set for us by the GridLayout; although, if we decide to use margin parameters, these will be "respected" by the GridLayout algorithm as well, as you will see.

Converting a RelativeLayout UI to a GridLayout

To get the best overview or perspective on how the two most often used layout containers, RelativeLayout and GridLayout, differ, let's convert the RelativeLayout that you created for your EditGalaxy.java Activity subclass to use a GridLayout parent layout container tag instead. In this way, we can build on the same Java code that we used in the previous chapter, allowing us to focus primarily on XML UI design in this chapter.

Open your **activity_edit.xml** file in the central editing pane of Eclipse, if it is not there as a tab already, and edit the <RelativeLayout> opening and closing tag, changing the work Relative to Grid, so that it now reads **<GridLayout>**.

After you do this, you need to have Eclipse "evaluate" the markup, and in the XML editor, this evaluation is invoked by using the **CTRL-S** (File Save) keystroke (hold down the **Ctrl** key on the keyboard while typing in an "**s**").

As you can see in Figure 8-1, Eclipse will place its wavy yellow warning highlighting under the RelativeLayout child widget tags that use relative layout parameters, which you will have to replace to utilize GridLayout parameters instead. There is also one wavy red error highlight under the <GridLayout> parent tag, and if you mouse-over this you will see that, as I mentioned previously in the chapter, GridLayout is an Android 4.0 class, and requires the use of API Level 14 or later. For this reason, you will have to edit your AndroidManifest.xml file in order to eliminate this wavy red error highlighting from your GridLayout parent tag.

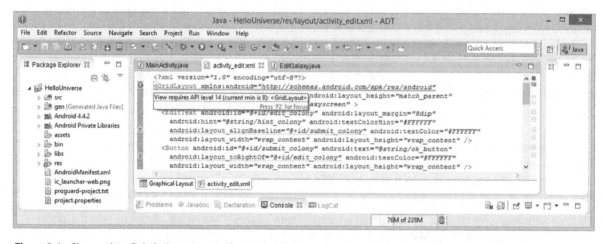

Figure 8-1. Change the <RelativeLayout> container parent tag to a <GridLayout> tag, and review error and warnings

It is important to note that Eclipse's Java editor does not require this CTRL-S work process to get Eclipse ADT to evaluate your Java code, as Eclipse will do this in "real-time," as you type. In contrast, the XML markup editor does require that you **Save** (CTRL-S) your markup before it will evaluate that markup for errors or warning highlights, and provide the necessary pop-up helper dialogs that explain what might be wrong.

To apply a concept which I have been trying to "drive home" thus far during the book, Eclipse's XML markup evaluation algorithm could be considered to be implemented in a "static" fashion, as it requires "submission" to Eclipse by using the "Save" function. In contrast, the Eclipse Java code evaluation algorithm could be said to be implemented in a "dynamic" fashion, as it does not require submission, but rather occurs in real time, evaluated by Eclipse's Java logic processing algorithm while the Eclipse software is running (performing other operations), and while you are typing in your Java programming logic structures. Before we can continue on, you will need to make an application **Minimum SDK Version** configuration edit in the <uses-sdk> child tag in your HelloUniverse application's AndroidManifest.xml file.

Upgrading Your HelloUniverse App to Android 4.0

Let's open up your **AndroidManifest.xml** file in the Eclipse central editing pane, by right-clicking on the file, and using the **Open** menu option, or left-click on the AndroidManifest.xml file, and use the **F3** function key. Change the **android:minSdkVersion** parameter from its current value of "8" to a value of "**14**," as is shown in Figure 8-2.

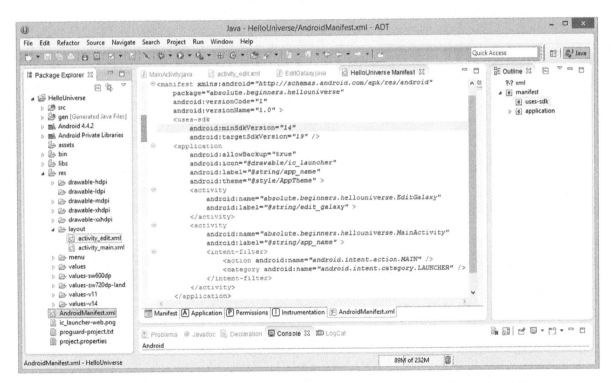

Figure 8-2. Change the <uses-sdk> child tag inside the parent <manifest> tag from a value of 8 to a value of 14

After making this change, use the **CTRL-S** keystroke combination, and **Save** the file, which will then evaluate the XML markup, as well as the effects of this markup across all of the XML markup and Java code in your entire project in Eclipse. This will remove the red error highlighting across your entire HelloUniverse project, which will remove error (and warning) highlights and icons from the Package Explorer pane, the Outline pane, and each of the editing tabs which might be open in the central editing pane.

This will also remove the errors from the error-related tabs at the bottom of the Eclipse IDE, which are located underneath the Outline and Editing panes. It is important that you become familiar with all of these areas of the Eclipse IDE and use each of them to the fullest development advantage!

As you can see in Figure 8-2, this Minimum Required SDK Version parameter change gives you a clean project again. Figure 8-2 also shows how your XML markup will look after you click on your activity_edit.xml editing tab, and remove all of the RelativeLayout class layout parameters, including: layout_margin, layout_toRightOf, layout_alignLeft, layout_alignBaseline, and layout_below, so you are reverting back to a "virgin" layout design.

We are doing this so that you can learn how to produce this same design, using (fewer) GridLayout parameters.

Removing these **RelativeLayout.LayoutParams** class's UI layout parameters will allow you to reduce your XML markup by 33%, from a lengthy 36 lines of markup, to a mere 24 lines of markup, as is shown in Figure 8-3.

Figure 8-3. *Deleting the 17 margin, baseline, toRightOf, below, and alignLeft relative layout alignment parameters*

You are about to see how much more efficient a <GridLayout> parent tag will be than a <RelativeLayout> tag will be for this type (grid-like) of UI layout design. By adding just a few key parameters into the parent layout container tag, and zero parameters into the child UI widget tags, we can achieve exactly the same result using far less XML markup.

You can even use the GridLayout parent tag with no parameters (except for the required layout_width and layout_height), and with zero child tag parameters, to achieve a LinearLayout type of UI design!

Once you remove the 17 RelativeLayout parameters from your <RelativeLayout> container XML markup, including the android:layout_margin parameter in the first child <EditText> UI widget, you would expect to again see all of your UI elements stacked on top of each other, in the upper-right corner of the screen, when you use the Graphical Layout Editor (GLE) tab to preview your UI design.

However, as you can see in Figure 8-4, because you are using the <GridLayout> container, the UI elements will actually be laid out in a horizontal grid, even with no parent tag or child tag (layout) parameters being specified whatsoever. This means that it would be possible for you to create a (horizontal) LinearLayout type of UI layout design in Android by using the GridLayout class with zero parent or child UI layout parameters.

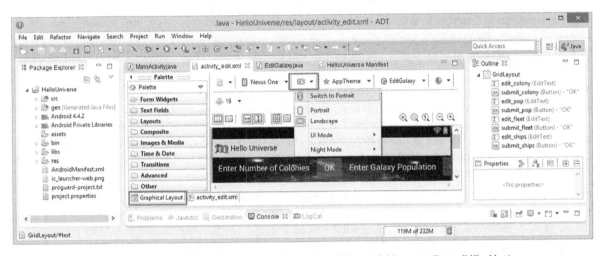

Figure 8-4. Using Graphical Layout Editor tab set in landscape mode to see how GridLayout aligns all UI widgets

There is a "layout orientation" toggle icon at the top of the Graphical Layout Editor preview (rendering) pane which will make this more obvious to you, once you select landscape mode to give you a wider view of what the GridLayout engine is doing with these (minimalist) parent tag configuration parameters. The icon shows a smart phone with an "arcing arrow" on it, which signifies flipping the UI layout design view between **portrait** (up and down, or a vertical screen orientation) and **landscape** (widescreen, or a horizontal screen orientation) **modes**.

Click on this icon, shown outlined in red in Figure 8-4, to toggle the screen preview orientation back and forth, or use the down-facing arrow to drop down a more detailed menu, allowing you to select the toggle, or the mode, specifically. There are also **UI Mode** and **Night Mode** sub-menus from which you can select GLE preview modes.

As you can more clearly ascertain in landscape mode, the GridLayout engine, using only default parameters, is going to arrange your child UI elements in a single-row grid, with a number of columns which matches up with the number of widgets defined inside of the parent GridLayout layout container structure. This is why I made the analogy to a <LinearLayout> parent tag with an android:orientation="horizontal" layout orientation or direction configuration parameter.

It is important to note that you can always get a better view of how a UI class will align UI elements in different screen orientations if you put the GLE into **landscape** mode, by clicking this icon at the top of the GLE.

Be sure and take the time to experiment with the drop-down menu, as well as the sub-menu hierarchy of options, which will allow you to control the **orientation**, **UI mode** (the normal, car dock, desk dock, television, and appliance options), and **Night Mode** (daytime or nighttime option).

This menu is also shown in Figure 8-4, with the "Switch to Portrait" toggle option highlighted, and current landscape mode icon highlighted. This is indeed a handy menu for all of you UI designers!

GridLayout Parent Parameters: Let's Experiment!

Experimentation is a fantastic way to ascertain what any given Android class, and its attributes or properties (in the form of XML parameters, in this case), are going to do. For this reason, I am going to add parent (first), and child (later) parameters, and then observe what these do by using the GLE after each major parameter addition.

The GLE has a lot of interesting functionality regarding GridLayout UI design, so it will be good to experiment with using some of these as well. We'll also experiment with the order that child (widget) tags take inside of the container, since the GridLayout has an "automatic" layout feature. For this reason, we'll create a UI design using only parent <GridLayout> parameters, and then we will add in child widget **GridLayout.LayoutParams** class parameters, such as layout_row or layout_column, to show you a more **memory-efficient** way to define a UI layout grid.

We know the android:layout_width and android:layout_height parameters will be set to a **wrap_content** default value by the GridLayout engine for any of your <GridLayout> child widget tags, as we saw in Table 8-4, which outlines default values that the GridLayout uses for cells in your grid.

However, layout_width and layout_height parameters in the parent <GridLayout> tag instruct the GridLayout engine how to expand to fit a View (layout), which is **above** it. This is usually the display screen itself, as it is in this particular case. Since you want the grid to fill this entire space (the entire application screen), we will leave the **match_parent** constant that we used for your <RelativeLayout> parent tag as the setting for the required layout_width and layout_height parameters for this parent <GridLayout> container tag configuration.

Next, we'll add in your ID and grid configuration parent tag parameters.

GridLayout Parameters: Configuring Your Grid

First, let's add in an **android:id** parameter named **gridLayout**, so we can control the GridLayout from our Java code, and add **android:rowCount** and **android:columnCount** parameters, defining the rows and columns for the grid which we are creating, which initially will replicate the RelativeLayout design that we created during Chapter 7.

Since your RelativeLayout design clearly used four rows and two columns to hold the EditText and Button UI widgets, the **rowCount** GridLayout engine parameter (GridLayout engine configuration attribute or data value) would be set to "**4**," and the **columnCount** parameter (attribute) would be set to a data value of "**2**." Do this using the following XML markup, which you can see inside of the <GridLayout> tag, in Figure 8-5:

```
android:id="@+id/gridLayout" android:rowCount="4" android:columnCount="2"
```

Figure 8-5. *Add the android:id, android:rowCount and android:columnCount parameters to the parent GridLayout*

Notice that I'm leaving the background image plate and the white textColor and textColorHint settings (parameters) to maintain the visuals of this UI design, and to show how to easily change a UI design while the graphic design elements remain unchanged, simply by changing a parent tag along with a few of its configuration parameters.

If you add the android:rowCount="4" parameter first, and then click the Graphical Layout Editor tab, you will not see any change in your GridLayout, which means you will see what is shown in Figure 8-4. This is because the default columnCount parameter for the GridLayout engine is one, and you have not specified any row and column layout parameters inside of the child UI widgets, which we are going to do a bit later on in this chapter.

Once you add in the android:columnCount="2" parameter, you will see the UI grid rendering results which are shown in Figure 8-6. As you can see, the GridLayout engine is getting amazingly close to the optimal UI design by using only two of the global (parent tag) GridLayout configuration parameters (these are listed in Table 8-2).

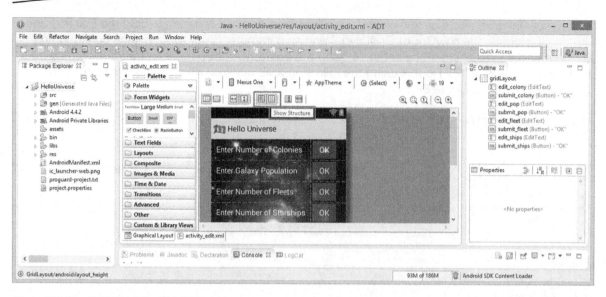

Figure 8-6. Use the GLE to show the GridLayout parent parameters and the Show Structure icon to show guides

It is important, not only for experimentation and learning, but also for memory optimization (using the smallest amount of memory needed to achieve your intended UI design result) to only use the configuration parameters which are needed to achieve the result you desire; in this case, that happens to be replicating the RelativeLayout UI design with a GridLayout UI design. Since we are getting pretty close here, I wanted to try implementing the **UseDefaultMargins** configuration parameter next, to see if this global parameter gives us a better UI alignment result than putting dozens of layout_margin tags in the eight UI elements inside of the GridLayout currently. If it does improve our layout visually, and give us a more professional end result, we will leave it in the UI design.

After we ascertain if the android:useDefaultMargins parameter is going to improve our GridLayout UI design, we will start experimenting with changing the UI widget order inside of the parent layout container, and learn about some of the other parameters which are important to know about relative to creating a GridLayout design.

GridLayout Alignment: The UseDefaultMargins Constant

Add a new line in your <GridLayout> parent tag after the required layout_width and layout_height and add in the **android:useDefaultMargins** parameter set to a boolean value of **true** to turn on this auto-alignment feature. The global alignment parameter is shown highlighted in Figure 8-7 along with seven other parameters.

Figure 8-7. *Add the android:useDefaultMargins parameter to the <GridLayout> tag to have the engine do your alignment*

Let's preview the new useDefaultMargins global GridLayout parameter by clicking the Graphical Layout Editor tab to "render" our GridLayout UI design's parameters visually. You can see the visual layout result in Figure 8-8, along with the green grid guides (toggle icon) turned on, to allow us to visualize these auto-margins much better!

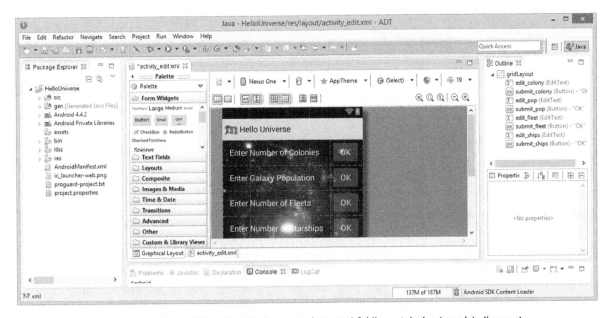

Figure 8-8. *Click the Graphical Layout Editor tab and observe an improved GridLayout design (margin) alignment*

As you can see in Figure 8-8, the result of this global (parent) margin spacing parameter is to more evenly space the UI design out, relative to the sides of the screen (the X dimension), as well as in the Y dimension (top to bottom), between the UI elements themselves, so we'll leave this parameter in place, and start to take a look at UI widget order and layout orientation next.

Changing the Widget Order Inside of the GridLayout

If you had originally designed the Edit Galaxy Info UI by using nested <LinearLayout> tags, all of the <EditText> UI elements would have been grouped together in a (left side) vertical LinearLayout and all of the <Button> UI elements would have been grouped together in a (right side) vertical LinearLayout. If you had designed this UI using <LinearLayout> tags, you would have renamed the outer (parent) <LinearLayout> to <GridLayout> and deleted the nested <LinearLayout> tags, yielding the resulting parent and child tag structure seen in Figure 8-9.

Figure 8-9. Changing the order of the UI widgets to group all of the <EditText> and <Button> widgets together

Let's simulate this "grouped UI widget type" collection of widgets inside of the <GridLayout> container and see if the child widget order changes how the GridLayout engine will auto-arrange the grid UI design. If it does, we will then ascertain if there are any "global" parameters which you can add into your parent <GridLayout> tag, in order to "correct" this new alignment back into the EditText fields on the left, Buttons on the right, result which we are looking to achieve. This exercise will allow you to better visualize how the GridLayout algorithm actually works!

To create this alternate UI widget order seen in Figure 8-9, you need to cut and paste the first three <Button> UI widgets underneath the last Button widget. Make sure to maintain the ID order of **submit_colony**, **submit_pop**, **submit_fleet**, and **submit_ships**.

It is important to note that once you add in the layout_row and layout_column child UI widget parameters, which you will be doing a bit later on in this chapter, the widget order inside of this GridLayout layout container will no longer matter, as you will be specifying the grid location or grid index values directly.

Now you are ready to use the Graphical Layout Editor tab to "render" or preview the new GridLayout and child widget order, which as you can see in Figure 8-10 is not what we are looking to achieve. The EditText widget UI elements are placed into the grid layout first and the Button widget UI elements are placed into the grid layout after that, which is probably what you were expecting to happen.

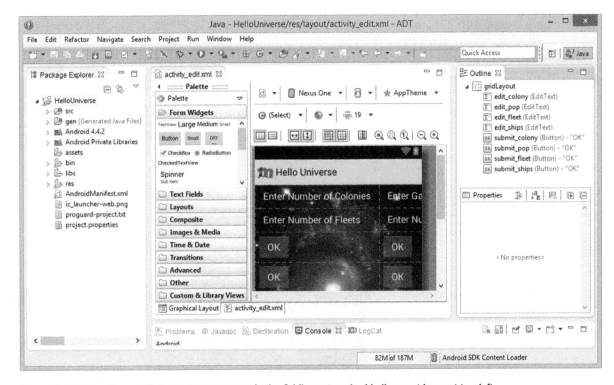

Figure 8-10. *The different UI element arrangement in the GridLayout, and grid alignment icons at top-left*

The question is, is there a simple (single) global parameter you can place in the parent <GridLayout> container, which will change the grid **widget distribution (placement) algorithm**, from placing UI widgets **from left to right, going in a top to bottom direction**, which is what was happening before, to using a different grid widget distribution (placement) algorithm, which would place the same UI widgets **from top to bottom, going in a left to right direction**?

In fact, there is such a global parameter, called **android:orientation**, which is supported with the GridLayout engine, just like it is with the <LinearLayout> parent (and child) tag. This makes these two UI layout container classes even more similar, because, as you now know, these two UI layout containers also share the **layout weight** parameter as well.

It is important to note that even though these two UI layout container (ViewGroup) classes are quite similar, the GridLayout class is not in fact subclassed from the LinearLayout class. This would be the assumption that one might make, due to the similarity between the two classes, as far as parameters (and visual results with no parameter specified) are concerned.

The GridLayout uses the default **android:orientation** value of **horizontal**, which is shown in Figure 8-10 as being set using the (selected) icon with the three columns on it, shown at the top-left of the preview area in the GLE (Graphical Layout Editor).

It is a bit confusing having the GLE icon for **Set Horizontal Orientation** using vertical columns, and the GLE icon for **Set Vertical Orientation** using horizontal rows, but you will get used to it as time goes on.

Click on the currently unselected **Set Vertical Orientation** icon, which depicts row layout ordering, as is shown in Figure 8-11. As you can see, this changes the distribution of the UI widgets, so that now they are placed into the grid cells in exactly the way you want them to be, and you are back to having the desired UI layout result.

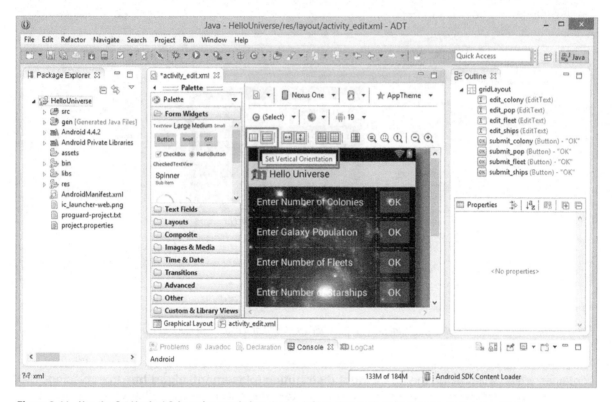

Figure 8-11.   Use the Set Vertical Orientation toggle icon (at top-left) to change the grid layout ordering algorithm

I have now shown you that with the type of UI widget ordering (every other one) you would use in a RelativeLayout UI container as well as the type of UI widget ordering (collected together) you would use in a LinearLayout UI container, there is an orientation setting (horizontal or vertical) in the GridLayout parent container which will organize them the way that you want them to display.

You can also specify your grid UI row and column positioning within each of the child tags inside of the parent GridLayout container, so you could have your child tags randomly specified, and still achieve this layout result. This is done using the layout_row and layout_column parameters shown in Table 8-1.

We are going to do this next, since this is the most memory-efficient way to specify a GridLayout UI design, and the most precise, since we are specifically defining the grid index locations for each of our child UI elements.

GridLayout Child Widget Parameters: Specifying Layout

Let's add **android:layout_row** parameters in the four <EditText> child tags, specifying row index values from 0 through 4, and **android:layout_column** parameters specifying the first column index, which is zero, since in computer programming things are numbered starting with zero.

Your XML markup for these four <EditText> child tags should look like the following, and you can see this markup in Figure 8-12:

```
<EditText android:layout_width="wrap_content" android:layout_height="wrap_content"
    android:id="@+id/edit_colony" android:hint="@string/hint_colony" android:layout_row="0"
    android:textColorHint="#FFFFFF" android:textColor="#FFFFFF" android:layout_column="0" />
<EditText android:layout_width="wrap_content" android:layout_height="wrap_content"
    android:id="@+id/edit_pop" android:hint="@string/hint_pop" android:layout_row="1"
    android:textColor="#FFFFFF" android:textColorHint="#FFFFFF" android:layout_column="0" />
<EditText android:layout_width="wrap_content" android:layout_height="wrap_content"
    android:id="@+id/edit_fleet" android:hint="@string/hint_fleet" android:layout_row="2"
    android:textColor="#FFFFFF" android:textColorHint="#FFFFFF" android:layout_column="0" />
<EditText android:layout_width="wrap_content" android:layout_height="wrap_content"
    android:id="@+id/edit_ships" android:hint="@string/hint_ships" android:layout_row="3"
    android:textColor="#FFFFFF" android:textColorHint="#FFFFFF" android:layout_column="0" />
```

Figure 8-12. Add layout_row and layout_column child widget parameters, defining precise UI element grid layout

Use the GLE to preview the android:layout_row and android:layout_column parameters, as can be seen in Figure 8-13.

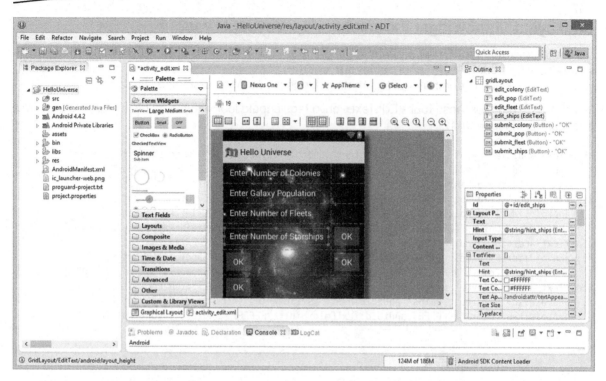

Figure 8-13. The <EditText> UI elements with the layout_row parameters, setting locations 0 through 3

As you can see in Figure 8-13, the GridLayout engine is now correctly placing the <EditView> UI widgets in the correct column index zero and row 0 through 3 grid locations, leaving the grid locations next to these EditText UI elements empty. The GridLayout algorithm auto-layout feature then places the Button UI elements after the EditText UI elements, since we have not yet specified the Button UI element grid index values of column index 1 and row 0 through 3, which we are going to do next.

The parameters for the <Button> child UI widgets will be similar to the ones you added in the <EditText> child tags. In fact, if you like, you can copy and paste these parameters from the <EditText> tags into the <Button> tags. Once you do this, make sure that you set the second series of layout_column index values to "1" and then use the same layout_row values, ranging from "0" to "3," as is shown in the following XML markup:

```xml
<?xml version="1.0" encoding="utf-8"?>
<GridLayout xmlns:android="http://schemas.android.com/apk/res/android" android:id="@+id/gridLayout"
    android:layout_width="match_parent" android:layout_height="match_parent"
    android:background="@drawable/editgalaxyscreen" android:orientation="vertical"
    android:columnCount="2" android:rowCount="4" android:useDefaultMargins="true" >
    <EditText android:layout_width="wrap_content" android:layout_height="wrap_content"
        android:id="@+id/edit_colony" android:hint="@string/hint_colony" android:layout_row="0"
        android:textColorHint="#FFFFFF" android:textColor="#FFFFFF" android:layout_column="0" />
    <EditText android:layout_width="wrap_content" android:layout_height="wrap_content"
        android:id="@+id/edit_pop" android:hint="@string/hint_pop" android:layout_row="1"
        android:textColor="#FFFFFF" android:textColorHint="#FFFFFF" android:layout_column="0" />
    <EditText android:layout_width="wrap_content" android:layout_height="wrap_content"
```

```
        android:id="@+id/edit_fleet" android:hint="@string/hint_fleet" android:layout_row="2"
        android:textColor="#FFFFFF" android:textColorHint="#FFFFFF" android:layout_column="0" />
    <EditText android:layout_width="wrap_content" android:layout_height="wrap_content"
        android:id="@+id/edit_ships" android:hint="@string/hint_ships" android:layout_row="3"
        android:textColor="#FFFFFF" android:textColorHint="#FFFFFF" android:layout_column="0" />
    <Button android:layout_width="wrap_content" android:layout_height="wrap_content"
        android:layout_column="1" android:layout_row="0" android:id="@+id/submit_colony"
        android:text="@string/ok_button" android:textColor="#FFFFFF" />
    <Button android:layout_width="wrap_content" android:layout_height="wrap_content"
        android:layout_column="1" android:layout_row="1" android:id="@+id/submit_pop"
        android:text="@string/ok_button" android:textColor="#FFFFFF" />
    <Button android:layout_width="wrap_content" android:layout_height="wrap_content"
        android:layout_column="1" android:layout_row="2" android:id="@+id/submit_fleet"
        android:text="@string/ok_button" android:textColor="#FFFFFF" />
    <Button android:layout_width="wrap_content" android:layout_height="wrap_content"
        android:layout_column="1" android:layout_row="3" android:id="@+id/submit_ships"
        android:text="@string/ok_button" android:textColor="#FFFFFF" />
</GridLayout>
```

The final XML markup is shown in Figure 8-14, and replicates the Edit Galaxy Information UI design that you created by using a RelativeLayout class in the previous chapter. If you want to see a screen shot of what the final design should look like, take a look at Figure 8-11. Now we need to take a closer look at those other major parameters that I outlined in Tables 8-1 and 8-2, including the layout_gravity and the concept of cell spanning.

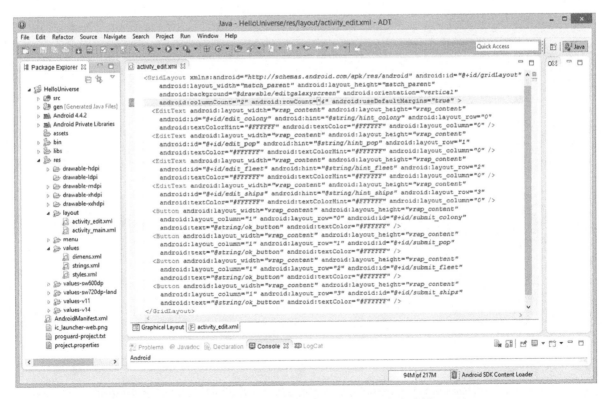

Figure 8-14. The XML markup which will replicate the RelativeLayout UI design using a GridLayout tag

Next, we are going to learn how to span multiple columns, by adding an <AnalogClock> UI widget, underneath the current Edit Galaxy Info UI design. We will do this so that users can reference their local Earth time, while they are utilizing the rest this UI design to update their Galaxy object data fields.

Combining GridLayout Cells: Using a Span

Let's add the <AnalogClock> at the top of the UI design, both in the XML markup and in the screen area itself. To do this, add a new line of space after the parent <GridLayout> tag, and add a child <AnalogClock> tag with the required layout_width and layout_height dimensioning parameters set to **wrap_content**, which is what you normally use for an AnalogClock. Since we are going to put the AnalogClock widget (object) at the top of the design, we'll use a row and column index of 1, a columnSpan of 2 (columns), and a CENTER layout_gravity parameter using the following XML markup, which is also shown in place at the top of your GridLayout in Figure 8-15:

```
<AnalogClock android:layout_width="wrap_content"
             android:layout_height="wrap_content"
             android:layout_row="0"
             android:layout_column="0"
             android:layout_columnSpan="2"
             android:layout_gravity="center_horizontal"  />
```

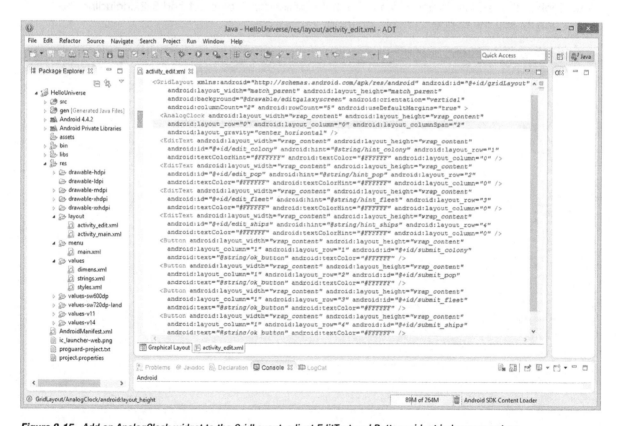

Figure 8-15. Add an AnalogClock widget to the GridLayout, adjust EditText and Button widget index parameters

Since you are placing the AnalogClock UI widget into the first row of the UI design, and **spanning** across the first and second columns by using the **android:columnSpan** parameter with a data value of "**2**," you will need to adjust the android:layout_row parameters for your EditText and Button class UI elements to be numbered from 1 through 4, which represents rows 2 through 5 of the design, whereas before they were numbered from 0 through 3, which represents rows 1 through 4 of the (previous) design.

The cell index changes to the four EditText and four Button child tags are shown in Figure 8-15, in addition to the addition of an AnalogClock UI widget child tag and the **android:layout_gravity** and **android:columnSpan** parameters, which are the parameters which we are focusing our learning process on in this part of the chapter.

Once you have added in the <AnalogClock> child tag and then updated the android:layout_row parameters so that your <EditText> and <Button> child tags will lay out in the grid below the <AnalogClock> UI element, click on the Graphical Layout Editor tab and render the new GridLayout UI design, which should now have an AnalogClock UI element centered at the top of the design (see Figure 8-16).

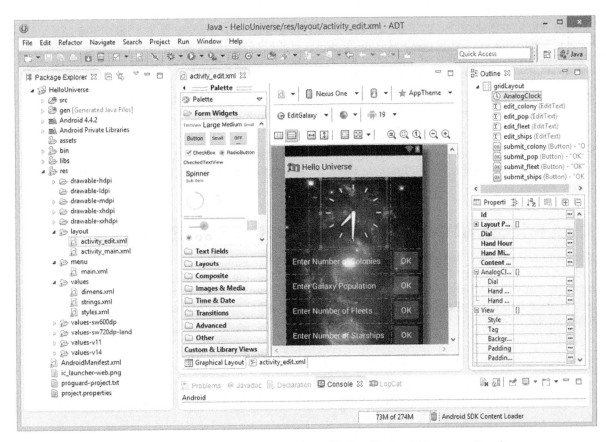

Figure 8-16. Using the Graphical Layout Editor to render the <AnalogClock> widget and GridLayout columnSpan

Notice that the green grid guidelines in the Graphical Layout Editor are not taking your columnSpan parameter into consideration, as a grid line is still showing to the right of the AnalogClock, showing both the left cell and the right cell. If the GLE was "rendering" the columnSpan attribute you added correctly, there would not be a green vertical dotted line in the top row, because you've defined a "span," and that should show as one big cell!

So, as you can see, Eclipse ADT is not 100% perfect, and there are still some code improvements for Google developers, as well as Eclipse ADT developers to implement, so that more and more of the XML parameters are visualized correctly inside of the GLE.

Still, there are some useful features in the GLE, especially for working with the GridLayout class, as you may have noticed from the dozen or so grid-related icons that are located above the preview area in Figure 8-13.

The "take away" here is not to expect Eclipse, ADT, or the Android SDK to be bug-free and to work perfectly; you have to work with what you have got with this development environment at any given point in time. Over time, the IDE (Eclipse) and SDK (Android Developer Tools Plug-In and Android SDK) will improve in both function and stability, as teams of people are working on these tools every day, just as you are working on developing your Android apps every day!

Despite the incorrect grid-rendering guides, the AnalogClock is centering in the top of the GridLayout correctly, so the android:columnSpan parameter has correctly spanned the top two columns into one single column, and the **android:layout_gravity="center"** parameter is centering the AnalogClock correctly within this single grid cell.

If you want to, you can toggle the grid guides icon back off and see that the design looks really professional at this point in time. The only thing I can think of trying to improve this design is right-aligning the EditText widgets!

Next, let's use some more android:layout_gravity parameters, in the <EditText> child UI widgets, to align them with the Button UI widgets on the right instead of left-aligning the labels with the left side of the display screen.

Align GridLayout Cells: Using the layout_gravity Parameter

You have already seen the android:layout_gravity parameter in action centering your AnalogClock widget; let's use it to right-align our EditText widgets with our Button widgets. The easiest way to do this is to copy the UI parameter from the <AnalogClock> tag, paste it into the first <EditText> tag, and change it to use the **right** constant, instead of the center_horizontal constant, as you can see in Figure 8-17.

Figure 8-17. Add android:layout_gravity="right" parameters to <EditText> child UI widgets to align them to Button

Once you have changed the parameter to invoke right-alignment of the widget, copy the parameter from the first <EditText> UI widget child tag and paste it into the other three <EditText> UI widget child tags, so that all of the EditText fields align in the same fashion.

If you have not done so already, click on the Graphical Layout Editor tab at the bottom of the Eclipse central editing pane, and render (preview) your UI design to see if you like the EditText fields aligning with the Button UI elements. I moused-over the second EditText UI element before hitting the PrintScreen button on my keyboard to "grab" the screenshot, so that you could see that the GLE actually gives you real-time UI usage feedback, just like you would get inside of the Nexus One AVD emulator.

As you can see from the moused-over EditText field, it aligns opposite the Button UI element perfectly, and looks quite professional. Left-aligning (the default) or right-aligning the EditText fields is largely a matter of taste, so simply let your client decide which look and feel is best.

It is also interesting to note that the GLE does not access your AndroidManifest.xml file to get your app title value, so you will see the Hello Universe at the top of this screen until you run it in the Nexus One AVD!

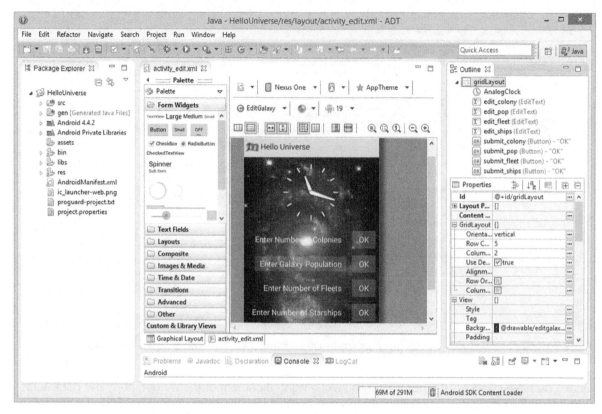

Figure 8-18. *Use the Graphical Layout Editor tab to render or visualize the EditText UI element, now right-aligned*

Go ahead and use the **Run As ➤ Android Application** menu sequence to check out your GridLayout in the AVD. Next, we are going to look at another advanced UI layout container class which was also added in Android 4.0, the **SlidingPaneLayout** class, which is another cool UI layout class that you can use to design impressive UIs!

Using the Android SlidingPaneLayout Class

The SlidingPaneLayout class was another recent class addition to the Android OS, as of the Android 4.0 Ice Cream Sandwich release. This UI layout class was designed to help Android developers to design a two panel, side-by-side, sliding-overlay UI design that can morph between different screen sizes, shapes, and orientations.

The SlidingPaneLayout class was utilized to create the UI foundation for the Google Hangouts application, so if you wanted to see the SlidingPaneLayout user interface in action on your own Android device, it is utilized in at least one of your Android OS-supplied applications, if not more.

What we are going to do with your Hello Universe application in the second part of this chapter is to create the SlidingPaneLayout "Sliding UI" design. This will allow users to slide your main content pane (home screen) to the right to reveal Galaxy selection **ImageButton** UI elements. Your users will be able to click on the alternate galaxy ImageButtons to create and display galaxy information about each of three well-known and popular galaxies in our Hello Universe.

The Android SlidingPaneLayout: Class Specification

The SlidingPaneLayout class is designed to provide a **horizontal**, **dual-pane** user interface layout, for use at the **top-level** of your application's UI design. By "top-level," I mean in your MainActivity. java class, which is really your top-level, or "Home" Activity, for your Android application.

We will implement the current Galaxy Information Screen as one of the two panes in this SlidingPaneLayout UI container, and then add some other UI functionality which will be accessed from the Hello Universe application home screen. This will be done by sliding (or swiping) the galaxy information pane, revealing a galaxy selector UI design. We will create the galaxy selector UI using a GridLayout, to keep the XML markup concise, and to practice what we learned in the first section of the chapter. We'll use ImageButton UI widgets, to introduce you to that popular UI widget class, because we're going to be expanding our knowledge regarding the ImageButton in the next chapter covering graphic design in Android.

Because of the nature of its sliding function or method of operation, a SlidingPane UI layout container is a good solution for creating UI layouts which smoothly adapt across different device screen sizes and different screen orientations. I believe this is a reason Android OS developers added this ViewGroup subclass, so that developers could easily implement a UI design which will expand out to a wider extent on large (tablet and iTV) screens, but which will be able to contract off-screen on small screen (smartwatch or smartphone) devices while still remaining usable.

The SlidingPaneLayout class hierarchy starts with the Java Object master class, and progresses from there to the View class, then to the ViewGroup class, and finally to the SlidingPaneLayout class. The SlidingPaneLayout is also part of a special **android.support.v4.widget** package, and is structured using the following class hierarchy:

```
java.lang.Object
  > android.view.View
    > android.view.ViewGroup
      > android.support.v4.widget.SlidingPaneLayout
```

The Android SlidingPaneLayout class is a **public static** class. It is referenced by using a specialized **support.v4** package by using an **import android.support.v4.widget.SlidingPaneLayout** statement, located at the very top of your Java Activity subclass; in this case, it will be used in your Hello Universe app's MainActivity.java class.

The left pane, which is the first pane to be defined in your SlidingPaneLayout UI XML definition file, is treated as the "**content list**" or as a "**content browser**." This left UI pane is designed to be subordinate to, or of a lower priority than, the "**primary detail view**," which is the right pane, and which should be used to display content.

The optimal use of this SlidingPaneLayout class would involve UI-Content "pairings," which require two panes to display the UI and content or information which you wish to be persistent (visible) on the display screen at all times. An example of this might be a phone contact list (on the right in the primary detail view) along with a UI design providing various types of interactions (call, text, e-mail, tweet, remove) applicable to contacts in the list.

Another example would be displaying a user's recent e-mail list (on the left, using the content browser scenario) with a primary content detail pane or view on the right displaying e-mail contents of an e-mail selected from the content list on the left. In the Hello Universe application, this could be a "visual" list of popular galaxies including the milkyWay galaxy in the left content browser pane, and the resulting display of their planetary information in the right pane primary detail view, once the ImageButton for each Galaxy object is clicked.

The primary objective of the SlidingPaneLayout UI layout container class is to have the UI and the content the UI controls **simultaneously visible**. The SlidingPaneLayout was not meant to be utilized to implement screen-switching UI designs, which allow your user to navigate between different functional Activity subclasses within your Android application.

Task-switching use cases for providing application Activity navigation should use Options Menu and ActionBar-based UI design approaches instead. The use of a SlidingPaneLayout should be for an app or Activity that keeps the user in **"single task mode,"** and optimizes the UI design to maximize the functionality between your UI and your content parts of the screen, which maximizes the user's ability to focus upon, and to complete, the task at hand.

The SlidingPaneLayout approach to UI design should therefore be considered when you require a more "niche" UI layout container, which would be considered to be a memory-efficient approach to implementing a dual-pane UI layout.

This UI layout container should target primary usage on large display screens (tablets, notebooks, and iTV Sets, including the 2K HDTV and 4K UHDTV), but which also needs to provide seamless user experiences for end users on smaller Android device screens (mini-tablets, eBook readers, smartphones, and smartwatches).

SlidingPaneLayout Technical Considerations: Layout Weight

Inside of your SlidingPaneLayout parent container (the parent XML tag), the child UI widget objects (child XML tags), in this case they will be <ImageButton> child tags, are allowed to overlap. This will only occur if the combined width of the UI elements exceeds the available width that you specify for a SlidingPaneLayout parent container.

Your parent SlidingPaneLayout container tag's android:layout_width and android:layout_height parameters will usually be configured using the **MATCH_PARENT** constant. This will define a SlidingPaneLayout to fit all of your Activity subclass's available screen real estate, so that it can "morph" between different device screen sizes and orientations, which is what it's designed to do, so you want this UI layout container to be in "full screen" mode.

When an overlap UI layout scenario is encountered on a smaller display screen size or on a portrait orientation display screen, your user will be able to slide the UI (first or top View child object) away from obscuring your content View. The user accomplishes this by dragging the UI pane, or using a keyboard to navigate in the direction of the overlapped View. If the UI (or content) for the child view is horizontally scrollable, then your user may also grab this content, using the edge of this content.

It is important to note that we are covering another UI container which supports the **android:layout_weight** parameter. The LinearLayout container, which we learned about in Chapter 6, also supports this concept of UI layout weight, so you should be sure to apply everything that you're about to learn about android:layout_weight parameter here to your LinearLayout UI design skills.

I was covering so many other foundational concepts back in Chapter 6 that I didn't have room to get into layout weight, but I will cover it here, while hoping to keep this chapter to a reasonable length!

The SlidingPaneLayout class implements the use of layout weight parameter constants by using its nested class **SlidingDrawerLayout.LayoutParams**. The nested class only contains this one single **android:layout_weight** attribute (or property, or parameter), so rather than adding an entire technical section on this nested class at this point in this chapter, I'll instead include a section discussing what the android:layout_weight parameter will do for the LinearLayout container and for the SlidingPaneLayout container.

UI Spacing in LinearLayout and SlidingPaneLayout: Using Layout Weight

The LinearLayout and SlidingPaneLayout classes are the only UI layout classes which support assigning a UI element weight to an individual child widget UI element within the UI layout container. This is done by using the **android:layout_weight** attribute, along with a **floating-point** (also known in Java as a **float**) numeric value.

This weight attribute, property, or parameter serves to assign a "spacing importance" value to a child widget UI element. This spacing importance is defined in terms of what numeric percentage of the total screen space that the UI widget should occupy within the overall UI layout design, which is usually the entire display screen due to the MATCH_PARENT layout constant.

The layout_weight parameter looks at all of the weights defined across the layout (in the case of the SlidingPane UI, it would be the two panes), but in the case of a LinearLayout, it could be more than two child UI design (nested layout containers or widget) elements. The android:layout_weight parameter uses these numeric weight definitions to determine exactly what percentage of the screen real estate each UI design element will occupy.

A relatively larger weight value will allow a UI element to be allocated more of the total screen real estate in the direction (X or Y dimension) for which that weight has been defined for that UI element. The default setting for the weight parameter, if no weight value is specified, is **zero**, which represents the very lowest priority.

If other UI elements have been assigned a higher weight value, then the default value of zero would be the equivalent of the **wrap_content** layout constant setting being applied to a UI element and no additional spacing will be added around that particular UI design element. If you remember, using wrap_content is like shrink-wrapping your UI widget.

If all of your child UI elements (widgets or nested layouts) specify layout_weight values, then all of the screen space in the parent ViewGroup (SlidingPaneLayout or LinearLayout) will be allocated to the children according to the **relative proportion** between all of the declared weights.

Since **floating-point** values are required, a logical way to approach this would be to use "**percentage of one**" data values. For instance, a floating-point value of **0.25** would represent **25%** of the total screen real estate.

When using this approach to defining screen layout weight percent values, make sure that all of your floating-point android:layout_weight values add up to an even 1.0 value (which would signify 100% of the screen area).

As an example, if you have three child Button UI elements within a parent LinearLayout container, and you set the weight to 1 in two of these, while the other is given no weight parameter (that is, set to 0), then your third Button UI element without any weight will not expand to fill any UI design space and will only occupy the area required by its content. This is why I made a "zero weight is equivalent to the Android wrap_content constant" analogy earlier.

Under this scenario, the other two Button UI elements will expand equally, and fill the remaining screen space. If the third UI Button element were to be given a weight of 2, instead of 0, that UI Button would be specified as being more important (or having more screen layout weight) than your other two UI Button elements. Under this scenario, that UI Button would get half of your total screen real estate, while the first two UI Buttons share the rest equally, that is, each would get one-quarter, or 25%, of the total UI design space.

The way that these relative weights would be calculated is as follows: to get the total weight, add 1+1+2=4 and then to calculate each relative weight percentage, divide the weight value by the total value, like so: 2/4 is 50% and 1/4 is 25% for the other two.

To give each UI Button an equal portion of the screen space, you would use a layout_weight value of 0.333.

As I mentioned previously, an easier way to set layout_weight would be to use **percentage of one** floating-point values, such as using 0.5 instead of 2, and 0.25 instead of 1, for this particular example. Doing it this way would allow you to numerically conceptualize the screen weight as **percentages** of the screen width (or height, if using a LinearLayout definition with orientation="vertical"), rather than using whole numbers relative to each other.

It is important to note that float (decimal) data values can accept integer (whole number) data values, since a value of 2 can also be considered to be a 2.0 value, so integer values will always be accepted in float value data fields.

The **layout_weight** parameter will be used by the SlidingPaneLayout "engine" (algorithm) specifically, in order to determine how Android will divide any leftover space between the two panes after a change in screen size or orientation has been detected by Android, and the new screen measurement data has been assessed. The weight parameter is not as critical (and not as useful) for the SlidingPaneLayout as it is for the LinearLayout container. The android:layout_weight parameter for the SlidingPaneLayout will be considered relevant by the SlidingPane algorithm (engine) only for the width dimension, whereas LinearLayout can use weight in the height dimension as well as in the width dimension.

When the two panes involved in a SlidingPane UI design do not overlap at all, the layout_weight will behave as it would in a LinearLayout. This allows developers to define the percentage of the screen that is used by each of the two panes. Remember, the two weight values need to add up to 100%, so the best approach is to use floating-point values that add up to one, such as 0.35 for 35% of your screen width, and 0.65 for the other 65% of screen width. This allows Android developers to assign very precise dual pane dividing values.

If the two panes (and the child UI widgets inside of them) are constrained by the device screen width, such as in a portrait display orientation, or smaller Android devices, such as smartwatches, the two panes will overlap, and a more complex weight assessment algorithm will be utilized.

As you might imagine, in this circumstance, your layout weight specification is not followed (applied) as precisely by the SlidingPaneLayout algorithm, and will instead favor your right-side primary content pane, and will allow the left-side UI pane to slide over the primary content only when the UI is needed by the user.

A weight assigned to the fixed (right) content pane that becomes covered by the (left) UI pane will be evaluated in such a way that the content pane will be sized to fill most of the available screen space. A small (minimized) strip of the UI pane will still be visible on the left, which will allow the user to grab the slideable pane and pull it back over the content view when the UI is needed by the end user for the application's intended functionality.

Besides SlidingPaneLayout.LayoutParams and its weight parameter, there are two other nested classes under the SlidingPaneLayout class. These include a **SlidingPaneLayout.PanelSlideListener** interface, which is an **event listener interface** that was specifically designed to be used for monitoring touchscreen (slide) events associated with your SlidingPaneLayout UI design implementations. You should utilize this interface for subclassing your own PanelSlideListener subclass, in order to create a customized MyPanelSlideListener class implementation.

There is also a **SlidingPaneLayout.SimplePanelSlideListener** nested class, which provides a **simple listener class**. What a simple listener class does is that it subclasses the SlidingPaneLayout. PanelSlideListener interface, and only implements the minimum amount of functionality for that class. This simply means that the subclass will add zero additional features and will contain only basic event listening functionality from the superclass.

You will create an **activity_slidingPane.xml** UI definition file, as well as a **SlidingPaneActivity. java** class, and then define the SlidingPaneLayout UI design and implement some digital image compositing techniques to make it look professional and exciting to the end user. After that, you'll test the UI design across different screen sizes and orientations to see it work!

Using SlidingPaneLayout: Galaxy Selector

Let's get down to business and implement a SlidingPaneLayout in your Galaxy Information Screen UI design so that you can choose from more than one popular galaxy, and have its information update in your information screen. To accomplish this, you will have to create and implement the following structural structures in your MainActivity.java code and your activity_main.xml markup for your Hello Universe Android application:

- Wrap an **<android.support.v4.widget.SlidingPaneLayout>** parent tag around the existing <LinearLayout> UI design structure, which will place that UI design structure inside of the SlidingPane UI engine as one of the two sliding panes for this SlidingPaneLayout class.

- Create another vertical <LinearLayout> UI layout design containing three <ImageButton> UI widgets, so you can get started at a beginning level with the ImageButton class, which we will be learning about in detail in the next chapter on graphic design for Android.

- Configure the <ImageButton> and <LinearLayout> XML tags with the minimum amount of parameters which will be needed to accomplish a three ImageButton UI for the second pane of the SlidingPaneLayout UI design.

- Add three new <string> constant XML parameters containing the galaxy names for the sight-impaired to use (hear) when they encounter the ImageButton. Note that Android requires the android:contentDescription parameter in all <ImageView> and <ImageButton> UI widgets.

- Run the SlidingPaneLayout UI design modification in the Nexus One AVD emulator to see the progress in the new sliding pane UI design.

- Swap the order of the <LinearLayout> structures to put the planet information pane as the top-most pane in the SlidingPaneLayout engine by copying the <LinearLayout> and nested <ImageButton> tags to the top of the UI design underneath the <SlidingPaneLayout> parent tag, which will swap the ImageButton UI pane with the Planet Information Screen pane.

- Run the revised SlidingPaneLayout UI design adjustments in the Nexus One AVD emulator to make sure that the panes have switched places in the final sliding pane UI design.

Creating a SlidingPaneLayout: Revising the XML

What we want to do is to make the Galaxy Information Screen UI design that you created in Chapter 6 one of the SlidingPaneLayout UI panes, so we are going to put your existing **<LinearLayout>** structure inside of this SlidingPaneLayout structure, which uses the parent tag from the android.v4 support package which uses the tag format:

<android.v4.widget.SlidingPaneLayout>

You will insert this parent tag at the top of the **activity_main.xml** file.

Add the <android.support.v4.widget.SlidingPaneLayout> tag at the top of your activity_main.xml file, and cut and paste the **xmlns:android**, **xmlns:tools** and **tools:context** parameters from the <LinearLayout> parent layout container into the (now) SlidingPaneLayout parent container, and add an **spLayout** ID, as shown in Figure 8-19.

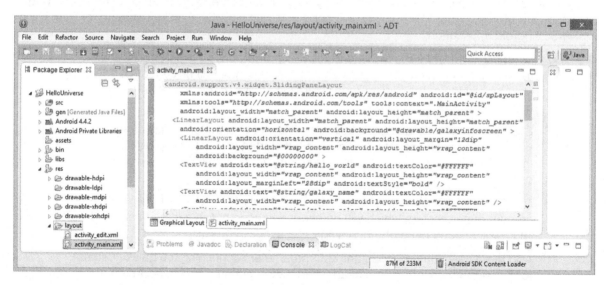

Figure 8-19. Add a SlidingPaneLayout parent layout container on the outside of your current LinearLayout design

Then copy and paste the required layout_width and layout_height parameters from the <LinearLayout> tag into the <SlidingPaneLayout> parent tag, so that the parameter configuration shown in Figure 8-19 is the following:

```
<android.support.v4.widget.SlidingPaneLayout
   xmlns:android="http://schemas.android.com/apk/res/android" android:id="@+id/spLayout"
   xmlns:tools="http://schemas.android.com/tools" tools:context=".MainActivity"
   android:layout_width="match_parent" android:layout_height="match_parent" >
```

Go to the bottom of the new UI definition, and add a <LinearLayout> container structure, right above the closing <SlidingPaneLayout> container closing tag, and add an <ImageButton> tag inside it, as is shown in Figure 8-20.

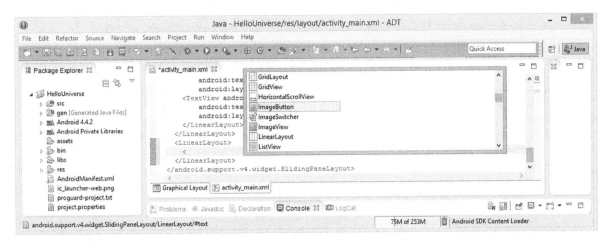

Figure 8-20. Add a <LinearLayout> at the end of the existing design and add an <ImageButton> child tag inside it

Since the <ImageButton> UI widget needs a digital image to use for its "source" or android:src parameter, let's copy the three galaxy images, named **galaxybutton1.png**, **galaxybutton2.png**, and **galaxybutton3.png** into the **/res** folder using the Windows Explorer file management utility next.

As you can see in Figure 8-21, I have copied these files, which are in the project files repository for the book, into the **/res/drawable-hdpi** folder.

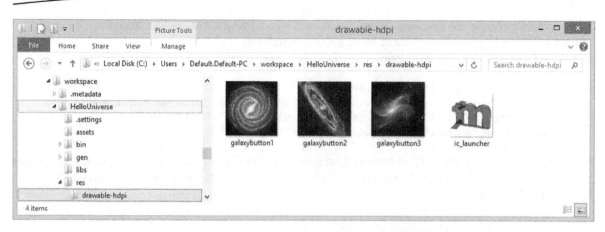

Figure 8-21. Copy the galaxybutton PNG24 images into your /workspace/HelloUniverse/res/drawable-hdpi folder

We will be learning how to support all of these different drawable folders in the next chapter when we cover the art of Android graphic design.

Name the <ImageButton> UI widget **galaxyOne** using the **android:id** parameter, and then set the **android:src** image source file parameter to reference the **@drawable/galaxybutton1** asset. Make sure to copy the required **layout_width** and **layout_height** parameters from the <TextView> tag (above), set to **wrap_content**, as is shown in Figure 8-22.

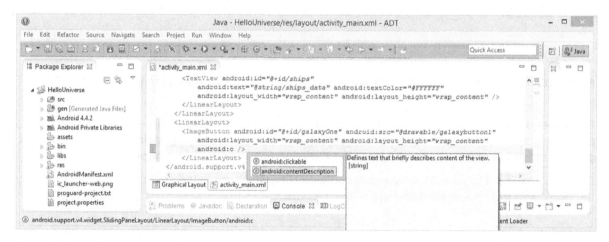

Figure 8-22. Configure the <ImageButton> tag with parameters and add a required contentDescription parameter

Remember that if you don't add an **android:contentDescription** parameter to any digital-image–related widget, such as <ImageView> and <ImageButton>, you will get a red error highlight in your markup. So next, type in the **android:c** part of this parameter, and then select the contentDescription parameter option, and set it to the value of **@string/galaxyone**, which will (soon) be a <string> constant with the data value of "Milky Way Galaxy."

Next, let's create three new <string> constants for our three galaxy name content description parameters, as is shown in Figure 8-23.

Figure 8-23. Adding <string> constants with the ImageButton's galaxy names for use with the contentDescription

The values for the three galaxy content descriptions should be "Milky Way Galaxy" for galaxyone, "Andromeda Galaxy" for galaxytwo, and "Spiral Galaxy M106" for galaxythree. As I mentioned previously in the book, I am using data and imagery from NASA, which is legally allowed to be utilized for educational purposes, as I am doing here in this book.

The completed <ImageButton> tag and parameters, shown in Figure 8-24, will look like the following markup:

```
<ImageButton android:id="@+id/galaxyOne" android:src="@drawable/galaxybutton1"
        android:layout_width="wrap_content" android:layout_height="wrap_content"
        android:contentDescription="@string/galaxyone"  />
```

Figure 8-24. Add a required layout_width and layout_height to <LinearLayout> and vertical orientation parameter

The easy way to create the next two <ImageButton> tags is to copy and paste the first <ImageButton> tag under itself two more times, changing the **galaxyOne** ID to **galaxyTwo** and **galaxyThree**, respectively, and changing the **galaxybutton1** to **galaxybutton2** and **galaxybutton3** and the **galaxyone** to **galaxytwo** and **galaxythree**.

Since the Graphical Layout Editor tab will not be able to correctly "render" the SlidingPaneLayout's algorithm (engine) (as you will see, it only previews your LinearLayout of ImageButton UI elements, which look great, by the way), let's use the **Run As ➤ Android Application** menu sequence (right-click on your project folder to get to this menu, if you forgot where to locate it) to test the current SlidingPaneLayout class UI design now!

As you can see in Figure 8-25, the SlidingPaneLayout class's engine (algorithm) is evaluating the ImageButton UI pane as the top pane, and, if you drag the pane to the right, you'll reveal the Galaxy Information Screen pane underneath it.

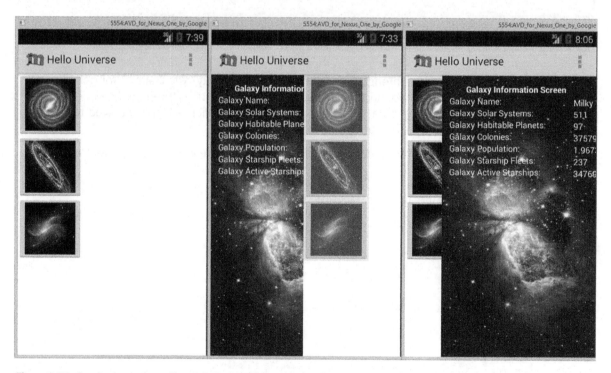

Figure 8-25. *Previewing an ImageButton (left), first SlidingPane configuration (center), and final SlidingPane (right)*

Notice how your top pane fades as it slides to the right, as can be seen via the (lighter) ImageButtons, in the center part of Figure 8-25.

Since you want your Galaxy Information Screen to be the prominent pane in the UI (that is, the top-most pane), which slides over the less-prominent (bottom-most) UI part of your sliding pane UI design, you will need to change the order of your <LinearLayout> containers within your <SlidingPaneLayout> parent container.

To achieve this change, you will need to cut and paste the <LinearLayout> construct which you just constructed at the end of the SlidingPaneLayout UI definition containing the three <ImageButton> UI elements to the top of the <SlidingPaneLayout> container, relocating it directly underneath the opening <SlidingPaneLayout> tag.

The SlidingPaneLayout algorithm (engine) will take the two highest-level (top-most) child layout container constructs and put them into the UI pane and the content panes, respectively. In pseudo-code, your two constructs are structured as follows:

```
<SlidingPaneLayout>
     <LinearLayout>
          <ImageButtons>
     </LinearLayout>
     <LinearLayout>
          <LinearLayout>
             <TextViews>
          </LinearLayout>
          <LinearLayout>
              <TextViews>
          </LinearLayout>
     </LinearLayout>
</SlidingPaneLayout>
```

Now that your <ImageButton> LinearLayout structure is at the top of your <SlidingPaneLayout> container, as shown in Figure 8-26, you can again use the **Run As ➤ Android Application** menu sequence so that you can see that you have achieved the intended result, shown on the right-hand side of Figure 8-25.

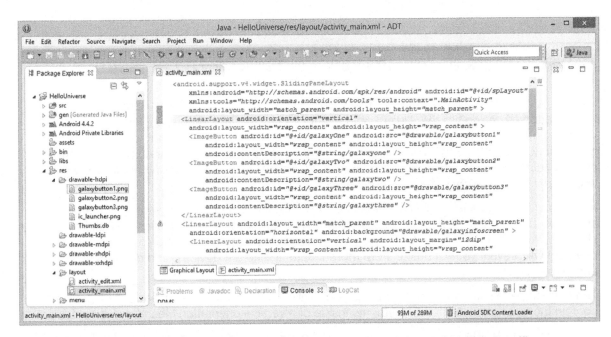

Figure 8-26. Move the <LinearLayout> containing the <ImageButton> UI widgets to the top of the SlidingPane UI

Before we finish learning about the Android SlidingPaneLayout class, which we will be customizing further in the next chapter on graphic design for Android, we should take a look at how to utilize the **android:layout_width** and **android:layout_weight** parameters inside of the two child UI panes. The panes underneath the <SlidingPaneLayout> tag can contain parameters defining what percentage of the screen should be used on widescreen (layout_weight), and how many device independent pixels (DIP) the UI pane should open up to be, when the user slides the content pane and uncovers the UI pane (layout_width). Once we have discussed these two key parameters, we will have covered everything that you should know about the SlidingPaneLayout class.

Set Pane Size: layout_width and layout_weight

Add an android:layout_weight="0.25" and also change the android:layout_width to a "hard-coded" DIP value of **110**, using an android:layout_width="110dip" parameter, and then change the android:layout_height to use a **match_parent** constant, as shown in Figure 8-27.

Figure 8-27. *Add a layout_weight parameter and change layout_height to match_parent and layout_width to 110dip*

Using a MATCH_PARENT constant will make sure that the height of your first <LinearLayout> ImageButton UI design fills the SlidingPaneLayout UI pane's height dimension, which is what you want it to do. Generally, for a SlidingPaneLayout class UI design, you will want to use a match_parent constant for the child UI layout containers underneath the <SlidingPaneLayout> parent tag, as the SlidingPaneLayout deals only with the width dimension in its processing engine (algorithm) and simply fills the height dimension completely.

It is interesting to note that if you define a fixed value for the android:layout_width parameter using an integer DIP (or dip or dp) value, you can control how far out your content pane will slide over your UI pane. You will generally want to avoid hard coding DIP values in your Android UI design, since doing so will prevent your UI design from morphing to fit different devices (and different screen sizes and screen shapes).

The content pane you now have defined as your Galaxy Information Screen, and the UI pane, now contain the three ImageButton UI elements inside of a vertical orientation LinearLayout container.

By defining a **110 DIP** layout_width value, you will constrain your users to dragging the Galaxy Information Screen just far enough to perfectly reveal the three ImageButtons which you created during this chapter, and which we will refine further, along with finishing the Java code for this SlidingPaneLayout UI design, in the next chapter.

The difference between defining the android:layout_width using an Android OS constant and using a fixed DIP value is shown on the left and right sides of Figure 8-28, respectively. As you will see when you play around with the XML markup a bit, the fixed DIP android:layout_width value allows you to constrain exactly how far the content pane will slide to the right and how much of the UI pane it will reveal.

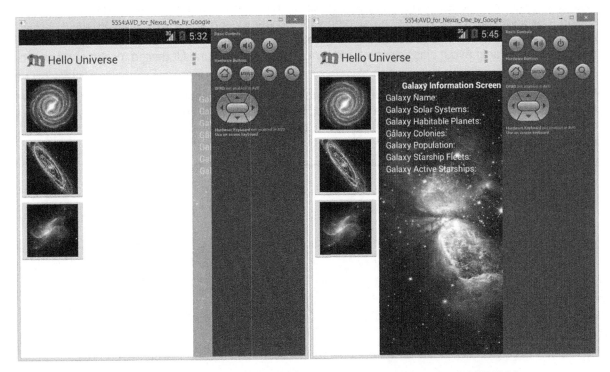

Figure 8-28. Test the UI design in the Nexus One AVD with layout_width as match_parent and as 110 DIP (right)

I determined a DIP setting that would show the ImageButton UI elements and leave an even amount of margin around them, giving the most professional visual result with the basic ImageButton parameter configuration. We will be changing and enhancing the ImageButton in the next chapter. As you can see, we're currently using this UI widget simply to display an image on top of a button element. As you'll soon see, it can do much more!

Summary

In this eighth chapter, you learned about some more advanced Android 4.0 layout container classes, including the **GridLayout** class and the **SlidingPaneLayout** class. You learned about how the "engines," or algorithms, behind these classes work, and what parameters you need to use in your child UI widgets to harness this power.

You learned about the seven global or parent configuration parameters which go in the parent <GridLayout> tag itself, as well as how to use the five local (child) grid cell definition parameters which you can use to affect how child UI widgets in the grid are positioned, aligned, and even span between grid cells. You upgraded your Hello Universe application to use the Android 4.0 API Level 14 in your AndroidManifest.xml file, so these UIs work.

You learned about how to leverage the most popular user interface widget, the **ImageButton** class, and how to set it up using its basic **android:src** digital image source parameter to reference some cool galaxy button images we are going to expand on in the next chapter. You also learned how to set-up a SlidingPaneLayout UI design using only XML markup, and (for now) using zero Java code changes. You learned how the **android:layout_weight** and **android:layout_width** parameters affect how the SlidingPaneLayout class's engine will render your sliding pane UI design for the end users of your application.

Next, in Chapter 9, you'll learn all about graphic design for Android, including foundational graphics theories and concepts, how to create a wide spectrum of resolution density image assets, how to create interactive multi-state ImageButton assets, how to use the NinePatch classes and the 9-patch tool, and about image compositing.

Android Graphic Design: Making Your UI Designs Visual

In the first half of the book, I tried to stay as much "inside" of Android OS, Android SDK, and Eclipse ADT as possible, to get a good "head start" on the dozens of core classes and concepts which the Android developer should have knowledge of and mastery of, in order to have a global overview of how everything in the Android OS fits together.

In the second half of the book, which will show you how to incorporate new media elements into your app's UI design, such as digital images, digital audio, digital video, and animation, we will venture "outside" of the core Android development tools, and use software packages outside of Eclipse ADT which are commonly used by application developers for new media content development.

You got a brief taste of this in Chapter 3 when we used the popular GIMP 2.8 digital imaging application software to create a custom application icon for the Hello Universe application which we had just created. We will also utilize GIMP in this chapter, to explore the graphics concepts for this chapter and get some hands-on experience in applying image compositing concepts and techniques we will be discovering during the course of the chapter.

There is no way I can cover all of the graphics concepts and topics that I would like to in one single chapter, at least not using less than a hundred pages! However, if you want to dive into this particular topic in Android app development specifically, Apress has the *Pro Android Graphics* (Apress, 2013) title that I wrote, which features approximately 620 pages dedicated to this popular Android graphic design concepts and techniques topic, and all of which applies to both Android 4.x as well as Android 5.x.

We will be covering several of the core Android classes which are used to implement graphic design elements, such as **ImageButton** (which we started on in Chapter 8), **ImageView**, and **NinePatch**. During this chapter, we will utilize these three Android graphics classes to "skin" the SlidingPane UI layout container design. **Skinning** the UI design using graphics elements will enhance the visual aspects of this UI design, and increase its interest to the end-user, as well as increasing its perceived level of professionalism. We will also finish what we started in the previous chapter and "wire up" the ImageButton widgets to make your SlidingPaneLayout UI interactive.

Imaging Concepts, Formats, and Techniques

The first thing that we need to do is to get a "knowledge foundation" regarding the concepts, formats, and terms which we are going to use during the rest of this book, regarding working with digital images. This area is most commonly called graphic design, although I am going to approach it from a more professional "digital imaging" and "image compositing" standpoint.

The concepts, formats, techniques, and terminology that I cover in this chapter will also apply to animation and digital video new media assets, as both of these are based on digital imagery in one way or another, so we will be able to build on the knowledge base created in this chapter in future chapters, which I am trying to do in each and every chapter in this book, so your knowledge of Android increases exponentially, and in a logical fashion.

First, we will cover the **pixel**, the foundational element of the digital image, and then the concept of **resolution**, or the size of the digital image, and then the concept of **aspect ratio**, or the shape of the digital image. Once we are done with the second dimension (2D) aspects, we will go into the third dimension (3D) and look at how the colors of each pixel are created using red, green, and blue (RGB) **layers** of color or color "plates" and then at how transparency is defined within an image using a fourth "**alpha**" layer which contains transparency values.

After that, we'll get into more advanced digital imaging concepts like **compositing** and pixel **blending**, and take a look at how all this knowledge is used when using digital image formats and **codecs** to compress image assets.

The Foundation of Digital Images: The "Pixel"

Digital Images are made up of two-dimensional, or **2D**, arrays (grids) containing "**pixels**." The industry term pixel is a conjugation of two words: **pictures** (commonly called **pix**) and **elements** (shortened to be just **els**).

The number of pixels in any digital image asset should be expressed using a term called **resolution**, which is the number of pixels in both the **width** (denoted using a **W** or an **X** for the **x-axis**) and the **height** (denoted using an **H** or a **Y** for the y-axis) image **dimensions**. The resolution of an image asset is usually expressed using two (X and Y) numbers with an "x" in the middle, such as **800x480**, or using the word "by," such as **800 by 480 pixels**.

To find the total number of pixels that are in a 2D image, simply **multiply** the width pixels by the height pixels. For instance, an HDTV resolution 1920 by 1080 image will contain 2,073,600 pixels, over 2 million pixels, also referred to as two **megapixels**. The more pixels which are in an image, the higher its resolution.

Just like with digital cameras, which range from 3 megapixel smartphone cameras to 75 megapixel DSLRs, the more megapixels that are in the digital image grid or array, the higher quality level the image will have. This is why 4K UHDTV screens, which have a resolution of 4096 by 2160, are becoming quite popular.

Android supports everything from **low-resolution** 320 by 240 pixel display screens on Android smartwatches, such as the Neptune Pine or entry-level flip-phones and small screen phones, to **medium-resolution** 854 by 480 pixel display screens on mini-tablets and smartphones, to **high-resolution** 1280 by 720 pixel display screens on HD smartphones and medium size tablets, to **extra high-resolution** 1920 by 1080 pixel display screens on large tablets and iTV sets, to the new **super high-resolution** 2560 by 1440 (such as on the Samsung Galaxy S5) and 4096 by 2160 (4K iTV Sets) pixel display screens on professional smartphones and 4K iTV sets. It's challenging to develop an app which can span from smartwatches to 4K iTV Sets!

The Shape of a Digital Image: The Aspect Ratio

A slightly more complicated aspect (no pun intended) of image resolution would be the image's **aspect ratio**, a concept which also applies to Android device (hardware) display screens. Aspect ratio is the **ratio of width to height** or **W:H**, or, if you like to think in terms of an x-axis and y-axis, it would be X:Y. The aspect ratio will define the **shape** of an image or display screen; that is, how square or rectangular (popularly called widescreen) the image or the display screen might be.

A **1:1** aspect ratio display screen (or digital image) is **perfectly square**. It is important to note that it is this **ratio** between these two numbers that defines the shape of the image or screen, and not these numbers themselves, and that's why it is called an aspect **ratio**, although it's often called "aspect" for short.

Many Android display screens these days use an HDTV widescreen aspect ratio, which is **16:9**. However, some use a less wide, or taller, **16:10** (or 8:5, if you prefer) aspect ratio. Even wider screens will also surely appear on the market soon, so look for **16:8** (or 2:1, if you prefer) ultra-wide screens, which will have a 2160 by 1080 resolution.

An image aspect ratio is usually expressed as the smallest set or pair of numbers that can be achieved (reached) on either side of the aspect ratio colon. If you paid attention in High School, when you were learning all about lowest (or least) common denominators, then this aspect ratio mathematics should be fairly easy to calculate and to understand.

I usually do this mathematical matriculation (say this five times rapidly, to make what we are about to do seem easier) by continuing to divide each side by **two**. Taking the fairly odd-ball 1280 by 1024 (called SXGA in the display industry) resolution as an example, half of 1280:1024 is 640:512, and half of that would be 320:256, half of that is 160:128, and half of that again is 80:64, half of that is 40:32, half of that is 20:16, half of that is 10:8, half of that is 5:4, so an SXGA screen uses a **5:4** aspect ratio.

Interestingly, all of the above ratios are the same aspect ratio, and all are valid. So if you want to take the really easy way out, replace the "x" in your image resolution with a colon and you have an aspect ratio for the image, although distilling it down to its lowest format, as we've done here, is far more useful!

Original PC screens used a "squarer" **4:3** aspect ratio, and early **3:2** aspect ratio CRT "cathode ray tube" TV sets were nearly square. The closer the numbers on either side of the colon are to each other in size, the more square an image or a screen will be (identical numbers, remember, are a square aspect), unless one of the numbers is a one!

A 2:1 aspect is a widescreen display, and a 3:1 aspect display would be downright **panoramic**! The current market trend is certainly toward wider screens and higher resolution displays; however, Android smartwatches could change this trend back toward square aspect ratios, which are certainly useful in a wide variety of applications.

Coloring Your Digital Images: RGB Color Theory

So now you understand digital image pixels, and how they're arranged using 2D rectangular arrays, at a specific aspect ratio which defines their rectangular shape! The next logical aspect (again, no pun intended) to look into is how each of those pixels assign their **color values**. Color values for pixels are defined by the amount of three colors, **red**, **green**, and **blue** (hence the term **RGB**), which are present in varying amounts in each pixel. Android display screens utilize **additive color**, which is where the wavelengths of light for each RGB color plane are **summed** together. Additive color can be used to create tens of millions of different color values, and is utilized in the popular LED displays used in iTVs, smartphones, laptops and tablets. Additive color is the opposite of **subtractive color**, which is utilized in printers.

To show the difference, under a subtractive color model, mixing a red color with a green (using inks) will yield a purple color, whereas in an additive color model, mixing a red color with a green color (using light) will yield a yellow color. Subtractive color models are limited in the spectrum of color that they can produce, whereas the additive color model can produce every color under the rainbow (or, I should say, every color in the universe!).

The amount, or numbers, of red, green, and blue "shades" or intensities of light that you have available to mix together will determine the total amount of colors which you will be able to reproduce. In today's digital device hardware capabilities, we can produce **eight bits** (8-bit) or **256 levels** of light intensity for each red, green, and blue (RGB) color.

We can generate this color for each pixel individually, so every pixel in your image can have 256 levels of color intensity variation, for each of these red, green, and blue values. Each of these RGB "plates" or "planes" will use one byte of data per red, green, and blue color. A byte uses an 8-bit data value, which allows it to represent the color intensity level from a minimum of zero (off, no color contributed, or black if all the RGB planes are using this value) to a maximum of 255 (fully on, maximum color contributed, or white if all RGB planes are using this value).

The Number of Colors in a Digital Image: Color Depth

The number of data bits which are used to represent the amount or number of colors in a digital image is referred to as the **color depth** of that image. It is important to note that in digital imaging, less than 8 bits can be used to represent the amount of colors in an image, but only when you are using an **indexed color** model, which we'll be learning about soon.

There are several common color depth levels used in the digital imaging industry, and I will outline the most common ones here, along with the digital image file formats used with each color depth in the Android OS. The lowest color depth exists using the **8-bit indexed color** digital image format. An indexed color image will have a maximum of **256** total color values per pixel and will use the **GIF** and **PNG8** image formats to contain this indexed color type of digital image data. An indexed color image will not have three (RGB) color planes, so it is generally three times smaller than a **truecolor** RGB image. Instead of the three (RGB) color planes, indexed color uses a "**palette**" of up to 256 color values to represent all of the colors in the digital image.

A medium color depth image, which is not supported in Android, but which I will discuss here, for continuity of learning, will feature the **16-bit "high color"** color depth. A high color image will contain **65,536** colors. This would be calculated as 256 times 256 (8-bit and 8-bit is 16-bit), and is supported using TARGA (TGA) and Tagged Image File Format (TIFF) image formats, as well as the Windows BMP digital image file format.

A 24-bit truecolor color depth image will feature the full 8-bit color data values for each RGB color plate (color plane) and will be capable of displaying more than 16.7 million potential colors per pixel. This is calculated as 256 times 256 times 256 (8-bit and 8-bit and 8-bit is 24-bit), and equals **16,777,216** colors. Android file formats which are capable of supporting 24-bit color include **JPEG** (using a **.jpg** file extension), **PNG24** and **PNG32** (using a **.png** file extension), and **WebP** (using the **.webp** extension).

Using 24-bit color depth will give you the highest digital image quality level, which is why Android prefers the use of the PNG24 or the JPEG image file format. Since PNG24 is **lossless**, which means that it loses no quality (and none of the original image's data) during the compression process, it has the highest quality compression (and the lowest original image data loss), along with the highest quality color depth. This is the reason why PNG24 is the preferred digital image format to use as far as the Android OS is concerned, because its usage will ultimately produce the highest quality visual result for your Android applications.

It is important to note that there are higher color depth images out there, called **HDRI**, or **High Dynamic Range Images**, that use 32-bit, 48-bit, and even 64-bit color depths. The hope is that the Android OS (and device hardware) will probably move to support these extremely high digital image color depth standards, which are currently being utilized for advanced i3D console games.

Representing Colors in Android: Hexadecimal Notation

Now that you know what color depth is, and that colors are represented as a combination of three different red, green, and blue (RGB) color channels within any given image, we need to look at how, as programmers, we are going to represent these three RGB color channel values inside of our Android applications to create any single one of these 16,777,216 colors.

It is important to note that in the Android OS, color is not only used in digital images, commonly called **bitmap** images, but also in **2D illustration**, which is commonly referred to as **shapes** or **vector** images, as well as in **color settings**, such as the background color value utilized in your user interface screen, or for your textColor values, for instance, that define what color your text will be.

In Android, different levels of RGB color intensity are represented as data values using **hexadecimal notation**. Hexadecimal notation is based on the original **Base-16** computer notation used decades ago to represent 16 bits of data value. Unlike Base-10, which counts from zero through 9, Base-16 counts from zero through F, where F would represent a Base-10 value of 15 (zero through 15 gives you 16 data values).

To tell the Android OS that we are giving it a hexadecimal value, we preface these Base-16 values using the **pound sign**, also known as a **hash tag**, like this: **#FFFFFF**. Because each slot in this 24-bit hexadecimal representation represents one Base-16 value, to get the 256 values we need for each RGB color will take **2** of these slots, as 16 times 16 equals 256. Thus, for a 24-bit image, we would need **6** slots after the hash tag, and for a 32-bit image, we would need **8** slots after the hash tag. We will be covering what these 32-bit type of digital images are, and what they are used for, during the next section of this chapter.

These hexadecimal data slots represent the **RGB values** in the following format: **#RRGGBB**. Thus, for the color white, all red, green, and blue channels in this hexadecimal color data value representation are at the maximum luminosity of fully on, or FF, which would be 16 times 16, or the full 256 data value for each RGB color **channel**. For this reason, the value #FFFFFF would represent the whitest white that is possible.

> **Note**   As you can see, I'm giving you all of the different industry terminology (color channel, color plane, color plate) that you will find currently being used in the graphics industry. All of these terms are used interchangeably.

When you "**additively**" **sum** all of these RGB colors together, you will get white light. As I have mentioned before, the color **yellow** is represented by the red and green channels being on and the blue channel being off, so the hexadecimal notation representation for the color yellow would be **#FFFF00**, where both red and green channel slots are on, using FF for a color intensity (level) value of 256, and the blue channel slots are fully off using 00, a zero value.

As I mentioned earlier in this section, there is also a **32-bit** image color depth whose data values are represented using the **ARGB** color channel model, where the **A** stands for **alpha**, which is short for **alpha channel**. We'll be going over the concept of **image alpha** and alpha channels in far greater detail during the next section of the chapter on alpha channels, and we will also cover the related concept of **pixel blending**. Let's get more advanced in Android graphic design so we can make our applications truly stand out!

The hexadecimal notation data slots for an ARGB color channel model data values will hold data in the following format: **#AARRGGBB**. Thus, to represent the fully opaque color white, all alpha, red, green, and blue channels in this hexadecimal color data value representation would be at a maximum luminosity (as well as opacity), and the alpha channel fully opaque, as represented by an FF value, so its hexadecimal value would be: **#FFFFFFFF**.

A **100% transparent** alpha channel is represented by the alpha channel slots being set to **zero**; thus, a fully transparent image pixel could be **#00FFFFFF**, or **#00000000**. It is important to notice that if an image alpha channel is set to be fully transparent, then each pixel's color value (represented by the last six hexadecimal data slot values) does not even matter, and thus you could put any color value in these last six data slots!

Image Compositing Transparency: Alpha Channels

In this section of the chapter, we'll take a look at how digital images are **composited** together, which is a process known as **image compositing**, which is usually done by a professional who is called a digital image **compositor**.

Digital image compositing is the process of **blending** together more than one **layer** of digital imagery, in order to obtain the resulting image. A composite image on a display screen will appear as though it is one single image, when in fact, it is actually a collection (a "stack") of more than one **seamlessly** composited digital image **layers**.

To be able to accomplish seamless image compositing using layers, the images used in each layer need to have an **alpha channel** (a transparency level) value associated with each pixel in the image. We can utilize this alpha value for each pixel in the image to precisely control the blending of that pixel with the other pixels in the same image **coordinate** or location, but which are on the other layers above and below that particular image layer. It is because of this stacked layer paradigm that I refer to this compositing as 3D, as the layers are stacked into place along or using a **Z-axis**, and can be said to have a particular **Z-order**. Don't get this confused with 3D modeling software such as Blender, as the end result of a digital image compositing (layer) stack is still a resulting 2D digital image asset.

Like the other RGB channels, the alpha channel also has **256 levels of transparency** which are represented via the first two slots in the hexadecimal representation for the **ARGB** data value, which has 8 slots (32-bits) of data, rather than the 6 slots used to represent a 24-bit image. A 24-bit image could thus be thought of as being a 32-bit image with no alpha channel data. Indeed, if there is no alpha channel data, why waste another 8 bits of data storage, even if that alpha channel is filled with F values, representing fully opaque pixel values. A 32-bit image with an alpha channel filled with F values has 25% more data than a 24-bit image with no alpha channel, and yet it would yield the same exact result, so don't use a 32-bit image unless you need to use transparency values for the pixels in that image (for compositing purposes).

So, to summarize, a 24-bit image has no alpha channel, and is not going to be used for image compositing, unless it is the **bottom plate** in the compositing layer stack, whereas a 32-bit image is going to be used as a compositing layer, on top of something else which will need the ability to show through (via transparency values defined in the image alpha channel) in some of the pixel locations in order to create the final seamlessly composited digital image.

How does having an alpha channel and using digital image compositing factor into my Android graphics design pipeline, you might be wondering. The primary advantage here is the ability to split what looks like one single image into a number of component layers. The reason for doing this is to be able to apply Java code logic to individual layer elements, in order to control various parts of a 2D image which you could not otherwise individually control, were the image simply one single 24-bit image, which can be transformed as a whole, but not on a per-subject (per pixel area) basis as it could be if each image element were on its own layer, and thus a separate element in memory, which could later be controlled using program logic.

Algorithmic Image Compositing: Blending Modes

There is another more powerful aspect of image compositing called **blending modes**. Any of you familiar with Photoshop or GIMP have seen that you can set each layer in an image composite to use different blending modes. Blending modes are **algorithms** that specify how the pixels contained within that layer are blended (mathematically) with the previous layers (underneath that layer). This pixel blending algorithm will take into account your transparency level. By combining blending modes and transparency, you can achieve virtually any digital image compositing result, or special effect, that you are trying to achieve. Since there are entire books written on using blending modes, and the effects you can create, I won't get into that too much here!

Interestingly, blending modes can be implemented in the Android OS by using Android's **PorterDuff** Class, which is a real tribute to, and an indicator of, the power that lies in the Android software development API. The PorterDuff class gives developers many of the powerful blending modes that Photoshop or GIMP 2.8 affords to digital imaging artisans. This class essentially allows Android apps to implement powerful image compositing features similar to the GIMP or Photoshop. The major difference, of course, is that you can control the blending modes interactively, using custom Java programming logic, which is the exciting part for Android developers. Some of the powerful Android PorterDuff class blending modes include: **ADD**, **SCREEN**, **OVERLAY**, **DARKEN**, **XOR**, **LIGHTEN**, and **MULTIPLY**. The Apress *Pro Android Graphics* title covers how to implement PorterDuff blending modes inside a complete digital image compositing pipeline, if you are interested in diving into this graphics compositing and blending area of Android in greater detail.

Masking Digital Imagery: Using Alpha Channels

One of the most popular uses of the alpha channel is to "**mask**" out an area of a digital image. This is usually done in order to create a layer which can be utilized in the digital image compositing **layer stack. Masking** is the process of extracting subject matter, essentially cutting that subject matter right out of the image, by placing it (pasting it) onto its own transparent layer. I will show you how this is done a bit later.

The masking process yields a part of your image on its own layer. The masked subject will be **isolated** from the rest of the source image, but because of the layer transparency, will look like it is still in the final image composite. The power is now you can do things to that subject matter, in GIMP, or later on in Android, and not have those operations, whatever they may be (rotate, tint, distort, and so forth) affect the rest of that image. If you export just one of these transparency layers that has subject matter on it in GIMP or Photoshop, the transparency layer will be converted into an alpha channel.

The masking work process allows you to put image elements (subject material) to use inside of other images, or in an animation, or to use in a special effects application. Digital imaging software (Photoshop, GIMP, Painter or Corel Draw) has many tools and features that are specifically there for use in masking images for use in image compositing. You can't really do effective image compositing without creating a mask, so it's an important area to master for graphic designers.

You can mask automatically, using blue screen or green screen backdrops and computer software that can automatically extract those exact color values, in order to create a mask using an alpha channel. You can also mask manually, by hand, using a digital imaging software package, and its wide array of pixel selection tools.

The most important consideration in the masking process is getting smooth but crisp edges around your masked object, so that when you "drop it into" a layer over a new background image, it looks as though it had been photographed there in the first place. The key to this is a proper "selection" work process. Using digital image software **selection tools** (and there are a half-dozen of these in GIMP 2.8) in the proper way, using an optimal work process, is the key to "**pulling**" a "**clean**" image mask (more cool graphics industry terms for you to throw around, to make you appear savvy and professional).

For instance, if there are areas of uniform color around the subject matter you wish to mask, maybe you shot it using a blue screen or green screen, you can use the **magic wand tool** along with a **threshold setting** to select everything except the object, and then **invert** that **selection set**, in order to obtain a selection set containing the object. Sometimes, the correct way to approach something is **in reverse**, as you learned way back in Chapter 3.

Other selection tools contain complex algorithms which can look at color changes between pixels, which can be very useful for **edge detection**, which you can use in other types of selection work processes. The edge detection selection tool will allow you to drag your cursor along the edge of the object which you wish to mask, while the edge detecting selection tool's algorithm lays down a precise, pixel-perfect placement of your selection edge, ultimately creating or "pulling" that object's mask for you.

Smoothing Edges: The Concept of Anti-Aliasing

Anti-aliasing is an imaging technique usually implemented using an algorithm where two adjacent colors in an image, which are on an edge between two color areas, are blended together along that edge. This will make that edge appear to be smoother when the image is zoomed out; that is, when the pixels are not individually visible.

What anti-aliasing does is it tricks your eyes into seeing a smoother edge, to eliminate what is commonly called "the jaggies." Anti-aliasing provides impressive results, by using only a few (usually seven or eight) **averaged** color values of the pixels which lie along the edge that needs to be made smoother. By averaged, I mean some color or spectrum of colors that are part of the way between two colors that are intersecting at the jagged edge in an image.

I created a basic example of anti-aliasing to show visually what I mean. In Figure 9-1, you will see that I created a (seemingly) smooth red circle against a yellow background. I zoomed into the edge of that circle, and grabbed a screenshot. I placed this alongside of the zoomed-out circle to show the anti-aliasing (orange) values of a color between (that is, made using) the red and yellow color values that border each other along the edge of the circle. If you are looking at black and white, you will see all of this in grayscale!

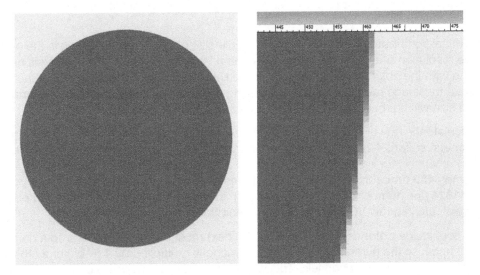

Figure 9-1. A red circle on a yellow background (left) and a zoomed-in view (right) showing the anti-aliasing

The best way to get good anti-aliasing is to use a proper image masking work process, and using the proper settings for any given selection tool that you might be using. One of the other tricks to implementing your own anti-aliasing is to use a **Gaussian Blur** tool with a very low blur value (0.15 to 0.35) on the (transparency) layer containing the object which has the jagged edges. This will provide the same effect that you see in Figure 9-1, and not only that, it will "blur" the transparency values for the alpha channel (mask) itself as well, allowing you to anti-alias that image object with any background imagery you may be attempting to seamlessly composite it against. I will be showing you these techniques using GIMP during the rest of the book, so get ready to learn!

Optimizing Digital Images: Compress and Dither

There are a number of technical factors which affect digital image **compression**, which is the process of using a "**codec**," which is short for **CO**der-**DEC**oder and is an **algorithm** which looks at your image data and finds a way to save it out as a file which uses significantly less image data. The codec's **encoder** essentially finds "**data patterns**" in an image, and then turns these data patterns into a form of data that the **decoder** part of a codec can reconstruct the original image from, many times with zero loss of image quality.

There are some approaches which you can use to get a better quality image compression result, which will result in a smaller file size, along with higher image quality. An image with a small file size and a high level of quality can be said to have a highly optimized **data footprint**. This is a primary objective in optimizing digital imagery, to get the very smallest data footprint possible, while at the same time achieving the highest-quality visual end result.

Let's start out by discussing all of the digital image attributes that affect the image data footprint the most, and later we can examine how each of these aspects will contribute to the data footprint optimization for any given digital image. Interestingly, the order of aspects that are important to data footprint optimization are similar to the order of the digital imaging concepts which we have covered thus far during this chapter.

The most critical contributor to the resulting image file size (that is, data footprint) is the number of pixels or the resolution of the digital image. This is logical because each of these pixels needs to be stored, along with the color values for each of the pixel's (RGB) color channels. Thus, the smaller you can make the image resolution, while still having the image still look detailed, the smaller the resulting file size will be, because there's less data that needs to be compressed.

You can calculate the raw uncompressed image size using the formula: **Width times Height times Color Channels**, so for 24-bit RBG images, there are three (RGB) color channels, and there are four (ARGB) color channels for a 32-bit image. Thus, an uncompressed, truecolor (24-bit) VGA image will have **640 times 480 times 3**, equaling **921,600** bytes of original uncompressed data. If you divide 921,600 by **1024** (the number of bytes in a kilobyte), this will give you the number of **kilobytes** (K or KB) which are in a raw VGA image, and that number is an even **900KB**.

As you can see, image **color depth** is therefore the next most critical contributor to a data footprint of an image, because the number of pixels in that image is multiplied by **1** (8-bit) or **2** (16-bit) or **3** (24-bit) or **4** (32-bit) color data channels. This is one of the reasons indexed color (8-bit) images are still being widely utilized, usually via the **PNG8** image format, which features a superior **lossless** compression algorithm to the one that the outdated GIF format utilizes. Lossless compression algorithms like PNG lose zero image data (quality), whereas a **lossy** compression algorithm, such as JPEG, throws away data, and therefore some of the image quality, to achieve more data compression at the expense of the visual quality result.

Using Indexed Color Imagery: Dithering Pixels

Indexed color images can simulate truecolor images, if the colors which are used to create the image do not vary widely. Indexed color images use 8-bit data to define the image colors, using a **palette** of 256 optimally selected colors, rather than 3 RGB color channels. Depending on how many colors are used in the image, using only 256 colors to represent an image can cause an effect called **banding**, where the transfer between adjoining colors is not smooth. Indexed color image codecs have an option to correct for this visually called "**dithering**." Dithering is the process of creating **dot-patterns** along the edges of two adjoining colors in an image. This tricks your eye into thinking there is a third color being used. Dithering gives us a maximum perceptual amount of colors of 65,536 colors, (256 times 256), but only if each of those 256 colors borders on each of the other 256 colors otherwise it would be less than 65,536 perceived colors.

You can see the potential there for creating additional colors, and you'll be amazed at the result an indexed color image can achieve in some scenarios (that is, with certain images). Let's take a truecolor image, such as the one that is shown in Figure 9-2, and save it as an indexed color image to show you a dithering effect. We'll take a look at this dithering effect on the driver's side rear fender on the Audi racecar 3D image, as it contains a smooth gradient of gray color.

Figure 9-2. A truecolor source image which uses up to 16,777,216 colors which we are going to optimize to 5-bit PNG5

I set the codec to encode a **PNG8** image, shown in Figure 9-3, using **5-bit** color (**32** colors), so that you can see this dithering effect. As you can see, dot patterns are made between adjacent colors, creating the perception that there are additional colors beyond the 32 being used to create the image.

Figure 9-3. The dithering effect in an indexed color image with compression set to 32 colors (5-bit color)

It is interesting to note that there is the option to use less than 256 colors when compressing your 8-bit indexed color image. This is usually done to reduce the data footprint even further. For instance, an image that can attain good results using **32 colors** would actually be a **5-bit** image, and thus is a **PNG5**, even though the format is termed **PNG8**. The **Colors:** "spinner" in Figure 9-3 is where you set this number of colors, and you can set any number from 2 (1-bit color, on or off, black and white) up to 256 colors (8-bit).

Also, notice that you can set a **percentage** of dithering to use. I usually select either the **0%** or **100%** setting, but you could fine-tune your dithering effect anywhere in between those two extreme values. You can also choose a **dithering algorithm** type; I use **diffusion** dithering, as it will yield a smoother gradient effect along an irregularly shaped gradient, such as the one that you see in Figure 9-3, on the Audi racecar's fender.

Dithering, as you might imagine, will add data patterns to an image which are more difficult for a codec's algorithm to compress. Because of this, dithering can increase the data footprint by a few percentage points. Be sure to check the resulting file size with and without dithering applied, and make sure the dithering provides improved visual results if it adds data weight to the resulting file size (data footprint).

The final concept that we have learned about so far that can increase the data footprint of the image is the alpha channel, as adding an alpha channel will add another 8-bit color channel containing pixel transparency data values to the image being compressed. If you need an alpha channel to define transparency, in order to support future compositing needs with the image, there is not much choice but to include this alpha channel data. Just make sure not to use a 32-bit image format to contain a 24-bit image with an empty (completely opaque, and not defining any transparency) alpha channel.

It is interesting to note that many alpha channels which are used to mask objects in an image will compress very well. This is because alpha channels contain large areas of white (opaque) or black (transparent), with very little grey value in the pixels along edges between the two colors to anti-alias the mask. These grey values in an alpha channel are essentially the anti-aliasing values, and as you now know, are used to provide visually smooth edge transitions between the masked object and the imagery which will be used behind it.

The reason for this is because in an alpha channel image mask, the 8-bit transparency gradient is defined using a white to black spectrum (gradient) which defines the alpha channel transparency. So these grey values along the edges of each object in the mask are essentially averaging, or blending, the color of the (RGB) object with color in the target background image. This essentially provides real-time anti-aliasing for the image element (object) on your transparency layer with any background image that is placed behind it.

Android Image Formats: Lossless Versus Lossy

Android supports several popular digital image file formats, some of which have been around for decades.

These range from the decades-old Compuserve **GIF** (Graphic Information Format) and the Joint Photographic Experts Group (JPEG) formats, to the more recent PNG (Portable Network Graphics) and WebP (Web Photo) formats. I will cover these in order of origin, from the older (and less desirable) GIF, to the newest WebP format.

Compuserve **GIF** is fully supported by the Android OS; however, it's not recommended for use! GIF is a lossless digital image file format, as it does not throw away any image data to achieve its better compression result. This is because a GIF compression algorithm (codec) is not as refined (read: powerful), and it only supports **indexed** color, which we covered earlier in the chapter. That said, if all your image assets are already created, and they use the GIF format, you will still be able to use them without any problems (other than the resulting quality to file size ratio) in an Android app.

The next oldest digital image file format which Android supports is **JPEG**, which uses the truecolor color depth, instead of an indexed color depth. JPEG is a **lossy** digital image file format, because it throws away the original image data in order to be able to achieve a smaller file size. The file sizes achieved by using the JPEG algorithm can be an order of magnitude (10X) smaller than the original raw uncompressed image data.

It is important to note that the original (often referred to using the term "**raw**") uncompressed image data is **unrecoverable** after compression by the JPEG codec's encoder has taken place. For this reason, you will want to make sure you have saved your original uncompressed image file before you "run" the image through the JPEG compression algorithm.

If you zoom into a JPEG image after compression, you will see discolored areas which clearly were not present in the original image. These "degraded" areas in the JPEG image data are termed **compression artifacts** in the digital imaging industry, and compression artifacts only occur when you utilize lossy image compression. This is the primary reason why the JPEG file format is not the most highly recommended digital image format for use in Android.

The most recommended image format for use in Android application development is called the **PNG**, or **Portable Network Graphic**, file format. PNG is pronounced **Ping** in the digital image industry. PNG has both an indexed color version, called PNG8, or PNG5, if you only needed to use 32 colors, as we saw earlier in the chapter, and a truecolor version, called PNG24, and a truecolor with alpha version, called PNG32.

The PNG8, PNG24 and PNG32 numbering extensions I am using represent the **bit-depth** of color support, so a truecolor PNG which has an alpha channel would technically be referred to as a PNG32. Similarly, a PNG using 16 colors would be said to be a **PNG4**, a PNG using 64 colors could be referred to as a **PNG6**, and a PNG using 128 colors could be referred to as a **PNG7**, and so forth. The reason PNG is the recommended format for use with Android is because it uses **lossless** compression, and yields high image quality along with a very decent (respectable) compression efficiency.

The most recent image format was added to Android when Google acquired ON2 and is called the **WebP** image format. The format is supported under Android 2.3.7 for image read, or playback support, and in Android 4.0 or later for image write, or file saving support. Image write support in Android, in case you might be wondering, would be used with the Android device camera, so that your users can save (write) images to their SD card or to the "cloud" via remote web server. WebP is a static image version of the WebM video file format, which is also known in the industry as the ON2 VP8 codec, which was acquired by Google and released as open source.

Creating Android NinePatchDrawable Assets

This section of the chapter will outline how to create a **NinePatch** graphic, using the Android Draw 9-patch tool. NinePatchDrawable objects are unique to Android, although there is some movement to add the format to the HTML5 standard as well. A NinePatch image uses the PNG image format, and is designed to be able to tile efficiently in either the X or the Y image dimension, or in both dimensions at the same time. This allows a NinePatch image to be able to morph to fit different size and shape UI widgets and/or display screens, if used as a border element.

You will need a source PNG image with which to create your **NinePatchDrawable** object. I have provided a PNG32 (truecolor with alpha channel) digital image asset, which you can find in the project assets repository for this book. The reason I am using an alpha channel to define transparency in the center area of the 9-patch that we're about to create is so that any image layers (intended composites) which are behind the image asset inside Android will composite perfectly with the 9-patch image asset in the image compositing stack that we will be implementing using XML UI layout design definition markup later on in this chapter.

Installing Your Android Draw 9-patch Software

Let's get started by locating the **Draw 9-patch** tool in your Android SDK folder hierarchy, in the **tools** sub-folder. Open your OS file navigation utility, for Windows 8 it is the Explorer, as shown in Figure 9-4. As you can see, I named my Android SDK folder **Android**, and inside of it is an **adt-bundle-windows-x86_64** folder that I unzipped to install the SDK. Under this folder is an **/sdk** sub-folder, and underneath that is the **/tools** sub-folder.

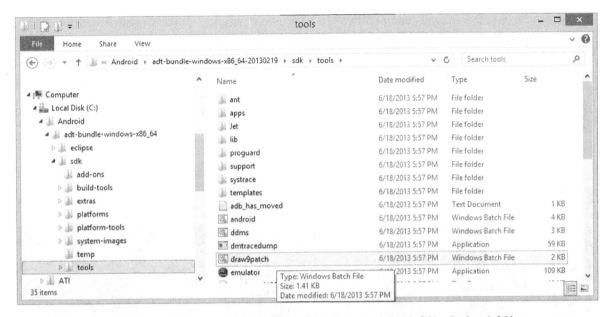

Figure 9-4. *Locate the draw9patch Windows Batch File in an adt-bundle folder, /sdk sub-folder, /tools sub-folder*

Once you click on the **tools** sub-folder, as is shown in Figure 9-4, you will see a **draw9patch.bat** Windows Batch File. This is what we'll need to launch to run the Draw 9-patch software utility. Right-click on the draw9patch file and select the **Run as administrator** menu option, as is shown in Figure 9-5. This will launch Windows 8.1 DOS terminal software, which is needed to run .bat batch files. Since this DOS batch file is executing the draw9patch batch file, it will subsequently launch the Draw 9-patch application from the tools folder. Please don't ask me why Android is using three-decades' old DOS technology, because I have absolutely no idea, but this Draw 9-patch tool certainly looks like it used to run under DOS, meaning it is extremely ancient technology!

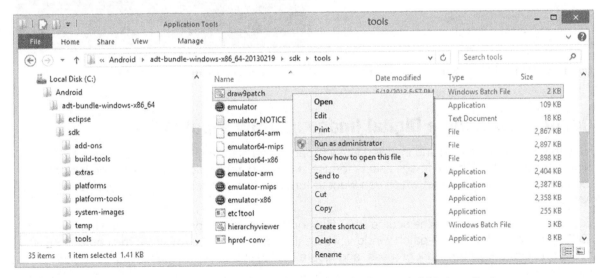

Figure 9-5. *Right-click on the draw9patch Windows Batch File and select the Run as administrator option to run*

If you intend to use the Draw 9-patch software a lot, you can also select the **Create shortcut** option on the menu shown in Figure 9-5 and drag the shortcut to your quick launch taskbar so you don't have to go through this work process more than once!

As you can see in Figure 9-6, the Windows Command Line Terminal software will open up, and will run the draw9patch.bat, which then opens a **Draw 9-patch** software editing window, on top of a cmd.exe Terminal window. You should minimize the Terminal window, and leave the Draw 9-patch editing tool open for use.

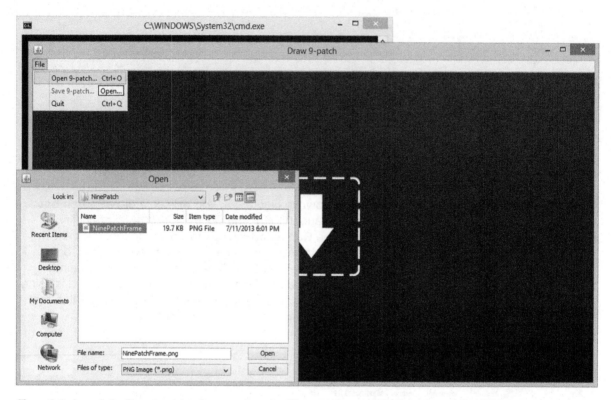

Figure 9-6. *Launch the Draw 9-patch software, and use the File menu to access the Draw 9-patch Open dialog*

Opening the Source Digital Image in Draw 9-patch

Now that you have located and installed Draw 9-patch, you are ready to use the software to create NinePatchDrawable (object) image assets for use in Android applications. The first step is to open the source digital image asset which you want to turn into a NinePatchDrawable object for use in Android.

There are two ways to open the source PNG files for 9-patch development. You can either drag the PNG image onto the Draw 9-patch window, where the "drop it here" arrow is, in the center, or use the **File ➤ Open 9-patch** work process, and locate the file in this book repository's NinePatch sub-folder.

Both of these approaches are shown in Figure 9-6; however, I'm going to use the conservative route, and use the **Open** dialog, which you can see in the bottom left-hand corner of the screenshot. For faster work process during production, you can simply drag your PNG file out of your file manager utility and drop it right into (onto) the Draw 9-patch tool.

Once you find the **NinePatchFrame.png** 32-bit PNG32 source image asset, select it, and click on the **Open** button. You will then see your Draw 9-patch software, with your PNG file in the editing and preview areas.

Exploring Your New Draw 9-patch Editing Software

The left pane is the NinePatch **editing pane**, where you can create your one-pixel wide black lines, which allows you to define "patches." These patches will tell the NinePatch class "engine" in Android what the scalable areas are for this NinePatchDrawable, as well as defining where your center (called the padding area in a NinePatch) content area will be.

The right pane is the resulting NinePatch **previewing pane**, as you can see on the right side in Figure 9-7, where you can see what your NinePatch drawable asset will look like when it is scaled according to the one-pixel black border line definitions which you are in the process of defining in the left editing pane of the software.

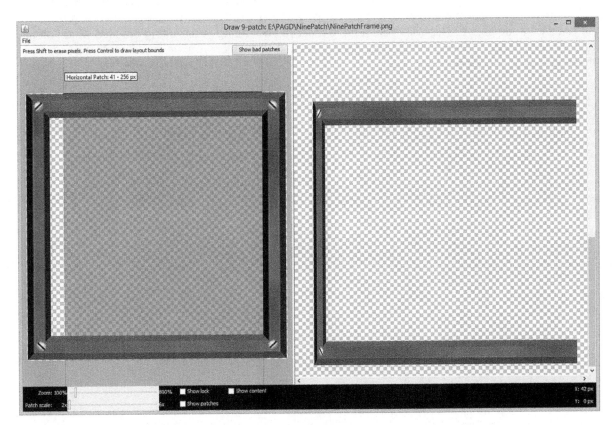

Figure 9-7. Draw out a horizontal patch at the top one-pixel black line segment to define the active X-axis area

Defining Your NinePatchDrawable Scalable Areas

To define how your NinePatchDrawable asset will scale from side to side (along the X axis), click in the top one-pixel transparent perimeter on the right side, near the corner, as shown in Figure 9-7, and drag to the left. This will draw out a one-pixel black line, which will define your X-dimension scalable patch. Once you draw in the rough approximation of what you want, you can fine-tune the line using the fine gray lines at each end of the one-pixel line segment. If you place the mouse over these gray lines, the cursor will change into a double arrow and you can then click and drag the grayed-out area, until it fits pixel-perfectly with the transparency area in the center of the NinePatchFrame PNG32 source image which you are using to create the NinePatchDrawable asset.

You can also right-click (or if you use a Macintosh, hold the Shift key and click) to erase any previously drawn lines. As you can see in the preview pane on the right side of Figure 9-7, you're still not getting the visual result that we are going for here, as the NinePatchDrawable asset is quite distorted. Let's continue on, and define your left side, one-pixel black border, Y-dimension scalable patch, to see if we can correct this Y-scaling distortion.

First, let's use one of the more colorful Draw 9-patch software options, the **Show patches** check box option. This is located at the very bottom of the Draw 9-patch editing pane. This option is there so that you can visualize the patch X and Y settings visually, using different colors. Look for the empty check box next to this Show patches option, and check it to turn this feature on. As seen in Figure 9-8, this option will provide coloration for your selected areas, by using a combination of purple and green colors. This will make it more clear to you during your editing process which areas of the image asset are being affected by the patch definition which you are implementing by using these one-pixel black perimeter lines.

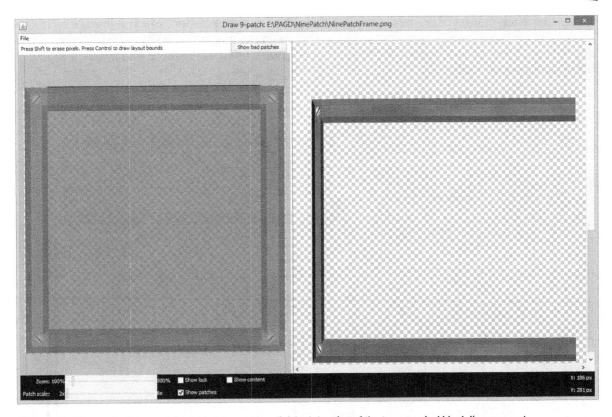

Figure 9-8. Turn on the Show patches check box option; finished drawing of the top one-pixel black line segment

As you can see in Figure 9-8, a number of other useful controls exist at the bottom of your editing pane. These include a **Zoom** slider, which will allow you to adjust the zoom level of your source graphic in the editing area.

The other slider in the bottom is the **Patch scale** slider, which will allow you to adjust the scaling of the actual NinePatchDrawable preview imagery which is being shown in the preview area on the right side of the display.

The **Show lock** option check box will allow you to visualize the non-drawable areas of the NinePatchDrawable when you mouse-over them. The **Show content** option check box highlights your content area in a preview pane image, where purple shows the area in which any Android View subclass (widget or layout container) content will be allowed to composite (to show through from other z-order "layers" in your user interface compositing stack) with your NinePatchDrawable.

A NinePatchDrawable can generally be contained (utilized) within any Android class that supports an Android Drawable asset referenced using either the source (android:src) image plate or the background image plate (android:background) parameter, including ImageButton, ImageView, ViewGroup, and so forth.

The Show patches option check box, which we have just enabled, allows us to preview our scalable patch definitions in real-time in the left pane editing area. The pink color will represent the area of the patch that is scalable.

Finally, at the top of the editing area, there is a **Show bad patches** button, which will add a red border around patch areas which may produce artifacts in the graphic when it is scaled. Visual excellence for your scaled images will be achieved if you strive to eliminate all bad patches in your NinePatchDrawable design.

Now it is time to draw in our left one-pixel border, as shown in Figure 9-9.

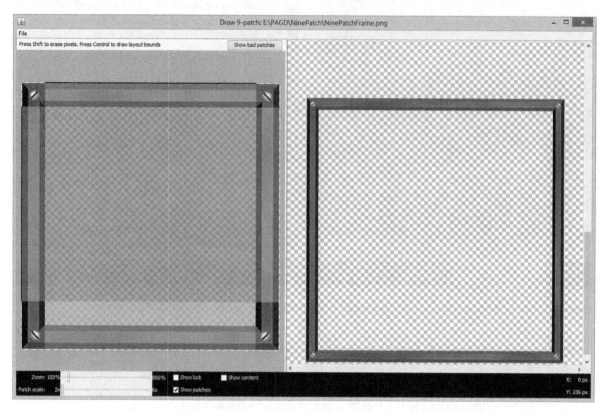

Figure 9-9. Draw down a vertical Y patch, using the left one-pixel black line segment to define the Y-axis patch scale

As you can see in Figure 9-9, I didn't draw this one-pixel black border line all the way down the left side. I did this so that you could visualize how well this Show patches option works. This option will allow us to visualize exactly what we are doing right down to the pixel level, as you can see in Figure 9-9, when you look at the color areas and how they "blend" with the transparency checkerboard pattern and the source PNG32 image asset. This precision is absolutely necessary if we want to define the perfect 9-patch image asset for use in our NinePatchDrawawble object.

Figure 9-10 now shows your NinePatchDrawable PNG32 image asset with both the top, as well as the left, one-pixel (border) black line definitions in place. As you can now visualize, thanks to the Show patches option, we have now defined our static areas, shown as clear (no coloration), which will not scale, and our scalable areas, shown using a green overlay. The Show patches option has allowed us to do this with surgical pixel precision.

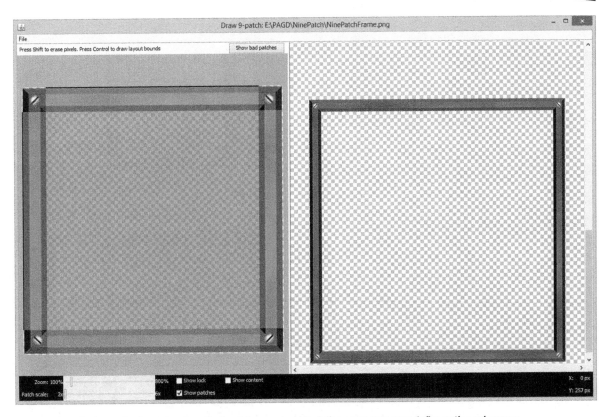

Figure 9-10. Both your horizontal and vertical patch one-pixel black line segments now define active axis areas

Also notice in Figure 9-10 on the right-hand preview side of the Draw 9-patch software tool that the results for your NinePatchDrawable PNG32 image asset patch scale definition is giving you a professional scaling result.

If you grab that **scrollbar** on the right side of the preview pane area of the screen and pull it up or down, you will see that the NinePatch scales in a portrait as well as in a landscape container shape, with perfect visual results, regardless of the aspect ratio (shape) of the container which is holding your NinePatch asset.

Defining Your NinePatchDrawable Padding Areas

Now that we have defined the **scalable areas** of the NinePatch image asset, it is time to define the **padding areas** for the NinePatch image asset. This is accomplished by using the one-pixel black border lines on the **right** and **bottom** of the editing pane.

As you can see in Figure 9-11, I have drawn in, on the right-hand side, the one-pixel black border line segment which is needed to define the Y image dimension for our center (padding) area for the 9-patch image asset. The center area in the case of the PNG32 asset contains an alpha channel value of #00000000, or 100% transparency, which you could also define, as you now well know, using any other color value, such as white, or #00FFFFFF.

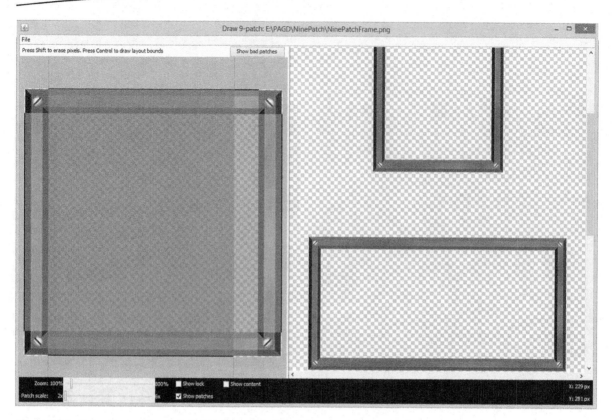

Figure 9-11. Define the padding areas using the one-pixel black line segments on the right and bottom

Also notice in Figure 9-11 that I am in the process of drawing in the second, one-pixel black border line segment at the bottom of the image. I am doing this in order to define the X dimension for the center padding area, which will define where other (composited) image assets in our user interface design can show through this NinePatchDrawable image asset. If I didn't have transparency in this graphic, image assets behind it (those on a lower z-order layer) would not show through. Due to the padding, images on top of it would draw inside the NinePatch image. So if your NinePatch had a white interior and you used it in the background UI plate, the image in the source UI plate would "respect" this padding (interior) area and be drawn on top of it (background is behind foreground).

Notice the muted colors in Figures 9-11 and 9-12, which are used to show different layers of the **scalable** versus **padding** area definitions. The padding definitions use a gray overlay on a green or purple (or pink, if you prefer) scalable area definition. As you can see on the right side, the NinePatchDrawable scaling result is giving us exceptionally professional results, regardless of the source image's orientation or dimensions, which the 9-patch image asset is being scaled into. Notice in Figure 9-12 that I'm pulling the right side one-pixel black border line segment up, showing the patch adjust guides, and how you can adjust padding parameters precisely.

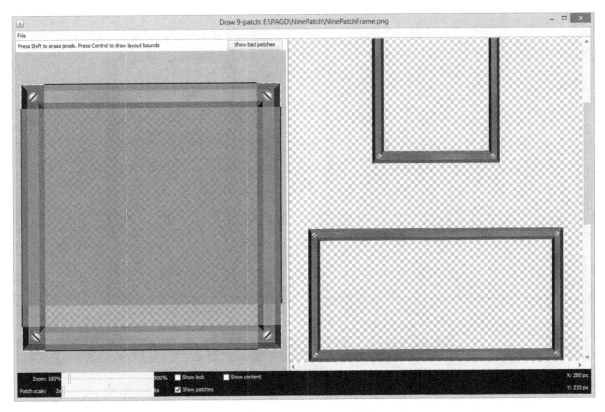

Figure 9-12. Adjust Padding area via the right side one-pixel black line segment (showing patch adjust guide)

Figure 9-13 shows a finished NinePatch image asset definition, with both a scaling set of border line segments, as well as a padding set of border line segments. We've utilized patch definition guides on four sides of a PNG.

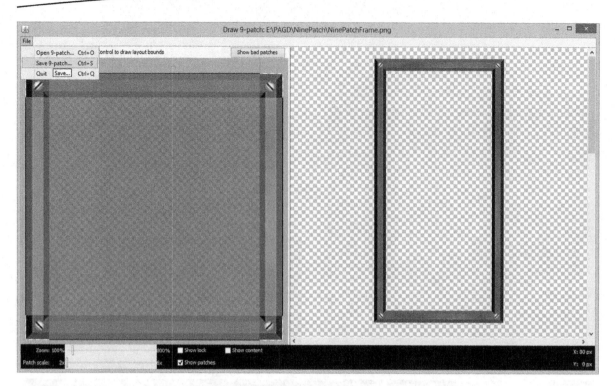

Figure 9-13. *Final patch definition and using the File menu and Save 9-patch menu option to save a 9-patch*

It's important to note that if you place the mouse in the left editing pane over the center section of the NinePatch definition, and then hold it there, a tool-tip pop-up will appear giving you the precise pixel patch coordinates for the final NinePatchDrawable definition, which you may want to know about for the XML markup or Java code.

In our case, this will show that you have utilized 256 pixels minus 26 pixels, or 230 pixels of our total 280-pixel image dimension, for our center scalable area. Note that 256 is a numeric value that scales quite well, as it is the "**power of 2**" data value (2, 4, 8, 16, 32, 64, 128, 256, 512, 1024). This means that you have used **25 pixels**, or half of the 50 remaining pixels, for the actual image assets (bars and screws) that will be scaled. The reason this is not 26 pixels is because the NinePatchDrawable image format uses that one-pixel border to define its patches.

This also means that the fixed areas of this 9-patch, in this case, it is a corner of the frame with a standard screw in it (to hold the frame in place, of course, or so it appears) will thus each be exactly **25 pixels square** in size. These corner areas of the NinePatchDrawable will not be distorted in the X or Y dimensions, although they may be uniformly scaled as needed. There are enough corner pixels (more than two dozen) to be able to scale up, if it is used on higher pixel density (resolution) screens, and to have the detail to appear photo-real if scaled down.

As you can see in Figure 9-13, on the right-hand side of the Draw 9-patch application preview pane, our scaling picture frame graphic looks extremely crisp, and quite realistic. If you scroll the preview pane, this holds across all of the scaling orientation previews. Now it is time to **Save** our NinePatchDrawable image asset. Do this by using the **File** menu and the **File ➤ Save 9-patch** menuing sequence, which you can see in Figure 9-13.

Saving Your NinePatchDrawable Asset in Android

Your Draw 9-patch software tool's File Save dialog will automatically save your 9-patch image assets with the required **.9.png** file name extension, which is required by Android OS, when using NinePatchDrawable assets.

When Android sees this type of PNG file in your **/res/drawable-dpi** folders, it automatically sets it up using the **NinePatch** class to load it, and converts it into a **NinePatchDrawable** image asset once it's referenced in XML.

It is important to note here that there is also an **Open 9-patch** menu option, seen in Figure 9-13, which opens a normal (non-9-patched) PNG file (*.png). We used this earlier to load the PNG asset and add the empty one-pixel border around the image, allowing us to create guides showing where to scale patches and place content.

If you use this menu command to open up previously saved 9-patch PNG files (*.9.png), the 9-patch PNG asset will be loaded into the Draw 9-patch tool as previously modified with no one-pixel border drawing areas added, because these one-pixel patch definition areas already exist within the file, due to the previous editing session!

One final caveat for the File Save dialog is that it **will not show (preview) this .9.png extension** in the dialog itself, but will insert it on your hard disk drive, when it saves your file out as the new NinePatchDrawable image asset. This can be somewhat confusing the first time that you utilize this software utility, as the file it says in the File Save dialog that it's going to save is **NinePatchFrame. png**, but what it actually saves out is **NinePatchFrame.9.png**.

Make sure to keep this caveat in mind when you go into the File Save dialog, so that you don't write out a **NinePatchFrame.9.9.png** file! Even if you do this, the next step in the work process would be to go into your OS's file management utility and simply rename the file to be filename.9.png. While you're there, take a look at your original file, as well as the new 9-patch version, and see how much data footprint "weight" the 9-patch definition has added to your file.

To find out your exact file size **delta**, or difference, between these two files, you will want to right-click on each of the two PNG file assets and use the **properties** option. This will allow you to see what the actual file size data footprint for each file actually is. Your original PNG32 was 19.7 kilobytes, and the new NinePatch PNG is 20.2 kilobytes. This means that the NinePatch definition guides added one-half of a kilobyte to this 280-pixel square image asset, or about 2.5% more data. This is really not too bad, considering that you just added an X-axis and a Y-axis (independent of each other) flexible image scaling capability right into the PNG32 image asset itself!

Now that you have created a usable NinePatchDrawable asset, let's go into your XML markup for the SlidingPaneLayout that you started creating in the previous chapter, and we'll finish learning what the ImageButton class can do. We will do this by implementing a NinePatchDrawable asset inside of a multi-state ImageButton which we will create next, so that you can learn not only how to create your own UI Button graphics, but how to make these graphics morph and animate relative to what the user of the application is doing on the screen at the time.

The ImageButton Class: Multi-state Buttons

Android's **ImageButton** class is a direct subclass of the **ImageView** class, which is itself a subclass of the View superclass, which, as you learned in Chapter 6, is a subclass of the java.lang.Object master class, and is primarily utilized to create UI widgets and layout containers (via the ViewGroup superclass). The Android class hierarchy for the ImageButton class would thus be structured as follows:

```
java.lang.Object
  > android.view.View
    > android.widget.ImageView
      > android.widget.ImageButton
```

The ImageButton class, like its parent class ImageView, is stored in a separate Android package for UI widgets, which is called the **android.widget** package. This is because the ImageButton is an often-used UI widget which can be leveraged to create custom button UI widgets which can be "skinned" using Android Drawable objects.

This makes the ImageButton class extremely powerful, as Android Drawable objects can be **BitmapDrawable** (images), **NinePatchDrawable** (asymetric tiling imagery), **AnimationDrawable** (animation), **ShapeDrawable** (illustrations), and any of the other Android Drawable subclasses. I wish I could cover all of these Android Drawable subclasses within this book; however, if you wanted to explore Android Drawables further, you should check out the Apress *Pro Android Graphics* title.

The ImageButton UI widget would be used when developers need to create a custom button UI element, which will display the button using an image instead of using a standard text label on a square gray background, as the standard UI Button element would do. We have already implemented both Button and ImageButton elements in previous chapters that covered user interface layout design classes, including the LinearLayout, RelativeLayout, GridLayout, and SlidingPaneLayout.

Just like the Android Button class UI widget, an ImageButton UI widget can be pressed, using a click or a touch event by the user, and can have button focus characteristics defined as well by implementing multi-state images.

As you saw in the previous chapter, if you don't utilize any of its custom parameters, your ImageButton widget will have a visual appearance of a standard Android Button UI object with a gray button background which changes color to blue when the button is pressed. The real power of the ImageButton class comes when you use it with alpha channel capable images, in conjunction with multiple image states, both of which you will be learning about in detail during this chapter.

The ImageButton UI widget can define up to four different ImageButton "states" which are defined using XML markup, which we will be doing a bit later on in this chapter. We will cover these ImageButton states in detail in the next section of this chapter, after I cover a couple of the key XML parameters and Java methods here in this section on the ImageButton class member methods and features.

The **default image** for your ImageButton UI widget, which defines its **normal state**, can be defined statically by using the **android:src** XML parameter in a <ImageButton> child tag, inside of your XML layout container UI definition, as you did for the ImageButton UI elements that you used in the SlidingPaneLayout in Chapter 8. You can also define a default image for the ImageButton UI widget, which defines its normal state, **dynamically** (at run-time) in your Java code; you can implement this by using the **.setImageResource()** method.

We will be using XML to define our UI designs, which the Android OS prefers that we do, for this book. If you use the android:src parameter to reference image assets, this will put an image on the ImageButton, as you saw in Chapter 8. It is important to note developers can use both the android:background parameter, which allows a background image plate, or layer, to be added to the ImageButton element, as well as the android:src parameter, which allows you to install the foreground image plate (layer). This enables you to perform image compositing inside of the ImageButton UI element itself.

If you do this, you will want to use alpha channels in your images, as we have been, and will be, doing in this chapter. This is why I have been getting into alpha channels so deeply, as they allow you greater flexibility inside of your Android graphic design pipeline.

The reason that you would want to define both a foreground image plate and a background image plate at the same time, in the same UI element, would be so that you could take advantage of the power of digital image compositing which Android affords you by allowing multiple image plates (parameters that support Drawable objects). You can also set the ImageButton background color value to transparent (#00000000) if you want to composite with other UI elements behind the ImageButton, such as using a background image asset for your parent layout container, for instance.

The States: Normal, Pressed, Focused, Hovered

An ImageButton class allows you to define custom image assets for each of the **states** for a UI button. States include **normal** (the default or not in use), **pressed** (a user touching, or pressing down on, device click selection hardware), **focused** (recently touched and released, or recently clicked and released) and **hovered** (a user is over an ImageButton with the mouse or navigation keys, but has not touched it, or clicked on it, as yet).

The hovered state was added recently in Android 4, API Level 14, possibly in anticipation of using the Android OS for the Google Chromebook product or in anticipation of the Amazon Fire TV or the Dell Wyse Cloud Connect Android HDMI PC product, or other products such as 2K (1920 by 1080) iTV sets or 4K (4096 by 2016) iTV sets that come with a mouse, keyboard and game controllers.

I've summarized the four currently supported ImageButton states as of Android OS 4.4.4, called KitKat, along with their mouse event programming equivalents that would be used on non-touchscreen devices, in Table 9-1.

Table 9-1. *The Android ImageButton Class Primary Image Asset State Constants and Mouse Usage Equivalents*

ImageButton State	Description of Button State along with its Mouse Event Equivalent
NORMAL	Default ImageButton State when not in use. Equivalent: **Mouse Out**
PRESSED	ImageButton State when touched or clicked. Equivalent: **Mouse Down**
FOCUSED	ImageButton State when touched and released. Equivalent: **Mouse Up**
HOVERED (API 14)	ImageButton State if focused (not touched) Equivalent: **Mouse Over**

ImageButton UI elements are time-consuming to create, because you will want to create a unique digital image asset for each ImageButton state. Different images will visually indicate to a user a different ImageButton state. The reason this can be difficult is not because of the XML markup that is involved, but rather due to extensive digital imaging work which you will need to do for each button, across several ImageButton states and across several different resolution densities.

We will be using GIMP 2.8.10 (or later, if it's out) in the next section of the chapter, to create your digital image assets for these ImageButton UI states for each of the three galaxy ImageButtons that we're going to implement.

We are going to create these **12** image assets, that is, 3 ImageButton graphics asset sets for each of 4 states, in each of the **5** mainstream resolution densities that are required by Android, as defined by the folder names which Eclipse ADT created for you when you created your HelloUniverse application bootstrap back in Chapter 3. So to do things correctly, and be able to span across all of the different device types, screen sizes, and resolutions from smartwatch to 4K iTV sets, you're about to create 60 (5 times 12) ImageButton assets.

After we learn the lengthy work process for creating the five dozen digital image assets, you will need to create your XML structures which will implement these multi-state ImageButton UI elements. We will then move on to learn the standard work process for defining each ImageButton state. This is done using an XML Drawable asset in the form of an **image selector** definition file, which lives in your "root" **/res/drawable** folder. This file will use the parent **<selector>** tag with child **<item>** tags. The <item> tags will define each of your ImageButton's states, using digital image asset references. Once this XML definition is set up, Android will handle changing the image state for you based on what the end-user is doing with the device hardware.

Creating Multi-State Imagery: Using GIMP

Let's launch GIMP and use a **File ➤ Open** menu sequence to access an **Open Image** dialog, seen in Figure 9-14.

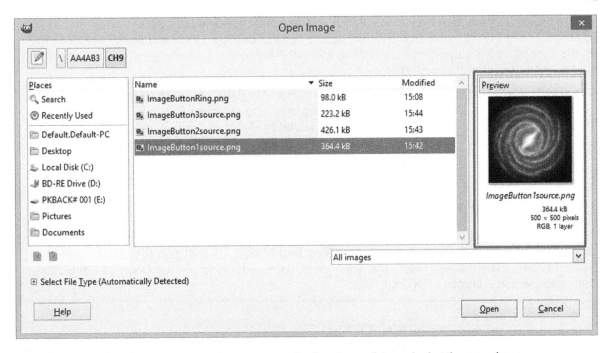

Figure 9-14. *Use the File ➤ Open menu sequence to access the Open Image dialog and select the source image*

Double-click on the **ImageButton1source.png** file in the book asset repository to **Open** it, as shown in Figure 9-15.

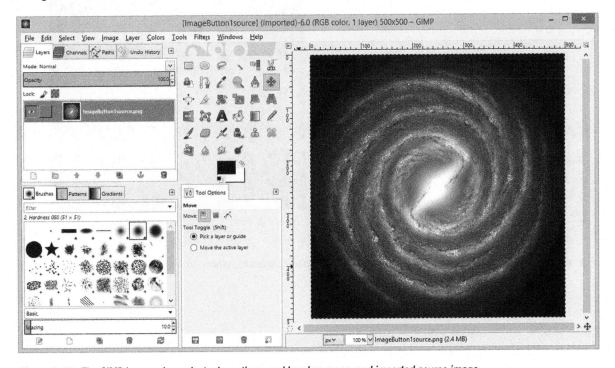

Figure 9-15. *The GIMP layers, channels, tools, options, and brushes areas, and imported source image*

Notice the primary functional areas in GIMP: the layers and channels palettes at the top-left, the tool icons palette to the right of that, the tool options palette underneath that, and the brushes palette to the left of that. Note that these are floating tool palettes, so you can arrange GIMP 2.8 in any way that might be best for the comfort of your particular work process.

The source image, which is the 500-pixel version of the Milky Way galaxy that I got from the NASA web site, is shown on the right in the image editing area, and the **layer** it is on is shown selected in blue on the left under the Layers palette, with its **visibility** (denoted using an eye icon) turned on. Later, we will be using this **eye icon** to toggle layer visibility on and off, once we add some more layers to your image composite, which we'll do next.

Using GIMP for Compositing: Importing a Layer

The easiest way to add a new compositing layer in GIMP is to import an image which already has an alpha channel in it, such as the **ImageButtonRing.png** PNG32 file shown at the top of Figure 9-14, which is going to be the next layer up in your image composite, is to use the **Open as Layers** menu sequence, which is shown in Figure 9-16.

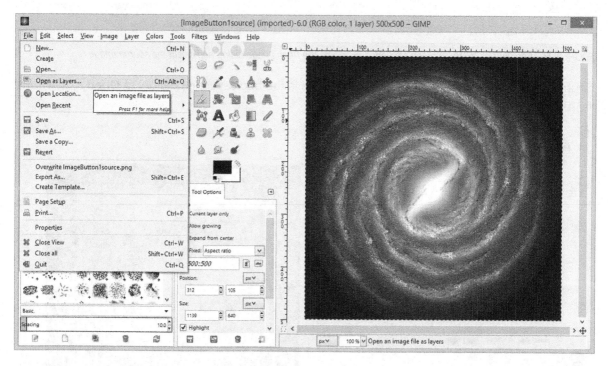

Figure 9-16. Using the File ➤ Open as Layers menu sequence to add the ImageButton ring decoration as a new layer

It is important to notice that GIMP also has **pop-up helper** features, which will describe what everything in the software will do for you. To invoke this interactive feature, you "**hover**" (interestingly, this is one of the ImageButton states that you just learned about in the previous section) your mouse over the tool icon, the palette layer or the menu option. This is shown under the selected menu option, in yellow, in Figure 9-16.

The **Open as Layers** function is useful because it combines the **File ➤ Open** and **Layer ➤ New Layer** operations into one seamless "move" that will open an image containing one or more layers, and will then place those layers **above** the current selected layer. In this case, as you can see in Figure 9-15 (the Layers palette tab is obscured by the File menu in Figure 9-16), the selected layer is the Milky Way galaxy source image that you originally imported (to see that "move," reference Figure 9-14).

As you can see in Figure 9-17, the **ImageButtonRing.png** layer is now selected and is now on top of your **ImageButton1source.png** layer in the **Layers palette** (top left), and the ring decoration for the ImageButton image asset, which you are in the process of creating, is compositing seamlessly with a Milky Way galaxy image underneath it (refer to the image preview area on the right of the screen shot).

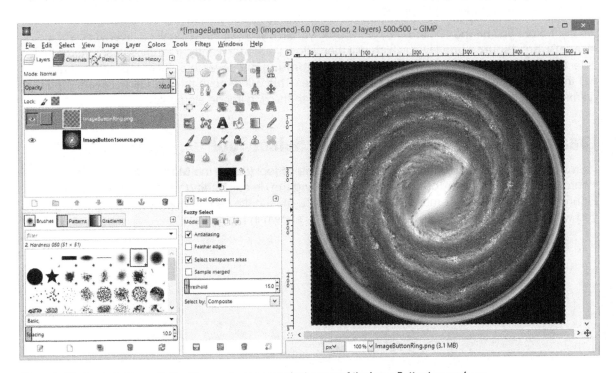

Figure 9-17. A selected ImageButtonRing.png layer composited on top of the ImageButton1source layer

You could simply have your ImageButton draw a ring on top of your galaxy imagery; however, this would allow the "corners" of the galaxy image to stick out beyond the ring, and that is not as professional of a result. Let's make this graphic that you are creating look completely "button-like," and teach you some advanced features of GIMP at the same time, since, after all, this is the graphic design chapter of the book, and I don't want to leave you wanting more!

What we are going to do in the next section is to go into detail regarding how to leverage the transparency inside of your ImageButtonRing.png image asset, in order to surgically cut the Milky Way out of the center of the original source galaxy image. This will point out to you the "**modal**" (or modes of operation) nature of the GIMP image editing software, and how to use this as an advantage, by selecting a "**selection set**" using one layer, and applying an operation to a different layer using that selection set, as it will still be actively selected. Pretty cool advanced graphics moves!

You will do this by selecting the ring image asset, as is shown in the Layers palette (in blue), in Figure 9-17, as well as the **Fuzzy Select Tool**, also shown selected in blue in the top-center of the screenshot, and Shift-clicking (which adds to the selection as you click different areas) in each corner of the ring image. Shift-clicking means holding down the Shift key on the keyboard to add selection areas each time you click. This will select the transparent (and unused, in the galaxy image) corner areas around the ring UI element.

Finally, before you hit the "Delete" key on your keyboard, you will strategically (cleverly) select the **ImageButton1source.png** layer, which will then allow you to (brilliantly, if I may say so) utilize that selection set that you "culled" from the **ImageButtonRing.png** layer in a delete operation that you will then apply to the ImageButton1source.png layer. This will remove the rounded corners from the galaxy image, and make it match up seamlessly with the ring image element.

Creating an Alpha Channel: Fuzzy Select Tool

I have encircled (ensquared, actually) the **Fuzzy Select** tool (called the **Magic Wand** tool in Photoshop), and the **Tool Options** palette containing the default setting which we will be using, in Figure 9-18. Since GIMP is modal, and because you must have certain operational modes selected, you will need to have GIMP "set up" exactly as it is shown in Figure 9-18.

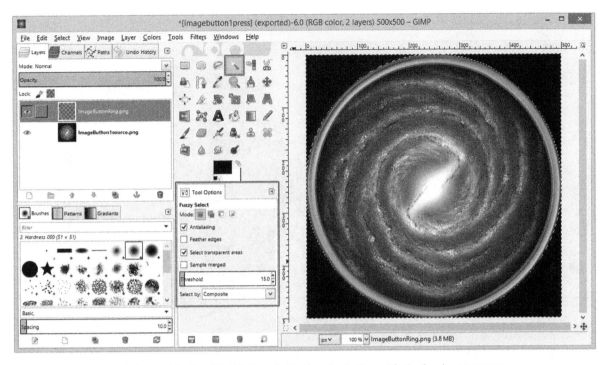

Figure 9-18. *The Fuzzy Select tool (top) and Tool Options (bottom) and selection set in the four image corners*

The "target layer" mode is set to ImageButtonRing.png, the tool or "pixel operation mode" is set to Fuzzy Select, and the "Antialiasing" mode and "Select transparent areas" mode for that tool are also selected. A **Threshold** of **15% variation** in pixel colors (which is the default, and does not apply here, as we are selecting transparency) is also shown on the Tool Options palette. You can use just about any Threshold setting, in this particular case.

Once all of your settings or "modes" of operation are defined, you can click in the upper-left corner of the image which will select that corner, as shown by the "marching ants" selection area. Next, you will want to hold down the **Shift** key on your keyboard, which tells GIMP that you want to **ADD** more areas to your "**selection set**." Next, click in the other three corners, making sure that you hold the Shift key down when you make each of these three strategic clicks!

Once you have marching ants in all of the corners, which at this point will look like marching ants around a square perimeter of the image composite, as well as around the circular part, which is outside of the ring image, you will then want to make sure to click on the other **ImageButton1source.png** layer, before hitting your **Delete** key on your keyboard. This is because you do not want to delete the transparency in the ring image, but instead, the black rounded corner areas that you have strategically selected, by using the ring image transparency in the ImageButton1source.png source image to easily define a round corner selection.

If you are doing this series of "moves" or operations using Photoshop, you will see the transparency immediately, which will look like what is shown in Figure 9-22 (if you want to look ahead). However, GIMP uses a white background for its layers, which once you hit the Delete key, you will see, and which is shown in Figure 9-19.

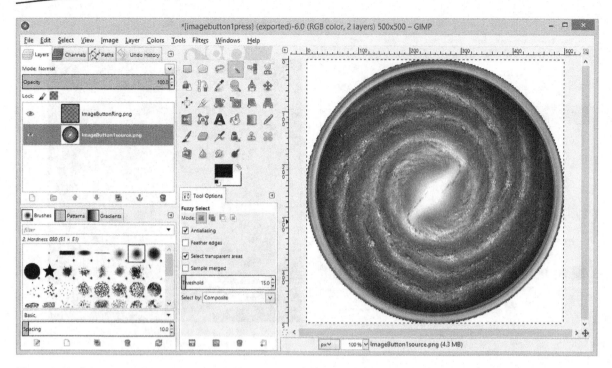

Figure 9-19. Select source image layer and use the Delete key to remove the corners revealing the layer background

Figure 9-19 also shows the ImageButton1source.png layer being selected for the delete operation, and that the selection is still "active" (that is, the ants are still marching). We need to get the remaining (circular) galaxy part of the image onto its own layer with transparency, so I am going to show you the work process to achieve that end result as well.

We are going to apply another clever technique as well as an often-used operation in digital image editing called "**inverting**" the selection set. The principle behind this, which we have already seen once in this book, way back in Chapter 3, is that it can often be easier to select what we don't want in the selection set, and then "invert" that selection to select what we do want in the selection (or as the selection set).

What's interesting in this case is that four different (separate) triangular selection areas are tuned into one single circular selection area by using the **Select ➤ Invert** menu sequence, which is shown in Figure 9-20. Notice that I have clicked on the **eye icon** next to the ImageButtonRing.png layer to turn that **layer visibility** off, so that I can see more clearly what I am getting as a result in the ImageButton1source.png layer. I have encircled the eye icon area in the Layers palette, showing that the eye icon is no longer visible next to the ImageButtonRing.png layer.

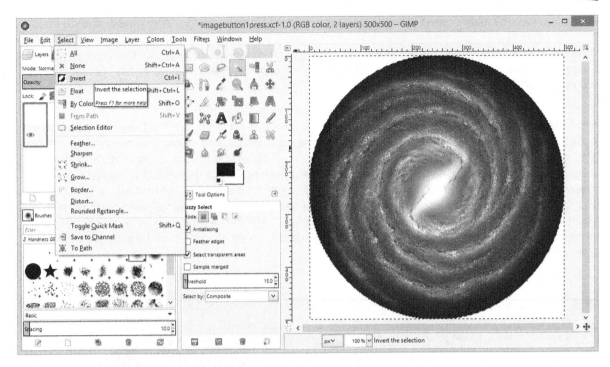

Figure 9-20. *Turn off ring layer visibility via the eye icon (shown off) and invert the selection using Select ➤ Invert*

This time, instead of using the Delete function, we are going to use the **Copy** function, either by using the **Ctrl-C** keyboard shortcut, or by using the **Edit ➤ Copy** menu sequence in GIMP. What this will do is to put those pixels which are inside of the circular selection area into your system memory's "**clipboard**," which is used to hold things in memory that you will want to use later, like text, if you're using a word processor, or pixels, if you're using GIMP.

Next, we are going to use the **Edit ➤ Paste as ➤ New Layer** utility in GIMP, to create a transparency layer using the alpha channel which is in the selected circular galaxy image area, which is now in your workstation's memory, in a reserved area of memory which is commonly called the "**clipboard**."

Creating a Composite Layer Using the Clipboard

GIMP has another really cool workflow feature which makes creating multi-layered image composites easier when you use the clipboard a lot to hold image elements which you have extracted from other image layers by using selection sets (and then copied into system memory). This menu sequence combines the **Edit ➤ Paste** and the **Layer ➤ New Layer** operations into one single unified **Edit ➤ Paste as ➤ New Layer** operation that will create a new layer for you, and then paste the pixels into that layer from your clipboard.

Since you have already copied this selected circular area from your Milky Way galaxy source imagery into the clipboard of your workstation, let's use this cool Paste As New Layer function next, to create the new layer which has our transparency already in it. The transparency in the new layer will be everywhere that there is no image data present in your clipboard, which is really the end result that we're looking to achieve.

The menu sequence is shown in Figure 9-21, and as you can see, the current **ImageButton1source.png** is still visible, as well as selected (which is signified using a light gray color). Thus, the clipboard image layer will be pasted above this, and below the ImageButtonRing. png layer, which is exactly where you want the new layer to be within your overall image compositing layer stack. This is because you want your ring UI element on top of the Milky Way galaxy image layer that has the transparency in it, so that when you export the project, it looks like a button. Remember to achieve this visual result that you will need to have the original galaxy image layer visibility turned off, as shown in Figure 9-22, which the GIMP File ➤ Export operation will "respect" during the image export process, and your end-result will be an ImageButton UI element with transparency all the way around it.

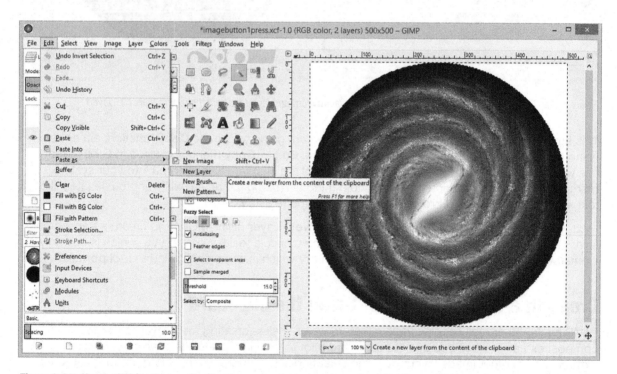

Figure 9-21. Use the Edit ➤ Paste as ➤ New Layer menu sequence to create a new layer with an alpha channel

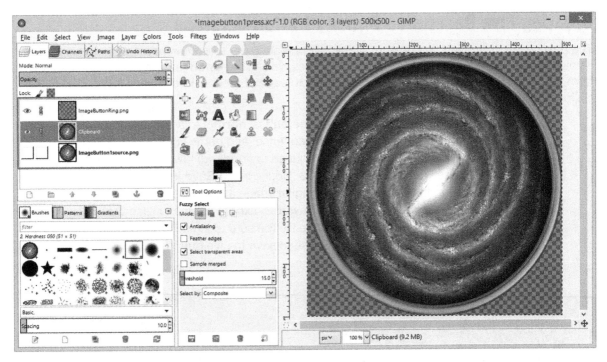

Figure 9-22. The final composite image result with the original source image turned off, showing layer lock icons

Once you paste in this new transparent layer, with this circular galaxy image component on (in) it, into the composite, as shown in Figure 9-22, you can click the eye icon next to the original ImageButton1source.png source image layer, and turn its visibility off. This will make the white layer background color for that layer invisible, and you will see only the **Clipboard** layer and the **ImageButtonRing.png** layer. You will also see that what we now have looks like a custom image button UI element. You can also use the **Select ➤ None** menu sequence if you wish, to remove the marching ants selection, as that selection set is no longer needed.

If you want to, you can now double-click on the word "**Clipboard**" in the middle layer, which will enable the layer name for editing, and you can type in **ImageButtonTransparency** and hit the **Enter** key to enter it, as is shown in Figure 9-27, where the Layers palette is finally not being obscured by GIMP menus anymore.

Now we are ready to enter the phase in our work process where we export (save out) the **imagebutton1normal** PNG file format in the various resolutions that Android OS will use to match different device resolution density screens. This 500-pixel source image will be the highest-resolution asset, and will go into the **/drawable-xxhdpi** resource folder. It will be used on super high-resolution screens such as the 2560 by 1440 Samsung Galaxy S5 and 4K iTV sets, which have the 4096 by 2160 screen resolution.

Creating Five Resolution Density Button Versions

The next series of "moves" in our work process for creating the five different resolution densities will involve using the **Image Scale** algorithm in GIMP, as well as the **Undo** feature, so that we can scale from the original 500-pixel version (XXHDPI) down to each of the lower resolution levels of XHDPI, HDPI, MDPI, and LDPI.

1. To save out the **XXHDPI** version of the **default** or **normal** ImageButton state, use the **File ➤ Export As** menu sequence, and name your file **imagebutton1normal.png** using the required (by Android) lowercase letters and numbers, as is shown in Figure 9-23. Notice in the **Save in folder** area of the dialog that I am saving the digital image asset directly into the HelloUniverse resource folder in the **/drawable-xxhdpi** subfolder. Use the **Export** button once you have named the file (be sure to include the .png file extension to tell GIMP what format to use to save the file during the export operation).

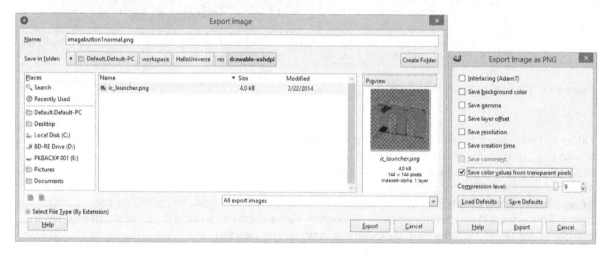

Figure 9-23. *Use a File ➤ Export As menu sequence to access the Export Image dialog, to save the first ImageButton*

2. Use the **Image ➤ Scale Image** menu sequence to open the **Scale Image** dialog and scale the image to **256 pixels** using **Cubic** Interpolation, as seen in Figure 9-24. Export the image to the **drawable-xhdpi** folder, using the file name that you used in Figure 9-23, as each different resolution version will need to have the **exact same file name**.

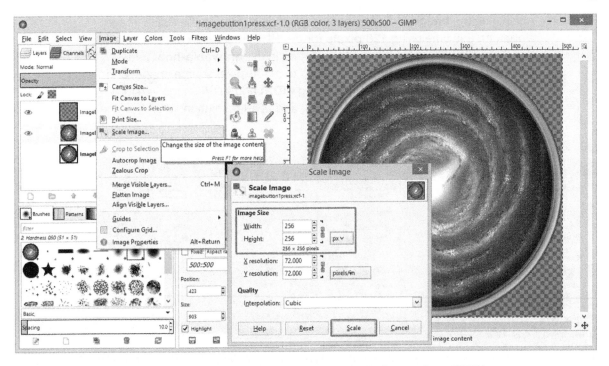

Figure 9-24. Use the Image ➤ Scale Image menu sequence to scale the XXHDPI image to be an XHDPI image

3. Use the **Edit ➤ Undo Scale Image** menu sequence after you have exported
    your **XHDPI** image asset, as seen in Figure 9-25, so when you scale down to
    the **HDPI** image, the GIMP Cubic interpolation algorithm will have the original
    XXHDPI 500 pixel image to work with!

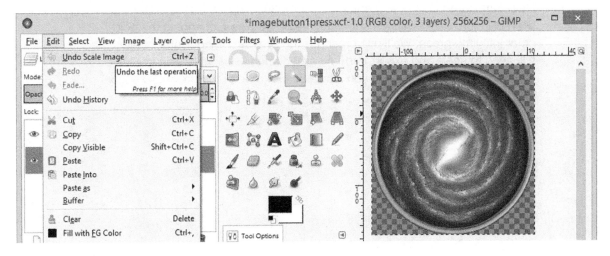

Figure 9-25. A 256-pixel XHDPI scaled image (right), and the Edit ➤ Undo Scale Image menu sequence

4. Again, use the **Image ➤ Scale** menu sequence to access the Scale Image algorithm, this time using **128 pixels** for the **HDPI** resolution density version, and Export the file using the same file name in the **drawable-hdpi** folder. Use **Edit ➤ Undo Scale Image** to return to a 500-pixel source image, and perform the same work process, creating **MDPI** and **LDPI** image versions. Scale Image dialogs for the HDPI, MDPI, and LDPI resolutions are shown in Figure 9-26.

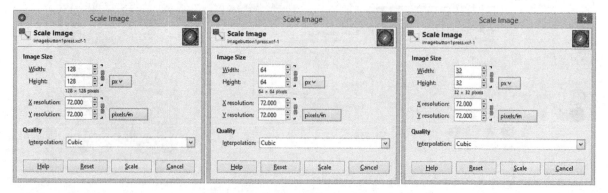

Figure 9-26. Perform a Scale Image operation, using the 500-pixel source, for HDPI (left), MDPI (center), LDPI (right)

Creating Your Other Three ImageButton States

Let's create the other states:

1. Use the **Colors ➤ Hue-Saturation** menu sequence to access the **Hue-Saturation** dialog, and enter a value of **30** next to the **Hue slider**, as seen in Figure 9-27. This will shift the Hue **30 degrees**, changing the gold color into lime green. We'll use green for the **pressed** ImageButton state, and will need to scale and export this lime green ImageButton version in all five resolution density folders, as you learned how to do in the previous section.

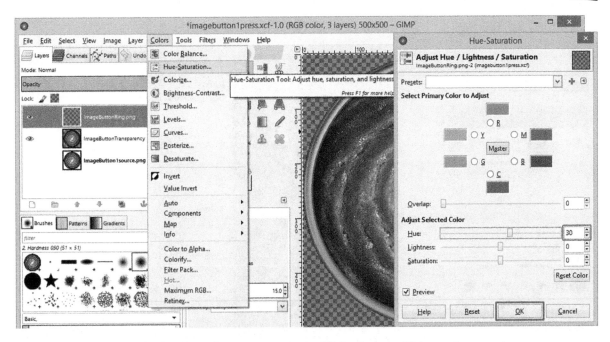

Figure 9-27. Use the Colors ➤ Hue Saturation menu sequence to shift the Hue value 30 degrees to a green hue

2. The work process to follow for this involves the same work process you undertook with the **imagebutton1normal.png** image asset, only you will name the (green) "pressed state" image button asset **imagebutton1press.png** instead. The work process is shown in Figures 9-23 through 9-26 and involves saving out the (XXHDPI) 500-pixel asset and then scaling from that asset down to an XHDPI (256 pixel), HDPI (128 pixel), MDPI (64 pixels), and LDPI (32 pixels) asset, saving to the appropriate resolution density folder each time using the **File ➤ Export As** menu sequence. Be sure to use the **Edit ➤ Undo Scale Image** command each time you scale (called "**downsampling**"), so that you give the GIMP cubic scaling algorithm the full 500 pixels of data to use to create an optimal image scaling result.

3. After you finish creating the five pressed state ImageButton digital image assets, you'll then need to create your five **focused** state ImageButton digital image assets, which we will color **red**, again by using the Hue-Saturation algorithm, with a **negative 80** Hue degree shift value, which you can see in the dialog shown in Figure 9-28.

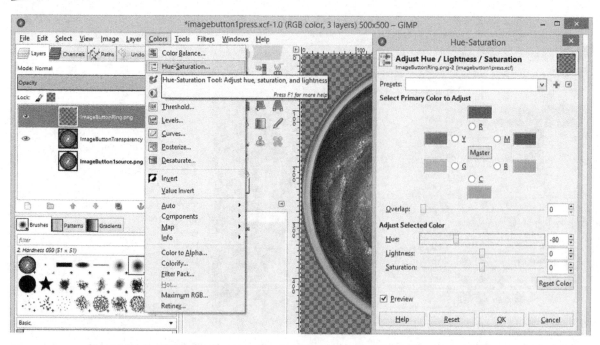

Figure 9-28. The green hue, and using Hue-Saturation dialog to shift the Hue value -80 degrees to a red hue

4. Implement the work process shown in Figures 9-23 through 9-26 a third time, saving out your (XXHDPI) 500-pixel asset, and then iteratively scaling down from the focus state asset four more times, using **Edit ➤ Undo Scale Image** between each iteration, to create your XHDPI (256 pixel), HDPI (128 pixel), MDPI (64 pixels), and LDPI (32 pixels) assets. Be sure to save each asset using the same **imagebutton1focus.png** file name in the appropriate resolution density folder each time by using the **File ➤ Export As** menu sequence.

Again, make sure to use GIMP's **Edit ➤ Undo Scale Image** command each time you downsample, so that you give the scaling algorithm the full 500 pixels to use to create an optimal image scaling result. Finally, you will need to create the ImageButton **hover** state asset, which we will color using a **purple** hue for the decorative ring. To create this purple hue for the hover ImageButton state, shift the Hue **-60 degrees**, as you can see in Figure 9-29, along with the red ring color, which you achieved using the previous Hue shifting operation.

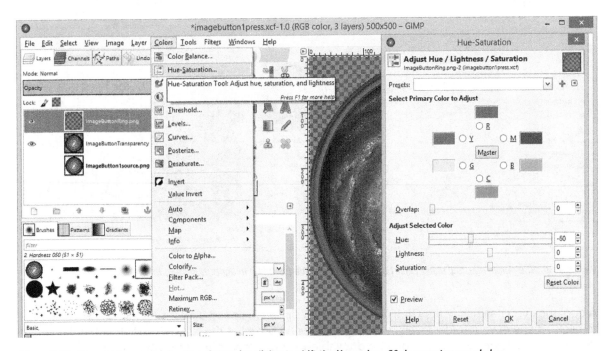

Figure 9-29. The red hue, and using Hue-Saturation dialog to shift the Hue value -60 degrees to a purple hue

I included a screenshot, shown in Figure 9-30, showing the **purple** hue, and the **Export Image** dialog, with the **hover** state file named **imagebutton1hover.png** being saved into the **/res/drawable-xxhdpi** resource folder.

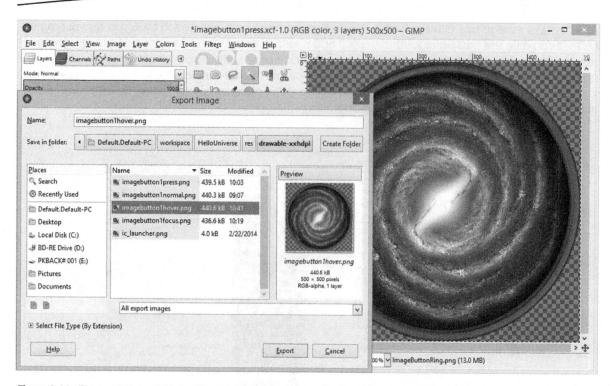

Figure 9-30. The purple hue, and using Export Image dialog to save the hover ImageButton state to XXHDPI

A cool trick you can use in the GIMP **File ➤ Export** dialog to speed up your folder navigation is to click on any of your folder levels, which are shown in boxes at the top of the dialog, to take you directly to that folder. So, to go from the drawable-xxhdpi folder to the drawable-xhdpi folder rapidly, click on the res box at the top between the HelloWorld box and the drawable-xxhdpi box, and then double-click to select drawable-xhdpi, in the center area of the dialog, and Voila! You will be in the next folder that you need to save in! Since your file name is the same, you do not need to edit the value in the **Name** field at all, simply click the **Export** button at this point and export the file. Then do the **Edit ➤ Undo Scale Image**, the **Image ➤ Scale** to create your next resolution assets, and perform the same rapid **File ➤ Export As** work process.

All of this might seem like a ton of work, but you will be amazed at how rapidly you can generate all these files, once you develop your optimal work process. I timed myself doing the **imagebutton3press.png** button state in all 5 resolutions, and it took me 3 minutes to go through this entire scaling process, so, 12 minutes for all 4 states times 3 buttons yields 36 minutes. So creating all 60 assets should take you around an hour, or a minute per image. I'd say that's an acceptable average! If you have any clients who are conceptualizing Android development as being a bit easier than it actually is, simply have them purchase and read this book!

An important take-away from this section of the chapter is that using any modern day digital image editing and compositing software, and even an IDE software such as Eclipse, is going to be a highly "modal" user experience. In GIMP, the **tool** that you have selected works on the **color channel** that you have selected inside of the **layer** that you have selected using **tool options** that you have specified, and all of these mode settings are then applied to the pixels in the image, which you "run through" this user-determined pixel selection and algorithmic processing pipeline. Because of all of these different modes which need to be set correctly in digital imaging, digital video editing, and in 3D modeling and animation, professional users really need to stay "on their toes" and realize exactly what they are doing with these software modes at all times during the content creation process. Content development, as well as software development, might appear to be quite simple, but in reality, they are actually a lot more difficult than they seem to be on the "surface!"

Now you have the image assets in place to be able to create the ImageButton XML definition files needed to implement a multi-state ImageButton which will access these 60 different digital image assets that you just created!

Creating Your ImageButton's XML Structure

The standard work process to define your ImageButton state is to utilize an **XML Drawable definition** file, which will be located in the **/res/drawable** folder. This file has a parent **<selector>** tag and child **<item>** tag which define each of your ImageButton states, using custom digital image asset references. Once the XML definition is set up, Android OS will select the correct image asset to utilize based on the hardware device resolution, and the ImageButton state that is needed (normal, pressed, focused or hovered) at the time.

The order of your state definitions inside of the <selector> parent selection container is quite important. This is because these states will be evaluated in the order that they are encountered in the XML Drawable definition file. This is why the normal image asset is referenced last, because it will be displayed after the android:state_hovered, android:state_pressed, and android:state_focused states are evaluated.

Let's get started by creating your **/res/drawable** folder to hold the NinePatchDrawable asset as well as the multi-state XML definition assets, which will then reference the 60 image state assets you just created for the 5 primary drawable-dpi resolution density folders. XML definitions and NinePatchDrawable assets will always go into this /res/drawable folder.

1. Right-click on the **/res** folder under the HelloUniverse project folder, and select the **New ➤ Folder** menu sequence, which will open the dialog shown on the left-hand side of Figure 9-31. Name the folder **drawable**, select the /res folder, and then click the **Finish** button to create the new /res/drawable folder to hold your XML definitions.

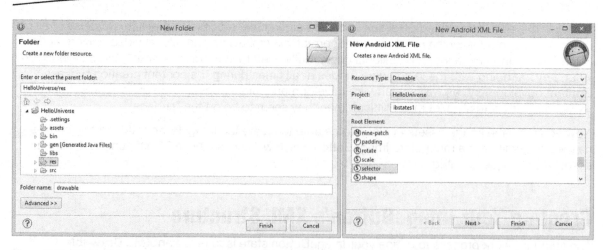

Figure 9-31. Right-click the /res folder and create a new folder (left) named drawable; create a new XML file (right)

2. Right-click on this new /res/drawable folder and select the **New ➤ Android XML File** menu sequence to get the dialog shown on the right-hand side of Figure 9-31. Name the file **ibstates1**, which stands for image button states, select the root element parent **<selector>** tag type, and then click the **Finish** button. This will open up an empty <selector> XML **state definition file** in Eclipse. A <selector> XML state definition will allow you to implement a selection set, much like the Java switch-case statement that you learned about earlier in the book. This selector will allow the Android OS to select amongst several different ImageButton drawable assets, based on the set of four android:state parameters that will define your basic ImageButton states. The child **<item>** tags inside of the parent <selector> tag will implement these **android:state** parameters, as well as reference the image assets using the **android:drawable** parameter. This is shown in the ibstates.xml tab in Eclipse in Figure 9-32, and uses the following XML mark-up format:

```xml
<?xml version="1.0" encoding="utf-8"
<selector xmlns:android=http://schemas.android.com/apk/res/android >
    <item android:state_hovered="true" android:drawable="@drawwable/imagebutton1hover" />
    <item android:state_pressed="true" android:drawable="@drawwable/imagebutton1press" />
    <item android:state_focused="true" android:drawable="@drawwable/imagebutton1focus" />
    <item android:drawable="@drawable/imagebutton1normal" />
</selector>
```

Figure 9-32. Create an ibstates1.xml file with a parent <selector> tag and four child <item> tags for button states

3. Perform the same work process outlined in Figures 9-31 and 9-32 to create
    an ibstates2.xml and ibstates3.xml file referencing the imagebutton2state
    and imagebutton3state assets. This will be quite easy if you copy the XML
    markup you created for ibstates1.xml into the ibstates2.xml and ibstates3.
    xml file, and change instances of the number 1 to 2 and 3, respectively. I am
    naming these files using this naming convention for a very good reason!

Referencing Multi-State XML via activity_main

To put these new multi-state ImageButton UI elements into play (place) in your **activity_main.xml**
UI design, you will need to edit the **android:src** parameter to reference the XML definition files that
you created in the previous section. Make sure not to use the **.xml** file extension in your reference
file name. This new markup is shown in Figure 9-33, along with an android:background="#00000000"
(transparency value) parameter for each <ImageButton> that will define the transparent background
color value. This background parameter will essentially remove that (default) square grey button
background from your ImageButton UI element, so that the image asset itself becomes the button,
which is why we are using the Android ImageButton class.

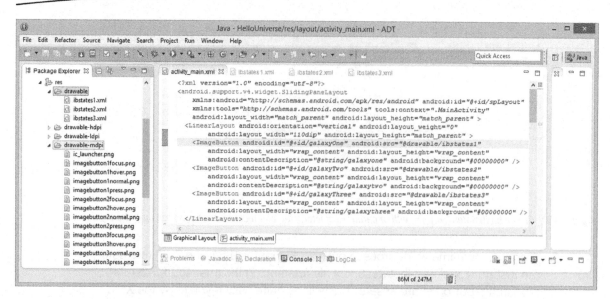

Figure 9-33. Change your android:src parameters for each <ImageButton> to reference the ibstates XML files

Now all we have left to do to upgrade the graphic design elements in your SlidingPaneLayout container that you created in the previous chapter is to use your **Run As ➤ Android Application** menu sequence, to make sure that your ImageButton UI elements will change color when you click on them, and add a reference to the NinePatch image asset that you created earlier in the chapter, so that you can see that new Drawable asset type in action as well in your SlidingPaneLayout UI!

It's important to note that not all of these interactive ImageButton states work in every AVD emulator, so if you want to test the **focused** or **hovered** states, be sure to use an Android hardware device that supports these to test your multi-state ImageButton XML markup. The reason I taught you the most extensive and complete work process, all four states across all of the different resolution densities that would be needed across any type or size device, is so that you know how to do this in case you want your application to span every possible hardware device type and configuration. If one of these states is not supported on a given hardware device, the Android OS will simply not access that image asset which is attached to that android:state parameter. I'd play it safe, and implement all of these ImageButton states in all of the resolution densities.

Adding a NinePatch to a SlidingPaneLayout

Finally, we need to implement the **NinePatchDrawalbe** asset that we created earlier in the chapter in your SlidingPane Layout container, to show you how to use this type of Drawable asset with your UI designs. If you've already run the app in the Nexus One AVD, you have seen that your ImageButton UI elements look great, as you can see in Figure 9-34, on the left-hand side. You can also see the NinePatchDrawable asset that we will be adding to the SlidingPaneLayout, as well as the margin spacing that we will have to add to refine and perfect the UI design to work with the NinePatchDrawable digital image asset.

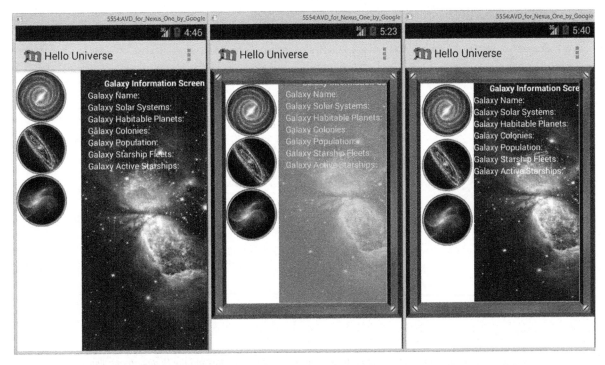

Figure 19-34. Test your multi-state ImageButtons (left) and the NinePatchDrawable (middle and right) in the AVD

To implement the NinePatchDrawable, you will add an android:background="ninepatchasset" parameter into your <SlidingPaneLayout> parent tag, as shown in Figure 9-35. This background plate parameter will reference a **ninepatchasset.9.png** file, which you will copy into the **/res/drawable** folder from wherever you saved it earlier, or from the book software repository, which contains all of this book's Java code, XML markup, and assorted new media assets.

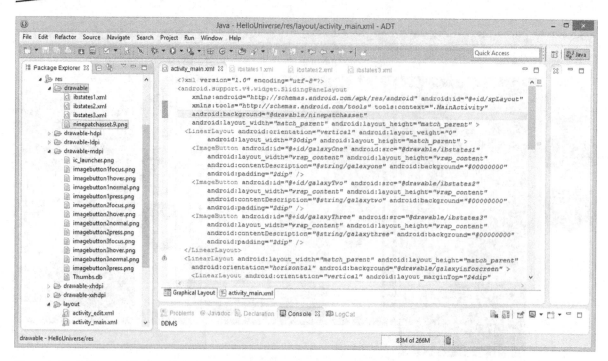

Figure 9-35. *Adding the NinePatchDrawable asset to the SlidingPaneLayout and adjusting the UI design margins*

I have opened the /res/drawable and /res/drawable-mdpi folders in Figure 9-35, to show all of the files which we have been creating during the chapter. I used a **Refresh** command to make them all visible to Eclipse after I had copied them (ninepatchasset.9.png), and saved them directly into my project resource folder hierarchy.

Also shown in Figure 9-35 are the android:padding="2dip" parameters in each of the <ImageButton> tags, and the modification to the android:layout_marginTop="24dip" parameter that I had to add into both of those nested LinearLayout containers in the second content pane, in order to push the text content down into the NinePatchDrawable asset's frame.

Congratulations, you have implemented a plethora of advanced, axis-independent scaling, interactive graphic design Android UI element attributes which aren't even covered in more advanced Android development books!

Summary

In this ninth chapter, you learned all about 2D graphic design concepts and principles, as well as about Android drawables and supported image formats, including the unique NinePatch image format used to create a type of "drawable" in Android called a **NinePatchDrawable**. You learned how to create a NinePatch using the Android **Draw 9-patch** software utility, and eventually implemented it inside of your SlidingPaneLayout UI design.

Next, you learned about the Android **ImageButton** class and used GIMP to create all of the assets, 60 of them in total, needed to implement three **multi-state** ImageButton UI elements, each having 4 UI states, across 5 resolution density levels or targets. You learned quite a bit about the proper way to utilize GIMP for a streamlined digital image editing and compositing work process, and got a lot of practice as well creating cool image assets for three ImageButtons for four interactive states (which animate the buttons on touch) across five resolution densities spanning smartwatches through 4K UHD iTV sets. My, we are impressive, aren't we? You also learned how to implement multi-state ImageButtons and NinePatchDrawables by using XML markup.

Next, in Chapter 10, you'll learn all about Animation for Android, including foundational animation theory and concepts, how to create a wide spectrum of resolution density animation assets, how to create frame animation assets for use with Android's **ImageView** class, and how to make the SlidingPaneLayout UI elements interactive.

Chapter **10**

Android Animation: Making Your UI Designs Move

In the previous chapter on graphic design, I covered two dimensional (2D) concepts, such as pixel arrays and aspect ratios, as well as three dimensional (3D) concepts, such as layer stacks and z-order. In this chapter, we are going to take all of that knowledge into the fourth dimension (4D), which is **time**, and discover concepts such as **motion** and **frame rate**. We are again going to build upon all of those fundamental graphic design concepts you learned about in the previous chapter, because you can also apply all of those core digital imaging concepts to animation. Thus, we will be taking "static" or motionless graphics from the previous chapter and turning them into motion graphics which can look even more realistic, because it looks like the subject matter is moving or animated.

You can use frame animation to create an illusion of motion using cels or frames, and you will be learning about all of those concepts, terminology, and techniques you can use to do this in the next section of the chapter. During this chapter, we'll take a look at exactly how to set up frame-based animation inside of your Android app, using an XML animation definition file containing a parent **<animation-list>** tag as your animation frames container. An <animation-list> parent tag allows you to add individual frames of an animation as child **<item>** elements, allowing you to create an XML frame animation definition you can use as a multimedia asset.

I will be covering more of the core Android classes which are used to implement graphic design elements, such as **ImageView**, as well as Android classes which are used to implement frame animation and procedural animation, **AnimationDrawable** (frame animation), and **Animation** (procedural animation).

During the chapter, we will utilize these three Android graphics classes to "**animate**" the SlidingPaneLayout UI layout container design. We'll install an ImageView UI widget underneath your Galaxy Info Screen to hold a spaceship animation, showing a different type of space vehicle for each galaxy listed in the SlidingPaneLayout container.

Frame Animation Concepts and Techniques

The first thing that we will always need to do is to get our "knowledge foundation" regarding frame animation's concepts, formats, and terminology, since we're going to use these during the rest of this chapter, in conjunction with working with Android animation. This new media type is commonly called 2D animation, and I'm going to cover 2D **vector** animation, also known as **procedural** animation or "**tween**" animation, later on in this chapter.

Frame Animation: Cels, Frames, and Terminology

Frame-based animation could be termed "cel-based" animation because of the original 2D animation created by Walt Disney. Disney animators drew on what at that time were called "**cels**," in order to represent each individual movement in their cartoon animation in its own cel. Interestingly, the original cels from these animation projects are now "framed," and sold to collectors for thousands of dollars! Thus, there are both physical and conceptual connections between these two animation terms, **frame animation** and **cel animation**.

Later on, with the advent of feature films, the term "frame" replaced the term "cel." This was because the analog film projectors which were used to display **24** frames per second used frames of film. These frames of film were displayed using one or more reels containing film frames, which would create the illusion of motion when light was projected through the moving frames using film projectors in a theater projection room behind an audience.

The technical term for digital frame-based animation is **raster animation**, as the frames or cels are made up of collections of pixels. Pixel-based imagery is commonly known in the industry as **raster imagery**. Raster images are also commonly called "**bitmaps**" because they are a map (array) of bits (pixels). In fact, there is the **bitmap (.BMP)** file format used in Microsoft Windows; however, this digital image file format is not currently supported for use under the Android OS. Because the bitmap file format has become so popular due to its use in Windows, raster animation is also frequently called **bitmap animation** within the multimedia production industry. Android has a BitmapDrawable class and creates a BitmapDrawable object for your bitmap image assets.

We will utilize these various animation industry terms interchangeably throughout this chapter, so that you will get used to using all of these different, but accurate, terms to refer to your frame-based 2D animation, which can also be called raster animation, bitmap animation, frame animation, cel animation, and digital image animation.

Frame Animation Formats: PNG, GIF, JPEG & WebP

The Android OS supports the same open source digital image file formats which you use for 2D imagery in the Android application for use within your frame-based animation assets. If you think about it, this is quite logical, as a 2D animation is defined by using those individual 2D digital image frames as the foundation for 4D motion.

The significance of this is that you can use indexed color images if you want to create an 8-bit frame animation, using the PNG8 or GIF formats. You can also use truecolor image formats to create your 24-bit, or 32-bit, frame animation. You would do this by using the PNG24, PNG32, WebP, or the JPEG digital image file formats.

Just like with digital image file formats, Android prefers the **PNG** data format over GIF, WebP, or JPEG when used in frame-based animation. This is due to the PNG **lossless** image quality, and reasonably good image compression results, which will result in a **higher quality end-user experience**, given a capable app developer.

It is also important to note that the Android OS does not currently support the **Animated GIF** format, which is also known as the **animGIF**, or **aGIF**, animation file format. There are some workarounds being discussed online for this until support for this format is added to Android. Given that PNG8 gives better compression results and that defining frames using XML and controlling them using Java code will give us far more control over the end result we are trying to achieve, I'm going to focus on **currently supported** Android frame animation solutions and methodologies, for now.

Android OS support for several mainstream digital image file formats gives us an impressive amount of latitude to be able to optimize the frame animation's data footprint. Because of Android's support for the PNG32 format, we will also be able to implement an image compositing work process in our frame animation endeavors. You can do this by using the 8-bit alpha channel transparency capability in the PNG32 format on a frame-by-frame basis.

Optimizing Frames: Color Depth and Frame Count

In frame animation, there are three primary ways to optimize your animation data in order to achieve a smaller **data footprint**. You can **reduce the resolution** of each frame, you can **reduce the color depth** used to define each frame, and you can **reduce the number of frames** utilized to create an illusion of motion in the animation.

Since we need to provide at least three different resolution density targets to support Android 4.4, we will focus on optimizing the color depth and the total number of frames as much as possible first, for practical purposes, as you're essentially going to want to provide frame resolution spanning from at least 120 pixels for MDPI through 240 pixels for HDPI to a maximum of 480 pixels for XHDPI. As you'll see during this chapter, you do have the option to provide fewer than five resolution density targets (we will use three) and have Android scale the rest. The hope is that Android will scale your assets down (termed: downsampling) rather than scaling assets up (termed: upsampling).

Since we have a choice between using a lossless PNG32, which as you now know is a true color PNG with a full 8-bit alpha channel, and an indexed color PNG8, which is many times smaller (per each frame), we will use this lossless PNG8 for animated elements which do not need to be composited (using a PNG32's 8-bit alpha channel) for our application's animated UI elements in this chapter. We can use the ImageView plates to implement our compositing pipeline by using a background plate for static graphics and a source (foreground plate) for the animation.

It is interesting to note that there is an advanced way around this compositing challenge, which is to use a white or a black background color for a PNG8 animation using no alpha channel and then composite with the Android PorterDuff class. This is because using certain PorterDuff **blending modes**, you can make white and black values become transparent using **blending algorithms** rather than alpha channels. Alpha channels are more efficient (but have a heavy data footprint, especially when used across multiple frames in an animation) because they are "**static**" (that is, pre-defined), whereas using a "**dynamic**" algorithm at runtime will use valuable CPU processor cycles (system hardware resources). This PorterDuff image blending algorithm class is covered in great detail in the *Pro Android Graphics* (Apress, 2013) title, which I wrote previous to writing this title.

If you are not going to have to composite your animation over other graphics (or are compositing with blending modes using the PorterDuff class), you can also consider using a JPEG format to get a far smaller per-frame data footprint. As you know, the JPEG codec does this by throwing away some of the image data (and thus throwing away some of the original image's quality).

It is important to note, however, that using JPEG for animation can increase image artifacts in each frame of the animation. If you apply too much image compression on each frame, causing artifacts, and you later animate the JPEG artifacts, this will cause an effect commonly termed in the industry as "dot crawl" or "pixel crawl."

With JPEG animation, not only do you have artifacts, but because the medium is animated, and the artifacts are on different pixels on each frame, it's like they are waving their hands in the air and saying: "Here I am, I'm an important artifact!" This doesn't lend itself to a good user experience if your JPEG frames are poorly optimized.

Just as you can optimize a 2D animation by using the indexed (8-bit) color depth, you can also optimize your 2D animation by **using fewer frames** to create the illusion of motion. As you will see in the next chapter on digital video, the same concepts hold true for bitmap animation as with digital video: fewer frames to store will yield a smaller data footprint, which ultimately will translate into a smaller Android application file size for your APK.

Also, the smaller the number of frames that will be used to achieve realistic motion, the fewer frames will have to be defined in our frame animation XML definition markup. It's also important to note that at runtime, fewer frames will require **less processing** power in order to play your frame animation, and **less memory** resources to hold the frames in, before they are displayed on the device display screen. In fact, we get professional results in this chapter by using only a few frames of animation for your ImageView UI's 3D animation new media assets.

Data footprint optimization becomes more important as the number of frame animations that are included in the application increases. New media applications such as games and eBooks tend to have several frame animations running at any given time inside the application Activity screen. Thus, you need to consider processor power and system memory as valuable resources! Animation assets will require careful optimization, so that the application does not use up your user's Android hardware device memory and CPU resources while your app is being used.

Animation Resolution: Pixels Add to File Size!

The **number of pixels** in each animation frame, or the **frame resolution** for your frame-based animation, is of tantamount importance to the optimization of a frame animation asset data footprint. Review the raw image data mathematics that we covered back in Chapter 9, and apply this to each frame in your animation, so that you can calculate the exact raw data **system memory footprint** you will need to hold your frame-based animation.

Just like you did with your static digital image button assets, you will need to provide (at most) five resolution density-specific raster animation image target resolutions to be able to span every popular Android device type screen density. For this reason, if you can make your animation a few dozen pixels smaller for each dimension, without affecting its visual quality, this will add up to memory savings in your endgame, no pun intended.

It is important to make sure to "trim" any unutilized pixels within your animation, so that the animated elements come as close (one pixel away) to touching the edges of your image container as possible. You will see that I've done this in all the animation frame assets we will be using in this chapter, so you'll be able to see what I mean.

Similar to what you learned about digital imagery in Chapter 9, Android will automatically handle the decisions regarding which of the 2D frame animation pixel densities to implement for each device screen which the OS is running on. Our largest 480 by 480 pixel resolution frame animation asset is for the XHDPI resolution density, and I will create a 240 by 240 pixel version for HDPI, as well as a 120 by 120 pixel version to use for MDPI.

The reason that I'm not creating an XXHDPI resolution version on the highend (4K TV) is because the XHDPI animation frames can be scaled up if needed for those devices, which represent 2% of the device market, and on the lowend (240 pixel flip-phone or smartwatch), the MDPI animation frames can be scaled down if needed for those devices, which also represent about a 2% market share amongst all the current Android hardware devices.

The Android AnimationDrawable Class

The Android **AnimationDrawable** class is used to create a frame animation type of Drawable object in Android, which holds a list of drawable assets which define the frames of the animation, as well as playback parameters.

Android's AnimationDrawable class is part of the **android.graphics** package, as you might imagine, and is kept with all of the other types of Drawable objects in Android, using the **android.graphics. drawable** sub-package.

The class hierarchy starts with the java.lang.Object master class, which is subclassed to create the **Drawable** class, which is subclassed to create a **DrawableContainer** class, which is subclassed to create an **AnimationDrawable** class. The Java class hierarchy for the AnimationDrawable class would thus look like the following:

```
java.lang.Object
  > android.graphics.drawable.Drawable
    > android.graphics.drawable.DrawableContainer
      > android.graphics.drawable.AnimationDrawable
```

The reason that this **DrawableContainer** class is between the Drawable and AnimationDrawable is because it was logical to create the DrawableContainer class for what you might consider "multi-drawables," or drawables with **more than one** state, level, frame, or other such drawable asset element. Examples of these ContainerDrawable subclasses include the **StateListDrawable**, used to create the **multi-state** ImageButton, the **LevelListDrawable** used for **level indicators**, such as the signal level meter on your smartphone, and the **AnimationDrawable**.

The simplest way to create one of these frame animation drawable assets is to define the animation frames using an XML file, which will be stored in the HelloUniverse project's **/res/drawable** folder. We will be creating three spaceship animations during this chapter, using the AnimationDrawable and Animation classes, after we discuss how the AnimationDrawable and Animation classes function. After we create the AnimationDrawable object(s), we'll set them up with background images, using an ImageView object. Later on in the chapter, when we write your Java code for the SlidingPaneLayout, we'll call the **.start()** method to start each AnimationDrawable object's playback cycle.

The XML animation definition construct which you are going to be specifying later in the chapter gets **inflated** by your Java code, and becomes an AnimationDrawable object. This object contains all information regarding your frame animation asset, including each actual animation frame image asset reference, as well as each frame's playback (duration) setting.

After the AnimationDrawable object has been instantiated and inflated, you can trigger it by using a .start() method from within your application Java code. This is usually done from the inside of your event handler, such as the one that we will be adding to the ImageButton UI elements later in the chapter. You would use an event handler if you wanted the frame animation to be triggered (started) interactively. You can also call the .start() method from the inside of your Activity subclass's on Create() method, if the animation is intended to simply run on your Activity startup screen somewhere once the Activity is created (started).

If you want to research more detailed information regarding the Android AnimationDrawable class, you can find more technical details on the Android Developer website at the following URL:

```
http://developer.android.com/reference/android/graphics/drawable/AnimationDrawable.html
```

Now that we have gone over the AnimationDrawable class basics, let's take a look at how to use XML markup to create your frame animation definition file(s), which will live in the Android application project's **/res/drawable** folder.

Creating Frame Animation Using XML Markup

The way that frame animation is defined in Android is by using an XML definition file containing markup that defines an **animation list** filled with **frame items**. This XML file should be stored in the **/res/drawable** folder, which you created in the previous chapter, and which holds Android Drawable asset XML definitions, such as multi-state (**StateListDrawable**) ImageButton elements, **NinePatchDrawable** asymmetrically scalable digital image assets, and **AnimationDrawable** frame animation assets.

In case you are wondering why this XML file is kept in your /res/drawable folder, and not in a **/res/anim** folder, this is because there are **two types** of animation in Android. Frame animation uses the /drawable resource folder hierarchy to hold the AnimationDrawable XML definitions (i.e. the /res/drawable folder) and their referenced digital imagery assets (in the /res/drawable-dpi sub-folders).

Procedural Animation object(s), which we will be covering later on in this chapter, use the /res/anim project folder, along with an Animation class constructor method to create Animation objects.

The frame animation XML file will specify the individual frames in your AnimationDrawable object definition (essentially, this XML file is a 2D AnimationDrawable object constructor) by using the <animation-list> parent XML tag. This frame animation XML construct essentially creates an AnimationDrawable objectcontaining references to numbered frames (your image files). The image file references represent the individual frames in your raster animation. A procedural (or vector) animation XML file, on the other hand, won't specify any frames, but will instead specify algorithmic or procedural transformations, that, when **interpolated**, will create an illusion of motion. We'll cover this type of animation a bit later on in this chapter.

The <animation-list> Tag: Your Frame Container

Most of the 2D frame-based animation assets will be created by using an**<animation-list>** XML parent tag and its playback and visibility configuration parameters. The primary configuration parameter that you will be using is the **android:oneshot** parameter. This is the parameter that controls whether the **animation playback** will be configured to **loop continuously** or **play forever** (using the oneshot="false" setting), or if it will be configured to **play just one single time** (using the oneshot="true" setting). One-single-time playback is usually used with an event handling setup, because you want the animation to play one time whenever it is clicked. The continuous playback method, on the other hand, is usually setup with a .start() method call inside of an on Create() method, so the animated design element continues playing (all the time, forever), somewhere on that Activity's display screen.

Later on, you will reference the XML file that contains this <animation-list> parent tag, and its children tags, by using its first name (that is, the first part of the filename) without the extension, just like you did with the multi-state ImageButton definition in the previous chapter. We will create a frame animation XML definition file that uses an **anim_milkyway.xml** file name, but which references this file in Android XML markup and Java code as: **anim_milkyway**. Once this <animation-list> is defined using XML, you will be able to reference the frame-based animation that you have defined in it from any of your UI or UX designs across your entire application.

Finally, there is an **android:visibility** parameter which you can utilize if you are going to control the visibility of your AnimationDrawable object within your Java code. You can use this parameter to set the **initial visibility** setting, which is usually going to be "true" or visible, until a user clicks it, or some other code function hides it.

As you'll see later, there is also a way to auto-start your animation via XML, so that you don't have to use an ID parameter, which is generally used to provide a way for your Java code to inflate and reference your XML tag constructs.

The <item> Tag: How to Add in Animation Frames

The <animation-list> tag will always be the parent tag, because it is designed to contain **<item>** tags, which will always be the child tags. The item tag is used to define the frames in your <animation-list> tag, with one <item> tag for each animation frame. There are two parameters used inside of the <item> tag: the **android:drawable** file name reference parameter, and the **android:duration** parameter which specifies a frame display duration integer value in milliseconds. A millisecond is one-thousandth of a second, so one second of frame duration would use a 1000 integer value. All these <item> tags exist inside of your parent <animation-list> container, in the order in which they are to be displayed, just like you are loading the animation frames into a data array in system memory, which, essentially, you are.

The math for calculating this duration value, which is ultimately going to represent the animation's **frame rate**, which is usually specified in **frames per second**, or **FPS**, is the **number of seconds** you want the animation to last **times 1000, divided by the number of frames** that you have in your animation. So if you want a Lunar Lander to rotate once every second, and you have 8 frames to create the smooth illusion of motion (45 degrees of rotation per frame), then **1 times 1000 divided by 8** gives you **125**, so you would use an android:duration="125" parameter for each <item> tag.

If you want a slower 2-second rotation, you would use a **250** value, a 3-second rotation would be 3000 divided by 8 or a value of **375**, and so forth. Using XML markup will make it easy to experiment or "tweak" these values, until you get the exact animation motion you're looking for.

Next, you will create your XML animation definition file using Eclipse ADT, using a very similar work process to what you did in the previous chapter in order to create the XML for the multi-state ImageButton UI elements.

Creating Frame Animation in MainActivity

The first thing you'll need to do is to copy these eight **lunarlander** PNG files from the book files repository into your project's **/res/drawable-xhdpi** folder. These are indexed color **PNG8** files, which are 320 by 320 pixels. I'll also include 160 by 160 (HDPI) versions and 80 by 80 (MDPI) versions for those of you who want to provide a range of resolution density assets in your application. Figure 10-1 shows the eight files, as well as a background plate ring image to composite behind them called **imageviewwhitering.png**, copied into the XHDPI folder. The animation XML asset we will be creating will be used in a source image plate for the <ImageView> composite.

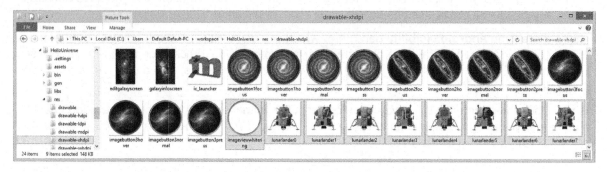

Figure 10-1. Copy the eight lunarlander PNG files and the imageviewwhitering.png background image to /res/drawable-xhdpi

Creating an anim_milkyway.xml File and Markup

Right-click on the /res/drawable folder and select the **New ➤ Android XML File** menu sequence to open a **New Android XML File** dialog, shown in Figure 10-2. Name the file **anim_milkyway**, select an **animation-list** root element from the center selector area, and then click the **Finish** button to create the bootstrap XML file.

Figure 10-2. Create an anim_milkyway.xml animation-list

Next, add the android:oneshot="false" parameter into the parent <animation-list> tag, as seen in Figure 10-3. Add eight **<item>** child tags with **android:drawable** parameters referencing the eight numbered file names for the animation frames, and add an **android:duration** value specifying how fast you want your spaceship to spin!

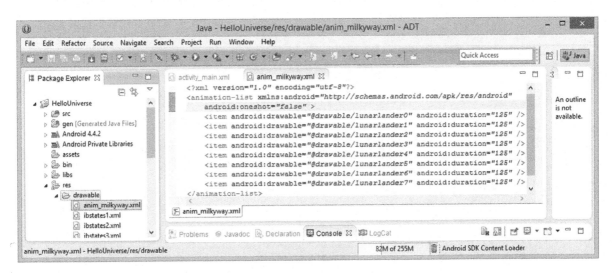

Figure 10-3. Configure the <animation-list> parent tag with a oneshot parameter, and add eight <item> child tags

Your frame animation XML definition markup should look like the following:

```xml
<?xml version="1.0" encoding="utf-8"?>
<animation-list xmlns:android="http://schemas.android.com/apk/res/android"
    android:oneshot="false" >
    <item android:drawable="@drawable/lunarlander0" android:duration="250" />
    <item android:drawable="@drawable/lunarlander1" android:duration="250" />
    <item android:drawable="@drawable/lunarlander2" android:duration="250" />
    <item android:drawable="@drawable/lunarlander3" android:duration="250" />
    <item android:drawable="@drawable/lunarlander4" android:duration="250" />
    <item android:drawable="@drawable/lunarlander5" android:duration="250" />
    <item android:drawable="@drawable/lunarlander6" android:duration="250" />
    <item android:drawable="@drawable/lunarlander7" android:duration="250" />
</animation-list>
```

Notice that the screen shot in Figure 10-3 shows a fast one second spin rate using a duration value of 125 milliseconds, while the XML markup above shows the slower two second spin rate, using a duration value of 250 milliseconds. Play around with this value to achieve the spin rate that you like best with this animation.

The next thing that you need to do is reference this animation definition file inside of the activity_main.xml file. Notice that once you do this, your animation will play using only XML; you don't have to call a .start() method!

Wiring-Up Your Animation: Referencing Your XML

Change the android:layout_height parameter for your second <LinearLayout> container to **wrap_content**, add an android:id="@+id/llh" so that you can reference it, and add a **<RelativeLayout>** parent tag on the outside of the SlidingPaneLayout content pane structure, as is shown in Figure 10-4, in the top screen.

Figure 10-4.   Change the horizontal LinearLayout to wrap_content in the height dimension and add <ImageView>

Add a closing </RelativeLayout> tag above the closing <SlidingPaneLayout>, as shown in Figure 10-4, and add an <ImageView> tag above it, with the required layout_width and layout_height parameters set to **wrap_content** and the required android:contentDescription set to a **galaxyone** string constant.

Reference the **anim_milkyway** XML file you created using the **android:src** parameter for a source foreground image plate for the ImageView, and use the **imageviewwhitering** PNG8 file using the **android:background** parameter in the background plate. If you use your **Run As ➤ Android Application** menu sequence now, you will notice that the animation overlays the top of the galaxy info screen, so use an **android:layout_below** relative layout parameter to reference an **ID** that you added to the first <LinearLayout> inside of your new <RelativeLayout> "wrapper" that you're using to install this animation underneath your existing design. The <ImageView> XML markup should look like this:

```
<ImageView android:layout_width="wrap_content" android:layout_height="wrap_content"
  android:src="@drawable/anim_milkyway" android:background="@drawable/imageviewwhitering"
  android:layout_below="@+id/llh" android:contentDescription="@string/galaxyone"  />
```

Now if you use the **Run As ➤ Android Application** menu sequence, you will see the results on the left side of Figure 10-5. As you can see, the Android OS is scaling the foreground image resource to match the size of your background image resource, even though we have provided assets with different pixel dimensions. I made sure (using imaging software external to Android) that these would match up perfectly, to the pixel, and Android is not "respecting" the pixel dimensions for my digital imaging assets. I am going to show you how to get around this problem next, so you can achieve the result shown in the other two panes (middle and right) in Figure 10-5.

Figure 10-5. Test markup (left), add adjustViewBounds parameter (middle), and add a padding parameter (right)

You will need to add in a parameter that tells Android not to scale our referenced drawable assets, but instead to "respect" their pixel dimensions and draw them "pixel-for-pixel." The android:adjustViewBounds="true" will perform this function for the <ImageView> UI widget, as you can see in the center pane of Figure 10-5. If you want to see the markup for this in the <ImageView>, take a look at Figure 10-6.

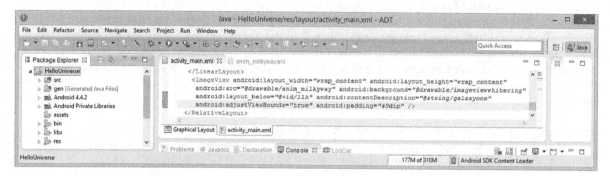

Figure 10-6. Add adjustViewBounds="true" and 40 DIP of android:padding value to shrink the source and center

Resizing Source Imagery: Using Padding Values

As you can see in the middle and right panes of Figure 10-5, the foreground and background image plates in the ImageView are now conforming the ImageView to the pixel dimensions of these images, except that the UI widget is still scaling up the source image to match the dimensions of the background image. We'll need another parameter to be able to get around this problem. Hopefully one day, Android OS developers will add in the android:maintainDrawablePixels parameter which, when set to true, will allow developers to do their relative pixel scale compositing (that is, different layers with different pixel dimensions, as we are using here) outside of the Android OS. For now, we are going to leverage the **android:padding** parameter, which installs space on the **inside** of the View container; in this case, it is an ImageView. An android:layout_margin parameter, on the other hand, installs space on the outside of the View container, which **moves** the entire container around on the screen. Padding, on the other hand, **scales** what is inside of that container. We'll use this to our advantage in order to fine-tune the effect of the ring background around the outside of our animation.

Fortunately, the android:padding parameter only affects the source (foreground) image plate, which in this case, is referencing the **anim_milkyway** XML animation asset that we have recently created, using <animation-list>.

We are going to use this fact that padding only scales (affects) the foreground image plate to our advantage, by adding an android:padding parameter, which will add the same amount of padding on all four sides (insides) of the ImageView container. This will serve to both **scale down** (technically this would be called downsampling) and **center** the Lunar Lander animation, allowing the background plate ring decoration element to show through from its lower z-order location (on the compositing layer underneath the foreground image).

The final XML markup for your <ImageView> UI widget child tag is shown in Figure 10-6, and should look like the following:

```
<ImageViewandroid:layout_width="wrap_content"android:layout_height="wrap_content"
 android:src="@drawable/anim_milkyway"android:background="@drawable/imageviewwhitering"
 android:layout_below="@+id/llh" android:contentDescription="@string/galaxyone"
 android:adjustViewBounds="true" android:padding="40dip" />
```

You can experiment with different padding values, until the corners of your animation asset stop overlaying the ring background element and the shading inside of its rim, so that the white values essentially hide any "seams" between these images. You can do image compositing using alpha channels, and in many instances in a more simple fashion simply by making sure that background and foreground colors match perfectly, eliminating any seam!

Next, let's use a different AVD emulator, so you can see the entire ImageView UI element. Use the **Run As ➤ Run Configurations** menu sequence to set the AVD to the **Galaxy Nexus**, which uses a 720 by 1280 resolution. The Nexus One AVD uses 480 by 800 resolution. If you want an image of the Run Configurations dialog, see Figure 4-9.

Testing Your SlidingPane in a Galaxy Nexus AVD

After you set the Galaxy Nexus as the active or default AVD emulator in the Run Configurations dialog, launch it from that dialog, or launch it using the **Run As ➤ Android Applications** menu sequence. As you can see in Figure 10-7, the **NinePatchDrawable** has scaled down so that the frame is thinner, and the entire background ring is visible, with the foreground animation composited over it. The 40 DIP padding setting is no longer perfect, as you can see, the very tips of the corners of the foreground animation overlaying the ring, so our composite is no longer "seamless." To fix this, we will need to scale down the foreground image another 10%, using the higher padding value of **44 DIP**. As you can now see, you also need to install an android:layout_marginLeft parameter to push the ImageView UI element into the center of the frame, as you can see on the right side of Figure 10-7.

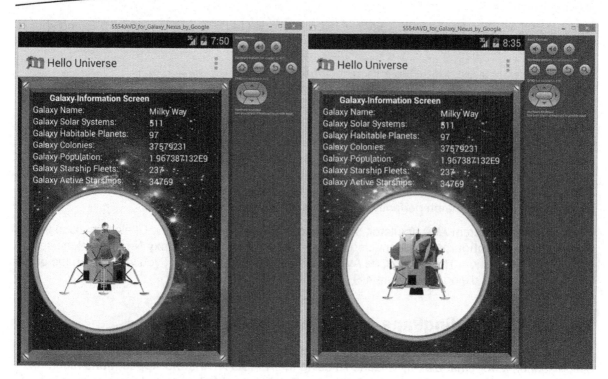

Figure 10-7. *Test UI design in Galaxy Nexus AVD (left) and add a 38 DIP left margin parameter to center (right)*

The final XML markup for the ImageView UI widget is shown in Figure 10-8, and looks like the following:

```
<ImageView android:layout_width="wrap_content" android:layout_height="wrap_content"
 android:src="@drawable/anim_milkyway" android:background="@drawable/imageviewwhitering"
 android:layout_below="@+id/llh" android:contentDescription="@string/galaxyone"
 android:adjustViewBounds="true" android:padding="44dip" android:layout_marginLeft="32dip" />
```

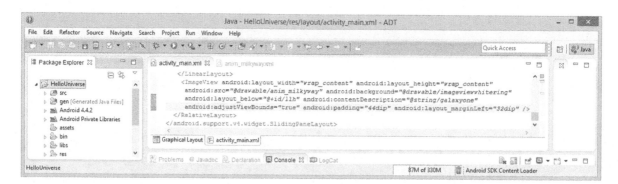

Figure 10-8. *Add an android:layout_marginLeft="32dip" parameter to center the <ImageView> in the SlidingPane*

Now that you have learned about frame animation, let's learn about the other major type of animation, called vector or procedural animation, which is supported in Android. The term in Android for this type of animation is "tween animation."

Tween Animation Concepts and Techniques

The patron saint of animation, Mr. Walt Disney, is also responsible for the animation term **tween**, as cels were "tweened" or "in betweened" by his junior animators. The senior animators would create the primary movement "key frames" and the junior animators would then create the "tweens." Be careful not to confuse this term with the popular term used to describe the pre-teen (twelve+teen) years, unless of course you know someone in this age range who is a very talented animator, like some of the artisans who are probably reading this book right now, so that they can take their work to the next level (interactive).

Tweening is now done **algorithmically** for you by the Android OS using something that's called **interpolation**. Interpolation algorithms are provided by the Android **Animation** class, which we will be learning all about after we get up-to-speed on all of our tween animation (or vector or procedural animation) concepts and terminology. One of the cool things that was added in Android 5 was additional interpolation algorithms, so be sure not to skip the final chapter in this book covering Android 5!

These procedural attributes are the types of attributes which can be interpolated, or more accurately, which can be "transformed" by using interpolation. They include **alpha** (transparency) which you've already learned about to some extent, as well as **translation**, which is the 2D industry term for movement; **scale**, which is the industry term for size; and **rotation**, which is the industry term describing which direction something is facing.

Each of these concepts (rotate, scale, and translate) has an XML tag and class in Android, so let's cover these new vector animation concepts next. In case you might be wondering, a "vector" is a "ray" that is traced out in two or three dimensions, starting at one point and shooting out through (or to, it if stops) another point. So, a line, basically.

Procedural Concepts: Rotate, Scale, Translate

Let's start out by learning about some of the concepts involved in vector imaging (illustration) and animation. First of all, there are two primary types of vector platforms, 2D or two-dimensional (flat) vector graphics such as we find in Illustrator or InkScape, and 3D, or three-dimensional (volumetric) vector graphics, such as what we find in 3D modeling software such as Blender 3D or Autodesk 3D Studio MAX.

Concepts that we cover in this section of the chapter will apply to both 2D and 3D imaging and animation, but we are sticking to 2D Animation in this Absolute Beginners book!

Both 2D animation and 3D animation utilize vectors. 2D vectors, which use x and y coordinates, are used in 2D, and 3D vectors, which use x, y, and z coordinates, are used in 3D. Both 2D and 3D animation involve these core concepts of translation (movement), rotation (direction), and scaling (size).

There is a z concept in 2D animation, but it is not a z-axis, but rather a z-**order**. z-order in 2D is akin to layers in digital imaging, as we have already discussed earlier in the book. z-order involves what layer order each 2D (flat) layer is in, and whether it is front of, or behind, other 2D layers, making the z-order a number which orders the layers in your 2D composite. This z-order number defines what is in front of, and what is behind, any given 2D layer. Changing this z-order numeric value in realtime using your Java programming logic can create flip-book special effects.

Translation in 2D involves movement along an x or y axis, and it is the most basic of the three transformations you can achieve in 2D animation. Translation is defined by the **starting point** for the movement, the **amount** or distance of that movement, in pixels or percentages, and the **direction** of movement, along either an x or y axis (or along some relative combination of both x and y axis values, which will create a diagonal movement).

Rotation in 2D involves rotation around a given x, y **pivot point** coordinate. The amount of rotation is defined using **degrees**, a **direction** (positive/clockwise or negative/counter-clockwise) of the rotation, and the pivot point (center) **location** of the rotation. Since there are **360** degrees in a full circle, rotational mathematics involves this 360 number specifically, like FPS calculations involve the number 1000 (number of milliseconds in a second).

Scale in 2D involves a size for a given shape, and is defined by a **decimal number** relative to the current size of the shape. For instance, a 0.5 scale would be half of the current size, and a 2.0 scale would be twice the current size of that shape. Like translation, scaling has an x and a y component. If the values are the same, this scaling can be said to be **uniform scaling**; if they're not the same, the scaling could be said to be **non-uniform** scaling.

To draw a parallel to something that you have learned about previously, uniform scaling maintains aspect ratio, and non-uniform scaling "skews" or "distorts" (that is, changes) the aspect ratio. Therefore, non-uniform scaling is most often used for animation special effects, such as making a ball "squash" when it bounces off the ground.

Interestingly, you can also define a **pivot point** for your scaling operation, which allows **skewed scaling** where the placement of the pivot point can influence your scaling operation. On irregular shapes, this can give a more precise level of control over the resulting shape-warping special effects for the scaling operation. Given that sometimes the 2D shapes being scaled contain bitmap images, you can obtain some very interesting results using a pivot point placement that is not at the exact center point of that image. The industry term for putting an image in a 2D shape or on a 3D object is called "texture mapping."

Procedural Data Values: Ranges and Pivot Point

In order to be able to **interpolate**, we need to specify more than a single numeric value, because interpolation, or tweening, involves creating new **interim values** between a starting and ending value. So, information learned in the previous sections (interpolation) will be applied to information found in this section (ranges), and then in the next section, we will cover alpha blending as well as the more complicated procedural animation parameters that are available to control animation start time offsets, looping characteristics, and how many times it loops.

To have any procedural animation, we will always need to specify a **range**, from a starting value, called a **From** value, to the ending value, called a **To** value. This seems logical, as we need to animate something over time from one value to another value!

Besides having a range, many of the more complex procedural animation transformations involve a **pivot point**. A pivot point tells Android how to skew a scale transform favoring a certain area or what point to rotate around, as you'll see in a future section when we get into implementing these different types of transforms using XML.

Like a value range, a pivot point will also require two values to establish. However, unlike a value range, which utilizes a From and To value, a pivot point uses a two dimensional location on your display screen, and uses **x** and **y** coordinates, just like pixels do, to define where the pivot point is to be placed within that 2D "**plane**." A plane in 2D is like a sheet of paper, or like a layer in compositing, and is an "infinitely flat" 2D (x and y) surface. By infinitely flat I mean that there is no z dimension "depth" to the 2D plane.

Pivot points are also used extensively in 3D animation, where setting the pivot point requires three (x, y, and z) data coordinates in order to be properly specified in 3D space. Currently, Android uses 2D procedural animation in its Animation class, with 3D animation being handled via a different **android.opengl** package. Discussion of 3D animation is best-suited for a Pro Android 3D title. In this book, we are covering 2D, as that is the best starting point to use for absolute beginners!

Let's take a look at a fourth type of procedural transform, **alpha blending**, next, and then we will look at advanced parameters.

Procedural Compositing: Alpha Blending

There is one other attribute which can be animated procedurally in Android, but it is not a transformation. **Alpha blending** is much more akin to a compositing feature; in fact, it is a crucial part of compositing. If you transform an object, the object changes physically in some way, moving it to a different location (translation), changing its size (scaling), or what direction it is facing or how it is oriented (rotated).

Alpha blending an object with its background to create procedural animation is done by specifying a change in the object alpha (transparency) value, with zero being transparent and one being opaque. This is usually termed as a **fade-in** or a **fade-out** in the content production industry, and technically is compositing. In Android, alpha blending is included with a procedural animation toolset, because alpha values are logical attributes to animate, especially if you are creating an animated children's ghost story, or a transporter beam special effect, or something similar.

You can finely control the Alpha attribute of an object that you are animating procedurally by using alpha parameters, and you can use an **AnimationSet** class to seamlessly combine alpha (transparency) blending with a translation, scale, or rotation transformation. Like most of the other procedural animation attributes, alpha blending amounts are set using real or floating-point (float) numbers between 0.0 (transparent) and 1.0 (visible). The exception to this is pivot points, which you specify using a percentage, such as 50%, and degrees, which you specify using decimal numbers (floating point, or float values) between 0 and 360 degrees.

It is important to note that using more than one decimal place is allowed when using real or float values. Thus, if you want the object to be exactly one-third visible, you could use 0.3333 or, for three-quarters visible, you could specify 0.75 as the starting or ending value for your object's alpha value.

Set alpha starting and ending values by using the **fromAlpha** and the **toAlpha** parameters; so to fadeout an object, you would set fromAlpha to 1.0, and toAlpha to 0.0, in order to achieve that fade-out special effect.

To combine multiple different types of procedural animation parameters together, you would create a "**set**" for the animation transformation parameters. Using a procedural **animation set** will allow you to group transforms and compositing together in a logical and organized fashion. This enables you to create more complex procedural animation. We will cover how to create procedural animation sets in detail a bit later on during this chapter.

Procedural Timing: Using Duration and Offsets

You might be wondering how you set the timing which is used between all of these different range data values. You actually have done this already for your frame animation using the android:duration parameter, which sets the duration for displaying one single frame. In procedural animation, duration sets the timing value for a range, and will also to some extent define how many interpolated data values are created by Android during that range, as well as the duration of each of the segments between the interpolated values.

It is important to remember that the Android Animation classes decide this value based on the device's processing power and what the algorithm (an animation engine) thinks will provide the most optimal (the smoothest) visual result, given the current processing power to applications in use ratio, or trade-off.

The duration for any given procedural animation range is set using the duration parameter, which like it does in frame animation, also takes an integer value in milliseconds. It's interesting to note that programming languages such as Java and JavaScript will utilize these millisecond values for all of their timing functions and operations.

Thus, if you wanted the fade-out we discussed in the previous section to take four seconds, the XML parameter would be android:duration="4000", since 4000 milliseconds equals 4 seconds. If you wanted this fade-out to take 4.352 seconds, you would use a millisecond value of 4352, and thus you have a one-thousandth of a second "granularity," or level of precision, available for your procedural animation timing accuracy.

Each transformation (or alpha blend) range that you define has its own separate duration setting, allowing for a great deal of precision in the XML markup definition of the effect which you are trying to achieve.

There is one other important timing-related parameter, which allows you to **delay** when the specified range will start playback. This is called an animation **offset**, and it is controlled using the **startOffset** parameter data value.

Say you wanted to delay the start of your four second fade-out by four seconds. All you would have to do is to add the android:startOffset="4000" to your **<alpha>** parent tag (which we will be using for real, a bit later on in the chapter), and this timing delay control would be implemented. A startOffset parameter is especially useful when utilized in conjunction with looping animation, which we're going to be covering next. The reason for this is that when used with animation loop scenarios, a startOffset parameter will allow you to define a **pause** during animated element loop cycles. Let's take a look at **loops** next, and parameters for controlling looping animation.

Procedural Loops: RepeatCount and RepeatMode

Like frame animation, procedural animation can play once, and then stop, or can play continuously in a loop. There are two parameters that control looping, one which controls whether an animation will loop or not and another which controls the way or "direction" in which the animation will loop back and forth. A procedural animation parameter that controls the number of times an animation, or component part of an animation set, will loop is called the **repeatCount** parameter. This parameter will require a whole number (integer) data value.

If you leave this repeatCount parameter out of (that is, unspecified in) the procedural animation definition, then an animation will play once and then stop. This means that the default setting is **android:repeatCount="1"** for this parameter. The exception to using an integer value for this parameter is the **infinite** constant. If you want to have an animation **loop forever**, you would want to use an **android:repeatCount="infinite"** parameter setting.

In case you're wondering, the value that the constant "infinite" defines is **-1**, so an **android:repeatCount="-1"** parameter definition should work just as well. The parameter which defines what **style of looping** is used is the **repeatMode** parameter, which you can set to one of two predefined constants. The most common of these two is **restart**, which will cause an animation to loop seamlessly (unless you've defined the startOffset parameter). In case you're wondering, the value that a "restart" constant defines is **1**, so **android:repeatMode="1"** works too!

The other type or mode of animation looping is the **reverse** mode, which is also called **"pong animation,"** as it causes the animation to reverse at the end of its range, and run backward, until it reaches the beginning again, at which time it runs forward, like the original video game called **Pong**. Back and forth, ad infinitum! In case you're wondering, the value that a "reverse" constant defines is **2**, so **android:repeatMode="2"** will also work.

All of these parameters may seem simple on their own, but when combined into complicated structures using an animation set, which we are going to take a look at later, these parameters can quickly become very complicated in combination with each other to produce some very detailed and impressive animation results. Don't underestimate the power of these parameters when they are put together by a savvy developer, in the right XML structure. By the end of this book, you will be that savvy developer! Next, let's take a look at the Android Animation class and its subclasses that implement tween animation, and then implement procedural animation using XML.

The Animation Class: Android Tween Animation

The Android Animation class is used to create tween animations of View objects in Android. This is done by the interpolation of data values within groups of predefined transform types. This creates the "frames" of procedural animation, although Android OS will decide how many frames are needed to create a smooth animation result.

Android's Animation class is part of the **android.view** package, and is kept with all the other Animation classes, subclasses, and methods, using the **android.view.animation** package. This is quite different from the bitmap or frame animation, which uses AnimationDrawable objects and is kept in the android.graphics.drawable package. The Animation class hierarchy starts with the java.lang.Object master object, which is then subclassed to create the **Animation** class. The Java class hierarchy for the Animation class would thus look like the following:

```
java.lang.Object
  > android.view.animation.Animation
```

The Animation class is used to create the subclasses which are actually used via the XML tags, which we will learn how to implement a bit later on in the chapter. There is one subclass for each of the four types of tween animation you learned about in the previous section, including the **AlphaAnimation**, **RotateAnimation**, **ScaleAnimation**, and **TranslateAnimation** classes. There is also an **AnimationSet** class which is used to create groupings of more complicated tween animation transforms called, you guessed it: **Animation Sets**.

Since we have already covered all of the XML parameters which can be used with the Android Animation class, and therefore with any of its subclasses, in previous sections of this chapter, let's jump right into some hands-on XML markup and create your /res/anim folder and a procedural animation asset to go inside of that folder that takes a spaceship image and applies a procedural animation transform to it to animate it, so you can start to learn about how to create tween animation in Android. After you create a tween animation spaceship, we will create a third spaceship, using both frame and tween animation together, for the ultimate in Android animation!

Creating Tween Animation Using XML Markup

The simplest way to create one of these tween animation assets is to define your procedural animation using an XML file, which will be stored in the HelloUniverse project's **/res/anim** folder. We will create this folder before we create an Animation object XML definition which will live inside of that folder. The work process is similar to what you did previously to create a /res/drawable folder and frame animation drawable XML asset definition.

Since we are creating three spaceship animations during this chapter, using both an AnimationDrawable object and an Animation object, we will create our second spaceship animation using an image of a different type of spaceship that one might find in the Andromeda galaxy and apply a rotate transform to that image procedurally to make it spin slowly through the galaxy. After that, I'll show you how to combine frame and tween animation together, providing you the ultimate 2D animation weaponry possible for your Android programming arsenal.

After we create the Animation object using an XML definition, we will attach the animation data to a spaceship digital image called **friendship.png**. I got this spaceship off of the NASA website in the 3D Studio .3DS format. I rendered the model in a simple black and blue color using 3D Studio MAX 2014. After you create a **/res/anim** folder and XML file containing procedural animation parameters, we will get back into Java coding and wire up ImageButton UI elements so I can show you how to setup and trigger frame animation and tween animation.

Create an /anim Folder: Tween Animation Assets

Right-click on your **/res** folder, select **New ➤ Folder**, and name the folder **anim**, as is shown in Figure 10-9.

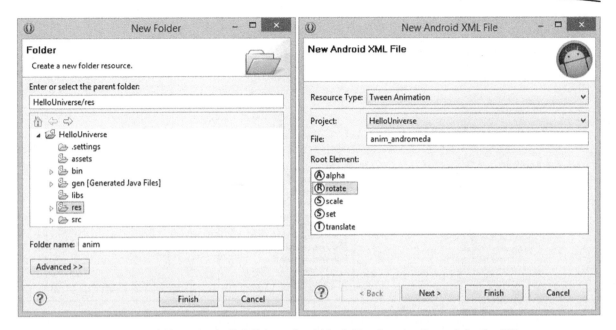

Figure 10-9. Create an /anim folder under the HelloUniverse/res folder (left) and create a Tween Animation XML

Once you have a **/res/anim** folder in place, seen in Figure 10-10 on the left, right-click on that folder and select the **New ➤ Android XML File** menu sequence to open the dialog shown on the right side of Figure 10-9. Since you right-clicked on the /anim folder, Eclipse will set the **Resource Type** to **Tween Animation**, so all you need to do is to name this file **anim_andromeda**, and select the **<rotate>** root element, as seen in Figure 10-9. Once you click the **Finish** button, you will see the bootstrap (empty) **anim_andromeda.xml** file seen in Figure 10-10.

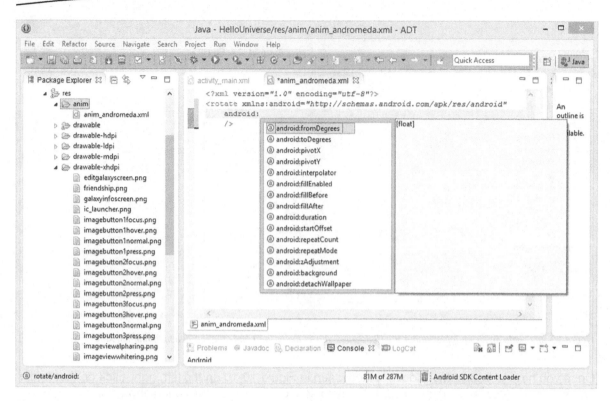

Figure 10-10. Use an android: work process inside the <rotate> tag to bring up helper dialog with all parameters

We will be using the first five of these parameters listed, as well as a **duration**, **repeatCount**, and **repeatMode** parameter to configure our rotate transform in the next section. Since we talked about all the primary parameters earlier in the chapter, we can get down to business and configure the rotate transform so we can rotate our Andromeda spaceship!

Rotate Transform: The Configuration Parameters

The first five primary parameters will define the From and To rotation degrees, as well as the pivot point x and y location and the method of interpolation which will interpret the speed at which the rotate transform is moved (accelerated or decelerated) over time. In this case, we want a friendship.png 3D spaceship image, that the XML animation definition will eventually be attached to (using Java), to rotate evenly and smoothly. This is achieved by using "**linear**" interpolation in Android. The XML markup for the five initial transform definition parameters are shown in Figure 10-11, and should look like the following:

```
<rotate xmlns:android="http://schemas.android.com/apk/res/android"
    android:fromDegrees="0.0"
    android:toDegrees="360.0"
    android:pivotX="50%"
    android:pivotY="50%"
    android:interpolator="@android:anim/linear_interpolator" />
```

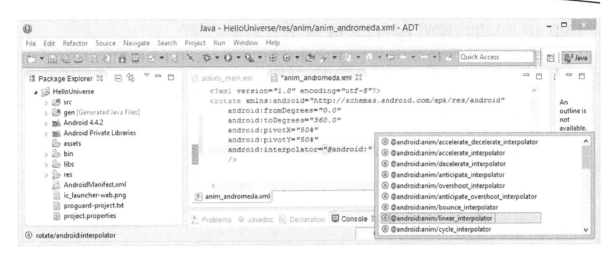

Figure 10-11. The first five primary rotation configuration parameters, and Android interpolator constants

Next, define your timing for the rotation by adding an android:rotation parameter set to a value of **9000**, or nine seconds, as shown in Figure 10-12, and define the looping behavior by setting the repeatCount to "**infinite**" and the repeatMode to "**restart**," which will allow the rotation to loop seamlessly rather than to pong (a pong, or back and forth animation, would be set by using the "reverse" constant).

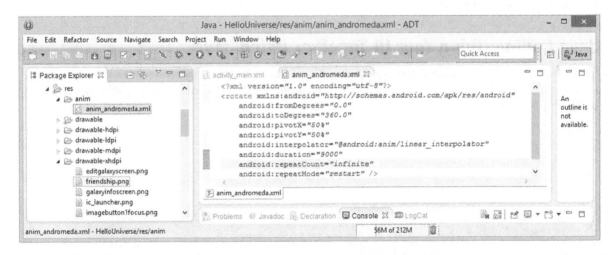

Figure 10-12. Add in the nine-second android:duration parameter, an infinite repeatCount, and a restart repeatMode

Now that you have defined a rotation transform using the <rotate> tag and configuration parameters, you'll need to reference this RotateAnimation object to the ImageView widget containing the spaceship you want to rotate.

SetUp an ImageView: Assigning an ID Parameter

Before we can use this <ImageView> UI widget in Java program logic, we will need to add an android:id value to it, which we can use to reference it from inside of the Java programming logic which we are about to create in the next section of the chapter. This parameter is shown at the top of the <ImageView> seen in Figure 10-13.

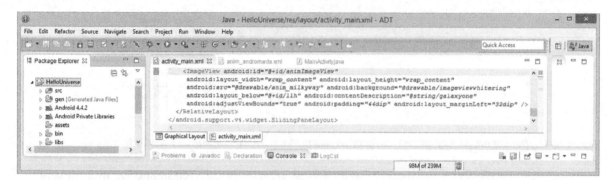

Figure 10-13. Add an android:id parameter and name the ImageView animImageView so you can reference it in Java

Since the <ImageButton> UI elements already have ID values, this is all you have to add in your **activity_main** XML file, so we are ready to get into some fairly extensive Java coding next, to make the UI design functional.

Java Coding: Tying Your UI Together Using Java

Since the <ImageView> is central to everything that we will be doing over the rest of this chapter, let's declare an ImageView object named **animImageView** at the top of your MainActivity class, under the TextView objects, as shown in Figure 10-14.

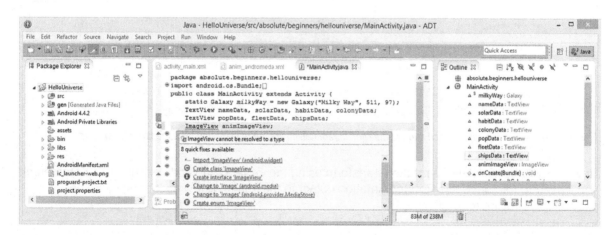

Figure 10-14. Declare an ImageView object and name it animImageView at the top of your MainActivity.java file

1. Mouse-over the error highlight and select **the Import 'ImageView' (android. widget)** option to have Eclipse write an import statement for you so that you can use the ImageView class in your code.

2. Next, instantiate this animImageView object inside of your on Create() method, as seen in Figure 10-15, so that Android will create the object when the application MainActivity starts. Reference your <ImageView> widget XML definition using a **findViewById()** method, using the **R.id.animImageView** reference path and ID value. Notice that you can use the **same naming values** for the XML definition ID that you can for your Java object.

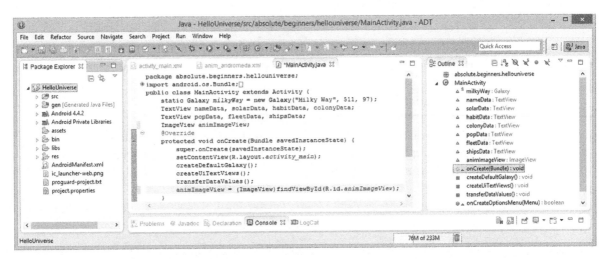

Figure 10-15. Instantiate the animImageView inside of the onCreate() method using the findViewById() method

3. The next object that you will need to declare and instantiate will be the **Animation** object which we will name **spaceShipAnim**, and which will hold the transform data that you defined in the previous section of the chapter. As you can see in Figure 10-16, you will again need to mouse-over the red error highlight and select the **Import 'Animation' (android.view. animation)** option, so that Eclipse ADT will write your import statement for you.

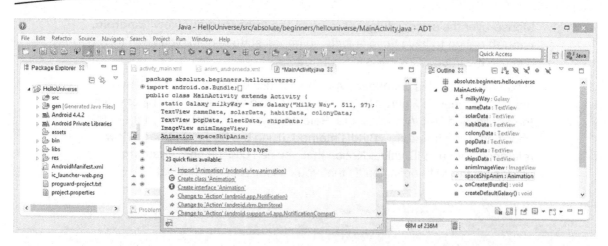

Figure 10-16. Declare an Animation object and name it spaceShipAnim at the top of your MainActivity.java file

4.   To instantiate this spaceShipAnim Animation object, you will use the
     .loadAnimation() method, rather than the **findViewById()** method.
     The .loadAnimation() method is in the **AnimationUtils** class, and is called
     off of this class using dot notation, using the method call **AnimationUtils.
     loadAnimation()**, as seen in Figure 10-17.

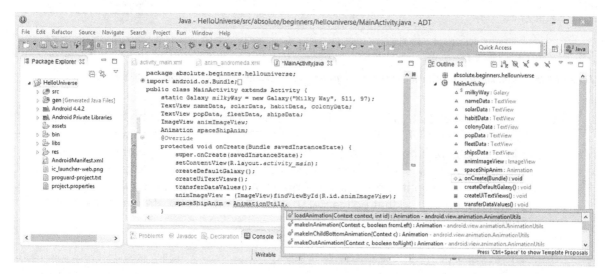

Figure 10-17. Instantiate the spaceShipAnim Animation object inside of onCreate() using a loadAnimation() method

5. To instantiate the spaceShipAnim Animation object, you will set it equal to the **.loadAnimation()** method call, chained off of the **AnimationUtils** class and configured with the current Activity Context object (**this**) and the reference to the **anim_andromeda** XML RotateAnimation object definition file which you created earlier. Do this using the following single line of Java programming logic, which is shown error-free in Figure 10-18:

```
spaceShipAnim = AnimationUtils.loadAnimation(this, R.anim.anim_andromeda);
```

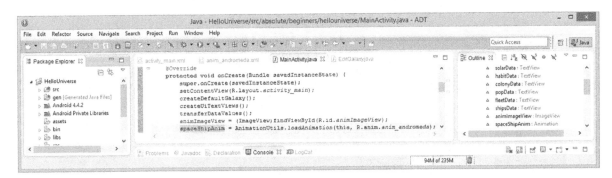

Figure 10-18. The spaceShipAnim object referencing the anim_andromeda XML transform definition file

Now your ImageView and Animation objects have been declared (created) and instantiated (loaded into system memory). Before we wire them together to make them work together as a team, let's continue with the basics and declare and instantiate your three ImageButton objects as well, since these are going to trigger the app to change between frame animation, tween animation, and hybrid (frame+tween) animation.

Just like you did with the TextView objects, declare one **ImageButton** class reference, and give it three names, **imageButtonOne**, **imageButtonTwo**, and **imageButtonThree**. As you can see in Figure 10-19, you will need to mouse-over the red error highlight and select the **Import 'ImageButton' (android.widget)** option from a dialog that pops up, so that Eclipse will write the ImageButton class import statement for you. Effortless Java coding!

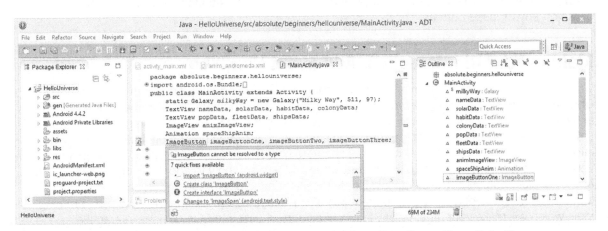

Figure 10-19. Declare ImageButton objects; name them imageButtonOne, imageButtonTwo, and imageButtonThree

Next, add a line of code (three actually, one per ImageButton object) under your **transferDataValues()** method call, that instantiates each ImageButton object and references it to a **galaxyOne**, **galaxyTwo**, and **galaxyThree** android:id value, which you assigned earlier when you were designing your XML UI layout definition. The Java code is written with the following three lines of Java code, which is shown error-free in Figure 10-20:

```
imageButtonOne = (ImageButton)findViewById(R.id.galaxyOne);
imageButtonTwo = (ImageButton)findViewById(R.id.galaxyTwo);
imageButtonThree = (ImageButton)findViewById(R.id.galaxyThree);
```

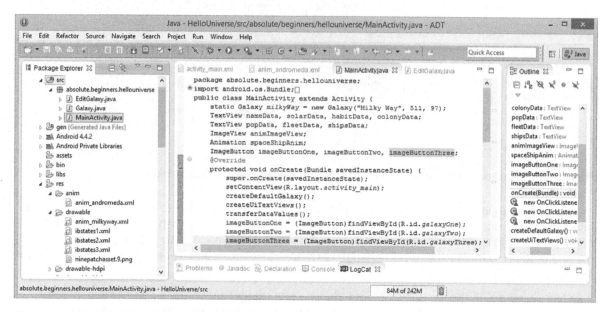

Figure 10-20. *Instantiate three ImageButton objects inside the onCreate() method using the findViewById() method*

Now we have created all of the objects that we need, so let's get even more complicated and add **event handler** logic to each of the ImageButton objects, so something will happen when our user clicks on any of these buttons!

Making Your UI Interactive: Add Event Handling

One of the reasons I covered event listeners and event handling early on in this book, during Chapter 7, was so that I had the option, when I wanted it, to show you how to create interactive aspects of an application. I want to do this here by making the ImageButtons control the animation I'm creating for the different galaxy information screens. I have been putting off finishing this galaxy information screen UI design for a couple of chapters now. Therefore, in this chapter, I'm going to show you how to add event handling to the ImageButton widgets and how to add Java logic inside of these event handler structures. The Java logic inside the event handlers will change depending upon which of the different types of animation you are using. We will also be completing the Java programming logic which will make your other galaxy information screen user interface designs interactive.

The easiest way to create these event handling structures is to copy one of the event handling structures from your EditGalaxy.java Activity subclass and paste it under the five instantiation lines of code for the ImageView, Animation, and ImageButton objects, as shown in Figure 10-21.

Figure 10-21. Add View.OnClickListener() event handling structures to each of the three ImageButton objects

1. Copy the colonyButton event handler structure, change colonyButton to imageButtonOne, and delete the Java code on the inside of the onClick() method, so that you have an empty event handling structure ready for your ImageButton elements.

2. Copy this empty structure two more times beneath it, and change imageButtonOne to imageButtonTwo and ImageButtonThree. The final Java code structure should look like the following, and is shown installed in the code in Figure 10-21:

```
imageButtonOne.setOnClickListener(new View.OnClickListener() {
    @Override
    public void onClick(View v)  { Java code will go in here to switch Animation assets
and TextView info }
});
```

3. Since the Animation asset that we designed in the previous section is for **imageButtonTwo**, open up this event handler structure as shown in Figure 10-22, call a **.setImageResource()** method, off of the animImageView object, and find the reference to the **friendship.png** asset that you copied into the **drawable-xhdpi** folder from the book assets repository.

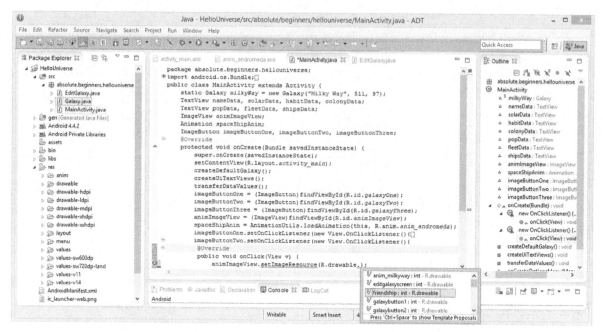

Figure 10-22. Set the animImageView ImageView to the friendship image using the .setImageResource() method

4. Once you complete the **animImageView.setImageResource()** method configuration, which is shown error-free in Figure 10-23, the next thing that you will need to do, once you have installed the correct foreground (source) image plate into the ImageView object, is to remove the **imageviewwhitering.png** background image, so that the friendship 3D spaceship can float freely in front of your galaxy image. Do this by setting the value for your background parameter to **null**, which signifies **unused** or not currently set, using a **.setBackground(null)** method call, as shown in Figure 10-23. When you do this, you will get an error highlight informing you that you need to set the Minimum SDK Level to 16 for your application, which we'll be doing in the next section of the chapter.

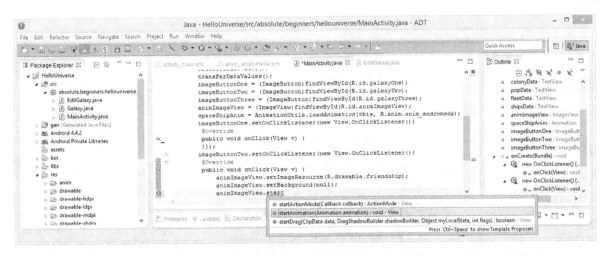

Figure 10-23. *Remove the background image via .setBackground(null) method call and call .startAnimation() method*

Note   If you want to see why I'm using a null (and SDK Level 16) to remove the background image plate, look ahead at Figure 10-24 on the left. This will show you what ImageView looks like after you use a .setImageResource() method call, but before you remove the background image, which was used by the AnimationDrawable object, and which is thus currently installed in the ImageView object, and needs to be removed when the user clicks on the second ImageButton UI element using this .setBackground(null) method call.

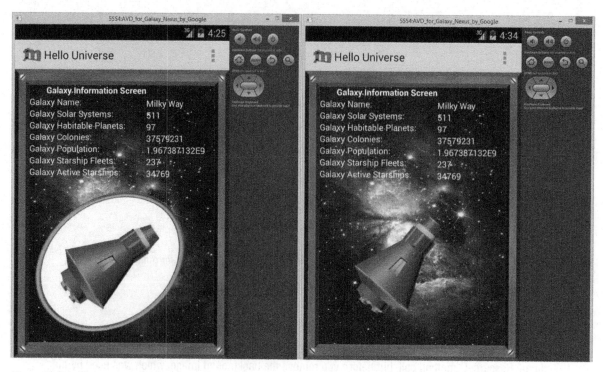

Figure 10-24. Test tween animation in the Galaxy Nexus AVD before (left) and after (right) removing the background

5.   The final thing once we install the correct foreground image (friendship.png) and remove the background image is to start the RotateAnimation object defined via the <rotate> tag in the anim_andromeda.xml file by using the **.startAnimation()** method call off of the animImageView object. This "wires" the ImageView object up to the Animation object using the following line of Java code, which is shown (under construction) in Figure 10-23:

```
animImageView.startAnimation(spaceShipAnim);
```

As you can see, if you type the **animImageView** object and a period and the word **start**, Eclipse will show you a pop-up helper dialog containing all method calls which are available for that object which begin with the word **start**.

6.   Once the three Java statements are in place, use a **Run As ➤ Android Application** menu sequence and test the app in the Galaxy Nexus AVD. As you can see in Figure 10-24 on the right, the new animation works perfectly.

Using .setBackground(): Upgrade App to SDK V16

Just to be thorough, I wanted to include a screen shot showing you the **AndroidManifest.xml** file, with the new Minimum SDK Version parameter set to **API Level 16**, which is shown highlighted in Figure 10-25. This will allow you to use the **.setBackground(null)** to remove any background image from the ImageView object, and later you will use a **.setAnimation(null)** to remove the procedural animation data from the ImageView as well.

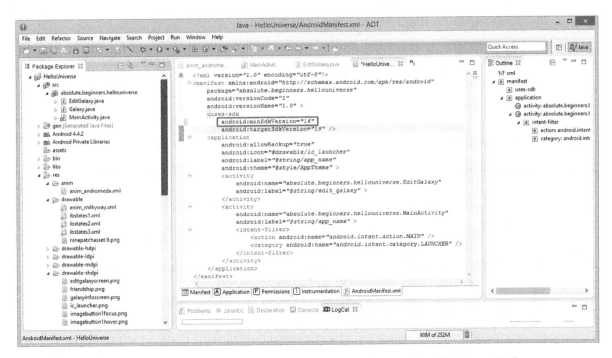

Figure 10-25. Upgrading the android:minSdkVersion parameter to 16 to be able to use the .setBackground(null)

As you can see in Figure 10-26, your code for the imageButtonTwo event handler structure is now error-free, and your Java programming logic that performs the three major "moves" that need to be done regarding your animation asset are in place. In pseudo-code, the three things that we will need to do for each ImageButton are:

```
Set the Source (foreground) Image Plate Asset by using the .setImageResource() method call
Set the Background Image Plate Asset by using .setBackgroundResource() or remove it using
.setBackground(null)
Set the Animation Asset by using the .startAnimation() method call or remove it using the
.setAnimation(null)
```

Figure 10-26. The second ImageButton event handler configured to remove the background and start the animation

Since imageButtonTwo removes the background image plate, installs an animation, and changes the foreground or source image plate, we need to add Java programming logic into the imageButtonOne event handler structure next, which restores these settings in case the user has clicked on the second (or third) ImageButton UI element.

The original AnimationDrawable would be setup by using the following code, which is shown in Figure 10-27:

```
animImageView.setBackgroundResource(R.drawable.imageviewwhitering);
animImageView.setImageResource(R.drawable.anim_milkyway);
animImageView.setAnimation(null);
```

Figure 10-27. The first ImageButton event handler, configured to remove the animation and replace the drawables

As you can see in Figure 10-27, the event handling code for imageButtonTwo is error-free, and is ready to test.

Now if you use the **Run As ➤ Android Application** menu sequence and test the app, you can click the first two ImageButton UI elements, which will allow you to switch back and forth between using the ImageView widget to hold an AnimationDrawable asset and an Animation asset animating a BitmapDrawable (image) asset. Pretty advanced stuff for an absolute beginner! I guess you are not an absolute beginner anymore! Next, let's get really advanced and combine frame animation and procedural animation, which will give you the maximum amount of power and creative opportunity to create any animation or special effect that you can imagine!

Hybrid Animation: Using Frames with Tween

To create the spaceship for our Spiral Galaxy M106, we will need to use both an AnimationDrawable object to hold frames of the pulsing LightShip and an Animation object to apply scale (pulsing), rotate (spinning), and alpha (fading in and out) transformations using an AnimationSet object. I am going to attempt to cover everything you'd ever want to know about Android animation in this chapter, so your apps will be amazing!

1. The first thing that you will need to do is to create the XML definition files for the Animation object as well as the AnimationDrawable object by right-clicking on the /res/drawable and /res/anim folders and using the **New ➤ Android XML File** dialog to create **anim_lightship.xml** and **anim_lightshipset.xml** files. The dialogs with these XML file names and root element settings of **<animation-list>** and **<set>** are shown in Figure 10-28.

Figure 10-28. *Right-click on /res/drawable to display the dialog on the left and right-click on the /res/anim folder to display the dialog on the right*

2.   Before you setup your AnimationDrawable object XML definition file which
     you created in the dialog shown on the left side of Figure 10-28, you must
     first copy the 11 lightship animation frames, which are optimized using the
     PNG8 format, into the **/res/drawable-xhdpi** folder for your HelloUniverse
     project. Use a Windows Explorer file management utility, shown in Figure 10-29
     with energyship0.png through energyship10.png files installed. Also shown
     are the ImageButton assets, galaxy background images, decorative ring
     background compositing elements, custom application icon, lunarlander
     animation asset, and the friendship spaceship PNG. You are getting quite a
     collection (three dozen) of drawable resources here!

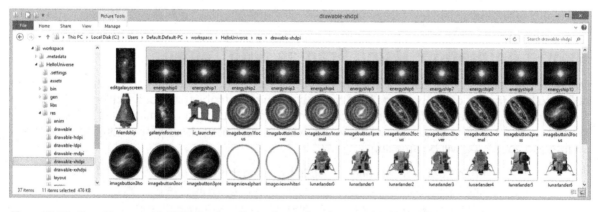

Figure 10-29. *Copy 11 energyship PNG8 files from the book repository into your /res/drawable-xhdpi folder*

3. Now you are ready to create the **anim_lightship.xml** file. The easiest way to do this is to copy the **<item>** tags from the inside of the **anim_andromeda.xml** file and change **lunarlander** to **energyship** and change the value for the duration parameter to **200** milliseconds, which is **5 FPS** (frames per second). Copy the eighth frame and paste it three more times underneath itself to create the ninth through eleventh frames, as seen in Figure 10-30.

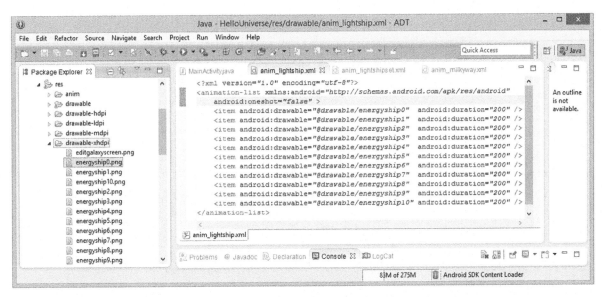

Figure 10-30. *Create 11 <item> child tags for the frames of the AnimationDrawable and set the duration to 200*

4. Now that the AnimationDrawable object is configured using XML, click on the **anim_lightshipset.xml** tab at the top of Eclipse, and switch over into editing the Animation object XML (bootstrap) definition file, shown in Figure 10-31. This Animation object is actually an **AnimationSet** object, as it uses the **<set>** parent tag to hold the child transform tags; in this case, these will be a <rotate> and <scale> transform as well as an <alpha> tag.

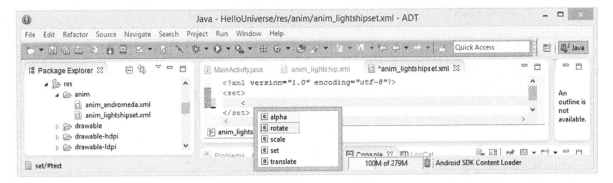

Figure 10-31. *Use the left-facing chevron < character inside of the <set> parent tag to open the transforms dialog*

5. In the space between the opening <set> and closing </set> tags, type a left-facing chevron character to open the child tag helper dialog, which shows five types of Animation class tags which can be child tags to the <set> tag.

6. Double-click on the <rotate> child tag, shown highlighted in Figure 10-31, and copy the parameters that you used in the anim_andromeda.xml RotateAnimation object definition file into the child tag, as shown in Figure 10-32.

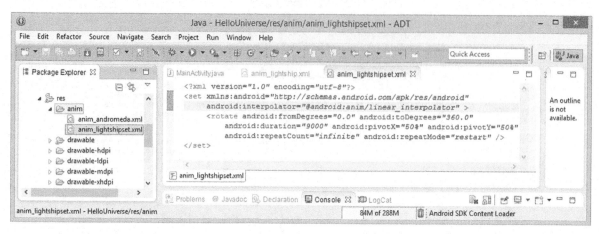

Figure 10-32. *Add the xmlns:android and android:interpolator to the <set> parent tag and copy over the <rotate> tag*

We will use the same parameters for this <rotate> tag that we used before, so we can move onto learning about the other types of transforms, but feel free to experiment with the values that you use for these parameters, as this is a great way to get a feel for what each of these parameters will do when you run the application in the AVD.

7. Next, add a line of space under the <rotate> tag and use the left-facing chevron to popup the helper dialog and double-click on the **<scale>** child tag option, or type the opening **<scale** and closing **/>** container characters, to prepare to add parameters to the **ScaleAnimation** object child tag container. If you want to see the parameters which are allowed inside of this tag, use the **android:** work process to popup the parameter helper dialog.

8. Next, you need to add in parameters that scale the animation on the x and y axis from 100% (**1.0**) to 50% (**0.5**), and back (repeatMode="**reverse**") over a **4500**-millisecond duration. Set the pivot point to the middle (**50%**), and set a repeatCount of **infinite**, using the following XML markup parameters, as shown in Figure 10-33:

```
<scale android:fromXScale="1.0" android:toXScale="0.5"
    android:fromYScale="1.0"  android:toYScale="0.5"
    android:pivotX="50%"  android:pivotY="50%"  android:duration="4500"
    android:repeatCount="infinite" android:repeatMode="reverse" />
```

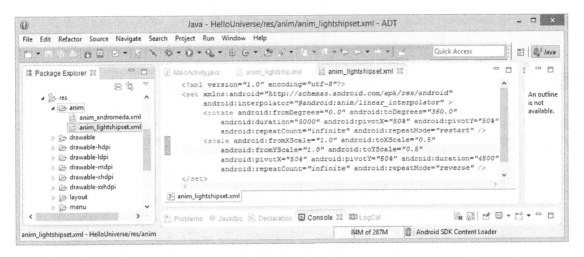

Figure 10-33. Add a <scale> child tag and configure to scale from 100% down to 50% and back up again (reverse)

9. Next, add a line of space under the <scale> tag, use the left-facing chevron
    to popup the helper dialog, and double-click on the **<alpha>** child tag option,
    or type the opening **<alpha** and closing **/>** container characters, to prepare
    to add parameters to the **AlphaAnimation** object child tag container. If you
    want to see the parameters which are allowed inside of the alpha tag, use the
    android: work process to popup the parameter helper dialog.

10. Next, you need to add parameters to animate opacity from 100% to 67%
    and back (repeatMode="reverse") over a **2250**-millisecond duration. Set the
    pivot point to the middle (50%), and set a repeatCount of infinite, using the
    following XML markup parameters, as shown in Figure 10-34:

```
<alpha android:fromAlpha="1.0" android:toAlpha="0.67" android:duration="2250"
        android:repeatCount="infinite" android:repeatMode="reverse" />
```

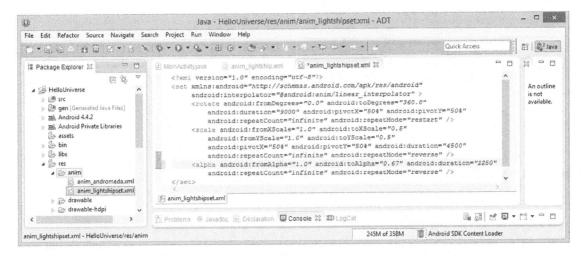

Figure 10-34. Add an <alpha> child tag and configure it to fade from 100% to 67% and then back again (reverse)

Notice that my animation duration values "sync" with each other; that is, 4500 goes into 9000 exactly twice and 2250 goes into 9000 four times and into 4500 exactly twice as well.

Setting up Your Hybrid Animation via Java Code

Let's add this new animation to your Java code next, first by adding an Animation object named **lightShipAnim** to hold the animation data that you just created, and then adding method calls inside of the third ImageButton's event handling structure to remove the other animation setup(s) and replace them with your latest creation.

1. Since you have an Animation object declared, add a comma after spaceShipAnim, and add the lightShipAnim to your list of declared Animation objects, as shown in Figure 10-35. Then copy and paste the spaceShipAnim instantiation line of code again underneath itself, change spaceShipAnim to lightShipAnim, and change the R.anim reference from anim_andromeda to reference anim_lightshipset instead. The new Animation object instantiation code should look like the following:

```
lightShipAnim = AnimationUtils.loadAnimation(this,R.anim.anim_lightshipset);
```

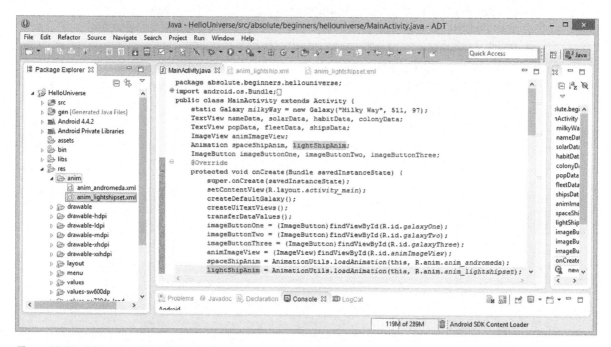

Figure 10-35. Add a second lightShipAnim Animation object declaration, and instantiate it using .loadAnimation()

2. Now you are ready to add the method calls off of the animImageView ImageView object, which will setup the source image plate using the **.setImageResource()** method call, clear out the background image plate using the **.setBackground(null)** method call, and start the animation using a **.startAnimation()** method call. This would be done in the third ImageButton event handling structure, using the following code, shown in Figure 10-36:

```
animImageView.setImageResource(R.drawable.anim_lightship);
animImageView.setBackground(null);
animImageView.startAnimation(lightShipAnim);
```

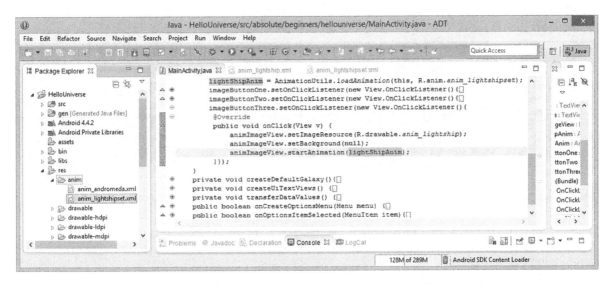

Figure 10-36. Add a Java statement to the imageButtonThree event handler setting image, background, and animation

3. Now we are ready to test the animation using the **Run As ➤ Android Application** menu sequence, and as you can see in Figure 10-37, the energy-based lightship animation pulses and twinkles as expected. If you want to, use the PorterDuff class to blend the black parts of the image. The Android PorterDuff class is too advanced to cover in this book.

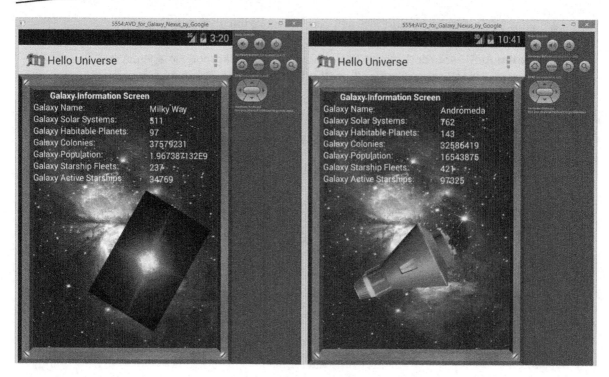

Figure 10-37. *Test the hybrid animation in Galaxy Nexus AVD (left) and add in the .setText() method calls (right)*

If you want to learn more about PorterDuff blending, how to accomplish this using the Android Canvas, Paint, and Bitmap classes is covered in my more advanced *Pro Android Graphics* (Apress, 2013).

You could alternatively use GIMP 2.8 and its advanced color selection tools to remove the black parts of these animation frames(images), replace them with alpha channel transparency, and save them as PNG32 instead, which you learned how to do earlier in the book in Chapter 3 and Chapter 9. Time for a little practice!

Next, we will take a quick look at how to use the **.setText()** method, inside of your ImageButton event handling structure to put different statistics on your galaxy info screen for the two other galaxy information screens using the TextView UI elements.

Completing the Galaxy UI Design: Using .setText()

You have already used this **.setText()** method in Chapter 6, to transfer data out of your Galaxy object into your TextView UI widgets, and you can also use it in your programming logic here, to set the text for your user interface elements. We will do this here, to reinforce how this is done. As you can see in Figure 10-38, all you need to do is to call this .setText() method off of the TextView object names declared at the top of your Activity and instantiated in your **createUiTextViews()** method, and pass over your new (made up) galaxy information inside of the quotation marks as text (**String**) data. You can copy the code from your **transferDataValues()** method into your imageButtonTwo onClick() handler if you want to speed up your code development work process.

Figure 10-38. Change the galaxy information screen text data using the .setText() method call to configure TextView

To be thorough, and finish up your SlidingPaneLayout UI design, create these .setText() method call structures in both of your imageButtonTwo and imageButtonThree event handling structures, and make up some similar values to the ones that you used for the Milky Way galaxy. When you test your app in an AVD, the information and animation will now change for each of the ImageButton UI elements when you click on them.

Procedural Animation or Frame Animation?

Finally, I wanted to discuss some of those higher-level theories, principles, concepts, and trade-offs which will serve to differentiate the frame-based AnimationDrawable approach from the procedural (vector) or tween Animation approach.

Frame or raster animation will tend to be **memory-intensive**, more than it is processing-intensive, as each frame that is going to be placed onto the screen will be loaded into memory, so that these frames can later be used in your application. Displaying these images from memory onto a View is fairly straightforward, and does not require any complex calculations, so the processing overhead is low, as it only involves moving each frame's image asset from memory over onto the display screen.

Frame animation will give you more control **outside** of the Android OS, because you can use production software, including 3D, digital imaging, digital video, digital illustration, special effects, particle systems, fluid dynamics, morphing, digital painting, and the like to manipulate all of your pixels into exactly the animation effect that you're looking to achieve.

Since Android does not yet include all of these advanced multimedia production tools, using frame animation will allow you to leverage powerful production tools, some of which we will be using within this book, outside of the Android development environment, and then bring the results into your Android app using the image assets defined as frames within in the AnimationDrawable object.

Procedural animation tends to be more **processing-intensive**, because there is numeric value interpolation, as well as the application of interpolator motion curves to those resulting interim data values. Additionally, if sets and sub-sets are utilized to create a complex animation structure, there can be a great deal more data processing involved, as well as the memory space which would be required to hold the plethora of settings, ranges, pivots, interpolation values, and similar animation processing data that will be needed by the Animation subclasses.

Procedural animation gives you more control **inside** of Android. This is because you are doing everything that controls your animation using Java code and XML markup, and your animation data and can made to be **interactive** within your Java programming logic. This is because Java code and data (and even your UI elements) can be crafted to interface with the procedural animation in real-time, allowing it to be made interactive, whereas frame animation, at least by itself, is not as interactive. Frame animation by itself is a more linear medium, like digital video, where frames are played sequentially to achieve the motion result.

Since you can apply procedural animation to just about any View object in Android, including your text, UI widgets, images, video, and frame animation, if you set things up correctly, such as using image compositing techniques to their best results, you can achieve some impressive interactivity by using frame animation in conjunction with procedural animation, as you have seen during this chapter.

If you are combining frame with procedural animation, as we did during this chapter, you will have a load on **both processor and memory resources**, so you must try and optimize what you are doing, so that you don't use up too much of the system resources needed to run the rest of your application code and UI. This is why we were concerned with our data footprint optimization in Chapter 9, and why we're learning about the same type of optimization principles here.

The Animator Class: Parameter Animation

There is another animation class in Android which I did not cover in this chapter, as it is not a new media asset, but rather a way to animate parameter changes in any Android class which uses XML to implement its objects. You can use Android's **Animator** class as a shortcut to animating object properties inside of Android that would usually be animated (changed over time) using Java iteration loops. To research this on your own, you can visit the following Android Developer website if this area is of interest for your app:

```
http://developer.android.com/reference/android/animation/Animator.html
```

Summary

In this chapter, you learned all about **2D animation** concepts and principles, expanding on the 2D graphics concepts and principles which you learned about in the previous Chapter 9, into the **fourth dimension** of **time**. Changing images over time is the foundation for both 2D animation as well as digital video media. We will be covering digital video in the next chapter, as a logical follow-on to subject material you learned in this chapter.

You learned about Android's **AnimationDrawable** object and frame-based animation and the supported digital image formats (PNG) utilized for animation frames. You learned about how to define frame animation, as well as how to implement it inside your SlidingPaneLayout UI design from Chapter 8, using the Android ImageView class, which is used to hold Android **Drawable** objects, such as images and frame animation XML definitions.

Next, you learned about the Android **Animation** class, used to implement the other major type of animation in Android, known as "tween" animation, procedural animation, or vector animation. Tween animation uses XML tags and parameters to create animation, using **alpha** blending, **scaling**, **rotation**, and **translation** (movement).

You learned how to define procedural animation, as well as how to implement it in your SlidingPaneLayout UI design from Chapter 8, using the Android **ImageView** class and Animation class, which you also declared and instantiated in your MainActivity.java Activity subclass to be able to "wire-up" your procedural animation data to a friendship.png 3D spaceship rendered image that you made spin slowly within your galaxy.

We finally got around to adding event listeners to the ImageButtons which you created in the previous chapter, and learned how to add and remove both image assets, or references to these assets, more accurately, and how to add or remove procedural animation data that you want to effect the assets using calls to the **.setAnimation()** method call. You learned how to use the **null** value in a method call to remove the reference to a media asset, whether that is an image (Drawable or AnimationDrawable object) or a tween animation (Animation object).

Next, you created **hybrid** animation, which used both frame animation and procedural animation to achieve the ultimate animation special effects. You finished up your SlidingPaneLayout by adding **.setText()** method calls to the three ImageButton event handling structures. Finally, we discussed basic trade-offs between frame animation's use of **system memory** and procedural animation's use of **CPU processing cycles**.

Next, in Chapter11, you'll learn all about **Digital Video** in Android, including foundational digital video theory and concepts, what digital video file formats are best to use in Android, how to create digital video assets for use with Android's **FrameLayout** container class, and how to use the Android **VideoView** class and widget. You'll also learn how that class works with the Android **MediaPlayer** class, the Android **Uri** class and the Android **MediaController** class.

Digital Video: Streaming Video, MediaPlayer, and MediaController classes

In the previous chapter on **2D Animation**, we covered implementing motion graphics in Android and using digital image file formats such as PNG or JPEG in conjunction with XML constructs to create frame-based animation.

There is another way that you can play a series of frames in Android, called "**digital video.**" Digital video assets are especially well-suited for situations when you have hundreds or even thousands of frames, and cannot easily handle them all using an Android AnimationDrawable class. Additionally, digital video can be "**streamed**" over a network connection, which 2D animation assets cannot, and thus your new media can be **external** to your application.

In this chapter, we are going to take all of the newfound knowledge that you gained in Chapter 10 regarding the fourth dimension (or 4D) of time, as well as concepts that you learned about such as frames and frame rates, and we'll again expand upon that knowledge, with new concepts such as **bitrates** and new digital video codec (file format) support in Android, including the popular **MPEG-4** and **Web-M** digital video formats which are also the formats that are used in HTML5.

We'll be covering several often-utilized Android classes you can use to implement video graphic design elements, such as the **VideoView** UI widget, a **FrameLayout** UI layout container, as well as three media-related Android classes which you can utilize to implement digital video (or digital audio) control and playback. These include the **MediaPlayer** (video or audio playback), **Uri**, and the **MediaController** (the transport control panel).

During this chapter, we will be utilizing these five Android digital video-related UI design (FrameLayout and VideoView) and playback (MediaPlayer, Uri, and MediaController) classes to create a digital video playback Activity for your application. We'll install a VideoView UI widget in a

FrameLayout container, accessed using the menu in the HelloUniverse application, and then we will create a **3D flythrough** of one of the planets in the Universe using the **Terragen 3** software. You will also learn how to **optimize** the digital video using **Sorenson Squeeze**, and finally learn about MediaPlayer, Uri, and MediaController objects when you stream your video using Java.

The FrameLayout Class: Framing DV Content

The Android **FrameLayout** class is the most basic layout container class, as it provides simple frame layout for content, usually digital video, which is why I waited until this chapter to cover this FrameLayout class in detail!

A FrameLayout is usually utilized to contain one single UI widget that contains some sort of new media content such as digital video. An example of a complex UI widget that would be perfect to use in conjunction with this FrameLayout container would be the **VideoView** widget. The VideoView widget (class), which we will go over in detail in a future section of this chapter, is designed to contain an **MPEG-4** (or a **WebM**) digital video asset.

The FrameLayout class is a **public** class that extends the ViewGroup superclass, which as you know is a master "blueprint" class which is used to create Android layout container subclasses. The FrameLayout class hierarchy, which starts with the Java language's Object "master class," and progresses down from View to ViewGroup to a FrameLayout class, would be structured using the following Java (and Android) class hierarchy:

```
java.lang.Object
  > android.view.View
    > android.view.ViewGroup
      > android.widget.FrameLayout
```

The FrameLayout class was designed by Android OS developers to specify the area on the display screen which is intended to display one single item. This is why it is named using the term "frame," as typically a frame holds a single image. For this reason, you should design the FrameLayout UI to hold one child UI widget. Because a FrameLayout class does not have a lot of methods defined which allow a lot of layout positioning attributes (or parameters), it is the simplest of the Android layout classes. This also makes this class quite **memory-efficient**!

If you try to use multiple child UI widgets inside of your parent FrameLayout container, you will find that it is difficult to position multiple elements accurately in a way that is scalable across different screen sizes, shapes, and orientations. This is due to the lack of layout position attributes, which is also what makes the FrameLayout class so very memory-efficient.

What happens if you attempt to use a FrameLayout container to organize multiple UI elements is that you will see a high occurrence of UI elements **overlapping** each other, which is not the professional result that you will be seeking for your UI designs. This is why I taught you about the Linear, Relative, and Grid layout container classes first!

The only way to control positioning of your child UI widgets within the parent FrameLayout UI container is by assigning a "**layout gravity**" parameter to each UI widget. This is done using the **android:layout_gravity** parameter inside of each UI widget's child tag in your FrameLayout XML user interface definition file, which we will be creating a bit later on in the chapter, after we learn all about the FrameLayout class as well as its nested classes that provide the layout parameters.

This layout_gravity design parameter does not allow developers to do any of the pixel-precise positioning that is possible using the other more advanced (and less memory-efficient) layout container classes. The FrameLayout class essentially allows Android OS to do all of your UI design positioning so that you can scale your UI design to fit all of the different Android device screen sizes and orientations, usually in a full-screen mode, which is the optimal mode for use with digital video assets. This gravity parameter for a FrameLayout class is provided by a nested class called **FrameLayout.LayoutParams**. We'll be covering this nested class in the next section of this chapter. It is identical to the gravity parameter that was used in the other layout container classes (ViewGroup subclasses) that we covered in Chapters 6, 7, and 8. I'm going to cover layout gravity again here, to reinforce your comfort with it, because it's very important to UI design.

Since it is a basic UI layout class, you can also utilize the FrameLayout class as a superclass, for the purpose of creating more specialized UI-related classes. Any classes which you create by subclassing a FrameLayout class would be termed **direct subclasses** of the FrameLayout class.

Some of the "**known**" direct subclasses of FrameLayout (that is, the FrameLayout subclasses which have already been coded for you, and which have been made permanent classes in the Android API) will include: DatePicker, TabHost, MediaController, CalendarView, ScrollView, TimePicker, ViewAnimator, HorizontalScrollView, GestureOverlayView, and AppWidgetHostView classes. The FrameLayout class also has several known indirect subclasses which are part of the Android API. These include: TextSwitcher, ViewFlipper, ImageSwitcher, FragmentTabHost, and the ViewSwitcher class. Next, let's take a look at the FrameLayout.LayoutParams class.

FrameLayout.LayoutParams Nested Class: Gravity

The FrameLayout.LayoutParams class is a nested class which subclasses the ViewGroup. MarginLayoutParams nested class, which, in turn, subclasses (or extends) the ViewGroup. LayoutParams nested class that was coded originally using the Java Object master class in order to create layout parameters for all ViewGroup subclasses.

Android layout parameter, or **LayoutParams**, nested classes are what provide the layout parameters for your UI designs, which are usually created via XML, as you'll see a bit later on in this chapter when you create the FrameLayout containing your VideoView UI widget.

The FrameLayout.LayoutParams class hierarchy starts out with a Java Object and progresses down the class hierarchy from **ViewGroup.LayoutParams** to **ViewGroup.MarginLayoutParams** to **FrameLayout.MarginLayoutParams**, and thus would be structured like the following:

```
java.lang.Object
   > android.view.ViewGroup.LayoutParams
     > android.view.ViewGroup.MarginLayoutParams
       > android.widget.FrameLayout.LayoutParams
```

FrameLayout.LayoutParams inherits all ViewGroup.LayoutParams as well as ViewGroup. MarginLayoutParams (margin parameters), and then the class adds the **layout_gravity** parameter and its constants, which we are going to cover in detail in this section, since these constants are specifically intended to be used with the FrameLayout UI container which we're going to be using for the digital video playback engine we are creating in this chapter.

The most often used gravity constant with the FrameLayout container is **fill**, as one usually wants content or UI elements, such as the VideoView, to be displayed "full screen." Your second most often used constant would be **center**, which is similar to fill, but does not scale the content; rather, it centers the content or UI element (the child widget) in the display. There are also constants provided to fill or center your UI widget or the nested UI layout container in only the horizontal (X-axis) or the vertical (Y-axis) dimension. These would be the **fill_vertical** or **fill_horizontal**, and the **center_vertical** or **center_horizontal** constants. These constants, shown in Table 11-1, will allow you to fine-tune how Android will position your UI widget inside of your FrameLayout UI container. It is important to note that using fill_vertical or fill_horizontal may change your content aspect ratio, which may distort that content in an undesirable way.

Table 11-1. These android:layout_gravity Constants Are Defined by the Nested Class FrameLayout.LayoutParams

Gravity Constant	The function which is specified by using this Gravity Constant
top	Aligns UI element to or at the **TOP** of a FrameLayout container
bottom	Aligns UI element to or at the **BOTTOM** of a FrameLayout container
left	Aligns UI element to or at the **LEFT** of a FrameLayout container
right	Aligns UI element to or at the **RIGHT** of a FrameLayout container
center_vertical	Centers the UI element (or UI layout container) vertically
center_horizontal	Centers the UI element (or UI layout container) horizontally
center	Aligns UI element to or at the **CENTER** of a FrameLayout container
fill_vertical	Scales UI element (or layout container) to fill Frame vertically
fill_horizontal	Scale UI element (or layout container) to fill Frame horizontally
fill	Scales UI element to **FILL** the FrameLayout container
clip_vertical	Clips the top and bottom edges of the UI element for FrameLayout
clip_horizontal	Clips the left and right edges of the UI element for FrameLayout
start	Aligns UI element to or at the **START** of the FrameLayout container
end	Aligns UI element to or at the **END** of the FrameLayout container

There are some more advanced constants, such as **clip_horizontal** and **clip_vertical**, which are conceptually a bit more challenging, as these will "clip" (that is, remove a portion of) your UI element or content, in either the horizontal (X-axis) or the vertical (Y-axis). In digital imaging, this operation is termed "cropping," and instead of scaling your content (or UI design) to fit any given screen dimensions, these **clipping** constants will instead **remove** (clip away) parts of your content or design, in order to make it fit the new screen size and dimensions.

Finally, you can use **start** and **end** constants to implement both **RTL** (Right To Left) and **LTR** (Left To Right) "directional" UI layouts. These would replace your left and right constants (for LTR), or right and left constants (for RTL). If you are developing for end users that use RTL languages, and you need your UI designs to be able to **mirror** these types of RTL language design scenarios, use a start and end constant instead of left and right.

These RTL (Right To Left) and LTR (Left To Right) layout constants were only recently added, in Android 4.2, to allow design support for languages which are read starting on the right side of the screen and moving toward the left side of the screen. Android will automatically reverse the value of the start and end constants, depending on whether a RTL or LTR screen direction is being used by the user (that is, depending on the language setting).

The gravity constants would only be used in a FrameLayout when there is more than one child widget (multiple UI widgets, or nested ViewGroup layout containers). This is similar to the way you will use the top, bottom, left, or right constants to "pin" UI widgets or layout containers to the sides of a FrameLayout (display) like you did with the GridLayout. Gravity is used for **generalized positioning**, not for precise positioning, like the parameters that you find in the RelativeLayout class, for instance, which can provide designs that are precise and at the same time are also scalable to different screen sizes and shapes.

Creating a Frame Layout Using XML Mark-Up

The first thing that we will need to do to add the "**Fly Over Planet**" video playback menu option to your app is to add a **<string>** constant, as shown in Figure 11-1, which you will use later to label your second menu item.

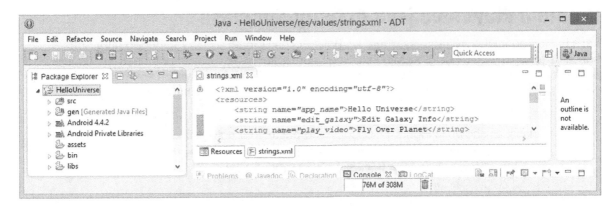

Figure 11-1. Add a <string> constant resource named play_video and give it a data value of "Fly Over Planet"

1. Name the constant **play_video** and give it a String data value of **Fly Over Planet** using the following markup:

    ```
    <string name="play_video">Fly Over Planet</string>
    ```

2. Next, right-click the **main.xml** file in the **/res/menu** folder and **Open** it.

3. Copy and paste the first child <item> tag underneath itself and change edit_galaxy to **play_video** and 100 to **200**.

4. Change the action_settings to **300**, as is shown in Figure 11-2, so that your parent <menu> tag now contains three **MenuItem objects**. Once you complete the XML menu definition file upgrade, you'll be ready to go into the Java code and access play_video.

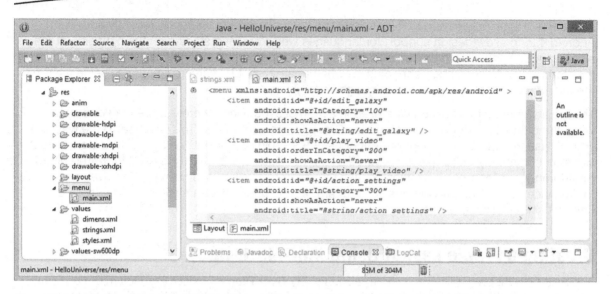

Figure 11-2. Add a MenuItem object using an <item> child tag named play_video inside of a parent <menu> tag

Create a PlayVideo.java Activity Subclass

Let's use an optimal work process where we have Eclipse create a new **PlayVideo.java** Activity subclass for us, by continuing on with installing your OptionsMenu object. We need to add in a switch-case statement structure for the new second MenuItem object, which you just installed in your /res/menu/main.xml folder and file in the previous section of this chapter.

1. The easiest way to accomplish this is to open up your **MainActivity.java** class, as shown in Figure 11-3, copy and paste your edit_galaxy switch-case statement, from case through break, underneath itself.Change the edit_galaxy to **play_video** and change the edit Intent to **playIntent**.

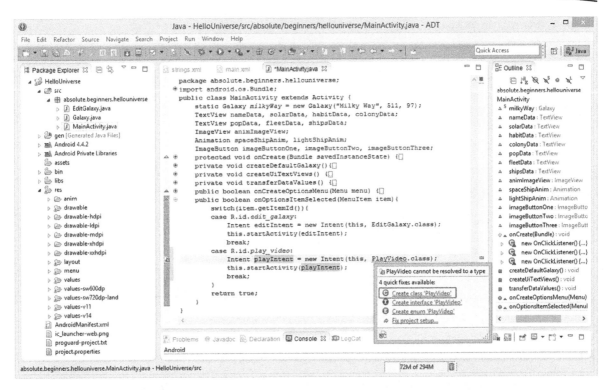

Figure 11-3. Add a second case statement to the switch construct referencing play_video and using a playIntent

Since there is no PlayVideo class as yet, once you make these editing changes, Eclipse will "throw" a wavy red error highlight underneath the PlayVideo class reference inside of your **Intent() constructor** method call.

2. Mouse-over this wavy red error highlight and select the first **Create class 'PlayVideo'** option, shown circled in red in the screenshot shown in Figure 11-3. This will instruct Eclipse ADT to create a "bootstrap" empty class for you to use to write your PlayVideo.java Activity subclass.

3. Before Eclipse can create this class for you, it will need to get some information from you regarding what you are going to use the class to do; in this case, we'll use it to create an Activity, so the **New Java Class** dialog, which is shown in Figure 11-4 on the left, will open up. Click the **Browse** button next to the **Superclass** selector and open up the **Superclass Selection** dialog shown on the right side of Figure 11-4, and select the **Activity** class.

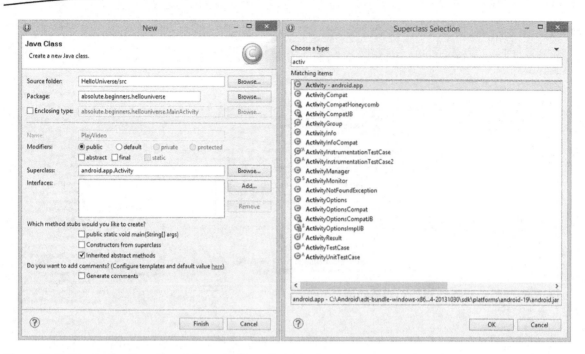

Figure 11-4. Fill out a New Java Class dialog and a Superclass Selection dialog to create a new PlayVideo class

4. Once you click the **OK** and the **Finish** buttons, you will get an empty
    PlayVideo.java tab opened up for you in Eclipse. Next, copy and paste the
    first four lines of the on Create() method from the MainActivity class inside
    of the PlayVideo class (inside of the curly brackets which contain the class's
    code), and then change the activity_main reference in the setContentView()
    method call to **activity_play** as shown in Figure 11-5.

Figure 11-5. Create a standard protected void onCreate() method referencing the activity_play in setContentView

Creating Your activity_play XML UI Design

To get rid of the wavy red error highlight, shown in Figure 11-5, which the pop-up options menu (interestingly) does not give us a correct solution for fixing (Eclipse is not perfect, as I mentioned earlier in the book), you will need to right-click on the **/res/layout** folder and select the **New ➤ Android XML File** menu sequence. This will open up a **New Android XML File** dialog, seen in Figure 11-6, where you'll name the UI layout **activity_play**, and select the **FrameLayout** root element (parent tag) for your video playback Activity UI design.

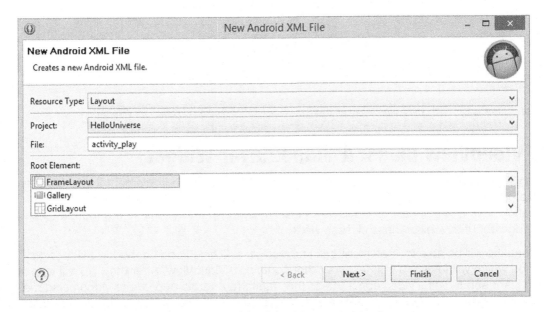

Figure 11-6. Create an activity_play.xml UI layout file using a FrameLayout root element

Once you click **Finish**, you will see the XML markup for the parent **<FrameLayout>** container which Eclipse will write for you, along with the required **layout_width** and **layout_height** parameters, shown in Figure 11-7.

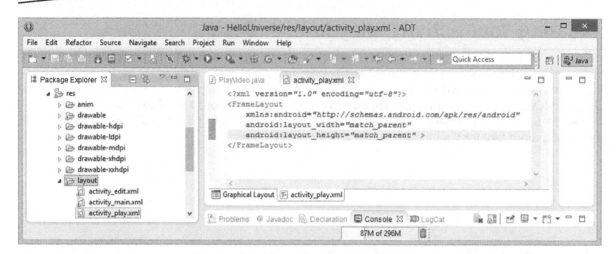

Figure 11-7. The activity_play.xml FrameLayout UI layout container XML definition file ready for VideoView

The VideoView Class: A VideoPlayer Widget

Before we get into all of the complex Java code and XML markup to implement this video player inside of the FrameLayout container that you have just installed in the HelloUniverse Android application, I want to get into the VideoView class in detail, so that you have the foundational knowledge about how all of these classes work.

After that, we will be able to implement this knowledge, and finish coding the XML UI design definition which will feature a FrameLayout that contains a VideoView. After that, we will take some time to learn about digital video concepts as they relate to Android and create video using the Terragen 3.0 virtual world creation software package. After that, we will learn about the MediaPlayer class and get into some more advanced Java programming.

Android's **VideoView** widget class is a direct subclass of the SurfaceView class, which is a direct subclass of the Android View class, which is a direct subclass of the java.lang.Object master class. Android's VideoView class hierarchy is structured as follows:

```
java.lang.Object
  > android.view.View
    > android.view.SurfaceView
      > android.widget.VideoView
```

The SurfaceView superclass (View subclass) is similar to the FrameLayout (ViewGroup subclass) in as much as it is intended to provide a class for creating View widgets that are used for one sole purpose: playing content on their surface. In the case of the VideoView subclass, this would be playing digital video content on the surface of the View object, as is evident in the naming of the class.

The Android VideoView class is stored in the **android.widget** package, making the VideoView a user interface element, which we know is called a UI widget in Android OS. For this reason, your **import statement** for using a VideoView class in an Android application would reference **android.widget. VideoView** as its package path.

This VideoView class is a **public** class and has two dozen method calls and callbacks that one might think of as actually being part of the Android **MediaPlayer** class, which we'll be covering in a future section of the chapter.

You can access these MediaPlayer functions (method calls) via the VideoView class, so, ultimately, you can view these two classes as inexorably bound together. You will see precisely how these two key Android classes intertwine as we progress through this chapter, especially when we get into the Java program logic a bit later on.

We will take a closer look here at some of the more useful video playback control method calls, so that you are familiar with them, in case you need to implement any of these extended digital video features in your own video playback applications. In the next section, we will also need to review Android VideoView's digital video **playback lifecycle**, so that you can see exactly how all of the various video playback "**states**" all fit together.

The basic VideoView method calls include .pause(), .resume(), .stop(), .start(), .suspend(), and .stopPlayback(). There's also a .setVideoURI(), and a .setMediaController() method call, as well as a .setVideoPath() method call which accomplishes much of the same end results as the .setVideoURI() call.

There are four **.get()** method calls for "polling" or "getting" information about digital video assets. They include .getDuration(), .getCurrentPosition(), .getBufferPercentage(), and .getAudioSessionId(), as well as the .isPlaying() method call to see if the video is playing back currently.

There are also three **.can()** method calls that ascertain what the VideoView can (or cannot) do, regarding the MediaPlayer class. These include the .canPause(), .canSeekBackward(), and .canSeekForward() method calls.

There are also all of your standard **event handling** method calls, which are **inherited** from the Android View superclass. These include the .onTouchEvent(), onKeyDown(), and onTrackballEvent() method calls, among all of the other event handlers. The event handler which is usually used with the VideoView, for instance to bring up the MediaControl "transport" UI panel, is the onTouchEvent() event listener.

Finally, there are specialized method calls, such as .resolveAdjustedSize() or .onInitializeAccessibilityEvent() that are included to allow developers to implement **accessibility standards** if needed for their video playback UI.

A VideoView Lifecycle: Eight Video Playback Stages

Before you start working with the Android digital video-related classes, learn about digital video concepts, and create custom 3D digital video assets, you'll need to understand the different "stages" which a digital video asset goes through in Android. Playing digital video may seem simple from the end user's perspective. **Play**, **Pause**, **Rewind**, and **Stop** all provide basic video transport functions. All these are involved in the overall video playback process or lifecycle. There are other "under the hood" stages which allow Android to load the video asset into memory, or to set parameters for playback and similar system-level considerations. These unseen digital video lifecycle stages will allow developers the flexibility to create an optimal digital video user experience, and give Android developers a wider variety of playback options.

When you implement a VideoView widget, you are also instantiating a MediaPlayer object, even though you do not have to write any XML markup, or even write any Java code, to create this MediaPlayer object! MediaPlayer objects are essentially video playback engines, and will play digital video assets associated with the VideoView UI element. This is done using a **URI** object, and a video asset reference, which the URI object contains. We'll cover URI and MediaPlayer classes later on in this chapter. The video playback states are shown in Table 11-2.

Table 11-2. Video Playback States and How They Affect the Android MediaPlayer Object and Its Video Playback

Video Playback State	What is happening with the MediaPlayer object (video playback)
Idle State	MediaPlayer object is **instantiated** and ready for configuration
Initialized State	MediaPlayer object is **initialized** with data path, using a **URI**
Prepared State	MediaPlayer object is **configured**, or "prepared," for playback
Started State	MediaPlayer object is **started** and is decoding the video stream
Paused State	MediaPlayer object is **paused** and stops decoding video frames
Stopped State	MediaPlayer object is **stopped** and stops decoding video frames
Playback Completed	MediaPlayer object is **finished** decoding the video data stream
Ended State	MediaPlayer object is **ended** and **removed from system memory**

I'll go through these eight states in the logical order in which they are used and in the order in which they are listed in Table 11-2.

1. When your MediaPlayer object is first instantiated, it's not actually doing anything. A MediaPlayer object would therefore initially be in what is termed the "**Idle**" state, much like a car idles when not "engaged."

2. Once you load your MediaPlayer object with the video data reference using your URI object, with a **Uri.parse()** method call or a **.setDataSource()** method call, a MediaPlayer object will enter what is termed an "**Initialized**" state. There is an interim state, between the Initialized MediaPlayer object state and the "**Started**" MediaPlayer object state, which is called the "**Prepared**" MediaPlayer object state.

3. The Prepared state is accessed using the MediaPlayer.OnPreparedListener, which is a nested class that we will be learning about in the MediaPlayer sections of this chapter, and which we will be using a bit later on inside of our HelloUniverse application Java code in the PlayVideo.java Activity subclass, which will play a video asset.

4. Once the MediaPlayer object has been Initialized, and loaded with video data, it is usually "**prepared**" (that is, configured using various playback option settings). After this is done, a MediaPlayer object can then be **Started**.

5.   Once Started, the video is playing, and can be "**Stopped**" by using the
     .stop() method call, or "**Paused**" by using the **.pause()** method call. These
     three video states, Started (Play), Stopped (Stop), and Paused (Pause) should
     be the most familiar to users of digital video, as they are represented by
     the three primary buttons that are found on the video transport bar. In the
     Android OS, the video transport bar is provided using the MediaController
     class.

6.   The final MediaPlayer object digital video playback state is called the
     "**Playback Completed**" state. When the MediaPlayer object reaches this
     state, it signifies that your video asset has stopped playing, and has reached
     the **EOF** (End Of File) marker inside your video asset. You can bypass this
     Playback Completed state if you have invoked the **.setLooping(true)** method
     call and flag. This would be called off of the MediaPlayer object. In this
     use-case, your digital video will continue to loop seamlessly forever, until you
     call the **.stop()** method to stop it.

Note   There are also **.start()** and **.reset()** method calls available for a MediaPlayer object, which can
start and reset the MediaPlayer object at any time, based on the needs of your Java program logic. If you call
a .start() method, your video asset will enter the started state; conversely, if you call a .stop() method, your
video will be stopped. Methods do to your video asset what their names suggest that they do.

7.   Finally, there's also a **.release()** method call, which invokes an "**Ended**"
     state for a MediaPlayer object. This will "terminate" your MediaPlayer object,
     which means that the Android OS will completely remove it from the Android
     device's system memory.

As you will see in the MediaPlayer sections of this chapter, there are other nested classes which
will also allow you to "**listen**" for errors (MediaPlayer.OnErrorListener), as well as for other
states of the MediaPlayer, such as when it reaches a Playback Completed state (MediaPlayer.
OnCompletionListener).

First, we need to create your <VideoView> widget inside of the parent <FrameLayout>, as that is
the next logical step in implementing video inside of the HelloUniverse application. Once that is
completed, we can review the MediaPlayer class and all of its related classes, and then get into
some serious Java coding to implement digital video setup and playback!

Creating a VideoView Widget in the FrameLayout

Let's get started:

1. Click the **activity_play.xml** tab to edit your XML UI definition, shown in
    Figure 11-8, and add a line of space after the opening <FrameLayout> tag.
    Use a left-facing chevron to open the pop-up widget helper dialog. Find
    the <VideoView> widget and double-click on it to insert it inside of the
    <FrameLayout> container.

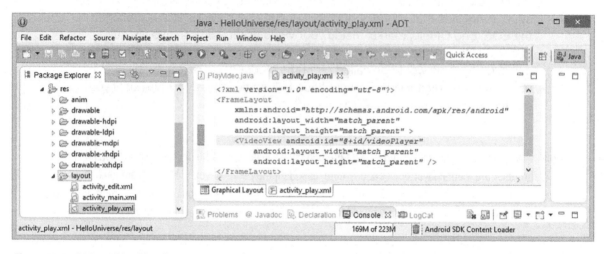

Figure 11-8. Add a child <VideoView> widget tag inside of the parent<FrameLayout> tag; add ID, layout parameters

2. Add an android:id parameter with a value of **@+id/videoPlayer**, and a
    required layout_width and layout_height parameter, set to the **match_parent**
    constant, so that the VideoView is scaled to fit inside of the FrameLayout.

Notice the <FrameLayout> is also configured to **match_parent**, so the VideoView will be scaled to
fit the screen as well, because both of these UI elements are set to match_parent and the top-most
parent is the display screen.

3. The next thing that we need to do to prepare this VideoView UI widget for
    use is to declare it in your PlayVideo Activity subclass, at the top of the code
    base, on top of (before) the onCreate() method, as seen in Figure 11-9.

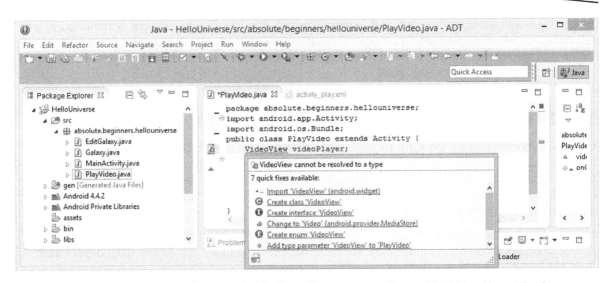

Figure 11-9. Declare the VideoView object, name it videoPlayer, then mouse-over the error highlight and import the class

4. Name the VideoView **videoPlayer** since that is what it is, and then mouse-over
    the wavy red error highlight and select the **Import 'VideoView' (android.widget)**
    option to have Eclipse write the VideoView import statement.

5. Next, you need to instantiate the videoPlayer VideoView object using the
    findViewById() method call and then reference to the **activity_play.xml** UI
    definition file that you just created inside of that method call, as shown in
    Figure 11-10. Once you've done this, you will be able to call methods off this
    videoPlayer VideoView object.

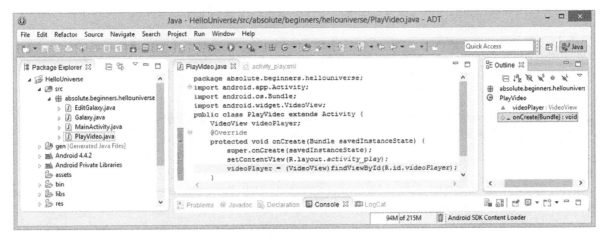

Figure 11-10. Instantiate the videoPlayer VideoView object the using findViewById() method referencing the videoPlayer ID

Before we start calling methods off of this videoPlayer VideoView object, let's get some background regarding the other classes (and thus objects) that we are about to use in our Java code next, including both the Uri and the MediaPlayer classes. We will cover the Android **Uri** class first, since we need it to reference our video data!

The Uri Class: Referencing the Video Data

URI is an abbreviation for **Uniform Resource Indentifier**. It's Uniform because it's standardized, it is a Resource because it references a data path to some data (content) which your applications will operate on (and utilize). It's an Identifier because it identifies where to go and load the data, which is also known as the content's **data path**. The Android **Uri** class only capitalizes the U, the industry term capitalizes all three (URI) letters in the term.

The URI has four parts. First is a URI **schema**, such as HTTP://. Next comes an **authority**, like apress.com. Next comes the **data path**, such as /data/video. Finally comes the **data object** itself, in its file format, such as asset.mp4.

The Uri objects in Android hold a reference to a data path which will be used to access raw or specialized data of one type or another. One example of such data would be a SQLite database, or in this case, a digital video asset. Other examples would include a website URL or similar types of content which an application might use.

The Android Uri class is a direct subclass of the java.lang.Object master class. Just so that you don't get confused when you look at the Android developer's site documentation, note that the **java.net.Uri** class exists alongside the **android.net.Uri** class. However, I suggest that you use the Android-specific version of the Uri class, since it is optimized for use within the Android OS.

The Uri class is a **public abstract** class, and has over three dozen methods which allow developers to work with Uri objects (and data path references). Since this is an Absolute Beginner's book, we will not be getting into this Uri class at a great level of depth, but you're welcome to research it yourself, on the Android developer website. The Android Uri class hierarchy is structured as follows:

```
java.lang.Object
  > android.net.Uri
```

The Android Uri class is kept in the **android.net** package, making it a tool for accessing data across a **network**. For this reason, the import statement for using the Uri class inside of your Android application would reference a package path of **android.net.Uri**, as you will see in the next section when we implement your Uri object.

The Android Uri class allows developers to create Uri objects that provide what is termed an **immutable** URI reference. In Android, you make your objects immutable by placing them into system memory for use, and we'll need to do this for our URI data path reference by using Android's Uri class and its **Uri.parse()** method.

Your Uri object reference includes a URI specifier, as well as a data path reference, which is the component of the URI which follows the ':// '. The Uri class will take care of the process of building and parsing a Uri object, which will then reference data in a manner which will conform to the popular RFC 2396 technical specification.

To optimize the Android operating system and application performance, the Uri class performs a minimal amount of data path validation. What this means is that methods are not specifically defined for handling invalid data input, so you will need to define your own. This means the Uri class is very forgiving in the face of an invalid input specification, but it also means that if the data is invalid, your user may not get the result that they desire!

This means that as a developer, you have to be very careful in what you are doing, as Uri objects could return data garbage, rather than throw an exception, unless you specify otherwise in your Java code. Thus, error trapping and data path validation are left up to the developer to do inside their code, which is why URI is an advanced area which we are only covering at an introductory level so that you can load your digital video data!

Now we can use this Uri class and configure our VideoView UI element so we will be able to access our digital video asset. Let's do that next, and then we can get into the MediaPlayer class and its related classes.

The Uri.parse() Method: Loading Your VideoView

Here's how to use the Uri class:

1. Let's declare a Uri object at the top of your PlayVideo.java Activity subclass underneath the videoPlayer object and name it **planetFlyOverUri**, using the following Java object declaration, which is shown in Figure 11-11:

    ```
    Uri planetFlyOverUri;
    ```

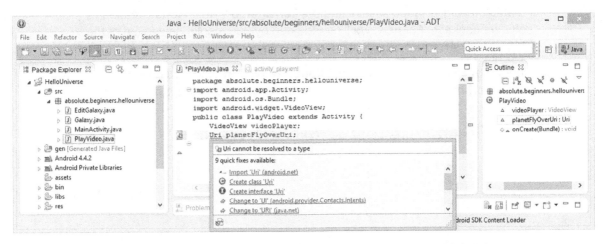

Figure 11-11. Declare a Uri object named planetFlyOverUri at the top of your PlayVideo.java Activity subclass

2.   Before loading the Uri object using the **.parse()** method, you'll need to create
     a **/res/raw** folder, which is used in Android to contain new media assets such
     as **digital video** and **digital audio** which are already optimized and simply
     need to be played back in their raw (unaltered) data format. Right-click on
     the **/res** folder, select the **New ➤ Folder** menu sequence to open the dialog
     shown on the left in Figure 11-12, and name this folder **/raw**.

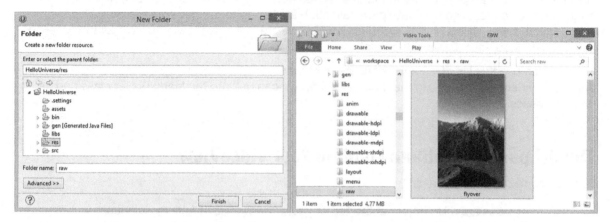

Figure 11-12. Use a New ➤ Folder menu sequence to create a /res/raw folder, then copy the flyover asset into it

3.   Once you have created the folder, copy the **flyover.mp4** file from the book
     repository into the folder. Later on in this chapter, I will show you how I
     created this digital video asset using the **Terragen 3** Virtual World Creation
     software package. For now, we'll use the 480 by 800 resolution version of the
     Planet Fly Over, so we can get right into our Java code!

4.   Now you are ready to configure the **planetFlyOverUri** object using the
     Uri.parse() method call and a URI reference to the **flyover.mp4** digital video
     asset, using the following line of Java code shown in Figure 11-13:

```
planetFlyOverUri = Uri.parse( "android.resource://" + getPackage() + "/" + R.raw.flyover );
```

Figure 11-13. Load the planetFlyOver Uri object using a Uri.parse() method and a data path to /res/raw/flyover

This sets the planetFlyOverUri Uri object to the result of the **Uri.parse()** method call. Inside of this method call is a **concatenation** using the **+** operator, which is used in Java to "concatenate" things together. What this concatenation inside of the Uri.parse() method parameter area does is create the URI path to the video data asset, referenced using this URI: **android.resource://absolute. beginners.hellouniverse/R.raw.flyover**.

5. Now that your planetFlyOverUri Uri object is loaded with the correct URI data path reference, you can "wire" this planetFlyOverUri Uri object to the videoPlayer VideoView object using the **.setVideoURI()** method call, using the compact line of Java code shown in Figure 11-14.

Figure 11-14. Configure the videoPlayer VideoView object to reference the planetFlyOverUri object with .setVideoURI()

This **sets** the VideoURI for the VideoView to the planetFlyOverUri object containing the URI reference to the digital video asset which needs to be played. This is fairly obvious, but I had to state it overtly! Next, let's go over some of the core concepts regarding digital video optimization before I get into showing you how to create and optimize your video assets using Terragen 3, VirtualDub, and Sorenson Squeeze Professional.

Digital Video Concepts: Bitrates & Codecs

Like the 2D animation we learned about in the previous chapter, digital video extends digital imaging into 4D, the fourth dimension of time, by using something called frames in the digital video (and film) industry. Video is thus also comprised of an ordered sequence of frames that are displayed rapidly over time. The difference from animation, at least in real-world usage inside of Android, is that digital video usually has a fairly massive number of frames (30 for every second of video playback time).

The optimization concept with frames in a digital video is very similar to the one regarding pixels in an image (the resolution of the digital image) because video frames multiply the data footprint with each frame used. In digital video, not only does the frame's (image) resolution greatly impact the file size, but so does the number of frames per second that the codec looks at to encode. This is commonly referred to as FPS, or the "frame rate." Standard industry video uses 30 frames per second, but you can use less if you want!

Since digital video is made up of a collection of thousands of digital image frames, the concept of digital video frame rate, expressed as frames per second, or more commonly referred to as FPS, is also very important when it comes to our digital video data footprint optimization work process. This is because with video optimization, lowering the frames per second that the codec looks at encoding will lower the total amount of data that is encoded, which in turn lowers the resulting file size.

In Chapter 8, we learned that if we multiply the number of pixels in the image by its number of color channels, we'll get the raw data footprint for the image. With digital video, we will now multiply that number again using the number of frames per second at which our digital video is set to play back, and again by the number of total seconds which represent the duration of the video "**clip**" which is being encoded into a digital video asset file. You can see why having a video codec that can compress this raw data footprint down is extremely important!

You will be amazed (later on in this chapter) at some of the digital video data compression ratios that we will achieve using the MPEG4 video file format, once we know exactly how to best optimize a digital video compression work process by using the correct bit rate, frame rate, and frame resolution for our digital video content. We'll also get into the concept of bitrates as well as video optimization during the next few sections of this chapter. First, in this next section, let's review the different digital video codecs that the Android OS currently supports.

Digital Video in Android: MPEG4 H.264 and WebM

Android supports the exact same open source digital video formats that HTML5 supports. This includes **MPEG-4 H.264** (MPEG stands for Motion Picture Experts Group) as well as the **ON2 VP8** format, which was acquired by Google from ON2 Technologies, renamed **WebM**, and then released into the open source environment. This is optimal from a content production standpoint, as the video content which a developer produces and optimizes can be used both in HTML5 engines such as HTML5 apps, browsers, and devices, as well as in the Android OS.

This open source digital video format cross-platform support thus affords us content developers with a "produce once, deliver everywhere," production scenario! This will reduce content development costs, thus increasing our revenues, as long as this "economy of scale in content development" is taken advantage of by app developers.

Since most Android devices these days have displays which are using a medium (854x480) to high (HD or 1280x720) resolution, if you are going to use the MPEG4 file format, you should utilize the **MPEG4 H.264 AVC** format, which is currently the digital video format most often used in the world today for Android and HTML5 apps.

The MPEG-4 H.264 AVC (**Advanced Video Coding**) digital video file format is supported across all Android OS versions for video playback, and under **Android 3.0** (and later versions) for **video recording**. It is quite important to note that recording video is only supported if the Android device hardware has video camera capabilities!

If you are a video content producer, you will find that the MPEG4 H.264 format has the best compression result, especially if you are using one of the more advanced encoding suites, like the **Sorenson Squeeze** Professional 9 software, which we will be using to optimize our 3D planet fly-over video asset later on in this chapter.

File extension support for MPEG4 video files includes **.3GP** (MPEG4 SP which stands for "Standard Play") and **.MP4** (MPEG4 H.264 AVC). I suggested using the latter (.MP4 AVC), as that is what I use for HTML5 apps, and MP4 is more common to stream in an AVC format, but either type of file should work just fine in an Android app.

A more recent digital video format that Android now supports is called the **WebM** (VP8) digital video format. This format also provides great quality results with a small data footprint. This is the reason why Google acquired ON2, the company that developed the VP8 codec. We'll learn about codecs later on in this chapter. WebM videoplayback was first **natively supported** in (and in versions after) **Android 2.3**. The term **native support** is used with code(in this case, it's a codec) which has become "natively" a part of the operating system software, which means it is included with the rest of the operating system (API) package.

WebM also supports something called **video streaming**, which we will also be learning about in a later section of this chapter. This WebM video streaming playback capability is supported only if your users have Android Version 4.0 and later. For this reason, I would recommend using WebM for your "**captive**" video assets, as Android 2.3 through 4.4 supports non-streaming WebM codec use. In case you are wondering, captive video is video that is not streamed, meaning video assets are "captive" inside of the **/res/raw** folder. Use an MPEG4 H.264 AVC if you are only going to be streaming video, as all of the Android versions, including Android 5, support that codec, both for captive video playback as well as for streaming video playback.

Digital Video Compression: Bitrate and Streams

Let's start out covering the **primary resolutions** used in commercial video. Before **HDTV**, or **High Definition TV**, came along, video was usually called **SD**, or **Standard Definition**, and used a standard vertical resolution of 480 pixels.

High Definition (or HD) video comes in two resolutions, **1280x720**, which I call "**Pseudo HD**," and the higher resolution **1920x1080**, which the industry calls "**True HD**." Both use a **16:9** widescreen aspect ratio, and are now used not only in film, television, and iTV sets, but also in smartphones (the Razor HD is 1280 by 720) and tablets (the Kindle Fire HD is 1920 by 1200). This **1920x1200** resolution is, by the way, a less wide, or taller, **16:10** pixel aspect ratio, and is becoming more common as a widescreen device aspect ratio, as is a **16:8** (or 2:1) aspect ratio, with 2160x1080 screens out now. There is even a 2560x1440 resolution screen on the Samsung Galaxy S5 smartphone. Why this resolution, you may be wondering? Power of Two (even) upsampling of the most common 1280x720 digital video content will provide the best viewing results. Multiply 1280 by 2 and 720 by 2 and see what resulting screen resolution you come up with!

There is also 16:10 Pseudo HD resolution, which features **1280 by 800** pixels. In fact, this is a common laptop, netbook, and mid-size tablet resolution. I would not be surprised to see a 16:8 1280 by 640 screen offered at some point in time as well. Generally, most content developers try to match their video content resolution to the resolution (and thus the aspect ratio as well) of each Android device upon which the video asset will be viewed.

Regardless of the resolution you use for your digital video content, your application can access video in a couple of different ways. The way I do it, because I'm a **data optimization** freak, is captive to the application. This means the data is inside of the Android application APK file itself, inside the **/res/raw** data resource folder.

The other way to access video inside your Android app is by using a **remote video data server**. In this case, the video is **streamed** from this remote server, over the Internet, and into your user's Android device as the video is playing back in realtime. Let's hope that this video server doesn't crash, which is one of the downsides of streaming.

Video streaming is inherently more complicated than simply playing back captive video data. This is because an Android device is communicating in realtime with remote data servers, receiving video data packets, decoding the data packets as the video plays, and writing the frames to the Android hardware display. Video streaming is supported via WebM on Android 4 and later devices, using the WebM format, or using MPEG4 on all of the Android OS versions.

The last concept that we need to cover in this section is the concept of **bitrate**. Bitrate is a key setting used in the video compression process, as you will see when we utilize Sorenson Squeeze Pro 9 later on in the chapter. Bitrates represent the **target bandwidth**, or data pipe size, which is able to accommodate a certain number of data bits streaming through it every second. Bitrates must also take into consideration CPU processing power within any given Android phone, making video data optimization even more important to the video playback quality.

This is because once bits travel through a data pipe, they also need to be processed and displayed on the device screen. In fact, captive video assets which are included in Android application APK files only need optimization for processing power. This is because if you're using captive video files, there is no data pipe for the video asset to travel through, and no data transfer overhead. Therefore, bitrates for digital video assets need to be optimized not only for bandwidth, but also in anticipation of variances in CPU capability. We'll look at optimization next.

In general, the smaller the video data file size you are able to achieve, the faster the data will travel through the data pipe, the easier it will be to decode the data using the codec and the CPU, and the smaller your APK file size will be, for obvious reasons. Single-core CPUs in devices such as smartwatches may not be able to decode high-resolution, high bitrate digital video assets without "**dropping**" frames, which is a playback quality issue, so make sure to thoroughly optimize low bitrate video assets if you are going to target older (or cheap) devices.

Digital Video Optimization: Codec and Settings

Digital Video is compressed using a software utility called a **codec**, which stands for **COde-DECode**. There are two opposing sides to each video codec; one **encodes** your video data (for captive or streaming), and the other **decodes** this video data (captive video or streamed video). A video decoder will be part of the OS (Android or HTML5), or the HTML5 browser, on other operating systems, which uses it.

The decoder side of the codec will always be optimized for **speed**, as smoothness of video playback is a key issue, and the encoder side will be optimized to **reduce data footprint** for the digital video asset that it is generating. For this reason, the encoding process may take a long time, depending on how many processing cores your workstation contains. Most video content production workstations should support 8, 12, or 16 processor cores.

Codecs (on the encoder side) are like **plug-ins**, in the sense that they can be installed into different digital video editing software packages, in order to enable them to encode different digital video asset file formats. Since the Android OS supports H.263 and H.264 MPEG-4 formats, and the ON2 VP8 WebM format for video, you need to make sure that you are using one of the codecs which encodes video data into these digital video file formats.

More than one software manufacturer makes MPEG encoding software, so there will be different MPEG codecs (encoder software) that will yield different (better or worse) results, as far as encoding speed and file size goes. The professional solution I recommend that you secure if you wish to produce professional video is called Sorenson Squeeze, which is currently at version 9. Squeeze has a professional-level version, which I will be using in this book, which costs less than a thousand dollars, and whose value is in excess of that suggested list price amount.

There is also an open source solution called **EditShare LightWorks 11.5** that is scheduled to natively support output using the MPEG4 and WebM VP8 codec sometime in 2014. So for now, I will have to use Squeeze Pro 9 for this book, until the codec support for Android and HTML5 is added to EditShare LightWorks 11.5 in 2014.

When optimizing for digital video data file size using encoder settings, there are a number of important settings which directly affect the data footprint. I'll cover these in the order in which they affect file size, from the most impact to the least impact, so you know which parameters to "tweak" or adjust in order to obtain the results that you are looking for.

As in digital image compression, the resolution, or number of pixels, in each frame of video is the best place to start your data optimizing process. If you are targeting 854x480 or 1280x720 smartphones or tablets, you don't need to use 1920x1080 resolution to get great visual results from your digital video assets.

With high-density (also termed high **dot pitch**) displays (HDPI, XHDPI and XXHDPI) currently common in the Android market, you can scale 1280 video up 33% and it will look reasonably good. The exception to this might be iTV apps for GoogleTV, which has a medium (or even low) dot pitch, due to large 55 to 75 inch screen sizes. In this use-case, if you are developing applications for iTV sets, you would want to use "True HD" 1920x1080 resolution.

The next level of optimization would come in the **number of frames** used for each second of video, called **FPS**, assuming the actual seconds contained in the video itself cannot be shortened by editing. This is known as your **frame rate**, and instead of setting the **video standard 30 FPS** frame rate, consider using a **film standard** frame rate of **24 FPS**, or the **multimedia standard** frame rate of

20 FPS. You might even be able to use a low **15 FPS** frame rate, depending upon your content. Note that 15 FPS is half as much data as 30 FPS, or a 100% reduction in data going into the encoder. For some video content, this will playback (look) the same as 30 FPS content; the only reliable way to test how low you can get the frame rate before you start to affect **video playback quality** is to set, encode and review with these standard video framerate settings during the content optimization (final video asset encoding) work process.

The next most optimal setting to tweak (experiment with settings for) in obtaining a smaller data footprint will be the **bitrate** that you set for a codec to try and achieve. Bitrate settings equate to an **amount of compression** applied, and thus sets the visual quality for video data. It is important to note that you could simply use 30 FPS, HD 1920x1080 video and specify a low bitrate ceiling. If you do this, the results would not look as good as if you first experimented with lower frame rates and resolutions using the higher (quality) bitrate settings.

The next most effective setting in obtaining a small data footprint is the number of **keyframes**. The codec uses your keyframe settings to know when to **sample** the digital video. Video codecs apply compression by looking at a frame, and then encoding only the **changes**, or **offsets**, over the next few frames, so that it does not have to encode every single frame in your video data stream. This is why a talking-head video will encode better than a video where every pixel moves on every frame, such as video with fast panning, or rapid zooming, for instance.

The keyframe setting in the encoder will force the codec to take a fresh frame sample of a video data asset every so often. There is usually an **auto** setting for keyframes; this allows the codec to decide how many keyframes to sample. There is also a **manual** setting which allows you to specify a keyframe sampling every so often, usually a certain number of times per second, or a certain number of times over the duration of the video (total frames). The more keyframes the codec needs to sample (and store in the file) the larger the resulting file size will be.

The next most effective setting in obtaining a small data footprint is the **quality** or **sharpness** setting, which is usually implemented using a slider. Sharpness controls the amount of blur that the codec will apply to the video pixels before compression. In case you are wondering how this trick works, so that you can apply it yourself in GIMP during your own digital image optimization work process, applying a slight blur to your image or video, which is usually not desirable, can allow for better JPEG compression. The reason for this is that a sharp transition in an image, such as sharp edges between colors, are more difficult for the codec to encode optimally (that is, using less data). More precisely (no pun intended), sharp or abrupt transitions in color will take more data to reproduce than soft transitions will. I would recommend keeping the quality or sharpness slider between an 80% and 100% quality setting, and try to get your data footprint reduction using the other variables that we have discussed here.

Ultimately, there are a significant number of different variables that you'll need to fine-tune in order to achieve the best data footprint optimization for each particular video data asset. Each video asset will be different (mathematically) to the codec, as each video asset is a different array or collection of pixel color data. For this reason, there is no "standard" collection of settings you can develop to achieve any given result. Your experience tweaking various settings will eventually allow you to get a better feel, over time, as to the settings you need to change as far as all the parameters go, to get your desired result with different types of uncompressed video source assets.

Creating Digital Video Content: Terragen3

The next thing that you need to learn is how to create digital video content that you can use to show the various concepts which you just learned about in the previous sections of this chapter. I'm going to use **Terragen 3.1**, a world creation 3D animation software package from **Planetside Software**, because it is not only an impressive 3D software package, but is also a professional-level 3D production software package. Fortunately, there is the free version as well as a paid Pro version, which I suggest that you purchase if you are serious about having all the primary production tools in your quiver. Go to their website at Planetside.co.uk and download the latest version of Terragen3. After you download and install the software:

1. Launch it with a shortcut icon, and you will see the Credits and Support tabs, shown in Figure 11-15, in the various rendered start-up screens for the software. You can see exactly what this software is capable of by viewing these startup screens!

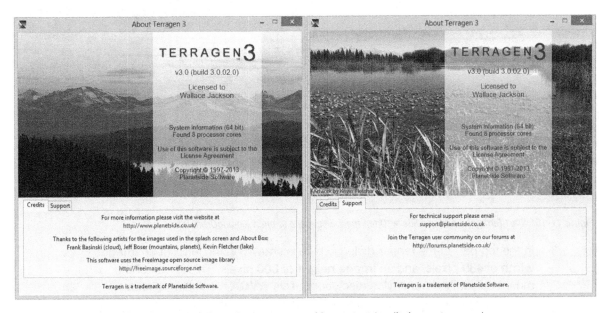

Figure 11-15. Using Terragen3 world building software to create video content (credits/support screens)

2. As you can see, this software package rocks in the hands of a seasoned user! Next, we will open a basic seamless looping camera fly-over of a basic world that you'll find in the book assets folder called **loopingOrbit_v03.tgd** (tgd is TerraGen Data). Use a **File ➤ Open** menu sequence to open it in the software, as shown in Figure 11-16.

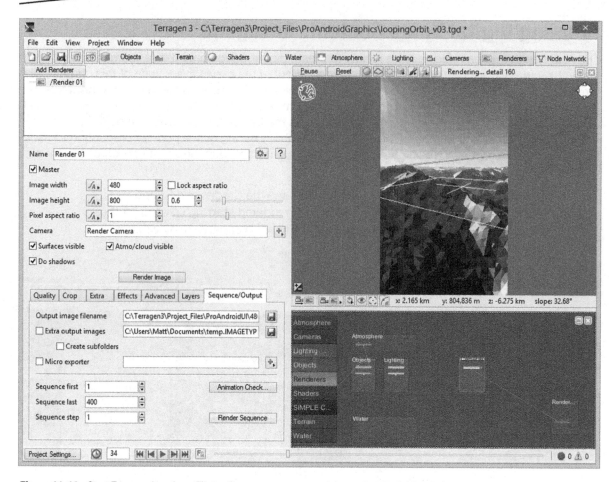

Figure 11-16. Start Terragen3 and use File ➤ Open menu sequence to open loopingOrbit_v03

3. In the top part of the render dialog, which is shown on the left, set an **image width** of **480** pixels, and an **image height** of **800** pixels. This is one of the more popular Android device resolutions. This **WVGA** resolution will have enough pixels to be able to scale up or down with good results. Leave all the other render settings at their default settings. If you just wanted to render one frame, you could use the **Render Image** button, which is in the middle of this dialog, but this will not create a **sequence of frames**, which you will need to create **motion video** data. At the bottom of this dialog, you will see seven tabs which control **advanced settings**.

4. Click on the seventh (the right-most) tab, which is labeled **Sequence/Output**, to set the output file specifications as well as the image sequence settings. Enter your **project files directory** in the **Output image filename** field, as shown in Figure 11-16. Mine is C:\Terragen3\Project_Files\ProAndroidUI\, as you can see in the screenshot.

5. Make sure that your **Sequence first** field is set to a value of **1**, and set a value of **400** in the **Sequence last** field. Set your **Sequence step** to **1 frame**.

6. Once you have set all of your parameters for the render, click the **Render Sequence** button, which will instruct Terragen to generate 400 frames of custom digital video fly-over for you. Since Terragen outputs numbered files instead of the AVI format that Sorenson Squeeze requires, we will need to learn about a cool software utility called VirtualDub next, so that we can generate an uncompressed AVI file.

Creating an Uncompressed AVI File: VirtualDub

The next software package we will need to use is VirtualDub 1.9, which will take the 400 frames we created in Terragen3 and load them into an AVI file format. Then we can import the AVI in Squeeze for our compression work process.

1. Download and install VirtualDub and launch it. You will see the empty screen, shown in Figure 11-17. Use a **Video ➤ Compression** menu sequence to set compression for the resulting file to **Uncompressed**.

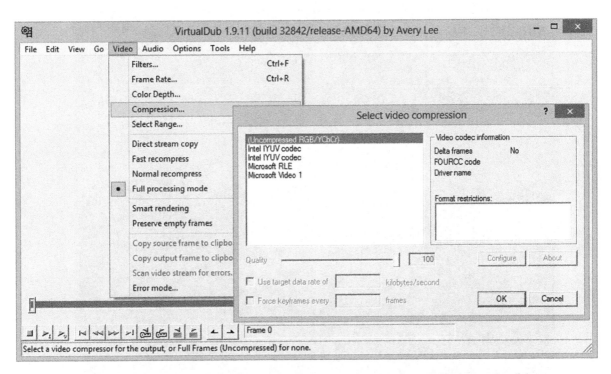

Figure 11-17. Launch VirtualDub and use the Video ➤ Compression menu sequence to open the compression dialog

2. Use the **Frame Rate**, **Color Depth**, and **Select Range** menu items, and set these compression parameters to be **10 FPS**, **24-bit color**, and **0 to 400**, respectively, as is shown in the series of dialogs in Figure 11-18.

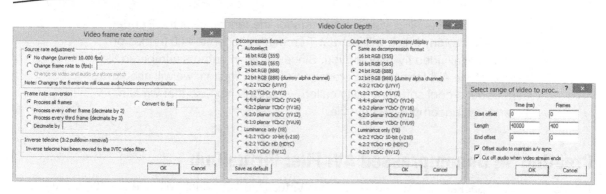

Figure 11-18. Setting the frame rate, video color depth, and frame range fora flyover.avi uncompressed file

3. Now you are ready to load your 400 frames, shown in Figure 11-19, using the **File ➤ Open** file menu sequence.

Figure 11-19. Use the File ➤ Open menu sequence to open the first frame in the 400-frame render sequence

4. Select the first frame in the 400-frame sequence and click the **Open** button to open all 400 frames in VirtualDub. You will see Frame 0 displayed in the software when all 400 frames are loaded, and there should be a 400-frame duration timeline at the bottom, as shown in Figure 11-19.

5. Next, use the **File ➤ Save AVI 2.0 File** menu sequence to open the dialog shown in Figure 11-20. Name the file flyover, and then use the **Save** button to save the AVI.

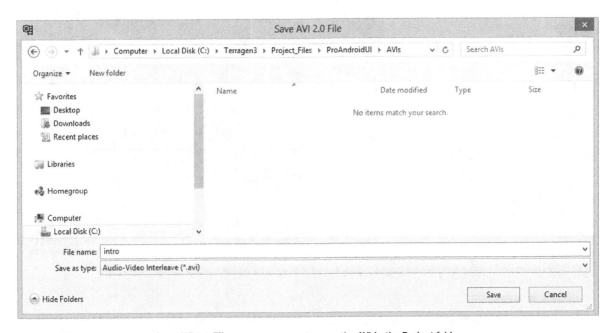

Figure 11-20. Use the File ➤ Save AVI 2.0 File menu sequence to save the AVI in the Project folder

6. After you click the **Save** button, you will see the processing start, and a progress dialog, shown in Figure 11-21.

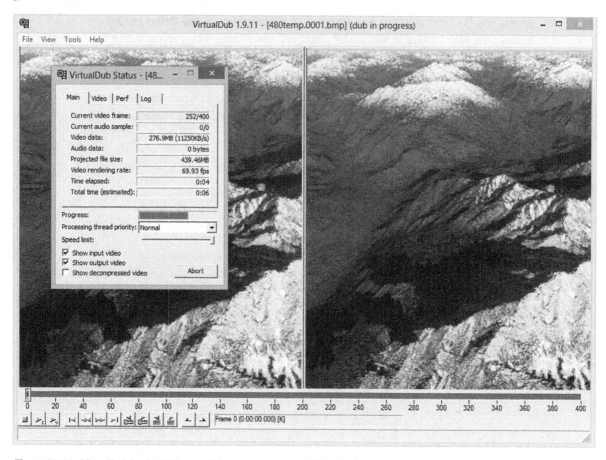

Figure 11-21. VirtualDub loads 400 frames into an uncompressed AVI, showing the progress stats

Now that you have your 400 frames of digital video data in an AVI format that Sorenson Squeeze can import, you can go into Squeeze and proceed with the video compression (data footprint optimization) work process.

Applying Video Compression: Sorenson Squeeze 9

Next, we're going to use Sorenson Squeeze Pro to compress the digital video asset. One of the reasons I utilized Terragen 3.1 and VirtualDub is to create completely uncompressed source video with zero compression artifacts. If you want this same pristine data using a camera, you would use Firewire, capturing full frame uncompressed (raw) video data to your hard disk drive, instead of going through the on-camera MPEG or Motion JPEG codec.

1.   Install Squeeze 9 and launch it.

2.   Next, click on the **Import File** icon on the upper-left, as seen in Figure 11-22. Notice the Squeeze software has left panels for holding **codec**, **filter**, and **publishing** options, a top preview area, and a bottom timeline area, which we will be using soon to apply our codec presets to your flyover.avi file.

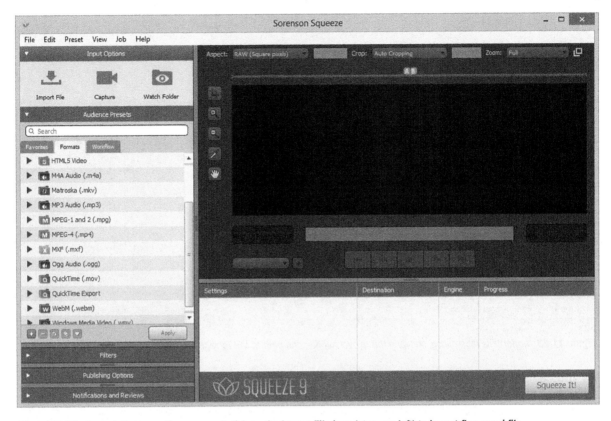

Figure 11-22. Launch Sorenson Squeeze and click on the Import File icon (at upper-left) to import flyover.avi file

3. Once you click the **Import File** icon, you'll see an **AVIs** dialog, shown in
    Figure 11-23. Navigate to the Terragen3/Project_Files/AndroidApps/AVIs
    folder and click on your **flyover** AVI file, and then on the **Open** button, to load
    your uncompressed AVI data into Squeeze 9. We are using uncompressed
    data to give Squeeze 9 the best, highest-quality source data to work with,
    going into the compression (optimization) process.

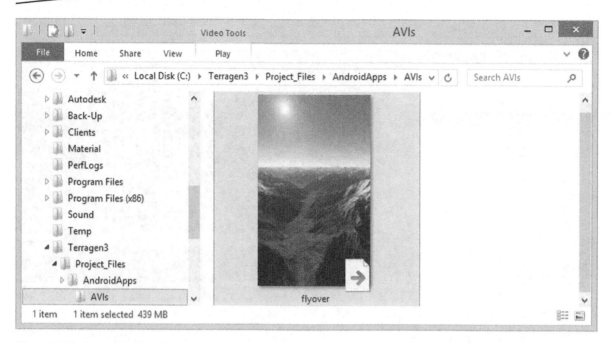

Figure 11-23. Import File AVIs dialog, showing the flyover.avi file, and path to the Terragen3 project folders

As you can see in Figure 11-24 on the left side, the video data loads into Squeeze, and displays the flyover.avi file in a bottom area of the window, where we will apply the codec presets once we create them.

Figure 11-24. Squeeze showing the AVI file loaded with the codecs (left), and right-clicking on the MPEG4 codec to Edit settings

4. Click on the right-facing arrow next to the **MPEG-4** codecs, and open up the MPEG-4 codecs, so you can right-click on the **768Kbps_360p** preset that comes with Squeeze.

5. Select the **Edit** menu option, so that we can edit these presets. Editing existing presets (and then giving them unique names, and saving them as your own) is the easy way to create your own custom data compression settings for the 480x800 flyover.mp4 file that you are creating here.

The Edit context-sensitive (right-click) menu option will open up the **Presets** dialog, as shown in Figure 11-25, where you can set all the different compression options which you learned about in the previous chapter section.

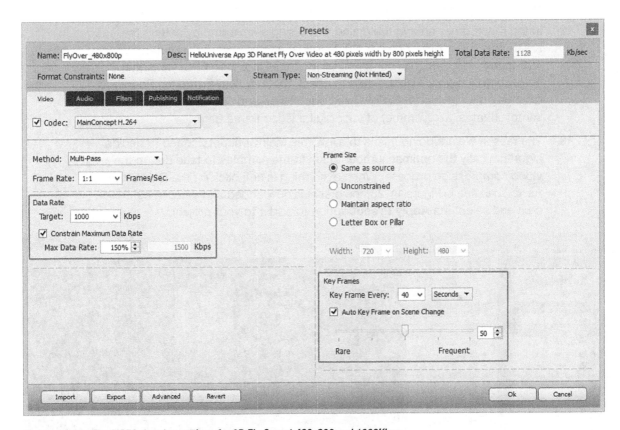

Figure 11-25. The MPEG-4 codec settings for 3D Fly Overat 480x800 and 1000Kbps

6. Name the preset **FlyOver_480x800p** and then enter a description of **HelloUniverse App 3D Planet Fly Over Video at 480 pixels width by 800 pixels height** at the top of the dialog, as shown in Figure 11-25.

7. Make sure that **Stream Type** is set to **Non-Streaming** and **Format Constraints** is set to **None**.

8. Select the **MainConcept H.264 MPEG-4** codec using the **Codec** drop-down menu, and using the **Method** drop-down, select the **Multi-Pass** option, which will take the longest time to compress your content, but will yield the very best compression to quality (ratio) result that is possible using the encoder's algorithm.

9. Leave the **Frame Rate** drop-down at **1:1**, and set your **Target Data Rate** to **1000 Kbps**.

10. Select the **Constrain Maximum Date Rate** checkbox and set a **Max Data Rate** of **150%**, which will give you a bitrate ceiling of **1500 Kbps**.

11. On the right side of the Presets dialog, set your **Frame Size** to match your source AVI resolution of 480x800 by selecting the **Same as source** option.

12. In the Key Frames area of the dialog, set a single keyframe by setting the Key Frame Every drop-down to 40 seconds, as this is your duration for your 400-frame video which is compressed in VirtualDub at 10 FPS, yielding a 40 second duration. Also, be sure to check the Auto Key Frame on Scene Change option, which will allow this codec to determine when to take a new sample (that is, a key frame) of your digital video frame data.

13. The reason we are doing this is to allow this MainConcepts codec to decide algorithmically the optimal number of keyframe samples to take during the video compression process. When everything is set, click on the **OK** button. As you can see in Figure 11-26, the preset is now added and you can right-click on it and select the **Apply Preset** option to add it to your project.

Figure 11-26. Right-click to Apply Preset (left), show applied preset (center), and Ready to Compress message (right)

14. Once you've applied the preset to your **flyover.avi** file, as shown in Figure 11-26, you can click the **Squeeze It!** Button to create the **flyover.mp4** file using the codec preset that you just designed. This will create the video asset, as you can see on the right side of Figure 11-27.

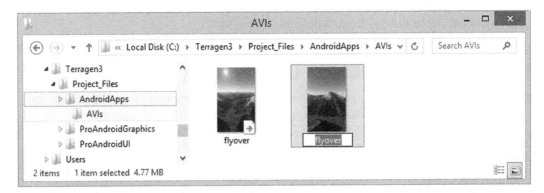

Figure 11-27. Go into AndroidApps\AVIs folder, and make sure .MP4 file is named flyover.mp4 (all lower case)

15. Open your operating system's file management software (on Windows 8.1 it's Explorer) and find your Terragen3 projects folder, and your **AndroidApps\AVIs** sub-folder, and rename the **FlyOver_480x800p** MPEG-4 file that Squeeze saved out for you **flyover.mp4** (using all lower case letters, as is required by Android OS), as is shown in Figure 11-28.

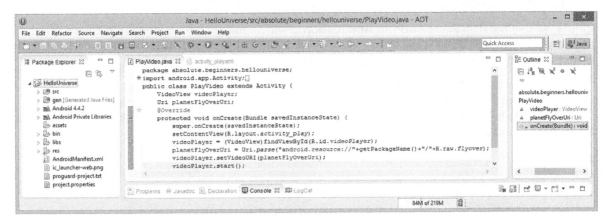

Figure 11-28. Add the videoPlayer.start() method call to finish implementation of a VideoView and start playback

16. Next, right-click on the flyover.mp4 file and **Copy** it to the OS clipboard, so that you can **Paste** it into the **/res/raw** folder, if you have not already done that using this book assets repository, that is!

Let's get back into Eclipse ADT and finish writing the Java code needed to implement this video asset using only a VideoView widget inside of a FrameLayout container in the PlayVideo Activity subclass in your Android app. I am going to show you how to use the .start() method before we get into the MediaPlayer class, so that you understand that you can implement video in Android (as an Absolute Beginner) without any knowledge of, or direct usage of, the MediaPlayer class or its related classes whatsoever! I am making sure to go from easy to difficult during this chapter, as using digital video assets in Android can range from simple to complicated.

Starting A Video Playback: Using .start()

Now that we have learned how to actually develop a video asset for use in your digital video UI designs within Android, we can finish writing the Java code which you have been writing to implement a digital video in your application's PlayVideo.java Activity subclass. The only line of Java code that we have not yet put into place is the call to the **.start()** method, which we will make off of the **videoPlayer** VideoView object, which you've already loaded with a URI for the /res/raw/flyover.mp4 video asset. We accomplished this using the Uri.parse() Uri class and the .parse() method. A call to this .start() method off of the videoPlayer VideoView object is done using the following simple line of Java code (more of a Java statement, actually) which is seen in Figure 11-28:

```
videoPlayer.start();
```

As you can see in Figure 11-28, you have implemented digital video playback in your Java code in a half-dozen lines of Java code, not including import statements, of course. Since we used a couple different emulators in the previous chapter, we can reset our Eclipse environment back to using the **Nexus One** emulator using a **Run As ➤ Configurations** menu sequence to open the **Configurations Editor**, and selecting and setting a Nexus One AVD for use.

Before we use the **Run As ➤ Android Application** menu sequence to launch the AVD, we will need to add the PlayVideo Activity declaration into our **AndroidManifest.xml** file, so that when the Intent object calls it, the Android OS knows that it is there.

This is because the PlayVideo Activity has been declared (and has been setup by the Android OS) for use in the application's Manifest. Copy the **EditGalaxy <activity>** tag structure in the Manifest, and then paste it underneath itself. Change EditGalaxy to **PlayVideo**, and edit_galaxy to **play_video**, **Save** the file, and you'll be ready to fly over your planet's surface!

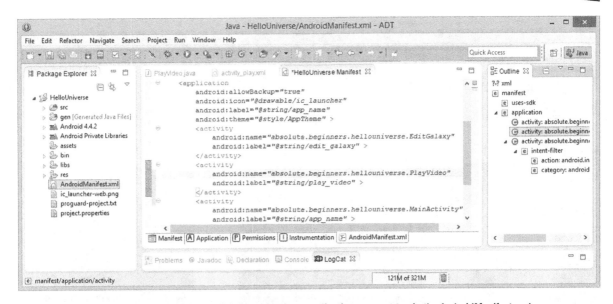

Figure 11-29. Add a PlayVideo <activity> child tag under the <application> parent tag in the AndroidManifest.xml

Run the application, and select the **Fly Over Planet** menu option, as seen in Figure 11-30, to watch the digital video play!

As you can see in the center pane of Figure 11-30, the digital video asset is maintaining its **480x800** resolution and aspect ratio, and is not scaling up to fill the screen even though we have specified a **match_parent** constant in both the X and Y dimensions in both the FrameLayout container and the VideoView UI widget. This is what the digital video (and imaging) industry terms as "**respecting**" the aspect ratio, and the Android FrameLayout class is coded so as to not distort an image or video asset, even if the match_parent constant has been specified.

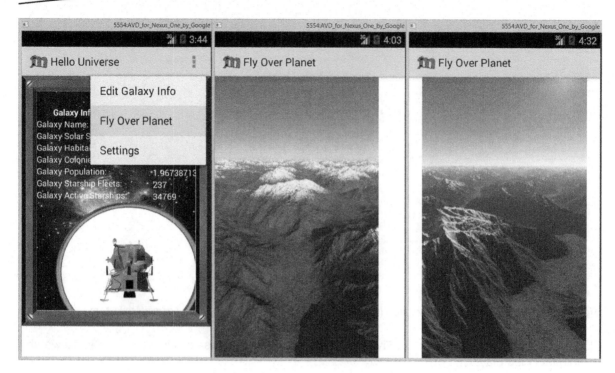

Figure 11-30. Test the VideoView and FrameLayout in the Nexus One (left and center) and layout_gravity (right)

What this means is that a FrameLayout container doesn't scale or otherwise alter what is inside of its container, which stands to reason, as it's the intent of this UI container type to frame or display a fixed result on the screen.

There is a way around this, a trick which I will be showing to you in a future section of this chapter, after I show you how to **center** this fixed aspect ratio digital video asset.

Let's get some hands-on experience with the one layout parameter which is supported by the FrameLayout class, the **android:layout_gravity** parameter. Next, we will take a look at how to make your current UI design look more professional, by centering the digital video asset inside of the display screen. If the user's display screen (device) size or shape changes across (between) devices, your video will stay attractively centered!

Positioning a Video Asset Using layout_gravity

Add a line of space under your layout_height parameter in your <VideoView> widget in the **activity_play.xml** file (tab) in Eclipse ADT, and add an android:layout_gravity="center" parameter, as shown in Figure 11-31.

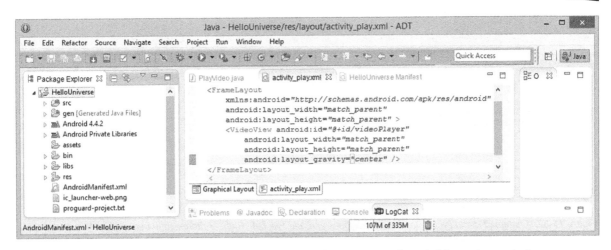

Figure 11-31. Add an android:layout_gravity parameter to the <VideoView> tag configured with a center constant

This will center the <VideoView> widget inside of the <FrameLayout> container. You can see the centering result on the right-hand side of Figure 11-30.

Scaling Video Non-Uniformly to Fit the Screen

Let's see if there is any method that we can use to force Android to scale our video to fit the display screen. We know that a <FrameLayout> container won't allow us to do this, so which of Android's layout container classes which we have learned about so far would allow this? The <RelativeLayout> container has **layout_alignParent** parameters, might we use those to "force" Android OS to scale this video non-uniformly, without respect to aspect ratio? Let's try it and see!

Change the **<FrameLayout>** and **</FrameLayout>** opening and closing parent tags to **<RelativeLayout>** and **</RelativeLayout>**, respectively, and remove the **android:layout_gravity** parameter and replace it with all four of the **layout_alignParent** parameters, using the following XML markup, as shown in Figure 11-32:

```xml
<?xml version="1.0" encoding="utf-8"?>
<RelativeLayout
  xmlns:android="http://schemas.android.com/apk/res/android"
  android:layout_width="match_parent" android:layout_height="match_parent" >
  <VideoView android:id="@+id/videoPlayer"
    android:layout_width="match_parent" android:layout_height="match_parent"
    android:layout_alignParentLeft="true" android:layout_alignParentRight="true"
    android:layout_alignParentTop="true" android:layout_alignParentBottom="true" />
</RelativeLayout>
```

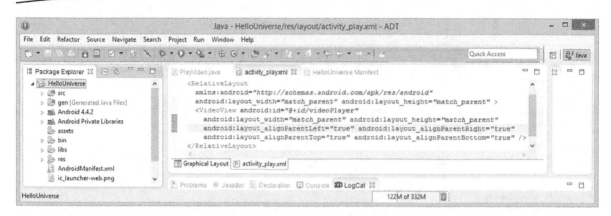

Figure 11-32. Change <FrameLayout> to <RelativeLayout> and add Top, Left, Right, Bottom alignParent parameters

This should scale the video asset up to meet each respective side of the user's display screen. Before we test this, we will also add a media control transport bar UI element into the mix using the MediaController class and its partner in crime, the MediaPlayer class.

Now that you know how to implement digital video using only the VideoView and Uri classes, it is time to get a bit more complicated and learn about the Android **MediaPlayer** class and **MediaController** class. Even though this is an Absolute Beginners book, I wanted to cover the topic of digital video thoroughly for all of our readers who might wish to implement advanced new media assets in their application user experience!

Android MediaPlayer: VideoPlayback Engine

The MediaPlayer class is a direct subclass of the java.lang.Object master class. As you know, this indicates that the Android MediaPlayer class was designedspecifically for the purpose of providing MediaPlayer objects. These MediaPlayer objects are a part of the VideoView widget, and you will learn how to make them "visible" to your Java code in the next section of the chapter.

The Android MediaPlayer class hierarchy would therefore be structured as follows:

```
java.lang.Object
  > android.media.MediaPlayer
```

The MediaPlayer class belongs to the **android.media** package. The import statement for using the MediaPlayer class in an app would reference the **android.media.MediaPlayer**.The MediaPlayer class is a **public** class, and features **nine nested classes**. Eight of the nested classes offer **callbacks** for determining information regarding operation of MediaPlayer's video playback engine. We'll be using one of these in the next section of the chapter.

The ninth nested class, a **MediaPlayer.TrackInfo** nested class, is utilized to return video, audio, or subtitle track metadata information. The MediaPlayer nested class callback that we'll be implementing later on in the chapter is the **MediaPlayer.OnPreparedListener**, which allows us to configure a MediaPlayer object before the digital video asset playback starts for the first time. Other often-used callbacks include the **MediaPlayer.OnErrorListener**, which responds to (or handles) error messages relating to the digital video asset (file) itself or the (lost) network connection, and the **MediaPlayer.OnCompletionListener**, which you can use to trigger other Java programming structures once your video asset playback cycle has completed.

There is also a **MediaPlayer.OnSeekCompletedListener**, which is called when a **seek operation** is completed, and a **MediaPlayer.OnBufferingUpdateListener**, which is called in order to obtain data buffering status for a video asset which is being streamed over a network. There are also a couple of less-often-utilized nested classes, such as the **MediaPlayer.OnTimedTextListener**, used when video **timed text** becomes available for display, and the **MediaPlayer.OnInfoListener**, used when **information** or **warnings** regarding video media being used become available for display. These nested class callbacks are not used that often, at least not to my knowledge, but they are available to you if you need them for specialized digital video implementation scenarios within your Android applications.

Now, let's continue with our Java programming, and implement a MediaPlayer.OnPreparedListener that will set the digital video asset to **loop** continuously. Fortunately, we learned about event listeners early on in the book in Chapter 7, so that I could cover more advanced callbacks, such as this one, during the second half of the book!

Loop Digital Video: Using .OnPrepareListener( )

Now we are going to implement one of the most-used nested classes for the MediaPlayer video playback engine class, the **MediaPlayer.OnPreparedListener()**, which will allow you to configure your videoPlay VideoView video asset to loop seamlessly. You do this by calling a **.setOnPreparedListener()** method off of your videoPlayer object, and inside of that Java programming construct, you use a **new** keyword to create an **OnPreparedListener()** method. This is accomplished via the following initial line of Java code:

```
videoPlayer.setOnPreparedListener(new MediaPlayer.OnPreparedListener()
{ onPrepared() method is in here });
```

As you can see in Figure 11-33, as you type in the **videoPlayer.setOnPreparedListener()** method call, off of your videoPlayer VideoView object, as you type in the **new** and the **MediaPlayer** and **the period** part of the statement, Eclipse will suddenly figure out what you are trying to do, and will popup a MediaPlayer nested class callback helper dialog, which is shown at the bottom-right corner of the screenshot that is shown in Figure 11-33.

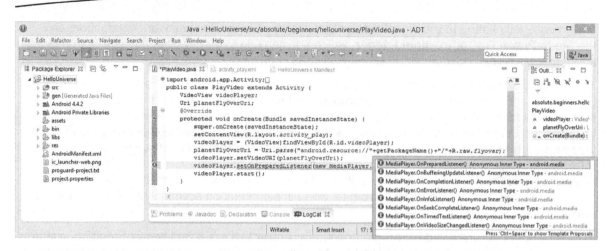

Figure 11-33. Type videoPlayer.setOnPreparedListener(new MediaPlayer. and then select OnPreparedListener

As you can see, this dialog contains all eight of the nested class callbacks that you learned about in the previous section of the chapter. Select the first **MediaPlayer.OnPreparedListener Anonymous Inner Type** option and double-click on it, which will insert it into your Java code structure. Not only does it insert the OnPreparedListener() method, but it also will add an unimplemented onPrepared() method structure, which you usually have to do via another mouse-over operation (this must be new in Android 4.4; Eclipse just keeps getting better at writing all of this Java code for you).

All you will have to do now is to add the operation that you want to happen during this preparation phase of your video asset. This would be to set the **looping parameter** to be **true**, so that the video will loop forever.

It is important to notice that I am calling the .setOnPreparedListener() method **before** I call the .start() method, because I don't want to start the video before I prepare (configure) it for use! Remember, the order of Java programming statements is extremely important, and putting method calls in the wrong order would generate unintended results!

Now all you have to do is to add a **.setLooping()** method call and parameter to the **public void onPrepared()** method inside of the OnPreparedListener() method, called off of the **MediaPlayer** object named **arg0**, which Eclipse has created for us. This is all done using the following Java program logic, shown in Figure 11-34:

```
videoPlayer.setOnPreparedListener(new MediaPlayer.OnPreparedListener(){
    @Override
    public void onPrepared(MediaPlayer arg0){
        arg0.setLooping(true);
    }
});
```

Figure 11-34. Adding the onPrepared() method to our new MediaPlayer.OnPreparedListener() callback structure

As you can see in Figure 11-34, the code is error-free, and ready to test using a **Run As ➤ Android Application** menu sequence. As you can see on the left side of Figure 11-35, thanks to that trick I taught you in the previous section on scaling video assets non-uniformly, your looping digital video asset now fills your screen, and (not in the screenshot, unfortunately) you can watch your 3D planet flyover digital video asset loop seamlessly on the screen. The right side shows the MediaController, which we'll be adding in the next section, but which I put in this screenshot to save space. You have implemented looping digital video in your application using only 12 lines of Java code, not counting the 3 import statements (which you can see at the top of Figure 11-34).

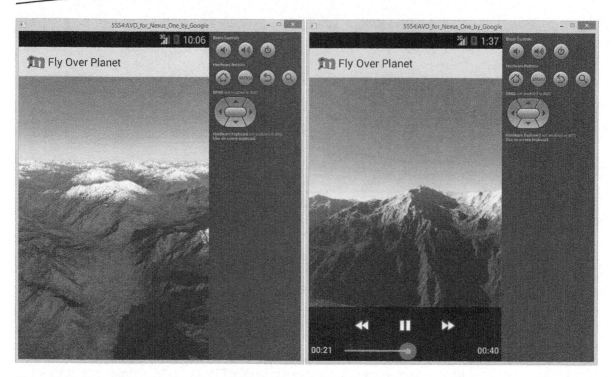

Figure 11-35. Non-uniform scaled (and looping) video (left) and MediaController transport control (right)

Next, I'm going to show you how easy it is to **stream** video, instead of using captive video assets in Android. All you have to do is change your Uri object to reference an **HTTP://** instead of an **android.resource://** in your URI data path referencing string.

Streaming Digital Video: Using HTTP URL in URI

Since Android handles all of the logistics regarding streaming video from the Internet into the hardware device, all we as developers really have to do is to provide a correct **HTTP:// URL**, or **Uniform Resource Locator**, in the place of the **R.raw.flyover** resource locator, which we have been using up until now.

Do this by replacing the **android.resource://absolute.beginners.hellouniverse/R.raw.flyover** URI path with an **HTTP://www.e-bookclub/flyover.mp4** reference to an external server. This is a gridserver that I happen to own, in this particular case. As you can see in Figure 11-36, the **Uri.parse()** method call will accommodate an **HTTP://** URL reference as easily as an android.resource:// URI reference. That makes it easy for us to switch our URI path references!

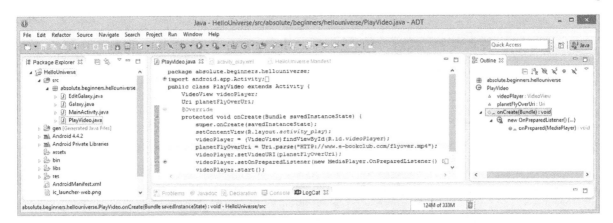

Figure 11-36. Streaming digital video into your Android application using an HTTP URL in the Uri.parse() method

Test the streaming video using **Run As ➤ Android Application**, and watch the video stream! It is important to note that once the video streams over the network the first time, it will loop out of the system memory thereafter.

Add a Video Transport UI Using MediaController

Finally, let's implement your MediaController UI transport controller, the buttons used to control the video.

1. The first step is to use a **new** keyword in conjunction with the **MediaController()** constructor method with a passed parameter containing a standard Java Context object, which in this case is passed using the Java keyword **this**. This powerful code will construct a MediaController object we will name **videoTransport**.This is accomplished using the following Java programming construct, as shown in Figure 11-37:

    ```
    videoTransport = new MediaController(this);
    ```

Figure 11-37. Declare a MediaController named videoTransport, and construct a new MediaController() object

2. Once you declare the `MediaController videoTransport;` statement at the
    very top of your PlayVideo Activity subclass, and mouse-over and **Import
    MediaController (android.media)**, you will be able to **instantiate** and
    construct your new MediaController object inside of your onCreate() method.

Notice in both Figures 11-37 and 11-38 that I've clicked on the videoTransport MediaController
object in the Java code, which tells Eclipse to highlight the (tan colored) tracking of the instantiation.
I did this in the next screenshot to show both the videoTransport MediaController object
declaration and instantiation (tan color) as well as the object use (gray color) for the videoTransport
MediaController object. This is a simple but effective technique to track an object's usage throughout
your Java programming logic.

Figure 11-38. Wire videoTransport to videoPlayer using the .setAnchorView() and .setMediaController() methods

The next thing that we will need to do is to "wire" the VideoView object to the MediaController object so that they know each other are there and so they will work together seamlessly.

In pseudo code speak, we need to tell the MediaController object that it is controlling the VideoView and tell the VideoView to use the MediaController object to control its media (in this case, digital video). This "cross-wiring" of the two objects will take two lines of Java code, which after they are in place, will give your user the ability to click (or touch) your video and bring up a MediaPlayer Transport UI element.

The MediaController, or the MediaPlayer Transport, whichever way you want to look at it, will always work regardless of whether you have your digital video asset set up to loop or to only play once.

3. As you can see in Figure 11-38 we will first use the **.setAnchorView()** method call, off of the **videoTransport** object, to wire the videoTransport and the videoPlayer objects together. This tells the videoTransport object: "the videoPlayer VideoView object is your AnchorView."

4. Then we will use the **.setMediaController()** method call, off of the **videoPlayer** object, to wire the videoPlayer and the videoTransport objects together. This will tell your videoPlayer object: "use the videoTransport MediaController object as the MediaController for the VideoView." These two simple lines of Java programming logic should look like the following:

```
videoTransport.setAnchorView(videoPlayer);
videoPlayer.setMediaController(videoTransport);
```

5. Use your **Run As ➤ Android Application** menu sequence to launch the Nexus One AVD, and click the three dots at the top-right of your ActionBar and select the Fly Over Planet option from the menu. Once your digital video starts playing, even if it loops, at any time you can click on the screen and bring up the video media transport controls.

After a few seconds, the transport controls will fade away if they are not being actively used to start, stop, pause, or shuttle the digital video asset's frames.

Congratulations, you have essentially mastered digital video for your Android application development during this chapter, doing everything from learning the fundamentals of video to creating and optimizing digital video assets to coding a video playback Activity with looping capabilities and a transport controller UI element for your users to use. Pretty comprehensive for one single chapter! If you want to venture more deeply into this subject, look for my titles *Pro Android Graphics* (Apress, 2013) and *Pro Android UI* (Apress, 2014) that get into this subject area and combine it with more advanced graphic design and user interface design topics.

Summary

In this chapter, you learned all about **digital video** concepts, formats, codecs, and principles, expanding even further on the 2D animation concepts, formats, codecs, and principles that you learned about in Chapter 10.

You learned about Android's **FrameLayout** UI layout container class, and how it **respects** or "locks" the aspect ratio of your Drawable object asset which it contains, to prevent unwanted skewing or warping of an asset. You also learned later on in the chapter how to force the Android OS to **non-uniformly scale** (to "unlock" the aspect ratio) by using the **RelativeLayout** layout container class, in conjunction with the **layout_alignParent** parameters.

Next, you looked at the **FrameLayout.LayoutParams** nested class and the concept of layout **gravity** and how it is the only way to generally position UI elements inside of a FrameLayout container, since that layout container type in Android is designed to usually hold only one or maybe two UI elements. In this chapter, this was your **VideoView** widget, and eventually a **MediaPlayer** transport UI element, called a **MediaController**.

Next, you created your FrameLayout UI XML definition file, as well as your **PlayVideo.java** Activity subclass, so that you had your foundation in place for adding in all of this digital video functionality. After doing that, you learned about the VideoView class and the video lifecycle stages, and then you added a VideoView to your FrameLayout. Next, you learned about the Android **Uri** class and its **Uri.parse()** method, used to implement the address or "**path**" to your digital video asset, as well as to other types of external assets as well, if you wish.

You learned about the foundational concepts of digital video encoding and optimization, including frame rates, bit-rates, codecs, resolution, quality (blur), and how these all work together to allow you to optimize your digital video asset's data footprint. After that, you learned how to use Terragen, VirtualDub, and Squeeze to create a 3D planet fly over video asset and optimize that asset from full frames uncompressed AVI format into MPEG-4 file format, taking data that was over 400MB and turning it into a usable 4MB digital video asset. Amazing stuff!

You finally got around to learning about the Android **MediaPlayer** class and its eight nested classes, used for callbacks which allow you to control your user's digital video experience. You added an **OnPreparedListener()** event listener to your videoPlayer VideoView object and used the **.setLooping(true)** method call, to tell your video asset to loop forever. Then you learned how to alter a URI so that you were **streaming video**, instead of using **captive video**, and finally you implemented a **MediaController** object named videoTransport, and wired it up to your videoPlayer VideoView, using the **.setAnchorView()** and the **.setMediaController()** method calls. You have learned a plethora of information, tricks, classes, methods, callbacks, and techniques relating to video!

Next, in Chapter12, you'll learn all about **Digital Audio** in Android, including foundational digital audio theory and concepts, what digital audio file formats are optimal to use in Android, and how to create digital audio assets for use with the Android **SoundPool** audio sequencing class. More advanced media concepts and implementation!

Chapter 12

Digital Audio: Providing Aural Feedback for UI Designs Using SoundPool

In the previous chapter on **digital video**, we covered the Uri, MediaPlayer, and MediaController classes, which you can also use with **digital audio**, which we are going to cover in this chapter. Since these classes are used in the same exact way with digital audio assets, I am going to show you how to use the Android **SoundPool** audio sequencing class in this chapter, so I can cover as many of Android's new media classes as possible in this book.

If you want to play **long-form** digital audio, such as songs, albums, or audio books, you would use the Android MediaPlayer class along with the Android MediaController and URI classes, using the **SeekBar** widget, instead of the VideoView. You could also loop long-form audio in the background, without using the SeekBar widget!

If you want to play **short-form** digital audio, however, such as **sound effects** for your games or UI elements for aural feedback, you would use the Android SoundPool class. The SoundPool "engine" is actually more versatile than the MediaPlayer class is when it comes to controlling digital audio assets. SoundPool is a powerful digital audio **sequencing** engine, and basically allows you to **composite audio**, in the same way that you use layers in digital image compositing to composite imagery. SoundPool is a complex and versatile digital audio class, upon which Android continues to improve, so it's a stretch for an Absolute Beginner!

Digital audio is a bit different from digital imagery and digital video as you can't see it; you have to rely on your ears. Instead of using waves of light, as color does, digital audio uses waves of sound, and as such, the technical fundamentals are completely different. If you are new to digital audio, Appendix A in this book will cover both the theory and the concepts behind digital audio, as well as a plethora of digital audio codecs and file formats that are supported in Android, as well as what each of them would be used for inside of an Android application.

In this chapter, we'll utilize Android's SoundPool digital audio sequencing class to add amazing sound effects to the ImageButton UI elements in your SlidingPaneLayout design. We will do this to add aural feedback for your users. We'll learn how to implement this SoundPool engine correctly in your Android applications, as this is no easy task. Digital audio sequencing and synthesis is an advanced topic indeed, but a key part of an Android app.

Audacity 2: Creating Digital Audio Assets

In this section of the book, you'll learn how to use the open source audio engineering software called **Audacity**, currently at version 2.0.5. First, we will make sure that Audacity has all of the plug-ins and codecs installed that are available (for free) for the software and which will make your audio editing environment far more powerful. Then we'll learn how to use the software to create digital audio assets in some of the Android OS audio formats.

Audacity Plug-Ins: Adding Codecs and Features

Assuming that you downloaded and installed **Audacity 2.0.5** back in Chapter 1, we will now need to add in some "plug-ins" which will greatly enhance the feature set of the software. We will also add in many of the popular codecs which are now supported in the Android OS.

Visit the **audacity.sourceforge.net** web site and **download Audacity 2.0.5** (if you haven't already), and install it. Click on the **Other Audacity Downloads for Windows** link, shown on the left in Figure 12-1, to access the **Optional Downloads** area of the web site, shown on the right side of Figure 12-1. The most important **.EXE installers** to focus on are the **LADSPA** plug-ins, the **LAME** MP3 encoder, and the **FFmpeg** import and export library (MPEG-4).

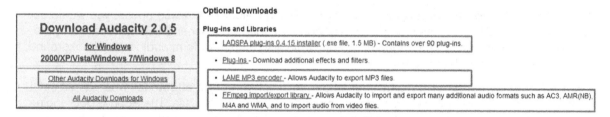

Figure 12-1. *Visit* audacity.sourceforge.net *and click on Other Audacity Downloads for Windows to display the Optional Downloads links*

Algorithms that add features and codecs to Audacity are kept in the Plug-Ins folder, so adding features to this software package is as easy as exiting the software (if it is running), copying a file or files into this folder, and restarting the software again. Figure 12-2 shows your **Audacity\Plug-Ins** folder, with 22 plug-in files installed.

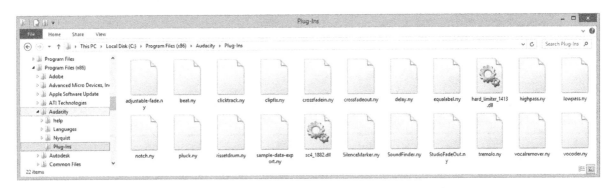

Figure 12-2. The 22 default (included) plug-in files included with the original installation of Audacity 2.0.5

When you are done with the LADSPA installation process, you will have added around a **hundred more** plug-in files to this folder; so many, in fact, that I won't even try to generate another screenshot containing all of these files!

Click on the LADSPA plug-ins 0.4.15 installer link shown in Figure 12-1 and download the 1.5MB .EXE file. When the download finishes, launch the file and select the language you are using (I chose **English**) and click the **Next** button to go through the dialog series. Be sure to accept the **license agreement** and use the suggested default **destination location** suggested in the right-most dialog shown in Figure 12-3. Once you proceed through the three dialogs, you can click on the **Install** button, initiating the LADSPA install.

Figure 12-3. LADSPA Setup series of dialogs; Welcome, License Agreement, and Destination Location

Once the LADSPA plug-ins are installed, click on the other two links, either of which will take you to another web site (the Audacity web site is not legally allowed to "host" these MPEG installers) where you can download the LAME (MPEG3) and FFmpeg (MPEG4) installation executable files for Windows. I am on Windows 8.1. Click on the two links seen in Figure 12-4 (in either order) and run the installers after they finish downloading.

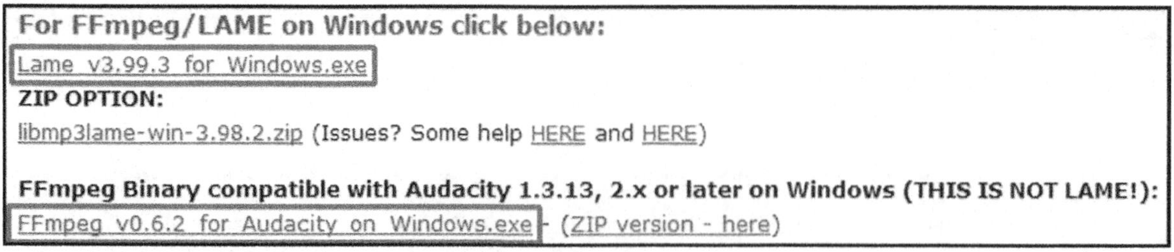

For FFmpeg/LAME on Windows click below:

Lame_v3.99.3_for_Windows.exe

ZIP OPTION:

libmp3lame-win-3.98.2.zip (Issues? Some help HERE and HERE)

FFmpeg Binary compatible with Audacity 1.3.13, 2.x or later on Windows (THIS IS NOT LAME!):

FFmpeg_v0.6.2_for_Audacity_on_Windows.exe (ZIP version - here)

Figure 12-4. FFmpeg/LAME download page download links section, and the two download links to click

The installer dialog sequences for both of these installers are so similar to what is shown in Figure 12-3 that I'm not going to include them here, as I don't want to spend much more than a page or two on this topic. However, I do need to make sure that you have Audacity 2.0.5 upgraded using all of these utilities that will maximize your Android application development workstation with these **supported codecs** and audio engineering features (algorithms) which are compatible with the digital audio features that are currently offered by the Android 4.x OS and Android 5.x OS.

The PCM (uncompressed) Wave (WAV) audio assets I'm going to use in your HelloUniverse application were given to me to use for educational purposes in this book by the internationally renowned sound designer Frank Serafine, a personal life-long friend and film and television production colleague of mine. In fact, we are working together on a film and a television series project this year, but it's nothing space-related! Just in case you want to get your own digital audio assets for your Android applications, I will include a short section on free digital audio sample searches next!

Free Digital Audio: Locate HelloUniverse Audio

To find some **free for commercial use** audio samples, I'm going to use the **Google** Search Engine, and type in a **query**, for something on the order of **Free Audio Samples**, **Free Digital Audio Samples**, **Free Audio Files**, or **Free Digital Audio Files**, and similar Google search term combinations. It's important to note that each of these Google searches will turn up completely different results due to **keywords** used in each of the different web sites that offer these digital audio assets. Be advised that many of the **paid audio sample** web sites will put the word "free" in their web sites (as an SEO tactic) so that they will come up on these types of free audio sample searches. To find word combinations, use the **plus** symbol, such as: **Free+Digital+Audio+Files** for instance. This will tell the search engine that you want to find sites where these words are located right next to each other.

There are dozens of good free audio sample web sites, all of which will fit the bill for your needs, so be sure and investigate these further when you have some spare time. Make sure that the ones that you use for your Android application development are free for commercial use, do not require any royalty payments, and do not have any copyright (usage) restrictions. What you want to look for is high-quality, uncompressed PCM (.wav file format) samples, using 16-bit or better (24-bit or 32-bit) sample resolution, with a 32 kHz, 44.1 kHz, or 48 kHz sample frequency (sample rates).

Note that if you download and use MP3 files (which most of these sites also offer), they will already have been compressed, and will be ready for use, but you will not have any control over the compression and optimization process. This is because much of the original audio sample data will have already been thrown away during the compression process, and you do not want to compress any kind of data which is already (lossy) compressed!

Digital Audio Optimization: Concepts & Formats

Let's launch Audacity 2.0.5 by clicking the Quick Launch icon on your Taskbar, and use the
File ➤ Open menu command sequence to open the **393KB button_sound_effect.wav** file from
the book assets repository.

The first time you open (or more accurately **"import"**) a Wave file format, you'll get the **Warning**
dialog shown in Figure 12-5. Select the **Make a copy of the files before editing (safer)** radio button
option, then select the **Don't warn again and always use my choice above** check box, and click
on the **OK** button to load the sample.

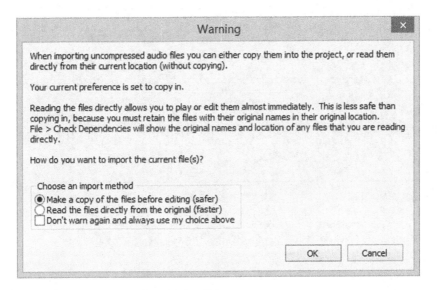

Figure 12-5. The importing compressed audio files Warning dialog

Using these audio file import settings, and using a copy of the file, instead of the actual file itself,
is called **non-destructive audio editing**, and is a common practice in the digital audio editing and
special effects industry.

The reason for using non-destructive audio editing practices is because if you mess up in your audio
sweetening and special effects application and damage the audio data, you can always go back to
square one by going back to loading the original audio data.

Once the button_sound_effect.wav sample data is loaded into Audacity 2.0.5, you will see a screen
exactly like the one shown in Figure 12-6. The upper-left corner contains the **audio transport
controls**, including **pause**, **play**, **stop**, **back**, **forward**, and **record**. Right next to that are the **editing
tools**, and on the far right are the **level meters** which will show green, yellow, and red **signal peak
indicators** when your audio is playing.

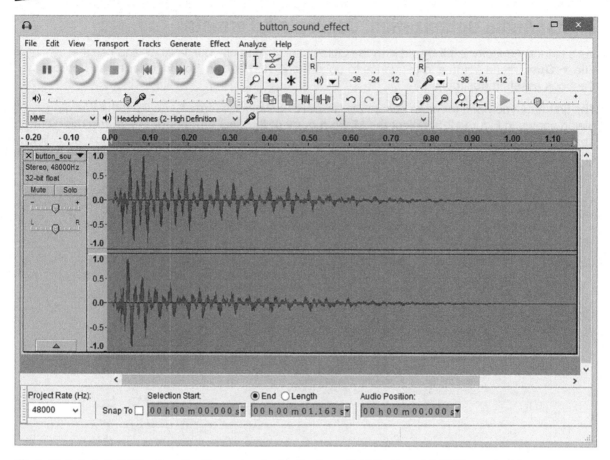

Figure 12-6. *Audacity 2.0.5 main audio editor screen showing the stereo 32-bit floating-point 48 kHz sample data*

Underneath these are settings for speaker and microphone volume, as well as system audio setting selector drop-downs. On the bottom of the Audacity window, you will find the project sample rate in Hz and hours, minutes, seconds, and milliseconds displays, for Selection Start, End or Length, and Audio Position, for micro-fine-tuning.

The first thing that you will want to do is to make sure your sample resolution and sample rate are set correctly, before you start to export to the various digital audio formats that you have learned about previously.

As you can see in Figure 12-6, the current sample rate is 48 kHz, which is high-quality and fine for our use, but the sample resolution is 32-bit, which is twice the amount of data that we need to get a great-quality sample data footprint result, regardless of the audio codec (format) that we use.

So our first step in our data footprint optimization work process is to change this raw audio sample data format from **32-bit 48 kHz** into a **16-bit 48 kHz** raw audio sample data format. This will reduce the amount of audio data going into the encoder (codec) by 100% right off the bat! You want to set a reasonable 16-bit 48 kHz audio file baseline, so that you can see the actual compression result that each audio codec can offer to the Android project. We will calculate this later as a percentage by dividing the baseline uncompressed audio file size by the compressed audio file size to see how many times, or what percentage, compression that codec is providing.

Setting Sample Rate and Resolution in Audacity

In the bluish-gray control panel located to the left of the visual display of your stereo audio sample, you will see your **button_sound_effect** sample file name, or the first part of it at least, and an arrowhead pointing down next to it. Click on this arrow to drop-down the **options menu**, select the **Set Sample Format** option, and then select the **16-bit PCM** option from its sub-menu, shown in Figure 12-7.

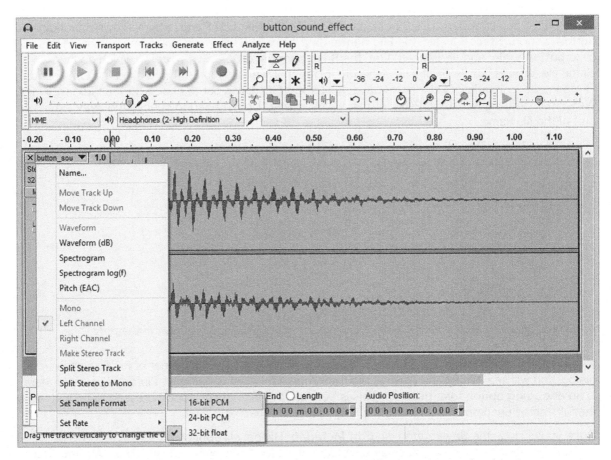

Figure 12-7. Setting audio sample resolution to 16-bit PCM (uncompressed) before you export to various formats

Setting the sample format using this menu will assure that you are exporting using the 16-bit sample resolution, for which audio playback is supported across all Android hardware devices. Next, export your baseline 16-bit uncompressed Wave audio .wav file format, which we will use to see what the largest possible audio file size (to use as your baseline) would be for this 16-bit 48 kHz audio sample of a 1.15 second button sound effect.

The new file size should theoretically be around **half** of the original file size that you opened (imported) into the Audacity 2.0.5 software, since 16-bits of data is half as much data as 32-bits of data. We will name the exported file **buttonaudio.wav**, as that is a simple file name which we're going to use for this audio asset using Android's lowercase-characters-only rule. We will reference the digital audio asset in the Java code that we'll be writing in the next section of the chapter, after we go through a data footprint optimization process using six audio formats which are supported in Android, including **WAV** (baseline), **FLAC**, **OGG**, **MP3**, **M4A**, and **AMR** (or **3GP**).

Exporting Uncompressed PCM Baseline WAV Format

To export a file in Audacity, we'll use the **File ➤ Export** menu sequence to open the **Export File** dialog shown in Figure 12-8. This dialog has several key areas, including the **Save in** folder specifier, which I have pointing to my CH12 book assets folder; the **File List Pane**, which shows the original **button_sound_effect.wav** file; the **File name:** data entry field where we will name our file, in this case **buttonaudio**; and underneath that, the **Save as type:** drop-down selector, which contains all the file formats that Audacity will export to, given that we have correctly installed the LAME and FFmpeg codec libraries. Notice that I have this Export File dialog set to export buttonaudio.wav in WAV (Microsoft) signed 16-bit PCM format, which is why I do not need to specify the **.wav** extension part of the file name.

Figure 12-8. Exporting a baseline 16-bit PCM WAV format file, and the Edit Metadata Dialog shown in all exports

If you click on the **Options** button, which is located in the bottom-right corner of the Export File dialog, you will see that for the Wave audio file format, you'll get a dialog that informs you that there is **no encoding option** for a PCM file. This is because Wave contains uncompressed data, just like the full frames uncompressed AVI file did in the previous chapter.

Once you click on the **Save** button, an **Edit Metadata** Dialog will appear, as shown in the middle in Figure 12-8. The dialog has data fields for text values for **Artist Name**, **Track Title**, **Album Title**, **Track Number**, **Year**, **Genre**, and **Comments**. Since I am optimizing here for the baseline data footprint, and our application does not require audio metadata, I am leaving these fields blank for now, so that we can get an accurate read on what the precise file size is; that is, the size of a file containing only the audio data. If you are wondering if Android OS can read, and therefore support, audio metadata if you did want to put this data into your audio files, the answer is a resounding YES!

Android has a **MediaMetadataRetriever** Class, which developers can utilize for this very specific purpose. If, for some reason, your audio application needs to leverage audio media metadata, you can use an **Edit Metadata** dialog, which will show itself every single time you save any type of audio file format in Audacity 2.0.5, along with the Android MediaMetadataRetriever Class, which you can research and learn about at the following URL:

`http://developer.android.com/reference/android/media/MediaMetadataRetriever.html`

If you look at the **buttonaudio.wav** 16-bit PCM Wave file that you just saved out, you will see that the file size, at **219KB**, is about half as large the original **button_sound_effect.wav** file, which was **393KB**. So, our baseline uncompressed data footprint for this 1.15-second button sound effect sample is 219KB. We can use this number to determine the amount of compression that we'll be getting with all these Android digital audio file formats.

Exporting via Lossless FLAC: FLAC audio files

The first format I am going to try out is the **FLAC** audio codec, because it uses **lossless** compression. This will give us a good idea of what kind of data footprint reduction we can get using compression which does not throw away any of the original audio data, and this will give us as perfect a result as the 16-bit PCM Wave audio does!

To do this, we'll again use the **File ➤ Export** menu sequence, and this time we will drop-down the **Save as type** menu and select the **FLAC Files** format, as is shown in Figure 12-9. Again, we will name the file **buttonaudio**, and I am going to save it into my CH12 folder for this book. Notice that there are no other files listed within the center area of this dialog; this is because now that we have selected the FLAC file format, this file save dialog region is now showing only FLAC files, and currently, there are none in the CH12 folder.

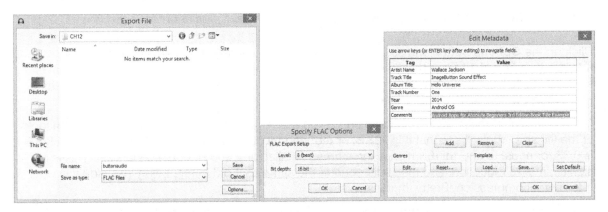

Figure 12-9. Export a FLAC file named buttonaudio.flac with Level 8 (best) quality and a 16-bit sample resolution

To set our **FLAC codec options,** click on the **Options** button and set the **quality level** to **8 (best)** and the **Bit depth** to **16-bit**. Note under the Bit depth drop-down that we can also use FLAC for a lossless 24-bit HD audio.

Once you've output your **buttonaudio.flac** audio asset, go into the file manager and take a look at the file size. You will see that it is **106KB**, or reduced by over 100% (106 divided by 219 is 0.484, or less than half as large).

Next, let's take a look at the other open source format, **Ogg Vorbis**, to see if it can give us an even smaller data footprint. Since Ogg Vorbis is a **lossy** file format, it should give us an even smaller file size than the FLAC did.

Exporting Lossy Ogg Vorbis: OGG audio files

Use the **File ➤ Export** work process, as we have been previously to open the **Export File** dialog, and select the **Ogg Vorbis Files** from the **Save as type:** drop-down menu. I named the file **buttonaudio**, which will produce a **buttonaudio.ogg** file name, and put it into the CH12 folder, as you can see in Figure 12-10.

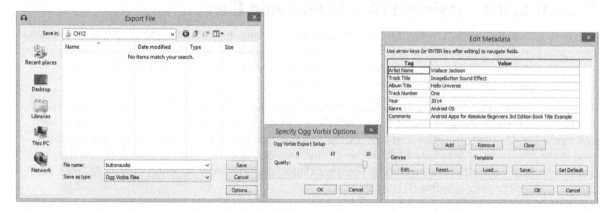

Figure 12-10. Export an OggVorbis file named buttonaudio.ogg with Level 10 quality and 16-bit sample resolution

Click on the **Options** button and select a **Quality** setting level between 0 and 10. I used the maximum setting of **10** to start with; during a real data footprint optimization, you would try several settings to see how the data footprint to quality trade-off was affected by the Quality slider setting. Play around with this, if you have time.

Once you have output your buttonaudio.ogg audio asset, go into your file manager and take a look at the file size. You will see that it is **72KB**, or reduced by **300%** in file size (72KB divided by 219KB is 0.33, or equal to one-third, which is three times smaller, or a 300% reduction in size). This is a significant size reduction, and the audio sounds the same as it did before using lossy (quality = maximum) compression. Pretty impressive stuff!

Next, let's take a look at MP3, the most common lossy audio format on the market. It should be interesting to see if MP3 can give us an even smaller data footprint than the Ogg Vorbis open source codec did.

Exporting Lossy MPEG3 Format: MP3 audio files

Use the **File ➤ Export** menu sequence again to bring up the Audacity **Export File** dialog, and set the **Save as type:** drop-down selector to **MP3 Files**, as is shown in Figure 12-11. I named the file **buttonaudio** and selected the CH12 folder, and then clicked on the MP3 Options button to open up the **Specify MP3 Options** dialog that is shown in the middle of Figure 12-11. I used the maximum Quality Bit Rate setting of 320 kbps, which is quite high for audio data, and a **Constant Bit Rate Mode** setting and a **Stereo Channel Mode**, since the file is in stereo. If you like, you can try different **Quality** Bit Rate settings, as well as **Variable** and **Average** Bit Rate Modes, to see how it affects the MP3 audio file data footprint. If you do this, to differentiate the files from each other, simply name the file with the settings in the file name. For instance, a file with a 320 kbps Quality setting and a Variable Bit Rate Mode could be named: **buttonaudio_320kbps_vbr.mp3**.

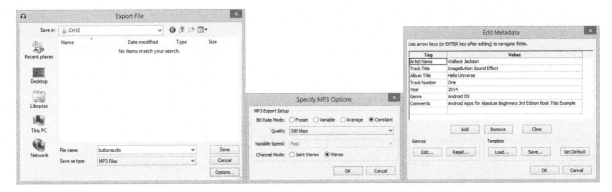

Figure 12-11. Export an MP3 audio file named buttonaudio.mp3 with 320 kbps Constant Bit Rate Mode encoding

In this way, you can compare your MP3 (or any other codec file format) audio file sizes, and do the simple math to figure out your percentage data footprint reduction, as we will do next for our buttonaudio.mp3, or rather, our **buttonaudio_320kbps_cbr.mp3** file (if you follow this naming convention), that you generated by clicking the **Save** button. Data footprint optimization is hard work, involving finding an optimal codec setting for each asset.

The buttonaudio.mp3 file size is **49KB**, representing a **447%** data footprint reduction. To figure this out, 49KB divided by 219KB is **0.223744**, which is **22%** of the original, uncompressed file size. 100% minus 22% equals the **78%** file size reduction. If you use the **1/x** (inversion) key on your PC calculator, you can get the percentage reduction, coming from the other direction. Inverting 0.223744 gives **4.469**, which means that you reduced your file size by 4.469 times, which equates to a **447%** reduction. This is a fairly impressive data footprint reduction!

Now that we have seen that our MP3 file size is smaller than the Ogg Vorbis, let's see how **MPEG4 AAC** in an **M4A** file format data compression improves your file size-to-quality ratio compared to MPEG3. Since MPEG-4 is a more recent and advanced codec technology, it should provide us a much better file size-to-quality ratio.

Exporting Lossy MPEG4 Format: M4A audio files

Follow the usual **File ➤ Export** work process to invoke the Audacity **Export File** dialog and select the **M4A (AAC) Files (FFmpeg)** from the **Save as type:** drop-down menu selector. As usual, name the file buttonaudio (which will be named buttonaudio.m4a by the Exporter after you click Save) in the CH12 directory (or whatever your digital audio assets folder name is), and then click on the **Options** button to open a **Specify AAC Options** dialog, as shown in Figure 12-12. I chose to ratchet the Quality setting up to 500 to see what a resulting MPEG4 file size would be when using a maximum quality level setting. Click **Save** to export the **buttonaudio.m4a** file.

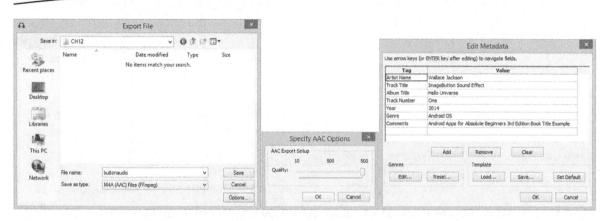

Figure 12-12. *Export an M4A AAC audio file named buttonaudio.m4a using the maximum quality setting of 500*

The buttonaudio.m4a file size is **47KB**, representing a **21%** data footprint reduction. To figure this out, 47 divided by 219 is **0.2146**, which is 21% of the original uncompressed file size. 100% minus 21% equals the **79%** file size reduction. Now that we've seen that our M4A AAC file size is the most impressive thus far, let's see if the more specialized **AMR-NB** (Narrow Band) data compression codec will give us any further data footprint improvements over MPEG4 AAC. Even though the MPEG-4 AMR-NB codec and format was designed and optimized specifically for voice applications, there may be some other applications, such as certain short-burst sound effects, which might obtain good if not great results using this codec. Let's find out!

As you know by now, any codec is simply a complex mathematical equation implemented as software and does not discriminate, so the only way to really find out what codec will give you the best result with any given asset is to run the original uncompressed audio data through the codec and see what happens. Let's do that next; then we will be finished comparing audio codecs which are supported in Android, and are also available in Audacity.

Exporting Narrow Band Format: AMR audio files

Follow the usual **File ➤ Export** work process to invoke the Audacity **Export File** dialog and select the **AMR (narrow band) Files (FFmpeg)** option from the **Save as type:** drop-down menu selector. Notice that the files you installed in the beginning of this section of the chapter have been added to the bottom portion of the menu.

As usual, let's name the file buttonaudio (which will be named buttonaudio.amr by the Exporter, after you click on the Save button) in the CH12 directory (or whatever your digital audio assets folder is called), and then click on the **Options** button to open the **Specify AMR-NB Options** dialog, shown in the middle of Figure 12-13. I chose to use the 12.20 kbps Bit Rate setting to get the maximum quality result that is possible with this codec.

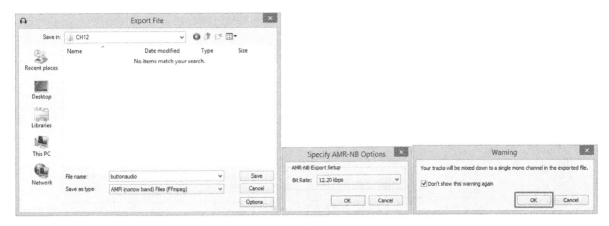

Figure 12-13. Export an AMR (narrow band) file named buttonaudio.amr with a Bit Rate setting of 12.20 kbps

This work process will allow me to see what the resulting AMR-NB file size would be when using a maximum quality level setting. Let's click on the **Save** button and export our **buttonaudio.amr** audio file now. As you can see, this is by far the smallest data footprint that we have obtained thus far, and yet when we play it back, it still sounds a lot like the button sound effect contained inside the other supported codec formats we have generated.

The buttonaudio.amr file size is **2KB**, representing more than a 99% data footprint reduction. To figure this out, 2KB divided by 219KB is **0.00913242**, which is 0.91% of the original, uncompressed file size. 100% minus 1% equals the 99% file size reduction. If you **invert** 0.00913242 you get **109.50**, which would represent a **10,950%** reduction in data footprint. I don't know about you, but my decision for a basic button sound effect would be to use a 2KB audio asset rather than a 47KB, 49KB, 72KB or 109KB audio asset, since it's just for aural feedback!

The only problem that you have now, and fortunately only with this last very niche codec and file format, is that Audacity wants to export put AMR-NB files with an .AMR file extension, whereas Android wants to see AMR-NB audio files using a 3GP file extension. It's always something, isn't it? Let's go back to the drawing board and look at the Audacity documentation. The Audacity manual File Export section tells us that we should be able to specify certain non-standard file extensions and get away with it, so let's go back into Audacity 2.0.5 and try it!

Let's follow the standard **File ➤ Export** work process, invoke the Audacity **Export File** dialog, and select the **AMR (narrow band) Files (FFmpeg)** from the **Save as type:** drop-down menu selector. This time, let's name the file **buttonaudio.3gp**. I'm using a CH12 directory for this book, you could use a C:\Android\Content\Audio folder, for instance. Next, click on the **Options** button and set the **12.20 kbps Bit Rate** (audio quality) option, using the **Specify AMR-NB Options** dialog, as shown in Figure 12-13. AMR Narrow band uses a **mono** audio channel format, as you probably noticed on the right-hand side of Figure 12-13, in the Warning dialog message.

Once you click on the **Save** button, you will see the **Warning** dialog shown on the right side of Figure 12-14. Click on the **Yes** button and save the file as buttonaudio.3gp so that you now have seven different audio assets.

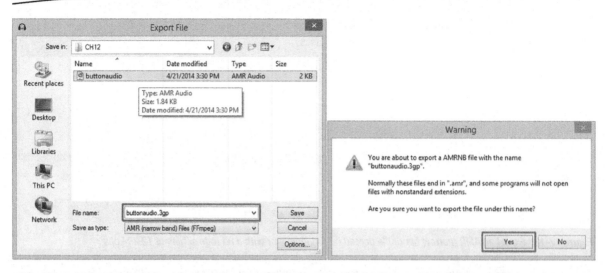

Figure 12-14. Warning dialog shown in the Export File dialog for a buttonaudio AMR file using a .3GP extension

Finally, you should copy and paste the six compressed audio assets into the proper asset location in the Android Project resource hierarchy, in the **/res/raw** folder, so you can access them later on in the chapter in your code.

> **Note**   We are about to get into the complexities of implementing the Android **SoundPool** digital audio **sequencing engine**. Remember that the appendix covers digital audio concepts and principles that are used in the remainder of this chapter. This information relates to what exactly digital audio sequencing is, as well as how it ties into digital audio **synthesis**, as this powerful SoundPool class not only allows you to sequence digital audio, but also to apply the effects afforded by digital audio synthesis to your digital audio sequences! So if you are unsure of any terms used, please refer to the appendix.

Android SoundPool: Audio Engine & Methods

The Android SoundPool class is a direct subclass of the java.lang.Object master class. It's important to note that SoundPool is not a subclass of the Android MediaPlayer class, as one might be liable to assume. However, like the MediaPlayer class, it is part of the **android.media** package, and thus, the complete path to the class (as used in an import statement) would be **android.media.SoundPool**. The Java class hierarchy looks like the following:

```
java.lang.Object
  > android.media.SoundPool
```

Since SoundPool is a subclass of java.lang.Object, we can infer that it is its own scratch-coded audio sequencing engine creation. It is also important to note that you can use SoundPool objects (SoundPool class) and MediaPlayer objects (MediaPlayer class) at the same time, if need be. In fact, there are distinct applications for both of these audio playback classes. You should use MediaPlayer for long-form audio (and video) data, such as albums, songs, audio books, or movies. SoundPool is best used for short-form audio snippets, especially when they need to be played in rapid succession and (or) combined together, such as in a game, eBook, or gamified application.

You can load your SoundPool collection of samples into memory from one of two places. The first, and most common, would be from inside the APK file, which I call **captive** new media assets, in which case, they would live in your **/res/raw** project folder, as they will for your HelloUniverse app. The second place you can load samples from is an SD Card or similar storage location. This is what one would term the Android OS file system.

The SoundPool uses the Android MediaPlayer Service to decode an audio asset into memory. We'll be covering Android Service classes in the next chapter in this book (are you starting to see the logical progression here?). It does this using uncompressed 16-bit PCM mono or stereo audio. This is the main reason that I've been teaching you a work process which optimizes the audio using a 16-bit sampling resolution, because if you use 8-bit audio, Android up-samples it to 16-bit, and you end up with wasted data that could have been "spent" on better quality.

This means that you should optimize your sample frequency but not your sample resolution (use 16-bit). Don't use stereo audio unless you absolutely need to. It is very important to conform your optimization work process to how SoundPool works to get optimal results across the largest number of consumer electronics devices. The 48 kHz is the best sample frequency to use if you can, with the 44.1 kHz coming in second, and 32 kHz coming in third. To optimize, keep a sample short and mono, and use a modern codec, such as MPEG4 AAC or FLAC, to retain the most quality and still get a reasonable amount of data compression for your APK file. Calculate memory use with raw audio size!

When the SoundPool object is constructed in Java, as you will be doing later on in this chapter, a developer will set a **maxStreams** parameter using an integer value. This parameter will predetermine how many audio streams you can composite, or render, at the same time. Be sure to set this parameter precisely, as it sets aside memory.

Setting the maximum number of streams parameter to as small a number as possible is a good standard practice. This is because doing so will help to minimize CPU cycles used for processing audio samples, and will reduce any likelihood that your SoundPool audio mixing will impact other areas of your application performance.

The SoundPool engine will track the number of active audio streams (samples) to make sure that it does not exceed the maxStreams setting. If this maximum number of audio streams is ever exceeded, SoundPool will **abort** a previously playing stream. It will do this based upon a **sample priority** value which you can specify.

If SoundPool finds two or more audio samples playing that have an equal sample priority value, it will make a decision regarding which sample to stop playing based upon **sample age**, which means the sample that has been playing the longest is the one that's terminated (playback stopped). I like to call this the **Logan's Run** principle!

Priority level values are evaluated from low to high numeric values. This means that higher (large) numbers will represent the higher priority levels. Priority is evaluated when a call to the SoundPool **.play()** method causes the number of active streams to exceed the maxStreams value which is set when a SoundPool object is instantiated.

In the case where the sample priority for the new stream is lower than all the active streams, the new sound will not play, and the .play() function will return a **streamID** of **zero**. For this reason, be sure that your application's Java code keeps track of exactly what is going on with your audio sample priority level settings.

Samples are looped in SoundPool by setting any non-zero looping value. The exception to this is that a value of **-1** will cause samples to loop **forever**, and under this circumstance, the application code must make a call to the SoundPool **.stop()** method to stop the looping sample. So a non-zero integer value will cause a sample to repeat itself that specified number of times; thus, a value of 7 will cause your sample to play back a total of 8 times, as computers start counting using the number 0 instead of 1.

You can change each sample playback rate using SoundPool, which as mentioned makes this class into an audio synthesis tool. A sample playback rate equal to 1.0 will cause your sample to play back at its original frequency. A sample playback rate of 2.0 will cause the sample to be played at twice its original frequency, which will shift it up a full octave higher, if it is a musical instrument note. Similarly, a sample playback rate set to 0.5 will cause SoundPool to play that sample at half of its original frequency, which will sound like it is a full octave lower.

The sample playback rate range of SoundPool is currently limited to 0.5 to 2.0; however, this could be upgraded in a future API revision to, say, 0.25 to 4, which would give developers a four octave sample playback range.

Now it's time to learn how to implement a SoundPool engine, and learn about a couple of other Android utility classes which are used with SoundPool. As you can see, I'm trying to cover as many key Android classes in this book as is humanly possible!

Adding a SoundPool Engine to the HelloUniverse

Now it is time to get into Java programming in your MainActivity.java Activity subclass and add a SoundPool engine so that you can add different aural feedback sounds to your three ImageButton UI elements.

Open Eclipse, open MainActivity.java in an editing tab, and declare a **SoundPool** object at the top of your class. Name it **buttonSamples** using the following **Java object declaration statement**, as shown at the top of Figure 12-15:

```
SoundPool buttonSamples;
```

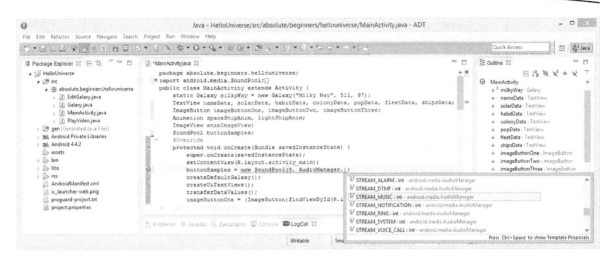

Figure 12-15. Declare a SoundPool object named buttonSamples and instantiate it in onCreate() using the new keyword

Next, you will instantiate this SoundPool object inside of the onCreate() method, so that when your application launches, the declared object gets set up (instantiated) for use in your application. Do this using the Java **new** keyword, in conjunction with the **SoundPool()** constructor method call, which accepts three parameters.

Here is the SoundPool() constructor method call format from the Android Developer web site documentation, so you can see it here more clearly before you start to use it in your code:

```
SoundPool( int maxStreams, int streamType, int srcQuality );
```

The parameters include a **maxStreams** value, an **AudioManager stream type**, and a **quality level**. If you type in the AudioManager class and a period, a pop-up dialog will list all of the constants available to you using this class. Construct the SoundPool object named buttonSamples using the following code, shown in Figure 12-15:

```
buttonSamples = new SoundPool(this, AudioManager.STREAM_MUSIC, 100);
```

Next, create a specialized Array object to hold your SoundPool audio sample references, using an Android **SparseIntArray** class and SparseIntArray object. The reason you are doing this is to be more professional in your coding by using an array structure to hold all of your sample references (that is, the data path resource locator information for your digital audio assets). Although we are only using a few digital audio samples during this chapter, often you will be using many more digital audio samples than this with the SoundPool engine, and therefore I am showing you how to keep all of these sample references in a SparseIntArray object.

As its name reflects, a SparseIntArray is highly efficient (a **sparse** use of memory and storage space) and holds **Integer** values in an **Array** programming structure used to hold data.

Declare a SparseIntArray object at the top of your MainActivity class named **buttonSampleArray**, and then in the **onCreate()** method, instantiate it using the Java **new** keyword and a **SparseIntArray()** constructor method, passing it the array size value of 3, using a standard Java object constructor method call shown in Figure 12-16:

```
buttonSampleArray = new SparseIntArray(3);
```

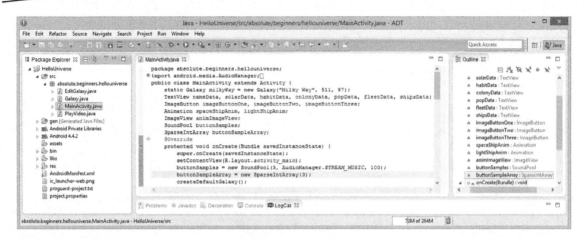

Figure 12-16.   Declare a SparseIntArray object named buttonSampleArray and instantiate it in onCreate() using new

Now that you've set up the two major Java objects needed to implement a SoundPool engine, all you need to do is to, you guessed it, wire them together using a SparseIntArray **.append()** method call and a SoundPool **.load()** method call. Before loading your SoundPool with these digital audio asset references, you need to install them!

In Explorer, seen in Figure 12-17, select the three audio assets you wish to use, **right-click**, and click **Copy**.

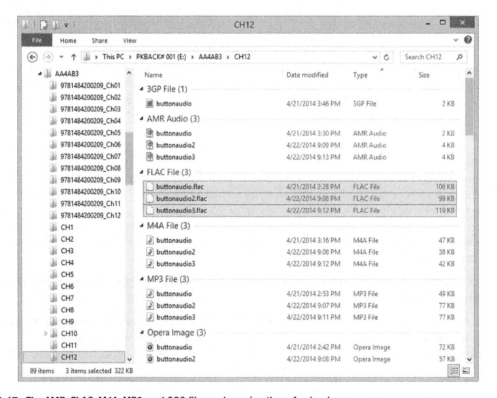

Figure 12-17.   The AMR, FLAC, M4A, MP3, and OGG files and copying three for /res/raw

Navigate to the project **/res/raw** folder, **right-click**, and click **Paste** to paste the three audio assets, as seen in Figure 12-18.

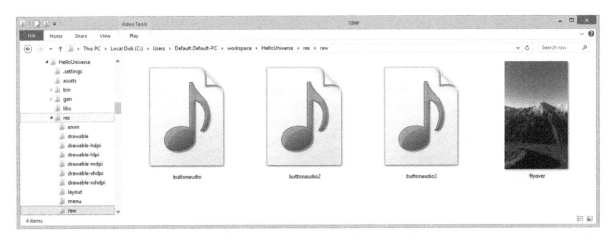

Figure 12-18. Paste any of the three buttonaudio samples of your choice into your HelloUniverse/res/raw folder

Notice in Figure 12-17 that even Windows Explorer gets things wrong, as it is listing Ogg Vorbis audio assets as being Opera browser audio assets! As developers, we must always be smarter than the tools that we utilize!

Make sure your buttonaudio, buttonaudio2, and buttonaudio3 files all use one codec type and that you don't have files of the same name with a different codec in the folder. I used FLAC and M4A to test the code for this chapter, but because Android only looks at the first part of the file name, if you have more than one codec version installed in your **/res/raw** folder at any given time for these file names, the Eclipse environment will throw an error message, or more than one error message, if you copy all of your codec versions into the /res/raw folder all at once. If you want to do this, be sure to rename the files first, using the **codec type** as part of the file name; for instance, you might name the unused files: buttonaudioflac, buttonaudiovorbis, or buttonaudiompeg4.

Now you have the Java objects and digital audio assets in place to be able to finish wiring up your SoundPool engine. Make sure that after you copy the three audio (codec) formats that you want to use, you right-click on your project folder, and use the **Refresh** command, so that Eclipse can see the new files. I was using MPEG-4 audio assets when I took the screenshot shown in Figure 12-19, as you can see on the left side of the screen, in the /res/raw folder. We are going to use a fairly complex Java construct to load our SparseIntArray object, while at the same time, loading the digital audio resource into the SoundPool object. As you may have noticed, I'm going to use more advanced concepts and constructs as this book progresses, so that you progress with it!

Figure 12-19. Load buttonSampleArray with three references to buttonSamples objects while also loading them

What we are going to do is to put a **buttonSamples.load()** method call inside a **buttonSampleArray.append()** method call. This **.append()** method call will add (append) SoundPool objects to a SparseIntArray object and will specify their order within that Array. The **.load()** method call will **load** your SoundPool object with the digital audio sample **reference** along with the **Context object** for MainActivity and finally the sound **priority**.

The Java programming constructs for loading the SparseIntArray object with three SoundPool objects, while at the same time loading the SoundPool object with the three audio assets which you just copied into the /res/raw folder, should look like the following Java programming structure, which is also shown in Figure 12-19:

```
buttonSampleArray.append(1, buttonSamples.load(this, R.raw.buttonaudio, 1));
buttonSampleArray.append(2, buttonSamples.load(this, R.raw.buttonaudio2, 1));
buttonSampleArray.append(3, buttonSamples.load(this, R.raw.buttonaudio3, 1));
```

Now that your SoundPool engine is declared, instantiated, and set up for use, we need to create another method, which will "trigger" the SoundPool engine when one of your ImageButton UI elements is clicked. We will call this method **.triggerSample()**, and this method will contain all of the **AudioManager** methods and **SoundPool** methods which will be needed to play the correct (selected) sample back out of the SoundPool engine using the volume the user has set for their Android device.

Creating a .triggerSample() Method: SoundPool .play()

The first step in creating the .triggerSample() method is to close up the other six methods in your MainActivity class, using the minus - icons at the left side of the Eclipse editing pane. Then, add a **public void triggerSample** method with parameters for **sound** and **pitch**, using the following line of Java code, as shown in Figure 12-20:

```
public void triggerSample (int sound, float pitch) { method code will go in here }
```

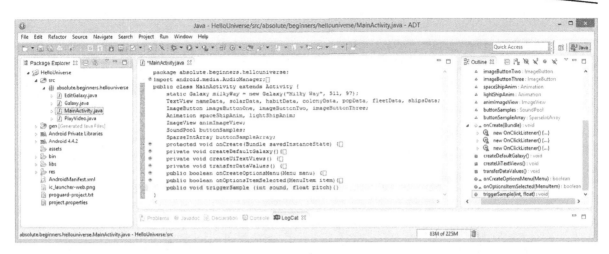

Figure 12-20. Add a public void triggerSample() method with a parameter int named sound and a float named pitch

When you call this custom method, you will pass the SparseIntArray number of the sound you want to use (1, 2, or 3) and the pitch you want to shift it to (1.0 for default octave, 0.5 for down an octave, or 2.0 for up an octave) using the following format triggerSample(1, 1.0), which would play your buttonaudio sample "as-is."

Inside of this .triggerSample() method, you will write all of the Java code to set up your sample playback, using the AudioManager class (and an AudioManager object) to access the **Android System Service**, which controls the audio playback hardware for your user's hardware device.

1. Declare and instantiate an **AudioManager** object named **audioControl** and set it equal to a method call to the **getSystemService()** method called off of the AudioManager class and pass a **Context object** into it, configured for the **AUDIO_SERVICE** by using the following single line of Java code, as is shown in Figure 12-21:

    ```
    AudioManager audioControl = (AudioManager)getSystemService(Context.AUDIO_SERVICE);
    ```

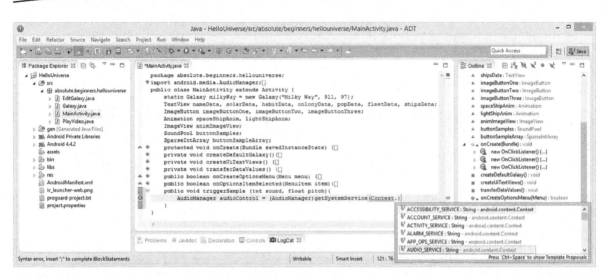

Figure 12-21. Declare and instantiate an AudioManager object named audioControl; configure as audio_service

As you can see in Figure 12-21, if you type in the **Context** object and a period, Eclipse will give you a pop-up helper dialog filled with all of the Android System Service types (**constants**) which are available for your app.

2. Next, create a floating-point variable named **currentSoundVolume** to hold the current audio stream volume and set it equal to a **.getStreamVolume()** method call off of the audioControl AudioManager object which you just created. If you type in the audioControl object and hit the period key, Eclipse will pop-up a helper dialog, which is shown in Figure 12-22, that contains all the method calls that you can utilize with an **AudioManager** object.

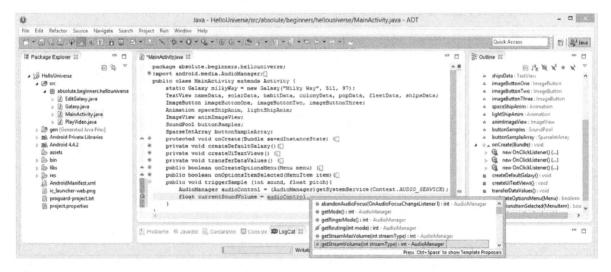

Figure 12-22. Add a currentSoundVolume float variable and call a .getStreamVolume() method off of the audioControl object

3. Inside of the **.getStreamVolume()** method, pass the **AudioManager. STREAM_MUSIC** constant to establish which StreamVolume you want to get (and then put) into your currentSoundVolume variable. This is shown in Figure 12-23, along with a **maximumSoundVolume** float variable that you are going to declare next, using a similar method call to a **.getStreamMaxVolume()** method, using the same STREAM_MUSIC constant. This will **configure** two (currently unused, as warning highlights indicate in Figure 12-23) **sound volume** variables.

Figure 12-23. Add a maximumSoundVolume float variable and call a .getStreamMaxVolume() method off of AudioManager

4. Once you have the two float variables declared and loaded with the current and maximum audio settings for the user's Android device, you can figure out a percentage value (divide current volume setting by a maximum) and give the SoundPool .play() method the value range (0.0 to 0.99) that it requires. Do this using the following block of Java code (I'll include all three statements here, in one place), which is also shown error-free in Figure 12-24:

```
float currentSoundVolume = audioControl.getStreamVolume(Context.STREAM_MUSIC);
float maximumSoundVolume = audioControl.getStreamVolume(Context.STREAM_MUSIC);
float volumeSet = currentSoundVolume / maximumSoundVolume;
```

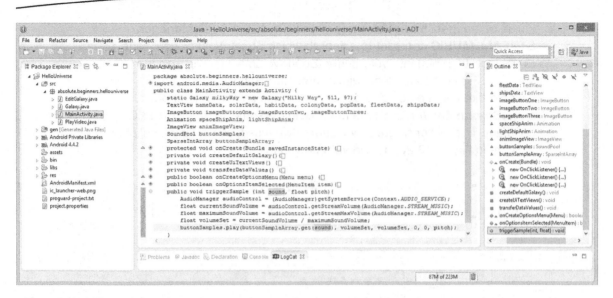

Figure 12-24. Call a .play() method off of the buttonSamples SoundPool object and pass in sound and pitch parameters

5. Once you have a **volumeSet** volume setting variable calculated, you can make a SoundPool **.play()** method call.

6. Call the **.play()** method off of your **buttonSamples** SoundPool object and then pass over parameters for the sample you want to play. These are denoted using the variable **sound** in the .triggerSample() method you are coding here, the **left volume** and **right volume**, the sample priority value, the **number of times** to play the sound (remember that zero means to play one time), and your **pitch shifting factor**, from 0.5 to 2.0 octaves, denoted using the variable **pitch**. This statement is coded using the following Java code shown in Figure 12-24.

```
buttonSamples.play( buttonSampleArray.get(sound), volumeSet, volumeSet, 0, 0, pitch );
```

This is the most important line of code in your .triggerSample() method, as everything else in the method goes into this line of code, from the sound and pitch parameters to the volumeSet variable, and the other lines of code that allow that variable to be calculated and established before it is passed into (used in) the .play() method call.

Now you have coded everything that you need to be able to call the .triggerSample() method inside of the event handling code that you have already created for your ImageButton UI elements. Let's do that next, so that you can hear how SoundPool will trigger your different sound effect samples for your different ImageButton UI elements.

Adding SoundPool to Your UI: Calling .triggerSample()

Let's call your **.triggerSample(int sound, float pitch)** method, which you wrote in the previous section of this chapter, inside of each of your three ImageButton onClick() event handler methods. This will invoke all of the code that you have been writing during the chapter to play your three sound effect samples using the SoundPool audio sequencing engine.

This is the easy part of the process, and involves writing three fairly simple lines of code, to be placed in each of your three ImageButton onClick() event handler methods, right after (or before, if you prefer) the object and method calls which set up your ImageView and TextView UI elements.

Add a **triggerSample(1, 1.0f)** method call to the imageButtonOne event handler, a **triggerSample(2, 1.0f)** method call to the imageButtonTwo event handler, and a **triggerSample(3, 1.0f)** method call to the imageButtonThree event handler methods, respectively.

As an example of what one of the three .setOnClickListener() event handler Java code structures should look like, here is the Java code for imageButtonOne, as is shown in Figure 12-25:

```
imageButtonOne.setOnClickListener(new View.OnClickListener(){
    @Override
    public void onClick(View v) {
        animImageView.setBackgroundResource(R.drawable.imageviewwhitering);
        animImageView.setImageResource(R.drawable.anim_milkyway);
        animImageView.setAnimation(null);
        nameData.setText("Milky Way");
        solarData.setText("511");
        habitData.setText("97");
        colonyData.setText("37579231");
        popData.setText("1967387132");
        fleetData.setText("237");
        shipsData.setText("34769");
        triggerSample(1, 1.0f);
}});
```

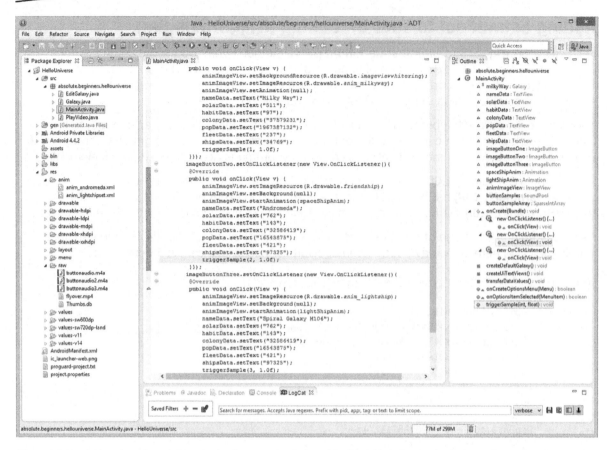

Figure 12-25. Add a triggerSample() method call to samples 1, 2, and 3 with 1.0f pitch value in the ImageButton handler

Now you're ready to use a **Run As ➤ Android Application** menu sequence to test your digital audio sequencer (your SoundPool engine implementation) and have some fun! As you click the ImageButton UI elements, you will hear some unique sound effects. Too bad I cannot include sound in a screenshot, or I'd put one in right here. Great Job!

Summary

In this chapter, you learned about how to use Audacity 2.0.5. You learned about the Android **SoundPool** digital audio sequencing engine class and how it allows you to add multiple audio samples to your Android application so that you can add digital audio sequencing capabilities to your applications.

You learned about all of the various ins and outs of the SoundPool digital audio sequencing and synthesis engine, as well as about all of its caveats and considerations regarding how it works. If you read the appendix in the book, as suggested during this chapter, you also learned all about the history of audio history, as well as about digital audio concepts, terminology, codecs and optimization techniques.

You learned how to implement the SoundPool engine as a SoundPool object in your application, and about how to use it with the **SparceIntArray** object and the **AudioManager** class (and Service) in the Android OS.

Next you added digital audio sound effects to each of your ImageButton UI elements, to make them way cooler, and to give your application's end-users some aural (audio) feedback regarding when they click on the app's ImageButton UI elements.

Next, in Chapter 13, you'll learn all about **Service** classes in Android, which you actually got some exposure to in this chapter when you implemented the AudioManager object. The next chapter is thus a logical extension to what you learned in this chapter. As you can see, I'm trying to cover things in the most logical, optimal fashion, as we progress through this long and complex journey to learn how to develop applications for the Android OS.

Chapter 13

Android Service Class and Threads: Background Processing

In the previous chapter on **digital audio**, you utilized the Android **AudioManager** class, which is a subclass of the Android **Service** class. You also learned about the Android **SoundPool** and the **SparseIntArray** classes. In this chapter, we will take a look at the Android Service classes and related processing concepts, such as **processes** and **threads**.

Developers use the Android **Service** classes to perform background **asynchronous** operations. Asynchronous means that these operations, or more accurately the Java code structures that define them, can go "off on their own," and process data streams, or perform complex computation, in the background. Background Service asynchronous operations can do this without having to synchronize with your application's user interface design, which is probably busy controlling how your application's content (the user experience) is being presented to your application's end-users.

Examples of using Android **Service** subclasses include the playback of long-form digital audio using the **MediaPlayer** class while your user is using other areas of the application, talking to servers or databases in the background, downloading data, managing file input-output streams, streaming new media content (digital video streams or digital audio streams), handling networking (SMTP and HTTP) protocol transactions, handling payment gateway transactions, real-time processing of GPS data, and similar complex computational or data-processing tasks.

This chapter looks closely at the Android **Service** class and all of the various characteristics of Android Service classes. We'll look at how their features, functions, settings, constants, and characteristics are declared in your Android application. As you may have surmised, declaring Services for usage is done in the AndroidManifest.xml file, by using the **<service>** tag. We will also implement a **Service** subclass in the **HelloUniverse** application, as you also might expect!

This is one of those complex, involved topics in Android, because it involves binding, synchronization, processes, processor cycles, threads, access control, permissions, and similarly advanced "OS layer" (OS level) topics, as these are all accomplished using the Linux Kernel (the lowest operating system layer) of the Android OS. We looked at these different levels of the Android OS back in Chapter 3, so you can refer to Figure 3-1 if you need another "refreshing" view of this Android application hierarchy!

Tasks that are delegated to an Android **Service** also tend to be very processor intensive, so keep your end-user's battery life in mind while you are developing processor-intensive applications. As you might guess, the two primary power drains on an Android battery are prolonged CPU processing and keeping the display screen lit (on) for long periods of time (which we covered in the video chapter).

Services are generally utilized to handle things that need to be running in the background of your app, in parallel with an Android user's real-time usage of your application, but not directly synchronized, or connected in real-time, with that application's user interface (or user experience) design.

Tasks that are generally delegated to an Android **Service** class are not typically tied to the user interface and user experience tasks, because forcing concurrent (synchronized) processing might cause that user interface task or user experience task to become stilted or jerky (that is, they won't portray a smooth user interface response or a good user experience).

Android Service Classes: Characteristics

A Service in Android can be defined as an **application component** that can perform CPU processor-intensive functions in the background. This is done without the need for any user interface design or any Activity display screen. A Service does not require any user interaction in order to accomplish its processing task.

An Android application "**starts**" a **Service** object by using an **Intent** object, and a **Service** object will continue to process in the background even if an Android device's owner switches over to a different Android application to do something else, such as answer a phone call, reply to an incoming email, or accept a social media connection request.

Any Android application component can "**bind**" to a **started Service** object and interact with it. It can even perform **interprocess communication**, which you may have heard referred to as **IPC**. We will be taking a closer look at processes and threads in the next section of the chapter, after the overview of Android Service class and object attributes.

Binding is an advanced programming concept that involves establishing a **real-time connection** between two separate application component processes. Once **bound**, the processes will alert each other whenever something has changed. The alerted process can then check and see if an update needs to be made based on that change. If you are a game programmer, you will commonly define a bind between your scoreboard UI design and your scoring engine, for instance, so your scoreboard numeric read-out will change in real-time, as your game is being played.

An Android Service usually will take one of two forms—either "bound" or "started." Let's start with the started Service, as it is the most common. An Android Service becomes "started" when the application component, such as an Activity, starts it. This is done by calling a **.startService()** method.

Once it has started, a Service can run in the background indefinitely, even in a scenario where a component that started the Service gets subsequently destroyed, either by the application program logic or by the Android OS. A **started Service** performs a single operation and does not return a result to the calling entity, much like a **void** method performs its task without returning anything to the calling method or object. As an example, the started Service might download or upload a data file over a network. Best practices dictate that when a started Service operation is completed, the Service object should automatically stop itself. This helps optimize Android operating system resources, such as CPU processor cycles and system memory usage, which should always be conserved.

A **bound Service** is created when an Android application component **binds** to a Service. This is accomplished by calling a **.bindService()** method. The bound Service offers a **client-server** interface that allows components to **interact** with the bound Service. Just like with a client-server relationship, you can send requests, get results, and you can even do all of this across (between) different processes, using interprocess communication (IPC).

A bound Service will remain in the system memory as long as other Android application components are still bound to it. Multiple application components can bind to a bound Service at the same time. When all of these application components unbind from the Service, that Service is "destroyed," or removed from system memory.

We will take a look at both of these types of Service formats, as well as a **hybrid** approach, where your Service can work in both of these ways at the same time. What this means is that you can start your Service (so that it is a started Service, and can run indefinitely) and later allow it to bind (or be bound to).

Whether an Android Service is specified as started or bound is determined by whether you have implemented a couple of the more often used **Service class callback methods**. For instance, the Service class **.onStartCommand()** method will allow components to **start** a Service, and the **.onBind()** method will allow components to **bind** to that Service.

Regardless of whether your application's Service is started, bound, or a hybrid (both started and bound), any other application component can use that Service, even from a separate application. This is similar to the way that any of your application components can start (launch) an Activity subclass by starting it using an **Intent** object. We covered using Intent objects in Chapter 7, so we could use them during the rest of the book. You will see how to use Intent objects to start Service subclasses during this chapter when you create your own **Service** subclass.

Controlling Your Service: Privacy and Priority

Service subclasses will run with a higher **priority** than inactive Activity subclasses. Because of this fact, it is far less likely that the Android operating system will terminate a **Service** class than it will an Activity class. I will be discussing the concept of priority in greater depth a bit later in this chapter. If an Activity subclass is "**active,**" or **currently in use** by your user on their display screen, it will obviously have the highest priority, as the assumption is that the user is currently and actively using it to interface (hence the term user interface) with the application and therefore with the Android hardware device.

It is important to note that you can declare your Service as **private** using your AndroidManifest XML file. This will **block access** to your **Service** subclass from other external Android applications. This is usually a good idea for security reasons, which I also discuss in this chapter. Android developers often do this as a programming or development "best practice," unless other applications absolutely need to use that Service.

A **Service** subclass, as a default, always runs inside the primary (UI) thread of the host application's primary process. Services that run inside of this primary process of your application are often termed **Local Services**. You will be reading about processes and threads in the next section of the chapter.

A misconception among Android programmers is that Android **Service** subclasses always run on their own separate threads. This is certainly possible, if you configure your **Service** subclass that way. The Service does not in fact by default create its own thread, and thus does not run in a separate thread unless you specify otherwise. You will read about processes and threads in the next section of this chapter, as these are very closely related topics.

What this means is that if your Service is going to do any CPU-intensive work (such as decoding streaming data in real-time) or blocking operations (such as real-time network access over busy network protocols), you should create a new thread within your Service in order to do that type of processing.

It is important to note that you may not need to use another thread for your Service class apart from the thread it is on (using already); for instance, in the example in this chapter we play a music file using the MediaPlayer in a Service without needing to spawn another thread.

The only way to really determine if this is needed is to first try using a **Service** class for your background processing, and then, if it affects your user experience, consider implementing the Android **Thread** class and a Thread object.

Processes and Thread: Foundational Information

When one of your Android application's components, such as your **MainActivity** class, starts and your application does not have any other components currently running, the Android operating system will launch a new Linux process for your application, using a single thread of execution called the **UI Thread**.

A process can generate or launch (I use the popular industry term "**spawn**") more than one thread. There is a **Thread** class (and therefore a **Thread** object can be created) in the Android OS. As a rule, all of your Android application components will run inside the same initial process and thread. This is generally termed the main thread, the primary thread, or the UI thread.

If one of your Android application components starts, and Android sees that a primary process already exists for your application, due to the fact that another component from your application already exists, that new component will also be started within that same application process, and will also use that same main thread.

To start your own thread, you must do so specifically within your Java code by creating a **Thread** object. You can also have different components in your application run in separate processes, and you can create additional threads for any process. This is what is usually done with Android **Service** subclasses. The process in Android is created using XML mark-up, unlike the **Thread** object, which is created using Java. You will be taking a look at creating a **<service>** using XML in the next section of the chapter. Creating a **Thread** object, and how and when to do so, is currently beyond the scope of this Absolute Beginner title, however.

As is the default functionality in the Android OS, all of your Android application components will run in the same process used to launch your application. Most of your basic Android applications will not need to change this behavior, and should not interfere with this default application launching and running functionality, unless there is a very compelling (and too advanced for this book title) functional reason for doing so.

For advanced applications (which we are not going to be covering in this book), I will cover this concept here, to be thorough regarding Android processes. If you happen to find yourself in a development situation where you absolutely need to control which Android process a certain application component belongs to and functions in, you can specify your own custom processes in, you guessed it, your application's **AndroidManifest.xml** file.

Let's take a look at how to spawn a process using the **android:process** parameter inside of the four major areas of Android. These are the Activity, the Service, the Broadcast Receiver (messaging), and the Content Provider (databases). These use the **<activity>**, the **<service>**, the **<receiver>**, and the **<provider>** parent tags, respectively.

Spawning a Process: The android:process XML Parameter

Your **AndroidManifest.xml** application component tags for each major type of application component, whether it is an **Activity <activity>** tag, a **Service <service>** tag, a **Broadcast Receiver <receiver>** tag, or a **Content Provider <provider>** tag, can include the optional **android:process** parameter. This parameter will allow you to control the process that a component will run inside of (or under, if you prefer to visualize it that way).

The **android:process** parameter should be utilized to specify the process under which the application component needs to run. You can set up this process parameter in such a way that each of the application's components run inside its own process, or you can "mix and match" components and processes in such a way that some of your application components will share a given process, while others will not share that process, or will even have their own process altogether.

If you wanted to get really complex, you could also set these **android:process** parameters so that components from different Android applications can execute together inside of the same Android process. This can only be accomplished when those particular applications share the same **Linux User ID**, and which are signed with the same certificates, so this topic is also a bit too complex for this book. I mention it here just so that you know about it in case you wish to research it further.

It is also interesting to note that the global **<application>** tag in your **AndroidManifest XML** file will also accept the **android:process** parameter. Using the **android:process** parameter inside of your **<application>** tag will set the default process value for your application, which would then be applied to all of your application's components inside of your XML application component definition (nested) hierarchy. Of course, this would not include those application components that then utilize their own **android:process** parameter.

In this situation, the application component child tag that utilized the **android:process** parameter to specify a different process for that particular application component would "override" the global or default process that you set as the process for your application to use via the **android:process** parameter inside the **<application>** tag. Thus, if you want all your components, except for one or two, to share the same custom process, define the process in your **<application>** tag and then override it selectively in one of the component child tags with **android:process**.

It is important to note that the Android OS has the option to shut down any of your processes at any given time. This is so that it can efficiently manage your system hardware resources (memory and processing cycles). This could be important when system memory is running low or if the memory used by your process is required by other processes that have a higher priority level or are receiving more usage (attention) from the end-user.

Application components running inside of a process that gets terminated by the Android OS are subsequently destroyed and are removed from memory. Not to worry, as any of these processes can be restarted again, at a later time, for any of those application components that still require something be accomplished for or by a user. In fact, that is exactly why that **savedInstanceState** Bundle object that you are now familiar with is always utilized!

When deciding which processes to kill, the Android system weighs their **relative importance** to the user. For example, it more readily shuts down processes that are hosting Activity subclasses that are no longer visible on screen, compared to a process hosting a visible Activity that is being used. The decision as to whether to terminate a process, therefore, depends on the **state** of the components running in that process. Since the rules Android uses to decide which processes to terminate are important to understand, you will read about them next.

The Process Lifecycle: Keeping a Process Alive

The Android OS will try to keep your application process in its system memory for as long as it can. However, it sometimes will need to destroy the older processes running in the OS. This is done in order to reclaim the system's memory resources for newer or higher priority processes. After all, so many Android devices ship with only one or at most two gigabytes of main system memory; this system memory can fill up fairly quickly, as users play games, launch apps, read eBooks, stream music, and place phone calls as the day goes on.

Even when devices start to ship with three gigabytes of main memory, you will still have memory management issues, and using processes and threads provide the tools for optimizing these memory management issues, so it is important that you understand how processes are handled in the Android OS. In case you are wondering, four megabytes of memory space in an Android device is out of the question, until Android releases the 64-bit version of its Android 5 OS, based on 64-bit Linux and 64-bit Java 7. This is because a 32-bit OS will only address 3.24MB of system memory.

The way that the Android OS determines which of its processes to keep and which of its processes to terminate is via a **priority hierarchy**. Android will place each running process into this priority hierarchy, which is based on each of the components running in the process queue, as well as the current status (running, idle, or stopped) of those application components. The way that Android removes processes from the process priority hierarchy, which is ultimately how memory is cleared and reallocated for the Android device, is that the process with the lowest priority (or least importance) is terminated first. Then the next lowest priority process is terminated, then the next lowest, until system resources that are needed for a higher priority process have been recovered for use.

There are **five process priority levels** within this priority hierarchy. Once you know what these are, you will see how practical the process priority hierarchy is, and you will also have a good overview of how **Service** subclasses (asynchronous background processing) or **Activity** subclasses (user interfaces) fit into a process priority schema, which is very important to understand as an Android developer, even if you don't implement custom processes. The five process priority levels are summarized in Table 13-1 for your quick reference.

Table 13-1. Android's five process priority levels, and what type of priority characteristics they exhibit on your app

Process Priority	Characteristics
Foreground process	A primary process that is currently actively processing your UI
Visible process	A secondary process that still affects what's visible on screen
Service process	A started process that contains a background processing service
Background process	A process containing an activity that's not visible onscreen
Empty process	A process that does not hold any active application components

Foreground Process

The highest priority process level is the **foreground process**. This is the primary process that is currently running (actively processing) and that is required for the application task that the user is currently engaging in. A process is considered a foreground process if it contains an activity (user interface) that a user is actively interfacing with or if it hosts a Service that is bound to an activity that the user is interfacing with. A process is also considered a foreground process if it is actively processing a Service that is running in the foreground, which means that the **Service** object has called the **.startForeground()** method.

If a **Service** object is currently executing one of the **.onCreate()**, **.onDestroy()**, or **.onStart()** Service lifecycle callbacks, which you will be learning about in this chapter, or is broadcasting a **BroadcastReceiver** object that is calling its **.onReceive()** method, it will be given a top foreground process priority level status by Android. In an optimal Android operating system scenario, only a few foreground processes will be running at any given time. Processes are terminated only as a last resort if memory gets scarce and the OS can't continue to run optimally.

Visible Process

The next highest priority process level is a **visible process**. This is a process that doesn't contain any foreground process components, but that can still affect what users are seeing on their displays. A process is deemed to be visible if it contains an activity that is not in the foreground, but that is still visible to the user display screen.—for example, an activity whose **.onPause()** method has been invoked. A great example of this is a foreground process activity that starts a dialog that permits another activity to be seen in the background.

A process that contains a **Service** subclass that has been **bound** to a **visible** process would also be able to get visible process priority! The visible process is considered to be almost as important as the foreground process, and thus a visible process is not terminated unless absolutely required to keep all foreground processes running in the operating system's memory space. Visible and foreground processes are thus extremely similar in the Android OS.

Service Process

The middle priority process level in these five levels is the **Service process**. This is a process that contains a Service that has been started with a **.startService()** method call, but that Android does not classify in either of the two higher process priority level categories. These Service class processes, because they have no user interface screen, and are running asynchronously in the background, are not directly tied to anything that a user sees on a display or is interacting with. They are still important to Android application development, which is why I have an entire chapter covering them.

Since a Service is still performing a task that the end-user wants to complete, such as playing an album of music in the background or downloading a file over the network, Android will keep a process that contains a Service object active, **unless** there is not enough memory to support them along with **foreground** and **visible** processes.

Background Process

The second lowest priority process level is a **background process**. This is a process that contains an Activity subclass that is not currently visible to the end-user. An example of this is when your Activity subclass's **.onStop()** method has been called. Since a background process has no detectible impact on the user experience, Android will terminate them whenever it becomes necessary to recover system memory for higher priority level processes (foreground, visible, or Service). There are often several background processes running, and Android keeps background processes in something called the **LRU** (Least Recently Used) list. This list guarantees that a process containing an Activity that was most recently utilized by the user is the last process to be terminated.

It is important to note that if your Activity subclasses implement their lifecycle methods correctly and save their current states using the now-familiar **savedInstanceState** Bundle object, then terminating that Activity subclass process will not have any discernible effect on the user experience. This is because when a user navigates back to the user interface screen for that Activity, a process will again be started for it, and your Activity subclass will restore all of its visible states by loading your **savedInstanceState** Bundle object contents.

Empty Process

The lowest priority process level is the **empty process**. This is a process that does not hold any currently active application components. If you are wondering why these empty process would be kept in system memory at all, the **strategic reason** to keep an empty process alive is for **memory caching** optimization, which improves the start-up time the next time a component, most probably an Activity, needs to run inside the process. The Android operating system will terminate these empty processes once the system memory is full, in an attempt to balance the overall system memory resources between the various process caches and with its underlying Linux kernel memory caches, which are so low level that developers cannot even access them.

Increasing Priority Level Rank

It is important to notice that process priority level rank might be increased because another process is dependent on a process. Any Android process that is currently servicing another process cannot be ranked lower than the process it is servicing. This is a logical behavior, if you think about it. Let's say the **Content Provider** (a database or a data store, covered in the next chapter) that is contained in process 01 is busy providing content to a user interface Activity in Process 02, or a Service object in process 01 is bound to an application component in Process 02. In these scenarios, Process 01 will always be considered as important as Process 02. This is also quite logical as the two processes are essentially acting together as one, and thus should be ranked or prioritized equally.

The next section looks at threads, which are even lower level than processes and can be used in a process (via Java code) to schedule processor-intensive or user interface tasks.

Thread Caveats: Don't Interfere with UI Thread

After Android launches an application using the **AndroidManifest.xml** file, the operating system spawns a thread of execution. This is usually termed the **main thread**. A main thread is in charge of dispatching and managing system-level and application-level events, which you learned about in Chapter 7. The events take place between the operating system and an app, such as an incoming phone call, as well as between your user interface widget event handlers and your application programming logic.

The main thread also controls drawing graphics, video, and animation (drawable) assets to the Activity display screen, so it is doing a lot of processing. This is a reason you might need to spawn your own thread, if something you want to do with your Android application might overload the heavy workload that is on the main (primary) thread. Unless and until you spawn a second thread, the main thread will be running your entire application.

The main or primary thread is also often referred to as the **UI thread** or user interface thread. This is because it's the thread inside of which the application components interact with components in the Android UI toolkit. The Android UI toolkit includes all the components, as classes, contained in the **android.widget** and the **android.view** packages, which you learned about in Chapters 6 through 11. All the Android UI toolkit components will run in the main process and are handled (managed) inside the UI thread.

For this reason, methods that respond to event handling callbacks, such as the **.onKeyDown()** event handler (used to report keyboard hardware interaction) or one of the lifecycle callback methods (such as a **.start()** method or a **.pause()** method) will always run inside the UI thread. This UI thread is contained within the main process for your Android application.

When an application dispatches intensive processing in response to user interface interactions, a single thread model can result in a slow user experience performance. This is why you must learn how to utilize threads properly, if you are going to do advanced Android application development.

The reason for this is obvious. If extensive processing is happening in the UI thread, performing long-winded operations, such as network access, complex calculations, or SQLite database queries, this will block some portion the user interface response processing. These more complex operations will reduce the amount of processing cycles available to your UI, and will essentially "block" the UI related events from being smoothly (that is, quickly) processed.

When the application UI thread becomes blocked, UI events cannot be dispatched for handling, and this includes drawing graphics and animation elements to the display screen. From a user experience standpoint, an application may appear to "hang," which is not desirable and is not at all professional.

It is important to note that if your application blocks the UI thread for more than a few seconds (for more than five seconds, actually) the user will be shown a dialog containing an undesirable (from a user experience standpoint) "**Application is Not Responding**" (called an **ANR**) dialog.

It is important to note that the Android UI toolkit isn't currently what is known as "**thread-safe**." For this reason, you should not at any time manipulate your application's user interface elements from inside a "worker thread."A **worker thread** is any non-UI thread, and is also commonly referred to as a **background thread**. In other words, it is a thread that you have spawned using your application Java code. This would be done in order to off-load intensive "worker bee" background processing so that the UI will continue to function smoothly. So remember the first rule in Android thread processing is that you must do all manipulation to your user interface elements from the inside of the UI thread, which is the app's main thread.

The second key rule is more general, and it is simply to not block the UI thread at any time for any reason. This is why you are able to create worker threads, in case you need to do something that may block the UI thread.

Should Your Android App Use Services or Threads?

An Android Service is an application component that can run in the background, even when your users aren't interacting with the application. If you need to perform work outside of your main UI thread, but only while the user is interacting with your application user interface, that is, when you should create an Android **Thread** object within that class of your application.

This would be done by instantiating a **HandlerThread** or **AsyncTask** object. You do not have to go to the trouble of declaring an entire Android **Service** subclass in your Manifest. If you look at it using the "static versus dynamic" standpoint that I have been teaching you over the course of the book, you are implementing a thread dynamically using Java code, whereas you implement a Service statically using XML mark-up to "declare it before use" in your **AndroidManifest** XML file, so the Android OS can optimize it!

Let's say that you wanted to stream some music from a music Service while your Activity is running. What you do is create a **Thread** object using the **.onCreate()** method, start it running using the **.onStart()** method, and stop it by using the **.onStop()** method. As mentioned, you would probably want to utilize a more refined Android Thread subclass such as the AsyncTask or HandlerThread class, instead of use a more general Thread class, which is generally used as a superclass to create more application-specific subclasses.

So when would you use Service subclasses over spawning Thread objects in existing classes, you might be wondering? If you remember from the previous section, Android processes that contain a Service subclass will always be prioritized higher than processes that utilize a background processing activity (Thread object). For this reason, if your apps are going to undertake extensive processing, access, or streaming operations, then you'd want to start a Service component subclass for that operation, rather than simply create a Thread object.

This is an especially relevant consideration if your background process is going to outlast your Activity screen. As an example, an Activity that is uploading a video that you created using the Android **Camera** class to a web server would want to utilize the Service subclass methodology to perform this upload. This is so that this upload process could continue in the background and finish uploading, even if the user leaves that Activity.

Thus, the primary reason that you would want to use a Service subclass over a Thread object is because using the Service component will guarantee that your processing operation will have at least a Service process priority level, regardless of what happens to your Activity subclass, which could drop below this process priority level based upon your end-user's usage or interaction with the Activity subclass that contains the Thread object.

Next, you'll learn how to write a Service subclass and how to call it using an Intent object. You will do this using the **PlayVideo.java** Activity subclass that you created in Chapter 11. You will implement the Android Service class lifecycle by creating an ambient planet audio player background Service component named **AmbientService.java**. This will be a Service subclass that will **extend** the Service class by utilizing the Java **extends** keyword inside of the class declaration to subclass the Android Service class.

You'll code Service class lifecycle methods in your Java code, including **onCreate()**, **onStart()**, and **onDestroy()** methods. You will leverage an Android Intent object in one of these to start the background Service, which will play background audio for the PlayVideo Activity created in Chapter 11. Finally you will also look at how to add the **<service>** tag to the **AndroidManifest.xml** file, and you will test your background audio Service subclass inside the Nexus One emulator. Since the video fly-over frames do not need to sync with the planet atmospheric ambient audio track, this will also show you a unique way to optimize your video and audio assets.

Creating a Service Subclass: AmbientService

Instead of having Eclipse create your class for you, you will create a class from scratch just like you did in Chapter 5 with your **Galaxy.java** class, in order to get some more practice with doing things using that work process.

1.   Open your **HelloUniverse** project in Eclipse and right-click on your **/src** folder, since that is where you want the file that you are creating to be placed.

2.   Next, select the **New ➤ Class** menu sequence and open the **New Java Class** dialog, shown in Figure 13-1.

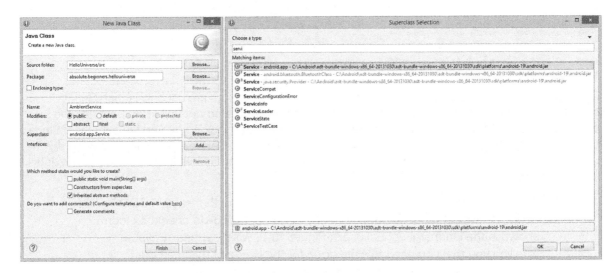

Figure 13-1. The New Java Class dialog with AmbientService name and the Superclass Selection dialog

3. Name the Service subclass **AmbientService** and click the **Browse** button next to the **Superclass** field to open the **Superclass Selection** dialog. Type in the letters "**servi**" to get a list of all the Service classes.

4. Double-click on the **Service - android.app** superclass option, at the top of the dialog, to select it as the Android superclass that you want to extend.

5. Once you are back in the New Java Class dialog, select the **absolute.beginners.hellouniverse** package in the **Package** field. Use the **Browse** button to access the selector dialog to find the package.

6. Leave all of the other New Java Class dialog settings at their defaults and then click the **Finish** button to create your bootstrap **AmbientService** Service subclass, which is shown in Figure 13-2. Notice that the **import statements** for the **android.app.Service** package and the **android.content.Intent** package are written for you.

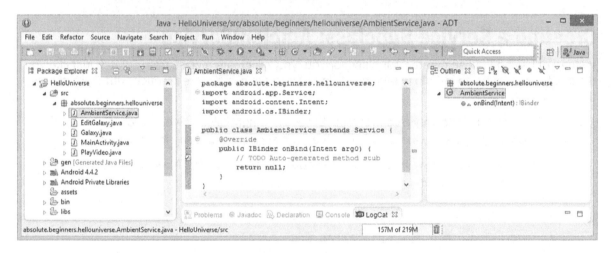

Figure 13-2. The bootstrap AmbientService Service subclass with required IBinder() method and imports

Both of these import statements are needed because Intent objects are used to launch Service objects. There is also an **android.os.IBinder** package **import** statement included, because the **public IBinder onBind()** method is **required** to be implemented inside any Service subclass. Since you are going to be creating a **started Service** and not a **bound Service**, you will be leaving this **.onBind()** method empty and unutilized, which is allowed, as long as it is there (as long as it exists in your Java code base).

7. If you want, you can delete the comment in the method that says "**TODO Auto-generated method stub**." When you do so, the **to-do** checkbox icon shown in the left margin of Eclipse in Figure 13-2, will disappear. Eclipse is telling you that you need to write code for the inside of this method, but unless you are creating a bind between your application logic and the Service, you don't really need to. Still, Eclipse is pretty cool, isn't it?

Now you can add the functionality that you want this **Service** subclass to have in the background. Since I didn't get a chance to show you how to play long-format digital audio assets in the previous chapter, I will take that opportunity here, and show you how to declare, instantiate, and utilize a MediaPlayer object, so that you know how to do this to playback long-form audio.

Using a Service to Carry Out a Task

This topic fits into the chapter's sequence perfectly, as it should probably be done as a Service object, so that the UI thread in your main process does not become overwhelmed (overloaded) with processing tasks, as it is already doing digital video decoding, multi-state **ImageButtons**, and hybrid (frame and tween) animation, among other things.

1. Declare a **MediaPlayer** object at the top of your **AmbientService** class and name it **ambientAudioPlayer**, as shown in Figure 13-3. I hope that you are getting comfortable declaring Android objects at the top of your class Java logic by now! Mouseover the red error highlight and select the **Import 'MediaPlayer' (android.media)** option so that Eclipse ADT will write the **import android.media.MediaPlayer;** Java statement for you.

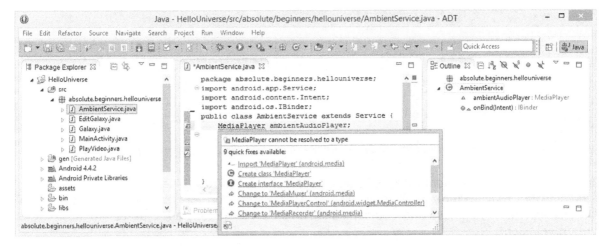

Figure 13-3. Declare a MediaPlayer object named ambientAudioPlayer and then mouseover the error and choose Import

2. The next step, as you are now familiar, is the **instantiation** and **configuration** of this **ambientAudioPlayer** MediaPlayer object. This is done using the **MediaPlayer.create()** method call, which you will use to pass your AmbientService **Context** object and a reference to an **ambient.m4a** MPEG-4 AAC ambient planet background audio file. You will copy that file into your **/res/raw** folder next.

3. Copy the **ambient.m4a** digital audio asset into your **HelloUniverse** project's **/res/raw** folder from the book assets repository. I omit the screenshots here, as you have seen how this is done in previous chapters. Once this is done, you are ready to write code!

4. Create an **onCreate()** method for the **AmbientService** Service subclass using the following Java code, shown in Figure 13-4. Then add the **MediaPlayer.create()** method call and **.setLooping()** method call to instantiate and configure your MediaPlayer object. That way, when your service is started, your MediaPlayer object will be as well:

```
@Override
public void onCreate() {
      ambientAudioPlayer = MediaPlayer.create(this, R.raw.ambient);
      ambientAudioPlayer.setLooping(true);
}
```

Figure 13-4. Add an onCreate() method, instantiate a MediaPlayer object, and then set it to loop using .setLooping()

If you do not see the **ambient.m4a** digital audio asset in the **/res/raw** folder, as shown on the left side of Figure 13-4, it simply means that you forgot to right-click on your project folder and select the **Refresh** menu command after you copied the ambient background audio asset into the **/res/raw** folder.

5. You will also have red error highlights under the **R.raw.ambient** part of the MediaPlayer object instantiation until you use the Refresh command (utility). Just as it is logical to instantiate (create) and configure your MediaPlayer object in an **.onCreate()** method for this **Service** subclass, it is logical to start the MediaPlayer object playback using the **.onStart()** method for the Service. The Java code, shown in Figure 13-5, looks like the following:

```
@Override
public void onStart(Intent intent, int startid) {
      ambientAudioPlayer.start();
}
```

Figure 13-5. Add an onStart() method and then start the ambientAudioPlayer MediaPlayer object playback loop using .start()

Notice that this is the only method of the three that takes two parameters—an **Intent** object named **intent**, which is needed to start the Service, and a **start ID integer** value, which you can use in your code inside the method if you want to have different types of Service objects starting the programming logic. Inside of the **.onStart()** method you have your code that calls the **.start()** method off of the **ambientAudioPlayer** MediaPlayer object.

Now that you have created methods that **create** and **start** your **Service** subclass, you only need to implement the method that **stops** and removes your **Service** subclass from system memory.

This is typically called the **.onDestroy()** method, and is one of the three methods that is required to be coded (implemented) when you create any Android **Service** subclass. Once you finish coding your **.onDestroy()** method, your **Service** subclass will be ready for use, and you can declare it for use in your **AndroidManifest.xml** file.

Just like you start your **ambientAudioPlayer** MediaPlayer object's playback loop in the **AmbientService** Service class's **.onStart()** method, you similarly stop the **ambientAudioPlayer** MediaPlayer object playback loop in your Service class's **.onDestroy()** method.

An **onDestroy()** method allows developers to control their own optimization of system memory usage, so that the Android OS does not have to do it by stopping the process. When the **Service** subclass is stopped via this **.onDestroy()** method, the MediaPlayer object is also stopped. Therefore, the ambient planet sound digital audio loop does not continue to play, as the MediaPlayer object exists independent of (or next to) the Service object.

6. The **onDestroy()** method is coded using the following Java logic, which is also shown in Figure 13-6:

```
@Override
public void onDestroy() {
    ambientAudioPlayer.stop();
}
```

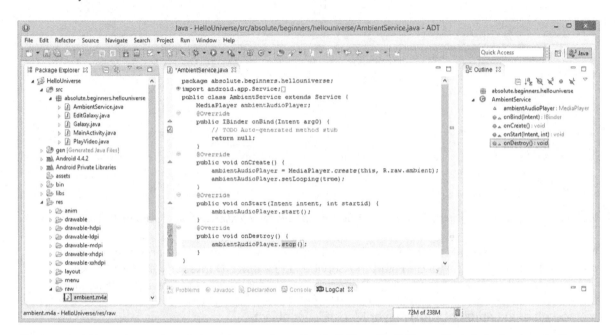

Figure 13-6. Add an onDestroy() method and then stop the ambientAudioPlayer MediaPlayer object playback using .stop()

Now that you have coded your first Android **Service** subclass, using about two dozen lines of Java code, you need to declare your **Service** subclass in your **AndroidManifest** file. Once you do this, you can start it using an Intent object from your PlayVideo Activity subclass, to add background digital audio ambient sound effects to your planet fly-over simulation.

Configuring AndroidManifest to Add a <service>

Whenever you add an Android Activity, Service, Content Provider, or Broadcast Receiver component to your Android application, you need to declare it for use inside of your **AndroidManifest** XML file, which is utilized to define, configure, and launch your Android application.

You will do that now, by opening your **AndroidManifest.xml** file, inside the central editing pane of Eclipse. At the top of the existing XML mark-up inside of the parent **<application>** tag add in a child **<service>** tag before the first **<activity>** tag for EditGalaxy. It is important to note that the order of the component child tags inside the parent **<application>** tag does not matter, as long as they are all in there somewhere.

Your <service> tag should implement the **android:enabled="true"** parameter. This parameter will enable your Service component for use inside of your application. Be sure to also include the **android:name=".AmbientService"** parameter, which is used to reference the **MusicService.java** class name. You will be creating this **Service** class in the next section of the chapter. The tag mark-up should look like this:

```
<service android:enabled="true" android:name=".AmbientService" />
```

The finished **AndroidManifest.xml** file and mark-up is shown in Figure 13-7.

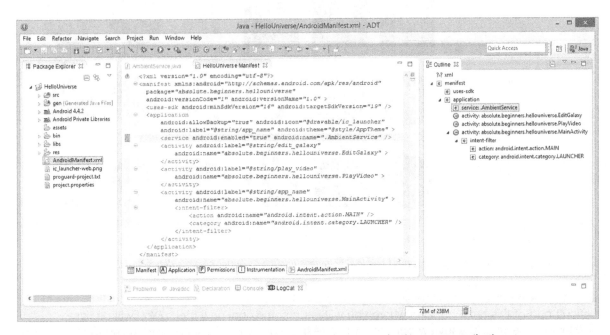

Figure 13-7. Open the AndroidManifest.xml file and add a child <service> tag under the parent <application> tag

Next, you will create the turn audio on and turn audio off icon UI elements. This UI design will overlay these icons over the digital video player surface, so that the user can click on these floating icons. These icons will use alpha channel transparency as well as allow users to click (or touch) them to turn on (start the Service) and off (stop the Service) the ambient planet background audio sound effects.

Starting a Service: Using .startService()

Now that you have created your **AmbientService** Service subclass and declared it for use in your **AndroidManifest** XML file, you are ready to start it using the **.startService()** method that you learned about earlier in the chapter. This is done using an Intent object in a very similar fashion to starting an Activity, which you have done already, so this should be familiar to you.

After you copy the **sound0.png** and **sound1.png** audio off and audio on icon graphics from the book repository into your **/HelloUniverse/res/drawable-hdpi** folder, as can be seen in Figure 13-8, you will begin working on adding to the user interface infrastructure that is currently in your

activity_play.xml user interface definition file. This file is used to hold the **<RelativeLayout>** container and the **<VideoView>** widget for your **PlayVideo.java** Activity subclass currently, and you will be adding the **<ImageView>**widgets to hold your audio control icon images.

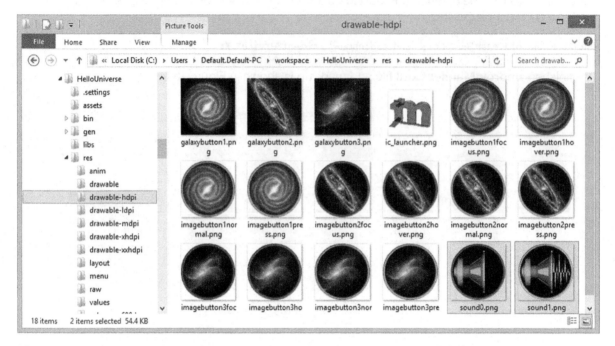

Figure 13-8. Copy the sound0.png and sound1.png PNG32 images into the /HelloUniverse/res/drawable-hdpi folder

After that is in place, you will be able to get into the Java programming part, which is the more difficult part of this task, but also where you will learn some cool new tricks. You will declare and instantiate your ImageView objects and "wire them up" with event handlers using the **.setOnClickListener()** method calls. Inside these (one for each audio control icon), you will have an **onClick()** event handler method, which will contain your **.startService()** method call for the playAudio icon and the **.stopService()** method call for the stop Audio icon.

Setting Up Your UI Design Using XML and Java

This section sets up the UI:

1. Since you are going to be using **ImageView** UI widgets, which like the **ImageButton** UI widgets require that you implement an **android:contentDescription** parameter for the sight impaired, the first thing that you need to do is add two **<string>**constants in your **/res/values/strings.xml** file named **play_audio** and **stop_audio**.

2. Set these with "Turn Audio On" and "Turn Audio Off" data values, as shown in Figure 13-9. When the sight impaired access the **playAudio** or **stopAudioImageView** UI elements used for the audio control icons, they will hear these phrases from the Android voice synthesizer, informing them what these UI elements are for.

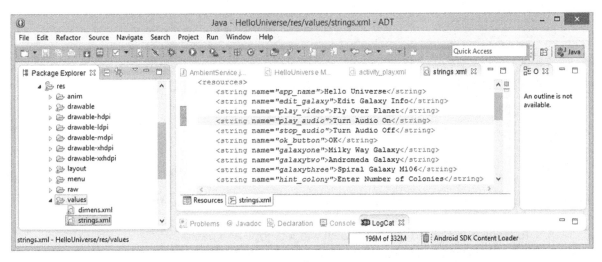

Figure 13-9. Create contentDescription parameter <string> constants for the sight impaired for audio on/off icons

3. Now that your **<string>** constants are in place, open the **/res/layout/activity_play.xml** file in Eclipse and add two child **<ImageView>** widget tags inside the parent **<RelativeLayout>** container tag. Configure the first with a **playAudio** ID and **sound1.png** image source reference and add some padding, say **60DIP** to compress the icon down in size a bit. Use the **marginLeft** and **marginTop** parameters with a **-50DIP** value to pull the icon up and to the left a bit.

4. Be sure to add the required **layout_width** and **layout_height** parameters, set to the value (constant) of **wrap_content**. Do this using the following XML mark-up, as shown in Figure 13-10:

```
<ImageView android:id="@+id/playAudio"  android:src="@drawable/sound1"
        android:contentDescription="@string/play_audio"  android:padding="60dip"
        android:layout_marginLeft="-50dip"  android:layout_marginTop="-50dip"
        android:layout_width="wrap_content"  android:layout_height="wrap_content"  />
```

Figure 13-10. Add<ImageView> child tags for the playAudio and stopAudio icons and configure them with parameters

5. To create the second **ImageView** UI widget, copy and paste the XML
    mark-up for the first **ImageView** child tag underneath itself and change
    the **playAudio** ID to be a **stopAudio** ID. Create a reference to **sound1** to
    reference a **sound0** asset. Next, add an **android:layout_alignParentTop**
    as well as an **android:layout_alignParentRight** parameter and set both of
    these to a value of "**true**." These will serve to force this audio off icon into the
    upper-right corner of your UI design. Everything else will remain the same, as
    shown in the following XML mark-up:

```
<ImageView android:id="@+id/stopAudio"  android:src="@drawable/sound0"
        android:contentDescription="@string/play_audio"  android:padding="60dip"
        android:layout_alignParentTop="true"  android:layout_alignParentRight="true"
        android:layout_marginLeft="-50dip"  android:layout_marginTop="-50dip"
        android:layout_width="wrap_content"  android:layout_height="wrap_content"  />
```

Since the **<ImageView>** widgets come after the **<VideoView>** widget, their compositing (layer)
z-order puts them on top of the digital video asset, so they will float above it. Since you are using a
PNG32 digital image asset, complete with an 8-bit anti-aliased alpha channel and 24-bit RGB image
data, you will get a perfectly seamless composite, complete with attractive icons made with 3D
software floating in the corners of your video screen!

6. Now you are ready to open your **PlayVideo.java** Activity subclass and
    declare two **ImageView** objects at the top of the class, named **soundOn**
    and **soundOff**. Use the following line of Java code to do so, as shown in
    Figure 13-11:

```
ImageView soundOn, soundOff;
```

Figure 13-11. Declare ImageView objects named soundOn and SoundOff and instantiate them using findViewById()

7. Next, add a line of space after the **setContentView()** method call in your
    PlayVideo class's **onCreate()** method and instantiate your **soundOn** and
    soundOffImageView objects by using the following two lines of Java code:

```
soundOn = (ImageView)findViewById(R.id.playAudio);
soundOff = (ImageView)findViewById(R.id.stopAudio);
```

Now that you have declared, instantiated, and loaded your two **ImageView** objects with references
to your XML definitions, which in turn reference your digital image assets as their source imagery,
you are ready to add event handling structures to each of these to "trap" click events (or touch
events) on each of them to turn the audio on or off. This is done by starting (or stopping) your
AmbientServiceService subclass, which will then start or stop the MediaPlayer object that is
referencing your ambient planet sound effect digital audio asset. Pretty cool!

8. Add a line of space underneath your **soundOn** object instantiation and type
    the **soundOn** object name again. Then press the **period** key and select the
    .setOnClickListener() method call using the Eclipse pop-up helper dialog.
    You can also simply type the name in.

9. Inside of the parameter area of the method, type the **new** Java keyword, and
    then the **View** object, and the **.OnClickListener()** method, called off of that
    object using **dot notation**. This can all be done using the following line of
    Java code (shown with comment and indenting), as shown in Figure 13-12:

```
soundOn.setOnClickListener(new View.OnClickListener() {
        //  Your event handling program logic will eventually go in here.
});
```

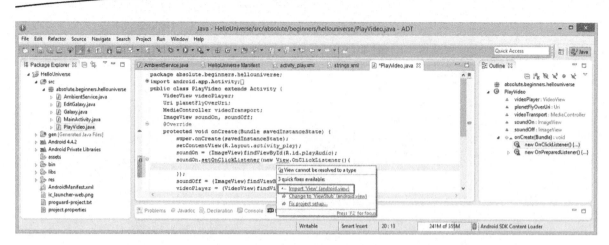

Figure 13-12. Add event handling to the soundOn ImageView object using .setOnClickListener() and new keyword

10.   As you can see in Figure 13-12, you will need to mouse over the reference to the **View** class and then select the **Import 'View' (android.view)** option, which will write your **import android.view.View;** line of code for you.

Once the **import** statement for the use of the View class is in place, you can continue to build the event handler.

Once you import the View class into your class, you will get a second wavy red error highlight, as shown in Figure 13-13, underneath the **View** object's method call to its **.OnClickListener()** method. If you mouse over this error, the Eclipse pop-up helper will tell you that you need to add the unimplemented **.onClick()** method, as shown in Figure 13-13.

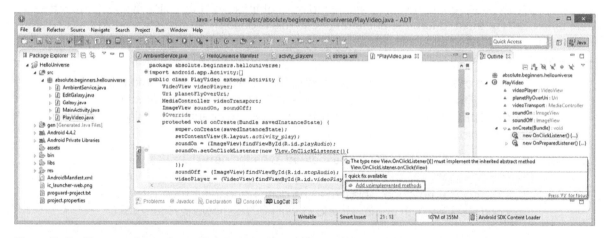

Figure 13-13. After you select an Import View (android.view) option, select an Add Unimplemented Method option

11. If you click the **Add unimplemented methods** option, Eclipse will write your "bootstrap" **onClick()** method code block (structure) for you. Once that is in place, you will be ready to add your **.startService()** method call, which will utilize an Intent object to start your **AmbientService Service** subclass. That will then start the Android MediaPlayer and start looping your **ambient.m4a** digital audio asset, which will then play your background audio.

12. Inside of the bootstrap **onClick()** method Eclipse created for you, which is shown in Figure 13-14, type in your **startService()** method call. Inside of that method call, use the Java **new** keyword to create an Intent object using the **Intent()** constructor method and reference to the current Context and your **AmbientService** class.

Figure 13-14. *Add startService() method call with a new Intent() method call inside it referencing AmbientService*

The **onClick()** event handling structure should look like this when you are done, as shown in Figure 13-14:

```
@Override
public void onClick(View arg0)  {
        startService( new Intent(this, AmbientService.class) );
}
```

13. As you can see in Figure 13-15, the code should be error-free; however, it isn't! Eclipse is showing a wavy red underline underneath the entire Java construct that you created inside the **startService()** method call. Mouseover the error and read the error message in the first line of the pop-up helper dialog. It reads "**The constructor Intent(new View.OnClickListener(), Class<AmbientService>) is undefined.**"

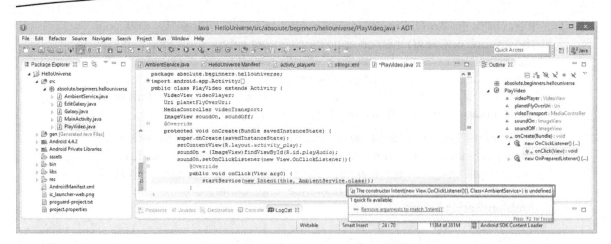

Figure 13-15. This error message shows that this Context object is the one for the View.OnClickListener() code structure

This error message tells you that the **Context** object that you are passing into the **Intent()** constructor method using the Java **this** keyword actually contains the Context for the **View.OnClickListener** structure, and not for the **PlayVideo** structure. The **PlayVideo** Context object is the Context (application component) that you want to be sending inside of the Intent object that you are constructing here when it gets delivered (sent over) to the **AmbientService** Service subclass. So the question becomes, how do you designate the PlayVideo Context object?

The way to specify the correct Context object, using the Java **this** keyword, is to preface it with the path to the **PlayVideo** class using dot notation. Therefore, **this** would become **PlayVideo.this** to solve this programming quagmire.

14.   The correct **startService()** method call would look like the following Java code, as shown in Figure 13-16:

```
startService( new Intent( PlayVideo.this, AmbientService.class ) );
```

Figure 13-16. Add a PlayVideo.this path reference to the this keyword using dot notation to fix the error

15. Now that you have an error-free **soundOn.setOnClickListener()** event handling structure that contains the correct **startService()** method call, you can copy and paste the entire structure to create your **soundOff** event handling structure. That structure will call the **stopService()** method call to stop the background audio playback.

The Java code blocks for both event-handling structures will look like the following, as shown in Figure 13-17:

```java
soundOn = (ImageView)findViewById(R.id.playAudio);
soundOn.setOnClickListener(new View.OnClickListener() {
@Override
public void onClick(View arg0)  {
startService( new Intent( PlayVideo.this, AmbientService.class) );
}
});
soundOff = (ImageView)findViewById(R.id.stopAudio);
soundOff.setOnClickListener(new View.OnClickListener() {
@Override
public void onClick(View arg0)  {
    stopService( new Intent( PlayVideo.this, AmbientService.class) );
}
});
```

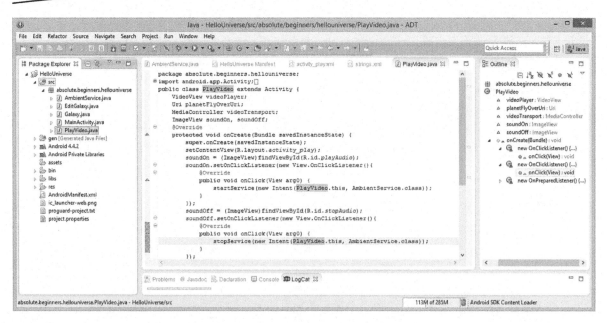

Figure 13-17. Now that the event handler code block is error-free, use it to create the soundOff stopService() call

Testing the PlayVideo Class with the Nexus One

Now that your Java code is in place in your **PlayVideo.java** Activity subclass and is error-free, you can test your **PlayVideo** Activity using the Eclipse Nexus One AVD emulator. Later, you will refine your play audio and stop audio icons by "tweaking" the XML UI design definition mark-up, and then you will be all done!

Right-click on the **HelloUniverse** project folder and use the **Run As ➤ Android Application** menu sequence to launch the Nexus One AVD. When the application launches, click the ActionBar Overflow Menu (three vertical dots on the right side of the ActionBar) and select the **Planet Fly Over** menu option to launch your **PlayVideo** Activity, shown on the left pane in Figure 13-18.

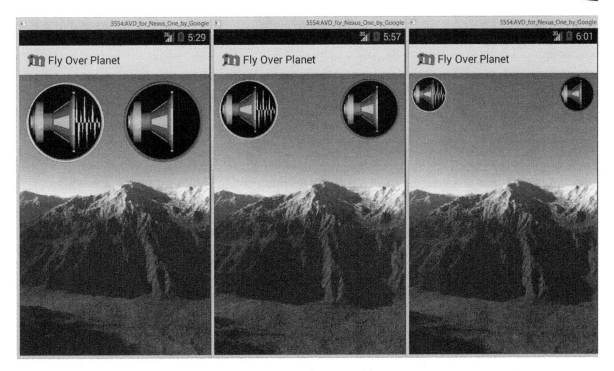

Figure 13-18. Use a Nexus One AVD to test your UI designs with padding and wrap_content and margin settings

Click on the **Turn Audio On** icon on the left and listen to the planet background audio loop play, as your video loop plays as well. Since these two new media assets do not need to "**sync**," you are now using the **VideoView** widget, which you learned about and installed in Chapter 11, to play digital video with one **MediaPlayer** object. The **AmbientService** Service subclass, which is using a second **MediaPlayer** object, loops your background audio at the same time that your digital video asset is looping.

If you wanted to sync the audio with the moving frames (moving picture for you film buffs) in the video, you would use a non-linear digital video editing software tool such as the open source EditShare Lightworks.

As you can see in the Nexus One AVD emulator, when you click on the Turn Audio On visual icon, the start Service Intent object is sent to your **AmbientService** class, and the MediaPlayer starts playback of your **ambient.m4a** digital audio asset, so that you have cool background audio special effects for your planet fly-over experience.

The next thing to test is the Turn Audio Off visual icon on the right side of the video screen, so click on that next to send a stop Service Intent object to your **AmbientService** class and stop the MediaPlayer play back. You should be able to use these two visual icons more than one time, to start and stop your audio effects as much as you want. Be sure to test this thoroughly and make sure that your code is working perfectly!

Also notice that when you click on the ImageView UI widgets that are on top of the VideoView UI widget, the events are "trapped" and are utilized only by those UI elements. They do not affect the VideoView, so the MediaController does not popup unless you click on the video part of the screen.

The next thing to do is change the configuration parameters, or attributes, of these **<ImageView>** child tags to reduce the size of these icon graphics, as well as push them up into the corners of the video.

This will allow more of the planet fly-over video to be seen, which will look more professional. The progression of what you are about to do in the **activity_play** XML mark-up can be seen in the middle and right panes of Figure 13-18. You will be using a couple of the layout parameters to downsample, or resize in a downward direction, the audio icon image assets that you installed in the **/res/drawable-hdpi** folder earlier in the chapter.

Let's remove the padding and negative margin parameters and use a much more simple **android:layout_margin** parameter with a value of **8dip** to push the icons away from the edges of the screen. To scale the icons down, you replace the **wrap_content** constant values in the **android:layout_width** and **android:layout_height** parameters with DIP values. Initially, we will try a setting of **100dip**, the results of which are shown in the center pane of Figure 13-18. The new XML mark-up should look like the following, as shown in Figure 13-19:

```
<ImageView android:id="@+id/playAudio" android:src="@drawable/sound1"  android:layout_margin="4dip"
android:contentDescription="@string/play_audio" android:layout_width="60dp"
android:layout_height="60dp" />
<ImageView android:id="@+id/stopAudio" android:src="@drawable/sound0"  android:layout_margin="4dip"
android:layout_alignParentTop="true" android:contentDescription="@string/play_audio"
android:layout_alignParentRight="true" android:layout_width="60dip" android:layout_height="60dip" />
```

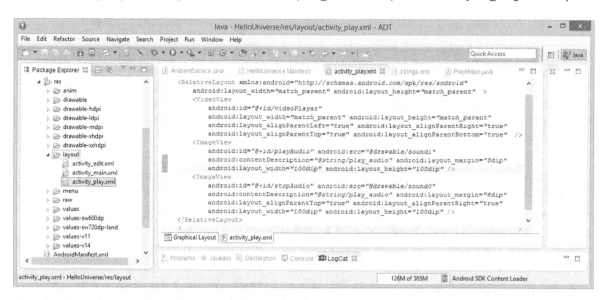

Figure 13-19. Change the wrap_content values to DIP values and change the padding values to margin values

The icons were still too big for my taste, so I reduced 100dip to **60dip** to scale the audio control icons down some more, and I reduced 8dip to **4dip** to pull the icons into the corners of the display more, as shown on the right pane of Figure 13-18.

Summary

In this chapter, you learned about the Android **Service** component subclasses as well as about **processing** concepts, principles, prioritization, and optimization. You learned about **Thread** objects and how these threads differ from Service components.

You learned all about different types of Android Services, including **started Services**, **bound Services**, and a **hybrid** between these two Service types, as well as about characteristics of Services, caveats about using Services, and when to utilize a **Service** subclass versus using a **Thread** object.

You learned about **processes** as well, and how to spawn your own process in your **AndroidManifest** XML file. You learned how to assign different application components to their own processes, by using the **android:process** parameter inside of your parent **<application>** tag or its child component tags, such as **<activity>**, **<service>**, **<provider>**, or **<receiver>**.

You created your own **Service** subclass called **AmbientService** to start a MediaPlayer object (and stop it) so that you could play ambient planet background audio effects while your digital video was looping. Then you created a new UI for your PlayVideo Activity to hold some audio control icons, and then wrote Java code that called the **Service** subclass from the **PlayVideo** Activity subclass using the **startService** and **stopService** methods.

In Chapter14, you will learn all about **Content Provider** classes in Android, which is an advanced area that includes database technology. I saved the most complicated chapter for last. As you can see, I am as always trying to cover things in the most logical, optimal fashion, as you progress through this journey to learn Android.

Android Content Providers: Providing Data to Applications

This chapter takes a look at how Android **provides content** in an application, using what the Android OS terms a **Content Provider**. This chapter covers how to share the provided content, as well as how to access, modify, update, and delete the data that these Content Providers provide. You will also take a look at some of the Content Providers that come installed with every Android OS.

The topics have become significantly more advanced as you have progressed from one chapter to the next over the course of this book, and this chapter is no different. Data structure access is significantly more complex than event handlers or UI design. This is because it involves **database design** and, therefore, you need to know how any given database is designed in order to be able to access its database structure correctly.

For this reason, I am going to provide you with the foundational basics of database design in this chapter, as I have often done for other core topics in Android, such as user interface design, digital imaging, 2D animation, digital video, digital audio, Services, threads and processes.

Content Provider (database) usage in Android also involves requesting **security permissions** for an application for different types of Content Provider (database) access, such as "**read**" and "**write**" access. As you're probably surmising by now, since you have been paying close attention during this book, this is accomplished by using your Android Manifest XML file, and adding in the appropriate Android **<permission>** child tags.

This chapter begins with a high-level overview of exactly what Android Content Providers are as well as what they can do for your Android application and its users. After that, you will learn some foundational information regarding database theory, and learn about the **SQLite** database used in Android. Then you will take a look at the various database structures provided with the Android OS, which you can use with your contact management and new media endeavors, since they have already been created and installed in the Android OS. After that, you will create a **ContactGalaxy.java** Activity subclass, that will allow you to install rulers for each of your galaxies!

An Overview of Android Content Providers

The term Content Provider is unique to Android development. It means nothing more than a **datastore** of data values, and is primarily found in the form of SQLite databases that are an integral part of the Android OS.

You can use Content Provider SQLite databases that are provided in the Android OS, and you can also create your own Content Provider databases for your application if you want, although that topic is too advanced for an Absolute Beginner's book. I am certain that there will soon be books that are dedicated solely to the topic of Android SQLite database design!

An Android Content Provider provides you with access to **sharable** data structures, commonly called databases, which the Android OS has chosen to use for their sharable data structures because they have the most high-level features, which unfortunately also makes them more complicated, hence this chapter. The general high-level procedure for utilizing a database management system (DBMS) is as follows:

1. Get **permission** to **read** from a given database. If you need to modify the database's content, you might also need to get permission to **write** to that database.

2. **Query** (search for and find) the data in the database management system (SQLite) using a "**key**," which in Android is the **_ID** data field. You will be learning about fields very soon.

3. **Access** (read into memory) the data in the database management system (SQLite) once you have located it using the query and **_ID** key.

4. **Modify** (over-write, append to, or delete) the data in the database management system (SQLite) once you have located it, read it, and ascertained that it needs updating.

When accessing data, you might read the data, write to the data (change the values of the existing data), append (add) new data onto the database structure, or delete existing data, based on the type of permission and level of security permission that has been established for your application in its **AndroidManifest.xml** file.

Data can be in Android internal (system) memory, in a SQLite database, or in an external storage location, such as an SD card, or even on an external database server, which would also be remote to the Android OS and to the Android device hardware.

Database Fundamentals: Concepts and Terms

A **database management system**, or **DBMS**, is a data storage system or engine that can store valuable data that can be easily accessed, read, and updated. This capability is quite desirable for a software development platform like Android.

If you have never been exposed to database technology, this section covers database fundamentals. Popular database software packages that you may be familiar with include Microsoft Access and Claris FileMaker Pro. The company that currently develops FileMaker is known as FileMaker, Inc.

As you know, there is a complete open source DBMS inside of the Android OS called SQLite, which is actually something called a **Relational DBMS**, or **RDBMS**. An RDBMS is based on **relationships** that can be drawn between data that is arranged using tables. These **data tables** support **rows** of data and **columns** of data. This is similar to a spreadsheet program like Excel, except that data in a relational database is not usually visible at the same time, like data in a spreadsheet is. It is important to note that you can generate reports using a database that can achieve this very same result if you want (once you learn about all of the programming that is involved).

Each database table **column** contains a similar type and classification of data within a given database record structure, which is generally called a **database field**. This means that, conversely, each **row** in your database table represents one entire **database record**. Generally when you are **writing** your database record, you will write **one entire row** or record of data when you first add that record. On the other hand, when you **search** a database for information, you are generally looking through just one of the data table's columns, or fields, for a specific piece of data or information.

Database columns (fields) can contain many different data types, such as numbers, text, or even references to data stored somewhere else. It is important to note that each data field needs to contain the same exact data type as the other data fields in that same column, as you can see in Figure 14-1.

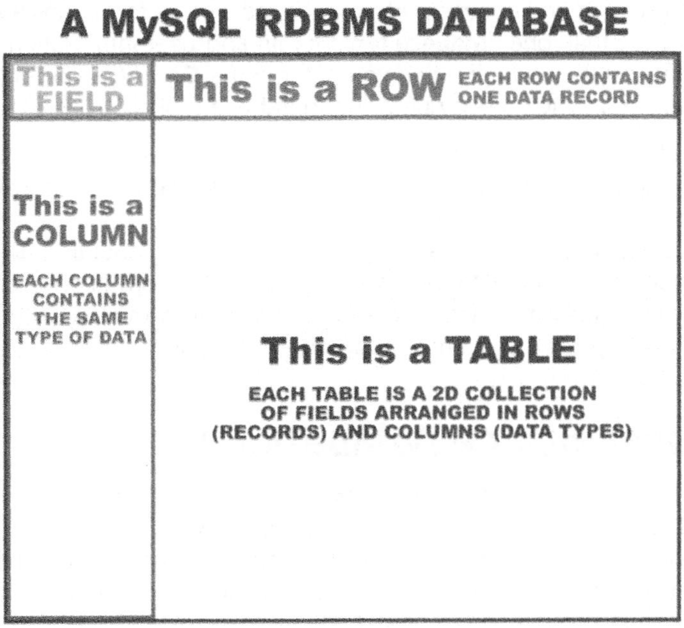

Figure 14-1. Basic overview of an RDBMS database (MySQL or SQLite)

Each row is a database record, and a database record will usually contain all sorts of different data types across the different data table columns. The classifications of data fields that a data record may contain usually spans names (text), numbers, and references (addresses) to things like emails, websites, social media profiles, passwords, and the like.

> **Caution**   Once the record structure and data fields that define your record structure are set up, don't change this record structure later, if you are designing your own databases. This is because currently loaded records (the fields) may not fit into the new data structure definition correctly! It is best to design your database structures **up-front**. The database design process is especially critical to the success of your RDBMS project over time.

One of the most popular database programming languages in the world is called **SQL**, which stands for **Structured Query Language**. You will be learning about SQL, as used in SQLite, later on in this chapter.

The **structured** part comes from the structured tabular format of a relational database, and the **query** part comes from the fact that these tables of data are designed to be searched through using a certain data value. The **language** part comes from the fact that SQL has evolved over time into a database programming language, which is so complex and involved, that there are probably more books regarding SQL RDBMS topics than there are on database programming for the Android OS.

If you have a massive amount of data fields (columns) in the database table, you will probably want to **optimize** your database using more than one table of data. In real-world database design, the theory of which is largely beyond the scope of an introductory book, you will want to have more than one database table for search and access performance, as well as for organization reasons. In fact the Android OS uses more than one database table for its end-user information storage and access, as you will soon see later in the chapter when you get into the **Contacts** database tables structure, which is quite complex, spanning quite a number of database tables.

The way to create multiple database tables that act together as one massive unified database is to have a **unique key** (unique index) for each record in each of the tables. That way, information for a single data record can span more than one database table using the unique key. In Android, this key is called an **ID** and is always designated using a system database constant **_ID** in Android's SQLite databases. For instance, if a key or **_ID** value is 154, your email information and phone information could be contained in two different tables, but stored under that same key (index) value, and thus accurately associated with your Android user account even though it spans across multiple tables.

SQLite: The Open Source Database Engine

As you know, the SQL in SQLite stands for Structured Query Language. The "Lite" part denotes that this is a "**lightweight**" version of a DBMS, intended for **embedded use** in consumer electronics devices, and not a full-blown DBMS, as would be used on an advanced computer system such as a database server. It is also interesting to note that SQLite is also included in all the HTML5 browsers! All you really need to know about SQLite is that it is a part of the Android OS, and that you can use it for data storage.

> **Note**   If you want to research SQLite a bit more on your own, which would be a good idea if your Android application needs to use SQLite databases extensively, SQLite has its own website that is kept up to date on a regular basis. Check it out at: `http://www.SQLite.org`.

There is a **SQLite API** in Android that contains all of the RDBMS functions needed to work with SQLite. These are contained in a series of classes and methods in the **android.database.sqlite** package. All you have to do is learn how to use them properly, which is not a simple task, due to the database structure complexity which has evolved during nineteen versions of Android (4.4 API Level 19).

SQLite is designed specifically for embedded systems use similar to JavaME (Micro Edition), and as such it has only a quarter megabyte, or 256KB, of total memory footprint. The memory space is utilized to host a relational database engine implementation. SQLite supports a minimum (standard) set of relational database functions and features, including the most common SQL syntax keywords, basic database operations like **READ**, **WRITE**, and **APPEND**, and prepared statements. These features are enough to provide robust Android database support.

SQLite supports three different data types: **TEXT,** which is known as a **String** value in Java, **INTEGER**, which is known as a **long** value in Java, and **REAL**, which is known as a **double** value in Java. When working in SQLite, all other data types must be converted into one of these compatible data types, before entering them into a database field.

It is important to note that SQLite doesn't validate any of the data types that may be written into its data fields (table columns) as being one of the required data types. This means that you can write an **INTEGER** value into a **TEXT** (String defined) data column, and vice versa, so you will always need to pay close attention to exactly what you are doing with SQLite for this reason. If you don't validate what you are doing using your Java code, you may get a wrong data type result written into one of your SQLite database fields!

To use SQLite in Android, you construct your SQLite statements for creating and (or) updating your database, which will then be managed by Android. When your app creates a database, the database structure will be kept in a specialized Android directory, which will always utilize the following Android OS database path address:

```
DATA/data/YOUR_APPLICATION_NAME/databases/YOUR_DATABASE_FILE_NAME
```

Next, you will take a look at the many different types of predefined Content Providers that come standard with the Android OS. You will also be looking at how these are accessed within the Android operating system and its **android.content** package. You will also be looking at the **Content Provider** and **Content Resolver** classes and methods used in Android to access its database structures.

There are a plethora of Android database structures for all of the different functional areas in the OS. This is why you are getting up to speed on this in the next section, because as you learned in the first part of the chapter, the first step in using a DBMS is understanding its database table structure.

Android Built-in Content Providers

A significant number of SQLite-based database structures are "hard-coded" into the Android OS, so that users of Android devices can handle things that they expect from a phone, iTV set, e-Reader, smartwatch, or tablet. These include contact directories, address books, calendars, camera picture storage, digital video storage, music albums, phone books, and so forth.

The most extensive of the SQLite database structures is the **Contacts** database, which contains many different tables (essentially acting as sub-databases) containing personal information, such as contact names, phone numbers, emails, preferences, social media settings, and so forth. These structures are very complex, and since this book is focused on programming for Absolute Beginners, and not database theory, you will be working with the primary contact name database, to keep it more about Java programming and Android Content Providers, rather than about database structure and theory.

The base-level interfaces of the **android.provider** package allow you to access those data structures that define the setup and personalization of each user's Android device hardware. Obviously, the data in each of these data structures will be completely different for each user's smartphone, smartwatch, tablet, phablet, e-Reader, or iTV Set.

Android 1.5 Contacts Database Contact Provider

Table 14-1 lists the now deprecated **Contacts** database interfaces for Android 1.5, 1.6, or 2.0, which can be found on the Android Developer site. Deprecated, in this case, means that this **Contacts** database has been replaced with a more modern **ContactsContract** database structure. However, the Contacts database structure is still valid, and will work just fine for those users who are still using Android OS versions 1.5, 1.6, or 2.0.

Table 14-1. *The Contacts database and its data table interfaces to be used for Android 1.5, 1.6 or 2.0 support*

Database.Table	Contents Held in this Database Table Structure
Contacts.OrganizationColumns	Organization
Contacts.GroupsColumns	Groups
Contacts.PeopleColumns	People
Contacts.PhonesColumns	Phone numbers
Contacts.PhotosColumns	Contact photographs
Contacts.PresenceColumns	IM presences
Contacts.SettingsColumns	Phone settings
Contacts.ContactMethodsColumns	Contact methods
Contacts.ExtensionsColumns	Phone extensions

The Contacts DBMS structure, shown in Table 14-1, was redone from scratch in Android 2.1. You will be taking a look at how the structure increased in complexity next.

As mentioned, if you browse the current Android Developer website documentation, you will find that these interfaces listed in Table 14-1 are all described as being deprecated. The reason that these are called **interfaces** is because they define how and where you are going to interface with the data, using the format **database.table**, so a table that has people in it is referenced using **Contacts.PeopleColumns**, as you can see in Table 14-1, row 3.

Deprecated Database Structures: Software Upgrades

Deprecated is a programming term that means that classes, methods, constants, interfaces, or databases have been replaced by other more modern programming structures. This usually happens during the release of newer versions of a programming language (such as Java) or an API (such as Android).

These newer structures replace the older structures and are usually more robust (fewer bugs) or more complex, but sometimes they differ only in how they are implemented. In the case of a database, they sometimes differ in the fields of data that are contained in the database tables.

This deprecation is exactly what has happened with the Contacts database interfaces between Android versions 1.x (1.0, 1.1, 1.5, and 1.6) and 2.0, and Android versions 2.1, 3.x, 4.x (2.1, 2.2, 2.3, 3.0, 3.1, 3.2, 4.0, 4.1, 4.2, 4.3, and 4.4) and 5.0. So database interfaces that work on Android 1.x and 2.0 phones are different than the ones that work on Android 2.1, 3.x, 4.x and 5.0 phones. The newer versions use more advanced, feature-rich database structures in **ContactsContract**.

If you are going to support 1.5, 1.6, or 2.0 phones, you need to use the database interfaces listed in Table 14-1. This book uses the Android suggested application support default settings of API Level 8 (Android 2.2) through API Level 19 (Kit Kat 4.4), as you learned in Chapter 3, so you need to use more advanced database structures that replace the original database structures in Android Level 7 (Android 2.1).

The good news is that deprecated does not mean disabled. In this case, it more accurately means, "not suggested for general use unless you need to support pre-2.1 versions for your Android users." So, if you need to support Android 1.5, 1.6, and 2.0 phones, you can use the interfaces listed in Table 14-1. Note that inside Eclipse, deprecated structures and method calls are **lined out** in the Java code, to show the developer that they are deprecated.

That can be a bit unnerving, since most devices these days are 2.3.7 through 4.4-compatible, so I suggest you take Android's "advice" and develop for API Levels 8 through 19 or later. This is suggested in the Create **New Android Application Project** series of dialogs, which you encountered in Chapter 3 (refer to Figure 3-3 to see the API Level defaults).

You will not be able to access data from newer database tables until you add support for the 2.1, 3.x, and 4.x DBMS structures in your code. You can do this by detecting which OS your user is using, and having code sections that deal with each (1.x and 2.0 versus 2.1, 3.x, 4.x or 5.x) database access structure differently, using different **ContentProvider** and **ContentResolver** code.

> **Note** If you want to be able to access every new feature, you can always have your Java code detect which version of Android a device is using, and then use custom code that delivers your optimal application functionality for each specific Android OS version.

Deprecation is a common programming situation that developers need to get used to. Hence, I am covering it here, so that as an Absolute Beginner, you can learn all about it now, and not be blind-sided by this advanced programming and application development concept later on down the line.

With Android, deprecation is especially prevalent, as different OS versions will feature different support for the hardware features that manufacturers add to their new smartphones, iTV sets, smartwatches, eBook readers, and tablets. These require new APIs, or changing the existing APIs, in order to support these new hardware features.

For instance, Android 1.5 was initially designed for use on smartphones. Android added touchscreen **gestures** in Android version 1.6, and **camera support** in version 2.0. Next, tablets and eReaders came along, and Android 3.0 added feature support for **large screen** consumer electronics devices.

Later, iTV sets came out, and so Android version 4.0 added GoogleTV support and the **TVDPI** constant for 1280 by 720p resolutions was added to the API. Next, Android game consoles, such as the nVidia Shield, came out, and faster screen refresh (60FPS) was added to Android 4.1. Likewise, faster touchscreen refresh (60FPS) was added to Android 4.2.

Recently, smartwatches and smartglasses have become popular, and so the faster Bluetooth 4.0 standard support was added into Android 4.3 and 4.4. Android 5.0 will feature new API additions that allow physical fitness hardware to be utilized with the Android OS, and so the version enhancements will go on and on, driven by the Android hardware manufacturers, which now number in the hundreds internationally, because Android is an "open" operating system platform.

Note   Over time, version functionality gets more and more difficult to keep track of. Indeed, Android already has nineteen different OS versions (API Levels) that your code must work across. Keeping track of all the current programming constructs, database structures, and logic mazes is enough of a challenge for most, without the layer on top that involves remembering which Java constructs and interfaces work, or do not work, with any given OS version. This is one of the primary reasons that Android programmers are so well compensated.

Table 14-2 lists some of the content providers that are compatible with the new Android versions (2.1 through 4.4) and that are used for manipulating contact information. A vastly different content provider database structure approach solidified in API Level 8 and beyond may well be the primary reason that the defaults in the **New Android Application Project** dialog (shown in Figure 3-3 in Chapter 3) suggests (that is, defaults to) API Level 8 through 19 support.

Table 14-2. *ContactsContract databases in the Android provider package and the type of data that they contain*

Database.Table Interface	Database Table Contents
ContactsContract.BaseSyncColumns	Generic columns used by sync adapters
ContactsContract.CommonDataKinds.BaseTypes	All typed datatypes supported
ContactsContract.CommonDataKinds.CommonColumns	Common columns across specific types
ContactsContract.ContactNameColumns	Contact name and contact name metadata columns in the RawContacts database
ContactsContract.ContactOptionsColumns	Columns of ContactsContract.Contacts that track the user preference for, or interaction with, the contact
ContactsContract.ContactsColumns	Columns of ContactsContract.Contacts refer to intrinsic contact properties
ContactsContract.ContactStatusColumns	Data used for contact's status info
ContactsContract.DataColumns	Columns (joined) from the data table
ContactsContract.DataColumnsWithJoins	Combines all Join Columns returned by ContactsContract.Data table queries
ContactsContract.DisplayNameSources	DataType used to produce display name
ContactsContract.FullNameStyle	Constant for combining into full name
ContactsContract.GroupsColumns	Data used for contact's grouping info
ContactsContract.PhoneLookupColumns	Data used for contact's phone lookups
ContactsContract.PhoneticNameStyle	Constants for pronunciation of a name
ContactsContract.PresenceColumns	Additional datalink back to **_ID** entry
ContactsContract.RawContactsColumns	Data used for the RawContact database
ContactsContract.SettingsColumns	Data used for contact's OS settings
ContactsContract.StatusColumns	Data used for social status updates
ContactsContract.StreamItemPhotosColumns	Columns in the StreamItemPhotos table
ContactsContract.StreamItemsColumns	Data columns in the StreamItems table

All of these Contact related database tables replace the deprecated versions listed in Table 14-1. If you want to look into these data tables in greater detail, detailed descriptions of these are available from the Android developer site at this link:

http://developer.android.com/reference/android/provider/package-summary.html

As you can see in Table 14-2, the **ContactsContract** database table structure is an order of magnitude more complex than the simple **Contacts** database table structure that was used prior to Android 2.1. With this complexity comes power and flexibility, but at the cost of more complex Java code needed to implement these databases and their features in your Android applications. This is a complex topic for the Absolute Beginner!

Next let's take a look at the **MediaStore** and **CalendarContract** databases and their tables, and then you will get into how to use the Uri object you learned about earlier in the book with the **content://** Content Provider URI.

The Android MediaStore Content Providers

The other collections of Content Providers that you may find important for new media content within the Android OS are the **MediaStore** Content Providers. These are listed in Table 14-3.

Table 14-3. Android MediaStore Content Providers

Database.Table Interface	Database Table Contents
MediaStore.Audio.AlbumColumns	Album information
MediaStore.Audio.ArtistColumns	Artist information
MediaStore.Audio.AudioColumns	Audio information
MediaStore.Audio.GenresColumns	Audio genre information
MediaStore.Audio.PlaylistsColumns	Audio playlist information
MediaStore.Files.FileColumns	Fields for master table for media files
MediaStore.Images.ImageColumns	Digital images
MediaStore.Video.VideoColumns	Digital video
MediaStore.MediaColumns	Generic media storage

Later in this chapter, you will look at how to declare content providers for use, access them, read them, modify them, and append to them. First, let's take a look at one more often used Android OS database, the **CalendarContract** database, and then you will look at how to use Uri objects to reference Content Providers.

The Android CalendarContract Content Providers

The **CalendarContract** databases include **eleven** calendar-related databases, each supporting various calendar functions, including events, attendees, alerts, reminders, and other similar calendar-related data support functions.

The reason that the Android operating system provides pre-built support, via its **android.provider** package, for your Android calendar database access is because it would be logical for applications that access these calendar features to be able to add customized, new capabilities to the existing Android calendar feature set.

Table 14-4 shows the **CalendarContract** Content Provider interfaces, as well as the different types of calendar functional data they access, and which they will allow you to reference directly using a Content Provider.

Table 14-4. CalendarContract databases in the Android provider package and the type of data that they contain

Database.Table Interface	Database Table Contents
CalendarContract.AttendeesColumns	Columns (joined) from attendees database
CalendarContract.CalendarAlertsColumns	Data used for calendar alerts function
CalendarContract.CalendarCacheColumns	Data used for calendar cache function
CalendarContract.CalendarColumns	Calendar columns that other URIs can query
CalendarContract.CalendarSyncColumns	Generic columns for use by sync adapters
CalendarContract.ColorsColumns	Data used for calendar colors function
CalendarContract.EventDaysColumns	Data used for calendar event day function
CalendarContract.EventsColumns	Columns (joined) from the events database
CalendarContract.ExtendedPropertiesColumns	Data Used in Calendar Extended Properties
CalendarContract.RemindersColumns	Data used for calendar reminders function
CalendarContract.SyncColumns	Sync info columns used by other databases

Next, you will take a look at how the **content://** area in Android OS is used to access these database structures using a Content Provider URI. Fortunately, you are already comfortable with Uri objects, so you have a head start!

Referencing a Content Provider: Content URI

If you want to be able to tell the Android OS what Content Provider you want to access, it is important that you understand the concept of the **Content URI**. You have used Uri objects before, so you are very familiar with the function they play in accurately referencing data (content) pathways in Android apps. Content Providers have a specialized path format. Just like the Internet's HyperText Transfer Protocol has a special format, **HTTP://**, content also has a special format that is very similar (and thus easy to remember), which is **content://**.

The complete URI for an Android Content Provider contained in a URI object will follow this data path format:

content://Authority/Path/ID

Consider in the following (hypothetical) Hello Universe Contact Galaxy database content URI:

content://com.hellouniverse.galaxydatabase/galaxy/andromeda/12345

In this imaginary URI, **com.hellouniverse.galaxydatabase** is the **Data Authority**, **galaxy/andromeda/** represents the **Data Path**, and **12345** represents the **_ID key** for the actual **Data Record**.

A Content URI will always contain four necessary parts: The **schema** to use, in this case, **content://** as well as a **data authority**, an (optional) **data path** to the data, and the **_ID** of the data record that you want to access.

The schema for Content Providers is always the word "**content**." A colon and a double forward slash (**://**) always appear in the front of the URI reference and separate the **data schema** from the **data authority**.

The next part of the URI is known as the **data authority** for the Content Provider. As you might have expected, the authority for each Content Provider must be **unique**. An authority naming convention usually follows your Java package naming conventions. Most organizations choose to use the backward dot-com domain name of their organization, plus a data qualifier for each content provider. Thus the previous example would assume that you own the **hellouniverse.com** domain name, which, of course, you do not.

Since the Android developer documentation recommends that you utilize the fully qualified class name of your **ContentProvider** subclass, you might then name your **ContentProvider** subclass **GalaxyDatabase.java** if you were following this example Content URI. I am going to use the **ContactGalaxy.java** Activity subclass name in the next section, to follow the Java class naming convention used throughout this book.

The third part of the URI standard is the **data path** to the data. Although it is optional, it is a fairly standard practice for **organizational purposes**. You would not usually put your data in the root folder of a server where it would get lost; instead, you place it in a **galaxy** folder, using sub-folders for each of the galaxy database tables. In this example, one subfolder would be a galaxy named **Andromeda**.

The Content Provider for the Android **MediaStore** (which you looked at in the previous section of the chapter) database, for example, will utilize different path names to make sure that the audio, image, and video files are kept in separate data type (data table) locations. By using different path names, one single Content Provider can accommodate many different types of data that are in some way related, such as the different new media content types, for example, kept in the **MediaStore** Content Provider in the different data tables.

For unrelated data types, it is standard programming practice that you would want to utilize a different Content Providers subclass, as well as a different data authority (and path, for that matter) for each database.

The last URI reference specification component is the **ID**, which, as you may have surmised, needs to be unique and numeric. This ID, or **_ID** in Android, is utilized whenever you want to access one single database record.

So, as you can see, the URI reference specification progresses from the most general or high-level (**content://**) specification, through the authority (server name), down through the pathway to the data (directory path), and ultimately, to the data record itself (**_ID**).

Since you are using the default OS support suggested in the New Android Application Project of API Level 8 (2.2) through API Level 19 (4.4), you will use the more modern (that is, not deprecated) Content Providers for the Android Content Provider example, which you will be creating during the rest of this chapter.

Let's get started by creating your new Activity subclass, called **ContactGalaxy.java**, and add it to your Android Manifest XML file, as well as to your application's **OptionMenu** object, using a **MenuItem** object with a menu label of "**Contact Galaxy Ruler**." For your UI design layout, take a look at the Android **TableLayout** container class, since databases use "tables" and since this is a UI layout container that you are likely going to want to use someday to format your data in a tabular format.

Creating the Activity: ContactGalaxy.java

Let's create a new Java class from scratch in the **HelloUniverse** project:

1. Right-click on the **/src** folder and select the **New ➤ Class** menu sequence to open the **New Java Class** dialog, which will allow you to access the **Package Selection** dialog and the **Superclass Selection** dialog shown in Figure 14-2.

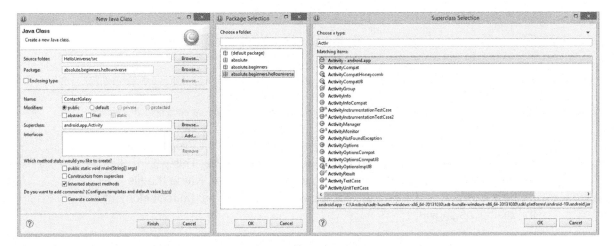

Figure 14-2. Use the New Java Class dialog to create a public ContactGalaxy.java activity subclass in Eclipse

2. Click on the **Browse** button, next to **Package,** and select the **absolute. beginners.hellouniverse** option shown in the middle of Figure 14-2. Click the **Browse** button next to **Superclass** and select the **Activity - android.app** superclass shown on the right side of Figure 14-2 to configure your new Java class for use. Name the class **ContactGalaxy**.

3. Once you click the Finish button, Eclipse will open up the empty **ContactGalaxy.java** class, shown in Figure 14-3. You can copy and paste the first four lines of Java from **MainActivity.java** and change your UI layout reference to the **activity_contact** file that you are about to create next, which for now will generate an error highlight.

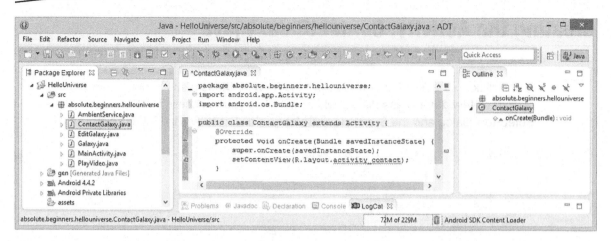

Figure 14-3. Copy an onCreate() method and change the setContentView() method to reference activity_contact

4. To generate the **activity_contact.xml** file, right-click on the **/res/layout** folder and select the **New ➤ Android XML File** menu sequence. This will invoke the **New Android XML File** dialog, shown in Figure 14-4. Name the file **activity_contact** and select the **TableLayout** container as the root element in the dialog, as shown.

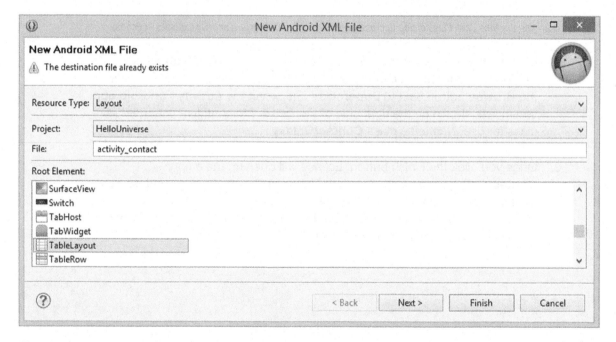

Figure 14-4. Use the New ➤ Android XML File dialog to create a <TableLayout> named activity_contact.xml

5. Once you click the **Finish** button, Eclipse will open the empty **<TableLayout>** user interface definition file, shown in Figure 14-5. As you can see, the required **xmlns:android** and **android:layout_width** parameters, as well as the **android:layout_height** parameters, are set to use the **MATCH_PARENT** constant. This will allow your UI design to be scaled up by Android to fill the display screen for your **ContactGalaxy** activity subclass.

Figure 14-5. Showing the <TableLayout> parent tag in place in the activity_contact.xml user interface definition

Next you need to add an **<activity>** tag to your **AndroidManifest.xml** file so that your application recognizes this new activity subclass. You will be doing even more configuration work in your Android Manifest XML file later on during the chapter, when you add **permissions** so that you can read and write data to a Content Provider.

Adding the ContactGalaxy Class to the Manifest

Right-click on your **AndroidManifest.xml** file and select **Open**. Add an **<activity>** tag under the **<service>** tag. Reference a **contact_galaxy** <string> constant, which you will be creating during the next steps in the work process. You will use this constant as the activity label (screen title). Set the constant up using the following XML tag and parameter, as is shown in Figure 14-6:

```
<activity android:label="@string/contact_galaxy" />
```

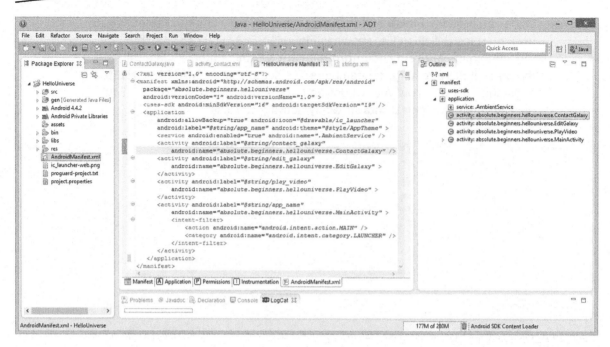

Figure 14-6. Add an <activity> child tag after the <service> child tag for the new ContactGalaxy activity subclass

Next, add in the **android:name** parameter, and reference your **ContactGalaxy** class by using your package name as the path resource qualifier. This will give the parameter the full resource path with which to reference the new class.

Your final **<activity>** tag XML markup with both of these configuration parameters installed inside of it should look like the following, as shown in Figure 14-6:

```
<activity android:label="@string/contact_galaxy"
        android:name="absolute.beginners.hellouniverse.ContactGalaxy"  />
```

Next you are going to create your MenuItem, which will allow your users to access this **ContactGalaxy** Activity subclass and its database functions using a menu title of "Contact Galaxy Ruler." This enables the application users to contact the emperor of each galaxy in their application directly. Contacting the emperors of each galaxy represents the ultimate in social media these days, as you might well imagine. Emphasis is on the word "imagine" here, of course. You will create a **<string>** constant, and reference it in the new **MenuItem** object XML definition, and finally, you will use an Intent object to access the **MenuItem** object inside of your **switch-case** statement, which is inside your **MainActivity.java** class Menu object event listening structure. Let's get started!

Adding a Contact Galaxy Ruler Item to the Menu

Right-click on your **strings.xml** file in your **/res/values** folder and **Open** it for editing. Add a **<string>** tag with the name **contact_galaxy** and a data value of **Contact Galaxy Ruler,** as shown in Figure 14-7.

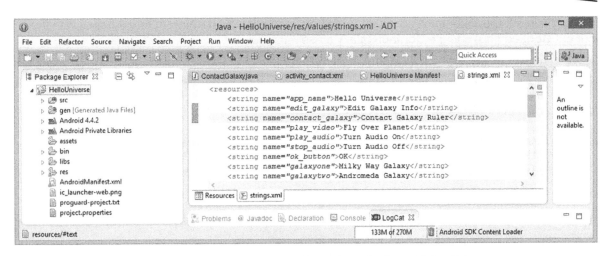

Figure 14-7. Add a <string> constant named contact_galaxy with the data value Contact Galaxy Ruler

Next, right-click on the **main.xml** Menu object definition file in the **/res/menu** folder and add a **contact_galaxy MenuItem** object. To do this, you use an **<item>** tag that is configured similar to your other menu items, as shown in Figure 14-8.

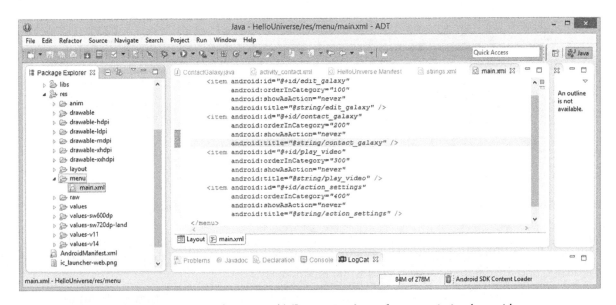

Figure 14-8. Add a MenuItem object using <item> tag with ID contact_galaxy, reference contact_galaxy <string>

Adding a Menu Intent in the MainActivity Class

Now that your **MenuItem** object is defined using XML, you can reference it in your **onOptionsItemSelected()** event handling structure in your **MainActivity.java** class. You will do this so that your users can switch over to the **ContactGalaxy** Activity subclass. Add a **case** statement for **R.id.contact_galaxy** and create a new **Intent** object named **dataIntent** using the Java **new** keyword.

Using the Intent class's **Intent()** constructor method, load this new **dataIntent** Intent object with the current **Context** (this) and the **ContactGalaxy.class** reference.

Next, you use the **.startActivity()** method call, called off your current Context object (**this**), which will then send your newly created **dataIntent** Intent object to the **ContactGalaxy** Activity subclass. This is all done using the following four lines of Java code, which create the Java switch-case structure that is shown in Figure 14-9:

```
case R.id.contact_galaxy:
        Intent dataIntent = new Intent( this, ContactGalaxy.class );
        this.startActivity( dataIntent );
        break;
```

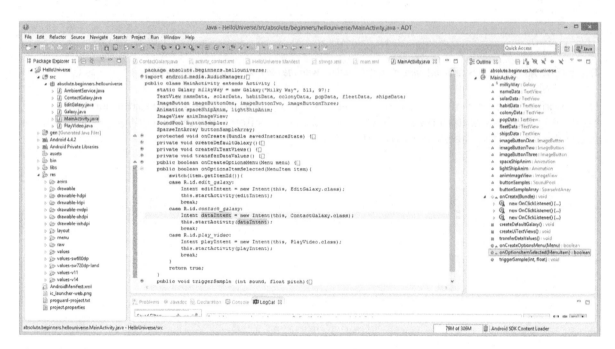

Figure 14-9. Add a case statement referencing contact_galaxy and instantiate an Intent object named dataIntent

Now that you have added the **MenuItem** object for your **Contact Galaxy Ruler** menu selection to your app's OptionMenu object structure, you have set up the infrastructure that is needed to add the UI design and the database access (and write) functionality.

Just to make sure that everything is error-free and working properly, use the **Run As ➤ Android Application** menu sequence and launch the Nexus One AVD. Click on the **OptionsMenu ActionBar Overflow Icon** (three vertical dots) and select the **Contact Galaxy Ruler** option, as shown on the left in Figure 14-10.

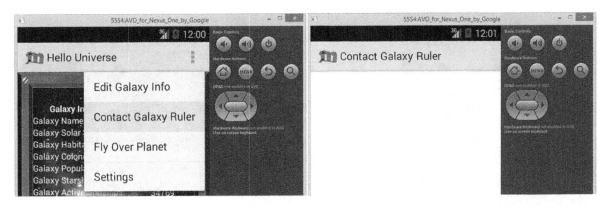

Figure 14-10. Test ContactGalaxy.java Activity subclass menu and TableLayout UI container in the Nexus One

On the right of Figure 14-10, you can see the empty (blank) TableLayout UI layout container, with the Contact Galaxy Ruler Activity screen label at the top of the app display screen that you defined in the Android Manifest XML file.

This last thing you need to do here to set up a database to use for your ContactGalaxy Activity subclass, before you write the Content Provider related Java code. Create some Galaxy Ruler contact data for your **ContactsContract** database table by using the Android Contacts utility, which you will learn how to use in the next section of the chapter.

Once you enter data into your **ContactsContract** database using the Nexus One AVD emulator, you will then be able to access the ContactsContract data table, using the Java code that you will be writing in the **ContactGalaxy.java** Activity subclass.

Creating Your Galaxy Emperor Contact Database

Now you are ready to add galaxy rulers (I hear Spock is the Emperor of Andromeda) to the Contacts database. In the Nexus One AVD, click on the Contacts Database icon, shown on the left side of Figure 14-11, to launch it.

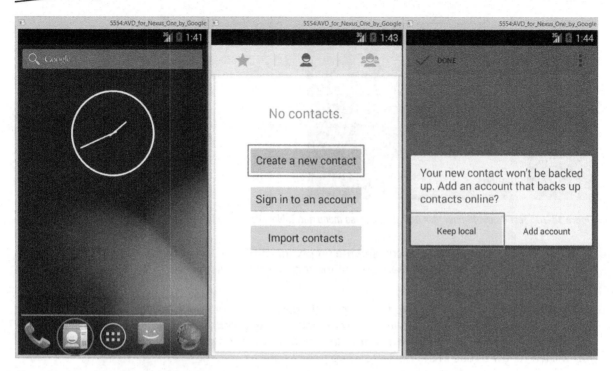

Figure 14-11. Launch the Nexus One and then click on the Contacts icon (left) and choose Create a New Contact (middle)

In case you are wondering how to get your Nexus One AVD emulator to show the standard launch screen instead of auto-running the application, remember that you can use the **Window ➤ Android Virtual Device Manager** menu sequence in Eclipse to launch your emulator without first referencing your Android development project.

Click on the **Create a new contact** button, shown in the middle pane of Figure 14-11, to add a new contact to the database table. When the "**Your new contact won't be backed up**" message, which can be seen in the right hand pane of Figure 14-11, appears, select the **Keep local** option, which will write this database table to your workstation hard disk drive.

Notice that you can use an AVD to populate your smartphone contact database by using the other **Add on-line account** option. I prefer to enter my contacts via my Galaxy Note 3 directly, so that I keep my development activities and my business contacts separate, but it is possible to bridge the two!

Now you are ready to enter your first Galaxy Ruler, **Emperor Spock** from Vulcan, into the contact database, as shown in the left pane of Figure 14-12. Use the virtual keyboard to type the name, and then click on the **Done** button to enter it. As you can see in the center pane of the figure, it will be entered into the **E** section of your **ContactsContract** database. At the bottom of that pane, you will see a smiling contact icon with a plus + sign next to it; click it to add the second contact—**Emperor James Tiberius the Fifth** of the Milky Way Galaxy.

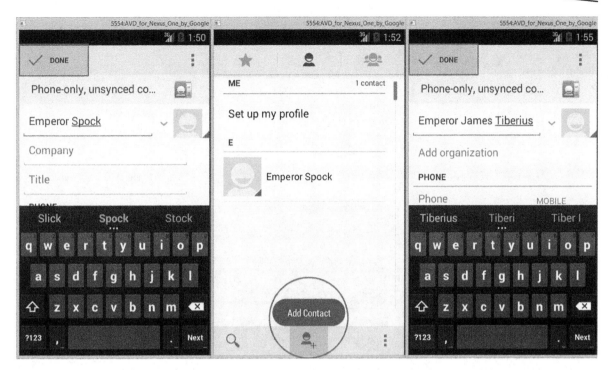

Figure 14-12. Enter Emperor Spock (left), choose Add Contact (middle), and then name the second contact Emperor James Tiberius

After you enter the USS Enterprise Captain James T. Kirk's great-grandson into your Galaxy Ruler Contacts database, click the **Done** button. Use the **Add Contact** button shown at the bottom of Figure 14-13 (left pane) to add the final ruler of the Spiral Galaxy M106, **Empress Nyota Uhura**, shown in the center pane of Figure 14-13.

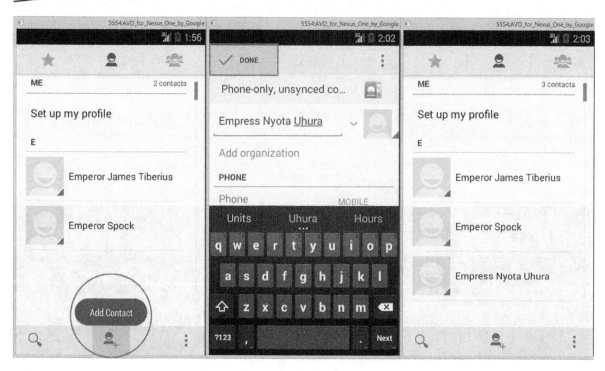

Figure 14-13. Add a third contact (left), name her Empress Nyota Uhura (middle), and view your contacts (right)

Once you have entered all three galaxy rulers, as shown in the right pane of Figure 14-13, you will have enough data to work with.

The next thing that you are going to learn how to do is to use the **Visual Android Manifest Editor** in Eclipse. Since this is an Absolute Beginner's book, you will look at how to do this the easy way. You will still look at the XML markup for the **<uses-permission>** child tags. You will do this because I am trying to get all of the readers to a more and more advanced place within your Android application development knowledge as this book progresses. I would like to take you all from being an Absolute Beginner to being a rock solid application developer, because there is an amazing amount of revenue to be generated out there in today's digital marketplace using the Android OS platform.

Adding Permissions in the AndroidManifest

Click on your **HelloUniverse Manifest** tab, shown in the middle of the five tabs you have open so far in Figure 14-14.

1. In the central editing area of Eclipse, click on the **Permissions** tab, this time at the bottom of the editing pane, to switch the editing pane into an **Android Manifest Permissions** Visual Editor mode. Click the **Add** button shown in Figure 14-14. Note that if you mouse over UI elements, you will get pop-up explanations of what they do.

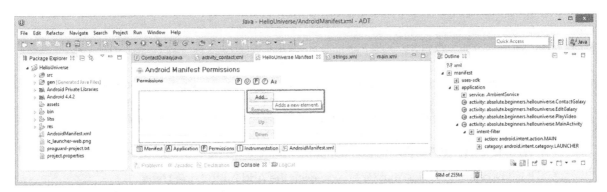

Figure 14-14. Click the HelloUniverse Manifest tab (top) and then the Permissions tab (bottom), and then click the Add button

2. Clicking the **Add** button will open this **Add Permissions** dialog, shown in Figure 14-15.

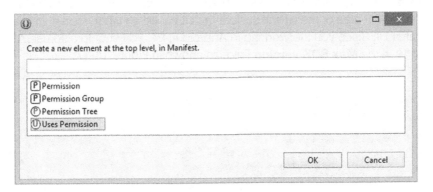

Figure 14-15. Select the Uses Permission option from the Add Permissions dialog

3. Select the **Uses Permission** tag, and click the **OK** button. This will add the **<uses-permission>** tag to your XML definition, and will insert it in the **Permissions** area of the visual editor, as can be seen in Figure 14-16. Select a **READ_CONTACTS** database permission constant from the permission type **Name** drop-down menu.

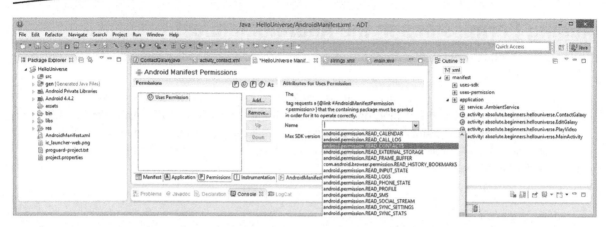

Figure 14-16. Select the READ_CONTACTS constant attribute for the Uses Permissions tag from the drop-down list

4. Now you have added a **READ** database permission for the **ContactsContract** database. While you are here, you might as well add the **WRITE** database permission for the **ContactsContract** database. Click on the **Add** button, and again add a **<uses-permission>** tag, this time selecting the **WRITE_CONTACTS** permission constant from the **Name** drop-down menu.

5. It is important to notice that when you click the **Add** button, the **Uses Permission** entry in the Permissions List area on the left changes to use the more detailed **android.permission** description entry of **READ_CONTACTS**. If you want the second Uses Permission entry to show a change after you select the drop-down menu option for **WRITE_CONTACTS**, simply click on the Uses Permissions tag in the list area. It will then update itself based on what you have set in the right side of this visual permissions editor. As you can see, any click in the left area of the UI will update the UI based on what you set in the right area UI. Since you are working in Android 4.4.4, you should also use **API Level 19** in the **Max SDK version** field, as shown in Figure 14-17.

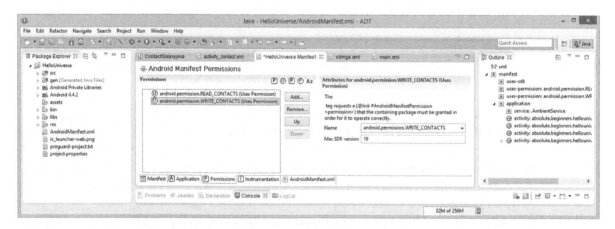

Figure 14-17. Click an Add button to add another Uses Permission tag and then set a WRITE_CONTACTS attribute

6. Once you have added your permissions, click on the **AndroidManifest.xml** tab at the bottom of the editing area and switch into XML editing mode. Take a look at the two new **<uses-permissions>** tags and the parameters that the Manifest Visual Editor has created for you. Your application now has "permission" to use this database. See Figure 14-18.

Figure 14-18. Click the bottom AndroidManifest.xml tab to show the XML mark-up for the <uses-permission> tag

Next, you are going to learn about Android's **TableLayout** class, so that you can create the ContactGalaxy UI design.

TableLayout: Creating Tabular UI Designs

The Android **TableLayout** class is a good layout container ViewGroup subclass to learn about in this chapter, as databases use a **tabular format**, and that is what the **TableLayout** class is optimized to provide. Even though it is subclassed from the **LinearLayout** class, as you will soon see, it is quite similar to the **GridLayout** container. The **TableLayout** class is most likely going to be used for applications that need to create "spreadsheet-like" tables of information. As such, it is a logical fit for use with databases, and a good UI layout container class to learn about in this chapter.

The **TableLayout** class is subclassed from the **LinearLayout** class, which you have already read about, so you will use this layout container to create a single-column table for the database access functions. You will use **Button** UI elements as the widgets inside of the table layout container, so that users can click on these Button UI elements to be able to invoke changes to the database.

The **TableLayout** class is a **public** class that extends **LinearLayout**, so its class hierarchy is as follows:

```
java.lang.Object
  > android.view.View
    > android.view.ViewGroup
      > android.widget.LinearLayout
        > android.widget.TableLayout
```

The **TableLayout** container arranges its child UI widgets by using **rows** and **columns**. A **TableLayout** UI design will usually contain a collection of **TableRow** objects, similar to how a **<Table>** tag in HTML contains **<TR>** tags. The **TableRow** object will define a **row** that will contain its own child widgets, again just like HTML.

Like the **GridLayout** container, the **TableLayout** container does not display border lines for its rows or columns. Each row has zero (which is one in programmer numbering) or more cells. Each cell will hold one View object. The number of **columns** that a **TableLayout** will have is defined by the row that has the most cells (columns). You can leave cells empty in a **TableLayout** if you like. **TableLayout** cells can **span** more than one column, just like they can in HTML. A width of a column is defined using the row with the widest cell.

A **TableLayout** can specify individual columns as shrinkable or stretchable using a **.setColumnShrinkable()** or **.setColumnStretchable()** method call. If it is earmarked as shrinkable, a column width can be shrunk to fit the table into its parent container. If it is earmarked as stretchable, it can expand its width to fit all extra space. The total width of a **TableLayout** will be defined by the parent container, which in this case is the **ContactGalaxy** activity's screen. Columns can be defined to be both shrinkable and stretchable. If you do this, the column changes size to always use any available space. You can also collapse (hide) a column by calling a **.setColumnCollapsed()** method.

Child widgets in a **TableLayout** may not specify a **layout_width** attribute. Width defaults to the **match_parent** constant. A **layout_height** attribute may be defined by child widgets; the default value will be **wrap_content**. If the child object is defined as a **TableRow** object, the height must be set to be **wrap_content**. Cells are added to rows using an increasing column order, both in Java code and XML. Column numbering is zero-based. If you do not specify column numbers for the child cells, they will be auto-incremented by the **TableLayout** engine (algorithm).

If you skip any column number, it will be considered to be an empty cell in that row. Although the typical child of a **TableLayout** is a **TableRow**, you can use a View subclass directly (without wrapping it in a **TableRow**) as a child widget in your **TableLayout** UI. A View will be displayed as a single row that spans all the table columns. Now you have the knowledge to be able to complete the inside of your **TableLayout** UI design in the next section.

Creating Your TableLayout UI for ContactGalaxy

First, create five **<string>** constants in your **strings.xml** file in the **/res/values** folder to serve as your Button UI element labels, as shown in Figure 14-19. These will list all of the galaxy rulers, add Viceroys for each galaxy, and return the user to the Home Galaxy (application home screen or the **MainActivity** class).

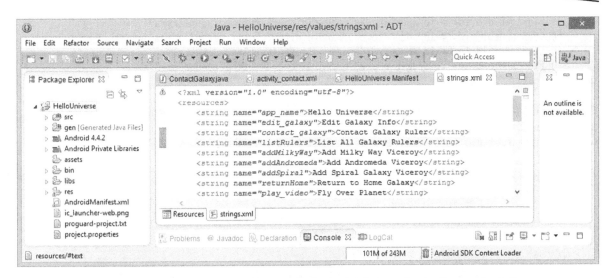

Figure 14-19. Add five <string> constants to the strings.xml file for the database read and write operation buttons

Next, add five child **<Button>** UI widgets in the **activity_contact.xml** file in the **/res/layout** folder to serve as your Button UI elements. Configure them using only the **android:id** and **android:text** parameters, as shown in Figure 14-20. Use ID names and reference values that match the ones you used in your **strings.xml** file. These **<Button>** configurations are quite simple, because the **TableLayout** class takes care of the layout parameter default settings!

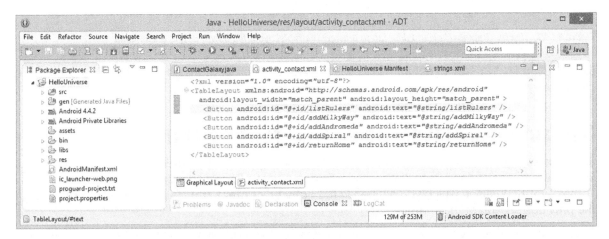

Figure 14-20. Add five child <Button> tags inside the <TableLayout> with only basic ID and text label parameters

The XML markup for the **<TableLayout>** parent tag and the five child **<Button>** tags looks like the following:

```xml
<?xml version="1.0" encoding="utf-8"?>
<TableLayout xmlns:android="http://schemas.android.com/apk/res/android"
    android:layout_width="match_parent" android:layout_height="match_parent" >
    <Button android:id="@+id/listRulers" android:text="@string/listRulers" />
```

```
        <Button android:id="@+id/addMilkyWay" android:text="@string/addMilkyWay" />
        <Button android:id="@+id/addAndromeda" android:text="@string/addAndromeda" />
        <Button android:id="@+id/addSpiral" android:text="@string/addSpiral" />
        <Button android:id="@+id/returnHome" android:text="@string/returnHome" />
</TableLayout>
```

Once this is all in place, click on the Graphical Layout Editor tab at the bottom of the editing pane and preview the **TableLayout** UI design. As you can see in Figure 14-21, the results are professional with very little markup.

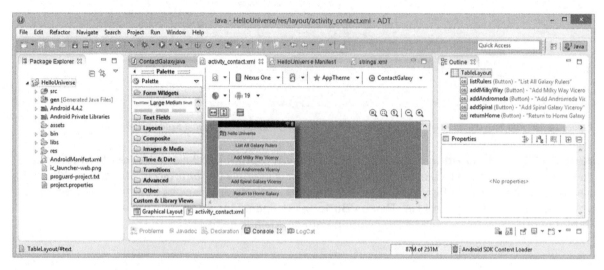

Figure 14-21. Use the Graphical Layout Editor tab to preview the TableLayout filled with Button UI elements

Now you are finally ready to get into Java coding, and write programming logic that will access these databases.

ContactGalaxy Class: Accessing Your Database

As you know by now, the first step in the process of coding your **ContactGalaxy.java** Activity subclass is to declare and instantiate your UI Button objects. These are contained inside the parent **TableLayout** container, which you defined in the **activity_contact.xml** file in the **/res/layout** folder in the previous section of the chapter.

Declare all five of your Button objects at the top of your **ContactGalaxy** class by using the one class declaration with multiple object names trick that I explained earlier in this book. This can be done by using the following single line of Java code, which is shown in Figure 14-22:

```
Button listButton, milkyWayButton, andromedaButton, spiralButton, homeButton;
```

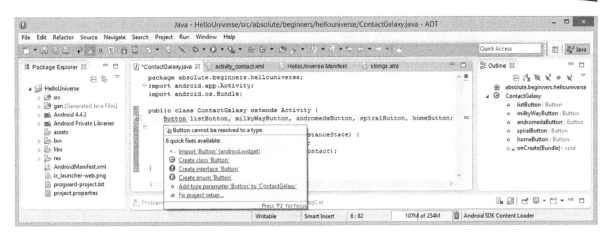

Figure 14-22. *Declare Button objects named listButton, milkyWayButton, andromedaButton, spiralButton, and HomeButton*

As you can see in Figure 14-22, you will first need to mouse over the wavy red error highlighting and select the **Import 'Button' (android.widget)** option to have Eclipse write the **import android. widget.Button;** statement that can be seen at the top of Figure 14-23. Once this is done, you can instantiate the **listButton** Button object by using the following two lines of Java code; the first instantiates an object and a second sets up an event handler:

```
Button listButton = (Button)findViewById(R.id.listRulers);
listButton.setOnClickListener( new View.OnClickListener() {  Your event handler onClick method will
go in here  });
```

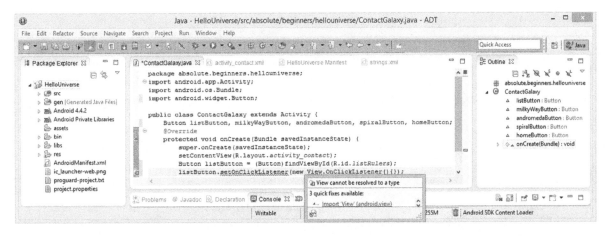

Figure 14-23. *Instantiate a listButton Button object and call a .setOnClickListener() method using the Java new keyword*

Once this infrastructure is in place, you can mouse over the wavy red error highlighting under the View class reference and select an **Import 'View' (android.view)** option. This will write the **import android.view.View;** statement. After this **import** statement is in place, you can again mouse over the remaining error and select the **Add unimplemented methods** option to write the bootstrap (empty) **onClick()** method for your event handler.

Inside the **onClick()** method, you are going to use the Activity class's **.finish()** method call. What this method call does, if your Activity was called from another Activity using an Intent object, is return you to that original Activity! See Figure 14-24.

Figure 14-24. Add an unimplemented method and replace the comment with a call to the Activity class's .finish() method

For now, you will use the .finish() method in all of the event handling methods, as seen in Figure 14-25. I'm doing this so there is functional code in the Button UI constructs, which will allow you to put all the Button event handling constructs into place. Then you can replace the **.finish()** method call with the database access programming logic as you implement the **listButton** through the **spiralButton**. This is a pretty cool coding trick!

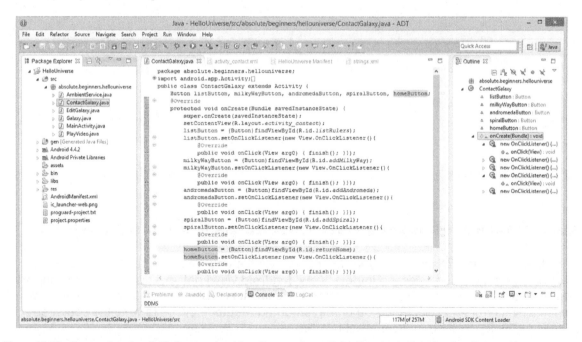

Figure 14-25. Copy and paste a listButton construct four times underneath itself to create the other four Button objects

Now it is time to get into the most difficult sections of this chapter—the Java code necessary to implement the **ContentProvider** and **ContentResolver** objects to access database structures in the Android OS.

Using the Android ContentResolver Class

Since resolving a Content Provider in Android takes more than one or two lines of code, in fact it, will involve a "do while" type of loop to read through the database records one by one, you should change the **.finish()** method call in the **listButton** object event handler to be a **listGalaxyRulers()** method call instead, as shown in Figure 14-26.

Figure 14-26. Replace the finish() method call with a listGalaxyRulers() method call and select Create Method in type

When you mouse over the currently nonexistent method and get the error message, "**The method listGalaxyRulers() is undefined for the type new View.OnClickListener()**", there are two options. The first—**Create method 'listGalaxyRulers()'**—will create an **inner private method** inside of your event handler structure. The second—**Create method 'listGalaxyRulers()' in type 'ContactGalaxy'**—will create the standard method type (outside of the event handler method) at the end of the class, as you have been doing thus far in the book.

You will use the **second option**, so that the event handler logic can call the **listGalaxyRulers()** method if it is needed. If you use the first option, only the **listButton** event handling structure will be able to see and access the method code block. If you use the first option, the method will be declared **private void listGalaxyRulers()** and it will be written underneath where it is being called in the event handler structure, you can try this option and see if you like it. The second option declares the method to be **protected void listGalaxyRulers(),** with visibility to the rest of your class. It places it at the bottom of your class, where all the other methods can access it if needed.

As you can see in Figure 14-27, Eclipse writes the bootstrap programming structure for the **listGalaxyRulers()** method for you at the end of the **ContactGalaxy** class, complete with a placeholder comment where your Java programming logic needs to be written. You will be replacing this comment with the database access Java code.

Figure 14-27.   The bootstrap method created by Eclipse at the end of the ContactGalaxy.java class listing

The first step will be to declare and instantiate a Cursor object named **rulerCursor** and load it with the database content you are going to list using the **getContentResolver().query()** method call chain. To do so, use the following line of Java code, which is shown in Figure 14-28 along with a URI pop-up helper dialog that contains the URIs:

```
Cursor rulerCursor = getContentResolver().query( ContactsContract.Contacts.CONTENT_URI, null, null,
null, null );
```

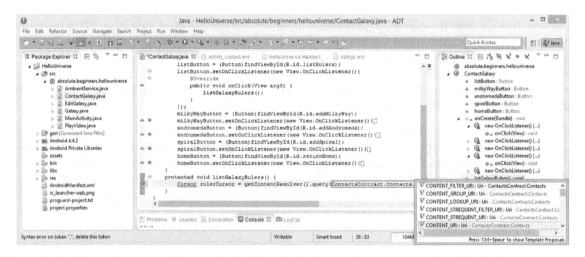

Figure 14-28.   Declare a Cursor object named rulerCursor and instantiate it using getContentResolver().query()

As you can see in Figure 14-28, once you type the **ContactsContract.Contacts** (database.table) reference in the **.query()** method parameter list, and then press the **period** key, a list of possible URIs will then appear. Find the **CONTENT_URI** option and select it by double-clicking it to insert that into your method call parameter. This will create the first ContactsContract.Contacts.CONTENT_URI parameter for your method parameter list.

As you can see in Figure 14-29, you will need to mouse over the error highlighting under the Cursor object, and choose the **Import 'Cursor' (android.database)** to import the Cursor class for use. Also notice that the four parameter options for the **getContentResolver().query()** method call have been named for you, and are also error underlined. This is to show you that there needs to be some valid data in these in order for the method call to be valid, even if this is a "**null**" (which will serve as an unused parameter indicator) data value.

Figure 14-29. Import the Cursor class; the projection, selection, selectionArgs, and sortOrder parameters

Since this chapter does not cover advanced SQL database concepts, such as projection, selection arguments, and sorting orders, you are going to be using **null** values in these optional database query parameters, as can be seen in the completed and error-free (but not warning-free) line of code seen in Figure 14-30. If you mouse over the warning, you will see the standard "**The value of the local variable rulerCursor is not used**" warning. Since you will be using the **rulerCursor** Cursor object in the next line of code, ignore this warning for now. It is now time to create a do-while loop construct, which will read through the now loaded **ContentResolver**.

Figure 14-30. The complete rulerCursor Cursor object configuration and the Eclipse warning message

In the Android OS, a do-while loop begins with the keyword **while** and then something to evaluate. In this case that will be whether your **Cursor** object, which is used to **traverse** or read through the database content, has reached the end of the database. This happens when the Cursor object reaches the last (final) record in the database and cannot read another record, much like reaching the EOF (End Of File) character when reading a file. In pseudo-code, the do-while loop structure, which you are going to write next, will equate to the following logic:

```
While (there is still another record to moveToNext to, and therefore to be able to read) Do the
things inside parens {
Create a String object to hold my Galaxy Ruler Name Data, and place the name data from a database
Column into it;
Use Android Toast Class, and its .makeText() method, to write this value to the display screen using
a long duration }
```

The first part of the **while** loop is the evaluation logic and is coded using the following line of Java code:

```
while (rulerCursor.moveToNext()) { the programming logic regarding what to do as the while loop is
in progress}
```

As you can see in Figure 14-31, if you type the **while** keyword, put the **rulerCursor** Cursor object inside of the evaluation parentheses, and then press the period key and type the letter "m," you will get a pop-up helper dialog with all of the Android Cursor class **.move()** method calls. The one that you use in a **while** loop is the **.moveToNext()** method call, which is highlighted for selection in Figure 14-31. Double-click on it to select it for use and you will be ready to code the inside of the **while** loop!

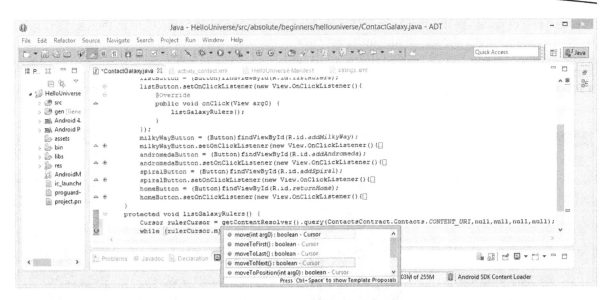

Figure 14-31. Create a while loop structure, and in the evaluation part of the loop, call .moveToNext() off rulerCursor

Inside of your **while** loop construct, inside of those **{}** curly braces, is the Java programming logic that will be executed during each "pass" of the loop. The **while** loop will continue to execute these statements as long as your Cursor object finds data records inside of a database that it can read, that is, until it reaches the last data record. The first line of Java code declares a String object. Name it **rulerName** and set it equal to the ruler name data in the database by calling a **.getString()** method, off of the **rulerCursor** object, and calling a **.getColumnIndex()** method off of the same object inside of the **.getString()** method call to read the database, as seen in Figure 14-32:

```
String rulerName = rulerCursor.getString(rulerCursor.getColumnIndex(ContactsContract.Contacts.
DISPLAY_NAME_PRIMARY));
```

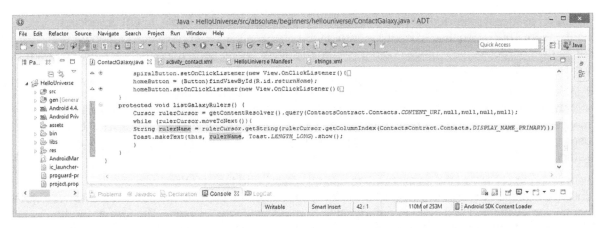

Figure 14-32. Inside the while loop create a String object named rulerName, load it with .getString(), and Toast it

The next line of code will use the Android **Toast** class to write the ruler name data to the user's display screen, as each record is processed. The **Toast** class is used to construct View object that contains a system broadcast message for your users. When this View object is displayed to your users, it will appear as an oval floating over the bottom of your application. If you want to look ahead and see what a **Toast** broadcast message looks like, there is one in Figure 14-33 on the bottom-right side.

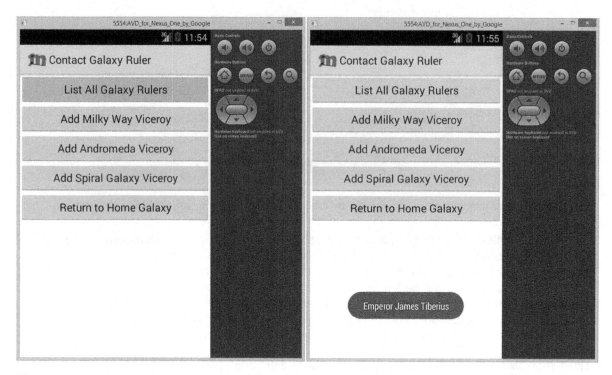

Figure 14-33. Use Nexus One AVD to test the List All Galaxy Rulers Button (left) and Toast of Ruler names (right)

A **Toast** broadcast message is unable to receive focus because it is simply an OS broadcast notification. This is because when the Android OS broadcasts a **Toast** message, which it often does for its own purposes, your users could be in the middle of typing something that requires constant focus (the OS kind, not the user's focus!).

The no focus for **Toast** broadcast messages concept here is to be as unobtrusive as possible while still showing the user the required information. Another example of the use of **Toast** broadcast message implementation is a brief message saying that your settings have been saved if the user uses your Setting menu option for your application and changes one of the global application settings.

I am going to show you the easiest way to use this class, and the standard way that it is used, by calling the static **.makeText()** method off of the **Toast** object itself. This will construct a **Toast** object containing everything you need to broadcast your messages to your users. The format for the **Toast.makeText()** method call and its three parameters, as well as a chained **.show()** method call off of the **Toast** object to show the message on the user's display screen, looks like the following Java code, also shown in Figure 14-32:

```
Toast.makeText( this,  rulerName,  Toast.LENGTH_LONG ).show();
```

This passes your **Context** object, using a Java **this** keyword, along with what you want to **Toast**, the **rulerName String** object, and the **LENGTH_LONG** duration constant, which is also accessed using dot notation off of the **Toast** object (class). I clicked on the **rulerName** String object in Figure 14-32 to show the object instantiation (initial tan highlight) and usage (second grey highlight) tracking. Eclipse will do this for you if you ask it to by clicking on any object declared in your Java code.

Now you are ready to test the List All Galaxy Rulers UI button in your ContactsGalaxy Activity subclass using the **Run As ➤ Android Application** menu sequence, as shown in Figure 14-33. Select the Contact Galaxy Rulers option from your OptionsMenu in the ActionBar Overflow (three dots) icon and run your TableLayout.

As you can see on the left side of Figure 14-33, your TableLayout does a good job creating your database access UI design, using only a half dozen lines of code. Click the **List All Galaxy Rulers** UI button element and you will see the Galaxy Ruler names that are currently in the database appear on the bottom of the screen in **Toast** broadcast message format. This can be seen on the right side of the figure at the bottom.

Writing to a Database: addGalaxyViceroy()

Now you are ready to go to the next level of database access and write new values into the Contacts database.

This is more complex, as well as more advanced, because the **WRITE** operation can change the database, and is thus termed a **destructive** database operation in the database industry. Conversely, a database **READ** operation is inherently **non-destructive**, as the data is only read, and does not change!

In this section of the chapter, you are going to create another custom method for your **ContactGalaxy** activity subclass, this time to write new **Viceroy** colony rulers into the Galaxy Ruler Contacts database, which you are creating here as an example of how to work with Android **ContentProvider** databases using **ContentResolver** objects.

Just like you did in the previous section, change the **.finish()** method call in the **milkyWayButton onClick()** event handler method to an **addGalaxyViceroy()** method call. This will force Eclipse to create your bootstrap method structure for you. As shown in Figure 14-34, you will select the second "**Create method in type ContactGalaxy.**"

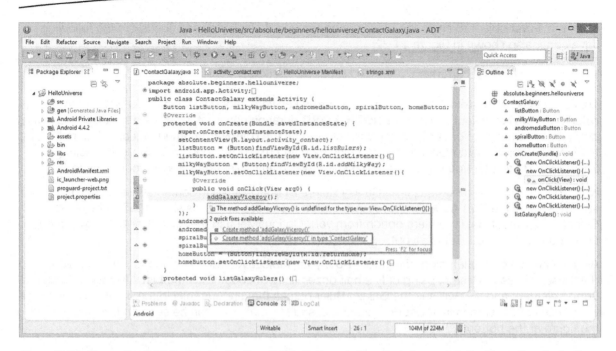

Figure 14-34. *Change the .finish() method call in the milkyWayButton event handler to be an addGalaxyViceroy() method call*

In the **addGalaxyViceroy()** method, declare a **ContentValues** object named **viceroyContact**
and then use a **new** keyword to call the **ContentValues()** constructor method to create the
ContentValues object, as shown in Figure 14-35.

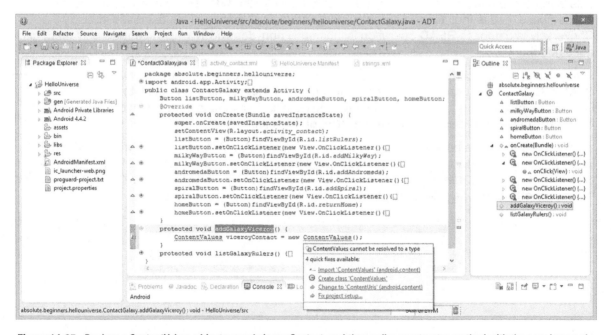

Figure 14-35. *Declare a ContentValues object named viceroyContact, and then call a constructor method with the new keyword*

Mouse over the wavy red error highlighting and select the **Import 'ContentValues' (android.content)** option. Call the **.put()** method off the **viceroyContact ContentValues** object to put a value in the **RawContacts** database. See Figure 14-36.

Figure 14-36. Call a .put() method off of the viceroyContact ContentValues object and load the RawContacts DB

Add a **String** object named **electedViceroy** to the **addGalaxyViceroy()** parameter list, and then reference this **electedViceroy** String object in the **.put()** method call to put the Viceroy's name into the **RawContacts** database. See Figure 14-37.

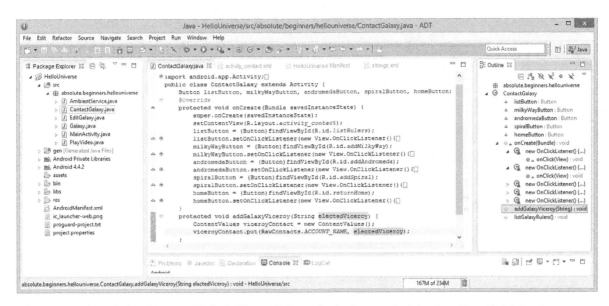

Figure 14-37. Add a String object named electedViceroy to the method call parameter list and .put() method data value

Since you added an electedViceroy name **String** to the **addGalaxyViceroy** method to pass it into the **RawContacts** database, let's also add new Viceroy names (using quotes) in your three method calls, as shown in Figure 14-38.

Figure 14-38. Add String values to the addGalaxyViceroy() method calls in the three button event handler structures

Copy the **.put()** method call that loads the **RawContacts.ACCOUNT_NAME** table with the Viceroy name and paste it underneath itself. Change **ACCOUNT_NAME** to **ACCOUNT_TYPE** in order to put the name into this data table. Next, create a **Uri** object named **newUri** and load it with the **getContentResolver().insert()** method call. Insert the **viceroyContact ContentValues** object into the **RawContacts** database using the **CONTENT_URI**. See Figure 14-39.

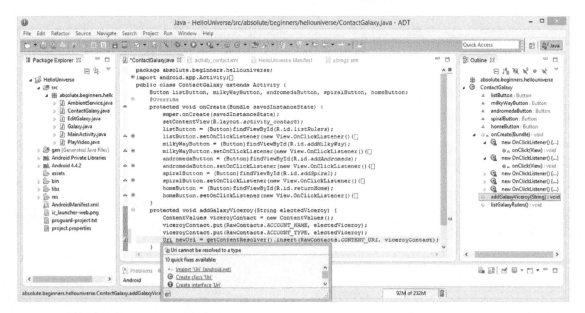

Figure 14-39. Create Uri object named newUri and use the getContentResolver().insert() method chain to load it

What you just accomplished, in a very complicated nutshell, was create a **ContentValues** object to hold your content values, load it with your **electedViceroy** name data, using the **.put()** method calls, and load these content values into the **RawContacts** database using the **getContentResolver(). insert()** method call. Finally, you loaded all of that into the Uri object named **newUri**, which you are about to convert into a different type of data value.

Now that you have a URI loaded with the **RawContacts CONTENT_URI** and Viceroy name String data, declare a long variable named **rawContactsId** and load it with the result (using the equals evaluator) of the **ContentUris** class's **.parseId()** method call. You will pass the **ContentUris. parseId()** method the **newUri Uri** object that you just created as its parameter. Finally, **clear** the **viceroyContact ContentValues** object by calling the **.clear()** method off of it, which will empty all of the data that you just loaded it with in the previous (first) four lines of Java code, and will thereby clear it for its next use (during the next four lines of Java code).

Your Java code should look like the following structure, which is shown in Figure 14-40:

```java
protected void addGalaxyViceroy(String electedViceroy) {
    ContentValues viceroyContact = new ContentValues();
    viceroyContact.put(RawContacts.ACCOUNT_NAME, electedViceroy);
    viceroyContact.put(RawContacts.ACCOUNT_TYPE, electedViceroy);
    Uri newUri = getContentResolver().insert(RawContacts.CONTENT_URI, viceroyContact);
    long rawContactsId = ContentUris.parseId(newUri);
    viceroyContact.clear();
}
```

Figure 14-40. Create a long variable named rawContactsId and set it equal to a result of ContentUris.parseId(newUri)

Next, you are going to use the **rawContactsId** long data value to put all of this Viceroy name data into the **Data** database using the **RAW_CONTACT_ID** key (_ID) constant. You will again use the **.put()** method, called off of your **viceroyContact** ContentValues object, as shown in Figure 14-41. Now the Viceroy is loaded in the data table.

Figure 14-41. Call the .clear() method and the .put() method off of a viceroyContact object. Import the Data class

Use another **.put()** method call to load the **Data.MIMETYPE** data field with the **CONTENT_ITEM_TYPE** MIME type using the **StructuredName** class, as shown in Figure 14-42. Mouse over and import this class for use.

Figure 14-42. Add another .put() method call and then mouse over to add Import statement for the StructuredName class

Next you will use the **.put()** method call again to place the Viceroy name into the **StructuredName** database. You use the **DISPLAY_NAME** constant, as shown in Figure 14-43, in the **StructuredName** pop-up helper dialog.

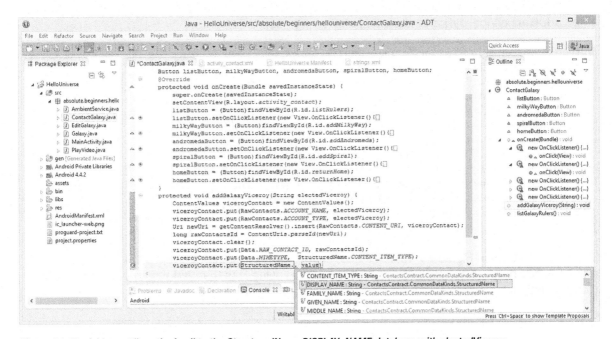

Figure 14-43. Add a .put() method call to the StructuredName.DISPLAY_NAME database with electedViceroy

Once the **viceroyContact** ContentValues object has once again been fully loaded for use, you will again use the **getContentResolver().insert()** method call chain to insert this **viceroyContact ContentValues** object into the **Data** database using the **CONTENT_URI** data field. The Java code is highlighted in Figure 14-44.

Figure 14-44. Call a getContentResolver().insert() method call chain with a viceroyContact ContentValues object

Finally, you will use another **Toast.makeText()** method call with the current Context object (this), the **electedViceroy** String data, and the **LENGTH_LONG** constant. This will tell the user that you have written your newly elected Viceroy's name into the database as requested. The final code for the entire **addGalaxyViceroy()** method is as follows:

```java
protected void addGalaxyViceroy(String electedViceroy) {
   ContentValues viceroyContact = new ContentValues();
   viceroyContact.put(RawContacts.ACCOUNT_NAME, electedViceroy);
   viceroyContact.put(RawContacts.ACCOUNT_TYPE, electedViceroy);
   Uri newUri = getContentResolver().insert(RawContacts.CONTENT_URI, viceroyContact);
   long rawContactsId = ContentUris.parseId(newUri);
   viceroyContact.clear();
   viceroyContact.put(Data.RAW_CONTACT_ID, rawContactsId);
   viceroyContact.put(Data.MIMETYPE,  StructuredName.CONTENT_ITEM_TYPE);
   viceroyContact.put(StructuredName.DISPLAY_NAME, electedViceroy);
   getContentResolver().insert(Data.CONTENT_URI, viceroyContact);
   Toast.makeText(this, electedViceroy + " has been elected", Toast.LENGTH_LONG).show();
}
```

The code is shown in Figure 14-45, error-free, and is ready to test in the Nexus One AVD emulator. You have written a database **WRITE** method using less than a dozen lines of Java code! Congratulations!

Figure 14-45. Add a Toast.makeText() method call with LENGTH_LONG constant and reference electedViceroy

Now use the **Run As ➤ Android Application** menu sequence and launch the Nexus One AVD. Select the **Contact Galaxy Rulers** menu item and fire up the **ContactGalaxy** Activity and your **TableLayout** UI design.

Click on each of the Add Galaxy Viceroy Button UI elements and make sure that the **Toast** broadcast messages appear on the screen. Then test the database write (add) by clicking the first List All Galaxy Rulers Button UI element. Make sure that all of the Emperors and Viceroys are listed, as they now should be. Finally, test the fifth UI Button element and make sure that the **.finish()** method call returns you to the **MainActivity.java** class. If it does, you have successfully implemented database reading and writing in your application. See Figure 14-46.

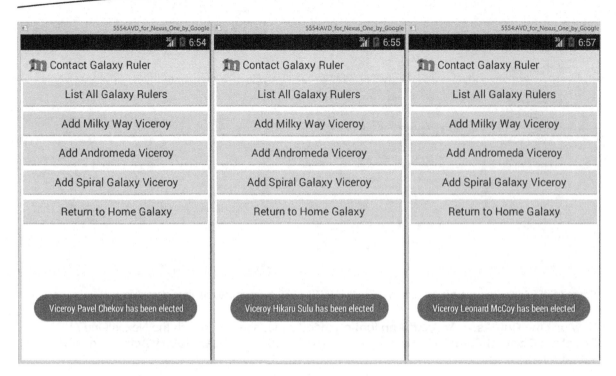

Figure 14-46. Test the middle three button elements in your UI design

Now you can get into developing for Android wearable devices and Android appliances in the next two chapters! Hooray!

Summary

In this chapter, you learned about Android **Content Provider** databases as well as about **database** concepts, principles, processes, and optimization. You learned about **ContentValues** objects and how to use the **getContentResolver()** method and its **.query()** and **.insert()** method calls. You learned all about different types of databases that come with Android, including **Contacts**, **ContactsContract**, **CalendarContract**, and **MediaStore**. You learned about **CONTENT_URI** and about what makes up a URI data path reference.

You created your own database access Activity subclass called **ContactGalaxy** to read from and write to the **ContactsContract** database in Android. You learned about the **TableLayout** container class and how easy it is to use to make tabular layouts using just a few lines of XML markup. Then you created the infrastructure for your **ContactGalaxy** class and created your **listGalaxyRulers()** database **READ** method and **addGalaxyViceroy()** database WRITE method. You used these methods inside your Button object event handlers to read and write the **ContactsContract** database in Android.

In Chapter 15, you will learn all about developing for Android wearables, which is an advanced area that includes all of the areas covered in the book thus far. I saved this most complicated chapter for last. You will be developing an application for the popular Neptune Pine SmartWatch product, so exciting times lie ahead!

Developing for Android Wearable Devices

This chapter looks at how to develop applications for Android **wearable** devices, which at the time of the writing of this book, is primarily dominated by the **smartwatch** product vertical. This market will eventually include **smartglasses** as well as other wearable devices, once the pricing of these smartglasses products becomes reasonable. Currently, smartglasses cost thousands of dollars!

This chapter covers the different types of wearables, the different manufacturer approaches to creating wearable products, and the different ways to develop for wearable devices that run Android. It is also important to note that there are other wearable OSs, so you will also encounter wearable products that run HTML5-based OSs such as Tizen OS. An example of a Tizen smartwatch is Samsung's Galaxy Gear 2. The Galaxy Gear 1 uses Android OS as its development platform, and a majority of the smartwatch products out there currently use Android 4.x as their core OS as well.

This chapter begins with a high-level overview of exactly what an Android wearable is. It explains what **True Android** wearable versus Android wearable **peripherals** means, the Android application development considerations for wearable products, how to optimize your Android application for the wearable environment, and the different kinds of Android wearable APIs, including the "normal" Android API, Android Wear SDK, and custom wearable SDK add-ons for wearables.

After that, you will create an **absolute.beginners.EarthTime** package and **EarthTime** application using the **New ➤ Android Application** series of dialogs, which will add the "planet" theme to your galaxy applications. Since you are allowed to use imagery from the NASA website for educational purposes, you will make a custom Earth smartwatch face for the popular Neptune Pine smartwatch. That smartwatch product does not require you to install the Wear SDK, or add any SDK add-ons, into your existing Android SDK installation. This way, you can simply continue using the Eclipse ADT installation that you have been using all along to develop your Neptune Pine smartwatch app. You will be installing the Wear SDK in Chapter 16, however, as it became available as I was writing that chapter on Android 5.0.

After you have created the EarthTime app and its EarthTime.APK using the standard **MainActivity. java** Activity subclass and **activity_main.xml** user interface design definition, you will create graphics design elements that are optimized for the Neptune smartwatch platform. You can develop this app for all Android devices, thanks to Neptune Pine using the Android 4.1.2 API Level 16. You will create the graphics at an even multiple of 240 pixels (for a square watch face), so that you will also have 480, 960, and even 1920 versions available for release on other device types, such as iTV Sets, tablets, eReaders, smartphones, car dashboards, game consoles and the like.

True Wearables versus Android Peripherals

In the world of Android wearables, and even in the world of Android appliances in some cases, which we will be covering in the next chapter, there can often be a distinction that you need to be aware of as an Android applications developer.

The manufacturers of Android wearable hardware products may have a vested interest in wanting to "hide" this distinction, as customers are looking at form and function, not how that form and function is being accomplished "under the hood." This is because the cost to manufacture one of these types of Android wearable devices will be quite high (computer miniaturization), while the cost to manufacture the other type of Android wearable device will be much lower. Lower manufacturing costs yield higher profit margins, especially if the purchasing public can be convinced the product is running the Android OS, when in fact, it may not actually be doing so!

This is quite evident in Android wearables product segments, which include smartwatches and smartglasses such as Google Glass. One of the smartwatches used in this book, the Neptune Pine, is a **True Android Device**. What this means is that a True Android Device will have a CPU, memory, an SD card, an OS, WiFi compatibility, and the like, right inside of the smartwatch itself! In this sense, a **True** smartwatch device is actually like having a smartphone on your wrist, and support is offered for telecommunications carriers, just like your smartphone currently offers.

This True Android smartwatch will be the only Android device that you need to wear. In case you are wondering, I borrowed this "True" Android description from the True HD (HDTV) industry term. True HD is 1920 by 1080 resolution, and is a necessary descriptive modifier, because of the fact that there is another lower 1280 by 720p resolution in the market that is also termed HD (I call it "pseudo-HD").

Most other smartwatches aren't currently True Android devices, although in my discussions with manufacturers, they are considering making this manufacturing leap in the future, probably due to the Neptune Pine. Currently, the other smartwatch products could be described as **peripherals** to an existing smartphone, phablet, e-Reader, iTV Set, game console, home media center or tablet.

The smartwatch products that use **Bluetooth** technology essentially become **screen extensions** for another True Android device, which has the CPU (processor), memory (application runtime DDR3), storage (an SD card), and the Internet and voice communication (WiFi and 4G cellular network access, respectively). These device hardware resources are the ones that actually process your smartwatch application logic, sending the results to the smartwatch screen. Android peripheral smartwatches obviously require a different application development work processes, as well as having a different data optimization and application testing procedure.

Optimization will be necessary to achieve the optimal performance and user experience, since the application is operating back and forth over a Bluetooth "wireless expanse" between the Android device running your application and the smartwatch peripheral that is displaying the application and processing the touchscreen event handling for your user interface. This is obviously going to slow down performance, due to the user experience (user interface event generation and event handling) having to travel back and forth through the air via a Bluetooth wireless data connection.

This is also most likely the reason why Android OS upgraded its Bluetooth support from Bluetooth 3.0 to Bluetooth 4.0 in a recent version (4.4) of the Android OS. This faster Bluetooth 4.0 allows the best performance possible between a peripheral and True Android device. I am covering this distinction up front, because I want you to be aware that there are two completely different ways that smartwatches can function (true or native, versus peripheral or remote). Android 5.0, which I cover in Chapter 16, upgrades Bluetooth even further, to Bluetooth 4.1, which puts Bluetooth devices in the cloud!

Now that the **Android Wear SDK** has been released with Android 5.0, there are actually three application development approaches to Android wearable applications development. I will cover them in the next section of this chapter.

Development Strategy: Android, Wear SDK, or Plug-In

There are three ways that Android wearable applications can be developed currently—by using the full or True **Android SDK** (true or native smartwatch apps), by using the recent Android **Wear SDK** (which was released in the Summer of 2014 along with the Android 5.0 API Level 20 OS, which is covered in Chapter 16), and by adding **SDK plug-ins**, usually called "**add-ons**" using the Android SDK Manager in Eclipse ADT (Android 4.4.4).

You learned about the Eclipse Android SDK Manager (from the Window menu) at the beginning of this book, when you installed and set up your Android SDK development environment in Eclipse ADT. A good example of a smartwatch that uses an SDK add-on approach is the Sony smartwatch. The **Sony Add-on SDK** is currently at version 2.1. You can access it from the following URL (the Sony smartwatch repository address). Enter it into the Android SDK Manager by using the **Tools ➤ Manage Add-On Sites** menu sequence:

```
http://dl-developer.sonymobile.com/sdk-manager/Sony-Add-on-SDK.xml
```

Don't do this, of course, unless you have a Sony smartwatch 2 or 3, and need to develop for it. I am developing for the Sony smartwatch 2 and 3 for my upcoming Pro Android Wearables book title. Figure 15-1 show the add-on once it is installed in the Eclipse ADT SDK Manager tool.

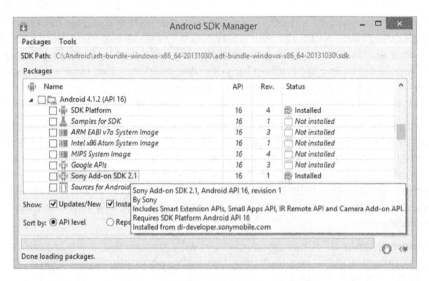

Figure 15-1. The Sony Add-on SDK 2.1 installation option in the Android SDK Manager

Once this add-on SDK is selected and installed, you have the additional APIs for developing for the Sony smartwatch platform. As you can see in Figure 15-1, if you mouse over the Sony Add-on SDK, it will tell you what API packages it contains, what version it is, and what Android API level (16) is required in order to implement it.

This light yellow pop-up shows part of the repository URL (but not the full URL that you will need, interestingly) used to access the Sony Add-on SDK Version 2.1. Expect a Sony Add-on SDK Version 3.0 to be released with Sony's smartwatch 3 product sometime during 2014, unless Sony adopts the Wear SDK, of course.

Hopefully the smartwatch 3 will have a higher screen resolution than the smartwatch 2, which had only a 220 by 176 pixel resolution for its smartwatch display screen.

The other popular SDK and API approach to developing for Android wearables—for now this is just smartwatches—is the **Android Wear SDK**, which is currently at Version 4.4W, and is now available in Android 5.0, and will be covered in Chapter 16. The Wear SDK will be covered in detail in my *Pro Android Wearables* title, which will probably be released sometime during early 2015. If you want to check out the Android Wear SDK, here is the Android developer website's Wear SDK URL:

```
http://developer.android.com/wear/index.html
```

The Wear SDK is similar to the Sony SDK, in that it will be installed on top of the IntelliJ IDEA Android SDK environment, and will provide a more generalized SDK (whereas the Sony SDK is specific to the smartwatch 2, smartwatch 3 and other Sony products) that more than one manufacturer can utilize. I will be covering the IntelliJ IDEA in detail during Chapter 16, when we will install Android Studio (IntelliJ IDEA), and then create a 64-bit Android 5.0 application.

It is important to note than any manufacturer can take this approach that Sony is taking, and provide their own customized SDK Add-on API plug-ins, which they might need to do to add features that are not currently supported in the Android Wear SDK.

Finally, there is the native or full SDK approach, which is obviously my favorite, and the most logical one to use in this book as you can get right into creating your smartwatch applications without doing anything extra to your Eclipse ADT installation. You simply have to create a new Android application, and make sure that the **<uses-sdk>** tags in your **Android Manifest** XML definition file will specify the correct minimum and target SDK versions, which for the Neptune Pine smartwatch are currently set at **Android 4.1 API Level 16**.

The reason that this is my favorite approach, and eventually the approach that all other smartwatch manufacturers will have to follow, is because the Neptune Pine is a full-blown Android device, just like a smartphone or a tablet or an iTV set. The economies of scale in software development should be readily apparent, but if you don't see them, I will outline them here.

Since Android already provides for different resolutions and aspect ratios in the way that it sets up its resource folders, especially the **drawable-dpi** folders, and the allowance for alternate resource folders on top of that, this allows the developer to create an application that spans from the True smartwatch (currently the Neptune Pine) up to the 4K iTV set using a single Android application project hierarchy structure.

The other reason I have chosen to use the Neptune Pine for this wearables chapter in this book is because you can simply take into account the Neptune Pine's 320 by 240 pixel screen in your graphic assets design, and jump right into developing an app for this smartwatch that also works across all of the other Android device types, from smartphones to e-Readers to tablets to iTV Sets.

You will be able to develop for the Neptune Pine without installing anything new using the Android SDK Manager, and without learning anything new regarding Android classes or development.

I am now going to cover some of the basic wearables development information, which I would normally include as foundational information at the beginning of any chapter in the book. In fact, in this case, this information will be included so that you will know how to optimize for peripheral wearables, since they require that level of optimization due to their operation across a Bluetooth wireless connection expanse. It is important to note that some of this type of optimization in built-in to how the Wear SDK operates.

Smartwatch Optimization Fundamentals: Display and CPU

To know how to optimize your applications for the smartwatch device type, you need to know the **limitations** of the hardware that you are developing for. Regarding smartwatch products, the current primary limitation is the **display size**, which is usually around 320 pixels, either in both dimensions such as the 320 by 320 Samsung Galaxy Gear, or in one dimension, such as the 320 by 240 Neptune Pine.

There are some lower resolution smartwatch displays still out there as well, such as the Sony smartwatch 2's 220 by 176 display, so be sure to know what the resolution is (in pixels) for the smartwatch that you are developing for! With higher pixel density LCD, LED, and OLED displays available for Wide HD (2160 x 1080) and UHD (2560 by 1440) smartphones that are coming out in 2014, you should see high-density 480 pixel (240 DPI), 640 pixel (320 DPI), and even 720 pixel (360 DPI) 2-inch screen smartwatch products coming out soon, probably during 2015 and 2016.

Another major limitation of smartwatches these days is the **CPU** (Central Processing Unit) support. Processor support is usually limited to a single core, although some smartwatches, like the Neptune Pine, feature powerful dual-core processors. Storage is usually implemented by using MicroSD cards, with the Neptune Pine coming with 8GB and offering affordable upgrades to 64GB storage, if needed.

I have already touched on some of the issues regarding optimizing for CPU and memory in other areas of this book; those apply just as importantly to smartwatches, if not more so. Be careful about using things such as data-heavy animation and special effects, if they are not absolutely needed, or if you do utilize these in your application, make sure to implement them 100% optimally!

It is important to note that both CPU and memory require power to run and to store your application data and code logic, and another limitation that you will find on smartwatches is **battery life**. A good example of this is the Sony smartwatch 2, which currently disables smartwatch Face Skinning in their API, because they are afraid that developers will create cool animated interactive watch faces (skins) that they think will drain the battery life of the smartwatch product.

Another important limitation relating to the smartwatch's CPU processing speed and power relates to smartwatch Peripherals. Is the smartwatch CPU processor on the smartwatch itself, or is the CPU processing your application's program logic remotely, over a Bluetooth 3.0 or Bluetooth 4.1 broadcast standard?

This is probably the biggest consideration of smartwatch peripheral application design and optimization, as the UI (the smartwatch's touchscreen) event handling will be initiated on the smartwatch peripheral, and then sent over Bluetooth 3.0 or 4.1 to a remote True Android device.

This device will then process these events in the **onClick()** or **onTouch()** event-handling structures, and then send the resulting user experience, that is, whatever program logic is inside of these event handlers, back over Bluetooth 3.0 or 4.1 to the smartwatch device, to be displayed on the smartwatch face (display screen) again.

There are three areas in smartwatch application development that you need to be very careful of in your wearables app optimization. First, how will your graphics perfectly fit the screen pixel-for-pixel?

Secondly, how smoothly will your user interface response and user experience function if you are developing for a smartwatch peripheral? This is not a concern at all for True smartwatches, as you now know the reasoning behind this since there is no external (wireless) communication going on.

Finally, how much of the smartwatch's battery life does your application use? All of these things point to well optimized Android applications; that is why I have been covering this optimization process, in one form or another, in many of the chapters in this book.

Optimization will continue to become more and more important, as some Android devices get bigger (for instance 4K iTV sets) and as others get smaller (smartwatches and smartglasses) or if they utilize Bluetooth 4.1 technology over a wider expanse (such as with the Android Auto SDK, for instance).

Creating Your EarthTime.APK Android App

Create a new Android application project called **EarthTime.APK** in the **absolute.beginners. earthtime** package using the **New ➤ Android Application Project** work process you learned about in Chapter 3.

The first thing that you will want to do is to close your **HelloUniverse** project folder in Eclipse. This is done by right-clicking on the project folder, and selecting the **Close Project** option from the menu, as shown in Figure 15-2.

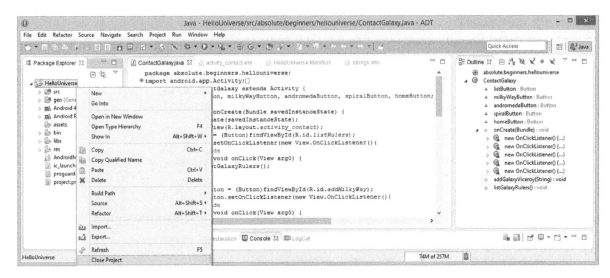

Figure 15-2. Right-click the HelloUniverse folder, and use the Close Project option to close the HelloUniverse project

Notice in Figure 15-3 that your project is still intact. It is just closed, so that you can create your new project. If you want to remove this project folder completely, you use the **Delete** menu selection, as shown in Figure 15-2.

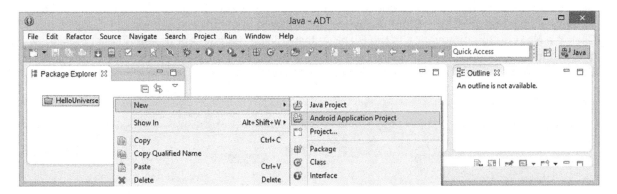

Figure 15-3. Right-click in blank area of the Package Explorer pane and select New ➤ Android Application Project

If you need to use Delete, make sure you **back up** your project folder hierarchy before you use this destructive (non-recoverable, like a DBMS **WRITE**) operation! Right-click in an open area of the Package Explorer pane, and select the **New ➤ Android Application Project** menu sequence (see Figure 15-3) to start the **New Android Application** series of dialogs, so you can create the app!

In the first **Create New Android Application** dialog, shown in Figure 15-4 on the left, name your application and project **EarthTime** and your package **absolute.beginners.earthtime.** Set the three SDK selection drop-down menus to the **API** Level **16** (**Android 4.1**) that the Neptune Pine smartwatch uses. Click the **Next** button, and accept the default checkboxes in the **Configure Project** dialog. This will create your launcher icon, a MainActivity Activity subclass, and the Project folder hierarchy in the Eclipse IDE workspace (Package Explorer pane), also shown in Figure 15-4, this time on the right side of the figure. Again, click the **Next** button to advance to the next dialog in the series.

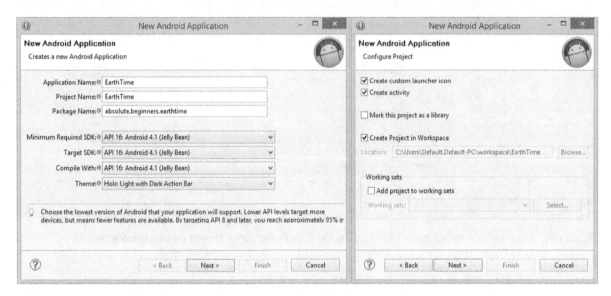

Figure 15-4.   Select API Level 16 for a Neptune Pine app and accept the defaults in the Configure Project dialog

Accept the defaults in the **Configure Launcher Icon** dialog, shown in Figure 15-5 on the left, as you will create your custom EarthTime icon later. Again, click the **Next** button to advance to the **Create Activity** dialog, and select the **Blank Activity** option shown in the middle section of Figure 15-5. Click the **Next** button to advance to the Blank Activity dialog, and accept the default settings shown on the right side of Figure 15-5. Finally, click the **Finish** button. Now you are ready to create your **EarthTime** application's UI design for the Neptune Pine!

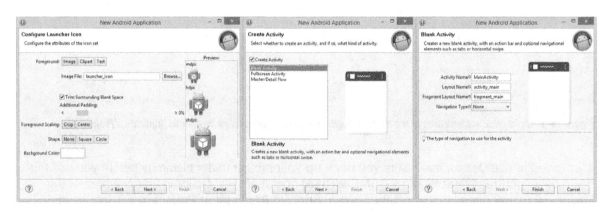

Figure 15-5.   Accept the default values for the Configure Launcher Icon, Create Activity, and Blank Activity dialogs

EarthTime UI Design: Styling an AnalogClock

Let's start with the easier XML markup, and design a low-memory watch face (a skin). You will do this using the **FrameLayout** class as the layout container, and the **AnalogClock** class as the UI widget. As you can see in Figure 15-6, I am using Eclipse in a new way, by minimizing the Package Explorer (far left) and Outline and Error views (far right) of the Eclipse UI, and using the entire area of the IDE for my editing pane.

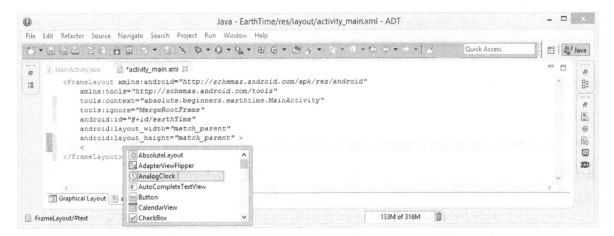

Figure 15-6. Add an <AnalogClock> child widget to a <FrameLayout> parent container to create the EarthTime clock

As you can see, the **<FrameLayout>** parent container is already coded for you, so change your **ID** to **earthTime** and add a **</FrameLayout>** closing tag. Then, use a left facing chevron **<** to open the pop-up helper, and select and insert the **<AnalogClock>** child tag for your user interface widget.

Add an **android:id** parameter, and name the **<AnalogClock>** widget **earthAnalogClock**. Copy and paste the two required **android:layout_width** and **android:layout_height** parameters from the **<FrameLayout>** parent tag in the lines that come right before the **<AnalogClock>** child tag. Now you are ready to add your background image!

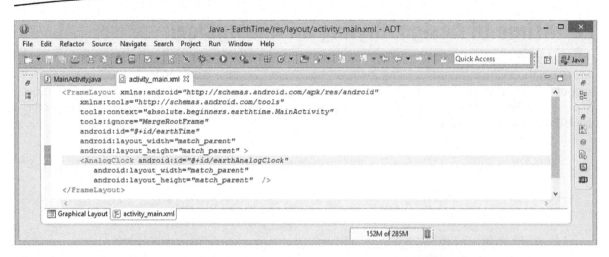

Figure 15-7. Add ID, set to earthAnalogClock, add required layout_width and layout_height, then set to match_parent

Adding the Background Image of Planet Earth

I have created an **earthtime240.png** for Neptune Pine. It is 320 by 240 pixels, since the watch will be square and centered, as well as **earthtime480.png** (HDPI) and **earthtime960.png** (XHDPI) versions, so this app can run not only on a Neptune Pine, but also on smartphones, tablets, and iTV Sets. Copy the **earthtime240.png** shown renamed (after copying) in Figure 15-8 into the **/res/drawable-mdpi** folder. MDPI is defined as 160 DPI, and the Pine 2-inch screen is 320 pixels. Copy **earthtime480** into the **HDPI** folder and **earthtime960** into the **XHDPI** folder.

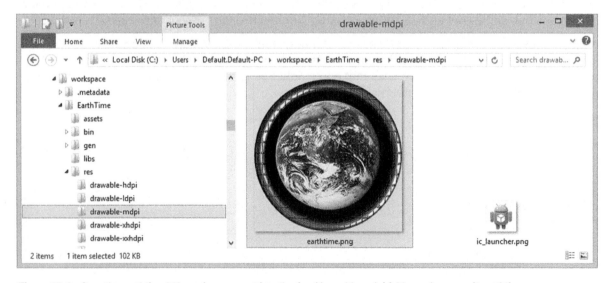

Figure 15-8. Copy the earthtime240.png image asset into the /res/drawable-mdpi folder and rename it earthtime.png

Next, add the **android:background** parameter, referencing the **earthtime** image asset, as shown in Figure 15-9.

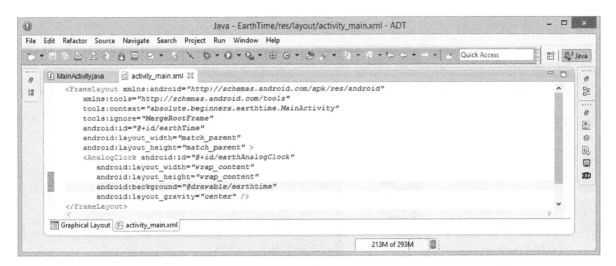

Figure 15-9. *Use the android:background parameter to reference the earthtime image and use layout_gravity to center it*

Make sure that you change the **layout_width** and **layout_height** parameter constants to **wrap_content** so that the watch face conforms to the square earth image background and to the AnalogClock widget's face, and not to your rectangular **FrameLayout** container. Finally, add an **android:layout_gravity** parameter and set it to use the **center** constant, so that the new watch face centers itself inside of the Neptune Pine smartwatch hardware (display screen).

Now you are ready to use the **Graphical Layout Editor** tab (at the bottom-left of the central editing pane) to preview your UI design. As you can see in Figure 15-10, the EarthTime AnalogClock widget is centering itself in the AVD emulator, and the widget's UI elements overlay the background image perfectly and quite professionally.

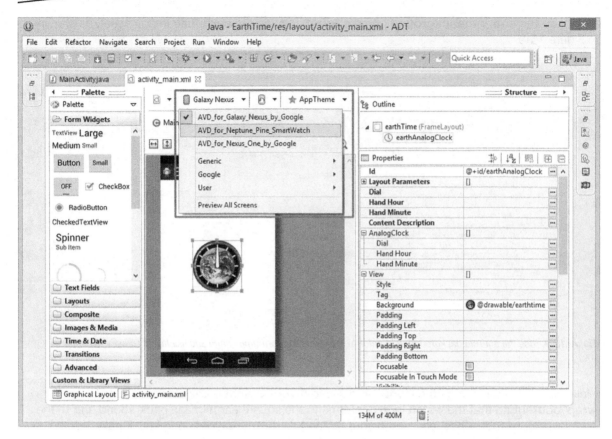

Figure 15-10. Click the Graphical Layout Editor tab, and then select the Neptune Pine AVD from the drop-down menu

There is one problem, however; the Graphical Layout Editor is set to use the Nexus One emulator. Let's set it to use the Neptune Pine AVD emulator that you created when you were learning about how to create custom AVD device definitions (those not included with Eclipse ADT) in Chapter 2.

Click the menu at the top of the Graphical Layout Editor that currently says **Galaxy Nexus** by clicking on the down (expand) arrow at the right, as shown in Figure 15-10. Notice that there is a portrait and landscape selector drop-down, as well as an Android Theme selector drop-down. Select the **Neptune Pine AVD** (shown highlighted) to switch the AVD emulator to the one you want to use to preview your EarthTime app in.

As you can see in Figure 15-11, the Graphical Layout Editor is now emulating the Neptune Pine smartwatch.

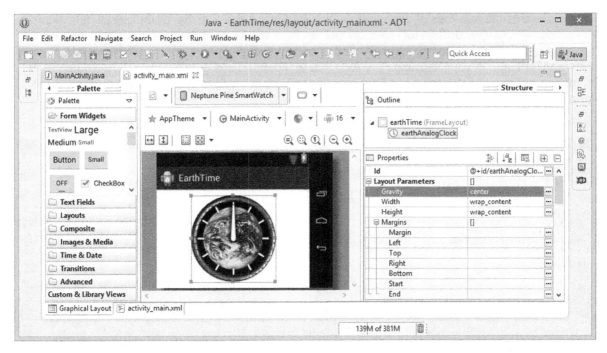

Figure 15-11. Preview the EarthTime clock UI design in the Neptune Pine AVD in the Graphical Layout Editor

EarthTime Code: MainActivity.java Class

Now you will install your standard **MainActivity.java** activity's minimum bootstrap code, as shown in Figure 15-12.

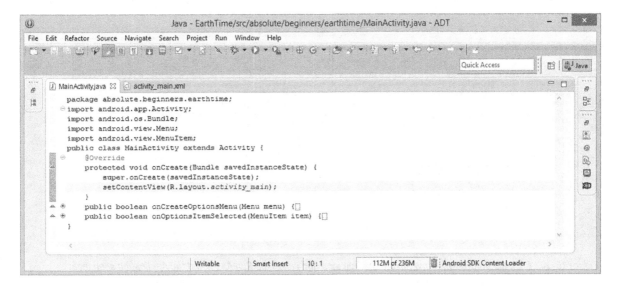

Figure 15-12. Create minimum Java methods: onCreate(), onCreateOptionsMenu(), and onOptionsItemSelected()

This represents the two lines of code that are required to get the **activity_main.xml** UI definition on the screen—the **super.onCreate()** method call, and the **setContentView()** method call—as you have been using throughout the book. After this code, which Eclipse wrote, you can get into testing the EarthTime app in your Neptune Pine AVD that you created earlier in Chapter 2. As you can see at the top of Figure 15-13, there is a **Run Icon** in the Eclipse toolbar. The icon uses a **green** video (or audio) **Play** transport button.

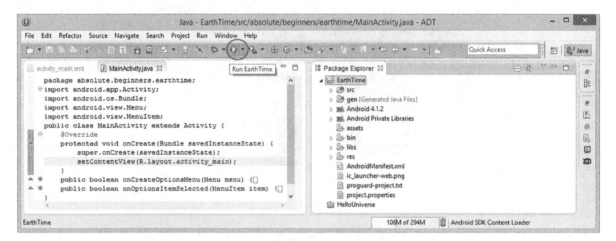

Figure 15-13. *The Run Application icon in Eclipse's icon bar and the Package Explorer pane on the right*

Click the drop-down arrow next to the Run (Play) Icon to access the same Run As and Run Configurations menu sequences that you have been accessing previously in the book by right-clicking on the project folder. Select the **Run As ➤ Android Application** menu sequence, as shown in Figure 15-14.

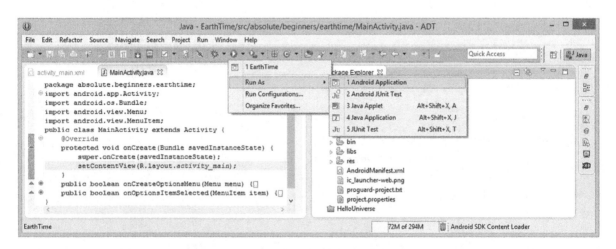

Figure 15-14. *Click the drop-down arrow next to the Run icon and select the Run As ➤ Android Application sequence*

If for some reason the Neptune Pine AVD emulator does not start, use the **Window ➤ Android Virtual Device Manager** menu sequence, and select the Neptune Pine AVD. Then click the **Start** button. In the Launch Options dialog that appears, shown in Figure 15-15 on the left, select the **Scale display to real size**, **Wipe user data**, and **Save to snapshot** options. Click the **Launch** button to start the AVD, shown on the right in Figure 15-15.

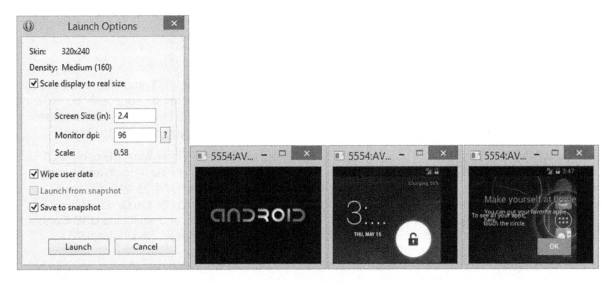

Figure 15-15. Use AVD Manager to launch Neptune Pine and then select Scale display to real size, Wipe user data

The Android OS loader animation is shown in pane two of Figure 15-15. After it finishes, and the OS loads, drag the dotted line to the left until it turns into a white lock, as shown in pane three of Figure 15-15. If you happen to get the "Make yourself at home" screen, shown in pane four of Figure 15-15, click the **OK** button, and the OS start up screen will load. This screen is shown on the far left (first) pane of Figure 15-16. Click the Open Apps button, which has six dots (representing app icons) in the middle. If you encounter the "Choose some apps" screen, shown in pane two of Figure 15-16, click on the **OK** button to enter the apps area, which is shown in the third pane of Figure 15-16. Pane three is what it looks like when you drag each app screen of six apps to the left to reveal the next six apps.

Figure 15-16. Click the open (six dots) icon, click OK to accept, and then drag the apps side to side. The right pane shows the launched EarthTime app

If you don't find the EarthTime icon on any of the screens, simply use the **Run Icon** drop-down menu, shown in Figure 15-14, to launch the application again, now that the Neptune Pine AVD emulator is restarted. You can use the **Run As ➤ Android Application** menu sequence to do this.

Once Eclipse writes the APK file to the AVD, you will see the application running, as shown in pane four in Figure 15-16. As you can see, it looks great. It is time to plug the Neptune Pine smartwatch into your PC, mount it, and test the APK! This will show you how to copy an .APK file over to a hardware device, so that you can do real-world Android smartwatch hardware device testing!

Attaching the Pine to the Workstation USB Port

To be able to follow along completely in this chapter, other than using the AVD emulator, you will need to purchase a Neptune Pine smartwatch. Luckily, they are extremely affordable, especially considering that they are a full-blown Linux computer that you can wear on your wrist! I highly recommend that you purchase one for your Android application development as soon as you are able to do so.

Next, plug your Neptune Pine into your workstation USB port, using the USB to MicroUSB cable that comes with the Neptune Pine. A window will pop open showing the Neptune Pine module and a folder named **Phone** (I told you it was basically a smartphone on your wrist!), which is actually the internal storage (**F:**) for the smartwatch. To be able to see this as an **F:** drive, and also see the **G:** drive (the SD card), you need to go into the **Settings Icon** in the Neptune Pine Apps area, and select the **USB Connect** section of the settings subheadings. Then select the **USB Mass Storage** option. See Figure 15-17.

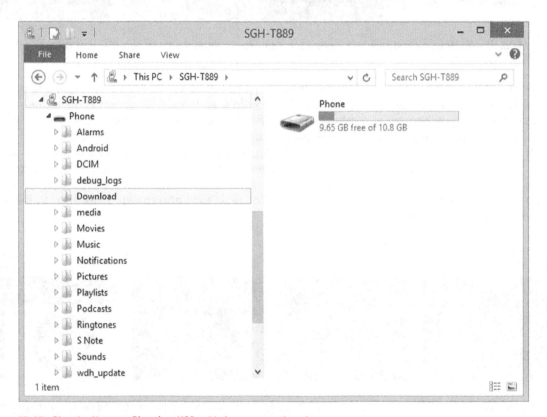

Figure 15-17. Plug the Neptune Pine via a USB cable into your workstation

Once you do this, you will get the **F:** and a **G:** drives and icons in your Windows Explorer, which you can see in Figure 15-19. If you have other drives, such as several hard disk drives, these letters may be a bit different.

Next, let's locate the **EarthTime.apk** file for the application. Since you ran it in the emulator, you know that this exists, so open your **/workspace** and **/EarthTime** folders. The logical place to store your executable would be in the binary (**/bin/**) folder, so let's look for it there first.

Click on the **/workspace/EarthTime/bin/** folder path, and look for the **EarthTime.APK** file. As you can see, it is there, and is less than 400KB, and therefore is currently quite well optimized. If you wanted to support smartphones and tablets and iTV sets, and put the HDPI and XHDPI image assets into those folders, this APK file size will grow even larger, probably to a couple of megabytes or more.

Right-click on the **EarthTime.apk** file in the **/bin** folder, shown in Figure 15-18, and select the **Copy** menu option. This will then put a reference to this file into your OS clipboard area in memory.

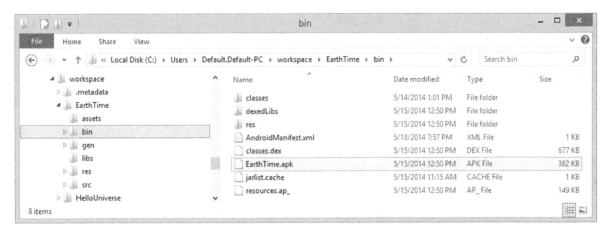

Figure 15-18. Find the .APK file for the EarthTime application, called EarthTime.apk, in the EarthTime project /bin folder

Now expand the view of Windows Explorer so that you can see the **F:** and **G:** drives that are on the Neptune Pine smartwatch. You are going to copy the **EarthTime.apk** file to the SD card (the **G:** drive) on the Neptune Pine. The source folder, file, and destination folder (**G:**) are shown in Figure 15-19. Once the file is in the **G:** drive, it has been transferred over the USB cable, from your workstation over onto your Neptune Pine smartwatch.

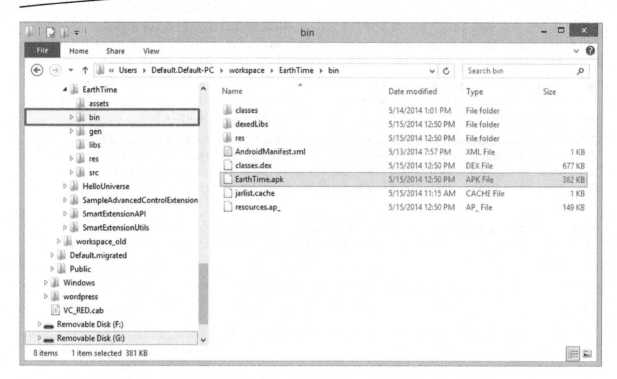

Figure 15-19. Find the Neptune Pine F: (internal storage) and G: (SD Card) mounted drives and copy APK over

Right-click on the **G:** drive, as shown in Figure 15-20, and use the **Paste** menu command to complete the APK file copy operation.

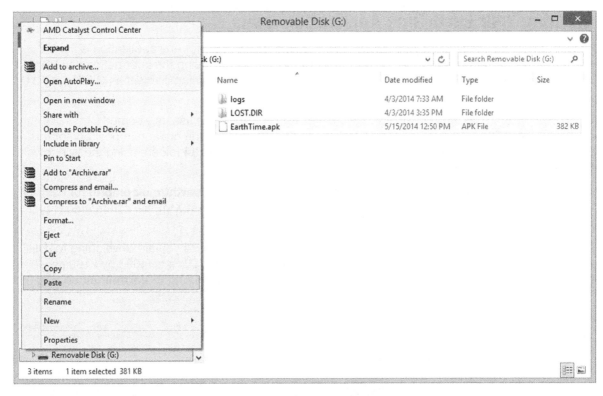

Figure 15-20. Right-click on the G: removable disk drive and select the Paste option to paste the .APK file

Once the APK file is on your Neptune Pine SD card, you can click on the EarthTime application icon and run the application on the smartwatch. Figure 15-21 shows the app on the Pine.

Figure 15-21. Run the EarthTime.APK application file from the Neptune Pine smartwatch SD card (G: Drive)

Creating Your EarthTime Application Icons

Now let's get into detailing the application. The first important detail for any application is its launcher icon, so let's create LDPI through XXXHDPI icon versions using the information you learned back in Chapter 4, in Table 4-1. You will use the process you are now familiar with in GIMP 2.8.10 to create the required six icon image assets.

If you don't want to go through all of this work, I have provided these assets—named **earthtimeiconLDPI.png** through **earthtimeiconXXXHDPI.png**—in the projects repository for this book. Copy these icon assets into their appropriate **/res/drawable-dpi** folders using the Windows Explorer file management utility.

Be sure to rename all of the **earthtimeiconDPI.png** asset names to **earthtimeicon.png** for each of the six folder names so that the XML markup in your **AndroidManifest.XML** file can reference just the one file name.

Remember that the XXXHDPI folder is for application icons only, unless you are developing for UHD devices such as the Samsung Galaxy 5 (2560 by 1440 pixels) or 4K iTV Sets (4096 by 2160 pixels). Figure 15-22 shows the renaming process, from **earthtimeiconMDPI.png** to **earthtimeicon.png**.

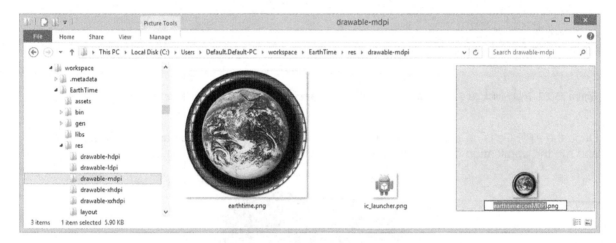

Figure 15-22.   Copy earthtimeiconMDPI.png into the /res/drawable-mdpi folder and rename it earthtimeicon.png

To install all of these new launcher icons into the **EarthTime.APK**—once you have copied the LDPI through the XXHDPI versions into the appropriate folders that the New Android Application Project sequence of dialogs created for you—all you have to do is one simple edit to your AndroidManifest XML application definition file.

This edit will change the launcher icon asset reference from pointing to the **ic_launcher.png** shown in the center of Figure 15-22 to the **earthtimeicon.png** image asset. You will find this digital image asset reference in the **<application>** tag, defined by the **android:icon** parameter, using the following XML markup, as shown in Figure 15-23:

```
<application  android:allowBackup="true"
        android:icon="@drawable/earthtimeicon"
        android:label="@string/app_name"
        android:theme="@style/AppTheme"  >
```

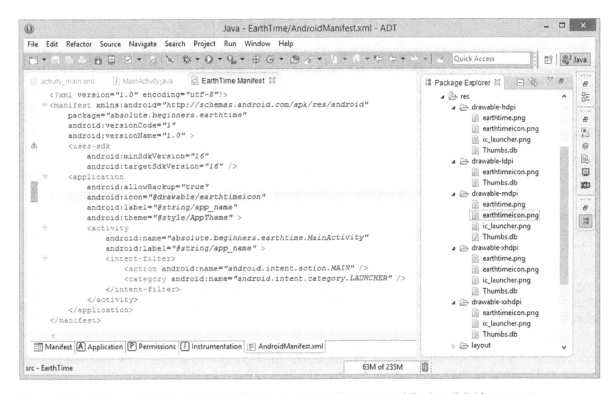

Figure 15-23. *Edit the <application> tag android:icon parameter to reference an earthtimeicon digital image asset*

Make sure after you copy all of the image assets into their respective folders that you use the **Refresh** command to tell Eclipse to register these digital image assets as part of your project. As you can see in Figure 15-23, the XML markup is error-free, and you are now ready to compile and run the new Neptune Pine application version.

There is one warning message that you should take a look at regarding the API level. Mouse over the wavy yellow underline warning highlighting under the **<uses-sdk>** child tag, underneath the parent **<manifest>** tag. As you can see in Figure 15-24, the warning is related to the targeting of the API Level 16, which is used by the Neptune Pine. What Android wants you to do is use the latest API Level 19, and allow the backward compatibility library (the Android Support Library installed and discussed in Chapter 2) to provide the API Level 16 support.

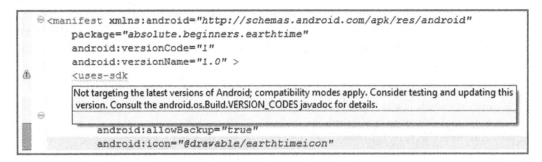

Figure 15-24. Mouse over the warning icon next to the <uses-sdk> tag and read the warning

There are two approaches to this—one is to depend on the Android Support Library and develop for the latest API level and the other is to "manually" develop for the exact API level the device needs. You target the exact device by doing what you are doing here in the AndroidManifest regarding using the **<uses-sdk>** tag. We will do it this way to show you both approaches, and because the Neptune Pine device uses Android 4.1.

Since you are testing on an actual Neptune Pine, you can try both settings and see how it works. If it works with the latest API, use that for the sake of cross-device compatibility if your app is going to run on smartphones, tablets, game consoles, phablets (phone-tablets) and iTV Sets as well.

The only thing that you as a developer will have to be careful of with this manual approach is to use classes, methods, and constants that are supported in API Level 16 (4.1.2) and prior API levels (1 through 15).

So you can ignore the warning, and use the **Run As ➤ Android Application** process to compile and run the app. In this way, you can generate the new **EarthTime.APK** file that has all of these new digital image assets in it. I also added the **earthtime480.png** (drawable-hdpi) and **earthtime640.png** (drawable-xhdpi) files into the **/res** folders.

As you can see in Figure 15-25, at the far left, the new icon is now in the ActionBar and the app looks much more professional. As you can also see on the right in Figure 15-24, the **EarthTime.APK** is now 2MB with all of the high-resolution image assets and icons installed.

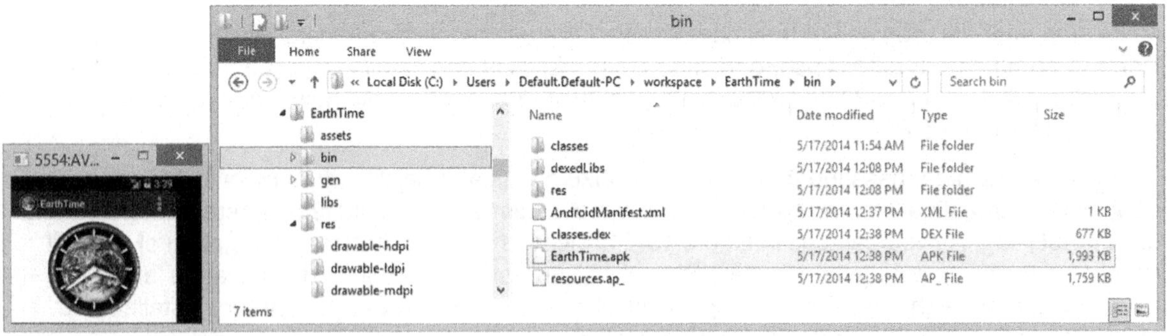

Figure 15-25. Compile the EarthTime.APK using the Neptune Pine emulator and locate the file in the /bin folder

This 2MB file is six times bigger, but also supports six types of Android devices (smartwatches, smartphones, tablets, iTV sets, eReaders, and game consoles). If you wanted to optimize this, you could remove the **launcher_ic** files that Android generated for you and you could use PNG8 format for the image assets rather than PNG32, although your edges would not be as smooth unless you used a uniform (pre-multiplied anti-aliasing) background color behind your analog clock background graphic. See Figure 15-25.

Next, let's take advantage of the Neptune Pine's rectangular screen area and add some other planets in the corner areas of the UI design. This will enable users to tap on each of the four corners to change the planet that's featured inside of the clock. You will use the **ImageView** class to add 60 pixel (one-fourth of 240 pixels) planet icons in the four corners of the current UI design using **layout_gravity** and **layout_margin** parameters. Since you don't need multi-state buttons, you will use **ImageView** instead of **ImageButton**, as it will take up less memory. Remember that the **ImageButton** class is subclassed from the **ImageView** class, which will add unneeded (in this implementation) code overhead. These are all things that you need to consider when thinking about your Android app's optimization: memory, APK size, CPU cycles used, battery power, screen sizes supported, and so on.

Adding Interactivity to the EarthTime App

Let's add some interactivity to this application by placing other planet icons in the corners of the display that the user can tap to change the planet that is used in the center of their clock design. I've created the necessary planet icon and clock background graphics, which you can copy from the book repository into the **/res/drawable-mdpi** folder. Multi-select (hold down the Ctrl key) the PNG32 files named **earthbutton**, **marsbutton**, **neptunebutton**, **jupiterbutton**, **neptunetime**, **jupitertime**, and **marstime**, and paste them into your **/res/drawable-mdpi** folder, as shown in Figure 15-26.

Figure 15-26. Copy jupitertime, marstime, neptunetime, and the four planet name button image assets to MDPI

Next, right-click on the **res/values/strings.xml** file to **Open** it. Add four **<string>** constants after the first **app_name** constant named **marsClock**, **earthClock**, **neptuneClock**, and **jupiterClock**, respectively. Then add descriptive text values for the sight impaired. The XML mark-up shown in Figure 15-27 looks like this:

```
<string name="marsClock">Use Mars Clock on Smartwatch</string>
<string name="earthClock">Use Mars Clock on Smartwatch</string>
<string name="neptuneClock">Use Mars Clock on Smartwatch</string>
<string name="jupiterClock">Use Mars Clock on Smartwatch</string>
```

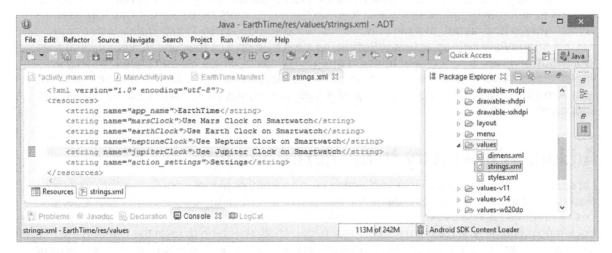

Figure 15-27. Add <string> constants for the contentDescription parameter of the four planet <ImageView> tags

Now that you have your image assets and string constants in place, you can add icons to your UI design.

Adding Four ImageView UI Icons to a UI Design

Since you are going to be positioning the planet icons using the **android:layout_gravity** parameter with the top, right, and bottom constants to position the planet icons in the corners of the UI design, you can simply add the **<ImageView>** child tags underneath the **<AnalogClock>** child tag. Add a line of space underneath your **<AnalogClock>** tag, and type a left facing chevron **<** character to bring up a supported child tag pop-up helper dialog, as shown in Figure 15-28. Double-click on the **ImageView** UI widget, which will insert it in your mark-up.

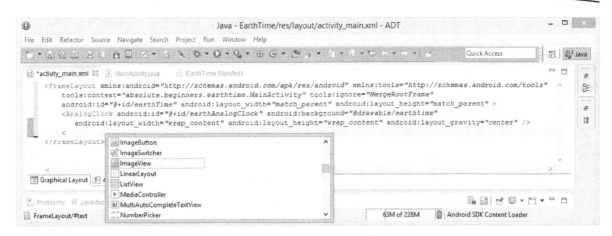

Figure 15-28. Add a line of space under the <AnalogClock> tag and use a left chevron < to open the tag selector

Name the **ImageView marsIcon** using the **android:id** parameter. Add an
android:contentDescription parameter, as required by all **ImageView** classes and subclasses,
referencing **marsClock**. Add the required **android:layout_width** and **android:layout_height**
parameters, set to a **wrap_content** constant.

Finally, add an **android:src** parameter referencing the **marsbutton** source PNG32 image that you
copied over. The XML mark-up for this first **<ImageView>** child tag should look like the following, as
seen in Figure 15-29:

```
<ImageView  android:id="@+id/marsIcon"  android:contentDescription="@string/marsClock"
    android:layout_width="wrap_content"  android:layout_height="wrap_content"
    android:src="@drawable/marsbutton"  />
```

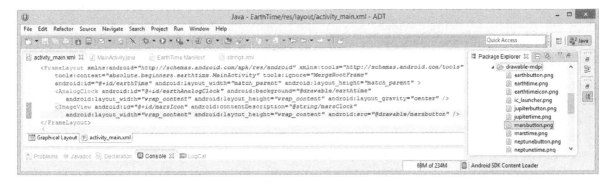

Figure 15-29. Configure an <ImageView> tag named marsIcon with a marsClock <string> and marsbutton image

It is important to note that you could have added an **android:layout_gravity="top|left"** parameter as well. Since this is the default setting, aligning objects at 0,0, or at the top left corner, this is not needed here. Preview the UI design using the GLE tab at the bottom of Eclipse, as shown in Figure 15-30, and add an **android:layout_margin** parameter, set to a value of **6 DIP** to center the planet icon in the gap between the clock and the screen corner.

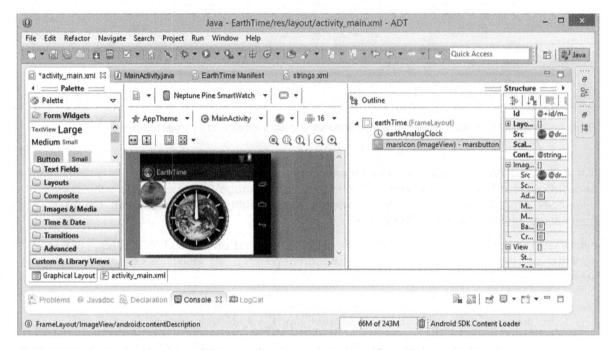

Figure 15-30. Use the Graphical Layout Editor to preview the marsIcon <ImageView> UI element's placement

Copy and paste the first **<ImageView>** tag structure underneath itself, as shown in Figure 15-31, to create your second **<ImageView>** planet icon UI. Change "**mars**" to "**neptune**" in the ID, content, and source parameters.

Figure 15-31. Copy and paste the marsIcon ImageView underneath itself and create a neptuneIcon ImageView

As you can see in Figure 5-31, the **android:layout_margin** parameters are in place for both **<ImageView>** tags, and the second **<ImageView>** will need to be set to **android:layout_ gravity="right"** (or **top|right**, if you want) to push the planet icon into the right corner. Since **top** is still the default, all you really need to accomplish this is the **right** constant! If you decide to use "**top|right**" as your constant pair, which is also allowed, make sure not to have any spaces in this constant, as the XML error system will think you are using a string and not a constant.

The final XML markup for the second **<ImageView>** structure will be copied two more times to create the bottom planet icons. The XML markup, which is shown in Figure 15-31, looks like the following:

```
<ImageView  android:id="@+id/neptuneIcon"  android:contentDescription="@string/neptuneClock"
      android:layout_margin="6dip"  android:layout_gravity="right"
      android:src="@drawable/neptunebutton"
      android:layout_width="wrap_content"  android:layout_height="wrap_content"  />
```

As you can see in the Graphical Layout Editor tab in Figure 15-32, the top two planet icons are now in place in the corners and are aligned perfectly thanks to the positioning fine-tuning provided by the 6 DP **layout_margin**.

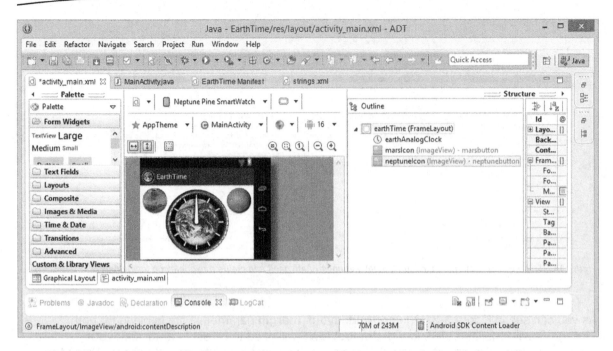

Figure 15-32. Use the Graphical Layout Editor to preview the neptuneIcon <ImageView> UI element's placement

Copy and paste the second **<ImageView>** tag structure underneath itself, as shown in Figure 15-33, and create the third **<ImageView>** planet icon UI element. Change "**neptune**" to "**jupiter**" for the ID, contentDescription, and drawable source parameters and change the **layout_gravity** constant from "**right**" to "**bottom.**"

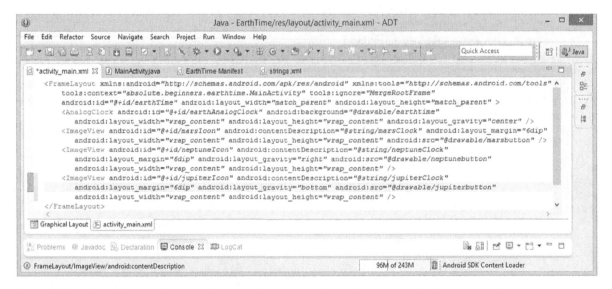

Figure 15-33. Copy and paste the neptuneIcon ImageView underneath itself and create a jupiterIcon ImageView

Again, since **"left"** is still one of the default (top,left or 0,0) alignments, all you really need to put in place to accomplish this bottom-left planet icon placement is the **bottom** layout gravity constant. Again, if you decide to use **"bottom|left"** as your layout gravity constant pair, make sure you do not have any spacing in the constant.

Now you can use the GLE tab to preview your planet icons UI design. As you can see, the app is starting to look pretty cool, with three other planets symmetrically spaced in three of the four corners of the application.

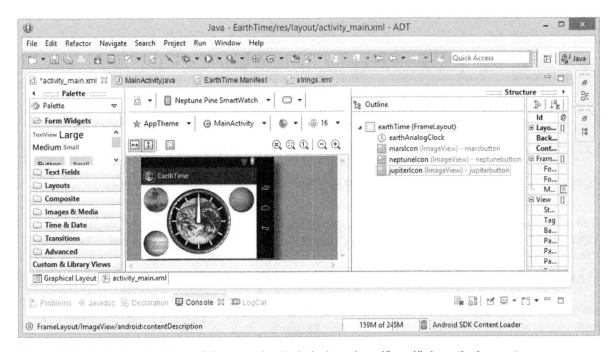

Figure 15-34. Use the Graphical Layout Editor to preview the jupiterIcon <ImageView> UI element's placement

Now you have three of the four planet icons in place; all you need to do is to add an Earth icon to your design.

Copy the Jupiter ImageView underneath itself and turn it into an **Earth ImageView**, as shown in Figure 15-35.

Figure 15-35. Copy and paste the jupiterIcon ImageView underneath itself and create an earthIcon ImageView

Edit all the parameters containing **"jupiter"** and change them to **"earth"**. Use the **"bottom|right"** layout gravity constant pair this time. This will place the Earth planet icon in the lower-right corner of the UI design.

In case you are wondering why I am putting the Earth planet icon in this corner, it is because there is an Earth icon in the ActionBar, in the top-left corner, and an Earth image in the center of the display, so using the Earth planet icon in the lower-right is thus symmetrical from a design sense. You can see what I mean in Figure 15-36 if you want to look ahead.

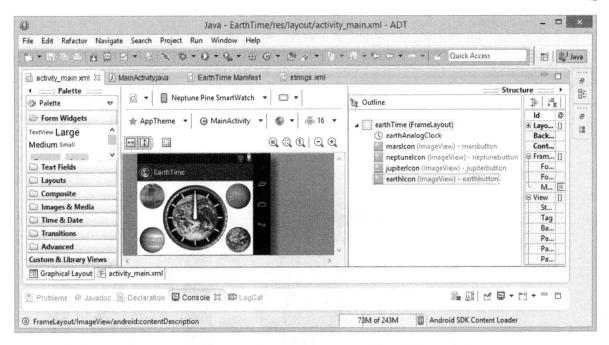

Figure 15-36. Use the Graphical Layout Editor to preview the earthIcon <ImageView> UI element's placement

The XML markup for the final **<ImageView>** UI widget structure for a planet Earth icon should look like this:

```
<ImageView  android:id="@+id/earthIcon"  android:contentDescription="@string/earthClock"
     android:layout_margin="6dip"  android:layout_gravity="bottom|right"
     android:src="@drawable/earthbutton"
     android:layout_width="wrap_content"  android:layout_height="wrap_content"  />
```

Notice that this time you need to use the **"bottom|right"** constant pairing inside of your **android:layout_gravity** parameter, because the default **"top"** and **"left"** parameters both need to be overridden to place the final planet icon into the bottom-right corner of the UI design. Also note that this is a perfect design for a memory-efficient **FrameLayout** container class, because you can use its basic **layout_gravity** and **layout_margin** parameter options to position this symmetrical smartwatch UI design, and it only uses around 16 lines of XML mark-up. See Figure 15-35.

Remember that the **FrameLayout** container inherits its margin and padding options from the **View** and **ViewGroup** superclasses, plus it has the **android:layout_gravity** parameter and its constants, which you learned about in Chapter 11.

Now use the Graphical Layout Editor tab to preview your final UI design, as shown in Figure 15-36. As you can see, you now have finger-tip-sized planet icons perfectly centered in your "available white space" corner areas.

Now use the **Window ➤ Android Virtual Device Manager** menu sequence to launch the Neptune Pine AVD, and use the **Start** button to access the **Launch Options** dialog shown in Figure 15-37, on the left side. Deselect the Scale to Real Size option in order to launch the larger (scaled up) version of the Neptune Pine AVD, shown in the middle of Figure 15-37. That way, you can see the overall UI element spacing more clearly, as you fine-tune your margin settings.

Figure 15-37. *Uncheck the Scale display to Real Size (left) box and launch the emulator (middle). The scaled display is shown on the right*

It is important to note that the Launch Options dialog is the only way to switch back and forth between the two different scales (sizes) of the Neptune Pine AVD. If you use the **Run As ➤ Android Application** menu sequence, it will use the last setting used in this Launch Options dialog, until you use the Window ➤ Android Virtual Device Manager ➤ Neptune Pine AVD ➤ Start ➤ Launch Options dialog sequence to change this setting.

Next, you will add a background space image, so that these planet icons (and planet clock) seem like they are where they belong—in space! You will use some of the image compositing techniques that you learned during the book to place a background image into the background image plate of the parent **FrameLayout** container object.

Enhancing the App: Adding Background Images

Copy the **earthtimebackground** PNG8 digital image asset from the book's files repository into your **EarthTime** project **/res/drawable-mdpi** folder, as shown in Figure 15-38. This image is 320 by 240 to fit the Neptune Pine screen resolution, and since it has a limited range of black, white, and yellow, I made it a dithered, indexed color PNG8 image, in order to save on the data footprint. This digital image adds only 58KB to your APK's file size.

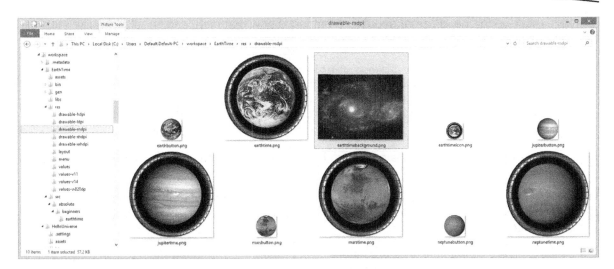

Figure 15-38. Copy the earthtimebackground.png digital image asset into the EarthTime/res/drawable-mdpi folder

Once you have copied the digital image asset, go into Eclipse, and right-click on the project folder. Use the **Refresh** menu item to make sure that Eclipse can now "see" this new image asset. Open the **activity_main.xml** file in a tab in Eclipse, and add an **android:background** parameter inside of the parent **<FrameLayout>** container that references this **earthtimebackground** drawable, as shown in Figure 15-39.

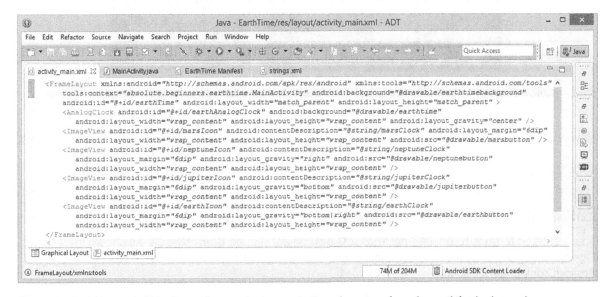

Figure 15-39. Add an android:background parameter to parent <FrameLayout> referencing earthtimebackground

The XML mark-up for the **<FrameLayout>** parent tag is now complete and should look like the following markup:

```
<FrameLayout  xmlns:android=http://schemas.android.com/apk/res/android
      xmlns:tools="http://schemas.android.com/tools"
      tools:context="absolute.beginners.earthtime. MainActivity"
      android:background="@drawable/earthtimebackground"  android:id="@+id/earthTime"
      android:layout_width="match_parent"  android:layout_height="match_parent"  >
```

Now your EarthTime application has a user interface and composited imagery just like an Android app should!

Use the **Run As ➤ Android Application** menu sequence to test the final user interface design. Depending on how you had your AVD scale to real world size set, the application should look similar to Figure 15-40.

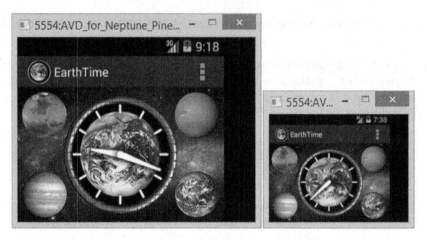

Figure 15-40.   Test the new background image with Scale to Real Size off (left) and Scale to Real Size on (right)

Now you are ready to add the Java code that will instantiate your UI elements and make them interactive. You will do this using the same Java object declarations, instantiations, and event handling structures you have learned about during the course of this book.

EarthTime Interactive: Adding Event Handling

The first thing to do is to declare an **AnalogClock** object named **planetClock**, as shown in Figure 15-41, and then mouse over the wavy red error highlight to have Eclipse import the AnalogClock class for you to utilize.

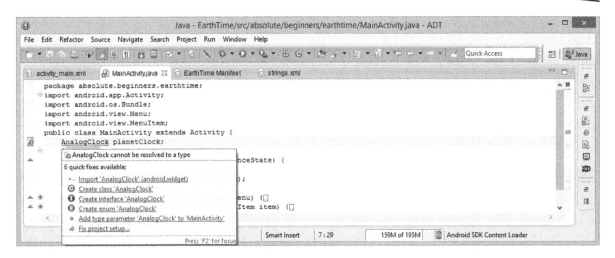

Figure 15-41. Declare an AnalogClock object named planetClock at the top of EarthTime app MainActivity class

Do the same thing for your four **ImageView** objects using a compound object declaration statement. Name the **ImageView** objects **jupiterIcon**, **neptuneIcon**, **earthIcon**, and **marsIcon**, as seen in Figure 15-42.

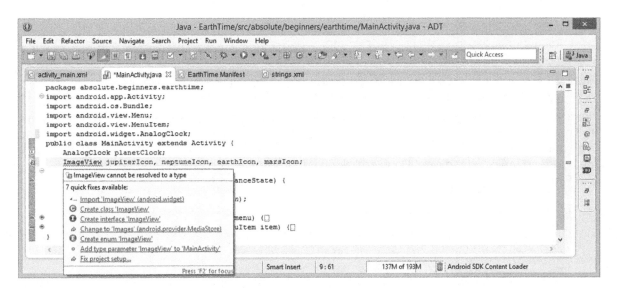

Figure 15-42. Declare an ImageView object series and name them jupiterIcon, neptuneIcon, earthIcon, and marsIcon

Make sure to mouse over the wavy red error highlighting, so that Eclipse will import the **ImageView** class for you.

Next, instantiate the AnalogClock and one of the ImageView objects using the **findViewById()** method. This will wire the object up to its XML UI definition, as shown in Figure 15-43, using the following lines of Java coding logic:

```
planetClock = (AnalogClock)findViewById(R.id.earthAnalogClock);
marsIcon = (ImageView)findViewById(R.id.marsIcon);
```

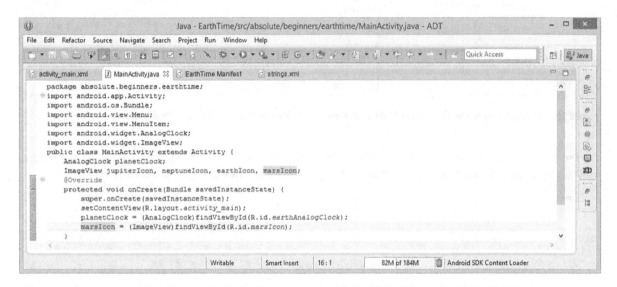

Figure 15-43. Instantiate planetClock AnalogClock object and marsIcon ImageView object using findViewById()

Next, you will add the event-handling structure to the **marsIcon** ImageView, and then you can copy and paste that icon structure to create the other three, as they are quite similar in form and function. Type the **marsIcon** object name and a period and then type "set" to find the **setOnTouchListener()** method from the pop-up dialog. Double-click on it to insert it as the method you are calling. See Figure 15-44.

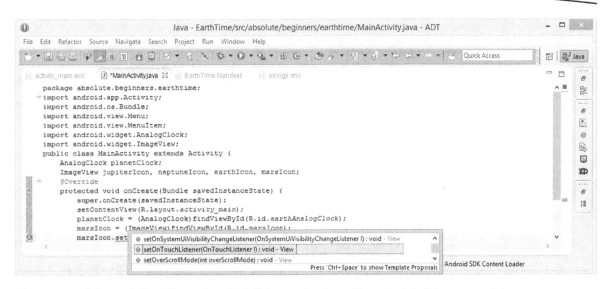

Figure 15-44. Call a .setOnTouchListener() method off the marsIcon ImageView object via Eclipse pop-up helper

Next, type the **new** keyword, the **View** class name, and a **period** inside the **.setOnTouchListener()**
parameter area. When the pop-up helper dialog appears, select a **View.OnTouchListener()**
anonymous inner type-android.view option, which will create the inside of the **OnTouchListener()**
structure. Then, simply add a method call to the **.setBackgroundResource()** method off of the
planetClock AnalogClock object inside of the **onTouch()** method, as shown in Figure 15-45. The
Java code structure should look like the following code:

```
marsIcon = (ImageView)findViewById(R.id.marsIcon);
marsIcon.setOnTouchListener(new View.OnTouchListener() {
     @Override
     public boolean onTouch(View arg0, MotionEvent arg1) {
          planetClock.setBackgroundResource(R.drawable.marstime);
          return false;
     }
});
```

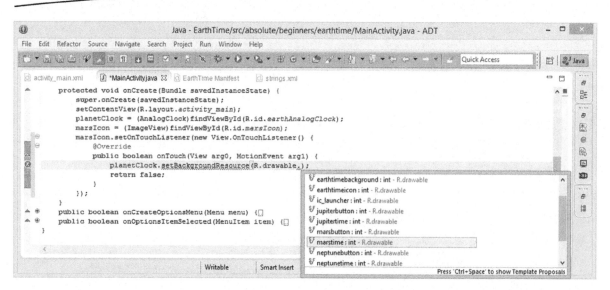

Figure 15-45. Add the onTouch() handler method inside of the OnTouchListener() by calling .setBackgroundResource()

As you can see in Figure 15-45, if you type in the **R.drawable** part of the asset reference, and then type a period inside of the **.setBackgroundResource()** method call's parameter area, Eclipse will show a helper dialog. This contains drawable assets that you have installed in the project thus far. Double-click on the **marstime:int - R.drawable** option to complete your **marsIcon** ImageView event-handling structure.

Copy the eight lines of code for the two **marsIcon** instantiation and event-handling structures, and paste them three more times underneath this structure. Change **"mars"** to **"earth," "neptune,"** and **"jupiter"** in each of the three eight-line Java code structures, creating the **earthIcon**, **neptuneIcon**, and **jupiterIcon** UI element Java code structures for the other three planet icons.

The four completed planet icon ImageView UI element code structures are shown in Figure 15-46, and are error-free. All that you have to do is use the **Run As ➤ Android Application** menu sequence and launch the AVD for the Neptune Pine. That way, you can test all four of the planet icons in the corners of your app to make sure that they change the planet image.

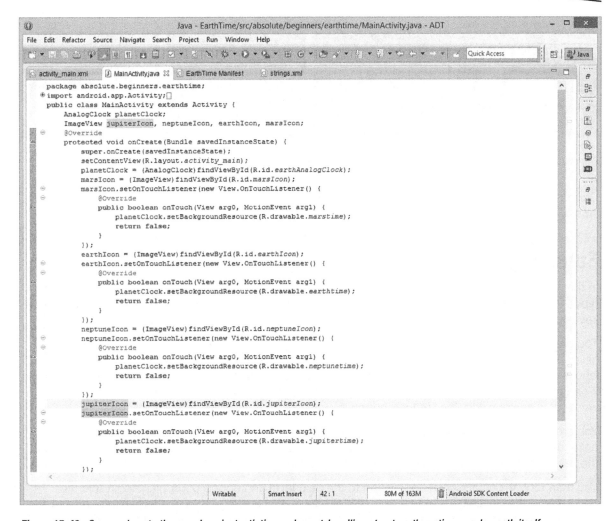

```
Java - EarthTime/src/absolute/beginners/earthtime/MainActivity.java - ADT
File  Edit  Refactor  Source  Navigate  Search  Project  Run  Window  Help

                                                                    Quick Access        Java

 activity_main.xml     MainActivity.java       EarthTime Manifest      strings.xml

    package absolute.beginners.earthtime;
  import android.app.Activity;
    public class MainActivity extends Activity {
        AnalogClock planetClock;
        ImageView jupiterIcon, neptuneIcon, earthIcon, marsIcon;
        @Override
        protected void onCreate(Bundle savedInstanceState) {
            super.onCreate(savedInstanceState);
            setContentView(R.layout.activity_main);
            planetClock = (AnalogClock)findViewById(R.id.earthAnalogClock);
            marsIcon = (ImageView)findViewById(R.id.marsIcon);
            marsIcon.setOnTouchListener(new View.OnTouchListener() {
                @Override
                public boolean onTouch(View arg0, MotionEvent arg1) {
                    planetClock.setBackgroundResource(R.drawable.marstime);
                    return false;
                }
            });
            earthIcon = (ImageView)findViewById(R.id.earthIcon);
            earthIcon.setOnTouchListener(new View.OnTouchListener() {
                @Override
                public boolean onTouch(View arg0, MotionEvent arg1) {
                    planetClock.setBackgroundResource(R.drawable.earthtime);
                    return false;
                }
            });
            neptuneIcon = (ImageView)findViewById(R.id.neptuneIcon);
            neptuneIcon.setOnTouchListener(new View.OnTouchListener() {
                @Override
                public boolean onTouch(View arg0, MotionEvent arg1) {
                    planetClock.setBackgroundResource(R.drawable.neptunetime);
                    return false;
                }
            });
            jupiterIcon = (ImageView)findViewById(R.id.jupiterIcon);
            jupiterIcon.setOnTouchListener(new View.OnTouchListener() {
                @Override
                public boolean onTouch(View arg0, MotionEvent arg1) {
                    planetClock.setBackgroundResource(R.drawable.jupitertime);
                    return false;
                }
            });

                        Writable      Smart Insert   42:1        80M of 163M      Android SDK Content Loader
```

Figure 15-46. Copy and paste the marsIcon instantiation and event-handling structure three times underneath itself

As you can see in Figure 15-47, the EarthTime application works perfectly, and all of the planet icons do their jobs. They seamlessly overlay the new background image in the AnalogClock UI widget with their respective planetary images.

Figure 15-47. Test each of the planet icon UI elements and make sure that the planetClock object shows a result

Congratulations! You have developed your first smartwatch app for the popular Neptune Pine smartwatch!

Summary

In this chapter, you learned about Android **wearable** development. You learned all about different types of wearables, including True Android devices and Android peripherals, as well as some of the key issues regarding wearables and how to optimize apps for this new Android platform.

You created your own Android wearables application for the popular Neptune Pine smartwatch, by using the New Android Application Project series of dialogs. You used the most memory efficient layout container, the Android **FrameLayout** class, and the **AnalogClock** widget to create a custom smartwatch face for the Neptune Pine using the public domain planet images from the NASA website, in keeping with the **HelloUniverse** theme.

You created the basic smartwatch **EarthTime** face and tested it on the Neptune Pine smartwatch using the USB cable. You copied the APK file onto the SD card for the Neptune Pine and then ran the Android application on the Neptune Pine hardware.

You then took the smartwatch application to the next level and added other planets around the perimeter of the UI design using the **ImageView** class. You added a cool space background image and then did some Java coding to declare and instantiate the **AnalogClock** and **ImageView** UI elements. You then added event handling to the **ImageView** planet icon UI elements that controlled the background resource of the **AnalogClock** widget using the **.setBackgroundResource()** method.

Finally, you tested your smartwatch application thoroughly, and made sure that it worked properly.

In Chapter 16, you will learn all about developing for Android 5.0, which is an advanced 64-bit OS that includes all of the functional areas of Android that we have covered in the book thus far. As I mentioned, I saved the most complicated chapter for last. You will be developing an application for the new 64-bit Android 5.0 operating system using the new IntelliJ IDEA, so exciting times lie ahead! It's time to time travel into the future, so onwards and upwards to the Future of Android: The 64-bit Android 5.0 OS!

The Future of Android: The 64-Bit Android 5.0 OS

As the third edition of this book was going to press, Google announced a 64-bit Android 5.0 L version of its popular operating system at the Google I/O trade show. Although Android hardware devices running this version of Android will not be available in large numbers until 2015, I decided to take this opportunity to add a "Future of Android" chapter covering what was different in the 64-bit Android 5 OS and how to develop applications for it. By doing so, this book covers developing for Android versions 1 through 5 and beyond!

Interestingly, all of the current Android classes, nested classes, methods, interfaces, constants, concepts, formats, codecs, and work processes that I covered in this book, which apply to Android 4, also hold true (that is, are applicable) to the 64-bit Android 5 operating system. For this reason, this final chapter is a fantastic opportunity to take the book to an even broader scope (or level) of coverage of the Android operating system than it already achieved!

In this chapter, I show you how I set up my production studio to handle both 32-bit Android 4.4.4 app development using Java 6 and Eclipse, as well as 64-bit Android 5.0 app development using Java 7 and IntelliJ using another Android 5.0 application development workstation. This new Android 5 development environment is called **Android Studio**, and it is currently in beta at version 0.8.

Since Android 4.x (4.0, 4.1, 4.2, 4.3, and 4.4.4) devices will be around for many years to come, you'll need to be able to develop for both 32-bit 4.x Android devices, with 3GB and less of system memory, as well as for 64-bit 5.0 or later Android devices, which support 4GB or more of system memory. If you have an Eclipse ADT workstation set up for developing 32-bit Android apps, you can continue to use that to develop for Android 4.4 and previous versions, and you can use IntelliJ on a different workstation to develop for Android 5.x. Alternatively, you can simply use Android Studio 5.0 to develop for all Android OS versions. Either way, by the time you are finished with this book, you will be able to develop Android apps with both the 64-bit IntelliJ (Android Studio 5.0) and Java 7, as well as with 32-bit Eclipse (ADT 4.4) and Java 6. This chapter covers the new features in Android 5.0, including the new development platform (IntelliJ IDEA), the new runtime (ART), the new 64-bit Linux

Kernel, the new Java 7 support, the new "materials" look and feel, and much, much more. Since Android 5 came out before this book was published, I cover it completely so that you have an up-to-date Android knowledge-base in one comprehensive book.

What's New in Android 5: New OS Features

This new version of Android has some fairly major changes and additions, both to the underlying platforms (Linux, Java, C++, and the runtime), as well as to the feature set for this new, 64-bit capable operating system.

It is important to note that these new 64-bit underpinnings, and the newly added features, will not "break" your current Android 4.4 application code and markup. Although there are two new View (subclass) widgets that you will be learning about during this chapter, there are zero changes to the existing "core" Android classes, nested classes, methods, constants, interfaces, codecs, new media file formats, XML definitions, project folder naming conventions, or to any of the related work processes that you might use when creating Android applications.

The significance of this is that everything that you learned regarding Android development during the first 15 chapters of this book is therefore still applicable to your Android 5.0 apps development. Thus Android 5.0 gives you even more speed, power, and capabilities, without taking anything away from your work process!

The first part of this chapter discusses all of the important changes and exciting additions, as well as their implications for your Android application development, in great detail. The second part of this chapter covers how to download, install, set up, and utilize the new Android Studio 5.0 environment based on the IntelliJ IDEA and Java 7 JDK. Finally, you'll develop an Android 5.0 application using Android Studio 5.0 beta 0.8.

Android 5.0 Platform: 64-Bit Linux and Java 7

One of the significant changes to the Android 5 platform that will not affect your application code or markup, but that makes your applications run up to 100% faster, is the use of the latest 64-bit Linux kernel and a more modern 64-bit Java 7 JDK. The reason for this is that the new 64-bit Android 5.0 OS matches up perfectly with the 64-bit central processing unit (CPU) hardware that is used in today's (and will be used in the future models of) consumer electronics devices like smartphones, tablets, eReaders, game consoles, and iTV sets.

The main advantage of a 64-bit OS is, as you probably know, the ability to address (or utilize) more than 3.24 Gigabytes of system memory. Since memory is manufactured using 1GB, 2GB, 4GB, and 8GB "modules" (or single chips), it is less expensive for manufacturers to "jump" from 2GB to 4GB memory support than to offer 3GB memory support. Since Android game consoles such as the nVidia Shield, Amazon Fire iTV, and the OUYA are quickly becoming popular, expect to see more Android hardware with 4GB, 6GB, or 8GB of primary system memory, as well as with powerful nVidia Tegra 3D processor support.

Additionally, certain Java or C++ programming constructs can also run more efficiently in the 64-bit processing environment, and there is less need for a Dalvik Virtual Machine optimization process, as full Java SE code can now run in the powerful 64-bit computing space. If 32-bit Android devices were like personal computers, then 64-bit Android devices are like the workstation on your desktop that you are using to develop i3D applications!

It is important to note that because the Android NDK (Native Development Kit) accesses the lower-level 64-bit layer of the Android 5 OS using the C++ programming language, it will take longer for NDK support to be added for Android 5.0. Since this is an Absolute Beginners title, this does not apply to what you are learning currently, and so you can proceed to learn how to use Java, XML, and IntelliJ IDEA to create Android 5 apps!

Android 5 Runtime: ART Will Become the Default

Back in Chapter 3, you learned all about how Android OS uses a runtime environment to launch and run your Android applications. Prior to Android 4.4, this was the Dalvik Virtual Machine. In Version 4.4, an option was added to use the ART, or Android Runtime, which provides faster and more efficient application launches at the expense of application (and data) storage "data footprint."

Since most of the new Android 5.0 devices will probably come with 64GB SD cards (or even 128GB or 256GB of data and application storage), ART has become the default runtime environment. Combine ART's pre-compiled, ready-to-load-into-memory predisposition with the new 64-bit OS speed, increased memory, and fast processors, like the nVidia Tegra K1 Quad-Core, and you have the recipe for workstation-like performance in the palm of your hand, which is clearly what Google is going for with Android 5.0 in order to increase its market dominance.

Enhanced 3D Support: OpenGL, Z-Layers, and Shadows

Android 5.0 adds a ton of impressive 3D-related features aimed at increasing the wow factor of the OS so that it can compete with the other 64-bit operating systems in the marketplace, such as Windows 8.1 and the upcoming Windows 9. It is said that "flat design" is a popular trend, but Android 5.0 seems to be bucking this trend by adding things like 3D ripple effects, fine-tune controls for drop-shadow (shadow height, Z-layer order, and the like), and OpenGL support, which puts Android 5.0 on the same level playing field (no pun intended) as the Xbox and PlayStation game consoles. Much of this capability is used in the new Android 5.0 Material Design schema, which I discuss a bit later in this chapter.

OpenGL ES 3.1 Upgrade: Enhanced Texturing and Shaders

One of the most powerful 3D features added in Android 5.0 is the inclusion of the latest version of OpenGL ES 3.1. This is the latest version of the real-time interactive 3D (i3D) rendering technology that is used in popular 3D video games. Most of the new features are related to the skin, called a **Texture Map** in the 3D modeling and animation industry, which makes a 3D object look realistic. These texture maps are made up of different shading attributes called **Shaders**, and advanced effects (animated or responsive to gameplay or position, for instance) can be created using a **Shader Language** in each shader "slot." This is somewhat akin to using layers in image compositing, only shaders are more complex and contain photorealistic attributes including transparency, luster (shininess), illumination (glow), reflectiveness (reflection), coloration (pixel color values), and the like.

Enhanced Texture Mapping functionality, such as Multi-Sample textures, can yield higher edge quality in texture maps (similar to the anti-aliasing you learned about in this book), and stencil textures can enhance the illusion of depth in a texture map that can be created using textures rather than actual 3D geometry (the underlying mesh or model). These advanced features allow 3D game output quality that rivals the traditional game platforms, such as PlayStation or Xbox, and it's clear that Google is going after the 3D game console space with Android 5 OS. There are already three Android-based game consoles on the market, ranging from $99 (OUYA and Amazon Fire TV) to $199 (nVidia Shield). These will be upgraded to Android 5 by 2015.

OpenGL ES 3.1 also supports something called a **Compute Shader**. These are not actually texture maps or shaders at all, but rather they are programming constructs that allow developers to use the GPU to perform non-3D related calculations (using the GPU, rather than the CPU). In game applications, a popular implementation of a compute shader is to offload game physics calculations onto the GPU. This is often done because current GPU technology is more powerful than CPU technology when it comes to solving complex mathematical calculations that are commonly utilized in i3D games applications.

Many new popular software packages, such as GIMP 3.0 and EditShare Lightworks 12, use this capability to make their 2D software perform complex special effects and pixel filter applications at lightning-fast speeds.

Your software can also utilize compute shaders, as long as you have an nVidia GeForce or AMD Radeon GPU in your system (or by now, in your Android devices). Android devices that feature the Tegra K1 microprocessor (manufactured by nVidia, and currently in the Shield and Fire TV) can thus use the GPU for non-3D-centric computation using these compute shaders.

OpenGL ES 3.1 is backward compatible with OpenGL ES 2.0 and OpenGL ES 3.0, so rest assured that none of your previous 3D or i3D code will be broken! OpenGL ES 3.1 will offer optional "extensions" that allow third-party manufacturers (such as nVidia) to add things like advanced blending modes (for texture layer compositing special effects) and fine-tuned shading effects, such as those found in the full OpenGL 4.4 specification. In fact, the Android Extension Pack (AEP), which you're going to examine next, is a prime example of this feature.

Extending OpenGL ES: The Android Extension Pack (AEP)

There is an additional extension to the OpenGL ES 3.1 standard called AEP, or Android Extension Pack. AEP allows features such as those found in the full OpenGL 4.4 release, so that console games with 3D graphics that are similar to those in Unreal 4 and Halo 4 will be able run on Android 5.0 and later hardware devices that support GPU hardware like the Tegra K1.

Three primary features of the AEP include Tesselation Shaders, Geometry Shaders, and Adaptive Scalable Texture Compression, or ASTC™, all of which are covered in this section of the chapter. Geometry shaders were the first feature to come out in OpenGL, so let's cover that concept first.

The geometry of a 3D object is the underlying 3D model (like a shape only in three dimensions instead of two), which is also sometimes referred to as the **mesh** because, without any texture mapping, that is exactly what it looks like. Another term that comes from this mesh-like 3D geometry is a **wireframe**. A mesh is made out of polygons, each of which are usually triangular (called "tris") or quadrilateral (called "quads").

A geometry shader allows an underlying mesh to become more refined, so that 3D models can be created using "low poly" modeling to save on data footprint (here it is again, this time in the creation of 3D assets). Geometry shaders allow low-poly meshes to be refined into higher-poly (polygon) meshes, which are smoothed on the client side using the GPU to apply what is termed **tesselation**, or the refinement of the mesh, by adding more vertices. A polygon is made up of vertices (points in space) connected by edges. A triangular polygon has three vertices and three edges, and a quad polygon has four vertices and four edges. It is important to note that a quad polygon can be split in half (diagonally) into two triangle polygons. An example of a quads modeler is the NeverCenter SILO software, and an example of a triangular modeler is the DAZ Hexagon or Blender software.

The rendering pipeline (a 3D layer stack, if you will) goes from the "Vertex Shader" on the top, or "skin" of the 3D mesh (model) down through the Tessellation Shader, which provides fine-tuned tessellation control over how the underlying geometry shader will be tessellated. How this all works is beyond the scope of an Absolute Beginner programming title, but I wanted to cover it briefly here so you have an idea of how advanced AEP is.

Finally, ASTC (Adaptive Scalable Texture Compression) is like a more advanced, 3D version of the WebM and WebP codecs added in Android 4. ASTC is in the full OpenGL 4.4 as well as in OpenGL ES 3.1, so it is an advanced technology that is used in the most popular 3D video games today. ASTC allows even better 3D texture map optimization, allowing developers to greatly reduce both the application data footprint and the amount of memory used for these texture maps to be applied to the 3D polygonal mesh. As I have been telling you all along, data footprint optimization is the name of the game these days, which is why I have been including this topic in all of my Android and Java 8 programming titles.

Z-Order and Z-Layers: The Third Dimension for UI Design

As you learned throughout this book, Android 4.4 and previous versions have a certain amount of support for the concept of Z-order, as it is necessary for implementing the compositing engine, which can be implemented using classes such as Android Canvas, View, RelativeLayout, FrameLayout, LayerDrawable, and PorterDuff. The concept of Z-order, sometimes called **Z-index**, can also be found in HTML5 and CSS3, as well as in JavaFX.

Besides using advanced Android classes such as Canvas, Z-index was not explicitly specified in the classes that used it. For instance, in some ViewGroup layout containers, you can use the **.bringToFront()** method to change the Z-order of the UI elements (View widgets) inside of the UI layout container. In Android 5.0, you can control the Z-index of each View widget in your ViewGroup layout container using a specific numeric value (Z-layer).

These classes, and the concept of Z-order, are also covered in my *Pro Android Graphics* book from Apress. Android 5.0 takes this Z-order concept to new heights (no pun intended) by specifically implementing a UI concept that I like to call Z-layers. Android 5.0 implemented this so that all of the Android 5.0 UI elements will have a specific Z-order, Z-index, or Z-layer value in the overall scheme of a now **Isometric** (2.5D) Android UI design space. This feature makes it easier for developers to add a 3D look and feel to their UI designs so that users can see things like stacked information "cards," as well as UI elements that float above the previously "flat" (2D) UI design paradigm.

Automatic Shadows: Shadowing Based on Z-Layers

Android also currently contains support for the application of drop-shadows, and this feature can even be implemented using XML in your user interface design definitions. It is important to note that you could apply drop-shadowing attributes to your TextView objects currently in Android 4, using four powerful XML parameters, including the android:shadowColor for setting the shadow's color, android:shadowDx for setting the shadow "delta" (offset) in the X direction (dimension), android:shadowDy for setting the shadow "delta" (offset) in the Y direction (dimension), and android:shadowRadius for setting a shadow blur radius (amount of shadow blur or softness). These shadow parameters currently exist in Android 4 and in previous Android versions as well, so feel free to add them to your TextView widgets.

In Android 5 and later, you should be able to use the shadow parameters with many of the other Android (View subclass) widgets as well, and the shadow parameters will automatically look at the Z information for the layer on which they reside (for at least some of their parameter settings). I imagine auto-shadowing parameters could be overridden by explicitly specifying (I call this hard-coding) that particular parameter. Taking shadowing to the next level in Android 5.0 is the next logical step or progression, giving Android what is called "isometric 3D" or faux-3D capabilities, which are also sometimes referred to as 2.5D (two and a half D). The 3D, 2.5D, and special effects capabilities, which have been added for the Android game development industry, are clearly going to be leveraged in the UI design areas in the OS, as these will contribute to the overall User Experience (UX).

The Camera 2 API: UHD with High Dynamic Range

Android 5.0 will unlock the unfettered power of the new ultra high definition (4096 by 2160 UHDTV) capable camera CCDs (charge coupled devices), which will capture UHDTV video at 8 megapixels (4096 times 2160 is actually 8,847,360 pixels, or 8.85 megapixels to be exact). The new Camera 2 API will unlock all of the power of the new UHD camera hardware that will be appearing in Android 5.0 devices. This Camera 2 API will allow developers to access each of the physical UHD camera features directly from the camera device hardware.

Android 5.0 device owners will be able to film their very own UHDTV shows or content and, on top of that, they will be able to stream uncompressed (raw) video frame data directly from the Camera hardware CCD data stream. The Camera 2 API will also support high dynamic range (HDR) digital video and high dynamic range digital images (HDRI). The Camera 2 API will also be able to access the more advanced YUV color space.

In case you are wondering what YUV color space entails, it is different from RGB (display) or CMYK (print) color spaces, and it allows color to be defined using a UV color plane. The YUV color model takes the human perception of color into account, and because of this, compression artifacts can be hidden more easily by making the artifacts not as noticeable to human perception. As you might imagine, this makes YUV a more complex color model than "straight" RGB, where every color is treated equally as a hexadecimal value. The YUV color representation is typically used where cameras are involved, such as in the film, videography, television, and digital photography industries. Clearly, Google is positioning Android 5.0 as a production tool.

In the world of digital cameras, "raw" means taking the raw pixel color data right out of the digital camera CCD hardware and using that untouched digital image data in your digital image-editing pipeline (workflow). There's a digital image data format, called **RAW**, and another open source lossless raw image format, introduced by Adobe in 2004, called **DNG** (Digital NeGative). Some popular digital camera smartphones, such as the Nokia Lumia 1020, already have this capability, so expect to see some Android 5.0 smartphones with lens assemblies on the back of the camera in 2015, probably introduced at the CES tradeshow in Las Vegas.

Another new feature of the Camera 2 API is **Burst Mode**, which allows photographers to take a series of rapid photographs, kind of like a second or so of video, so that they can select the best picture from a series of similar shots. The Camera 2 API also allows access to all manual exposure related digital camera controls, such as F-stop, depth of field, exposure time, and tonal mapping curves. These features show that Google is trying to encourage camera manufacturers such as Nikon, Pentax, Olympus, and Canon to put their Android 5.0 OS inside future digital camera products. This is one of the advantages of an open source OS that a proprietary (closed) OS platform is not going to be able to leverage in today's competitive consumer electronics market. An Android-based consumer electronics device is an open consumer electronics device, yielding a happy customer.

Project Volta: Control Power Use Optimization

The new power conservation initiative for Android 5.0, called **Project Volta**, is driven largely by the wearables industry verticals, as they have smaller batteries and are thus "power challenged" compared to large devices such as tablets, phablets, and devices that are plugged in, such as iTV sets and home media centers.

Android 5 has a new Job Scheduling API, which allows you to specify when your application's background processing tasks will take place. This essentially allows you to control power usage for the Android device. As you know from previous discussions in this book, you must continually be cognizant of the ways that apps might drain power from a user's device.

The new Job Scheduler API allows developers to specify when their tasks are processed during the various "use states" that a user has for their Android device. The most optimal use of processing power is when the device is charging, and thus is plugged in, like an iTV set is at all times! The next most optimal time to spawn processing tasks using the Job Scheduling API is when the device is idle and not being used for anything else (that is, not multitasking, which can overload the CPU and increase power usage).

There is also a new tool called the **Battery Historian** that allows developers to analyze their application's usage of power over time so that they can optimize power use. Another tool, called the **Battery Saver**, optimizes power usage by the Android OS and installed apps. For example, some front-facing features on the Android 5.0 estimate the time remaining until the Android device loses power and determine how long it will take to charge the Android device once it's placed on the charger.

Android Peripheral: Bluetooth Low Energy (BLE)

Recall that the previous chapter on Android wearables development explained what an Android peripheral is (versus a true Android device). Android 5.0 devices will soon be able to function using something called **peripheral mode**, using BLE, which stands for Bluetooth Low Energy (expenditure) hardware technology. Some of the more common market terminology for BLE includes "Smart Bluetooth" and "Smart Ready," and the major feature of BLE is greatly reduced power usage with the same range of operation and data transfer speed.

Bluetooth 4.1 support will also be added in Android 5.0 and later, which will extend the Bluetooth 4 range from 100 feet (30 meters) to worldwide (no range limit)! How is this possible, you may be wondering? This unlimited range is now accomplished via the cloud. Bluetooth 4.1 devices can talk to the cloud, via any Bluetooth-capable device, such as an iTV set in your living room or at the gym, an Android set-top box (STB, used for eSignage or digital signage), an Android Game Console, such as the Amazon Fire TV, an Android Home Media Center, and so on.

It is interesting to note that a Bluetooth 4.1-capable device does not necessarily need to be tethered to a tablet or to a smartphone to talk to the cloud. These Bluetooth 4.1-compatible devices can communicate with the cloud via any public Bluetooth hub. These public Bluetooth stations are popping up in gyms and malls now. It is important to note that Bluetooth 4.x peripherals, such as smartwatches, still need to be tethered to their parent device in order to accomplish their applications processing, as discussed in Chapter 15.

Enhanced Notifications: Notify via Lockscreen

Android 5.0 has upgraded and enhanced notifications, making then more visually appealing and enabling them to go "where no notification has gone before" (in keeping with our universe theme for the book). Notifications no longer require you to stop what you are doing to attend to them; you don't have to leave your app or swipe the screen to deal with a notification.

Android 5.0 implements what Google calls Head's Up! (dude) notifications, which overlay whatever activity screen your users happen to be on with a small floating window that is managed by the Android OS. There are capabilities to customize this behavior, of course, so that you don't bother users ensconced deeply in your i3D gameplay or for those watching a movie, for instance. Notifications can be "skinned" using material themes, which is covered a bit later in this chapter. These allow you to brand (customize) your Head's Up! notifications with custom UI design colors, patterns, shadows, fonts, borders, drawables, shapes, and the like.

These notifications distribute more than just text messages and updates; they can also "surface" content and even suggest actions for users to take. This can be done without the user having to unlock their phone or tablet. This is called **lockscreen notification**, and there are also powerful visibility controls that allow you to control precisely what types of information will be shown on the end user's lockscreen.

USB Audio Port: Connect Audiophile Equipment

Another exceptionally forward-looking feature that Google added to Android 5.0, which integrates it seamlessly with other types of consumer electronics devices such as home media centers and home stereo system products, is Micro USB Port audio data transport. I would not be surprised to see Micro USB Port video data transport either, based on the features that Google added to Android via the Camera 2 API.

While Apple is again promoting its Lightning audio connector as a proprietary media port, Google is doing the exact opposite of this "closed" or proprietary play, using a standard $1 USB-to-Micro USB cable for audiophile audio hardware connection, rather than a $20 Lightning-to-USB cable.

The difference between using the USB port for audio data and the headphone jack is that the headphone jack is for analog audio signals, while the USB Audio Port uses digital audio data. This means that other types of data, in addition to the audio data, could be sent over this connection as well, allowing metadata as well as transport control data to be sent from the Android 5.0 device to the home audio hardware product.

Android 5 Support: New CPU Hardware and Search

There are some other super cool features that I mention in this section before I cover the new Google Play 5.0 Store and server-side features. One really cool feature that would be expected from Google, the king of search, is the ability to search apps—and even content inside of your apps—and have that content appear on the results of a public Google search engine search query. This feature is no joke, and it is a massive opportunity for Android developers who understand Search Engine Optimization (SEO) and Social Media Marketing (SMM).

Not only is Google expanding the external hardware that will either be running the Android 5.0 OS or connect to it in some way, it is expanding support for the major hardware brands that will be found inside of the Android 5.0 OS devices. New CPU support will become available for ARM CPUs, nVidia GPUs, and x86 support for AMD, Cortex, and Intel CPUs, with most CPU manufacturers eager to support this uber-popular OS.

Another cool feature is the **Smart LockScreen**. It can use your smartwatch to unlock your smartphone or tablet, or it can use location-based (GPS) information that the user programs into it to tell it where it needs to be locked (out in public) and where it does not need to be locked (such as at home).

Another new feature is the **Recents** screen, which organizes applications by task rather than by software. This screen contains a list of documents that users can peruse for a specific task, allowing them to auto-launch applications directly into the activity screen that handles accomplishing that task.

Android 5.0 has the unique ability to seek out specialized types of network connections wherever the Android device might travel. Android 5.0 can scan all available networks and then automatically connect only with the type of network in which your application is interested, such as a transaction (electronic billing) network, a health information system network, or a digital signage network, for instance. This versatile capability allows for specialized dedicated networks to be created by banks, stores, bars, restaurants, gyms, and similar businesses.

Before I get into the new Material Design Themes information regarding Android 5.0 user interface design, I want to cover the new Google Play 5.0 service. Even though it is not "inside" of the Android 5.0 OS, it is an extension of the user experience (UX) for the Android 5.0 OS, so it's appropriate to cover in this chapter.

Google Play 5.0: New Server-Side 5.0 Services

In sync with the Android 5.0 operating system rollout, Google will be rolling out **Google Play Services 5.0** to bring the new Google Play (store) server-side capabilities to the Android 5.0 user experience. These include the new **Google Cast**, which allows you to use media tracks to enable closed-captioning support for Google's new Chromecast platform, as well as **Google Wallet** to facilitate in-app transactions. The Google Wallet allows you to use in-store notifications to prompt a user to show or scan digital cards, and you can create a Save to Wallet UI element for purchase offers within your applications. You can even allow payments to be split between a Google Wallet account and a credit (or debit) card using the split tender transaction. The **Google Drive API** provides cloud storage, and it now supports MIME types, query sorting, and offline folder creation.

Security has been improved via a **Dynamic Security Provider**, which now offers an alternative to the current secure networking APIs. This allows security patches to be updated more rapidly (to keep ahead of hackers). I mentioned the **App Indexing API** in the previous section. It allows content inside of your tablet or mobile applications to be accessible to Google search, which will drive end user engagements with your application.

There is a new set of APIs targeting wearable devices, called the **Android Wearable Services** APIs. These make it easier to interface with an app that is running on an Android wearable product. These APIs are designed to be "low latency" (fast and efficient), as well as to sync the peripheral automatically with the parent device.

There are also **Enhanced Ecommerce Analytics** features that developers can analyze to determine where in the overall purchasing process an end user may be abandoning an initiated transaction. Developers can measure product clicks, add to carts, checkout initiations, transactions, refunds, promotions, and reviews of product details.

Finally, there is a new set of Google Play **Game Services** APIs that include the **Quests** APIs and **Saved Game Snapshot** API, which take features that are normally "inside" of your (client-side) game programming logic and transfer them to the server side so that they can take on social media (friend and public view) attributes. There is also a new **Game Profile** feature, which allows developers to provide "experience points" for their game players, similar to a public-facing top score list on physical arcade game hardware in the arcade.

The Quest APIs provide developers with the ability to set up time-based "goals," or quests, for their players, and to provide rewards to these players on the "server side" without having to update the game on the "client side." This means that the Quest Engine is a service on the Google Play Services 5.0 server that runs independently of your game (or any other type of app) and receives information from your game when your players achieve your predefined milestones, such as reaching a new level or finding rare hidden treasure, for instance.

The Saved Game Snapshot API is also a service, which I like to call an "engine," that runs on the server side and that will save a player's progress in your game (or any other type of app) to "the cloud" (a server) so that the user can use the game across the different types of screen types (consumer electronic device categories) such as smartphones, iTV sets, tablets, game consoles, eReaders, smartwatches, home media centers, and the like. You can also store the game splash screen (or cover image), gameplay description, and minutes played, along with the game snapshot (progress) information, for re-engagement and viral marketing purposes. The next section covers the new UI design features that Google added to Android 5.0.

Material Design: Multi-Platform UI Design

There's another new UI Design feature that Google is calling **Material Design** and it will replace the concept of styles and themes, but that is essentially the same thing other than for the new terminology and additional features. The reason I give it its own section is because it allows developers to take an entire OS User Experience (UX), which is essentially the OS User Interface (UI), across all Google's platforms, including Android OS, Chrome OS, Chrome Browser, Google Apps, Gmail, Google+, and Google Voice.

Materials will probably be implemented in much the same way as styles or themes, using XML definition files, and thus the work process will be quite similar, if not identical, to style and theme definition. In fact, since themes are backward compatible, as you learned in this book, your existing UI themes will still work. You can just enhance them further using the new material capabilities. It is said that Google is adding 5,000 new code additions (classes, methods, interfaces, constants, and so forth) to Android 5, and the key here is the word "adding," since existing core classes will still function as they do under 32-bit versions of Android. In fact, I expect Google to continue to release 32-bit Android OS versions using the 4.x.x numbering schema, so look for a 4.5 and even a 4.6 version of Android to be released some time in the future.

This new material design leverages all of the new Android 5 capabilities, including new motion curve interpolators (enhanced UI animation), Z-index layers for Isometric 3D (enhanced 3D UI design), new ripple effects (enhanced UI touch feedback), a new home screen design, new lockscreen design, "skinnable" notifications, a Rolodex-like information organization paradigm, and a couple of cool new (View) widgets to allow developers to implement these features easily. Now that you have looked over some of the many new features in Android 5.0, it's time to download, install, configure, launch, and use Android Studio 5.0 (and Wear SDK and Android TV SDK) to develop some of your own 64-bit Android 5 applications!

Developing 64-Bit Android: The Android 5 IDE

You'll start by putting together a 64-bit Android Studio 5.0 integrated development environment to use as the foundation for your Android 5.0 application development. I strongly suggest using a 64-bit OS for your Android 5.0 development workstation. These days, it's hard not to purchase 64-bit hardware and software! You know that if Android smartphones are 64-bit, the computer workstations for sale are certainly all 64-bit "clean."

I am going to use one of my Windows 7, 64-bit quad-core systems that has 4GB of DDR3, which currently is set up for development for Android 1.5 through 3.0. I am going to "reform" this workstation from scratch for 64-bit Android 5.0 development by removing Java 6 and Eclipse ADT and installing the latest Java 7 and the IntelliJ IDEA, which are used for the new Android Studio 5.0 integrated development environment. In case you may be wondering, IntelliJ IDEA stands for "Intelligent Java Integrated Development Environment for Android," and a company called JetBrains created it. Don't let anyone tell you that Java development isn't rocket science!

The new IDEA supports the Wear SDK (wearables are covered in Chapter 15) and will soon support the Auto SDK and Android TV SDK, using repository updates. This means that you will only need to go through the process you are about to embark upon once, and Android Studio will update itself over the Internet as new versions become available. In fact, later in this chapter, I show you how I updated my beta 0.8.0 version to 0.8.2 and how I installed the Android TV SDK once it became available.

Since Java is the foundation for IntelliJ IDEA, you will install that first, after you use the Programs and Features control panel utility to remove any trace of Java or Eclipse. Then you will get the Android Studio 5.0 Bundle, which will give you the IntelliJ IDEA and Android 5.0 SDK as one unified install, so that you don't have to go through dozens of steps like you did back in those Android 1.x, 2.x, and 3.x development days.

Removing Java 6: Prepare a System for Android 5

Open the Control Panel, shown in Figure 16-1, and use **Programs and Features** to uninstall old versions of Java. On my system, this was Java 6u45, so I selected what I wanted to uninstall and clicked the **Uninstall** button.

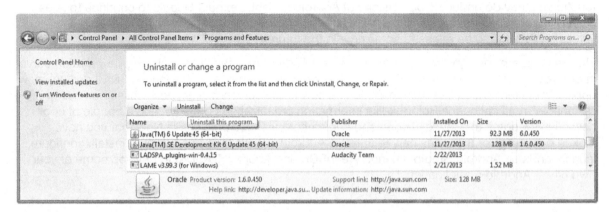

Figure 16-1. Use Control Panel ➤ Programs and Features to select Java 6 JDK and JRE and click the Uninstall button

Your workstation is now ready to install the latest Java 7 SE JDK (Java Development Kit), so let's do that next!

Java 7 SE: The Foundation for Android Studio 5

Google the term "Java 7 JDK download" and get the latest link to the Oracle TechNetwork Java SE 7 download page, shown in Figure 16-2. Select the **Accept License Agreement** radio button and download the latest Java 7 version. If you have a 64-bit workstation, use the x64 version; otherwise, use the x86 (32-bit) version.

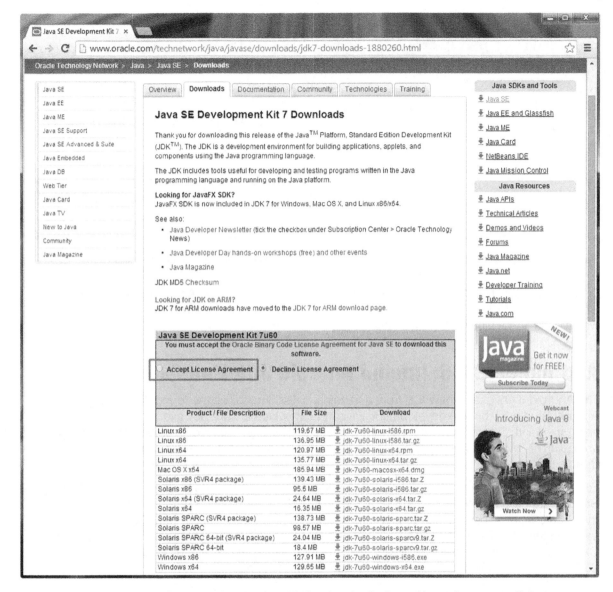

Figure 16-2. Download the 64-bit (x64) version of Java 7 JDK after choosing the Accept License Agreement radio button

Once the download is complete, right-click on the installer file and select the **Run as Administrator** menu option to install the software. Accept the default program folder (directory) shown on the left in Figure 16-3. The progress bar, shown on the right in Figure 16-3, will track your Java 7 environment installation.

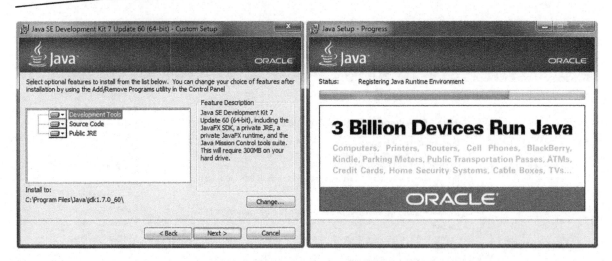

Figure 16-3. *Right-click the 64-bit Java 7 installer and use the Run as Administrator option to run the installer*

Once Java 7 is installed, you will be ready to download and install the Android Studio 5.0 bundle, which uses Java 7 both as a platform to run the IntelliJ IDEA as well as the Java SDK for Android 5.0, which uses 64-bit Linux OS Kernel and the Java 7 platform.

Android Studio 5: IntelliJ Android SDK Bundle

The Android 5 OS uses a new IDE from JetBrains, called IntelliJ, as the foundation for a new Android Studio 5.0 bundle development environment, which is currently available in beta on the developer.android.com web site. Currently, this is at developer.android.com/sdk/installing/ studio.html, but this could change, so it's best to use Google to search for "Android Studio Bundle download".

Figure 16-4 shows the Android Studio BETA page, which contains information about this Android Studio beta program, software, and what the new Android Studio will offer to developers, including the Gradle build system, expanded template support for the new Google Play Services 5.0 covered earlier in this chapter, the Lint tool and ProGuard, as well as other advantages, such as Google Cloud Platform support and Rich (graphical) Layout Editor support. When I downloaded Android Studio, it was at beta version 0.8.0, as you can see in the image.

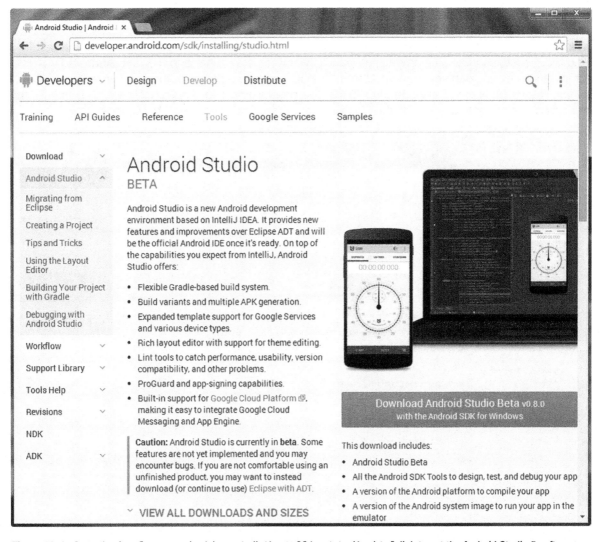

Figure 16-4. Go to the developer.android.com/sdk/installing/studio.html link to get the Android Studio 5 software

Since I downloaded the software, a version 0.8.2 has come out with some bug fixes, so instead of redoing these images, I will instead add a section after we download, install, and tour Android Studio that shows how to update the Android Studio IDE to the latest version by accessing the Google Android Studio code repository.

Click the blue **Download Android Studio** button and download Android Studio to your workstation hard drive. If you want to download other OS versions, you can click on the View All Downloads and Sizes link, shown at the bottom of Figure 16-4, which you will look at a bit later after you examine the rest of this page.

If you scroll down the page shown in Figure 16-4, you will see the IDE comparison table shown in Figure 16-5, which will show you the differences between the IntelliJ IDEA and the Eclipse ADT IDE. As you can see, Ant (an older, command-prompt-driven build system) is used for Eclipse ADT, while Android Studio uses a Gradle build system, as well as supporting Apache Maven, a software project management tool and repository. There are also a couple of other features supported by Android Studio (IntelliJ), such as advanced code completion and refactoring, as well as the ability to generate more than one (multiple) APK (Android Package) file, each of which will support a different type of Android device, such as a smartwatch (Wear SDK), tablet, smartphone, or iTV set (Android TV SDK), for instance. As you can see at the bottom of this IDE comparison chart, there is currently no NDK (which stands for Native Development Kit) for C++ programmers for Android 5.0, which is fine for the purposes of this book, since NDK development is not applicable to absolute beginners!

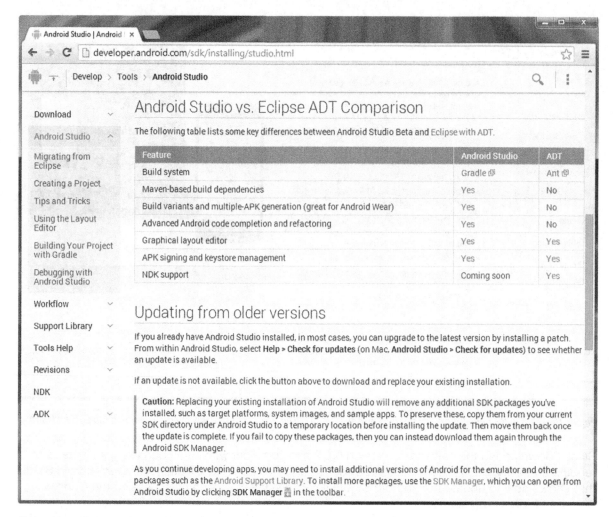

Figure 16-5.   Check out the Android Studio versus Eclipse ADT comparison of IDE features and updating caveats

The bottom part of Figure 16-5 explains how to update to the latest version of Android Studio by using the **Help ➤ Check for updates** menu sequence inside of IntelliJ to access the repository and to install update "patches." A software patch is a partial or incremental update to a software package, usually to fix bugs or to add minor features.

Since Android Studio 0.8.2 came out as I was writing this chapter, I will show you how the update process works. But first, I will show you how to install Android Studio and take a tour of some of its features, as well as show you how to create a New Android Application Project using the new Android Studio IDE.

First, scroll all the way down to the bottom of the Android Studio page and take a look at the Revisions section of the page, which lists all of the revisions of Android Studio, from 0.1.0 in May of 2013 through the current version 0.8.0 released more than a year later. Extrapolating from the three months per version timeline, version 0.9.0 should come out in September 2014 (Q3), and Version 1.0.0 should come out sometime around the end of 2014 (Q4).

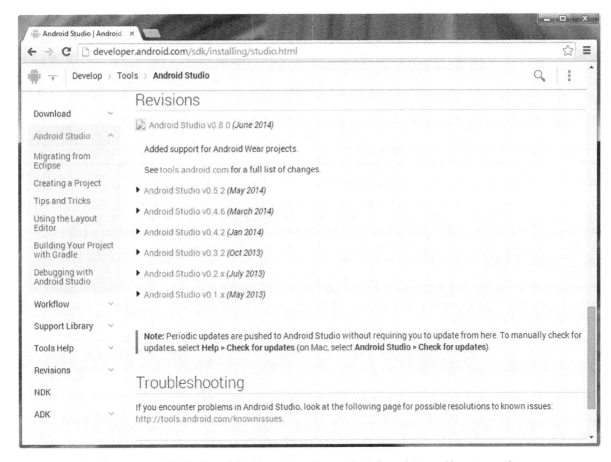

Figure 16-6. *Check out the Android Studio revision history, learn how to check for updates, and learn to use the troubleshooting help*

Downloading and Installing Android Studio

I have a particular work process for downloading software, since I use a lot of open source software. I install this software across a number of different production workstations, since it is free and I am allowed to use it on as many different systems as I wish.

Click on the **VIEW ALL DOWNLOADS AND SIZES** screen to slide open the "drawer" containing the Windows OS, Mac OS X, and Linux OS download files, along with their file sizes, MD5 checksum information, and their links, as shown in Figure 16-7. In case you are wondering how the checksum information is used, it verifies the accuracy of the download. Essentially, if the installer claims that it has been corrupted, this means the checksum of the downloaded file does not match the one that is listed.

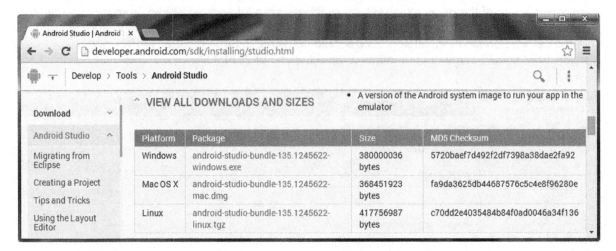

Figure 16-7. *Click the View All Downloads link, right-click an OS package link, and choose Save Link As to download the installer*

You can right-click on any of these links and select the Save File As, Save a Copy As, or Save Link As options, which will allow you to select the area on your hard drive, or in my case on a USB key, which I can transport among any of the workstations in my production facility, installing the software via an external drive.

Figure 16-8 shows the Save As dialog for 64-bit Windows 7 and the Android_5.0 folder I created to hold the android-studio-bundle Windows installer file, which I downloaded using the right-click Save As work process.

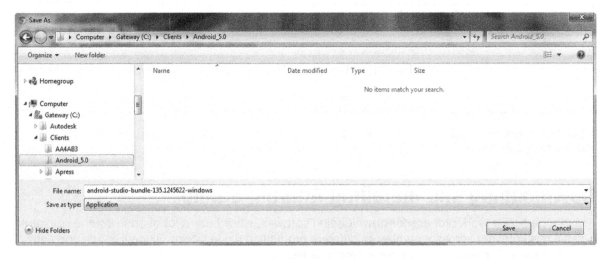

Figure 16-8. *The Save Link As menu item will open the Save As dialog; save android-studio into an Android 5.0 folder*

Once the download has completed, right-click on the file and use the **Run as Administrator** context-sensitive menu option to launch the installer, as shown in Figure 16-9. It is always safer to run and install the software package as the system administrator, so that the installer has the permissions it needs to create any of the necessary folders, sub-folders, or files.

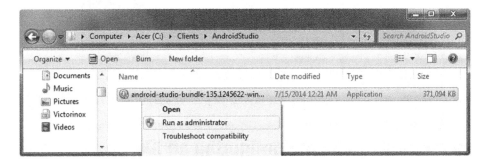

Figure 16-9. Right-click the android-studio-bundle installer and select Run as Administrator to launch it

As you can see in Figure 16-9, I used my trusty USB dongle (key) to transport the downloaded android-studio-bundle Windows installer file from my 64-bit 8GB HexaCore Gateway system, shown in Figure 16-8, to my 64-bit 4GB QuadCore Acer system, which is shown in Figure 16-9.

Once you launch the installer, you will get a Welcome dialog, as shown on the left in Figure 16-10. Click the **Next** button and choose your user base in the Choose Users dialog shown in the middle. Click **Next** and then accept the default installation destination folder in the Choose Install Location dialog, as shown on the right side of Figure 16-10. Notice that the space required, as well as the space available, is listed in this dialog.

Figure 16-10. The Welcome, Choose Users, and Choose Install Location dialogs for the Android Studio installer

Click on the **Next** button and accept the default Android Studio folder name in the Choose Start Menu Folder dialog, shown on the left side of Figure 16-11. Click the **Install** button to install the Android Studio software.

Figure 16-11. *The Choose Start Menu Folder (left), Installation Progress (center), and Installation Complete (right) dialogs*

Exploring Android Studio 5: Configuring an IDE

If you left the (default) **Start Android Studio** option checked in the final installation dialog, shown on the right side of Figure 16-11, once you click on the **Finish** button Android Studio will launch, as shown in Figure 16-12.

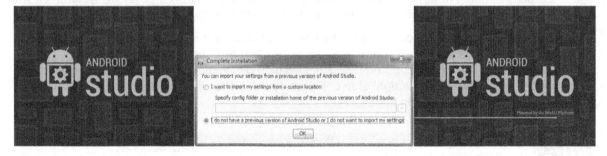

Figure 16-12. *Launch Android Studio using the Quick Launch shortcut on your taskbar and load IntelliJ IDEA*

I chose not to import any previous settings, installing a "virgin" Android Studio installation. Once I clicked the **OK** button, an Android Studio loader screen and progress bar, shown on the right side of Figure 16-12, appeared. Once the Android Studio IDE has loaded into system memory, the Welcome to Android Studio dialog appears, as shown in Figure 16-13. I decided to investigate the Configuration options for Android Studio first by clicking on the **Configure** option, which gave me another list of configuration options from which to select.

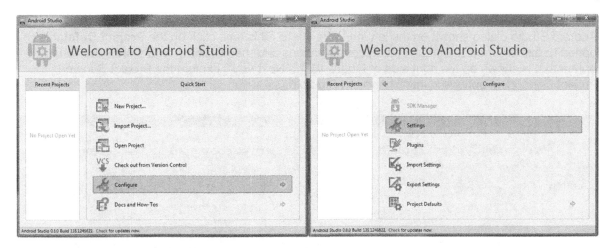

Figure 16-13. Showing the Configure ➤ Settings Android Studio dialog sequence

Let's take a look at how to configure your settings for this Android Studio 5.0 (IntelliJ IDEA) software first by clicking on the **Settings** option. As you can see in Figure 16-14, the Settings dialog for IntelliJ Android Studio is exceptionally complex and detailed, allowing you to click Project and IDE Settings categories on the left side of the dialog, which allows you to set up detailed configuration settings on the right side of this dialog. Take some time, click through the various categories on the left, and see what options are available on the right side of the dialog. That way, you'll know what you can configure when you revisit this dialog.

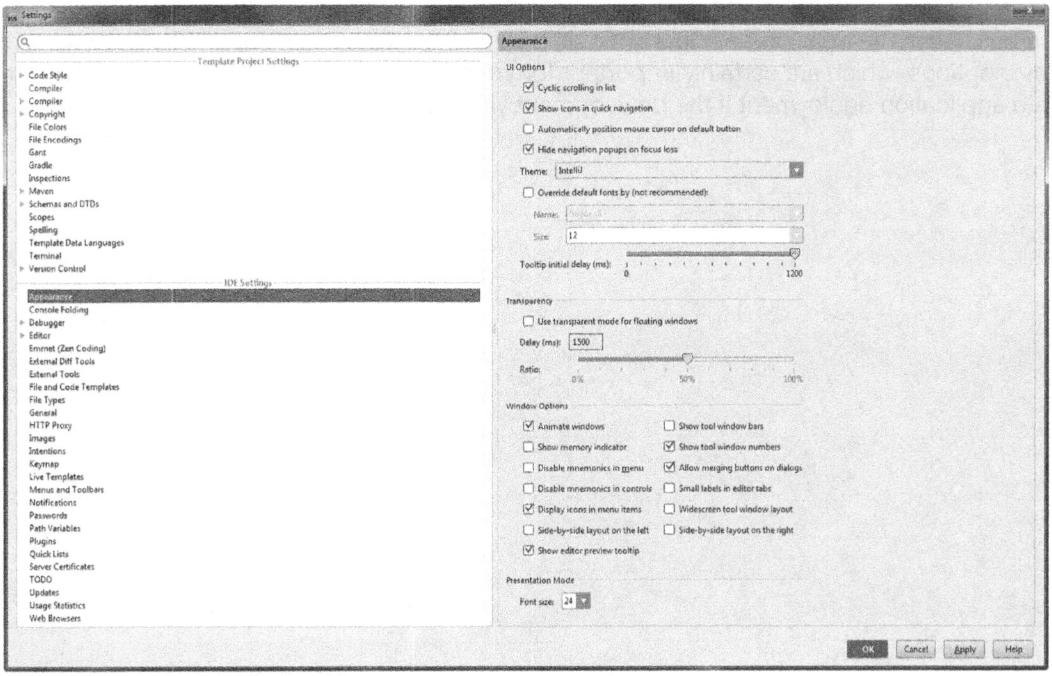

Figure 16-14. Take a look at the various ways you can customize the IntelliJ IDEA

Click the **Cancel** button in the Settings dialog shown in Figure 16-14 and return to the Configure Android Studio dialog shown on the left in Figure 16-15. This time click on the **Project Defaults** option to explore Project Default setting configurations and then click the **Run Configurations** option that is shown on the right side of Figure 16-15. Next you'll explore the Project Run and Project Debugging options in IntelliJ Android Studio 5.0.

Figure 16-15.   Click on the Project Defaults option (left) and then on the Run Configurations option (right)

This will open up the Run/Debug Configurations dialog, shown in Figure 16-16, where you can set Project Run and Project Debugging options for a number of different IntelliJ areas, the most important of which is obviously the Android Application option, shown on the top-left of the dialog. As you can see in the right side of Figure 16-16, this is where you select your APK, Activity, and Emulator options, which are certainly important for your app testing work process as well as for the ultimate application deployment if the development work is finished.

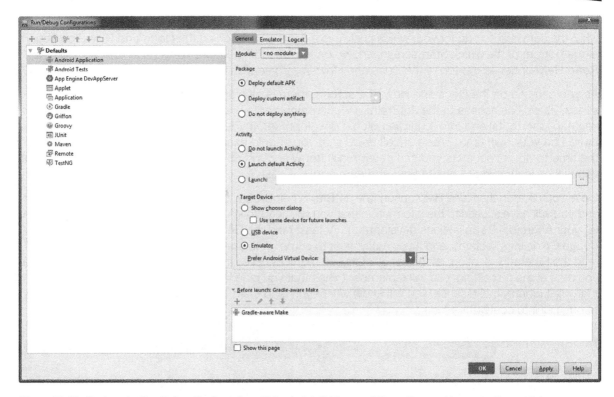

Figure 16-16. Explore the Run/Debug Configurations dialog in IntelliJ to see all the options and to access the emulators

Click the **Cancel** button after you are done exploring this dialog and then use the left-facing "back" arrows on the top of the Project Defaults and Configure screens (shown at the top of Figure 16-15) to return to the main Quick Start screen, which is shown in Figure 16-17.

Figure 16-17. Click the Docs and How-Tos option and then click the Read Help option to open the IntelliJ help docs

Next let's take a look at how to get to the IntelliJ IDEA documentation in case you want to read about what the software can do for you, which is always a good idea. Click on the **Docs and How-Tos** option at the bottom of the Quick Start screen, shown on the left side of Figure 16-17, and then click on the **Read Help** option at the top of the Docs and How-Tos screen, shown on the right side of Figure 16-17.

As you can see on the Docs and How-Tos screen, there is also access to the Tips of the Day dialog series, as well as access to the JetBrains TV eLearning content and reference materials regarding keymap (shortcuts) and info regarding plugin development, if you want to expand the capabilities of IntelliJ on your own time. These are all areas that you should examine more closely when you have the time to do so, because you can never really know enough about your IDE, since it is the tool that you will be leveraging to create your software applications!

Once you click on the Read Help option, the JetBrains help web site will open, as shown in Figure 16-18, and you will have access to the information that you will need to know about how to use the IntelliJ IDEA for your Android 5.0 applications development. At least read the Getting Started, Basic Concepts, and Usage Guidelines sections, and if you really want to come up to speed on IntelliJ IDEA, you will want to read the Reference section, as well as all of its sub-sections. Even if you don't understand everything that you read at the first sitting, you will remember things that you read later as you are using Android Studio that will suddenly make sense, you will know where you read them, and you can return there again later to put it all into context!

Figure 16-18. Peruse the IntelliJ IDEA documentation at www.jetbrains.com/idea/webhelp/intellij-idea.html

Since we are here in the Quick Start dialog and one of the choices is the New Project (creation) option, let's take a look at how to create a new Android 5.0 application. Then you will take a look at how to upgrade your IDE to the latest revision (0.8.2) as well as how to add a custom SDK, such as Android TV.

Creating Your First Android 5 Project

The first option listed on the Quick Start screen after you launch Android Studio 5.0 is the New Project option, which is shown on the left side of Figure 16-19. This is the equivalent of a New ➤ Android Application Project menu sequence in Eclipse ADT, which you used in Chapter 3 to create your Android 4.4 application. As you will soon see, this New Android 5.0 Project process is quite similar to the New Android 4.4 Project process. The knowledge that you gained developing for 32-bit Android 4 devices will transfer over to Android 5.

Figure 16-19. Select the New Project option, which will access the New Project: Configure Your New Project dialog

Click on the **New Project** option to open a New Project (Android Studio). The Configure Your New Project dialog is shown on the right side of Figure 16-19. Let's use an Application Name of HelloAndroid5 and the Company Domain of beginners.absolute.com, as is shown in the first two data entry fields in Figure 16-19.

This will create a package name of com.absolute.beginners.helloandroid5, as shown ghosted in the next line of the dialog. IntelliJ will set a project location to C:\Users\SystemName\ AndroidStudioProject\HelloAndroid5, as shown in the bottom Project location data entry field, which you should accept as is using the default folder location that is suggested by Android Studio 5.0. Once everything is configured the way you want it, click **Next**, which will take you to the second dialog in the New Android 5.0 Application Project series of dialogs. This will be the select Android device form factor dialog, which you will look at next.

Once you click the **Next** button, you will see the Select the Form Factors Your App Will Run On dialog, which is shown in Figure 16-20. This dialog has the default option selected for developing your Android 5.0 application for Phone and Tablet, which I would call the default form factor for an Android app, as this is currently the "sweet spot" in the market, with at least a billion of each of these device types currently in use worldwide.

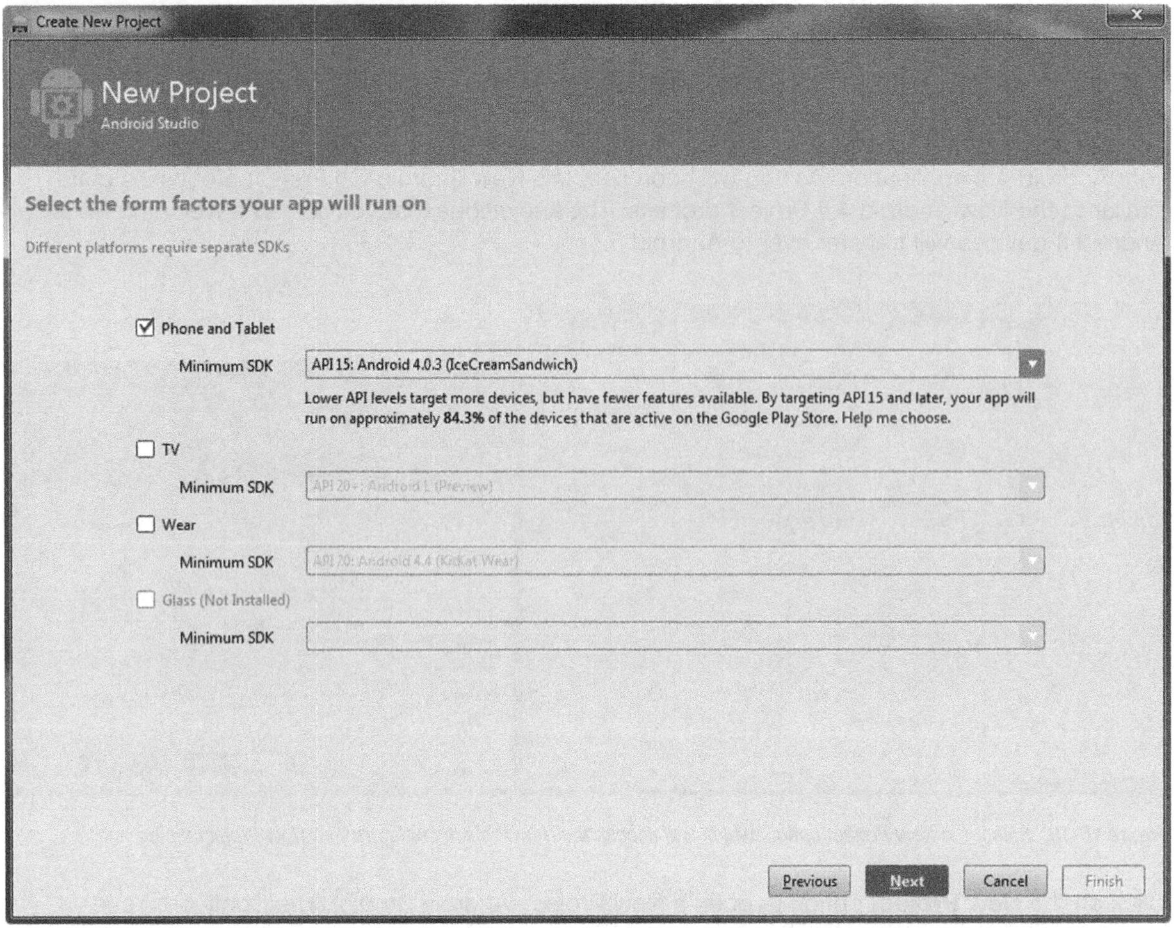

Figure 16-20. Select the Phone and Tablet option and then the Android 4.0.3 API Level 15 Minimum SDK option

Once you install the Android TV SDK, you can select that option and then select the Wear SDK option if you have an Android wearable device for which you are developing, or the Glass SDK if you have a pair of Google Glasses. When you install additional SDKs later, I show you how to install these other niche SDKs.

You can always go back later in the IntelliJ IDEA and add devices at any time that you need to do so, as you may have already surmised. For instance, once the Auto SDK becomes available, you can install it and then select it as a form factor for your app later. I will be showing you how to do all of these work processes throughout the remainder of this chapter, so that you are as up to speed on 64-bit Android 5.0 as you are on 32-bit Android 4.4.

Once you select your device form factors and click the **Next** button, you will be taken to the third dialog in this series, the Add an activity to Mobile dialog, which can be shown in Figure 16-21. This dialog contains almost a dozen "snapshots," or graphical icons, showing the different types of bootstrap application code configurations that this New Android 5.0 Application Project series of dialogs can automatically create for you.

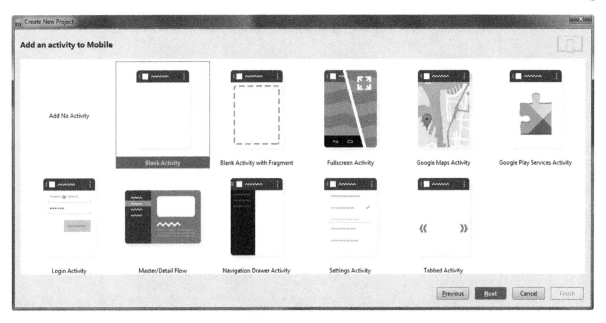

Figure 16-21. Select the Blank Activity template from the template options and then click the Next button

These set the app up for different types of applications, such as full screen (iTV set), Google Maps (smartphone), Google Play Services (game console), Master/Detail Flow (tablet), Tabbed (smartwatch), and the like. You'll use the default Blank Activity to see the minimum bootstrap code that IntelliJ IDEA will create and then build your Android 5.0 application on top of that, from scratch, so that you can learn how to do it.

Click the **Next** button and proceed to the fourth Choose Options for Your New File dialog in the series, shown in Figure 16-22. Use an Activity Name of **HelloActivity** and a Layout Name of **activity_hello** for the XML UI definition file. Make the application Title read **Hello Android 5.0!** at the top of the Android 5.0 app.

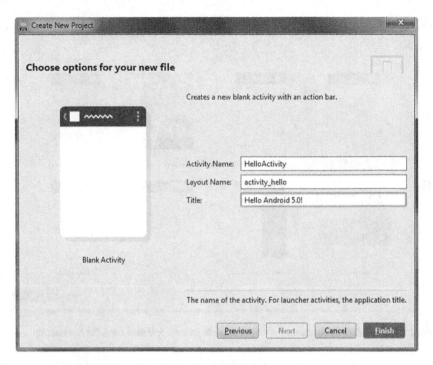

Figure 16-22. Name the Activity HelloActivity and the Title Hello Android 5.0!

As you can see, the same naming convention that you learned about in Android 4.4 regarding the Activity Java code, and for the XML UI definition markup, applies to your Android 5.0 app development.

Once you have all of this set up correctly, click on the **Finish** button and IntelliJ IDEA will build your bootstrap Android 5.0 application for you, just like Eclipse ADT did for you with your Android 4.4 application. As you can see in Figure 16-23, the first thing that IntelliJ will do is create the Gradle build environment for the project. The first time you do this, IntelliJ IDEA may need to download the latest version of Gradle from the gradle.org web site, which is what the progress bar is showing you in Figure 16-23.

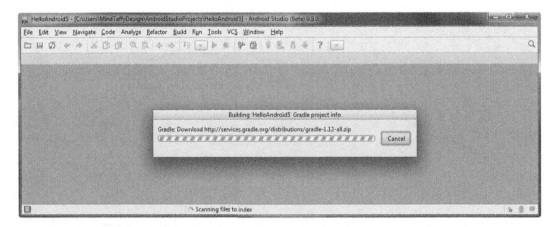

Figure 16-23. Building the HelloAndroid5 project Gradle progress bar on top of unused (blank) IntelliJ IDEA

Once the Gradle build is finished, you'll see the screen shown in Figure 16-24, which will tell you in the lower-left corner that the Gradle build finished, and how long the build process took. A Tool Windows Quick Access message will tell you how to access tools in IntelliJ using the icon in the lower-left corner of the IDE, and you can click the **Got it!** button. There is also some useful keyboard shortcut information in the center of the screen, which you can memorize (or write down) if you are on the fast track to becoming an IntelliJ power user. Notice how you can drag and drop files into IntelliJ using your OS file manager!

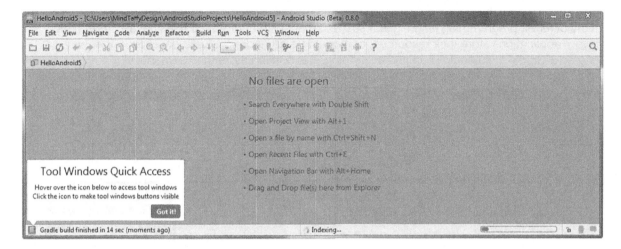

Figure 16-24. Gradle build finished screen; to access tool windows, click the icon to make tool window buttons visible

Once you click the Got it! button, you will be presented with the Tip of the Day dialogs (series), which you can peruse if you like. This will give you more information on tips, tricks, and shortcuts that will make using IntelliJ faster and more efficient. I created a composite image from a few of these, which you can see in Figure 16-25.

Figure 16-25. Explore the Tip of the Day dialog series to learn more about how to use IntelliJ IDE keyboard shortcuts

Once you use the **Close** button and exit the Tip of the Day series of dialogs, you will see your HelloAndroid5 project hierarchy as well as the Java code and XML markup that IntelliJ created for your bootstrap Android 5.0 application. Let's take a look at that next and see how it differs from your Android 4.4 bootstrap Java code, XML markup, and the project hierarchy that you are used to in the Eclipse ADT IDE.

Exploring Your Android 5.0 App in IntelliJ

The first thing that you will probably notice in the Project pane, on the left side of IntelliJ, is that the project folder hierarchy for your HelloAndroid5 project is organized differently than it is in Eclipse ADT, as you can see in Figure 16-26. This might take you a few minutes to get used to, but is not a material difference (no pun intended) from what you learned about in this book, since the /res (resource) folders are named in the same way. The Android 5.0 resource folder is in the HelloAndroid5/app/src/main/ folder hierarchy, which is logical, as resource folders are often kept in the source code folder in many different programming languages. I suspect that since Android 5.0 uses Java 7, this is how Java 7 applications store their resources, or it could be an Android Studio decision. Either way, as long as a Gradle build engine can find everything, it is nothing more than semantics!

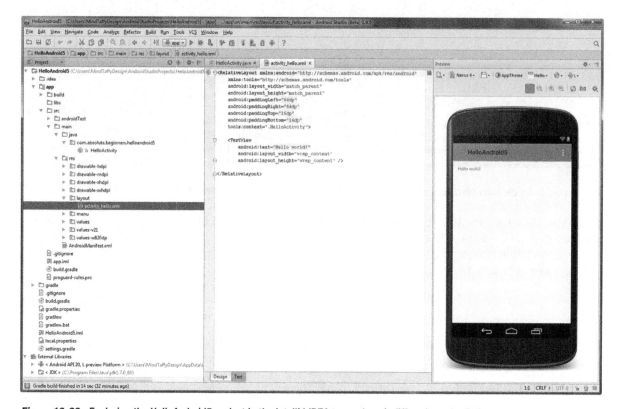

Figure 16-26. Exploring the HelloAndroid5 project in the IntelliJ IDEA to see how it differs from the Eclipse ADT

Also notice that the AndroidManifest.xml file is now located in the HelloAndroid5/app/src/main/res/ folder hierarchy, rather than in the root of the project folder as with Android 4. The Gradle build and ProGuard files are in the HelloAndroid5/app/src/main/ folder. Take some time to explore this new Android 5.0 project folder hierarchy by using the Project pane navigation icons, which work the same way as they do in Eclipse ADT.

Notice in the activity_hello.xml tab in the central code editing pane of IntelliJ that the <RelativeLayout> parent tag and <TextView> child tag are maked up in exactly the same way that they are in Android 4.4 (and earlier), which is what I was talking about when I said that most of what you will learn in this book will not change with Android 5.0 application development. Notice that the AVD emulator, shown on the right side of Figure 16-26, is now an integral part of the IDE, which will make the code-design-test work process faster. It's important to note that how quickly the code is compiled and run in an AVD is still dependent on CPU speed.

Next, click on the HelloActivity.java tab to see how similar the Java code for a bootstrap Blank Activity is to 32-bit Android 4 (and earlier) OS versions. I suspect that it will be identical, as the same core classes used for 64-bit Android 5.0 are used for the Android 1.x, 2.x, 3.x, and 4.x OS versions.

As you can see in Figure 16-27, the Java code that is used for Android 5.0 is identical to what you have been learning about in the first 15 chapters of this book—essentially making this book an Android 5 for Absolute Beginners title! The Java code starts with the Java package declaration, the import statements for the Activity, Bundle, Menu, and MenuItem classes, and the public class HelloActivity extends Activity class declaration.

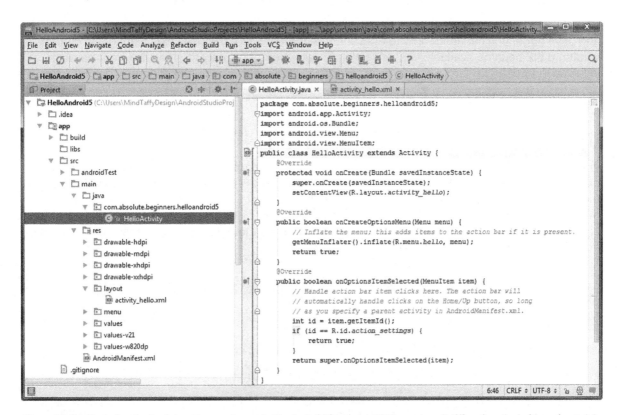

Figure 16-27. Exploring the bootstrap Java code created by Android Studio IntelliJ to see how it differs from Android version 4.4.4

Inside of the activity, you have the standard Android protected void onCreate() method with its super.onCreate() method that creates the activity passing up the savedInstanceState Bundle object and setContentView() method referencing the R.layout.activity_hello XML user interface design definition that you saw in the activity_hello.xml tab.

To create your menu object, you have the "standard" (across 32-bit and 64-bit Android OSs) public boolean onCreateOptionsMenu() method, which calls the .inflate() method off of the Menu class getMenuInflater() method and passes the XML Menu object definition using the standard /res/menu/hello.xml definition file and a Menu object named menu, just as you learned how to do during the course of this book.

Finally, you have the public boolean onOptionsItemSelected() method that passes in the MenuItem object named item. The only difference in this code from what you have used before is that the MenuItem object is evaluated using an if-then-else evaluation code construct rather than a switch-case code construct. The reason this was done is that most switch-case statements use constant expressions, whereas if-then-else statements can use variables, as you can see by the **int id = item.getItemId();** line of code in Figure 16-27. If you like using the switch-case approach, this should work in Android 5.0 and later as well, as both decision logic structures are supported in Java. A primary difference is that switch-cases use constants, whereas if-then-else statements can use variables.

Now that you have created and explored a new Android 5.0 application project, structure, markup, and Java code, you can learn how to upgrade the Android Studio. While I was writing this chapter, version 0.8.2 became available, so I am going to take the opportunity to show the work process involved in updating Android Studio using an IntelliJ IDEA, which is slightly different than how this is done using the Eclipse ADT IDE.

Updating the Android Studio IntelliJ IDEA

The Check for Updates feature is in the same place in IntelliJ and Eclipse (and every other software package), which is on the Help menu, as shown in Figure 16-28. You use a **Help ➤ Check for Update** menu sequence to invoke the IDEA updates from the repository, and you can use the **Help ➤ About** menu sequence to see the number of your current IDEA version, which you'll do right before you check for Android Studio updates. This will allow you to see the before and after result of the update from 0.8.0 to 0.8.2, which you are going to apply next.

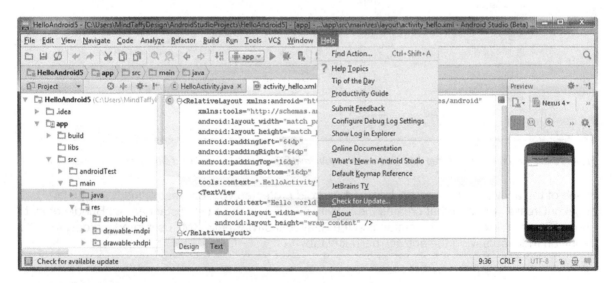

Figure 16-28. Use the Help ➤ Check for Update menu sequence in Android Studio (IntelliJ) to check for updates

As you can see on the left in Figure 16-29, the Android Studio IDE was at 0.8.0 when I used the Help ➤ About menu sequence. The Update Info dialog is shown in the middle of Figure 16-29, which is what I got when I used the Help ➤ Check for Update menu sequence. On the right (shown here in advance to save space) is the updated IDEA About screen showing the freshly updated 0.8.2 Android Studio, which is the ultimate goal for this section. Whether the update from 0.8.0 to 0.8.2 will be as smooth as you would expect is the primary issue at this point, because you are going to be dealing with beta versions of Android 5.0 Studio for some time to come, and until all of the bugs get ironed out of this aggressive new operating system incarnation, anything can happen! If anything does go awry, I will show you the correct work process for solving unanticipated problems.

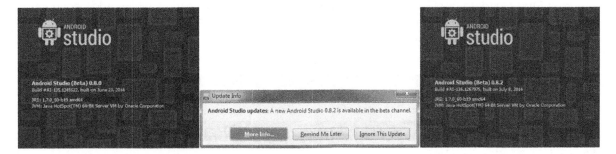

Figure 16-29. Use a Help ➤ About menu sequence to confirm the current version (left); click the More Info button (center)

Once you click on the **More Info** button in the Android Studio Update Info dialog shown in the center of Figure 16-29, you will be taken to the tools.android.com/recent site, which details recent changes to the Android Studio beta. As you can see in Figure 16-30 on the left, Android Studio 0.8.2 has been released, which enables me to show you how an update is performed and how simple (or difficult) it can be.

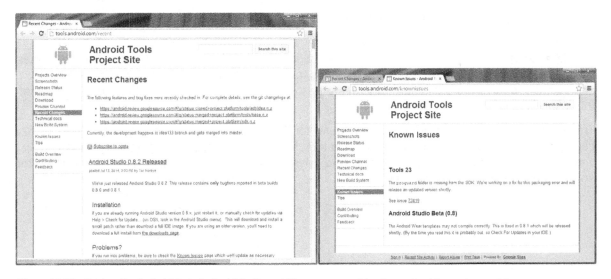

Figure 16-30. Review the Android Tools Project Site Recent Changes page at tools.android.com/recent/

I right-clicked on the known issues link at the bottom of the screen and opened it in a tab (see the right side of Figure 16-30). This shows that there is an issue with the ProGuard folder and it provides a bug-tracking number.

Since there is an update available, I used the **Help ➤ Check for Update** menu sequence again, and I got a quick pop-up message—about the size of a tool-tip message—that said that my Internet connection is faulty. To check on this, I started the Google Chrome browser and went to the Google.com web site, which worked fine. Thinking the Android Studio repository was down, I tried the Help ➤ Check for Update menu sequence a few more times, with the same result. To ascertain if other any other developers were experiencing this problem, I used Google to search for the string "Android Studio update fails" and got a hit on a stackoverflow.com question, which addressed this very issue. I show the top of the stackoverflow.com web site in Figure 16-31, as the entire thread of this widespread issue was several pages long.

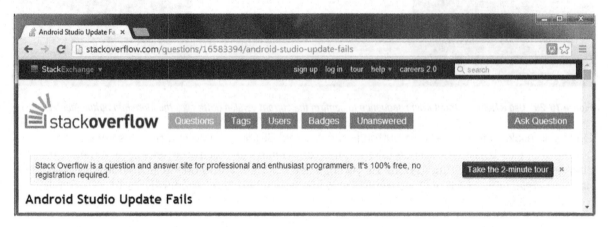

Figure 16-31. Google the string "Android Studio update fails" and go to the stackoverflow.com *Q&A web site*

I found a technical solution in one of the answers suggesting that I add Djava.net.preferIPV6Addresses, which is a network configuration switch that needs to be set to **true** in a **studio64.exe.vmoptions** configuration file in order to fix this problem. I will show you the work process that I used to implement this solution next.

The first thing that I did was search my computer for the studio64.exe file, as shown in Figure 16-32. I searched because Android Studio was not in the usual ProgramFiles folder. I right-clicked the vmoptions file and selected the **Open** option to open the studio64.exe.vmoptions file in a **text editor** so that I could add the needed switch.

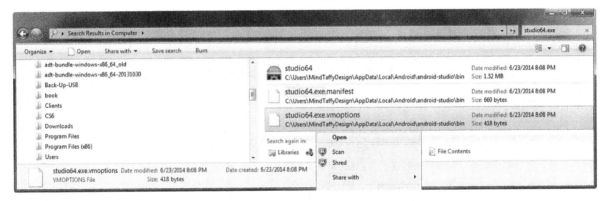

Figure 16-32. Search your computer for studio64.exe and right-click and then open the studio64.exe.vmoptions file

Windows didn't know how to open this type of file, so I chose the **Select Program from a List** option, as shown on the left in Figure 16-33. Then I selected the **Notepad** software (shown in the center) and clicked **OK**.

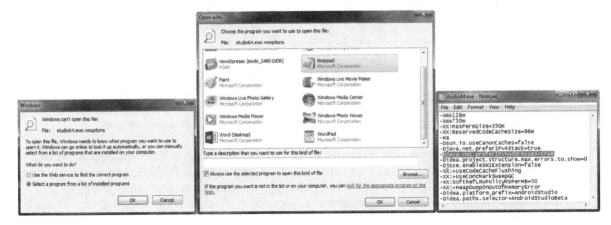

Figure 16-33. Select a program (left), find Notepad.exe (center), and add the switch -Djava.net.preferIPV6Addresses=true (right)

I added a **-Djava.net.preferIPV6Addresses=true** switch, shown in Figure 16-33, and I got the dialog shown in Figure 16-34, the next time that I ran IntelliJ and used the update feature.

Figure 16-34. Once you obtain the repository connection Update Info dialog (left), click the Update and Restart button

Once I was able to click the **Update and Restart** button, shown in Figure 16-34 on the left side of the screen shot, the update was performed, as indicated in the progress bar shown on the right side of Figure 16-34.

Once the progress bar is fully green and the update is completed, the IntelliJ IDEA will automatically restart and you will get your HelloAndroid5 project on the IntelliJ IDEA screen again, as shown in Figure 16-35.

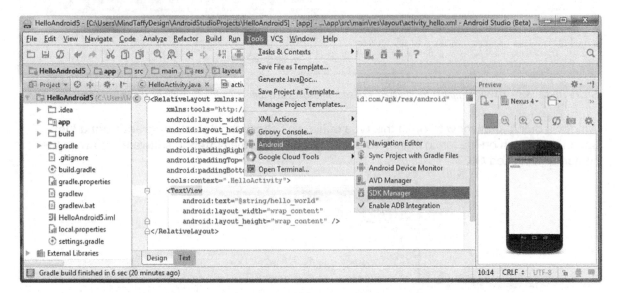

Figure 16-35. The Android SDK Manager in IntelliJ IDEA is on the Tools ➤ Android ➤ SDK Manager submenu

Now it is time to use the Android SDK Manager to take a look at what is in this new update as well as to get any other SDK tools, such as those for Wear SDK and Android TV SDK, as well as any that you don't have for Android 5.0 API Level 20. In IntelliJ, you access the Android SDK Manager by using the **Tools ➤ Android ➤ SDK Manager** menu sequence, which is shown highlighted in blue in Figure 16-35.

Once you invoke this menu sequence and fire up the Android SDK Manager, you will see the familiar dialog. I told you that Android 5 was not that different than what you are (now) used to with Android 4.4! The dialog will be empty, except for a few core Android 5.0 API and SDK tools that you installed and just updated. Initially, at the bottom of the dialog when you first open it, you will see a progress bar shown in Figure 16-36, which will tell you what the SDK Manager is "fetching," just as it did when you used it to update the 32-bit Android 4 SDK.

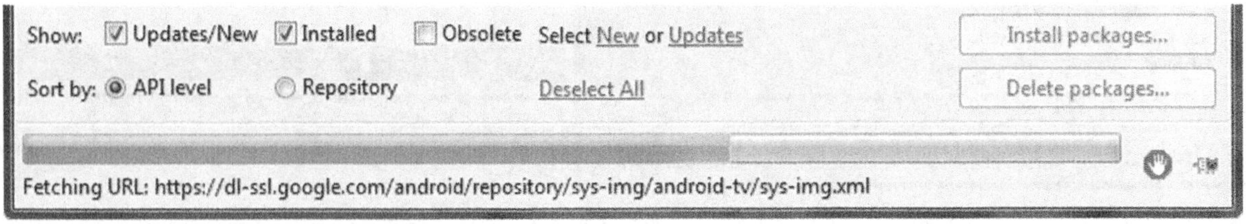

Show: ☑ Updates/New ☑ Installed ☐ Obsolete Select New or Updates   Install packages...

Sort by: ◉ API level ◯ Repository   Deselect All   Delete packages...

Fetching URL: https://dl-ssl.google.com/android/repository/sys-img/android-tv/sys-img.xml

Figure 16-36. When you initially invoke an SDK Manager utility, it fetches all of the files you need from a repository

Once the fetching process is complete, the Android SDK Manager will make suggestions to you about what to install, in the form of checked boxes, as shown in Figure 16-37.

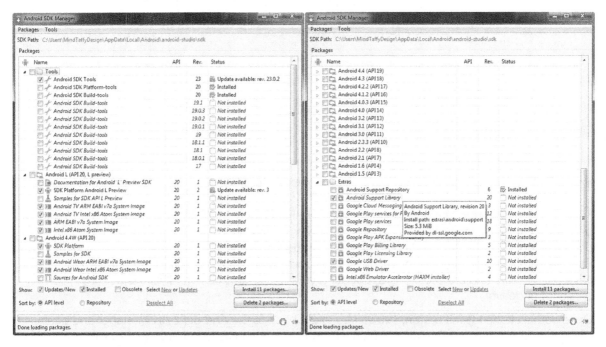

Figure 16-37. After a repository is accessed, the SDK Manager will show the installed SDK and suggest additional SDK installs

The dialog was so tall (long) and thin that I had to cut it into two halves to fit it into the screenshot, as shown in Figure 16-37. As you can see, the Android SDK Manager is suggesting that you install Android SDK Tools update 23.0.2 (Revision 23), Android TV, Android Wear, the Android 5 Support Library (API Level 20), and the latest Google USB driver. Agree to install all of these suggested packages and click the **Install Packages** button.

After you click the Install Packages button, you're presented with a Choose Packages to Install dialog, as shown in Figure 16-38, where you can read and accept the License agreement by clicking a radio button on the right that says **Accept License**. Finally, click on the **Install** button.

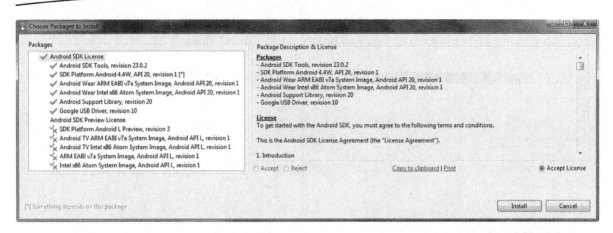

Figure 16-38. After you click the Install Packages button, you select the Accept License option. Finally, click the Install button

Notice that the left side of the Choose Packages to Install dialog will show you which of the selected packages can be installed (green checkmark) and have no dependencies, and which ones are dependent on other SDK or API packages that need to be installed first (green checkmark with a red X next to it). If you see this red X, you will be doing more than one round of updates and, as you have seen before and are seeing here, updating your IDE (in this case an IDEA) is not always a one-shot endeavor.

Once you click the **Install** button, you will be taken back to the Android SDK Manager and again see the progress bar at the bottom, which will show you the installation progress as well as what is being downloaded, the revision, the percentage completed, the bandwidth speed, and the estimated amount of time left for that particular package to download. As you can see, my new ViaSat Exede Internet Satellite system is quite fast!

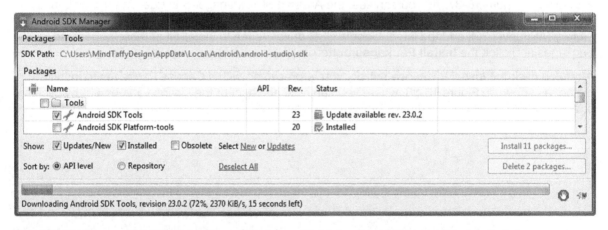

Figure 16-39. After you click the Install button, a progress bar will show you what SDK tool is being downloaded

Everything was going along very smoothly when suddenly the Android SDK Manager Log and an error dialog popped up on the screen, and my entire smooth update world fell apart. I clicked Yes (trying again to create that folder) several times, knowing in the depths of my soul that Windows 7 was not going to give permission to the Android SDK installer to create, move, or delete folders, as it was trying to do, and that I should have probably started IntelliJ IDEA using a trusty Run as Administrator work process before invoking these SDK updates.

Who knew? Clearly I was not thinking far enough ahead and I was not anticipating this problem. So I acquiesced to this current failure and clicked the No button. This allowed the Android SDK package installer to finish the package installations, which did not involve file or folder creation, deletion, or movement.

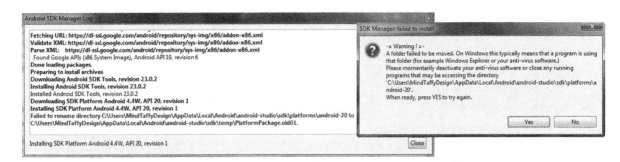

Figure 16-40. *Monitor an SDK Manager Log (left) for problems (right), such as the "failed to install" warning dialog*

I have thus created some more updater problems, but I can fortunately show you the work process I used to fix them, if you inadvertently do the same thing at some point in the future. As you can see in Figure 16-41, the installs continue and the Android Support Library (API 20) and Google USB Driver (r10) install successfully. However, the Android Wear SDK packages (System Image emulators for ARM and Intel hardware) fail because Android 4.4W (Wear) API 20 failed to install, and these packages are predicated on that package installing successfully, so you are going to have to go back and run IntelliJ as an administrator (some operating systems call this mode superuser) at some point in time after you finish taking a look at what did install successfully.

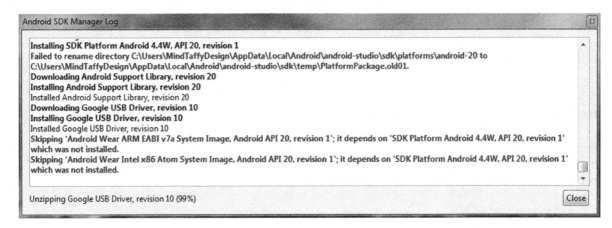

Figure 16-41. *An SDK Manager Log tells you that the Android Wear system images are not installed due to the previous error*

Click the **Close** button on the Android SDK Manager Log dialog to close it, and click the **OK** button on the info dialog shown in Figure 16-42, which tells you that the Android Tools Update is complete. Notice that this dialog also suggests that you close the Android SDK Manager utility window and then reopen it, which you will do before you run IntelliJ as an administrator so that you can see exactly what installed and what failed to install.

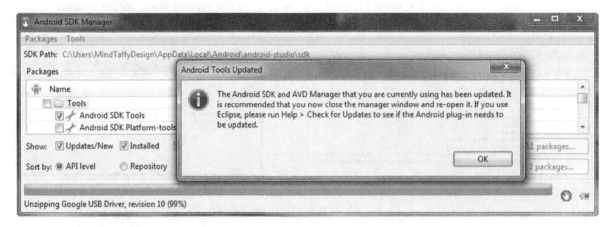

Figure 16-42.   Once the install is complete, you'll get an Android Tools Updated dialog suggesting you use the SDK Manager

Use the familiar **Tools ➤ Android ➤ SDK Manager** menu sequence to open SDK Manager and confirm that SDK Tools, Platform-tools, Build-tools, Support Library, and Repository are installed, as shown in Figure 16-43.

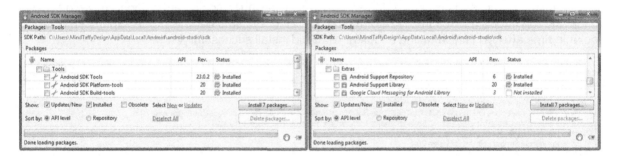

Figure 16-43.   Open the Tools ➤ Android ➤ SDK Manager dialog and confirm that the latest SDK Tools were installed

Exit IntelliJ and go back into your OS file manager utility search results for studio64.exe, as shown in Figure 16-44. This time, however, right-click on studio64.exe and use the **Run as Administrator** option to launch the IDEA.

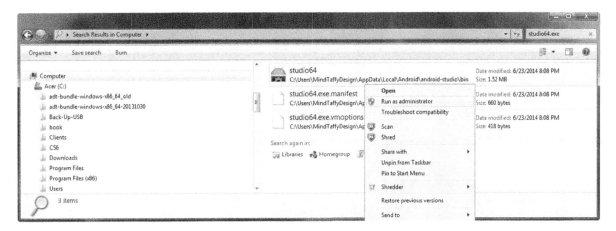

Figure 16-44. This time, you're going to run your updates by right-clicking Android Studio and choosing Run as Administrator

After you launch Android 5 Studio as an administrator, you will find that your HelloAndroid5 project has been seriously compromised, as can be shown in Figure 16-45, by no (project code-based) fault of your own! Click the blue **Open Android SDK Manage**r link at the bottom next to the error message to run the SDK Manager.

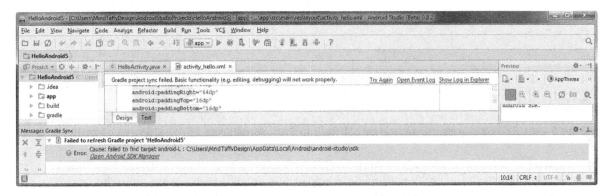

Figure 16-45. Relaunch Android Studio to discover that the failed installs from the previous update compromised the project

As you can see in your SDK Manager utility window in Figure 16-46, Android 5.0 Studio is suggesting that you install Android 5.0, code-named L API Level 20, Android 4.4W (Wear) API Level 20, and Android TV, which is what is currently available. In case you are wondering why wearables are at 4.4W, my guess is that the SDK is still at the 32-bit level, and thus it will use a 4.x numbering scheme, which will probably come to signify a 32-bit platform.

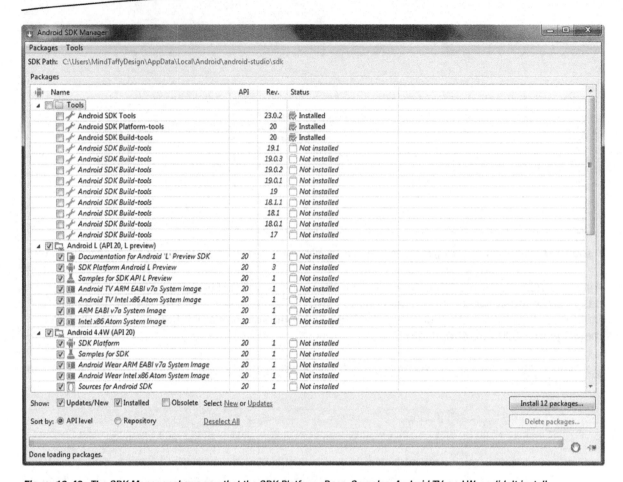

Figure 16-46. The SDK Manager shows you that the SDK Platform, Docs, Samples, Android TV, and Wear didn't install

Let's leave the selected packages as Android Studio suggests and click the **Install Packages** button. Since you've launched IntelliJ as an administrator, it will now have the authority to create, delete, rename, move, or launch any files or folders on your OS. This time there should be none of the problems that you encountered previously (see Figure 16-41).

Once you click the **Install** button, you will see the Choose Packages to Install dialog, with the selections (some ready to install, and some predicated on other installs) that will require you to select the **Accept License** radio button and click on the **Install** button. As you can see in Figure 16-47, there are five packages that can be installed right away, and another seven that require those five packages to be installed in order to install. This tells you that you will have to go through this SDK Manager ➤ Install ➤ Accept License work process again.

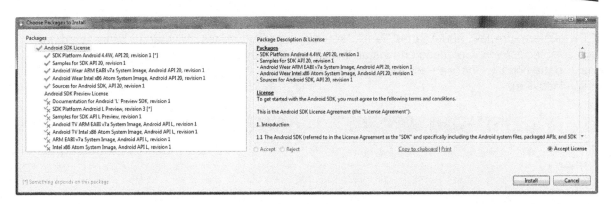

Figure 16-47. Select the Accept License radio button again and click the Install button to install API 20 and Wear

Once you click the Install button, you will get the progress bar at the bottom of the SDK Manager that will tell you which package is being downloaded, unzipped, or installed. That bar includes progress and speed statistics (see Figure 16-48).

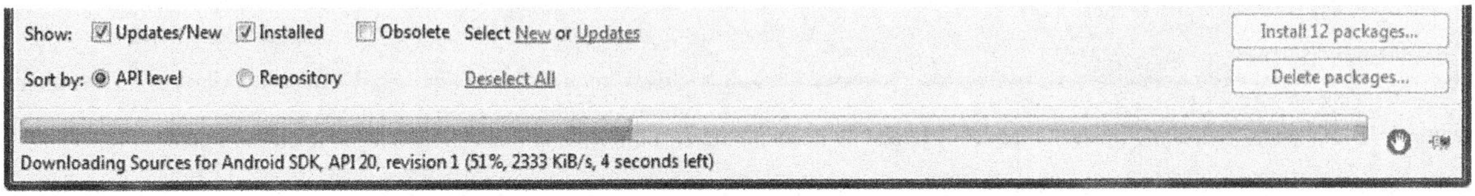

Figure 16-48. Once you click the Install button, IntelliJ will again attempt to download and install your selections

When the installation is complete, check the SDK Manager in the Status column, as shown in Figure 16-49, to make sure that the packages in the Android 4.4W section have all installed successfully, which they now have.

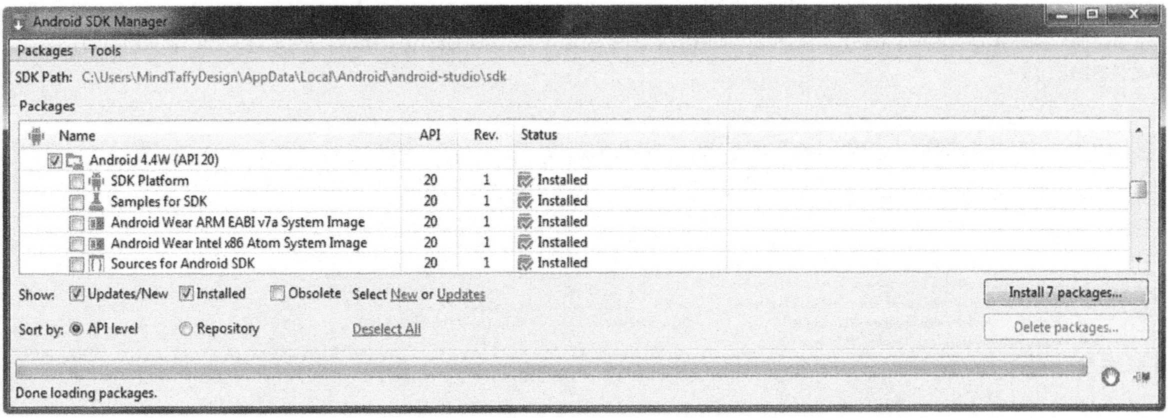

Figure 16-49. Go into the Tools ➤ Android ➤ SDK Manager utility again and confirm that the SDKs were all installed

As you can see in Figure 16-50, the Android 5.0 L API Level 20 preview documentation, samples, SDK platform preview, and Android TV (iTV set) development utilities still need to be installed and are selected for you. Go ahead and install these now, as they should now have green checkmarks next to them in the Choose Package to Install dialog (since the 4.4W API Level 20 packages have all been installed).

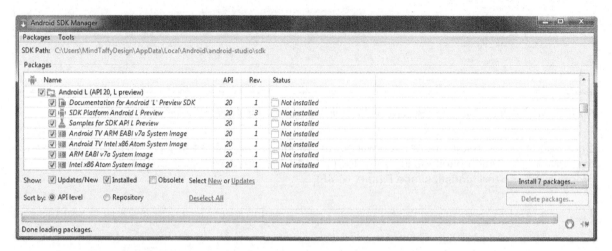

Figure 16-50. *Now that the SDK required for Android TV is installed, run the Android SDK Manager and install again*

Notice that this time the 4.4W packages installed successfully, as the IntelliJ IDEA that is installing them is now running with administrator level OS privileges and thus is able to create, move, or delete files or folders that were needed to complete the 4.4W installs that failed earlier. BE sure to notice that the Run as administrator work process can solve these types of problems with other types of software packages, not only with IDEs.

As you can see in Figure 16-51, the other seven packages are now cleared for installation, and all that you have to do is click the **Accept License** radio button and the **Install** button to finish installing all of the latest goodies that are available for the Android 5.0 platform on your new IntelliJ IDEA workstation!

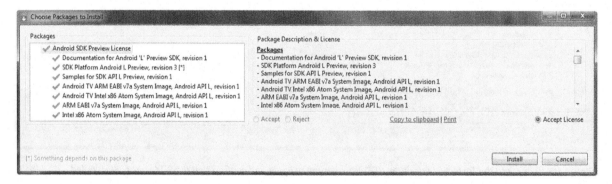

Figure 16-51. *Select the Accept License radio button and click the Install button to install Rev 3 and Android TV*

The final step in this lengthy and challenging "update and install the latest SDK" work process is to use the Status column of the SDK Manager to confirm that everything has installed correctly, as shown in Figure 16-52.

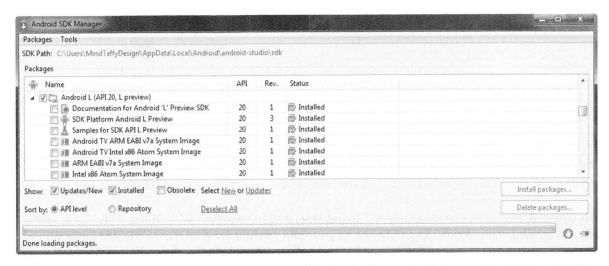

Figure 16-52. Go into the SDK Manager one final time to confirm that revision 3 of the SDK platform and Android TV are installed

As you can see, everything has now been installed, and it is time to exit and restart the Android Studio (IntelliJ) IDEA, load all of the new software into memory, and see if that fixes the currently broken Android project.

It is important to note that you do not need to start IntelliJ as an administrator this time around, as you are done updating software packages, SDKs, APIs, system images, and the like, so you don't need this level of power simply to run the IntelliJ IDEA and develop Android 5.0 applications (or Android TV or Wear apps).

As you can see in Figure 16-53, your HelloAndroid5 project is back—and in working condition to boot! Notice that if you click on the drop-down selector in the graphic-oriented Preview area on the right, as I did before I captured this figure, you will see that the Android Wear as well as the Android TV application preview capabilities have now been added to the Android Studio IDEA. Sometimes success can take some persistence!

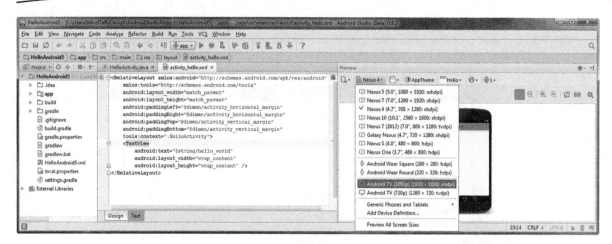

Figure 16-53. Exit and re-enter Android Studio "normally" using the Quick Launch Icon; the project is now restored!

Throughout this book, I have been trying to get you used to problems with SDKs, APIs, IDEs, and even with a build environment like Gradle, as you just experienced here. I'm doing this because programming is a marriage of the code and the programming platform (this includes SDKs, APIs, build environments, IDEs, runtimes, and system images).

It is important to take note, as you have throughout this chapter, that this platform and programming environment code does not work all of the time, as the platform developers (Google with Android or Oracle with Java) are always updating their code, just like you are with your applications.

Next you will learn how to set your application up to work with the new Android TV platform, which is newly available!

Android TV: Setting Up Android 5 Apps for iTV

Since Android TV just came out, this section looks at how to create an application that runs on an iTV set; thus this book titles spans from the smallest Android devices (smartwatches) to the largest (iTV sets)! If you wanted to research everything there is on Android TV, search Google for "Android TV" and click on the link for the Android TV preview located at developer.android.com/preview/tv/start/index.html, which is shown in Figure 16-54. Notice that you have already accomplished the Set Up the Preview SDK part of the Android TV prerequisites, so all you have to do is modify the project using the Android Manifest XML file and you will be off and running, developing Android applications for the Android TV platform!

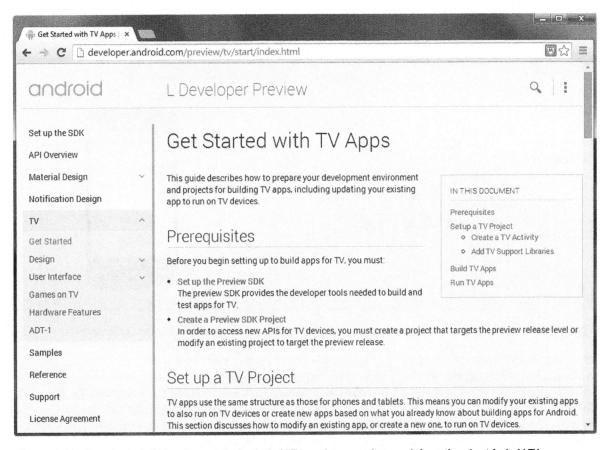

Figure 16-54. Go to the Android Developer web site, Android TV preview page, for more information about Android TV

You'll start with something that you have learned how to do already: editing your AndroidManifest. xml file. This file is located in the HelloAndroid5/app/src/main folder in the Android Studio (IntelliJ) project structure, so right-click on that now, as shown in Figure 16-55, and see if there is an Open option, just like there is in Eclipse ADT. As you can see, the Android Studio (IntelliJ) IDEA uses a different **Jump to Source** option, rather than an Open option. Now that you know that, you know how to open files for editing in IntelliJ IDEA!

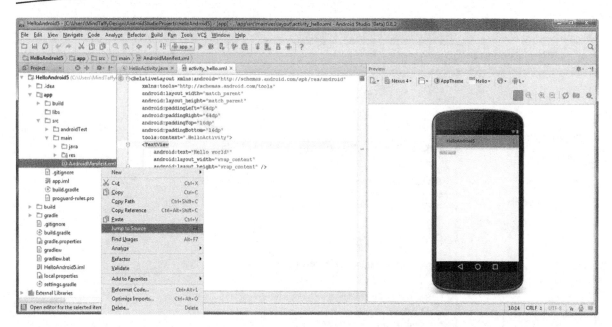

Figure 16-55. Right-click the AndroidManifest.xml file (in the /app/src/main folder) and use the Jump to Source option

Once the AndroidManifest.xml file is open in the central editing pane of the IDE, you can upgrade a <category> child tag under the <intent-filter> tag inside of your <activity> tag inside of your <application> tag to reference the **LEANBACK_LAUNCHER**, which is used for Android TV, rather than the default **LAUNCHER**, which is used for smartphones and tablets. As you can see in Figure 16-56, IntelliJ will help you as you are typing in the new constant value. You can type it in yourself, double-click the suggestion, or use **Control+Period** to select.

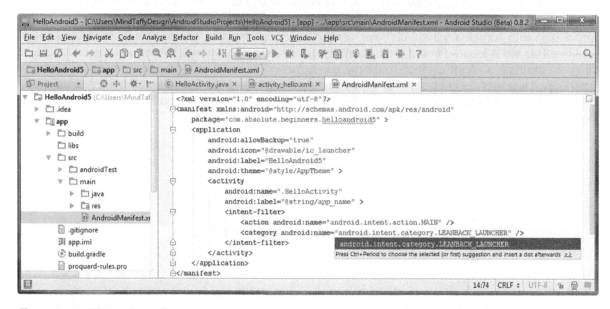

Figure 16-56. Edit the <intent-filter> structure <category> tag; change LAUNCHER to LEANBACK_LAUNCHER

Now you have to make sure that your Android app is shown as an Android TV app by the Google Play store, which will look for this <category> tag in your Android Manifest XML to make the decision regarding how and where to list your Android TV application. If you want to research information on how to design for the iTV set platform and hardware, you can go to the developer.android.com/preview/tv/ui/index.html page, which covers the UI Design layout and navigation guidelines and offers suggestions for Android TV, as shown in Figure 16-57.

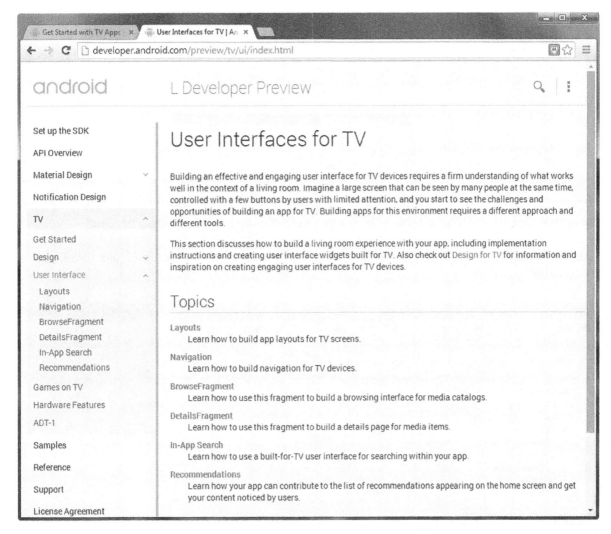

Figure 16-57. Be sure to peruse information on Android's Developer web site regarding iTV UI design guidelines

Notice that under the User Interface section on the left navigation pane for the preview site, there's a Games on TV section. You'll take a look next at how to list your Android TV application automatically as a game on the Google Play store, as this is something that you may want to do. Add a line of space after the android:theme parameter in the <application> tag and start typing the word "android." As you can see in Figure 16-58, IntelliJ implements an automatic tag parameter pop-up helper dialog, just like Eclipse does.

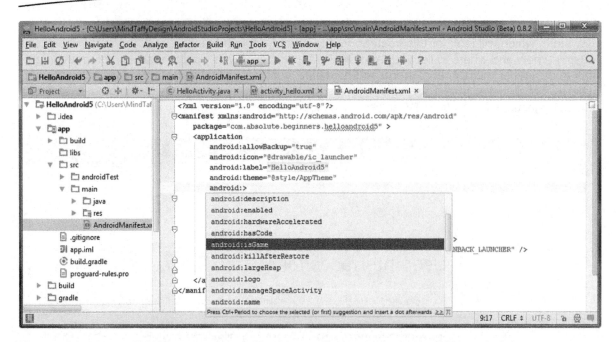

Figure 16-58. Add an android:isGame parameter inside of the <application> tag by double-clicking on the helper

Add the **android:isGame="true"** parameter using the helper. As you can see in Figure 15-59, you're ready to go!

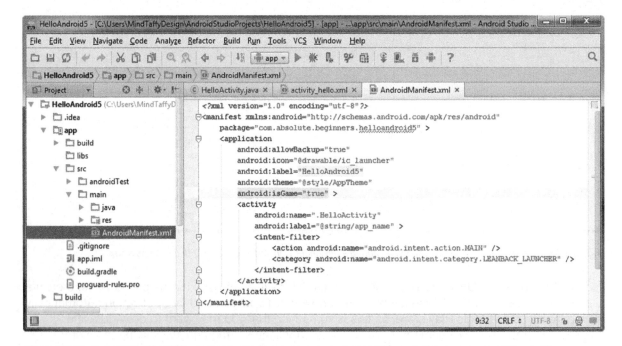

Figure 16-59. Android Manifest XML markup to display your app as an Android TV app in the games area of Google Play

Now you can close the AndroidManifest.xml tab or leave it open and click on the activity_hello.xml tab, which will open the Preview pane shown on the right side of Figure 16-60. Use the drop-down selector to select the TV (720p) preview mode selection, and you will see the HelloAndroid5 application running in a TV 720p preview.

Figure 16-60. *Select the TV (720p) option from the Preview area drop-down menu to see your app in Android TV*

Now you'll take some Android 4.1 code that you wrote earlier and drop it into the Android 5.0 Studio environment and run it—just to prove my point that 32-bit Android 4.x code and assets run identically in 64-bit Android 5.0. You will port the EarthTime application to run in IntelliJ IDEA next and run it in a TV 720p AVD.

Porting the EarthTime App to Android TV

Copy your EarthTime drawable assets into the /app/src/main/res/drawable-mdpi folder, as shown in Figure 16-61.

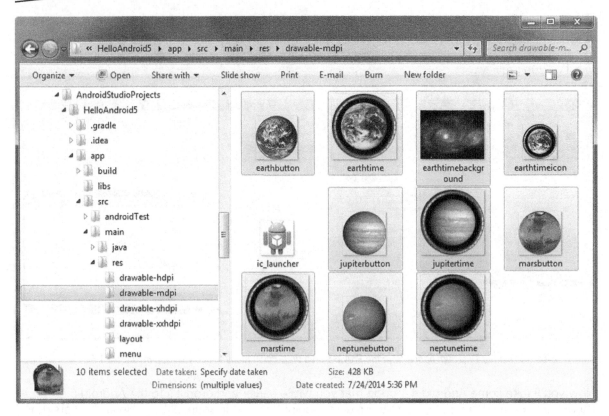

Figure 16-61. Copy the EarthTime drawable assets to /app/src/main/res/drawable-mdpi

It is important to note that IntelliJ IDEA does not require that you refresh like Eclipse ADT does. In fact, if you look ahead at Figure 16-64, you will see that these assets are in place without having to refresh during this work process.

Next, copy the entire <FrameLayout> UI design XML construct from your EarthTime /res/layout folder and paste it into the activity_hello.xml UI design bootstrap XML definition, as shown in Figure 16-62. As you can see, the IntelliJ IDEA highlights the @string constant references in red to show that these are not found.

Figure 16-62. Copy the <FrameLayout> structure from the EarthTime UI layout container into activity_hello.xml

To remove these error highlights, copy the three planetClock <string> constant XML definitions from your Eclipse project's /res/values/strings.xml file and add them into your IntelliJ project's /res/values/strings.xml definition file, as shown in Figure 16-63. As you can see, there are many similarities between the way that an Android project is set up in 32-bit Android 4 and the way that a project is set up in 64-bit Android 5.

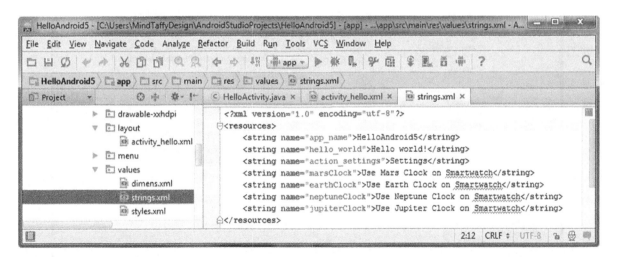

Figure 16-63. Copy the planetClock <string> constants from EarthTime into HelloActivity strings.xml

Now you can copy the Java code from the EarthTime.java tab in the Android 4.1.2 project that you created in Chapter 15 and paste it into the HelloActivity.java file under the package statement, as shown in Figure 16-64. Remember that the package needs to stay the same, as does the HelloActivity class, the R.layout.activity_hello reference, and the R.menu.hello reference. Other than that, the EarthTime code should run as is! Notice that even the latest 4.x version of Eclipse has switched from using switch-case statements for Menu Item selection to using if-then-else statements.

Figure 16-64. Copy the Java code from EarthTime.java and switch R.menu.hello and R.layout.activity_hello

Next, click on the activity_hello.xml tab and size the Preview pane as I have in Figure 16-65 to see that the app and assets are rendering correctly in the Graphical Preview pane (equivalent to the Eclipse Graphical Layout Editor pane). Now that you have the Android 4.1 application put together as an Android 5.0 project, you can start the AVD creation process so that you can finally run the Android 5.0

project in an emulator. This means you'll complete the entire Android 5.0 application development work process (from install, to update, create, port, emulate, and finally run) in one chapter (albeit a long one). You will see even more similarities with the AVD creation work process!

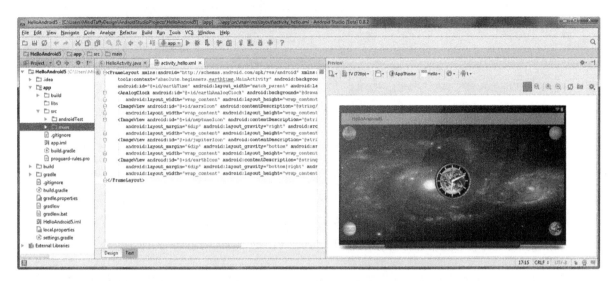

Figure 16-65. Click the activity_hello.xml tab and look at Android TV app in preview

Use the **Tools ➤ Android ➤ AVD Manager** menu sequence shown in Figure 16-66 to launch the AVD Manager.

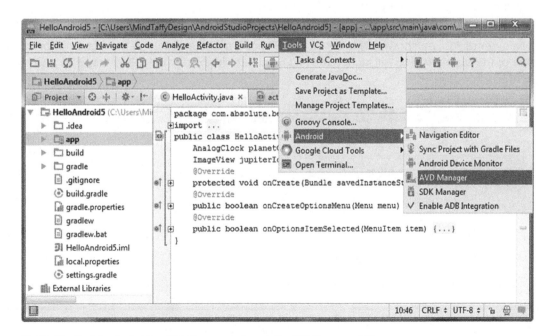

Figure 16-66. Use Tools ➤ Android ➤ AVD Manager to launch the AVD Manager utility

Select the Android TV 720p Device Definition, Create AVD, and configure the AVD, as shown in Figure 16-67.

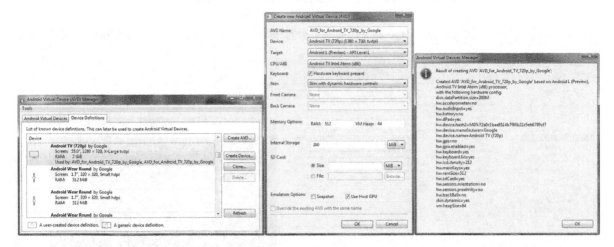

Figure 16-67. *Select the Android TV Device Definition (left), configure it (center), and finally, create it (right)*

Notice in Figure 16-67 in the middle that I selected Android 5.0 L Preview as the target and the Intel Atom x86 processor as the CPU, since you have installed the System Image for that hardware emulator. I selected the Skin with Dynamic Hardware Controls and 512MB of RAM, since my workstation only has 4GB of DDR3. I Use the Host GPU as well, since I have an AMD 64-bit workstation with GPU support. Once you click the **OK** button, you get the Result of Creating AVD dialog, which is shown on the right side of Figure 16-67.

Once an AVD is created, it will appear in the Android Virtual Devices tab of the Android Virtual Device (AVD) Manager dialog, as shown in Figure 16-68. Select it and then click on the **Start** button on the right side of the dialog, which will launch the AVD emulator in exactly the same way that it works in Eclipse ADT.

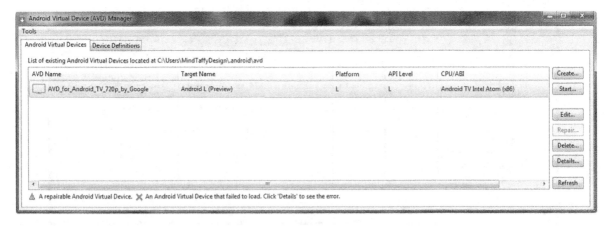

Figure 16-68. *Select the AVD_for_Android_TV_720p_by_Google and then click on the Start button*

Once you click the Start button, you will get the Launch Options dialog, as shown on the left side of Figure 16-69. I selected the **Scale Display to Real Size** so that I could see actual pixels, and then I set the Screen Size to **15.3** inches at 96 DPI to get a 1:1 pixel scale. I also selected the **Wipe user data**, more for future use than for a first time launch, as you have already learned all about previously in this book. Once you click the **Launch** button, you'll get a Starting Android Emulator dialog, as shown on the right side of Figure 16-69, showing the launch progress.

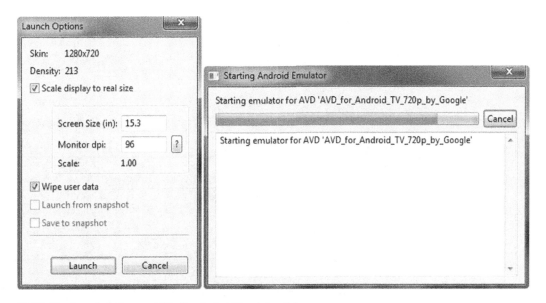

Figure 16-69. *The Launch Options and Starting Android Emulator dialogs*

On my workstation I could not at this point get the AVD to launch: it launched on the loading screen and then hung. I will give you one guess as to how I got the emulator to run in the end. I exited IntelliJ and used the **Run as Administrator** trick (shown in Figure 16-44) to launch IntelliJ, and only then did an AVD launch work. Did you guess correctly?

Now let's go into the Run/Debug Configurations dialog (under the **Run ➤ Run Configurations** menu sequence) and use the **Target Device** area of the dialog that you looked at earlier in the chapter to set the AVD emulator that you just created. Select the **Emulator** radio button, as shown in Figure 16-70, and select your new AVD.

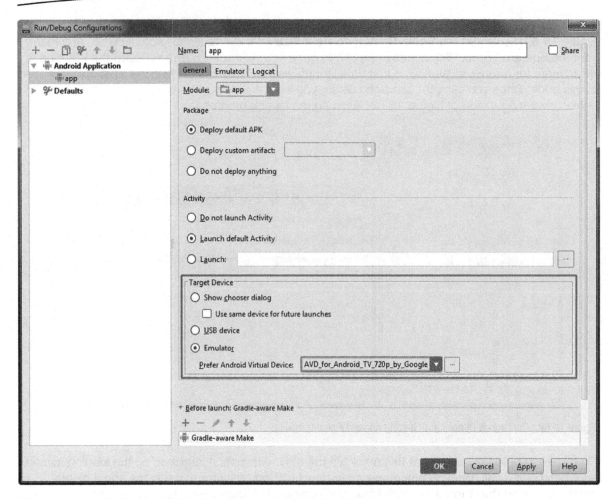

Figure 16-70. Go into the Run Configurations (Run menu) and select the Emulator option

Now when you use the **Run ➤ HelloActivity** menu sequence, you will see IntelliJ using the AVD, as shown in Figure 16-71 in the bottom "error, messages, and runtime feedback" pane (same as it works in Eclipse ADT).

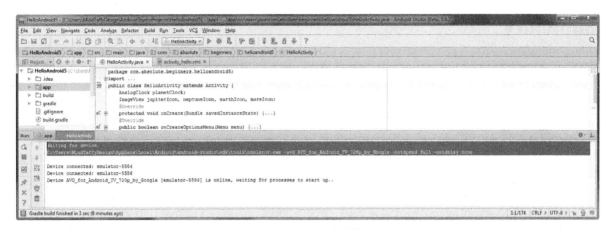

Figure 16-71. The bottom portion of IntelliJ shows error and progress messages, just like Eclipse ADT

When the Android TV 720p AVD emulator appears, click on the planet icons in the corners and make sure that the application code that you wrote for Android 4.1 works under Android 5 for Android TV! Pretty cool stuff, right?

Figure 16-72. The Android TV AVD launches and runs the EarthTime application perfectly—all the buttons work great!

Congratulations, you have created an Android 5.0 application for the Android TV platform, meaning that you've learned how to develop for everything from smartwatches to iTV sets during the course of this 700-page book!

Summary

In this sixteenth and final chapter, you learned about 64-bit Android 5.0 OS development. You learned all about the new features and attributes of the Android 5.0 L OS released this summer at the Google I/O show. Some think this OS will end up with the name "Lollipop," while others think that it will be named "Licorice."

You updated the 0.8.0 SDK to 0.8.2, and you learned about some of the pitfalls of using a beta version of the 64-bit OS version, which will certainly exist until this 64-bit OS and its IDEA are refined as much as the 32-bit Android OS was between the years of 2010-2014, so expect a stable Android 5.x OS sometime during 2015 or 2016.

Then you learned about the newly-released Android TV platform, and you learned where to access information regarding how to develop iTV set applications, as well as converting your very first HelloAndroid5 Android 5.0 application to be Android-TV compatible using the AndroidManifest.xml file. You learned how to designate the Android TV application as a game, so that it is listed in the games section of the Google Play store instead of in the apps section. You learned how to create an Android TV AVD and tested your Android TV app in that AVD.

I hope you have had a fun, insightful time during the lengthy journey that you have undertaken through Android 4.4.4 and 5.0, including the Wear SDK and Android TV, through sixteen chapters in this book! Be sure to check the Android 5 repository soon to see if the Auto SDK is available and get started developing amazing Android 5 applications across nearly a dozen different consumer electronics device type verticals! Android is taking over the consumer electronics industry! Have fun and be sure to enhance your knowledge of UI and graphics in Android with my *Pro Android UI* and *Pro Android Graphics* books, both from Apress! Happy developing!

Audio Concepts, Terminology, and Codecs

This appendix will help get you to get up to speed on the foundation of audio, as well as on digital audio concepts, terminology, and codecs (file formats) supported in the Android OS.

I added this appendix to make sure that you have a deep understanding of the digital audio new media assets that you will be creating, optimizing, and eventually "rendering" using Android's digital audio compatible classes such as SoundPool, MediaPlayer, Uri and MediaController.

Analog Audio and Digital Audio: History, Concepts, and Theory

For developers to use digital audio assets wisely and optimally, they will need to know the basic foundation of both analog audio and digital audio—where they came from, why they do what they do, and how to harness them. I felt that this book would not be complete without an in-depth discussion of analog and digital audio.

Foundation of Analog Audio: Sound Waves of Air

Those of you who are audiophiles already know that sound is created by sound waves pulsing through the air. This is the reason you see sub-woofers with massive 18- to 30-inch cones rapidly pushing out thunderous sound waves into audiences containing thousands of screaming fans at rock concerts. Before the digital audio industry existed, the analog audio industry was a major consumer electronics force. In fact, it still is today, with sound waves being controlled by complex analog electronics products, featuring capacitors, resistors, oscillators, crystals, vacuum tubes, circuit boards, mylar speaker cones, cardiod microphones, and similar analog audio creation technologies.

As mentioned, digital audio is quite complex, and part of this complexity comes from the need to bridge analog audio technology and digital audio technology. Analog audio is usually generated using speaker cones of different sizes, manufactured using resilient membranes made out of one space-age material or another. These speakers generate sound waves by vibrating or pulsing them into existence. Our ears receive this analog audio in exactly the opposite fashion, by catching and receiving those pulses of air, or vibrations with different wavelengths, and then turning them back into "data" that our brains can process. This is how we "hear" sound waves, and our brains interpret different audio sound wave frequencies as different notes or tones.

Sound waves generate various tones depending on the frequency of a sound wave. A wide or infrequent (long) wave produces a lower (bass) tone, whereas a more frequent (short) wavelength produces a higher (treble) tone. It is interesting to note that different frequencies of light produce different colors, so there is a close correlation between analog sound (audio) and analog light (colors), which also carries through into digital content production.

The volume of a sound wave will be predicated on the amplitude, or height, of that sound wave. The frequency of the sound waves equates to how closely together the waves are spaced along the X axis. The amplitude equates to how tall the waves are as measured along the Y axis. Sound waves can be shaped uniquely, allowing them to "carry" different sound effects. A baseline type of sound wave is called a **sine wave**, which you learned about in high school math with the sine, cosine, and tangent math functions. Those of you who are familiar with audio synthesis are aware that there are other types of sound waves used in **sound design**, such as the **saw wave**, which looks like the edge of a saw (hence its name), and the **pulse wave**, which is shaped using right angles, resulting in immediate on and off sounds that translate into pulses.

Even randomized waveforms, such as **noise**, are used in sound design to obtain edgy sound results. As you may have ascertained using previous knowledge regarding data footprint optimization, the more "chaos" or noise that is present in your sound waves, the harder they will be to compress for a codec, resulting in a larger digital audio file size for that particular sound.

The next section takes a closer look at how an analog audio sound wave is turned into digital audio data using a process called **sampling**, which is a core tool of sound design and synthesis.

Digital Audio: Samples, Resolution, and Frequency

The process of turning analog audio (sound waves) into digital audio data is called *sampling*. If you work in the music industry, you have probably heard about a type of keyboard (or rack-mount equipment) called a "sampler." Sampling is the process of slicing an audio wave into segments so that you can store the shape of the wave as digital audio data using a digital audio format. This turns an infinitely accurate analog sound wave into a discreet amount of digital data, that is, into zeroes and ones. The more zeroes and ones that are used, the more accurate the reproduction of the infinitely accurate (original) analog sound wave. The sample accuracy determines how many zeroes and ones are used to reproduce the analog sound wave, which is also the data footprint, so I will get into that discussion next.

Each digital segment of a sampled audio sound wave is called a **sample**, because it samples that sound wave at that exact point in time. The precision of a sample is determined by how much data is used to define each wave slice's height. Just like with digital imaging, this precision is termed the resolution, or more accurately (no pun intended), the **sample resolution**. Sample resolution in digital audio is usually defined as 8-bit, 12-bit, 16-bit, 24-bit, or 32-bit. HD audio uses 24-bit audio samples.

In digital imaging and digital video, the resolution is quantified in the number of colors, and in digital audio, this resolution is quantified in how many bits of data are used to define each of the audio samples taken. Just like in digital imaging (more colors yields better quality), a higher sample resolution yields better sound reproduction. The only difference between the two is that digital audio supports 12-bit sample resolution. I often wish than digital imaging formats supported 12-bit color!

Thus, higher sampling resolutions—using more data to reproduce a given sound wave sample—will yield a higher audio playback quality at the expense of a large data footprint. This is the reason that 16-bit audio, termed CD-quality audio, sounds better than 8-bit audio, just like truecolor images look better than indexed color images.

In digital audio there is now 24-bit audio sampling, known as **HD audio** in the consumer electronics industry. HD digital audio broadcast radio uses a 24-bit sample resolution, so each audio sample or slice of a sound wave contains 16,777,216 units of sample resolution. Some newer Android devices now support HD audio, such as the smartphones you see advertised featuring "HD quality" audio. This means they have 24-bit audio hardware, that is, a 24-bit capable audio decoder chip installed.

Beside a digital audio sample resolution, there is also a digital audio **sampling frequency**. This is how many of these samples at a particular sample resolution are taken during one second of sample time. In digital image editing, the sampling frequency is analogous to the number of pixels contained within an image. More pixels in an image would equate to the analog image being sampled more frequently.

Sampling frequency can also be called the **sampling rate**. You are probably familiar with the term CD-quality audio, which is defined as using a 16-bit sample resolution and a 44.1kHz sampling rate. This is taking 44,100 samples, each of which contains 16-bits of sample resolution, yielding 65,536 bits of audio data in each sample.

Let's do some math and find out how many bits of data provide one second of raw or uncompressed digital audio data. This is calculated by multiplying a 65,536 sample resolution by a 44,100 sample frequency. This gives you a maximum potential value of 2,890,137,600 bits to represent one second of CD quality audio. Divide this by eight to get 361,267,200 bytes, and by 1,024 to get 352,800 kilobytes, and by 1,024 again to get 344 megabytes.

Not every CD quality 16-bit sample will use all of these potential data bits, however, so your original raw (uncompressed) audio samples will be smaller than this, usually only a few dozen megabytes.

So to figure out raw data in an audio file you would multiply the sampling bit rate by the sampling frequency by the number of seconds in that audio snippet. You can see that it can often be a huge number! Audio codecs are really great at optimizing this data down to an amazingly small data footprint with very little (audible) loss in quality, as you will see during the course of this book.

So the exact same trade-off that you have in digital imaging and in digital video exists with digital audio as well. The more data you include, the better quality result you get, but at the cost of a larger data footprint.

In the visual medium, this is defined using color depth and pixels. With digital video, it's defined in frames. In the aural medium, it is defined via the sample resolution in combination with the sampling rate. Common sampling rates in the digital audio industry include 8kHz, 22kHz, 32kHz, 44.1kHz, 48kHz, 96kHz, 192kHz, and even 384kHz.

Lower sampling rates, such as 8kHz, 22kHz, and 32kHz, are optimal for sampling any "voice-based" digital audio, such as a movie dialog or ebook narration track, for instance. Higher audio sample rates are more appropriate for music and other sound effects such as rumbling thunder, which needs a high dynamic range (high fidelity). High sample rates are best for movie theater (THX) sound quality.

Some sound effects, such as the ones that you will use in your **HelloUniverse** app, can get away with using a lower 22kHz or 32kHz sampling rate, as long as the sampling resolution used is 16-bit quality. Ultimately, you will have to use your ears during the digital audio optimization process to ascertain the quality-to-file-size trade-off.

Digital Audio Attributes: HD, Stream, and Bit Rate

As mentioned, an industry "baseline" for superior audio quality is known as CD-quality audio and it is defined as a 16-bit data sample resolution at a 44.1kHz data sample frequency. This was used to produce audio CD products way back in the 20th Century, and it is still used as a minimum quality standard today. There is also the more recent HD audio standard, which uses a 24-bit data sample at a 48kHz or 96kHz sample frequency. This is used today in HD radio as well as in HD audio-compatible Android devices such as "Hi-Fi" HD audio smartphones.

If you are going to use HD audio in your Android applications, you need to make sure that your target users will own the HD audio-compatible hardware that will be required to utilize a higher level of audio fidelity. Just like with digital video data, digital audio data can either be captive within the application, with data files in the **/raw** folder, or digital audio can be streamed using remote data servers. Similar to digital video, the upside to streaming digital audio data is that it can reduce the data footprint of the application, just as streaming digital video data can. The downside is reliability. Many of the same concepts apply equally well to digital audio and digital video assets.

Streaming audio will shrink the size of your application's data footprint, because you do not have to include all of that heavy new media digital audio data inside of your .APK files, so if you are planning on coding a digital Jukebox application, you may want to consider streaming your digital audio data. Otherwise, try to optimize your digital audio data so that you can include it (captive) inside the .APK file. This way, digital audio will always be available to your application's users when they need to play it.

The downside to streaming digital audio is that if your user's connection (or the audio server) goes down, your audio file may not be available for your users to play and listen to! The reliability and availability of your digital audio data is the key factor to be considered on the other side of this streaming audio versus captive digital audio data trade-off. The same trade-offs which are discussed in this book for digital video assets can also be applied to digital audio assets.

Just like with digital video, one of the primary concepts in regards to streaming your digital audio is the **bit rate** of that digital audio data. As you learned in Chapter 11, the bit rate is defined during your compression process. As with digital video, digital audio files that need to support lower bit rate are going to have more compression applied to the data, which will result in a lower quality level.

These lower bit-rate files will play back smoothly across a greater number of devices, because fewer bits can be processed (and transferred) more easily. As a processor gets faster, it can process more bits per second. As a data bandwidth connection gets faster, it can more comfortably send or receive more bits per second as well.

Android Digital Audio: Digital Audio Formats

There are considerably more digital audio codecs in Android than there are digital video codecs, as there are only two video codecs—MPEG and WebM. Android audio support includes **.MP3** (MPEG3) files, WAVE (PCM or Pulse Code Modulated) **.WAV** files, **.MP4** (or .M4A) MPEG4 audio, OGG Vorbis **(.OGG)** audio files, Matroska (**.MKS**) audio files, FLAC (**.FLAC**) audio files, and even **MIDI** (.MID, .MXMF and .XMF) files, which technically aren't really even digital audio data at all.

Let me explain what MIDI is first, since it is not a format that you are going to be using in your **HelloUniverse** application.

MIDI stands for **Musical Instrument Data Interface**, and it is one of the very first ways that digital audio and computers worked together, dating all the way back to ancient times (the 1980s). The very first computer to feature the MIDI data port hardware was the Atari ST1040. This computer allowed me to plug my keyboard synthesizer, at the time it was my Yamaha DX-7, into that MIDI port. MIDI allowed me to play and record performance data into the computer using the MIDI data format along with an audio software genre called a MIDI sequencer and MIDI Sequencing software called FinalTrack.

A MIDI file contains zero sample data—that is, it contains no audio data, only the **performance** data. When this performance data is played back into the synthesizer using the MIDI hardware (cable and ports), the synthesizer generates the audio tones using this MIDI performance data. MIDI will record which keys on the synth or sampler keyboard were pressed, and when, along with the keypress duration, how hard it was pressed (called after-touch), and similar performance nuances.

When MIDI files are played back through a synthesizer, the synth replicates the exact performance of the performer or composer, even though that person is no longer playing that performance track; the computer is now playing that performance data exactly the way that it was originally performed.

The way that MIDI data was used in MIDI sequencing software is that you can play an instrument track, record it as MIDI data, and the sequencer will then play it back for you, while you play another instrument track right alongside of it. This enables digital songwriters to assemble complex musical arrangements using the computer, instead of hiring a studio full of musicians. You can download open source MIDI software called Rosegarden at **rosegardenmusic.com**; it not only contains a full MIDI sequencer, but also contains a music notation (scoring) program as well. Rosegarden was originally for Linux OS but is being "ported" to the Windows OS as well currently.

Android supports playback of MIDI files, but does not implement a MIDI class. It would not be an easy task to code a MIDI sequencer for Android, although some on the code forums are talking about it. For that reason it is beyond the scope of this book, and I mention it here only to educate you as to the history and scope of digital audio. MIDI played an important role early on in the evolution of digital audio, and is still part of digital audio today, especially if you are a songwriter or a sound designer.

The most common digital audio format supported by Android is the popular MPEG3, or MP3, digital audio file format. Most of you are very familiar with MP3 digital audio files, due to the music download websites like Napster. Most people collect songs in this format to use on popular MP3 players and via CD-ROM- and DVD-ROM-based music collections.

The reason the MP3 digital audio file format is popular is because it has a fairly good compression-to-quality ratio, and because the codec needed to play audio back can be found almost anywhere, even in the Android OS. MP3 is an acceptable format to use in an Android application, as long as you get the highest quality level possible out of it by using an optimal encoding work process.

It is important to note that MP3 is a lossy audio file format, like JPEG is for images, where some of the audio data (and thus quality) is thrown away during the compression process and cannot be recovered. Android does have a lossless audio compression codec, called FLAC, which stands for **Free Lossless Audio Codec**. FLAC is an open source audio codec whose support is as widespread as MP3, due to the free nature of the software decoder.

FLAC is also very fast, so the decoder is highly optimized for speed, it supports 24-bit HD audio, and there are no patent concerns for using it. This is a great audio codec to use if you need very high-quality audio within a reasonable data footprint. FLAC supports a wide range of sample resolutions, from 4-bits per sample up to 32-bits. It also supports a wide range of sampling frequencies—from 1Hz to 65,535kHz (65kHz), in 1Hz increments—so it is extremely flexible.

From an audio playback hardware standpoint, I would suggest using the 16-bit sample resolution and either a 44.1kHz or 48kHz sample frequency. FLAC is supported in Android 3.1 and later, so if your users are using modern Android devices, you should be able to safely utilize a FLAC codec.

Therefore, it is possible to use completely lossless new media assets in your Android application, using PNG32 and FLAC, as long as you are targeting Android Version 3.1 and later OS revisions.

Another open source digital audio codec supported by Android is the **OGG Vorbis** codec, another lossy audio codec from the **Xiph.Org** Foundation. The Vorbis codec data is most often held in an .OGG data file container, and thus Vorbis is commonly called OGG Vorbis digital audio data format. The OGG Vorbis supports sampling rates from 8kHz up to 192kHz, and supports up to 255 discrete channels of digital audio (as you now know, this represents 8-bits worth of audio channels). OGG Vorbis is supported in all versions of the Android OS.

Vorbis is quickly approaching the quality of HE-AAC and WMA (Windows Media Audio) Professional, and is superior in quality to MP3, AAC-LC, and WMA. It is a lossy format, so the FLAC codec is superior to OGG Vorbis, as it contains all of the original digital audio sample data (as it is lossless).

Android supports most popular **MPEG4** AAC (Advanced Audio Coding) codecs, including AAC-LC, HE-AAC, and AAC-ELD. These can all be contained in MPEG4 containers (**.3gp**, **.mp4**, and **.m4a**) or file extensions, and can be played back across all versions of Android.

The one exception to this is the AAC-ELD, which is supported only after Android 4.1. ELD stands for Enhanced Low Delay, and this codec is intended for usage in a real-time, two-way communications application, such as a digital walkie-talkie.

The simplest and most widely used AAC codec is the **AAC-LC** or Low Complexity codec. It should be sufficient for most digital audio encoding applications. An AAC-LC should yield a higher quality result at a lower data footprint than the MP3 format. The next most complicated AAC codec is the **HE-AAC** or High Efficiency AAC codec. This codec supports sampling rates from 8kHz to 48kHz, and both Stereo and Dolby 5.1 channel encoding. Android supports decoding both the v1 and v2 levels of this codec, and Android will also encode audio using the HE-AAC v1 codec in Android devices later than Version 4.1 (Jelly Bean). Use the AAC-LC codec to support the earlier versions of the Android OS.

For encoding speech, which usually features a different type of sound wave than music, there are two other **AMR** or **Adaptive Multi-Rate** audio codecs. They are highly efficient for encoding things like speech or short-burst sound effects that do not need high-quality reproduction (such as a bomb blast sound effect). There is also the AMR-WB (Adaptive Multi-Rate Wide-Band) standard in Android, which supports nine discrete settings from 6.6 to 23.85kbps audio bit-rates, sampled at 16kHz. This is a high enough sample rate where voice is concerned. This is the codec to use for a narrator track, if you were creating interactive ebook applications, for instance.

There is also an AMR-NB (Adaptive Multi-Rate Narrow-Band) standard in Android, which supports eight discrete settings, from 4.75 to 12.2kbps audio bit rates sampled. This can be an adequate sample rate if the data going into the codec is high quality, or if the resulting audio sample does not require a high quality due to the noisy nature of the content (such as a bomb blast).

Finally, there is **PCM** (**Pulse Code Modulated**) audio, commonly known as the **WAVE** or .WAV audio format. Many of you are familiar with this lossless digital audio format, as it is the original audio format used with the Windows operating system. It is lossless because there is no compression applied whatsoever! PCM audio is commonly used for CD-ROM content, as well as for digital telephony applications. This is because PCM WAVE audio is an uncompressed digital audio format, and therefore has no CPU-intensive compression algorithms applied to the data stream. Thus, decoding (CPU overhead) the data is not an issue for the telephony equipment or for affordable CD players.

For this reason, when you start compressing digital audio assets into the various file formats, you can use PCM as a "baseline" file format. You probably won't put it into your .APK file, however, because there are other formats (such as FLAC and MPEG4 AAC) that will give you the same quality using an order of magnitude less data.

Ultimately, the only real way to find out which audio formats supported by Android have the best digital audio codec result for any given audio data instance is to actually encode your digital audio in the primary codecs that you know are well supported and efficient. This process is covered in Chapter 12, where you can observe the relative data footprint results between the different formats using the same source audio sample.

Digital Audio Optimization: Device Compatible

Optimizing your digital audio assets for playback across the widest range of Android devices in the marketplace is easier than optimizing your digital video or digital imagery (and thus animation) across Android devices. This is because there is a much wider disparity of screen resolutions and display aspect ratios than there is a disparity of digital audio playback hardware support across Android devices, except for some Android hardware which features 24-bit (HD) audio playback hardware compatibility.

This is because our ears can't perceive the same quality difference in audio that our eyes can with digital imagery, animation, or digital video. Generally, there are three primary "sweet spots" of digital audio support, across all Android devices, that you should target for support for your high-quality audio.

Lower-quality audio, such as narration tracks, or short sound effects, can use a 22kHZ or 32kHz sampling rate with 8-bit, 12-bit, or 16-bit sampling resolution. The high-quality audio targets include CD-quality audio, also known as 16-bit data sampling at 44.1kHz. HD-quality audio is at the other end of this high-end audio spectrum, using a 24-bit data sampling resolution and a 48kHz audio data sampling rate. There is also an unnamed "somewhere in the middle" specification, using 16-bit data sampling at a 48kHz sampling rate, which is what THX used to use in movie theaters.

Ultimately, however, it comes down to the quality-to-file-size results that emerge from your digital audio data footprint optimization process, which can yield some amazing results.

Thus, the initial process for optimizing your digital audio assets across all of the Android devices is going to be to create 16-bit assets at 44.1kHz and 48kHz, and then optimize (compress) them using the different formats supported in Android. Once that process is completed, you can then see which digital audio assets provide the highest quality digital audio playback in conjunction with the lowest possible data footprint.

You will do this by using the latest version of the open source Audacity 2.0.5 digital audio editing and engineering software package. This software package is freely available on SourceForge.net, and is accessible to all readers, no matter which OS platforms they prefer, whether it be Windows 8.1, Macintosh OS/X, or SUSE Linux.

Audio Sequencing: Concepts and Principles

Recall that the earliest forms of digital audio sequencing actually utilized MIDI.

MIDI sequencers such as the Rosegarden software mentioned earlier are still popular, and allow performance data sequencing. This is where a composer plays each instrumental part into a computer using a synthesizer set to use a given instrument sample, say a guitar, bass, or piano sample, and then the computer plays back this performance data later on, while the composer accompanies the computer-replayed version of that performance.

Eventually MIDI sequencing software added digital audio capabilities alongside MIDI playback capabilities, as increased computer processing power, as well as specialized digital audio adapters, such as Creative Labs' X-Fi, became available to consumers at affordable prices. It turns out that this concept of audio sequencing is applied equally well to digital audio samples that are manipulated directly by a computer, as long as this computer is powerful enough. My Samsung Galaxy Note 3 has a 2.3GHz Quad-Core processor, so that time has certainly arrived!

Computers—in this case, Linux-based Android devices—keep getting more and more powerful, and are featuring four to eight processor cores, and one, two, or even four billion bytes of system memory.

This means that Android devices can hold several digital audio samples in memory, and this memory optimization is an issue with Android SoundPool, as you will soon see. I wanted to cover SoundPool, an admittedly advanced audio sequencing engine class in Android, in this book, even though this book is for "Absolute Beginners."

The reason for this is because if you want to utilize digital audio assets in your application, especially using samples or audio snippets, rather than just playing back songs, SoundPool is the way to go.

Digital Audio Synthesis: Concepts and Principles

Some of the very first MIDI keyboards were digital audio samplers. These played back digital audio samples, pre-recorded (sampled) by digital audio sample design professionals like Frank Serafine, using a range of sample resolutions and sample frequencies.

You learned about samples in a previous section in the Appendix, so what you are going to focus on here is how those samples are taken to the next level using **audio synthesis** (via algorithmic processing). Synthesizers can also apply these algorithms to raw waveforms, such as **sine**, **saw**, or **pulse** waves.

Synthesizers take digital audio—whether it's a generated wave borne out of an oscillator on a circuit board in a consumer electronics device, or a more complex sampled waveform, such as a sample of a plucked instrument string—and apply algorithmic processing to the waveform to create a different tonality, sound, or special effect. We're all familiar with the synthesized instruments in popular music today; these virtual instruments are created solely by using math and programming code!

One of the foundational mathematical manipulations that can be applied to audio waveforms within the digital audio domain is called **pitch-shifting**. This was the core technology that made keyboard samplers viable, as one sample could be used up and down the keyboard, simply by shifting its pitch!

Pitch-shifting algorithms can take a sound wave up or down an octave (or even a small fraction of an octave, known as pitch) to create a usable range of that sample, much as though you were playing it up and down the keys of a sampler keyboard or a synthesizer keyboard.

As you learned previously, the tone of a waveform can be determined by the frequency of that waveform itself, so it becomes a fairly straightforward mathematical computation to be able to accurately shift that pitch (wave) up an octave by shortening that wavelength by cutting it in half, or shift the pitch down an octave by doubling that wavelength. Any fraction between these two extremes changes the pitch of the audio sample, which is how you get different notes along a keyboard using a single waveform. You can even create fractions between "known" pitches (common notes such as A, B, D, F and G) which can be used to create "micro-tonal" music. Digital audio synthesis is amazing!

SoundPool can perform pitch-shifting on your digital audio samples, which is why you are learning about these concepts in this appendix, and it does have some impressive audio synthesis capabilities and will probably add even more features in future versions of the Android OS.

You need to know these digital audio synthesis concepts in order to leverage what SoundPool can do for your application effectively and optimally. If you need to use SoundPool, you will know how to do it correctly, and you will now understand why you need to do it that way in the first place.

Another core audio synthesis mathematical manipulation is the **combination**, or **compositing**, of two digital audio waveforms. This will allow the playback of two sounds at the same time, using a single oscillator, or using the speaker hardware. Just as with digital imaging, 2D animation or digital video compositing, this involves adding two different sample data values to arrive at the final data value.

Today's Android audio hardware features impressive multi-channel support, and probably has the capability of playing Stereo (two channels) or Quadrophonic (four channels) quality audio (effects, music, vocal tracks, and so on) using the audio hardware that is inside any given consumer electronics device.

But what if you want to combine six or eight tracks of digital audio in real-time, like an audio sequencer can? This is why SoundPool is important to master, because it can provide you with a digital audio sequencing engine right inside your Android application.

The Android SoundPool audio sequencing and synthesis engine is a complex class, as you might well imagine, and to make it work properly, you need to give it the most highly optimized samples possible. This class is in Android to stay, and its code will continue to be debugged, refined, and improved, so if your Android app is going to be audio-centric, you need to master it. Chapter 12 gets you up to speed on how to best use SoundPool, as well as what it can accomplish for your apps.

Raw Audio Data Optimization: Memory Footprint

What is important, if you are going to attempt the real-time audio compositing of six or eight audio samples, is that each of these samples is well optimized. This makes what you learned about digital audio data optimization extremely relevant when it comes to using SoundPool.

For instance, if you don't really need HD (24-bit sample resolution) audio in order to get the quality result, you should use CD-quality 16-bit audio, or even 12-bit audio, as you will save valuable memory and get the same result. If you can get the same audio quality using a 32kHz sample rate instead of a 48kHz sample rate, you are using 50% less sample memory!

For voiceover or sound effects audio, the memory savings are there for the taking, as often you can sample a bomb or laser blast effectively by using 8-bit resolution with an 8kHz sample rate. You often won't be able to detect much difference between 16-bit 48kHz Stereo audio and the lower bit-rate Mono audio, as you saw earlier in Chapter 12 between your WAVE and AMR samples, with a 200 fold memory savings (400KB down to 2KB).

If you don't absolutely need Stereo samples, and can mix them down into Mono samples, you will save 100% in memory. Combine this with lowering bit rates for the sample resolution and sampling frequency, and you can get the same audio result, at least from the user's perspective, using a hundred times less data (in many circumstances).

It is important to remember that the users don't hear the "before" (uncompressed) and the "after" (compressed) audio samples like you do. As long as they sound similar, you are good to go!

The other significant variable you can optimize is the length (in time) of the sample. Notice, in Figure A-1, that there is a significant portion of the sample after 0.8 seconds that does not have much data in it. Reducing the sample duration from 1.2 seconds or 1,200 milliseconds to 0.8 seconds or 800 milliseconds results in a 50% reduction in raw audio data that is being sampled in the first place. This kind of data savings can add up with several digital audio samples.

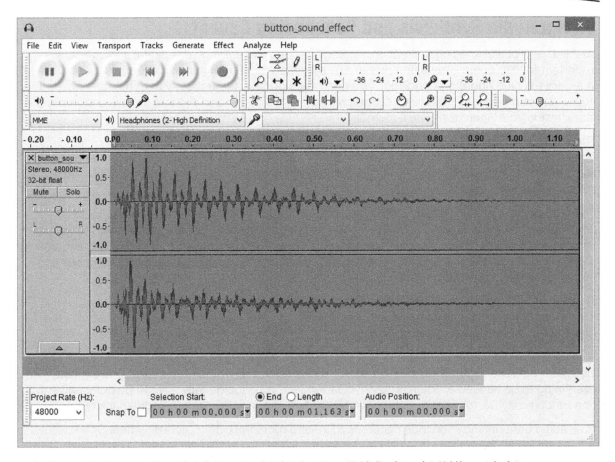

Figure A-1. Audacity 2.0.5 main audio editor screen showing the stereo 32-bit floating point 48 kHz sample data

I went into Audacity and further reduced the 32-bit 48kHz (393KB) sample to 16-bit 48kHz (219KB) and then used the Audacity Tracks ➤ Stereo Track to Mono menu sequence to create a Mono 16-bit 48kHz (110KB) raw data footprint for this audio data. Then, I selected the last portion of the sound wave, between the 0.8 and 1.15 duration, and pressed the Delete key, removing that unused data. I saved that out and it was 76KB of data. I reduced the raw audio data that will be recreated in system memory by Android, by 517% (81% less data).

I just showed you three different levels (sample resolution, stereo vs. mono, and sample duration) of raw audio data reduction (you can think of this as memory usage once the digital audio data has been decompressed by the Android OS into system memory). And this is before you even get into file size optimization using various encoders.

Codec optimization will affect your app's APK file size, but when the audio sample needs to play back inside your app, this audio sample still needs to be recreated in (decompressed into) system memory, before it can be "triggered" by the SoundPool engine.

Therefore, there are really two stages to audio optimization—what you do to the raw audio wave sample prior to encoding, relating to sample resolution, sample frequency, sample duration, and mono versus stereo sample playback, and what you do as you export into various codecs using settings to ascertain how much APK file size they can save your app.

Digital Audio Synthesis and Sequencing Caveats

Just like with digital imaging, animation, and digital video, optimizing your digital audio assets is important for two completely different, but related, reasons. With digital audio samples, especially in regard to using Android SoundPool, you must consider the amount of system memory needed to hold each sample once it has been decompressed by the codec and put into its raw, uncompressed state, inside your Android device's memory.

The second reason that well-optimized audio is important is the CPU processing part of the equation. It's pretty obvious that with less audio (duration, resolution, frequency, and number of stereo/mono tracks) to process, even if that is just sending the audio data to the audio hardware, there are less CPU cycles used.

Therefore, if you can get the same basic audio quality results using a lower sample resolution (fewer bits per slice of audio) or a lower sample frequency (fewer slices of the audio waveform per second), or fewer tracks (mono or one audio track instead of stereo or two audio tracks), and shorter playback duration, you will be saving both your Android operating system memory resources and your user's Android CPU processing power resources.

The reason I am going into all of this audio sample optimization information in such great detail in this appendix is because the Android SoundPool class will often get a "bad rap," because the raw audio sample sizes that developers provide to SoundPool are too data-heavy. The SoundPool engine gets blamed for this, rather than the developer's lacking data footprint optimization skillset.

Google the phrase "SoundPool doesn't work" and you will see what I mean. Everyone expects everything to be handed to them on a vinyl platter! Yes, you would really have to be quite ancient, or a modern day DJ, in order to get that last joke! Actually, vinyl is making a comeback currently.

Raw audio data optimization thus becomes more and more important, at least where SoundPool is concerned, as the number of digital audio samples that you require increases. This is again true for both system memory and system processing cycle usage considerations, because as you add samples, both of these resources are utilized more and more. Don't forget that there are other things that your application is doing, like user interface event handling, imaging, animation, digital video, and possibly even 3D rendering.

Another reason providing highly optimized digital audio samples is so important when using a SoundPool class is because there is currently a one megabyte limit on digital audio sample data when using a SoundPool engine. Although this limit might be increased in future Android API revisions of this digital audio sequencing class, it is still always best practice to optimize any digital audio assets effectively and efficiently.

Digital audio synthesis and sequencing using SoundPool in your Android app is a balancing act, both within the device that you are testing it on at the moment, as well as across all devices that your application will ever be run on.

If a given hardware platform (smartphone, tablet, ereader, iTV set, or smartwatch) cannot handle playing a given audio data load, then it may simply not play a given sample. As time goes on this will happen less and less due to better code and faster device processor and memory hardware. As you have learned thus far, digital audio synthesis, sequencing, and compositing is heavily predicated on the speed of the processor, the number of processor cores available, and the amount of memory available to hold all of the digital audio samples needed in their uncompressed format.

The bottom line is that you need to be extremely smart in how you are doing things with SoundPool. This is not as much about how you write your code (although that is certainly important), but more about how you set up your audio samples so that they use less memory and can be leveraged farther in your application.

A common mistake many Android developers make regarding SoundPool is trying to use it more like a sequencer than as an audio synthesizer. Users focus on SoundPool's ability to load multiple audio file waveforms into memory, but do not leverage its processing capability for creating a myriad of new waveforms, by using a few basic waveforms with SoundPool's pitch-shift capability.

Here you are again, back to that same **memory vs. processor** trade-off that you invariably have in the Android OS, regarding the use of almost all of these new media capabilities which Android offers.

If you use SoundPool as an audio sequencer, system memory can overload, and this can shut down SoundPool's functionality. Android developers must harness all of SoundPool features optimally, and at the same time, they must optimize each of their digital audio samples as much as possible.

Here is a great example of this. SoundPool allows pitch-shifting across two full octaves, from a setting of 0.5 (down one full octave, or half of your original sample waveform) up to 2.0 (or up one full octave, or twice of your original waveform width). Remember that the waveform height equates to amplitude, which is commonly referred to as volume.

Most users don't use this pitch-shifting feature, but instead, use different samples to achieve different notes. This fills up memory rapidly, and the end result is the app works less and less well across older devices. The correct way to use SoundPool is to take your samples—say a one string pluck from a guitar, one horn blow from a saxophone, one piano key strike, and three different drum samples—and using only six short Mono 48kHz 16-bit high-quality samples, make a basic synthesizer that has all four basic Jazz instruments.

Using this basic synthesizer set-up, your user could play instruments up and down two full octaves. This application would use only a few hundred kilobytes of memory to hold these 16-bit 48kHz uncompressed samples. If you used a high-quality microphone for your sampling process, you would be amazed at the high-quality results that you can obtain these days using a 16-bit 48kHz Mono sampling format. If you wanted to save memory, you could also use a Mono 16-bit 44.1kHz CD-quality audio or Mono 16-bit 32kHz audio with similarly acceptable results.

I hope I have covered enough digital audio sampling and synthesis concepts in this appendix to give you some insight as to how to optimize your digital audio assets for use with the SoundPool engine!

Index

H

I

Get the eBook for only $10!

Now you can take the weightless companion with you anywhere, anytime. Your purchase of this book entitles you to 3 electronic versions for only $10.

This Apress title will prove so indispensible that you'll want to carry it with you everywhere, which is why we are offering the eBook in 3 formats for only $10 if you have already purchased the print book.

Convenient and fully searchable, the PDF version enables you to easily find and copy code—or perform examples by quickly toggling between instructions and applications. The MOBI format is ideal for your Kindle, while the ePUB can be utilized on a variety of mobile devices.

Go to www.apress.com/promo/tendollars to purchase your companion eBook.

Apress®
THE EXPERT'S VOICE™

CPSIA information can be obtained at www.ICGtesting.com
Printed in the USA
LVOW03s1546180115

423347LV00001B/2/P